Visual C++5:
The Complete Reference

Chris H. Pappas
and
William H. Murray, III

Osborne **McGraw-Hill**

Berkeley New York St. Louis San Francisco
Auckland Bogotá Hamburg London Madrid
Mexico City Milan Montreal New Delhi Panama City
Paris São Paulo Singapore Sydney
Tokyo Toronto

Osborne/**McGraw-Hill**
2600 Tenth Street
Berkeley, California 94710
U.S.A.

For information on translations or book distributors outside the U.S.A., or to arrange bulk purchase discounts for sales promotions, premiums, or fund-raisers, please contact Osborne/**McGraw-Hill** at the above address.

Visual C++ 5: The Complete Reference

234567890 AGM 9987

ISBN 0-07-882391-9

Publisher
  Brandon A. Nordin

Editor-in-Chief
  Scott Rogers

Acquisitions Editors
  Wendy Rinaldi
  Lisa Lucas

Project Editor
  Heidi Poulin

Editorial Assistant
  Ann Sellers

Technical Editor
  Joe O'Neil

Copy Editor
  Gary Morris

Proofreader
  Stefany Otis

Computer Designer
  Jani Beckwith

Illustrator
  Lance Ravella

Series Design
  Roberta Steele

Cover Design
  Adrian Morgan

To Richard N. Aswad,

with gratitude

About the Authors...

Chris H. Pappas and William H. Murray are professors of Computer Science at the B.C.C. S.U.N.Y. campus in Binghamton, New York. They are authors of more than three dozen highly acclaimed computer books, including *The Visual C++ Handbook* and *Borland C++ In Depth*. Pappas and Murray are the Chief Executive Officers for Ninevah National Research, a New York-based company committed to software research and instructional materials. Pappas holds a Master's Degree in Computer Science from S.U.N.Y. Binghamton. Murray holds advanced degrees in Engineering and Secondary Education.

Contents

Part IV

Windows Programming Foundations

Part VI

Appendixes

Introduction

This book was written with two main goals; to help you become more familiar with the Microsoft Visual C++ compiler package, and to help people with different programming backgrounds become more proficient in C, C++, and 32-bit Windows programming. This is quite a task, even for a book containing hundreds of pages, but it was written with you in mind.

Our two major goals encompass a number of specific aims:

- This book introduces you to the powerful programming tools provided in your Microsoft Visual C++ compiler package. These include the compiler, debugger, and various Windows 95 and NT development tools. This book compliments your Microsoft reference manuals and online help to provide a quick start with each of the components in the compiler package.

- Programmers need a thorough understanding of each programming language they intend to use. You will find that this book covers all the important programming concepts in the C, C++, and Windows languages, including the Microsoft Foundation Class Library (MFC). If you are a novice programmer, early chapters will help you build the solid foundation you need to write more sophisticated programs. For advanced programmers, early chapters will serve as a reference source and will introduce you to exciting C++ concepts.

- You will learn how to debug program code and write programs that are free of syntax and logical programming errors.

- You will gain an understanding of how procedural programming differs from object-oriented programming and how to develop simple OOPs programs.

- You will explore the exciting world of Microsoft Windows programming. Chapters are devoted to helping you understand Windows concepts and how to write simple to intermediate programs.

We believe in teaching by example. We have made every effort to make each example in this book simple, complete, and bug-free. You can study these examples, alter them, and expand them into programs tailored to fit your needs.

This book will serve as a lasting reference to the Microsoft Visual C++ compiler and the tools it supports.

How This Book is Organized

Chapters 1 through 4 introduce you to the programming tools contained in the Microsoft Visual C++ compiler package.

Chapters 5 through 15 teach the foundational programming concepts needed for the C and C++ languages. These are procedure-oriented chapters that teach traditional C and C++ programming concepts.

Chapters 16 through 19 give you a complete introduction to object-oriented programming with C++. Here you will find terminology, definitions, and complete programming examples to help you with your development of object-oriented programs.

Chapters 20 and 21 introduce you to Microsoft Windows 95 and NT programming concepts and show you how to use the Microsoft Visual C++ compiler to develop applications that include GDI primitives, cursors, icons, menus, and dialog boxes. The applications in these chapters are traditional message based programs.

Chapters 22 and 23 are devoted to programming with the Microsoft Foundation Class Library (MFC). By using the power of C++ classes, the MFC will shorten both your Windows application development cycle and your program length.

Chapters 24 and 25 continue working with the MFC and introduce powerful Wizards that will automatically generate program code for you. You'll also learn important OLE concepts and you'll use Wizards to build OLE applications.

The MFC and Wizard works finishes with Chapter 26 where you'll be introduced to the concepts of ActiveX control design.

Appendix A provides you with a reference table of ASCII character codes. Similarly for your reference use, Appendix B lists DOS 10H, 21H, and 33H Interrupt parameters. Finally, Appendix C discusses the fundamentals of Dynamic link library (DLL) design.

How the Book's Material Was Developed

The material in this book was developed and tested on two Dell Pentium Pro computers running at 200 MHz and on two Toshiba Tecra 730CDT computers running at 166 MHz. All computers contained 32 MB of RAM. The computers were operated under Windows 95 and NT. The entire manuscript was prepared with Microsoft Word for Windows. All screen shots were taken with Collage, a Windows capture utility.

Part I

A Quick Overview of Visual C++

The
Complete
Reference

Visual
C++ 5

Chapter 1

The Visual C++ Compiler,
Version 5

Whe new Microsoft Visual C++ provides you with a comprehensive, up-to-the-minute, production-level environment for developing all Windows 95 and Windows NT applications. Microsoft's Visual C++ version 5 ships in three different configurations: the Learning, Professional, and Enterprise Editions. The following section presents the purpose and special features of each edition. This text was prepared using the Enterprise Edition; however, all of the material covered (except where noted in the text) is portable to all three editions:

Learning Edition

The Learning Edition allows you to easily master the C++ language while using the professional Visual C++ toolset. This edition contains all of the features of the Professional Edition except code optimizations, the Profiler, and static linking to the MFC library. It is a perfect choice for students and is priced low to make learning C++ affordable for a single individual. The license for the Learning Edition explicitly prohibits using the product to develop software for distribution.

Professional Edition

The Professional Edition provides developers with the license to distribute programs developed under it. It surpasses the Learning Edition in horsepower by adding services and controls for Win32 platforms, including Windows 95 and Windows NT. These features allow you to target the operating system's graphical user interface or console APIs.

New features added to the Professional Edition include:

- New C++ keywords: bool, explicit, false, mutable, true, and typename, for improved C++ performance
- Use of __declspec to declare whether the specified storage-class attribute applies to a type or to a variable of a type
- Compiler support for COM files
- New compiler optimization options
- Updated AppWizard that automates the dialog class in a dialog-based application
- MFC Asynchronous (URL) monikers (providing asynchronous-application Internet communication)
- Active Documents, displayed either in the entire client window of a web browser (e.g., Internet Explorer), or in an OLE container (e.g., Microsoft Word)
- Win32 Internet API (WinInet), making the Internet an integral part of any application, simplifying Internet services FTP, HTTP, and gopher
- Active Template Library (ATL)

- C Run-time library
- ANSI Standard C++ library
- ERRLOOK, which looks up system error messages

Enterprise Edition (used for this manuscript)

The Enterprise Edition has all of the capabilities of the Professional Edition and, further, allows developers to create and debug client/server applications for the Internet, or even an intranet. This edition ships with additional tools for working with SQL databases and debugging SQL stored procedures. The Visual SourceSafe source-code control system simplifies developing in a team environment. Features unique to the Enterprise Edition include:

- Specialized Microsoft transaction server
- Visual database tools
- Extensive SQL data type support

NOTE: *Unless specifically mentioned, the applications in this book can be compiled with any version of the compiler. For example, the applications in Chapters 1 through 19 are standard command-line C or C++ applications that can be run under MS-DOS or in a compatibility box under Windows 95 or Windows NT. Likewise, the Windows applications developed in Chapter 23 will run under Windows 95 or Windows NT.*

These latest Visual C++ compiler releases incorporate many new and upgraded features. Some of the most important include support for the AT&T C++ 2.1 standard, precompiled headers, auto-inlining, and p-code (packed code).

The Microsoft Visual C++ compiler packages also provide tools for building Windows programs targeted for other platforms. Your code can even be leveraged for both Apple Macintosh and other RISC machines. The C++ compiler includes all the header files, libraries, and dialog and resource editors necessary to create a truly robust Windows application. Microsoft has also incorporated the resource editors for bitmaps, icons, cursors, menus, and dialog boxes directly into the integrated environment. And speaking of integration, new class wizards help you build OLE applications using the Microsoft Foundation Class (MFC) libraries in record time.

In this chapter you will learn about the various components of the C++ compiler, the system requirements, and recommendations for setting up the development environment. This chapter explains the Microsoft Visual C++ system and shows you how to fine-tune it to your particular needs.

Many of the subjects discussed in this chapter are dealt with in greater detail throughout the remainder of the book. For example, there are chapters on the MFC library, class wizards, OLE, and so on.

Recommended Hardware

This section provides hardware and software recommendations that will help you get the most out of the Microsoft Visual C++ compiler. Many of the suggestions are intended to improve overall system performance, while others are meant to make the product more enjoyable to use.

Minimum Hardware and Software Requirements

Microsoft's standard Visual C++ compiler package will operate on a wide range of Intel-based computers.

 NOTE: There are special versions of the Visual C++ compiler for the MIPS & DEC Alpha AXP and Macintosh systems.

The following is a list of Microsoft's minimum hardware and software requirements necessary to run the 32-bit version of the Microsoft Visual C++ compiler package:

- Microsoft Windows 95 or Windows NT 3.51 or later
- Microsoft Visual C++ 1.5 or later
- Intel 486 or greater
- 8MB of RAM
- 800 x 600 or greater resolution display
- 10MB free hard disk space
- Mouse or other pointing device
- InstallWizard is designed for a typical developer's computer, which means a Pentium® processor and 800 x 600 resolution or better. You can run InstallWizard on a 640 x 480 screen, but you may need to arrange the windows differently to see all the information.

Recommended Hardware and Software

Minimal hardware and software requirements are not always the optimal choice for ease of use, performance, and overall product enjoyment. We recommend the following system profile to optimize the development cycle of C and C++ programs:

- Pentium-based PC, running at 150 MHz or higher
- 20MB of RAM
- 1GB hard disk space

- Super VGA monitor
- One high-density floppy disk drive (3.5-inch)
- One CD-ROM drive (for online documentation)
- Microsoft IntelliPoint Mouse

You will want a fast microprocessor that can handle the size and complexity of advanced Windows applications. Having a lot of memory maximizes the overall performance of both Microsoft Visual C++ and the Windows environment. (You can also obtain these performance enhancements by having a large amount of free disk space.)

Two operating systems are emerging as the new standard for 32-bit PC-based computers: Windows 95 or its more robust cousin, Windows NT. Unless you specifically need to develop applications for MS-DOS or Windows 3.*x*, we recommend moving away from these platforms when developing new applications. If you have not upgraded to either Windows 95 or Windows NT, you should do so before installing your Microsoft C++ compiler package.

The improvements made to Windows 95 and Windows NT provide you with the features and performance necessary to create state-of-the-art Windows applications. As you develop these applications in a graphical environment, your eyes will appreciate Super VGA resolution monitors. Buy a monitor with as large a screen as possible.

A Typical Windows Installation

The Microsoft Visual C++ compiler package installs almost automatically. However, there are some questions that you will need immediate answers for. In this section we'll take a look at a typical installation for the 32-bit version of the compiler.

1. Run the SETUP.EXE program on your first Visual C++ diskette or CD-ROM, while operating under Windows 95 or Windows NT.

2. You will be given a choice of install options, such as Typical, Custom, Minimum, or CD-ROM. The amount of hard disk space you must have depends upon the option you chose. We recommend the Typical installation. It is also possible to set the hard drive and/or subdirectory in which the installation will take place under Step 3. You will be prompted for your Name, Organization, and Product ID; enter this information carefully.

3. At this point, files will be copied from your diskettes or CD-ROM to your hard disk. You can view the progress by watching the File Copy Process dialog box. This installation took over 20 minutes on a 200MHz Pentium machine using an 8x CD-ROM drive.

4. When all files have been installed, you will be prompted as to whether your configuration should be changed now or later. We recommend the first option: Make Changes Now and Backup Current Version.

5. You will receive a prompt to register environment variables. This is in the form of a checkbox, with the box already checked. At this time, accept the default: And Register the Environment Variables. By registering the environment variables, you will provide your compiler with important information about your system.

6. With the installation complete, choose Reboot. This will reboot your entire system to allow all changes to go into effect.

Directories

Table 1-1 shows a typical subdirectory group for the Visual C++ compiler installation made in the MSVC subdirectory.

You will also find several README files located in the MSDEV subdirectory. These files are used to provide the latest release (and bug) information for the compiler.

Documentation

Visual C++ online documentation consists of Quick Reference and Books Online. Quick Reference allows you to quickly look up information while you program. Books

Location	Purpose
BIN	Executable files and build tools needed to build 32-bit applications
HELP	Help files
INCLUDE	C++ run-time and header files
LIB	C++ run-time and Win32 SDK libraries
MFC	Microsoft Foundation Class (MFC) library files
OLE	Files for building OLE applications
PROJECTS	Subdirectory used to organize your development projects
TEMPLATES	Subdirectory used to organize object templates
SAMPLES	Sample programs

Table 1-1.   *Important Visual C++ Subdirectories*

Online is the documentation set for Visual C++ in online format. Every Quick Reference topic has a link to Books Online, where complete information is available.

Depending on which install option you choose, Visual C++ will set up Quick Reference files on your hard disk, while Books Online files may remain on the CD-ROM. (Note: Choose this install configuration if you need to conserve hard disk space.) You can customize where to set up files or where to get information, or go directly to Books Online for context-sensitive (F1) help. Topics covered include:

- How to use Books Online
- User's guides
- Microsoft Foundation Classes (MFCs)
- Programming with the Microsoft Foundation Class library
- Class library reference
- MFC samples
- MFC technical notes
- C/C++
- Programming techniques
- C language reference
- C++ language reference
- Run-time library reference
- I/O stream reference
- Preprocessor reference
- C/C++ samples
- Win32 Software Development Kit (SDK)
- API 32 functions
- Win32 programmer's reference
- Windows sockets
- OLE Software Development Kit (SDK)

The Development System

The Microsoft 32-bit Visual C++ compiler for Windows 95 and Windows NT incorporates new, fully integrated Windows development tools and a visual interface. For example, the debugging capabilities of Microsoft's original CodeView are now directly accessible from within the compiler's integrated debugger. The following sections list those stand-alone utilities that are now incorporated directly into the Microsoft Visual C++ compiler.

The New Integrated Debugger

Microsoft pulls the horsepower of its original CodeView debugger directly into the Visual C++ platform with its new integrated debugger. The debugger is accessed from the Debug menu. The integrated debugger allows you to execute programs in single steps, view and change variable contents, and even back out of code sections. You will find it a big help when programs compile but don't seem to perform as expected.

The New Integrated Resource Editors

These editors are accessed from the Resource menu. The resource editors allow you to design and create Windows resources, such as bitmaps, cursors, icons, menus, and dialog boxes. Resources allow you to create visually appealing user interfaces to your applications. In the next sections, we'll look at some specific information on four of the most popular resource editors.

The Dialog Box Editor

The Dialog Box editor is a slick graphical development tool that allows you to easily and quickly create professional-looking dialog boxes. The Dialog Box editor allows you to customize a dialog box's labels, framing, option and checkbox selections, text windows, and scroll bars.

The Dialog Box editor allows you to combine numerous controls into your custom dialog boxes. Controls combine a visual graphical representation of a feature with a predefined set of properties that you can customize. For example, checkboxes, radio buttons, and list boxes are all forms of Windows controls.

The Image Editors

The graphical image editors allow you to easily create custom bitmaps, icons, and cursors. A *bitmap* is a picture of something—for example, an exclamation point used in a warning message. An *icon* is a small color image used to represent an application when it has been minimized. Visual C++ even allows you to use an image editor to create custom cursors. For example, you could design a financial package with a cursor that looks like a dollar sign. Custom icons, cursors, and bitmaps can be saved with a .RC file extension and used in resource script files. You'll learn how these resources are used in Chapters 20 through 23.

The Binary Editor

The Binary editor allows you to edit a resource at the binary level in either hexadecimal or ASCII format. You can also use the Find command to search for either ASCII strings or hexadecimal bytes, and use regular expressions with the Find command to match a pattern. You should use the Binary editor only when you need to view or make minor changes to custom resources or resource types not supported by the Microsoft Developer Studio environment.

The String Editor

The String editor allows you to edit string tables. A *string table* is a Windows resource that contains a list of IDs, values, and captions for all the strings of your application. For example, the status bar prompts are located in the string table. An application can have only one string table. String tables make it easy to localize your application into different languages. If all strings are in a string table, you can localize the application by translating the strings (and other resources) without changing source code.

Additional Tools

Additional Visual C++ tools that are integrated into the compiler's package are located under the Tools menu. These include Spy++, MFC Tracer, Control Wizard, and the Test Container. You'll find the Spy++ utility a great help when working on 32-bit Windows applications.

Spy++

Spy++ is a utility that gives a graphical view of the system's processes, threads, windows, and windows messages.

MFC Tracer

MFC Tracer is a tool that allows the programmer to set the trace flags in AFX.INI. These flags are used to define the category of Trace messages that are sent from the MFC application to the debugging window. Tracer is thus a debugging tool. You'll want to use the MFC Tracer tool when you build MFC applications in Chapters 23 and 26.

Control Wizard

The Control Wizard tool allows developers using the MFC library to incorporate and modify custom controls. This tool is normally used in conjunction with applications being created with the ClassWizard (see Project Menu) for building applications via a dynamic template.

Test Container

The Test Container tool is an application designed by Microsoft that allows you to quickly test custom controls. Properties and features of the control can be altered while in the Test Container.

Outside the Integrated Environment

There are several tools located outside the integrated environment, too. Some tools, such as Spy++ and MFC Tracer, are available within and outside the compiler's IDE.

The Process Viewer

The Process Viewer allows you to quickly set and view all of the options necessary to track current processes, threads, and processor time-slicing. To start the Process Viewer, simply double-click on the Process Viewer icon in the Visual C++ group box.

The Process Viewer can help answer questions such as:

- How much memory does the program allocate at various points in its execution?
- How much memory is being paged out?
- Which processes and threads are using the most CPU time?
- How does the program run at different system priorities?
- What happens if a thread or process stops responding to DDE, OLE, or pipe I/O?
- What percentage of time is spent running API calls?

WinDiff

The WinDiff utility is also found in the Visual C++ group. This tool allows you to graphically compare and modify two files or two directories. All of the options within WinDiff operate much like their counterpart commands in the Windows 95 Explorer or Windows NT File Manager.

What's New

The new Developer Studio has added many new and improved features to make it easier than ever to develop world-class applications. New additions include the ability to host Visual J++ 1.1 and Visual InterDev, as well as Visual C++ 5 and MSDN.

Automation and Macros

With Visual Basic Scripts you can automate routine or repetitive tasks. While macro recording allows for quick and easy authoring, the Developer Studio lets you manipulate Studio components as objects, allowing you to automate tasks that include opening, editing, or closing documents, or sizing windows. You can also create integrated add-ins using Developer Studio's object model.

ClassView

The new improved ClassView now works with Java classes as well as C++ classes. You can create new classes using MFC, ATL, or your own classes. ClassView also now provides the ability to view and edit interfaces for COM objects implemented in MFC or ATL. You can also use folders to organize classes the way you want.

Customizable Toolbars and Menus

Developer Studio makes it easy to customize toolbars and menus to fit the way you work. For example, you can:

- Change a menu to a toolbar
- Add or delete menu commands or toolbar buttons
- Change a toolbar button into a menu command
- Clone a menu or toolbar button from one toolbar to another so it is always accessible
- Design new toolbars or menus
- Personalize an existing toolbar or menu
- Reassign a menu command, making it a toolbar button

Internet Connectivity

Viewing World Wide Web pages in Developer Studio is a snap with the all-new InfoViewer or your own registered web browser to view Microsoft on the Web. With a web address in the URL window, you can click the address to view the web page. This feature allows Visual Studio users assurance of the latest breaking news, documentation, fixes, and/or upgrades as they become available.

Project Workspaces and Files

The new Developer Studio's flexible project system makes it easy to have a workspace with different project types. For example, you can create a workspace containing a Visual InterDev project *and* a J++ applet.

 NOTE: Workspace files now have the extension .DSW (formerly .MDP). Project files now have the extension .DSP (formerly .MAK).

There are now two Build file types: internal (.DSP) and external (.MAK). All DSP files are created when you create a new project within the Developer Studio environment or when you convert a project from a previous version. (Note: DSP files are not compatible with NMAKE.) You can create an external MAK file, compatible with NMAKE, by clicking Export Makefile on the Project menu.

Projects can now include active documents, such as spreadsheets and Word document files. You can even edit them without leaving Visual Studio's integrated development environment.

When you start a new workspace, the Developer Studio creates a file by the name yourWorkspaceName.dsw, which has a new extension, .DSW. Workspace files no longer include data specific to your local computer. At this point you may:

- Add the workspace file to a previously defined source control project
- Copy a workspace from another computer or a network directory and open the workspace copy directly, without creating a new workspace file for your local computer
- Use resource editors
- Use the WizardBar with dialog boxes to hook up code to the visual elements of your program

Wizards

The new Microsoft Developer Studio incorporates many new wizards, including some for the new integrated Visual J++ and Visual InterDev packages (available if you have these packages installed). You can use these wizards to create files, controls, and new types of projects.

Important Compiler Features

The Visual C++ compiler package contains many useful enhancements, new features, and options. The following sections introduce you to these improvements and briefly explain their uses.

P-Code

P-code (short for "packed code") is geared toward optimizing code speed and size. P-code can significantly reduce a program's size and execution speed—by as much as 60 percent. Better yet, all of this is accomplished simply by turning on the specific compiler option. This means that any code written in C or C++ can be compiled either normally or with p-code.

This technology compiles an application's source code into "interpreted object code," which is a higher-level and more condensed representation of object code. The process is completed when a small interpreter module is linked into the application.

The most efficient use of this technology does require some expertise, however. Since the interpreter generates object code at run-time, p-code runs more slowly than native object code. With careful use of the #pragma directive, an application can generate p-code for space-critical functions, and switch back to generating native code for speed-critical functions.

The best candidates for p-code generation are those routines that deal with the user interface, and because many Windows applications spend 50 percent of their time handling the user interface, p-code provides the optimum performance characteristics.

Precompiled Headers and Types

Visual C++ places generic types, function prototypes, external references, and member function declarations in special files called *header* files. These contain many of the critical definitions needed by the multiple source files that are pulled together to create the executable version of your program. Portions of these header files are typically recompiled for every module that includes the header. Unfortunately, repeatedly compiling portions of code can slow down the compiler.

Visual C++ speeds up the compile process by allowing you to precompile your header files. While the concept of precompiled headers isn't new, the way that Microsoft has implemented the feature certainly is. Precompilation saves the state of an application's compilation to a certain point and represents the relationship that is set up between the source file and the precompiled header. It is possible to create more than one precompiled header file per source file.

One of the best applications of this technology involves the development cycle of an application that has frequent code changes but not frequent base class definitions. If the header file is precompiled, the compiler can concentrate its time on the changes in the source code. Precompiled headers also provide a compile-time boost for applications with headers that comprise large portions of code for a given module, as often happens with C++ programs.

The Visual C++ compiler assumes that the current state of the compiler environment is the same as when any precompiled headers were compiled. The compiler will issue a warning if it detects any inconsistencies. Such inconsistencies could arise from a change in memory models, a change in the state of defined constants, or the selection of different debugging or code-generation options.

Unlike many popular C++ compilers, the Microsoft C++ compiler does not restrict precompilation to header files. Since the process allows you to precompile a program up to a specified point, you can even precompile source code. This is extremely significant for C++ programs that contain most of their member function definitions in header files. In general, precompilation is reserved for those portions of your program that are considered stable; it is designed to minimize the time needed to compile the parts of your program under development.

The Microsoft Foundation Class (MFC) Library

Windows applications are easy to use but not as easy to develop. Many programmers get waylaid by having to master the use of hundreds of Windows API functions required to write Windows applications.

Microsoft's solution to this steep learning curve is the object-oriented Foundation Classes library. The reusable C++ classes are much easier to master and use. The Microsoft Foundation Class (MFC) library takes full advantage of the data abstraction offered by C++, and its use simplifies Windows programming. Beginning programmers can use the classes in a "cookbook" fashion, and experienced C++ programmers can extend the classes or integrate them into their own class hierarchy.

The MFC library features classes for managing Windows objects and offers a number of general-purpose classes that can be used in both MS-DOS and Windows applications. For example, there are classes for creating and managing files, strings, time, persistent storage, and exception handling.

In effect, the MFC library represents virtually every Windows API feature and includes sophisticated code that streamlines message processing, diagnostics, and other details that are a normal part of all Windows applications. This logical combination and enhancement of Windows API functions has ten key advantages:

- *The encapsulation of the Windows API is logical and complete*   The MFC library provides support for all of the frequently used Windows API functions, including windowing functions; messages; controls; menus; dialog boxes; graphics device interface (GDI) objects such as fonts, brushes, pens, and bitmaps; object linking; and the multiple document interface (MDI).

- *The MFC functions are easy to learn*   Microsoft has made a concerted effort to keep the names of the MFC functions and associated parameters as similar as possible to their Windows API parent classes. This minimizes the confusion for experienced Windows programmers who want to take advantage of the simplified MFC platform. It also makes it very easy for a beginning Windows programmer to grow into the superset of Windows API functions when he or she is ready or when the application requires it.

- *The C++ code is more efficient*   An application will consume only a little extra RAM when using the classes in the MFC library compiled under the small memory model. The execution speed of an MFC application is almost identical to that of the same application written in C using the standard Windows API.

- *The MFC library offers automatic message handling*   The MFC library eliminates one frequent source of programming errors, the Windows API message loop. The MFC classes are designed to automatically handle every one of the windows messages. Instead of using the standard switch-case statements, each window message is mapped directly to a member function, which takes the appropriate action.

- *The MFC library allows self-diagnostics*   Incorporated into the MFC library is the ability to perform self-diagnostics. This means that you can dump information about various objects to a file and validate an object's member variables, all in an easily understood format.

- *The MFC library incorporates a robust architecture*   Anticipating the much-needed ANSI C throw/catch standard, the MFC library already incorporates an extensive exception-handling architecture. This allows an MFC object to eloquently recover from standard error conditions such as "out of memory" errors, invalid option selection, and file or resource loading problems. Every component of the architecture is upward compatible with the proposed ANSI C recommendations.

- *The MFC library offers dynamic object typing* This extremely powerful feature delays the typing of a dynamically allocated object until run-time. This allows you to manipulate an object without having to worry about its underlying data type. Because information about the object type is returned at run-time, the programmer is freed from one additional level of detail.

- *The MFC library can harmoniously coexist with C-based Windows applications* The most important feature of the MFC library is its ability to coexist with C-based Windows applications that use the Windows API. Programmers can use a combination of MFC classes and Windows API calls within the same program. This allows an MFC application to easily evolve into true C++ object-oriented code as experience or demand requires. This transparent environment is possible because of the common naming conventions between the two architectures. This means that MFC headers, types, and global definitions do not conflict with Windows API names. Transparent memory management is another key component to this successful relationship.

- *The MFC library can be used with MS-DOS* The MFC library was designed specifically for developing Windows applications. However, many of the classes provide frequently needed objects used for file I/O and string manipulation. For this reason, these general-purpose classes can be used by both Windows and MS-DOS developers.

- *The MFC library and wizards* The Class and Control Wizards only create code compatible with the MFC. These dynamic program developers are a must when developing OLE applications.

Function Inlining

The Microsoft Visual C++ compiler supports complete function inlining. This means that functions of any type or combination of instructions can be expanded inline. Many popular C++ compilers restrict inlining to certain types of statements or expressions—for example, the inline option would be ignored by any function that contains a switch, while, or for statement. The Visual C++ compiler allows you to inline your most speed-critical routines (including seldom-used class member functions or constructors) without restricting their content. This option is set from the Project menu by selecting Settings..., then the C/C++ folder, and finally Optimizations from the Category list.

Compiler Options

Microsoft Visual C++ compilers discussed in the book are global optimizing compilers that allow you to take advantage of several speed or code size options for every type of program development. In this section we will discuss those options directly related to the 32-bit version 4.0 Microsoft C++ compiler. If you are using the 16- and/or 32-bit version 2.0 compiler, your options will be similar, but located under different tabs.

The following compiler options allow you to optimize your code for executable size, speed, or build time. If you do not see an appreciable performance boost, it is possible that your test application does not contain enough code. All options are set from the Build menu by selecting the Settings menu item.

General

From the General tab you can specify the use, or nonuse, of the MFC library. Output directories can also be given for intermediate and final C/C++ compiled files.

Debug

From the Debug tab, the location of the executable file can be specified along with the working directory, optional program arguments, and a remote executable path name and filename. Furthermore, by using the Category list, additional dynamic link libraries (DLLs) can be specified.

Custom Build

From the Custom Build tab you can specify custom tools for use in building projects. This includes tools to run on the output file of the project configuration.

C/C++

The C/C++ tab allows you to select from the following categories: General, C++ Language, Code Generation, Customization, Listing Files, Optimizations, Precompiled Headers, and Preprocessor.

General

The General category permits you to set the warning level, specify debug information, set compiler optimizations, give preprocessor definitions, and list project options.

C++ Language

The C++ Language category lets you specify the representation method, set exception handling, set run-time type information, set constructions displacements, and list project options.

Code Generation

The Code Generation category allows you to target the microprocessor (80386 to Pentium), give calling convention, specify run-time library, note structure member alignment, and list project options.

Customization

The Customization category allows the following items to be enabled or disabled:

- Language extensions
- Function-level linking
- Duplicate strings
- Minimal rebuild
- Incremental compilation
- Banner and information message suppression

Listing Files

The Listing Files category allows the generation of browse information. Additionally, the browse file destination can be set. Local variables can be allowed in the browse file. The file types can also be optionally set. Project options are listed.

Optimizations

The Optimizations category allows various code optimizations to be set, such as speed, size, and so on. Inline function expansion can also be given. Project options are listed.

Precompiled Headers

The Precompiled Headers category allows the use of precompiled header files. These are files with PCH extensions. Precompiled header files speed the compile and link process, but should be eliminated from your directory upon project completion because of their large size. Project options are listed.

Preprocessor

The Preprocessor category allows preprocessor definitions to be given. It is also possible to include additional directories and ignore standard paths. Project options are listed.

Link

The Link tab allows you to select from the following categories: General, Customization, Debug, Input, and Output.

General

From the General category the name of the file and extension can be specified. Most frequently, the extension will be .EXE. However, you'll learn how to develop applications with DLL and SCR file extensions in this text. Object/library modules can also be entered. These are very important for multimedia applications, where specific libraries are not assumed. The following items can also be included:

- Debug information
- Incremental linking

- Profiling
- Ignoring default libraries
- Map file generation

Customization

The Customization category allows the following items to be included:

- Incremental linking
- Program database
- Output filename
- Process message printing
- Startup banner

Debug

The Debug category allows the generation of a map file and debug information in various formats.

Input

The Input category allows the specification of object/library modules. Additionally, symbol references and MS-DOS stub filenames are given.

Output

The Output category allows the base address, entry-point, stack allocation, and version information for the project to be set.

Resources

The Resource tab permits the resource file (usually a file with a .RES extension) to be given additional features including the language, resource include directories, and preprocessor definitions.

OLE Types

The OLE Types tab permits the output filename, the output header filename, preprocessor definitions, and startup banner to be specified.

Browse Info

The Browse Info tab allows the Browse Info filename to be specified. Additionally, the Browse Info file and startup banner can be checked.

Chapter 2

A Quick Start Using the IDE

The Microsoft Visual C++ IDE (integrated development environment) allows you to easily create, open, view, edit, save, compile, and debug all of your C and C++ applications. As an integral part of the Microsoft Development Studio, the C/C++ environment operates as a cohesive component within the entire Microsoft family of languages, including Visual Basic and Visual J++. The advantage of this language development suite is the ease of learning and use provided by such a cohesive set of development features and tools. To a very large degree, except for the specific language's syntax, once you have learned one environment's features—for example, Visual C++—you automatically know how to use the others! With Microsoft Development Studio's language integration, you can easily develop and combine multilanguage source files into one program.

Like all of the Development Studio components, the Visual C++ IDE contains options for fine-tuning your work environment according to your personal preferences and to comply with application-specific hardware requirements. Many of the features discussed in the next sections are demonstrated in Chapter 3.

Starting the Visual C++ IDE

Launching the Visual C++ IDE is easy. If you are using a mouse, you can double-click on the Visual C++ icon, which is found in the Microsoft Visual C++ group. Figure 2-1 shows the initial screen for the Visual C++ IDE.

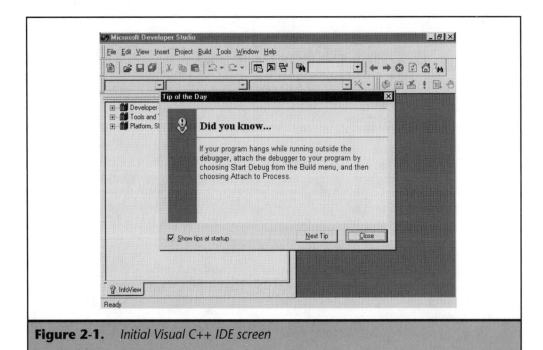

Figure 2-1.   *Initial Visual C++ IDE screen*

Accessing Context-Sensitive Help

Help for each Visual C++ IDE feature is easily accessed because all of the compiler's documentation is online. Tapping into this valuable resource is as simple as placing the cursor on the feature in question and pressing F1.

However, context-sensitive help is not restricted to Visual C++ IDE features. If you place the cursor on a C/C++ language construct and press F1, the help utility will automatically display a description of the construct's syntax, an explanation of its use, and often a clarifying, executable example.

This chapter is designed to give you a broad overview of each Visual C++ IDE option. Don't become discouraged by the number of features and options available. You can use the default settings of many of the Visual C++ IDE's capabilities, which make it easy to get an application up and running.

As your experience grows and your application requirements increase in complexity, you will gradually gain hands-on experience with the more sophisticated capabilities of this powerful environment. While you are reading this chapter, take a pencil and check those Visual C++ IDE features that sound interesting. When the need arises to use one of these features, you can easily refer back to this section for an explanation of how to use the option.

Understanding Menus

Before beginning a discussion of each Visual C++ IDE feature, let us examine a few traits that all menu items have in common. For example, there are two ways to access menu items. The most common approach is to place the mouse pointer over the preferred option and click the left mouse button. The second approach is to use the underscored hot key. For example, you can access the File menu directly from the keyboard by simultaneously pressing the ALT key and the letter F.

Menu items can be selected using the same sequences just described, and there is often one additional way to select them. You can directly activate some menu items from anywhere within the integrated environment by using their specific hot-key combinations. If a menu item has this capability, the option's specific hot-key combination is displayed to the right of the menu item on the menu. For example, the first option listed on the File menu is New.... This option can be invoked immediately simply by pressing CTRL-N, without having to first select the File menu.

Additional comments concerning menus: First, if a menu item is grayed, the integrated environment is alerting you to the fact that that particular option is currently unavailable. This means that the integrated environment is lacking some necessary prerequisite for that particular option to be valid. For example, the File menu's Save option will be grayed if the edit window is empty. The option knows that you cannot save something that does not exist, and it indicates this by deactivating and graying the Save command.

Second, any menu item followed by three periods (...) indicates an option that, when selected, will automatically display a dialog box or a submenu. For example, the File menu's Open... command, when selected, causes the Open dialog box to appear.

Finally, you can activate some menu items by clicking on their associated buttons on the toolbars, which are below the main menu bar.

Let's look at the interesting IDE features that are usually available via a menu choice.

Docking or Floating a Toolbar

You can make the Standard toolbar (found just under the Visual C++ title bar), or any other toolbar docked or floating. In *docked* mode, a toolbar is fixed to any of the four borders of the application window. You cannot modify the size of a toolbar when it is docked.

In *floating* mode, a toolbar has a thin title bar and can appear anywhere on your screen. A floating toolbar is always on top of all other windows. You can modify the size or position of a toolbar when it is floating.

To change a docked toolbar into a floating toolbar:

- Click (keep left mouse button depressed) on the title bar or on a blank area in the toolbar.

- Drag the toolbar away from the dock to any position you desire.

To dock a floating toolbar:

- Click (keep left mouse button depressed) on the title bar or on a blank area in the toolbar.

- Drag the toolbar to any of the four borders in the application window.

To position a floating toolbar over a docked toolbar:

- Click (keep left mouse button depressed) on the title bar or on a blank area in the toolbar.

- Depress the CTRL key, and drag the toolbar over any docking area within the application window.

The File Menu

The Visual C++ IDE File menu localizes the standard set of file manipulation commands common to many Windows applications. Figure 2-2 shows the command options available from the File menu.

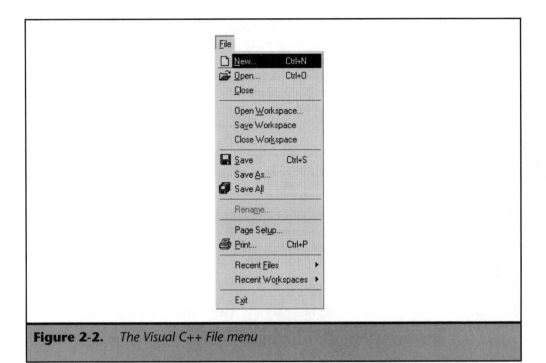

Figure 2-2.   *The Visual C++ File menu*

New...

The New... menu item opens a new edit dialog box window. You usually begin any new application at this point. The IDE automatically titles and numbers each window you open. Numbering begins at 1, so your first window title will always be *xxx*1, your second window title *xxx*2, and so on. The *xxx* is a label identifying the type of file you are working with (code, project, resource, bitmap, binary, icon, or cursor).

If you have windows titled *xxx*1 through *xxx*6 open and decide to close the one titled *xxx*2, the next time you invoke the New... option, that title (in this case, *xxx*2) will not be reused. Windows automatically supplies the next higher number (for this example, *xxx*7).

The quickest way to open a new edit dialog box is to click on the leftmost button on the toolbar. This button has a picture of a file on it. You can invoke the New... option directly by clicking on this control.

Open...

Unlike New..., which opens an edit dialog box window for a previously nonexistent file, the Open... menu item opens a dialog box that requests information on a previously saved file. This dialog box is the standard Open File dialog box, which displays the default drive, path, and file search parameters, and allows you to select your own.

The dialog box has a timesaving feature that automatically remembers your preferences and makes them the defaults each time you use the Open... command. Attempting to open an already opened file automatically invokes an audible alert and warning message. This useful reminder prevents you from accidentally opening two or more copies of the same file, editing only one of them, and then resaving the nonupdated version!

The second button from the left on the toolbar, which has a picture of a folder with an open arrow on it, can be used to invoke the Open... option directly.

Close

The Close menu item is used to close an open file. If you have multiple files opened, this command will close the *active* or *selected* window. You can tell which window is active by looking at the window's border. Active or selected windows have the keyboard and mouse focus (meaning the window actually receives keyboard and mouse input) and are displayed with your system's selected color preferences. These preferences usually include colored title bars and darker window borders. Inactive windows usually have grayed title bars and window borders.

If you accidentally attempt to close an unsaved file, don't worry. The integrated environment automatically protects you from this potentially devastating scenario by warning you that the file has not been previously saved, and it asks you if you want to save the file at this point.

Save

The Save menu item saves the contents of the currently selected or active window to the file specified. You can distinguish the previously saved contents of a window from the unsaved contents of a window by simply checking the window's title bar. If you see a default title, such as *xxx*1, you will know that the window's contents have never been given a valid filename and saved. Saving a previously unsaved file will automatically invoke the Save As dialog box.

You can also use the Save button on the toolbar. The third from the left, this button has the image of a floppy disk on it. If a file was opened in read-only mode (see the description of the Edit | Properties command), the control's image will be grayed, indicating that the option is currently unavailable.

Save As...

The Save As... menu item allows you to save a copy of the active window's contents under a new name. If you are wondering why you might choose this option, here's a possible scenario. You have just finished a project. You have a working program. However, you would like to try a few changes. For the sake of security, you do not want to tweak the current version. By choosing the Save As... option, you can copy the file's contents under a new name, and then you can tweak the duplicate. Should disaster ensue, you can always go back to your original file.

Save All

If you have never written a C, C++, Windows 95, or Windows NT application, you will be surprised at the actual number of files involved in creating a project's executable file. The problem with the Save option is that it only saves the active window's contents. The Save All menu item saves every window's contents. If any window contains previously unsaved text, the Save All command will automatically invoke the Save As dialog box, prompting you for a valid filename for each window.

Rename

The Rename command takes the file in the active edit window and allows you to give it a new name. For example, you may have imported an old C source file, modified it to bring it inline with C++ language features, and now wish to save it with a .CPP file extension, instead of a .C extension.

Page Setup...

The most frequent use for the Page Setup... menu item is to document and format your hard copies. The Page Setup dialog box allows you to select a header and footer for each printed page, and you can use it to set the top, bottom, left, and right print margins.

Table 2-1 lists the formatting codes available for selecting the type of header and footer.

Print...

Obtaining a hard copy of the active window's contents is as simple as selecting the Print... menu item. The Print dialog box provides you with several options. First, you can choose between printing the entire window's contents or printing only selected text by clicking on the appropriate radio button. You can also select which printer to use and configure the selected printer by choosing the Setup option.

If you wish to print only a portion of a window's contents, you must first select the desired text. Selecting text is as simple as placing the mouse pointer on the first character in the text you want to print and holding the left mouse button down while you drag the mouse to the right and/or down through the text. This causes the selected text to be displayed in reverse video. When text is selected, the Print dialog box will show the Print Range Selection radio button in normal type (not grayed), indicating the option's availability.

Formatting Code	Associated Use
&c	Center text
&d	Add current system date
&f	Use the file's name
&l	Left-justify text
&p	Add page numbers
&r	Right-justify text
&t	Add current system time

Table 2-1. *Page Setup Formatting Codes*

Recent Files List

Right below the Print... menu item is a list of the most recently edited files. The nice feature about such lists (often called *history lists*) is that they are context sensitive. History lists save you time by remembering the last several items you have selected for a particular option. For this menu, the items remembered are previously opened files. The first time you use the Visual C++ IDE, this portion of the File menu is empty, because there is no history of opened files.

Recent Workspaces List

The recent project list is immediately below the recent file list on the menu. This history list is similar to the recent file list, except that the recent project list contains only project files. To open any file, in either list, double-click the left mouse button on the selected item.

Exit

The Exit menu item allows you to quit the Visual C++ IDE. Do not worry if you have forgotten to save a window's contents before selecting Exit. The IDE will automatically display a warning message for each window containing unsaved text, allowing you to save the information before exiting.

The Edit Menu

Edit menu items allow you to quickly edit or search through an active window's contents in much the same way you would with any standard word processor. Figure 2-3 shows the Visual C++ IDE Edit menu with the Advanced pop-up menu.

Undo

The Undo menu item allows you to reverse the most recent editing change you made. You can also use the Undo option from the toolbar. The Undo option is the left-pointing arrow on the toolbar. This is the seventh icon from the left on our system.

Redo

The Redo menu item allows you to reverse the action of the last Undo. Use this option to reinstate a valid editing change that you thought was an incorrect change. The Redo option can also be used from the toolbar. On the toolbar, the Redo option is the right-pointing arrow. This is the eighth icon from the left on our system.

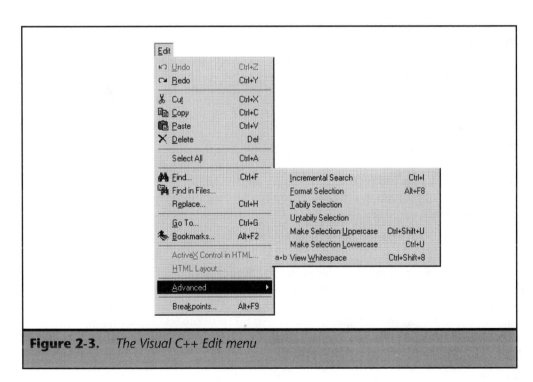

Figure 2-3.   *The Visual C++ Edit menu*

Cut

The Cut menu item copies the selected text, in the active window, to the Clipboard and then deletes it from the active window. Selecting text is as simple as placing the mouse pointer on the first character in the text you want to cut and holding the left mouse button down while you drag the mouse to the right and/or down through the text. This causes the selected text to be displayed in reverse video.

The Cut command is often used in conjunction with the Paste command to move text from one location to another. When the cut text is placed on the Clipboard, all previous Clipboard contents are destroyed.

The Cut option can also be used from the toolbar. On the toolbar, the Cut option is the scissors icon. This is the fourth icon from the left on our system.

Copy

Like Cut, the Copy menu item places the selected text on the Clipboard. However, unlike Cut, Copy leaves the original selected text in place. A good use for this option would be to reproduce intricate code sequences or clarifying comments needed in multiple source files.

The Copy command is often used in conjunction with the Paste command to copy text from one location to another. When the copied text is placed on the Clipboard, all previous Clipboard contents are destroyed.

The Copy option can also be used from the toolbar. On the toolbar, the Copy option is the dual-page icon. This is the fifth icon from the left on our system.

Paste

The Paste menu item is used to insert the contents of the Clipboard at the current cursor location. The Clipboard can only paste information that has been previously placed on the Clipboard by the Cut or Copy command.

The Paste option can also be used from the toolbar. On the toolbar, the Paste option is the clipboard-page icon. This is the sixth icon from the left on our system.

Delete

The Delete menu item deletes selected text without copying the information to the Clipboard. Selecting text is as simple as placing the mouse pointer on the first character in the text you want to delete and holding the left mouse button down while you drag the mouse to the right and/or down through the text. This causes the selected text to be displayed in reverse video.

Even though deleted text is not copied to the Clipboard, you can still undo a Delete by choosing the Edit | Undo command.

Select All

The Select All menu item is used to select the entire contents of the active window for cutting, copying, or deleting.

Find...

The Find... menu item works very much like a standard word processor's search option. However, since the C/C++ language is case sensitive, the Find... command can be tailored to search for case-sensitive, case-insensitive, and whole-word-only matches. The Find dialog box also allows you to set the direction for the search (up or down) from the current cursor location.

One very useful and sophisticated Find... option that is not usually associated with any word processor's search capabilities is the Regular Expression option. Table 2-2 lists and describes the Regular Expression search pattern symbols that can be used in the Find What: window.

Find in Files...

Find in Files... is one of the most valuable tools you'll ever use once you understand its capabilities. While identical in horsepower to Find..., Find in Files... adds one special advantage: the search has multiple-file scope! You may ask yourself, "Why would I ever need such a feature?" Here's the answer: If you are learning a new C/C++ language feature, use this option to scan for all programs containing it. If you are modifying a program, use Find in Files... to make certain you have caught all occurrences of the older syntax. If you are working on a large project, use Find in Files... to locate all of the code authored by a particular group or programmer. And remember, Find in Files... isn't just capable of searching one subdirectory or one hard drive; it can scan an entire network, intranet, or the Internet, tracking down any name, string, keyword, method, and much more.

Replace...

The Replace... menu item invokes the Replace dialog box, which allows you to replace text. Simply type in the string to search for, then type in the replacement string, and finally select from several matching criteria. Matching options include whole words only, case-sensitive or case-insensitive matches, and Regular Expressions (see the previous explanation).

Be careful when selecting the Replace All option, because this can have disastrous results. There are two things to remember when doing a replace: first, save the file

Pattern	Meaning
*	Substitutes for any number of characters
	Example: Data*1
	Finds: Data1, DataIn1, DataOut1
.	Substitutes for a single character
	Example: Data.
	Finds: Data1, Data2 but not DataIn1
^	Starts a search at the beginning of a line for the string
	Example: ^do
	Finds: each line beginning with "do"
+	Substitutes for any number of characters preceding the string
	Example: +value
	Finds: i_value, fvalue, lng_value
$	Starts a search at the end of each line for the string
	Example: some_var_n);$
	Finds: each line ending with "some_var_n);"
[ ]	Starts a search of the given character subset
	Example: Data[A..Z]
	Finds: DataA not Data1
	Example: Data[1248]
	Finds: Data2 not Data3
\	Starts a search for strings where the preceding character must be exactly matched
	Example: Data[A..Zi\0..9]
	Finds: DataAi1 not DataDo3
\{\}	Starts a search for any sequence of characters placed between the braces
	Example: \{no\}*_answer
	Finds: answer, no_answer, nono_answer, nonono_answer

Table 2-2. *Regular Expression Search String Patterns*

before you invoke the command; second, if something goes wrong with the replace, remember that you can always use the Undo option.

Go To...

You can quickly move the cursor to a specified location within an active edit window with the Go To... menu item. Choosing this option invokes a Line dialog box that allows you to enter the line number for the line of code you wish to jump to. Entering a line number greater than the actual number of source code lines available causes the command to place the cursor at the bottom of the window's text file.

Bookmarks...

The Bookmarks... option allows you to set bookmarks to mark frequently accessed lines in your source file. Once a bookmark is set, you can use menu or keyboard commands to move to it. You can remove a bookmark when you no longer need it. You can use both named and unnamed bookmarks. Named bookmarks are saved between editing sessions. Once you create a named bookmark, you can jump to that location whether or not the file is open. Named bookmarks store both the line number and the column number of the location of the cursor when the bookmark was created. This location is adjusted whenever you edit the file. Even if you delete the characters around the bookmark, the bookmark remains in the correct location.

ActiveX Control in HTML... and HTML Layout...

These two options allow you to edit either an embedded HTML ActiveX control or the HTML layout itself.

Advanced

The Advanced options allow you to fine-tune your source code. Useful options include the removal of tab stops, viewing of whitespace, and incremental searches.

Breakpoints...

The Breakpoints... option allows you to set breakpoints at specific locations, on selected data items, or on messages.

View Menu

The View menu contains commands that enable you to change your view of the Query Designer (see Figure 2-4).

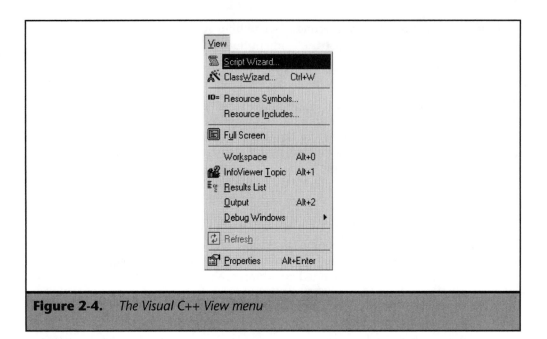

Figure 2-4. *The Visual C++ View menu*

Script Wizard...

An easy way to get started with scripting is by using an HTML authoring tool like Microsoft ActiveX Control Pad. The ActiveX Control Pad is freely available for downloading from the authoring tools section in the Microsoft Site Builder Workshop, accessible through www.microsoft.com. You use the Script Wizard... option to begin the design of a VBScript or JavaScript. Once the Script Wizard is launched, you first select the Default Script Language, next you Select an Event, Load, and then Insert Event.

ClassWizard...

The Microsoft C++ ClassWizard makes it easier for you to do repetitive tasks such as creating new classes, defining message handlers, overriding MFC virtual functions, and gathering data from controls in a dialog box, form view, or record view. One very important note: The ClassWizard only works with applications that use MFC classes, unlike ClassView and WizardBar, which work with MFC, ATL, or your own classes. Also, ClassView does not recognize classes unless they are registered in the ClassView database file. These are files with a CLW file extension. With ClassWizard, you can:

- Attach Automation methods and properties when creating a new class
- Author new classes from many of the main framework base classes that handle Windows messages and recordsets

■ Author new message-handling member functions

■ Declare member variables that automatically initialize, gather, and validate data entered into dialog boxes or form views

■ Delete message-handling member functions

■ Map messages to functions associated with windows, dialog boxes, controls, menu items, and accelerators

■ See which messages have message handlers already defined and jump to the handler program code

■ Work with existing classes and type libraries

Resource Symbols... and Resource Includes...

You will quickly discover that as your programs grow in size and sophistication, so will the number of resources and symbols. This makes tracking an ever-increasing number of symbols scattered throughout several files difficult. The Resource Symbols... and Resource Includes... options simplify symbol management by offering a central tool through which you can:

■ Modify the name and value of a symbol that is not in use

■ Define new symbols

■ Remove a symbol if it is not being used

■ Quickly locate the appropriate resource editor where the symbol is being used

■ Scan existing symbol definitions to see the value of each symbol, a list of symbols being used, and the resources assigned to each symbol

Full Screen

If you are like most programmers, when it comes to intense code authoring and/or editing, you like to see as much code at one time as possible. The Full Screen option is ideal for these situations, allowing you to zoom your edit window (or any other window, e.g., help screens) for maximum viewing.

Workspace

Imagine a desktop development environment. You have editors, compilers, manuals, Post-Its, textbooks, phone messages, and e-mail scattered across your desk and monitor, all of it relating to the project at hand. Try to think of the Workspace as an electronic secretary trying to organize some of this information. The Workspace option opens the Workspace view (usually the upper-left portion of your screen), giving you instant access to the current classes, files, resources, and reference manuals most recently accessed. Switching layouts is as simple as clicking on the tabs found at the bottom of the Workspace view.

InfoViewer Topic

Anytime you want to instantly flip back to the last help topic or sample program you were viewing, choose the InfoViewer Topic command, or even better, press ALT-1.

Results List

You use the Results List command to view query results. This option opens up a tabbed window allowing you to view search, lookup, see also, and history lists.

Output

The Output menu item brings the Output window to the foreground. The Output window contains progress reports on build, compile, and link processes, and it displays any generated warning or error messages.

Debug Windows

Choosing this option pops up a menu providing access to various integrated debugger options, including watch window, register window, call stack, memory, variables, and disassembly code.

Refresh

You use Refresh to repaint and update the currently active view pane in a similar manner to how pressing F5 in the Windows Explorer repaints and updates its contents.

Properties

If applicable, the Properties command displays current file statistics such as date created, file size, file type, editing characteristics, and much more depending on the file's type.

Insert Menu

The Insert menu accesses a list of commands for including new files, resources, or objects into your workspace (see Figure 2-5).

New Class...

When you select this option, the IDE creates a new MFC, ATL, or generic class. The New Class dialog appears in which you define the class name and the base class. It creates a header file and an implementation file for the class.

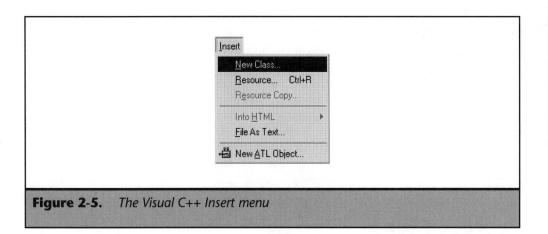

Figure 2-5.   *The Visual C++ Insert menu*

Resource...

This option allows you to add one of several resources to your workspace, including accelerator, bitmap, cursor, dialog, icon, menu, string table, toolbar, and version identifier.

Resource Copy...

Visual C++ allows you to copy resources while changing the resource's language, its property condition, or both. When you create or copy a resource with a different language or condition, this is displayed after the symbol name in the Project window. The Language identifies the language used for text in the resource. The Property Condition is a symbol that identifies a condition under which this copy of the resource is used. (Note: You can also copy from a template.)

Into HTML

The Into HTML option allows you to insert resources to enhance a web page.

File As Text...

Usually used to add source code, the File As Text... option first asks you to name the new file, and launches a clean edit window ready for text input.

New ATL Object...

The New ATL Object... allows you to add an Active Template Library class to your worskspace. ATL objects are a set of template-based C++ classes that allow you to easily create small, fast component object model (COM) objects. They provide special support for key COM features, including stock implementations of IUnknown, IClassFactory, IClassFactory2, and IDispatch; dual interfaces; standard COM enumerator interfaces; connection points; tear-off interfaces; and ActiveX controls. ATL code can be used to create single-threaded objects, apartment-model objects, free-threaded model objects, or both free-threaded and apartment-model objects.

Project Menu

The Project menu commands enable you to manage all of your open projects.

NOTE: The Data Connection command is added to the Add To Project submenu when Microsoft Visual Database Tools is active—Data Connection launches the Select Data Source dialog box so that you can add a data connection to your current database project—see Figure 2-6.

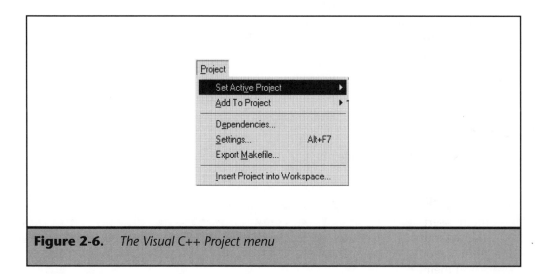

Figure 2-6. *The Visual C++ Project menu*

Set Active Project

In advanced program development there comes a time where it is best to break a large project down into subprojects. A *subproject* establishes a dependency of one project on another in a hierarchical fashion. Subprojects are used in Visual C++ projects, for example, when a project builds an executable program that depends on a static library. If the static library is a subproject of the project that builds the executable program, then the library will be updated before the executable program is built. The Set Active Project determines which project or subproject is currently active.

Add To Project

You use this option whenever you wish to add a file to a project. The file is added to a specified project and to all project configurations in that project. For instance, if you have a project named myFirstProj, with Debug and Release configurations, and an additional project configuration named myFinalProj based on the Release configuration, adding a file adds it to all those project configurations. If you add files from directories above the project workspace directory, Microsoft Developer Studio uses absolute paths in the filenames for those files in the project's .DSP file. Because of the absolute paths, it is difficult to share the project (DSP) file.

Dependencies...

In advanced program design, where a project is made up of several subprojects, you use the Dependencies... command to view this hierarchical relationship.

Settings...

The Settings... command opens up a very sophisticated dialog box allowing you to totally define your project's configuration settings, from classes used, to C/C++ compiler options, to link options, browse, OLE types, resources, browse settings, and build options.

Export Makefile...

The Export Makefile... option stores all the information required to build the project and can be used from the command line. Makefiles define the same project build settings you set in the Developer Studio environment.

Insert Project into Workspace...

This option inserts a project into your workspace. However, this might be slightly confusing without the following comparison between what a project is and how it differs from a workspace. A *project workspace* is the area defined that contains your projects and their configurations. A *project* is defined as a configuration and a group of files that produce a program or final binary file(s). On the other hand, a workspace can contain multiple projects, even projects of different types (for instance, Microsoft Visual C++ and Microsoft Visual J++ projects).

Build Menu

The options in the Build menu provide access to the IDE features that are involved in actual code generation, debugging, and running your program (see Figure 2-7).

Compile

Choosing this option instructs the IDE to compile the active window's contents. Compiling in this sense is asking the environment to check the syntax of the active file, for example C or C++ source code.

Build

Typical C/C++ programs are comprised of many files. Some of these files may be supplied by the compiler, the operating system, the programmer, or even third-party vendors. It can get even more complicated if the project's files are created by several programming teams. Because there can be so many files, and because the compile process can take a very long time, the Build menu item becomes an extremely useful tool. Build examines all of the files in the project and then compiles and links only those dependent files displaying dates and times more recent than the project's executable file.

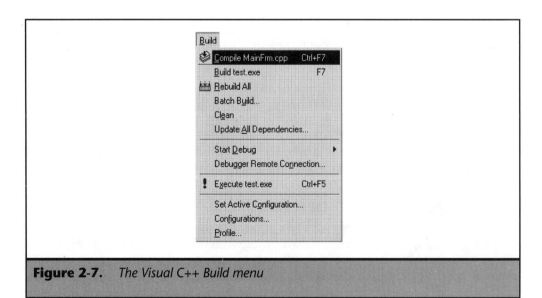

Figure 2-7. *The Visual C++ Build menu*

One decision you must make when selecting Build is whether the resulting file is to include debugging information (Debug mode) or not (Release mode). These modes are selected from the Project | Targets... menu item. Once you have a program up and running, you should usually choose a Build without the Debug option, since inclusion of the information makes the resulting executable file unnecessarily large.

If the Build process detects any syntax errors, either nonfatal warnings or fatal errors, these are displayed in the Output window. Use the Next Error or Previous Error menu items to search forward or backwards through this list.

If you have the toolbar visible, you can use the sixth button from the right to invoke Build. This button has a picture that looks like a bucket with two dark-colored, downward-pointing arrows on it.

Rebuild

The only difference between Build and Rebuild All is that Rebuild All ignores the dates of all of a project's files and painstakingly compiles and links all of them.

Imagine the following scenario. Your company, for the sake of economy, has decided to go without any systems maintenance personnel. This decision, coupled with the seasonal time change, system down time, and so on, results in your discovery that the systems on your network all have different system clock settings. Because of this, newly created files are being stamped with the previous day's date! Choosing the Build option in this case could leave these current, updated files out of the final executable file. However, by choosing Rebuild All, you avoid any date/time stamp checks, creating an executable file that truly reflects the current state of all included files.

If the Rebuild All process detects any syntax errors, either nonfatal warnings or fatal errors, these are displayed in the Output window. Use the Next Error or Previous Error menu items to search forward or backwards through this list.

If you have the toolbar visible, you can use the fifth button from the right to invoke Rebuild All. This button has a picture that looks like a bucket with three light-colored, downward-pointing arrows on it.

Batch Build...

This option is similar to the Build menu item except that it builds multiple project targets.

Clean

With the Clean command you can easily remove all files from the intermediate directories in any project configuration in your project workspace. Removing the files forces the development environment to build these files if you subsequently click the Build command.

Update All Dependencies...

Choosing this option instructs the IDE to read the compiler-generated dependencies and to scan non C/C++ source files for dependencies. Therefore, the dependency information for C/C++ files will not reflect any changes made since the last build.

Start Debug

Unlike a full-speed program execution, this option instructs the IDE to begin executing your program line by line, or up to any set breakpoint.

Debugger Remote Connection...

After you have configured a connection on both ends, you can begin remote debugging by choosing this option.

Execute

Once you have built your project with 0 errors, the Execute command allows you to run the program full speed.

Set Active Configuration...

With large projects being combinations of many subprojects, you need to instruct the Build or Rebuild command as to which project's executable needs creation. The Set Active Configuration... command performs this task.

Configurations...

The Configurations... option allows you to add or remove configurations from the active build cycle. For example, you may have begun with only a debug configuration and now wish to add a release version.

Profile...

This option is only available under the Professional and Enterprise Editions. Before using the profiler, you must build the current project with profiling enabled. If you want to perform function profiling only in the current project, you only need to enable profiling for the linker. If you want to do line profiling, you also need to include debugging information.

You use the Profiler to examine the run-time behavior of your programs. The Profiler allows you to determine which sections of your code are working efficiently by producing information showing areas of code that are not being executed or that are taking a long time to execute.

Tools Menu

The Tools menu accesses commands that enable you to work with your query. The Tools menu commands as described next apply to the Query Designer (see Figure 2-8).

Source Browser...

You use this option to browse your information files. You can instruct the compiler to create a .SBR file for each object file (.OBJ) it compiles. When you build or update your browse information file, all SBR files for your project must be available on disk. To create a .SBR file with all possible information, specify Generate Browse Info in the Project Settings dialog box (or /FR). To create a .SBR file that doesn't contain local symbols, specify Generate Browse Info, and then check Exclude Local Variables from Browse Info (/FR on the compiler command line). If the SBR files contain local symbols, you can still omit them from the .BSC file by using BSCMAKE's /El option.

Close Source Browser File

This option closes the currently active .SBR file.

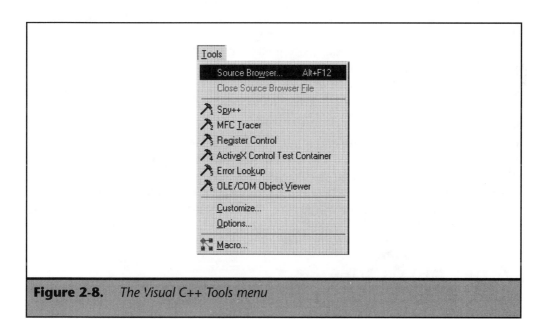

Figure 2-8. *The Visual C++ Tools menu*

Spy++

The Spy++ option activates a Win32-based utility that gives you a graphical view of the system's processes, threads, windows, and window messages. The Spy++ utility provides a toolbar and hyperlinks to help you work faster. Spy++ also allows you to refresh the active view, supplies a Window Finder Tool to make spying easier, and provides a Font dialog box to customize view windows.

MFC Tracer

To help debug Windows programs, MFC provides the MFC Tracer command. This will display, to a debugging output window or console, messages about the internal operation of the MFC library as well as warnings and errors if something goes wrong in your application.

Register Control

OLE controls, like other OLE server objects, can be accessed by other OLE-aware applications. This is achieved by registering the control's type library and class. You use the Register Control command for this purpose.

ActiveX Control Test Container

This command launches the Test Container application, shipped with Visual C++. The program is an ActiveX control container for testing ActiveX controls. Test Container allows the control developer to test the control's functionality by changing its properties, invoking its methods, and firing its events. In addition, Test Container can display logs of data-binding notifications and provides facilities for testing ActiveX control's persistence functionality.

Error Lookup

You use the Error Lookup command to retrieve a system error message or module error message based on the value entered. This option retrieves the error message text automatically if you drag-and-drop a hexadecimal or decimal value from the Developer Studio debugger or other OLE-enabled application. You can also enter a value either by typing it in or pasting it from the Clipboard and clicking Look Up. The accelerator keys for Copy (CTRL-C), Cut (CTRL-X), and Paste (CTRL-V) work for both the Value and Error Message boxes if you first highlight the text.

OLE/COM Object Viewer

The OLE/COM Object Viewer displays the ActiveX and OLE objects installed on your computer and the interfaces they support. It also allows you to edit the registry and look at type libraries.

Customize...

The Customize... menu item selects the Customize dialog box, which allows you to add, delete, and customize tools used by the Tools menu. Additional options allow you to assign shortcut keys to various commands.

Options...

The Options... menu item brings up the Options submenu, which offers commands that allow you to customize the Visual C++ IDE itself or modify how your application is developed. If you are a first-time user of Microsoft Visual C++, feel free to examine the contents of the Options submenu. However, until you fully understand the ramifications of changing install defaults, look but don't touch. Many of the changes that can be made at this level have global effects, and an incorrectly set option can literally halt all further application development.

Macro...

You use this option to create VBScript macros. The macros are procedures you write in the Visual Basic Scripting Edition language. With VBScript macros, you can simplify your work in Developer Studio. For example, in a macro you can combine several commands, speed up routine editing, or automate a complex series of tasks.

Window Menu

With the possible exception of the Docking View command, you will see that the remaining Window menu options are similar to those found in all standard Windows products (see Figure 2-9).

New Window

The New Window command provides one of many ways to begin entering and editing a new file.

Split

The Split option places a four-quadrant pane over the Edit view, allowing you to determine both a horizontal and vertical split point.

Docking View

A dockable toolbar can be attached, or docked, to any side of its parent window, or it can be detached, or floated, in its own miniframe window. Not all views are dockable, but if the active window is, for example the Workspace view, this is one method for docking and undocking the pane.

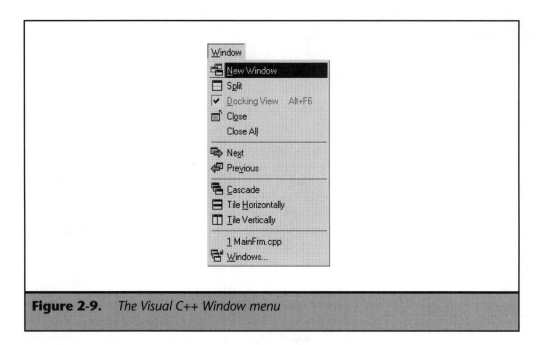

Figure 2-9. *The Visual C++ Window menu*

Close

This option closes the active window. You are prompted if the window's contents have not been previously saved.

Close All

This option closes all open windows. The IDE prompts you if any of the individual files have not been previously saved before actually closing and deleting its contents.

Next

Rather than clicking on a window to make it active, you can choose the Window | Next command to cycle through all open window contents.

Previous

This is similar to the Next command, only it works in reverse.

Cascade

This option displays all open windows in a manner similar to a splayed deck of cards. This allows for easy viewing of window titles.

Tile Horizontally

Tiles open windows with a wide but squat configuration. Best used for source code viewing.

Tile Vertically

Tiles open windows with a tall and narrow configuration. Best used for hierarchy analysis.

History List

This is a dynamic list of open windows, by name, at the bottom of the menu. It allows you to make the highlighted window active.

Help Menu

The Help menu begins with the standard online documentation Contents and Search... options and then diverges into several new help features, for example, the Documentation home page (see Figure 2-10).

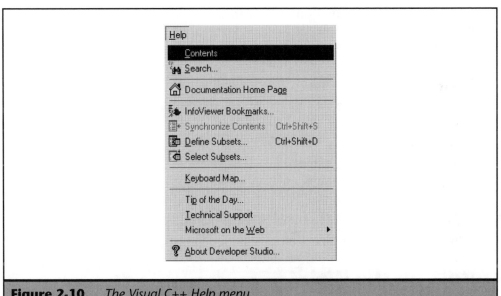

Figure 2-10.   *The Visual C++ Help menu*

Contents and Search...

These standard online documentation navigation controls provide the expected access to Microsoft's extensive online documentation.

Documentation Home Page

The Documentation Home Page command takes you to the highest-level page for the currently active help topic. It is similar to choosing the first page of a chapter that begins with an overview outline. Documentation Home Page topics are hot-links to topic-specific help files.

InfoViewer Bookmarks...

This option provides a quick way to relocate previously marked locations of interest whether they are online documentation files or even Internet sites.

Synchronize Contents

This option automatically synchronizes the table of contents to the currently open topic.

Define Subsets...

An information subset lets you focus your searches or your browsing on topics in a particular category. For example, if you are interested only in the Win32 API, you could define a subset that contains only the documentation from the Win32 SDK.

Select Subsets...

This command allows you to activate any user-defined subset.

Keyboard Map...

This option allows you to display the current keyboard shortcuts, including custom key settings and editor emulations.

Tip of the Day... and Technical Support

These two options speak for themselves.

Microsoft on the Web

This option is active if your computer can connect to the World Wide Web; it allows you to view web pages through the InfoViewer. Web access is available from the following locations in Developer Studio:

■ An URL address in a source window

■ Hypertext jumps in the InfoViewer Topic window

■ Microsoft on the Web on the Help menu

■ The Current URL box on the InfoViewer toolbar

You should take any steps necessary to prepare your computer to connect to the World Wide Web. For example, you must have the appropriate communications hardware installed, connected to a telephone jack or other communications line, and properly configured. You must establish access to the World Wide Web through an Internet service provider. If you are working within a corporate network with a security firewall, you need to take the necessary steps to communicate with other computers beyond the firewall.

About Developer Studio

A standard About box displaying the version, product ID, and installed component ID numbers.

The Complete Reference

Visual
C++ 5

Chapter 3

Writing, Compiling, and Debugging Simple Programs

The Visual C++ component of the Microsoft Developer Studio, like any new state-of-the-art development environment, can on first encounter be a very intimidating product. While the initial window seems straightforward, as soon as you begin peeking and poking around submenus and their related dialog windows, you can become easily overwhelmed by the options and apparent complexity of this new world.

You see, developing a multitasking, object-oriented, GUI (graphical user interface), multimedia, Internet-aware application really is no easy task—that is, if you had to do all of this from ground zero. However, today's language development environments automate the code generation for the majority of these goals. This text is designed to give you both a thorough understanding of the C and C++ languages and experience in today's number-one development environment—i.e., Microsoft's Visual C++—while learning the logic, constructs, and tools necessary to develop state-of-the-art programs.

This chapter is designed to give you hands-on experience with those commands needed to create, edit, save, compile, and debug simple programs. At this point, if you haven't done so already, you may want to take out a highlighting pen. Since the integrated environment offers so many ways to initiate each operation, you might want to highlight the text where you see the method that you prefer. For example, some people prefer to use keyboard commands, while others like the point-and-click mouse/menu interaction.

Starting the Developer Studio

In Chapter 2, you learned that starting the Visual C++ IDE (integrated development environment) is easy. If you are using a mouse, you can double-click on the Visual C++ icon, which is found in the Microsoft Visual C++ group.

Alternatively, you can access the Windows menu system with the following steps:

1. Press CTRL-ESC.

2. Enter **P** for Programs group.

3. Repeatedly press the CURSOR-DOWN key until the Microsoft Visual C++ group is highlighted.

4. Press the RIGHT-ARROW cursor key.

5. Repeatedly press the CURSOR-DOWN key until the Microsoft Visual C++ program is highlighted.

6. Press the ENTER key.

Here's the first opportunity to highlight your personal preference! Use the method you prefer, and start Microsoft Visual C++ now.

Creating Your First Program

The first thing you need to do before you enter a program is open a new file. From the File menu, choose the New... menu item. This option opens the New dialog box shown in Figure 3-1.

This dialog box is used to select the type of file you wish to create. For our example, click on the Text File option and then click on the OK button.

With a clean editing area, you are ready to begin entering a program. Enter the following example program:

```c
/* NOTE: This program contains errors     */
/* entered for the purpose of teaching     */
/* you how to use the Integrated Debugger! */

#include <stdio.h>

/* The following symbolic constant is used to
   dimension the array */
#define SIZE 5

/* Function Prototype   */
void print_them(int offset,char continue,int iarray[SIZE]);

void main( void )
{
  int offset;         /* array element selector     */
  int iarray[SIZE];  /* integer array              */
  char continue = 0; /* used to hold user's response */

/* First function call prints variable's "as is"     */
  print_them(offset,continue,iarray);

/* Welcome message and input of user's response      */
  Printf(\n\nWelcome to a trace demonstration!");
  printf("\nWould you like to continue (Y/N) ");
  scanf("%c",continue);

/* User-input of new integer array data              */
  if(continue == 'Y')
    for(offset=0; offset < SIZE; offset++) {
      printf("\nPlease enter an integer: ");
```

```
        scanf("%d",&iarray[offset]);
    }

/* Second function call prints user-entered data     */
  print_them(offset,continue,iarray);

}

/* Function outputs the contents of all variables     */
void print_them(int offset, char continue, int iarray[SIZE])
{
  printf("\n\n%d",offset);
  printf("\n\n%d",continue);
  for(offset=0; offset < SIZE, offset++)
    printf("\n%d",iarray[offset]);
}
```

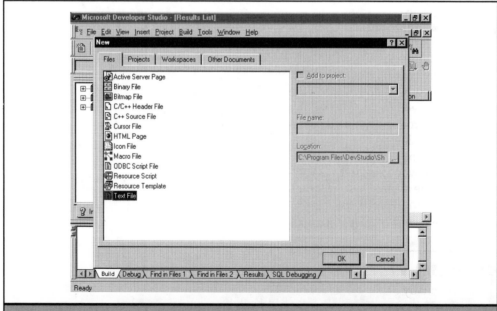

Figure 3-1.   *The New dialog box allows the programmer to start a new program*

Enter the program exactly as you see it. If you are familiar with the C language, you will notice that there are errors in the program. Do not correct them. The errors were placed there specifically to give you hands-on experience with various features of the integrated environment.

Editing Source Code

One of the main reasons for the success of Microsoft Windows is the graphical user interface (GUI). Windows 95 has introduced a modified GUI, but one that is intuitive to the experienced Windows user. A consistent user GUI means that when a particular feature appears in two different applications—for example, a Windows word processor and the Visual C++ IDE editor—that feature usually has the same menu and keyboard commands, in the same locations, in both applications.

This means that even if you have never used the Visual C++ IDE editor, you should find that correcting mistakes or moving to the end of a line, the beginning of a line, or the bottom of the edit window is just as easy and familiar as it is in your favorite Windows word processor.

Here are some helpful tips for working with the Visual C++ IDE editor. To move quickly through a line, hold down the CTRL key while pressing the left or right cursor key. This causes the edit cursor to move to the right or the left (depending on the cursor key pressed) one whole word at a time. (A word is defined as anything delimited by a blank space or punctuation.)

To delete an entire word instead of a single character, place the cursor on the space before or after the word to be deleted and press either CTRL-DEL (to delete the word to the right) or CTRL-BACKSPACE (to delete the word to the left).

To allow for the maximum amount of editing workspace, the horizontal and vertical scroll bars can be turned off (see Tools | Options). If you chose this option, the mouse cannot be used to scroll the window either horizontally or vertically. For this reason, you need to know two key combinations: CTRL-PAGE UP, which moves you to the top of a program; and CTRL-END, which moves you to the bottom of a program. How are you doing with that highlighter?

Perhaps you are wondering why we have made no mention of the horizontal movement keyboard equivalents. There is a reason: most professionally written code fits within the standard monitor's 80-column width. This makes for easy reading and code debugging—since each line of code is completely visible, there can be no hidden bugs in column 95.

Saving Files

There is usually a major conflict between you and the compiler. You think that you write flawless code, while the compiler believes otherwise. If that insult is not bad enough, there's the linker's impression of your algorithmic genius. However, the final blow to your ego comes from the microprocessor itself, which, after being passed an executable file filtered by both the compiler and the linker, chokes on your digital instructions.

Although disagreements between you and the compiler or the linker are not catastrophic, disagreements between you and the microprocessor are. The moral is: Save your file before you compile, before you link, and definitely before you try to run a program. Many a sad story has been told of a programmer who runs an unsaved file, crashes the application or the system, and then has to reenter the entire program.

If you have not already done so, save the example program you are working with. You can do so by either clicking on the third button from the left on the toolbar (the picture on this button looks like a 3.5-inch floppy disk), using the File | Save command, or pressing CTRL-S.

The first time you save a file, the IDE will present you with a Save dialog box. Save this file under the name ERROR.C.

Figure 3-2 shows the edit window as it looks just before the file is saved. After the file is saved, the title in the title bar will show the saved file's name.

Creating the Executable File

Most Windows 3.*x*, Windows 95, and Windows NT programs contain many files. Initially, however, most simple C/C++ programs start with just one file, the main( )

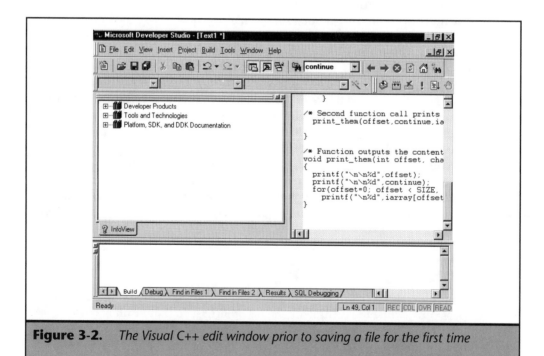

Figure 3-2. *The Visual C++ edit window prior to saving a file for the first time*

C/C++ file. As you become a more experienced programmer, this introductory approach will prove to be inefficient.

As your understanding of C/C++ and Windows application development increases, you will begin to break your solutions into multiple, logically related C/C++ files. To these you will add your own header files (header files have a .H file extension). By the time you reach the end of this book, you will be creating applications with source code files, header files, resource files, and so on.

So, even though the sample program contains just a single file, the following sections explain the steps necessary to build a fully formed C/C++ application under Windows.

Using Workspaces

Before you can compile a typical C/C++ program, the Visual C++ IDE needs to be informed of the names of all of the C/C++ and resource files needed to create the executable file. In the past, this process was typically done in a *make* file (make files have a .MAK file extension).

Make files are text files that follow a special syntax that details file dependencies. In other words, the syntax of the make file defines the files that must be present and compiled before the target file can be used in another phase of the compile or link process. By the way, due to the sophistication of this process, it is no longer called "compiling and linking." The word now used to describe these steps is "building."

Traditionally, make files had to be executed from the command line by a stand-alone utility program known as NMAKE. Microsoft has streamlined this entire process in the Visual C++ compiler by including a substitute utility called the Project utility. This utility can be accessed from within the IDE.

Whereas a programmer previously had to create a separate .MAK text file and run the NMAKE utility, the Project utility now allows you to achieve the same result without having to quit the Visual C++ IDE. The Project utility creates, edits, and uses make files with a .MAK file extension. What's even better is that creating the project file is an easy process.

Starting a New Project

To create a new project, choose the File | New... menu item. This command opens up the New File dialog box. This time select the Projects tab (see Figure 3-3). After you have selected this item, you will see the New Projects dialog box, which is the first step in creating a project file.

The first piece of information that the Project utility requires is a name for the project file. This is important since the name is the label that will be used to identify the final executable file.

Many first-time C/C++ programmers are surprised that the name of the program's executable file does not match the name of the source file containing the main( ) or WinMain( ) function. Remember, all project files must have a .MAK file

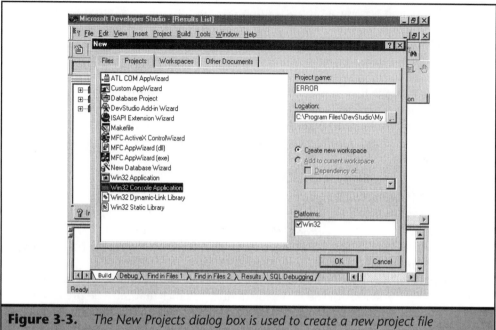

Figure 3-3. *The New Projects dialog box is used to create a new project file*

extension, but their actual name may be different from your source code files. For our sample program, use the project filename ERROR.MAK.

The second piece of information required is the project type. Options include dynamic link libraries (DLLs) and various executable formats. For this example, the Win32 Console Application option should be selected.

If you place an entry in the Location: category, this option instructs the Visual C++ IDE to automatically create a new subdirectory for your new project.

A fourth option involves the project's target platform. For the 32-bit version of the Visual C++ compiler, the Win32 option is active. Figure 3-3 holds information for a completed sample project file. To accept this information, click on the OK button.

Adding Files to a Project

Once a new project file is defined, the Project utility allows you to easily add files. Figure 3-4 shows the Add Files to Project... menu item highlighted. Accessing this pop-up menu is as simple as clicking the right mouse button within the ClassView.

Selecting this option opens a standard File Manager window allowing you to easily locate and then include all of the files necessary to create the executable program. One note about the types of included files: Header files (those with .H extensions) are *not* inserted into a project's file list; they are incorporated directly into the build process by #include preprocessor statements.

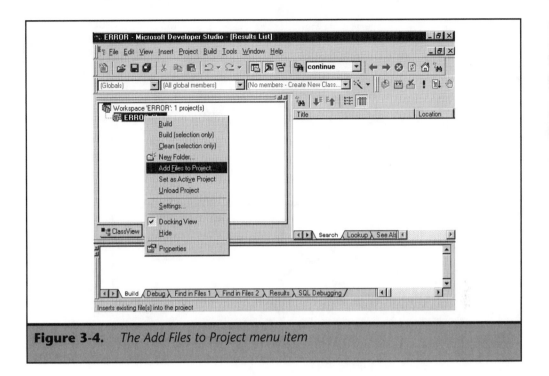

Figure 3-4.   *The Add Files to Project menu item*

The Insert Files into Project dialog box is very similar to the standard Windows File dialog box. It allows you to select a default drive and path, and it automatically lists the target path's filenames. For our sample program, simply double-click on the ERROR.C filename in the File name: list (see Figure 3-5). This will automatically insert the filename into the project file.

If this were a more fully formed project file, such as one that would be used for Windows application development, at this point you would continue to select files needed by the project. For our sample program, however, one file will do. At this point you are ready to formally end the project file's definition by clicking on the OK button.

Choosing Build or Rebuild All

Now that the project file has been created, you are ready to instruct the IDE to create the executable file. Remember, under Visual C++ this process is called a *build*.

Figure 3-6 shows the Build menu with the Rebuild All command highlighted.

In Chapter 2, you learned that the only difference between the Build and Rebuild All commands is that Rebuild All does not check the dates of any of the files used by the project. This command always recompiles and links every file in the project.

Because a poorly maintained system can have inaccurate internal clock settings, it is always safest to choose the Rebuild All option for small applications. Now, activate

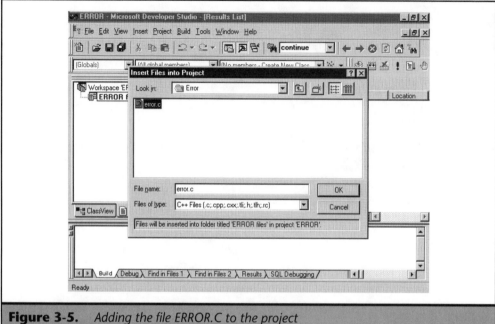

Figure 3-5. *Adding the file ERROR.C to the project*

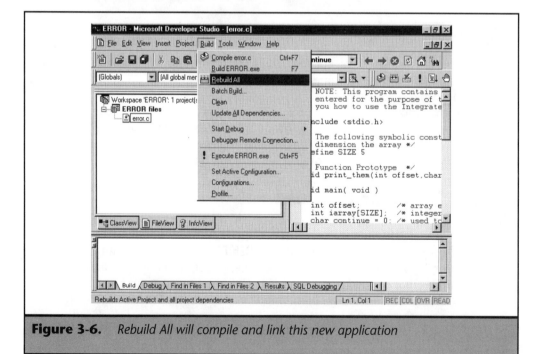

Figure 3-6. *Rebuild All will compile and link this new application*

the build process by clicking on the Rebuild All command or pressing ENTER when the command is highlighted.

Debugging Programs

If your program contains syntax errors, executing a Build or Rebuild All command automatically opens the compiler output message window, as seen at the bottom of the screen in Figure 3-7.

Each message begins with the source file's name, which for this example is C:\Program Files\DevStudio\MyProjects\Error\Error.c. This filename is important, because the typical Windows application contains many source files.

NOTE: *You will probably have your monitor's screen resolution set high enough to actually view the entire error or warning messages described in the following text.*

Immediately to the right of the source file's name is the line number, in parentheses, in which the warning or error was detected. In our example, the first error message was generated on line twelve (12). To the right of the line number is a

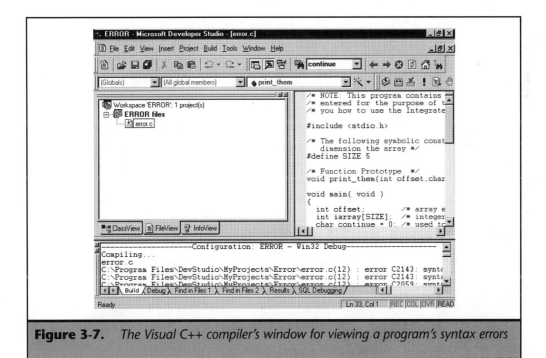

Figure 3-7. *The Visual C++ compiler's window for viewing a program's syntax errors*

colon, followed immediately by the word "error" or the word "warning," which is then followed by the associated error number.

Programs can run with warning messages, but not with error messages. The last piece of information found on each message line is a brief description of the detected syntax error.

Differences Between Warning and Error Messages

Warning messages might flag the use of a standard C/C++ automatic rule. For example, an automatic rule might be invoked when having a float value automatically truncated when assigning it to an integer variable. This does not mean that the code was written incorrectly, only that the statement is using some sort of behind-the-scenes feature of C/C++.

For example, all of the functions prototyped in MATH.H have formal arguments of the type double and return the type double. If your program passes to one of these functions an argument of the type float, the compiler will generate a warning. This warning will inform you that a conversion is taking place from the type float to the type double as the argument is pushed onto the call stack.

You can remove many warning messages by overriding automatic language defaults. You can do this by placing in the foreground those operators or functions designed to perform the behind-the-scenes operation. The example warning message described in the preceding paragraph would be removed by doing an explicit cast of the argument from the type float to the type double.

Your First Unexpected Bug

The first error message, shown earlier in Figure 3-7, shows what might happen when you are using a new language for the first time. Here the programmer tried to give a variable the name of a reserved, or language, keyword. If you are using a programming language that you *are* familiar with, you will probably not have this problem.

In C/C++, the word "continue" is a reserved, or language, keyword. In the sample program, the variable's name was chosen for self-documenting, readability reasons; however, it bumped into a language restriction. Chapter 6 contains a table of these reserved words for you to refer to when initially creating your source code.

Viewing Output and Source Windows

Once you have viewed your list of warning and error messages, you will want to switch back to the edit window to make the necessary code changes. You can select the edit window by either clicking on the mouse inside the edit window itself or by going to the Window menu and clicking on the filename, ERROR.C. Using whichever approach you prefer (has the highlighter dried out yet?), make the edit window the topmost window.

Using Find and Replace

There will be times when you will want to quickly locate something within your program. You could do this by bringing down the Search | Replace... dialog box, but the Visual C++ IDE provides a quicker option. If you look closely at the toolbar in Figure 3-7, you will see the word "continue" in the Quick Find list box.

To use Quick Find, simply click the left mouse button anywhere within the control's interior and type the label you want to find. Quick Find can now be activated by pressing ENTER. Figure 3-8 shows the results of this action. The first occurrence of the *continue* variable is highlighted.

This approach is fine for locating first occurrences, but in our case it is inefficient because we need to locate all occurrences of the *continue* variable. For this reason, the Edit | Replace... dialog box, shown in Figure 3-9, is a better choice.

The easiest way to use Replace... is to first place the cursor on the word to search for *before* you invoke the Edit | Replace... option. If you follow this sequence, the word being searched for will be automatically entered into the Find what: list when you invoke the command.

In Figure 3-9, you see this approach used by first placing the cursor on the variable *continue*, which was highlighted in the previous figure. Practice this sequence and see if you can get your screen to appear like the one in Figure 3-9.

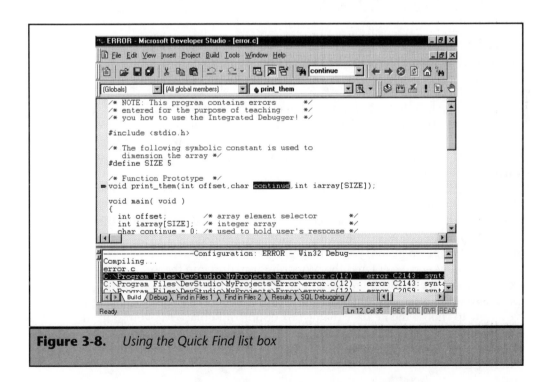

Figure 3-8. *Using the Quick Find list box*

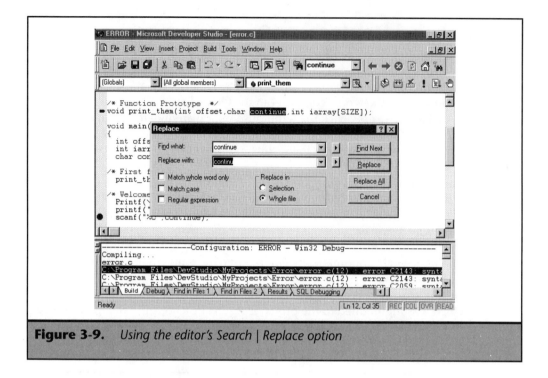

Figure 3-9. *Using the editor's Search | Replace option*

For our sample program, we want the variable that is currently named *continue* to still be readable, but it needs to be spelled differently than the reserved word. At this point, you need to manually enter the word "continu" into the Replace dialog box's Replace with: list.

Notice that this dialog box contains many of the standard word processor search-and-replace options, such as the ability to match whole words and designate case sensitivity. If you are new to the C/C++ language, you will be surprised to find out that C/C++ is case sensitive. For this reason, variables named *TOTAL* and *total* are treated as different.

One word of advice: Before you perform any search-and-replace operation, save the file. This will allow you to easily recover from a disastrous pattern match. Another approach is to use the Edit | Undo command. However, if your Undo buffer is not sufficiently large to hold all the changes the search-and-replace operation made, Undo might not be able to restore your whole program.

Now that you have entered the proper information into the Replace dialog box, you are ready to execute the replacement. However, there is one problem. The program contains the output statement "\nWould you like to continue (Y/N)". If you were to choose the Replace dialog box option of Replace All, your output statement would have a spelling error in it, because a Replace All would misspell the word "continue" in the program's screen output. For this reason, click now on the Find Next button.

Using Replace Options

The Replace dialog box presents you with several search options. Find Next searches for the search string's next occurrence. Replace inserts the substitute string. The Replace All option races through your code without interruption, finding and replacing the targeted text.

In this example, you need to repeatedly choose Replace, followed by Find Next, until you have replaced every use of the variable *continue* with the new spelling, *continu*. Remember, do not change the spelling of the word "continue" in the printf( ) statement.

Shortcuts to Switching Views

Earlier you saw that switching between the output message window and the edit window required some keyboard or mouse gymnastics. There is an easier way to get these two windows to interact. But first, if you are following the example development cycle, you need to stop and rebuild your program. If you made all of the necessary *continu* substitutions described previously, your output message window should look like the one in Figure 3-10.

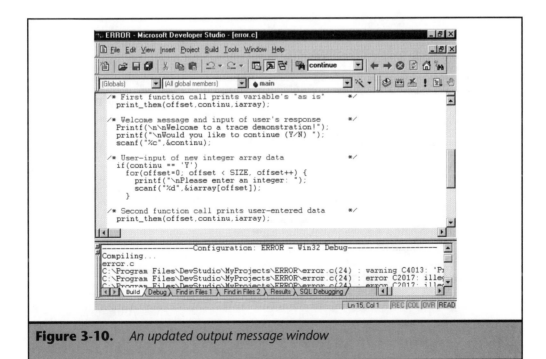

Figure 3-10.   *An updated output message window*

The improved way to interact with these two windows is very straightforward. First, place the cursor on the warning or error message of interest. For our example, pick the first message in the new output message window:

```
warning C4013: 'Printf' undefined;...
```

Now press ENTER. Voilà! The integrated environment automatically switches to the edit window and automatically highlights the suspicious code segment (with an arrow), as shown in Figure 3-11.

Useful Warning and Error Messages

When you learn a new language, you actually encounter two major learning curves. First, there's the time it takes to learn the syntax and nuances of the new language itself. But the second, more subtle learning curve involves understanding this new environment's help, warning, and error messages. In other words, you have to learn how this new compiler processes source code.

The good news is that the Visual C++ compiler produces some of the most accurate messages ever produced by any language environment. In our example, the compiler adroitly detected the misuse of a language keyword, continue.

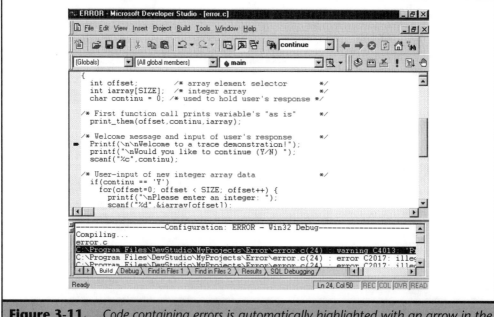

Figure 3-11. *Code containing errors is automatically highlighted with an arrow in the edit window*

As you now know, C/C++ is case sensitive. Once again, the compiler correctly detected an error. The function printf( ), supplied with your compiler, was defined in all lowercase letters. Because this function was accidentally entered with an uppercase "P," the compiler was unable to locate a matching library function Printf( ). With this word highlighted in the edit window, make the edit change by replacing the uppercase "P" with its lowercase equivalent. Don't forget to save your file.

More Work with the Debugger

At this point the program is ready for another attempt at building an executable file. Return to the Project menu and select the Rebuild All menu item. Figure 3-12 shows the updated output messages.

Do you remember how to easily switch to the edit window and automatically locate the illegal escape sequence identified in the error message? (All you need to do is place the cursor on the error message and press ENTER.)

As it turns out, the same statement that contained the misspelled printf( ) function has a second error. In C/C++, all format strings must begin with a double quote. Edit the line by placing a double quote (") after the opening parenthesis in the printf( ) function—that is, after printf(.

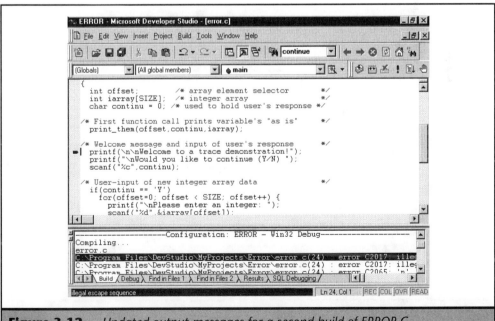

Figure 3-12. *Updated output messages for a second build of ERROR.C*

Make sure that your first printf( ) statement matches the one in Figure 3-13. Now, save the file and attempt another rebuild. Figure 3-13 shows the third updated output message window.

Our last error message was

```
syntax error : missing ';' before ')'
```

Place the cursor on the message and press ENTER. In the C/C++ language, unlike in Pascal, a semicolon is considered to be a statement terminator, not a statement separator. For this reason, the second statement within the for loop expression needs a terminating semicolon, not a comma. Change the comma after the constant SIZE to a semicolon, save the file, and execute a Rebuild All once again.

Success? According to the output message window, you should now have no warnings and no errors, and the Rebuild All command has successfully generated the executable file, ERROR.EXE. (Note: At this point if your compiler's errors and warnings message window does *not* show 0 errors and 0 warnings, you have inadvertently added a few typos of your own. Simply retrace your steps and edit the necessary code statements.)

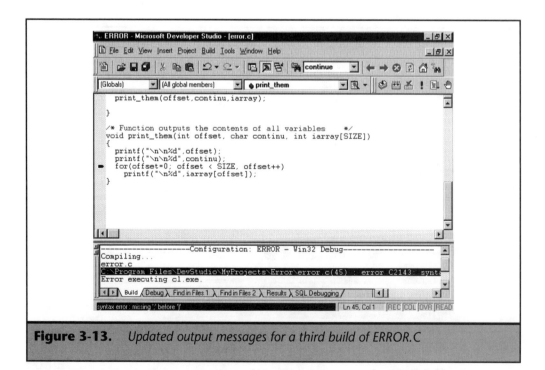

Figure 3-13.   *Updated output messages for a third build of ERROR.C*

Running Your First Program

To run a program after you have completed a successful Build or Rebuild All
operation, simply click on the Project menu's Execute command. If you do this with
the sample program, and enter a **Y** when asked if you would like to continue, your
screen should display something like the following:

```
-16173

0
32754
-16173
217
386
11

Welcome to a trace demonstration!
Would you like to continue (Y/N) Y

-16173

0
32754
-16173
217
386
11
run-time error R6001
```

Figure 3-14 illustrates what happens after you type **Y** and press ENTER.

Using the Integrated Debugger

The sample program's output begins by dumping the uninitialized contents of the
array. It then asks if you want to continue. A "Y" (yes) answer logically indicates that
you would now like to fill the array with your own values and then reprint the array's
contents to the screen.

In this sample execution, you responded with a "Y". However, if you examine
the program's output, you can easily see that you were never prompted for input.
In addition, the array's contents have not been changed, as evidenced by the
duplicated output.

In other words, although you have a program that appears to be syntactically
correct—there are no syntax errors—the application fails to perform as expected.

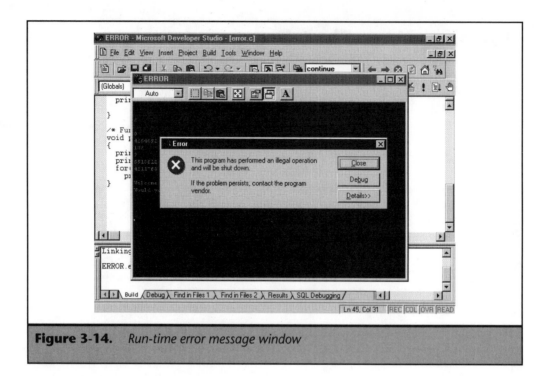

Figure 3-14.   *Run-time error message window*

These types of errors are called *logical* errors. Fortunately, the Visual C++ IDE integrated debugger has several features ready to come to your rescue.

Although the integrated debugger has many features, you will regularly use only a small subset of the commands. Basically, a debugger provides two powerful capabilities. First, it allows you to execute your program line by line, instead of at full speed. Second, it allows you to examine the contents of any variable at any point in your program.

When used correctly, these capabilities allow you to quickly locate an offending line of code. Unfortunately, the debugger does not automatically correct the code. (So, for the moment, your job security as a programmer is still not threatened!)

The Subtle Differences Between Step Into and Step Over

Figure 3-15 shows the Start Debug menu. When you start the debugger, usually by pressing F11, a Debug toolbar appears. Two of the more frequently used buttons represent the options Step Into (fifth button from the left on the Debug toolbar) and Step Over (sixth button). Both commands execute your program line by line.

The appearance of the edit window is different if you are using either one of these commands. When you are debugging a program using Step Into or Step Over, the integrated debugger highlights the line of code *about* to be executed.

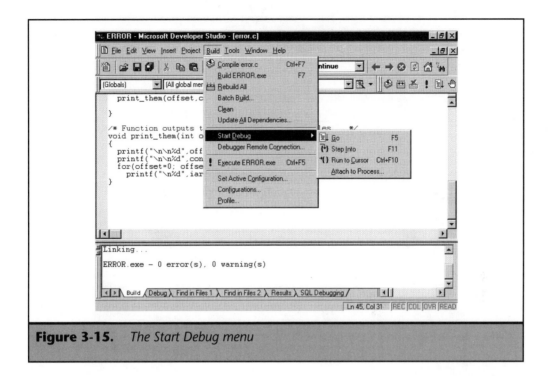

Figure 3-15. *The Start Debug menu*

The only difference between Step Into and Step Over occurs when the statement about to be executed is a function call. If you select Step Into on a function call, the debugger jumps to the function header and continues debugging the code inside the function. If you select Step Over on a function call, the debugger executes the associated function at full speed and then returns to the statement following the function call. You should use this command whenever you are debugging a program that incorporates previously tested subroutines.

Using either Step command, invoke the command three times. Figure 3-16 shows the sample program as it will appear after you have invoked Step Into or Step Over three times.

As you can see from Figure 3-16, the single-step arrow (also called a *trace* arrow) is positioned next to the call to the print_them( ) function.

For now, we want to execute the function at full speed. To do this, choose the Step Over command. If you watch closely, you will notice that the function executes and the trace arrow stops on the first printf( ) statement. So far, so good. Now press F8 four times, until the trace arrow stops on the scanf( ) statement.

At this point, you need to switch the program's execution window. You can do this by pressing the ALT-TAB combination. (You may need to use this key combination several times, depending on the number of tasks you have loaded.) When you are in ERROR.C's window, as shown in Figure 3-17, answer the question "Would you like to continue (Y/N)" with a **Y** and press ENTER.

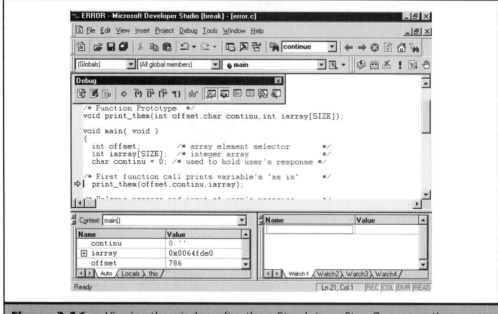

Figure 3-16. *Viewing the window after three Step Into or Step Over operations*

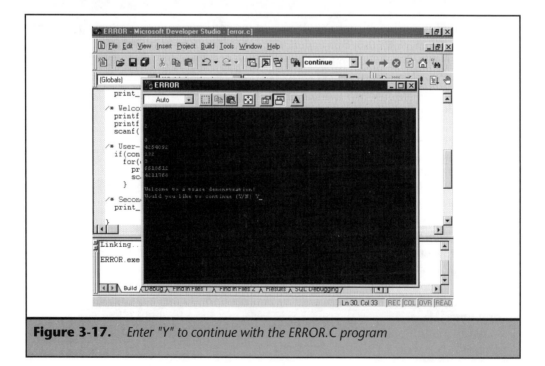

Figure 3-17. *Enter "Y" to continue with the ERROR.C program*

The integrated debugger immediately responds with the error message shown in Figure 3-18.

This message relates to the scanf( ) statement just executed. See if you understand enough of the C language to figure out what the problem is.

The problem relates to the incorrect use of the scanf( ) function. The scanf( ) function expects to receive the address of a memory location to fill. Examine this statement:

```
scanf("%c",continu);
```

As you can see, this statement does not provide an address. The solution is to place the address operator (&) in front of the variable *continu*. Correct the statement so that it looks like this statement:

```
scanf("%c",&continue);
```

Save the change, and execute a Rebuild All.

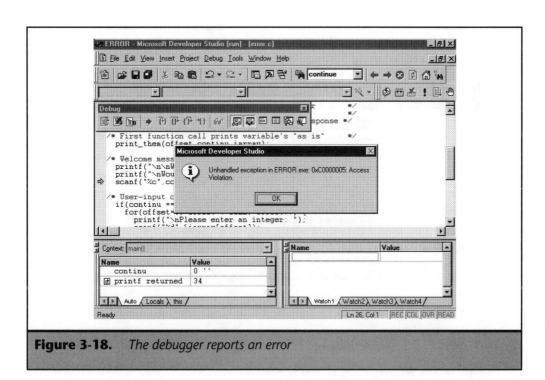

Figure 3-18. *The debugger reports an error*

Advanced Debugging Techniques

You can think of a breakpoint as a stop sign for the integrated debugger. Logically, breakpoints tell the debugger that all statements prior to the breakpoint are OK, so the debugger shouldn't waste time single-stepping through them.

The easiest way to set a breakpoint is to click on the breakpoint control, which you can do if the toolbar is visible. This button is the second from the right on the toolbar. The picture on it resembles a hand signaling "stop."

The Breakpoint button is a toggle. If the line that the cursor is on when you click on the button does not contain a breakpoint, the command sets one. If the line already has a breakpoint set, the command removes it. You can set as many breakpoints as you need by repeating this sequence. The Go command, when selected, will always run your program from the current line up to the next breakpoint.

For the sample program, you know that all statements prior to the scanf( ) function call are OK. You have just edited this line and are now interested in seeing if the new statement works properly. For the sake of efficient debugging, you are going to set a breakpoint on line 21, at the scanf( ) function.

Figure 3-19 illustrates another approach to setting breakpoints: using the Edit | Breakpoints... command.

This menu item opens up the Breakpoints dialog box. The default breakpoint type is Break at Location. All you need to do is type in the line number in the Location: box.

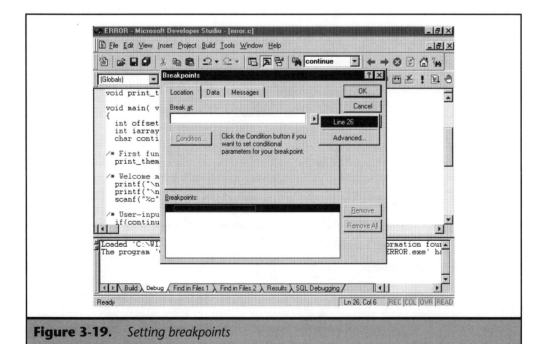

Figure 3-19.   *Setting breakpoints*

For our example, this is line 26. (If your scanf( ) statement is on a different line number, possibly because there are extra blank lines in the source code, enter your source file's line number for the scanf( ) statement.) Now choose the OK button.

Using Breakpoints

To debug a program at full speed up to, but not including, the breakpoint, you can use the Debug | Go menu item, as shown in Figure 3-20.

Assuming that you have the previously described breakpoint set, invoke the Go command. (Either select the command with the mouse, use the keyboard to access the command via the menus, or press F5.) Notice that the trace arrow speeds quickly to the statement containing the scanf( ) function call and then stops.

Once the debugger stops at a breakpoint, you can return to single-stepping through the program or even pause to examine a variable's contents. For now, we are interested in seeing if the syntax change made to the scanf( ) statement works. Choose the Step Into option, switch to the program's execution window, type an uppercase **Y**, and press ENTER.

Success! The integrated debugger no longer flags you with warning message windows. But does this really mean that the code problem is fixed? The simplest way to answer this question is to examine the current contents of the variable *continu*.

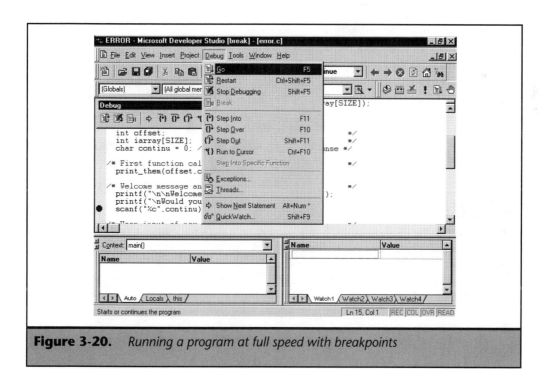

Figure 3-20. *Running a program at full speed with breakpoints*

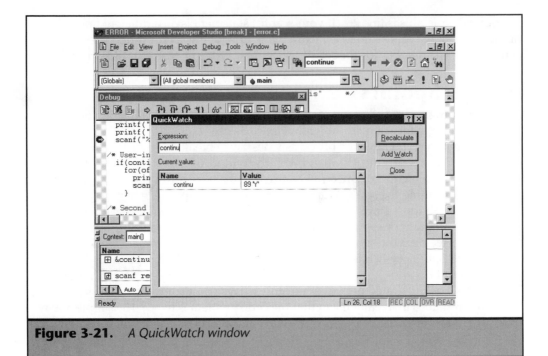

Figure 3-21. *A QuickWatch window*

An Introduction to QuickWatch

The QuickWatch... command opens up the QuickWatch dialog box, which allows you to instantaneously view and modify the contents of a variable. The fastest way to put a variable in the QuickWatch window is to place the cursor on the variable in your source code and press SHIFT-F9. If you do this with the sample program, you will see a QuickWatch dialog box similar to the one in Figure 3-21.

Now that you know that the contents of *continu* are correct, you can run the program at full speed to the end, using the Debug | Go command.

What's Coming?

In this chapter, you rehearsed the day-to-day commands necessary to create, edit, save, build, and debug a simple C program. In Chapter 4, you will learn about programming issues specific to more sophisticated Windows applications.

Visual
C++ 5

Chapter 4

Advanced Visual C++ Features

The Microsoft Visual C++ compiler includes several advanced tools that are useful for program development. This chapter examines the creation of bitmaps, cursors, and icons from within the Visual C++ IDE (integrated development environment), and it discusses several stand-alone utilities, such as Books Online, Spy++, Process Viewer, and WinDiff.

As you begin developing programs in C, C++, and Windows, you will find that the Visual C++ compiler helps you locate syntax errors during the build (compile and link) operation. Syntax errors are often the easiest to fix because of the detailed help provided by the online help facilities. However, just because an application is free of syntax errors does not mean that it will perform as expected.

Perhaps you wanted to print the time to the screen, but it didn't show up; or you may have wanted to see a file in a particular format, but you got it in another format. Maybe the screen was supposed to have a blue background with a white figure drawn on it, but what you got was a white screen and a white figure—kind of difficult to see. It may even be a performance issue: The program runs correctly when it is the only application loaded, but it crashes if more than one program is running. All of these situations fall outside the scope of simple syntax errors. Advanced development tools are needed to correct these problems.

This chapter introduces you to the tools designed to help locate these types of problems. You will learn the purpose of each tool and how to use it. As you work through the programming examples later in this book, you will find these tools very useful.

Creating System Resources

Customizing a Windows application with your own icons, cursors, bitmaps, and dialog boxes is easy with Microsoft's Visual C++ IDE. This is not just a compiler; it is also an easy-to-use, powerful resource editor.

Designing Bitmaps

This section teaches you how to use the Visual C++ IDE to draw a bitmap. All other graphic figures, such as icons and cursors, can be created in a similar manner.

The Visual C++ IDE allows you to design device-independent color bitmap images. These bitmaps are functionally device independent with respect to resolution. The image file format allows you to create a bitmap that always looks the same, regardless of the resolution of the display on which it appears.

For example, a single bitmap might consist of four definitions (DIBs): one designed for monochrome displays, one for CGAs, one for EGAs, and one for VGAs. Whenever the application displays the bitmap, it simply refers to it by name; Windows automatically selects the icon image that is best suited to the current display.

Figure 4-1 shows the initial Visual C++ IDE window. The first step you must take to create an application resource such as a bitmap is to click on the Insert | Resource... menu item.

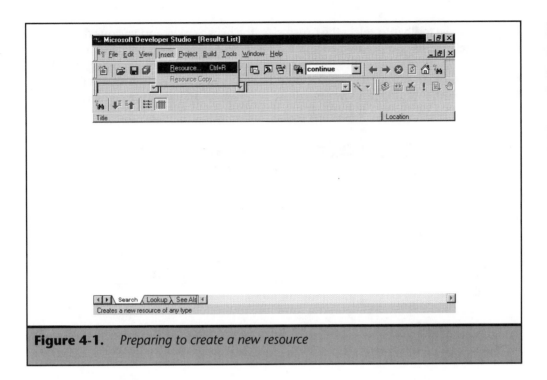

Figure 4-1. *Preparing to create a new resource*

The resulting dialog box, shown here, shows the drop-down list that displays the kinds of resources available. Because we want to create a bitmap, this resource is highlighted. Simply press ENTER to confirm your selection.

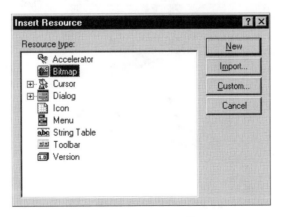

Creating a bitmap with the Visual C++ resource editor is about as easy as creating a picture with Windows Paintbrush. The Visual C++ resource editor first presents you with a blank bitmap grid and the drawing tools toolbar.

You use the toolbar to select the brush size, the brush color, and various drawing modes, such as fills and predefined shapes. Figure 4-2 shows a completed bitmap.

To set a resource's properties, begin by pressing ALT-ENTER. This step displays the particular resource's Properties dialog box. The following illustration shows the Bitmap Properties dialog box with the details of the bitmap's width, height, colors, filename, and save compressed properties.

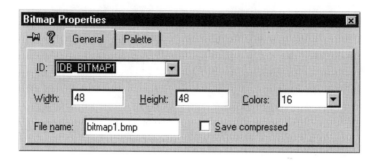

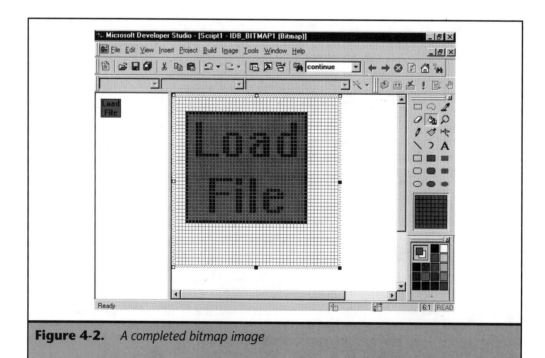

Figure 4-2.   *A completed bitmap image*

Designing Dialog Boxes

The initial steps required for creating a dialog box resource are identical to those described previously for creating a bitmap resource. First, choose the kind of resource you wish to create as shown earlier. However, this time, select the Dialog option.

Figure 4-3 shows a completed dialog box, the dialog box objects toolbox (on the right side of the screen), and the Text Properties dialog box.

The objects toolbox allows you to place a variety of controls in your dialog box design. These include (starting at the top and proceeding from left to right, not including the "arrow" selection control): bitmap, label, edit box, frame, button, checkbox, radio button, combo box, list box, horizontal scroll bar, vertical scroll bar, and a user-defined control.

Figure 4-3 shows the company name label object selected. The Text Properties dialog box is brought to the foreground simply by double-clicking on the label object itself. This is a convenient alternative to returning to the main resource window. Each kind of control has its own set of properties.

Setting Resource HotSpots

A cursor resource differs slightly from a bitmap or an icon resource in that it can contain a *hotspot*. A cursor's hotspot represents the part of the image that registers the cursor's screen coordinates.

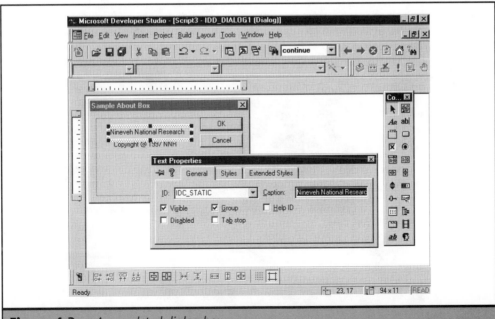

Figure 4-3.   *A completed dialog box*

Creating a cursor involves the same initial steps used for creating bitmaps and dialog boxes. This process is started by first selecting the Insert | Resource... menu item command, and then choosing the cursor resource. Figure 4-4 shows a finished cursor design resembling a stylized up arrow.

A cursor's hotspot is set by first clicking on the hotspot button to the right of the Hotspot: label in the design toolbar. Once you have clicked on the button, simply move the mouse pointer into the cursor's bitmap design and click on the appropriate cell.

For this example, the pencil's point at column 16, row 8 has been marked as the hotspot. The Visual C++ resource editor acknowledges this selection by placing the coordinates 16, 8 to the right of the Hotspot: label.

Online Documentation

Books Online (found either in the Visual C++ IDE Help menu or in the Visual C++ group) has an easy-to-use graphical interface that allows you to access hundreds of pages of Microsoft magazine and book articles. Figure 4-5 shows the initial Books Online window. (Your window might look different, depending on the latest update supplied with your compiler.)

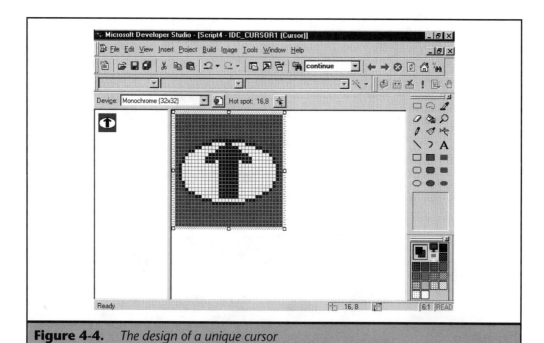

Figure 4-4.   *The design of a unique cursor*

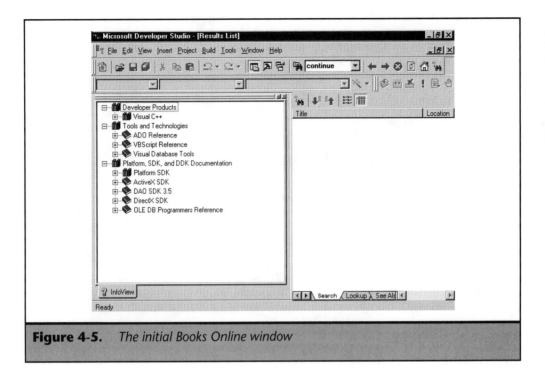

Figure 4-5.   *The initial Books Online window*

Notice that each entry has a closed-book icon followed by the book's title. Take a moment to study the previous figure, making a mental note of those books you feel you might need to refer to in the near future. Part of doing an efficient topic search, such as looking up keywords or C/C++ topics, involves knowing the type of information that is available.

Opening Reference Materials

One way to do a topic search is to first double-click on the book title you are interested in. Figure 4-6 illustrates what happens to the Books Online window when you double-click on the *What's New | What's New For Visual C++ Version 5* book title.

When you double-click on a book's title, the graphical display of the Books Online dialog box changes. First, the closed-book icon to the left of the book's title turns into an open book. Listed underneath the title is an expanded drop-down list of associated titles.

Notice that the subtitle's icon changes to an open book. Listed underneath this subtitle are all the names for the pages or chapters available. At this point, once you have found a page or chapter of interest, simply double-click on the item's title. Figure 4-7 shows the Visual C++ home page.

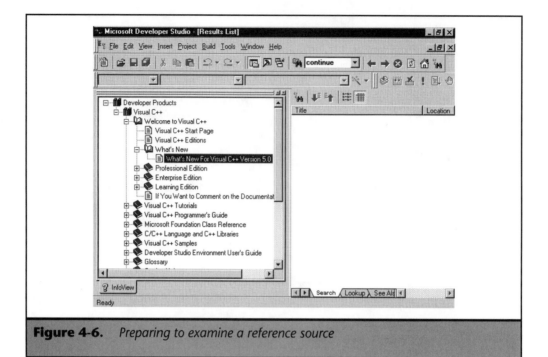

Figure 4-6. *Preparing to examine a reference source*

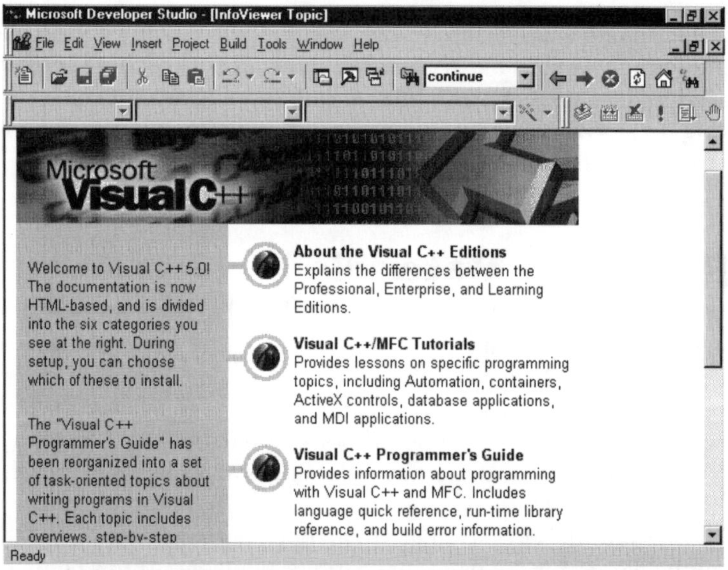

Figure 4-7. *A new title is brought to the foreground*

Searching for Specific Topics

A second approach to executing a search begins with double-clicking on the Help |
Search button. When you select this option, the dialog box presents you with a
standard Windows Search dialog box, shown in the following illustration. It shows
the dialog box set up to begin a search on Visual C++ System requirements category
features.

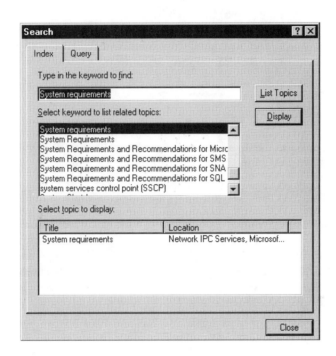

Simply select the List Topics button to update the workspace to show the
requested topic.

Getting a Hard Copy

Although it is definitely true that Books Online and its associated views make for
efficient searches, the utility pair may leave your eyes crossed. Besides, what if you
want some hard copy documentation, or you want to further analyze something after
your system is shut down? For these and other reasons, many people still prefer
reading a printed page over staring endlessly at a computer monitor.

Books Online uses a straightforward approach to document printing. Simply use
the File | Print Topic command. Books Online will print the topic that is displayed in
the active window when this command is selected.

Printing Single Topics

Often you will not need to print an entire topic, especially if the selected title is an entire chapter. By choosing the Edit | Copy command, you can decide which portions of a topic to print.

First, select the portion of the help text that you want to print. You select text by placing the mouse pointer inside the text window at the beginning of the text you want to select, holding down the left mouse button, and dragging the mouse until it highlights (shows in reverse video) the desired text.

Clicking the Edit | Copy button completes the operation. Copy places the information on the Windows Clipboard. Clipboard contents can be pasted into any Windows-based word processor for printing and editing.

Diagnostic Tools

The following sections explain the use of Microsoft's debugging and testing utilities. These utilities are used to locate an application's logical errors or errors that are generated when the application is executed simultaneously with other programs.

Spy++

Spy++ is one of the most dynamic tools shipped with Microsoft Visual C/C++. This utility allows you to "spy" on one or all of the currently loaded Windows applications. This utility's Window option allows you to view each application's name, class, module, parent, display window's rectangular screen coordinates, window style (for example, WS_CHILD), and window ID number.

Spy++ also lets you view the messages being sent throughout the environment. There are nine checkboxes that allow you to predefine the reported message types:

Mouse	Input	System
Window	Init	Clipboard
Other	DDE	Non-Client

Generated output can be displayed in synchronous or asynchronous mode and sent to a Spy++ window, a file, or to COM1 for remote debugging.

The following illustration shows the Spy++ Message Options dialog box with window selection data entered.

A QUICK OVERVIEW OF
VISUAL C++

```
Message Options                                          [X]

  Windows    Messages   Output

 ─Window Finder Tool───────    ─Selected Object──────────────
  Drag the Finder Tool over a   Window:    00000080
  window to select, then        Text:      ""
  release the mouse button.     Class:     #32769 (Desktop)
                                Style:     96000000
  Finder Tool:      ⊕           Rect:      (0, 0)-(640, 480) 640x480
                                Thread ID: FFFF55F9
   ☐ Hide Spy++                 Process ID: FFFF5161

 ─Additional Windows──────────────────────────────────────
   ☐ Parent        ☐ Windows of Same Thread    ☐ All Windows in System
   ☐ Children      ☐ Windows of Same Process

   ☐ Save Settings as Default

      OK          Cancel        Help
```

After you have selected the types of windows you want to watch, you use the Window menu to decide if these messages are to be watched for one window only or for all windows.

Process Viewer

Figure 4-8 shows a sample Process Viewer window. The Process Viewer dialog box allows you to quickly set and view all of the options necessary to track current processes, threads, and processor time-slicing.

To start the Process Viewer, simply double-click on the PView icon in the Visual C++ group. The Process Viewer can help you answer questions such as:

■ How much memory does the program allocate at various points in its execution, and how much memory is being paged out?

■ Which processes and threads are using the most CPU time?

■ How does the program run at different system priorities?

■ What happens if a thread or process stops responding to DDE, OLE, or pipe I/O?

■ What percentage of time is spent running API calls?

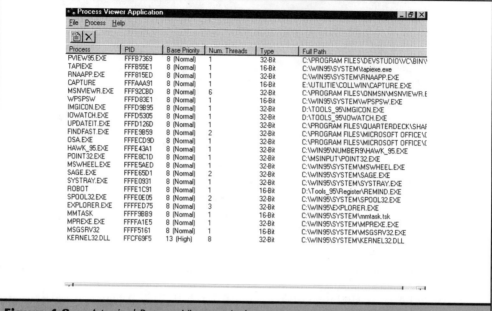

Figure 4-8. *A typical Process Viewer window*

CAUTION: *Since the Process Viewer lets you modify the status of processes running on your system, you can stop processes and potentially halt the entire system. Make sure that you save edited files before running the Process Viewer.*

WinDiff

The WinDiff utility, found in the Visual C++ group, allows you to graphically compare and modify two files or two directories. All of the options within WinDiff operate in a manner similar to those commands found in the File Manager.

Figure 4-9 shows a WinDiff dialog box with selections made to begin the process of locating the first file to be compared.

What's Coming?

In this chapter you have learned the fundamentals of using Microsoft's development and debugging tools. Unless you are already an advanced user, you will probably not need to use these tools until you reach the latter portion of this book.

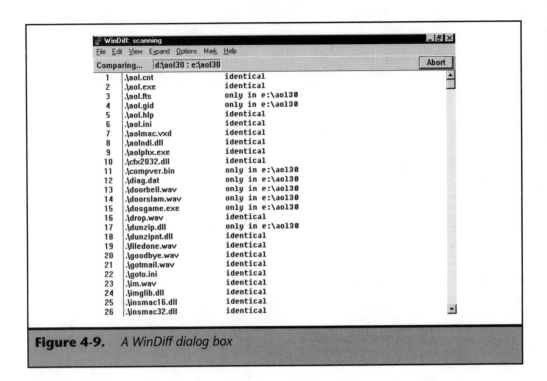

Figure 4-9. *A WinDiff dialog box*

The next chapter gives a formal introduction to the C/C++ language. The chapter looks at the early development of the C language up to its current state-of-the-art components.

Part II

Programming Foundations

The Complete Reference

Visual C++ 5

Chapter 5

C and C++ Programming

Beginning with this chapter, you will explore the origins, syntax, and usage of the C and C++ language. A study of C's history is worthwhile because it reveals the language's successful design philosophy and helps you understand why C and C++ may be the language of choice for years to come. Before you proceed, you should be comfortable with the Microsoft Visual C/C++ development environment. By now you should have installed the package, configured it to your personal requirements, and practiced using the compiler and the integrated debugger.

C Archives

Our archeological dig for the origins of the C language begins with a discussion of the UNIX operating system, since both the system and most of the programs that run on it are written in C. However, this does not mean that C is tied to UNIX or any other operating system or machine. The UNIX/C codevelopment environment has given C a reputation for being a *system programming language* because it is useful for writing compilers and operating systems. C is also very useful for writing major programs in many different domains.

The UNIX OS was originally developed in 1969 on what would now be considered a small DEC PDP-7 at Bell Laboratories in Murray Hill, New Jersey. UNIX was written entirely in PDP-7 assembly language. By design, this operating system was intended to be "programmer friendly," providing useful development tools, lean commands, and a relatively open environment. Soon after the development of UNIX, Ken Thompson implemented a compiler for a new language called B.

At this point it is helpful to examine the origins and history behind Ken Thompson's B language, a direct predecessor to C. Following is a comprehensive C lineage:

Language	Origins/Inventor
Algol 60	Designed by an international committee in early 1960
CPL	(Combined Programming Language) developed at both Cambridge and the University of London in 1963
BCPL	(Basic Combined Programming Language) developed at Cambridge by Martin Richards in 1967
B	Developed by Ken Thompson, Bell Labs, in 1970
C	Developed by Dennis Ritchie, Bell Labs, in 1972

Then in 1983, the American National Standards Institute (ANSI) committee was formed for the purpose of creating ANSI C—a standardization of the C language.

Algol 60 was a language that appeared only a few years after FORTRAN was introduced. This new language was more sophisticated and had a strong influence on the design of future programming languages. Its authors paid a great deal of attention to the regularity of syntax, modular structure, and other features usually associated with high-level structured languages. Unfortunately, Algol 60 never really caught on in the United States. Many say this was due to the language's abstractness and generality.

The inventors of CPL (Combined Programming Language) intended to bring Algol 60's lofty intent down to the realities of an actual computer. However, just as Algol 60 was hard to learn and difficult to implement, so was CPL. This led to its eventual downfall. Still clinging to the best of what CPL had to offer, the creators of BCPL (Basic Combined Programming Language) wanted to boil CPL down to its basic good features.

When Ken Thompson designed the B language for an early implementation of UNIX, he was trying to further simplify CPL. He succeeded in creating a very sparse language that was well suited for use on the hardware available to him. However, both BCPL and B may have carried their streamlining attempts a bit too far; they became limited languages, useful only for dealing with certain kinds of problems.

For example, no sooner had Ken Thompson implemented the B language than a new machine, called the PDP-11, was introduced. UNIX and the B compiler were immediately transferred to this new machine. While the PDP-11 was a larger machine than its PDP-7 predecessor, it was still quite small by today's standards. It had only 24K of memory, of which the system used 16K, and one 512K fixed disk. Some thought was given to rewriting UNIX in B, but the B language was slow because of its interpretive design. There was another problem as well: B was word oriented, but the PDP-11 was byte oriented. For these reasons, work was begun in 1971 on a successor to B, appropriately named C.

Dennis Ritchie is credited with creating C, which restored some of the generality lost in BCPL and B. He accomplished this through a shrewd use of data types, while maintaining the simplicity and direct access to the hardware that were the original design goals of CPL.

Many languages developed by a single individual (C, Pascal, Lisp, and APL) contain a cohesiveness that is missing from those created by large programming teams (Ada, PL/I, and Algol 60). It is also typical for a language written by one person to reflect the author's field of expertise. Dennis Ritchie was noted for his work in systems software—computer languages, operating systems, and program generators.

Given Ritchie's areas of expertise, it is easy to understand why C is a language of choice for systems software design. C is a relatively low-level language that allows you to specify every detail in an algorithm's logic to achieve maximum computer efficiency. But C is also a high-level language that can hide the details of the computer's architecture, thereby increasing programming efficiency.

C Versus Older High-Level Languages

At this point, you may be asking, "How does C compare to other programming languages?" A possible continuum is shown in Figure 5-1. If you start at the bottom of the continuum and move upward, you go from the tangible and empirical to the

Cyborg Neural Path Symbiosis
•
•
•

Artificial intelligence
Operating system command languages
Problem-oriented languages
Machine-oriented languages
Assembly language
•
•
•

Actual hardware

Figure 5-1.   *Theoretical evolution of programming languages*

elusive and theoretical. The dots represent major advancements, with many steps left out. Early ancestors of the computer, like the Jacquard loom (1805) and Charles Babbage's "analytical engine" (1834), were programmed in hardware. The day may well come when we will program a machine by plugging a neural path communicator into a socket implanted into the temporal lobe (language memory) or Broca's area (language motor area) of the brain's cortex.

The first assembly languages, which go back to the original introduction of electronic computers, provide a way of working directly with a computer's built-in instruction set, and are fairly easy to learn. Because assembly languages force you to think in terms of hardware, you had to specify every operation in the machine's terms. Therefore, you were always moving bits into or out of registers, adding them, shifting register contents from one register to another, and finally storing the results in memory. This was a tedious and error-prone endeavor.

The first high-level languages, such as FORTRAN, were created as alternatives to assembly languages. High-level languages were much more general and abstract, and they allowed you to think in terms of the problem at hand rather than in terms of the computer's hardware.

Unfortunately, the creators of high-level languages made the fallacious assumption that everyone who had been driving a standard, so to speak, would prefer driving an automatic. Excited about providing ease in programming, they left out some necessary options. FORTRAN and Algol are too abstract for systems-level work; they are *problem-oriented languages,* the kind used for solving problems in engineering, science, or business. Programmers who wanted to write systems software still had to rely on their machine's assembler.

In reaction to this situation, a few systems software developers took a step backward—or lower, in terms of the continuum—and created the category of *machine-oriented languages.* As you saw in C's genealogy, BCPL and B fit into this class of very low level software tools. These languages were excellent for a specific machine but not much use for anything else; they were too closely related to a particular architecture. The C language is one step above machine-oriented languages but still a step below most problem-solving languages. C is close enough to the computer to give you great control over the details of an application's implementation, yet far enough away to ignore the details of the hardware. This is why the C language is considered at once a high- and a low-level language.

Advantages of C

Every computer language you use has a definite look to its source code. APL has its hieroglyphic appearance, assembly language its columns of mnemonics, and Pascal its easily read syntax. And then there's C. Many programmers encountering C for the first time will find its syntax cryptic and perhaps intimidating. C contains very few of the friendly English-like syntax structures found in many other programming languages. Instead, C presents the software engineer with unusual-looking operators and a plethora of pointers. New C programmers will soon discover a variety of language characteristics whose roots go back to C's original hardware/software progenitor. The following sections highlight the strengths of the C language.

Optimal Code Size

There are fewer syntax rules in C than in many other languages, and it is possible to write a top-quality C compiler that will operate in only 256K of total memory. There are actually more operators and combinations of operators in C than there are keywords.

Terse Set of Keywords

The original C language, as developed by Dennis Ritchie, contained a mere 27 keywords. The ANSI C standard (discussed later in this chapter in "American National Standards Institute—ANSI C") has added several reserved words. Microsoft C/C++ further enhances the instruction set and brings the total Microsoft C/C++ keyword count to over 70.

Many of the functions commonly defined as part of other programming languages are not included in C. For example, C does not contain any built-in input and output capabilities, nor does it contain any arithmetic operations (beyond those of basic addition and subtraction) or string-handling functions. Since any language missing these capabilities is of little use, C provides a rich set of library functions for input/output, arithmetic operations, and string manipulation. This agreed-upon library set is so commonly used that it can almost be seen as part of the language itself. One of the strengths of C, however, is its loose structure, which enables you to recode these functions easily.

Lightning-Fast Executables

The C code produced by most compilers tends to be very efficient. The combination of a small language, a small run-time system, and the fact that the language is close to the hardware makes many C programs run at speeds close to their assembly language equivalents.

Limited Type Checking

Unlike Pascal, which is a strongly typed language, C treats data types somewhat more loosely. (Typing is explained in more detail in "Limited Type Checking," later in this chapter.) This is a carryover from the B language, which was also a loosely typed language. This looseness allows you to view data in different ways. For example, at one point in a program, the application may need to see a variable as a character and yet, for purposes of uppercasing (by subtracting 32), may want to see the same memory cell as the ASCII equivalent of the character.

Top-Down Design Implementations

C contains all of the control structures you would expect of a modern-day language. This is impressive when you consider C's 1971 incubation period, which predated formal structured programming. For loops, if and if-else constructs, case (switch) statements, and while loops are all incorporated into the language. C also provides for the compartmentalization of code and data by managing their scope. For example, C provides local variables for this purpose and calls-by-value for subroutine data privacy.

Modular Structure

C supports *modular programming*, which is the concept of separate compilation and linking. This allows you to recompile only the parts of a program that have been changed during development. This feature can be extremely important when you are developing large programs, or even medium-size programs on slow systems. Without support for modular programming, the amount of time required to compile a complete program can make the change, compile, test, and modify cycle prohibitively slow.

Transparent Interface to Assembly Language

There is a well-defined method for calling assembly language routines from most C compilers. Combined with the separation of compilation and linking, this makes C a very strong contender in applications that require a mix of high-level and assembler routines. C routines can also be integrated into assembly language programs on most systems.

Bit Manipulation

Often in systems programming it is necessary to manipulate objects at the bit level. Naturally, with C's origins so closely tied to the UNIX operating system, the language provides a rich set of bit-manipulation operators.

Pointer Data Types

One of the features an operating system requires of a language is the ability to address specific areas of memory. This capability also enhances the execution speed of a program. The C language meets these design requirements by using pointers (discussed in Chapter 10). While it is true that other languages implement pointers, C is noted for its ability to perform pointer arithmetic. For example, if the variable *student_record_ptr* points to the first element of an array *student_records*, then *student_record_ptr + 1* will be the address of the second element of *student_records*.

Extensible Structures

All arrays in C are one-dimensional. Multidimensional arrangements are built from combinations of these one dimensional arrays. Arrays and structures (records) can be joined in any manner desired, creating database organizations that are limited only by the programmer's ability. Arrays are discussed in more detail in Chapter 9.

Memory Efficient

For many of the same reasons that C programs tend to be fast, they tend to be very memory efficient. The lack of built-in functions saves programs from having to carry around support for functions that are not needed by that application.

Cross-Platform Portability

Portability is a measure of the ease of converting a program running on one computer or operating system to another computer or operating system. Programs written in C are among the most portable in the modern computer world. This is especially true in the mini- and microcomputer worlds.

Powerful Library Routines

There are many commercial function libraries available for all popular C compilers. Libraries are available for graphics, file handling, database support, screen windowing, data entry, communications, and general support functions. By using these libraries, you can save a great deal of development time.

Disadvantages of C

There are no perfect programming languages. Different programming problems require different solutions. It is the software engineer's task to choose the best language for a project. On any project, this is one of the first decisions you need to make, and it is nearly irrevocable once you start coding. The choice of a programming language can also make the difference between a project's success and failure. The following sections cover some of the weaknesses of the C language to give you a better idea of when to use and when not to use C for a particular application.

Limited Type Checking

The fact that C is not strongly typed is one of its strengths, but it is also one of its weaknesses. Technically, *typing* is a measure of how closely a language enforces the use of variable types. (For example, integer and floating-point are two different types of numbers.) In some languages it is illegal to assign one data type to another without invoking a conversion function. This protects the data from being compromised by unexpected roundoffs.

As discussed earlier, C will allow an integer to be assigned to a character variable, and vice versa. What this means to you is that you are going to have to properly manage your variables. For experienced programmers this will present no problem. However, novice program developers may want to remind themselves that this can be the source of side effects.

A *side effect* in a language is an unexpected change to a variable or other item. Because C is not a strongly typed language, it gives you great flexibility to manipulate data. For example, the assignment operator (=) can appear more than once in the same expression. This flexibility, which you can use to your advantage, means that expressions can be written that have no clear and definite value. Restricting the use of the assignment and similar operators, or eliminating all side effects and unpredictable results, would have seriously lessened much of C's power and appeal as a high-level assembly language.

Limited Run-Time Monitors

C's lack of checking in the run-time system can cause many mysterious and transient problems to go undetected. For example, the run-time system would not warn you if your application exceeded an array's bounds. This is one of the costs of streamlining a compiler for the sake of speed and efficiency.

"C Is Not for Children!"

C's tremendous range of features—from bit manipulation to high-level formatted I/O—and its relative consistency from machine to machine have led to its acceptance in science, engineering, and business applications. It has directly contributed to the wide availability of the UNIX operating system on computers of all types and sizes.

Like any other powerful tool, however, C imposes a heavy responsibility on its users. C programmers need to acquire a discipline very quickly, adopting various rules and conventions in order to make their programs understandable both to themselves, long after the programs were written, and to others trying to analyze the code for the first time. In C, programming discipline is essential. The good news is that it comes almost automatically with practice.

American National Standards Institute—ANSI C

The ANSI (American National Standards Institute) committee has developed standards for the C language. This section describes some of the significant changes suggested and implemented by the committee. Some of these changes are intended to increase the flexibility of the language, others to standardize features previously left to the discretion of the compiler implementor.

Previously, the only standard available was the book *The C Programming Language* by B. Kernighan and D. Ritchie (Prentice-Hall, Murray Hill, NJ: 1988). This book was not specific on some language details, which led to a divergence among compilers. The ANSI standard strives to remove these ambiguities. Although a few of the proposed changes could cause problems for some previously written programs, they should not affect most.

The ANSI C standard provides an even better opportunity than before to write portable C code. The standard has not corrected all areas of confusion in the language, however, and because C interfaces efficiently with machine hardware, many programs will always require some revision when they are moved to a different environment. The ANSI committee that developed the standard adopted as guidelines some phrases that collectively have been called the "spirit of C." Some of those phrases are:

- Trust the programmer
- Don't prevent the programmer from doing what needs to be done
- Keep the language small and simple

Additionally, the international community was consulted to ensure that ANSI (American) standard C would be identical to the ISO (International Standards Organization) standard version. Because of these efforts, C is the only language that effectively deals with alternate collating sequences, enormous character sets, and multiple user cultures. Table 5-1 highlights just some of the areas the ANSI committee addressed.

From C to C++ and Object-Oriented Programming

Simply stated, C++ is a superset of the C language. C++ retains all of C's strengths, including its power and flexibility in dealing with the hardware/software interface; its low-level system programming; and its efficiency, economy, and powerful expressions.

Feature	Standardized
Data Types	Four: character, integer, floating point, and enumeration.
Comments	/* for the opening, */ for the closing; // alternatively, meaning that anything to symbol's right is ignored by the compiler.
Identifier Length	31 characters to distinguish uniqueness.
Standard Identifiers and Header Files	An agreed-upon minimum set of identifiers and header files necessary to perform basic operations such as I/O.
Preprocessor Statements	The # in preprocessor directives can have leading white space (any combination of spaces and tabs), permitting indented preprocessor directives for clarity. Some earlier compilers insisted that all preprocessor directives begin in column 1.
New Preprocessor Directives	#if defined (expression) and #elif (expression).
Adjacent Strings	The committee decided that adjacent literal strings should be concatenated. For example, this would allow a #define directive to extend beyond a single line.
Standard Libraries	The proposed ANSI standard specifies a basic set of system-level and external routines, such as read( ) and write( ).
Output Control	An agreed-upon set of escape codes representing formatting control codes such as newline, new page, and tabs.
Keywords	An agreed-upon minimum set of verbs used to construct valid C statements.
sizeof( )	The committee agreed that the sizeof( ) function should return the type size_t, instead of a system-limiting variable of size integer.

Table 5-1.   *ANSI C Recommendations*

Feature	Standardized
Prototyping	The committee agreed that all C compilers should handle programs that do/do not employ prototyping.
Command Line Arguments	In order for the C compiler to properly handle command line arguments, an agreed-upon syntax was defined.
void Pointer Type	The void keyword can be applied to functions that do not return a value. A function that does return a value can have its return value cast to void to indicate to the compiler that the value is being deliberately ignored.
Structure Handling	Structure handling has been greatly improved. The member names in structure and union definitions need not be unique. Structures can be passed as arguments to functions, returned by functions, and assigned to structures of the same type.
Function Declarations	Function declarations can include argument-type lists (function prototyping) to notify the compiler of the number and types of arguments.
Hexadecimal Character Constants	Hexadecimal character constants can be expressed using an introductory \x followed by from one to three hexadecimal digits (0-9, a-f, A-F). For example, 16 decimal = \x10, which can be written as 0x10 using the current notation.

Table 5-1. *ANSI C Recommendations* (continued)

PROGRAMMING FOUNDATIONS

However, C++ brings the C language into the dynamic world of object-oriented programming and makes it a platform for high-level problem abstraction, going beyond even Ada in this respect. C++ accomplishes all of this with a simplicity and support for modularity similar to Modula-2, while maintaining the compactness and execution efficiency of C.

This new hybrid language combines the standard procedural language constructs familiar to so many programmers and the object-oriented model, which you can exploit fully to produce a purely object-oriented solution to a problem. In practice, a C++ application can reflect this duality by incorporating both the procedural programming model and the newer object-oriented model. This biformity in C++ presents a special challenge to the beginning C++ programmer; there is not only a new language to learn, but also a new way of thinking and problem solving.

C++ Archives

Not surprisingly, C++ has an origin similar to C's. While C++ is somewhat like BCPL and Algol 68, it also contains components of Simula 67. C++'s ability to overload operators and its flexibility to include declarations close to their first point of application are features found in Algol 68. The concept of subclasses (or derived classes) and virtual functions is taken from Simula 67. Like many other popular programming languages, C++ represents an evolution and refinement of some of the best features of previous languages. Of course, it is closest to C.

Bjarne Stroustrup, of Bell Labs, is credited with developing the C++ language in the early 1980s. (Dr. Stroustrup credits Rick Mascitti with the naming of this new language.) C++ was originally developed to solve some very rigorous event-driven simulations for which considerations of efficiency precluded the use of other languages. C++ was first used outside Dr. Stroustrup's language group in 1983, and by the summer of 1987, the language was still going through a natural refinement and evolution.

One key design goal of C++ was to maintain compatibility with C. The idea was to preserve the integrity of millions of lines of previously written and debugged C code, the integrity of many existing C libraries, and the usefulness of previously developed C tools. Because of the high degree of success in achieving this goal, many programmers find the transition to C++ much simpler than when they first went from some other language, such as FORTRAN, to C.

C++ supports large-scale software development. Because it includes increased type checking, many of the side effects experienced when writing loosely typed C applications are no longer possible.

The most significant enhancement of the C++ language is its support for object-oriented programming (OOP). You will have to modify your approach to problem solving to derive all of the benefits of C++. For example, objects and their associated operations must be identified and all necessary classes and subclasses must be constructed.

Object Code Efficiency

What follows is an example of how an abstract data object in C++ can improve upon an older language's limited built-in constructs and features. For example, a FORTRAN software engineer may want to keep records on students. You could accomplish this with multiple arrays of scalar data that represent each set of data. All of the arrays are necessarily tied together by a common index. Should there be ten fields of information on each student, ten array accesses would have to be made using the same index location in order to represent the array of records.

In C++, the solution involves the declaration of a simple object, *student_database*, that can receive messages to *add_student*, *delete_student*, *access_student*, or *display_student* information contained within the object. The manipulation of the *student_database* object can then be performed in a natural manner. Inserting a new record into the *student_database* object becomes as simple as this:

```
student_database.add_student(new_recruit)
```

Assuming the *student_database* object has been appropriately declared, the add_student( ) function is a method suitably defined in the class that supports *student_database* objects, and the *new_recruit* parameter is the specific information that is to be added. Note that the class of objects called *student_database* is not a part of the underlying language itself. Instead, the programmer extends the language to suit the problem. By defining a new class of objects or by modifying existing classes (creating a subclass), a more natural mapping from the problem space to the program space (or solution space) occurs. The biggest challenge comes in truly mastering this powerful enhancement.

Subtle Differences Between C and C++

The following sections detail the minor (non-object-oriented) enhancements to the C language.

Comment Syntax

C++ introduces the comment to end-of-line delimiter //. However, the comment brackets /* and */ can still be used.

Enumerated Variables

The name of an enumeration is a type name. This streamlines the notation by not requiring the qualifier enum to be placed in front of the enumeration type name.

Structure Versus Classes

The name of a structure or class is a type name. This class construct does not exist in C. In C++ it is not necessary to use the qualifier struct or class in front of a structure or class name.

Block Scope

C++ permits declarations within blocks and after code statements. This feature allows you to declare an identifier closer to its first point of application. It even permits the loop control variable to be declared within the formal definition of the control structure, as shown here:

```
// C++ point-of-use variable declaration
    for(int index = 0; index < MAX_ROWS; index++)
```

Scope Resolution Operator

You use the new scope qualifier operator :: to resolve name conflicts. For example, if a function has a local declaration for a variable *vector_location* and there exists a global variable *vector_location*, the qualifier *::vector_location* allows the global variable to be accessed within the scope of the local function. The reverse is not possible.

The const Specifier

You can use the const specifier to lock the value of an entity within its scope. You can also use it to lock the data pointed to by a pointer variable, the value of the pointer address, or the values of both the pointer address and the data pointed to.

Anonymous Unions

Unions without a name can be defined anywhere a variable or field can be defined. You can use this ability for the economy of memory storage by allowing the sharing of memory among two or more fields of a structure.

Explicit Type Conversions

You can use the name of a predefined type or user-defined type as a function to convert data from one type to another. Under certain circumstances, such an explicit type conversion can be used as an alternative to a cast conversion.

Unique Function Capabilities

C++ will please many a Pascal, Modula-2, and Ada programmer because it permits the specification by name and type for each function parameter inside the parentheses next to the function name. For example:

```
void * dupmem(void *dest, int c, unsigned count)
{
    .
    .
    .
}
```

The equivalent C interface, under the ANSI standard, would look exactly the same. In this case, C++ influenced the ANSI standards committee.

The C++ translator will perform type checking to ensure that the number and type of values sent into a function when it is invoked match the number and type of the formal arguments defined for the function. A check is also made to ensure that the function's return type matches the variable used in the expression invoking the function. This type of parameter checking is missing in most C systems.

Overloading Functions

In C++, functions can use the same names if you use the specifier overload, and each of the overloaded functions can be distinguished on the basis of the number and type of its parameters.

Default Parameter Values

You can assign default values to trailing sets of C++ function parameters. In this case, the function can be invoked using fewer than the total number of parameters. Any missing trailing parameters assume their default values.

Varying-Length Argument Lists

You can define C++ functions with an unknown number and type of parameters by employing the ellipsis (...). When you use this feature, parameter type checking is suppressed to allow flexibility in the interface to the function.

Reference Argument Types

Through the use of the ampersand operator (&), a formal function parameter can be declared as a reference parameter. For example:

```
int i;
increment(i);

  .

  .

  .

void increment(int &variable_reference)
{
  variable_reference++;
}
```

Because &*variable_reference* is defined as a reference parameter, its address is assigned to the address of *i* when increment( ) is invoked. The value of *i* that is sent in is incremented within function increment( ) and returned to variable *i* outside of function increment( ). It is not necessary for the address of *i* to be explicitly passed into function increment( ), as it is in C.

PROGRAMMING FOUNDATIONS

Inline Functions

You can use the inline specifier to instruct the compiler to perform inline substitution of a given function at the location where the function is invoked.

The new and delete Keywords

The new and delete operators that are introduced by C++ allow for programmer-controlled allocation and deallocation of heap storage.

void Pointers

In C++, the type void is used to indicate that a function returns nothing. Pointer variables can be declared to point to void. They can then be assigned to any other pointer that points to an arbitrary base type.

Major Differences Between C and C++

The most significant major enhancement to C involves the concept of object-oriented programming. The following sections briefly explain all of the C++ enhancements that make object-oriented programming possible.

Class Constructs and Data Encapsulation

The class construct is the fundamental vehicle for object-oriented programming. A class definition can encapsulate all of the data declarations, the initial values, and the set of operations (called *methods*) for data abstraction. Objects can be declared to be of a given class, and messages can be sent to objects. Additionally, each object of a specified class can contain its own private and public sets of data representative of that class.

The struct Class

A *structure* in C++ is a subset of a class definition and has no private or protected sections. This subclass can contain both data (as is expected in ANSI C) and functions.

Constructors and Destructors

Constructor and destructor methods are used to guarantee the initialization of the data defined within an object of a specified class. When an object is declared, the specified initialization constructor is activated. Destructors automatically deallocate storage for the associated object when the scope in which the object is declared is exited.

Messages

As you have seen, the object is the basic fabric of object-oriented programming. You manipulate objects by sending them messages. You send messages to objects (variables declared to be of a given class) by using a mechanism similar to invoking a function. The set of possible messages that can be sent to an object is specified in the class description for the object. Each object responds to a message by determining an appropriate action to take based on the nature of the message. For example, if *Palette_Colors* represents an object, and *SetNumColors_Method* represents a method with a single-integer parameter, sending a message to the object would be accomplished by using the following statement:

```
Palette_Colors.SetNumColors_Method(16);
```

Friends

The concept of data hiding and data encapsulation implies a denied access to the inner structures that make up an object. The class' private section is normally totally off-limits to any function outside the class. C++ does allow other functions outside methods or classes to be declared to be a friend to a specified class. Friendship breaks down a normally impenetrable wall and permits access to the class' private data and methods.

Operator Overloading

With C++, the programmer can take the set of predefined operators and functions supplied with the compiler, or user-defined operators and functions, and give them multiple meanings. For example, different functions typically have different names, but for functions performing similar tasks on different types of objects, it is sometimes better to let these functions have the *same* name. When their argument types are different, the compiler can distinguish them and choose the right function to call. What follows is a coded example; you could have one function called total( ) that was overloaded for an array of integers, of floating points, and of double values.

```
int total(int isize, int iarray[]);
float total(int isize, float farray[]);
double total(int isize, double darray[]);
    .
    .
    .
```

Since you have declared the three different functions by the same name, the compiler can look at the invoking statement and automatically decide which function is appropriate for the formal parameter list's arguments:

```
   total(isize,iarray);
    total(isize,farray);
....total(isize,darray);
```

Derived Classes

A *derived class* can be seen as a subclass of a specified class, thereby forming a hierarchy of abstractions. Derived class objects typically inherit all or some of the methods of the parent class. It is also common for a derived class to then incorporate these inherited methods with new methods specific to the subclass. All subclass objects contain the fields of data from the parent class as well as any of their own private data.

Polymorphism Using Virtual Functions

Polymorphism involves a tree structure of parent classes and their subclasses. Each subclass within this tree can receive one or more messages with the same name. When an object of a class within this tree receives a message, the object determines the particular application of the message that is appropriate for an object of the specified subclass.

Stream Libraries

An additional library stream is included with the C++ language. The three classes cin, cout, and cerr are provided for terminal and file input and output. All of the operators within these three classes can be overloaded within a user-defined class. This capability allows the input and output operations to be easily tailored to an application's needs.

Fundamental Components for a C/C++ Program

You may have heard that C is a difficult language to master. However, while it is true that a brief encounter with C code may leave you scratching your head, this is only due to C's foreign syntax, structure, and indentation schemes. By the end of this chapter, you should have enough information to have developed a working knowledge of the C language that enables you to write short but meaningful code. In the next section you will learn about the five fundamental components of a "good" program.

Five Elements of Good C Program Design

You may be familiar with a problem-solution format called an IPO diagram. *IPO diagrams* were a stylized approach to the age-old programming problem of input/process/output. The following list elaborates on these three fundamentals and encapsulates the entire application development cycle. All programs must address the following five components:

1. Programs must obtain information from some input source.

2. Programs must decide how this input is to be arranged and stored.

3. Programs use a set of instructions to manipulate the input. These instructions can be broken down into four major categories: single statements, conditional statements, loops, and subroutines.

4. Programs must report the results of the data manipulation.

5. A well-written application incorporates all of the fundamentals just listed, expressed by using good modular design, self-documenting code (meaningful variable names), and a good indentation scheme.

A Simple C Program

The following C program illustrates the basic components of a C application. It is suggested that you enter each example as you read about it to help you understand new concepts as you encounter them.

```
/*
 *   simple.c
 *   Your first example C program.
 *   Copyright (c) Chris H. Pappas and William H. Murray, 1997
 */

#include <stdio.h>

int main( )
{
  printf(" HELLO World! ");

  return(0);
}
```

There is a lot happening in this short piece of code. Let's begin with the comment block:

```
/*
 *   simple.c
 *   Your first example C program.
 *   Copyright (c) Chris H. Pappas and William H. Murray, 1997
 */
```

All well-written source code includes meaningful comments. A meaningful comment is one that neither insults the intelligence of the programmer nor assumes too much. In C, comments begin with /* and are terminated with */. Anything between these unique symbol pairs is ignored by the compiler.

The next statement represents one of C's unique features, known as a *preprocessor statement:*

```
#include <stdio.h>
```

A preprocessor statement is like a precompile instruction. In this case the statement instructs the compiler to retrieve the code stored in the predefined STDIO.H file into the source code on the line requested. (The STDIO.H file is called a header file. *Header files* can include symbolic constants, identifiers, and function prototypes and have these declarations pulled out of the main program for purposes of modularity.)

Following the #include statement is the main function declaration:

```
int main( )
{
    .

    .

    .
    return(0);   /*   or return 0;   */
}
```

All C programs are made up of function calls. Every C program must have one called main( ). The main( ) function is usually where program execution begins, and it ends with a return( ) from the main( ). The int to the left of main( ) defines the function's return type, in this case integer, and explains why the return statement contains a number inside the parentheses. A value of 0 is interpreted as meaning a successful program termination. It is also legal to use return( ) statements without the parentheses.

Following the main( ) function header is the body of the function itself. Notice the { and } symbol pairs. These are called *braces.* You use braces to encapsulate multiple statements. These braces may define the body for a function, or they may bundle together statements that are dependent on the same logic control statement, as is the case when several statements are executed based on the validity of an if statement. In this example, the braces define the body of the main program.

The next line is the only statement in the body of the main( ) function and is the simplest example of an output statement:

```
printf(" HELLO World! ");
```

The printf( ) function was previously prototyped in STDIO.H. Because no other parameters are specified, the sentence will be printed to the display monitor.

A Simple C++ Program

The example that follows performs the same function as the one just discussed, but it takes advantage of those features unique to C++.

```
//
//   simple.cpp
//   Your first C++ example program.
//   Copyright (c) Chris H. Pappas and William H. Murray, 1997
//

#include <iostream.h>

int main( )
{
  cout << " HELLO World! ";

  return(0);
}
```

There are three major differences between this example and the last. First, the comment designator has been changed from the /* */ pair to //. Second, the #include filename has been changed to IOSTREAM.H. The third change involves a different output operator call, cout. Many of the examples in the book will highlight the sometimes subtle and sometimes dazzling differences between C and C++.

Adding a User Interface to a C Program

The following program is a slightly more meaningful example. It is a little more complete in that it not only outputs information but also prompts the user for input. Many of the components of this program will be elaborated on throughout the remainder of the book.

```
/*
 *   ui.c
 *   This C program prompts the user for a specified length,
 *   in feet, and then outputs the value converted to
 *   meters and centimeters
```

```
 *    Copyright (c) Chris H. Pappas and William H. Murray, 1997
 */

#include <stdio.h>

int main( )
{
  float feet, meters, centimeters;

  printf("Enter the number of feet to be converted: ");
  scanf("%f",&feet);

  while(feet > 0 ) {
    centimeters = feet * 12 * 2.54;
    meters = centimeters/100;
    printf("%8.2f feet equals\n", feet);
    printf("%8.2f meters \n",meters);
    printf("%8.2f centimeters \n",centimeters);
    printf("\nEnter another value to be \n");
    printf("converted (0 ends the program): ");
    scanf("%f",&feet);
  }
  printf(">>> Have a nice day! <<<");

  return(0);
}
```

Declaring Variables

The first thing you will notice that's new in the program is the declaration of
three variables:

```
float feet, meters, centimeters;
```

All C variables must be declared before they are used. One of the standard data
types supplied by the C language is float. The syntax for declaring variables in C
requires the definition of the variable's type before the name of the variable. In this
example, the float type is represented by the keyword float, and the three variables
feet, meters, and *centimeters* are defined.

User Interaction

The next unconventional-looking statement is used to input information from the keyboard:

```
printf("Enter the number of feet to be converted: ");
scanf("%f",&feet);
```

The scanf( ) function has a requirement that is called a format string. *Format strings* define how the input data is to be interpreted and represented internally. The "%f " function parameter instructs the compiler to interpret the input as float data. In Microsoft C and C++, a float occupies 4 bytes. (Chapter 6 contains a detailed explanation of all of the C and C++ language data types.)

An Introduction to the Address Operator

In the previous statement you may have noticed that the float variable *feet* was preceded by an ampersand symbol (&). The & is known as an *address operator*. Whenever a variable is preceded by this symbol, the compiler uses the address of the specified variable instead of the value stored in the variable. The scanf( ) function has been written to expect the address of the variable to be filled.

A Simple while Loop

One of the simplest loop structures to code in C is the while loop:

```
while(feet > 0) {
   .
   .
   .
}
```

This pretest loop starts with the reserved word while, followed by a Boolean expression that returns either a TRUE or a FALSE. The opening brace ({) and closing brace (}) are optional; they are only needed when more than one executable statement is to be associated with the loop repetition. Braced statements are sometimes referred to as *compound statements, compound blocks,* or *code blocks.*

If you are using compound blocks, make certain you use the agreed-upon brace style. While it doesn't matter to the compiler where the braces are placed (in terms of skipped spaces or lines), programmers reading your code will certainly appreciate the style and effort. An opening loop brace is placed at the end of the test condition, and the closing brace is placed in the same column as the first character in the test condition.

Screen Output

In analyzing the second program, you will notice more complex printf( ) function calls:

```
printf("%8.2f feet equals\n", feet);
printf("%8.2f meters \n",meters);
printf("%8.2f centimeters \n",centimeters);
printf("\nEnter another value to be \n");
printf("converted (0 ends the program): ");
```

If you are familiar with the PL/I language developed by IBM, you will be right at home with the concept of a format or control string. Whenever a printf( ) function is invoked to print not only *literal strings* (any set of characters between double quote marks), but also values, a format string is required. The format string represents two things: a picture of how the output string is to look, combined with the format interpretation for each of the values printed. Format strings are always between double quote marks.

Let's break down the first printf( ) format string ("%8.2f feet equals\n", feet) into its separate components:

Control	Action
%8.2f	Take the value of feet, interpret it as a float, and print it in a field of eight spaces with two decimal places.
feet equals	After printing the float feet, skip one space and then print the literal string "feet equals."
\n	Once the line is complete, execute a new line feed.
,	The comma separates the format string from the variable name(s) used to satisfy all format descriptors. (In this case there is only one %8.2f.)

The next two printf( ) statements are similar in execution. Each statement prints a formatted float value, followed by a literal string, and ending with a newline feed. If you were to run the program, your output would look similar to this:

```
Enter the number of feet to be converted: 10
   10.00 feet equals
    3.05 meters
  304.80 centimeters

Enter another value to be
converted (0 stops program): 0
```

The C *escape sequences*, or *output control characters*, allow you to use a sequence of characters to represent special characters. Table 5-2 lists all of the output control symbols and a description of how they can be used in format strings. All leading zeros are ignored by the compiler for characters notated in hexadecimal. The compiler determines the end of a hex-specified escape character when it encounters either a non-hex character or more than two hex characters, excluding leading zeros.

Also on the subject of format strings—though this is a bit advanced—are the scanf( ) formatting controls. Table 5-3 describes the scanf( ) formatting controls and their meanings. If you wish to input a string without automatically appending a terminating null character (\0), use %nc, where *n* is a decimal integer. In this case, the c format symbol indicates that the argument is a pointer to a character array. The next *n* characters are read from the input stream into the specified location, and no null character (\0) is appended. If *n* is not specified, the default character array length is 1.

As you learn more about the various C data types, you will be able to refer back to Tables 5-2 and 5-3 for a reminder of how the different controls affect input and output.

Using the Integrated Debugger

To examine the actual operation of the C code presented in this section, you can use the integrated debugger. When you compile your program, make certain you have turned on debug information. This is done in conjunction with the Project utility. Once your application is compiled and linked, use the debugger to keep an eye on the variables *yard*, *feet*, and *inch*.

Sequence	Name	Sequence	Name
\a	Alert (bell)	\?	Literal quotation mark
\b	Backspace	\'	Single quotation mark
\f	Form feed	\"	Double quotation mark
\n	Newline	\\	Backslash
\r	Carriage return	\ddd	ASCII character in octal notation
\t	Horizontal tab	\xdd	ASCII character in hex notation
\v	Vertical tab		

Table 5-2. *Output Control Symbols*

Character	Input Type Expected	Argument Type
d	Decimal integer	Pointer to int
o	Octal integer	Pointer to int
x, X	Hexadecimal integer	Pointer to int
I	Decimal, hexadecimal	Pointer to int or octal integer
u	Unsigned decimal integer	Pointer to unsigned int
e, E	Floating-point value	Pointer to float
f g, G	Consisting of an optional sign (+ or −), a series of one or more decimal digits possibly containing a decimal point, and an optional exponent ("e" or "E") followed by an optionally signed integer value	
c	Character. Whitespace characters that are ordinarily skipped are read when c is specified; to read the next non-whitespace character, use %1s	Pointer to char
s	String	Pointer to character array auto create NULL string
n	No input read from stream or buffer	Pointer to int, into which is stored the number of characters read from the stream or buffer up to that point in call to scanf
p	In the form xxxx:yyyy, where x digits and y digits are uppercase hexadecimal digits	Pointer to far; pointer to void

Table 5-3. *Format Control Symbols*

Adding a User Interface to a C++ Program

The following C++ example is identical in function to the previous C example except for some minor variations in the syntax used.

```
//
//  ui.cpp
//  This C++ program prompts the user for a specified length,
//  feet, and then outputs the value converted to
//  meters and centimeters.
//  Copyright (c) Chris H. Pappas and William H. Murray, 1997
//

#include <iostream.h>
#include <iomanip.h>

int main( )
{
  float feet,meters,centimeters;

  cout << "Enter the number of feet to be converted: ";
  cin  >> feet;

  while(feet > 0 ) {
    centimeters = feet * 12 * 2.54;
    meters = centimeters/100;
    cout << setw(8) << setprecision \
         << setiosflags(ios::fixed) << feet << " feet equals \n";
    cout << setw(8) << setprecision \
         << meters << " meters \n";
    cout << setw(8) << setprecision \
         << centimeters << " centimeters \n";
    cout << "\nEnter another value to be \n";
    cout << "converted (0 ends the program): ";
    cin >>  feet;
  }
  cout << ">>> Have a nice day! <<<";

  return(0);
}
```

There are six major differences between the C++ example and its C counterpart. The first two changes involve the use of cin and cout for I/O. These statements use the << ("put to," or insertion) and >> ("get from," or extraction) iostream operators. Both operators have been overloaded to handle the output/input of all the predefined types. They can also be overloaded to handle user-defined types such as rational numbers.

The last four changes are all related to formatting C++ output. To gain the same output precision easily afforded by C's "%8.2f" format string, the program requires four additional statements. The file IOMANIP.H is included in the program to give access to three specific class-member inline functions: setw( ), setprecision( ), and setiosflags( ). As you look at the code, you will notice that the calls to setw( ) and setprecision( ) are repeated. This is because their effect is only for the next output value, unlike setiosflags( ), which makes a global change to fixed output.

C++ programmers who like the power and flexibility of the C output function printf( ) can use printf( ) directly from library STDIO.H. The next two statements show the C and C++ equivalents:

```
printf("%8.2f feet equals\n", feet);
cout << setw(8) << setprecision \
      << setiosflags(ios::fixed) << feet << " feet equals \n";
```

Adding File I/O

Of course, there will be times when an application wants either its input or output, rather than the keyboard and display monitor, to deal directly with files. This brief introduction serves as an example of how to declare and use simple data files:

```
/*
 *    file1a.c
 *    This C program demonstrates how to declare and use both
 *    input and output files. The example program
 *    takes the order_price from customer.dat and generates
 *    a billing_price that is printed to billing.dat.
 *    Copyright (c) Chris H. Pappas and William H. Murray, 1997
 */

#include <stdio.h>
#define MIN_DISCOUNT .97
#define MAX_DISCOUNT .95

int main( )
{
  float forder_price, fbilling_price;
  FILE *fin,*fout;

  fin=fopen("a:\\customer.dat","r");
  fout=fopen("a:\\billing.dat","w");
```

```
    while (fscanf(fin,"%f",&forder_price) != EOF) {
      fprintf(fout,"Your order of \t\t$%8.2f\n", forder_price);
      if (forder_price < 10000)
          fbilling_price = forder_price * MIN_DISCOUNT;
      else fbilling_price = forder_price * MAX_DISCOUNT;
      fprintf(fout,"is discounted to \t$%8.2f.\n\n",
              fbilling_price);
    }
    return(0);
}
```

Each file in a C program must be associated with a file pointer, which points to information that defines various things about a file, including the path to the file, its name, and its status. A file pointer is a pointer variable of type FILE and is defined in STDIO.H. The following statement from the example program declares two files, *fin and *fout:

```
, FILE *fin,*fout;
```

The next two statements in the program open two separate streams and associate each file with its respective stream:

```
fin=fopen("a:\\customer.dat","r");
fout=fopen("a:\\billing.dat","w");
```

The statements also return the file pointer for each file. Since these are pointers to files, your application should never alter their values.

The second parameter to the fopen( ) function is the file mode. Files may be opened in either text or binary mode. When in text mode, most C compilers translate carriage return/linefeed sequences into newline characters on input. During output, the opposite occurs. However, binary files do not go through such translations. Table 5-4 lists all of the valid file modes.

The r+, w+, and a+ file modes select both reading and writing. (The file is open for update.) When switching between reading and writing, you must remember to reposition the file pointer, using either fsetpos( ), fseek( ), or rewind( ).

C does perform its own file closing automatically whenever the application closes. However, there may be times when you want direct control over when a file is closed.

Access Type	Description
a	Opens in append mode. It creates the file if it does not already exist. All write operations occur at the end of the file.
a+	Same as previous, but also allows reading.
r	Opens for reading. If the file does not exist or cannot be found, the open call will fail.
r+	Opens for both reading and writing. If the file does not exist or cannot be found, the open call will fail.
w	Opens an empty file for writing. If the file exists, all contents are destroyed.
w+	Opens an empty file for both reading and writing. If the file exists, all contents are destroyed.

Table 5-4. *Valid C File Modes*

The following listing shows the same program modified to include the necessary closing function calls:

```c
/*
 *   file1b.c
 *   This C program demonstrates how to declare and use both
 *   input and output files. The example program
 *   takes the order_price from customer.dat and generates
 *   a billing_price that is printed to billing.dat
 *   Copyright (c) Chris H. Pappas and William H. Murray, 1997
 */

#include <stdio.h>
#define MIN_DISCOUNT .97
#define MAX_DISCOUNT .95

int main( )
{
  float forder_price, fbilling_price;
  FILE *fin,*fout;
```

```
  fin=fopen("a:\\customer.dat","r");
  fout=fopen("a:\\billing.dat","w");

  while (fscanf(fin,"%f",&forder_price) != EOF) {
    fprintf(fout,"Your order of \t\t$%8.2f\n", forder_price);
    if (forder_price < 10000)
       fbilling_price = forder_price * MIN_DISCOUNT;
    else fbilling_price = forder_price * MAX_DISCOUNT;
    fprintf(fout,"is discounted to \t$%8.2f.\n\n",
fbilling_price);
  }

  fclose(fin);
  fclose(fout);

  return(0);
}
```

The following program performs the same function as the one just examined but is coded in C++:

```
//
// file2.cpp
// This C++ program demonstrates how to declare and use both
// input and output files. The example program
// takes the order_price from customer.dat and generates
// a billing_price that is printed to billing.dat
// Copyright (c) Chris H. Pappas and William H. Murray, 1997
//

#include <fstream.h>
#include <iomanip.h>
#define MIN_DISCOUNT .97
#define MAX_DISCOUNT .95

int main( )
{
  float forder_price, fbilling_price;
  ifstream fin("a:\\customer.dat");
  ofstream fout("a:\\billing.dat");
```

```
  fin >> forder_price;
  while (!fin.eof( )) {
    fout << setiosflags(ios::fixed);
    fout << "Your order of \t\t$" << setprecision \
        << setw(8) << forder_price << "\n";
    if (forder_price < 10000)
      fbilling_price = forder_price * MIN_DISCOUNT;
    else fbilling_price = forder_price * MAX_DISCOUNT;
    fout << "is discounted to \t$" << setprecision \
        << setw(8) << fbilling_price << ".\n\n";
    fin >> forder_price;
  }

  fin.close( );
  fout.close( );

  return(0);
}
```

Disk file input and output are slightly different in C++ than in C. C++ has a two-part design to its stream library; a streambuf object and a stream. This same model performs I/O for keyboard and terminal as well as disk I/O. The same operators and operations perform in precisely the same way. This greatly simplifies a programming task that has always been difficult and confusing. To facilitate disk file I/O, the stream library defines a filebuf object, which is a derivative of the standard streambuf type. Like its progenitor type, filebuf manages a buffer, but in this case, the buffer is attached to a disk file. You will learn more about files in Chapter 11.

Visual
C++ 5

Chapter 6

Working with Data

H ere is a true statement: "You will never truly be a C/C++ programmer until you stop thinking in some other language and *translating* into C/C++!" You may have formally learned either COBOL, FORTRAN, Pascal, or PL/I, and then with brute force, taught yourself one or more of the other languages listed, and been quite successful at it.

The same approach will *not* work with C and C++. The reason for this is that these new state-of-the-art languages have unique features, constructs, and ways of doing things that *have no equivalent* in the listed, older, high-level languages. If you attempt to do a mental translation, you will end up not taking advantage of all that C and C++ have to offer. Even worse, in the presence of a truly experienced C/C++ programmer, you will look like an obvious novice. Technically and philosophically correct C/C++ source code design has many nuances that quickly expose fraudulent claims of expertise!

Fully appreciating all that C and C++ have to offer takes time and practice. In this chapter, you begin your exploration of their underlying structures. The great stability of these languages begins with the standard C and C++ data types and the modifiers and operators that can be used with them.

Identifiers

Identifiers are the names you use to represent variables, constants, types, functions, and labels in your program. You create an identifier by specifying it in the declaration of a variable, type, or function. You can then use the identifier in later program statements to refer to the associated item.

An identifier is a sequence of one or more letters, digits, or underscores that begins with a letter or underscore. Identifiers can contain any number of characters, but only the first 31 are significant to the compiler. (However, other programs that read the compiler output, such as the linker, may recognize even fewer characters.)

C and C++ are *case sensitive*. This means that the C compiler considers uppercase and lowercase letters to be distinct characters. For example, the compiler sees the variables *NAME_LENGTH* and *Name_Length* as two unique identifiers representing different memory cells. This feature enables you to create distinct identifiers that have the same spelling but different cases for one or more of the letters.

The selection of case can also help you understand your code. For example, identifiers declared in #include header files are often created using only uppercase letters. Because of this, whenever you encounter an uppercase identifier in the source file, you have a visual clue as to where that particular identifier's definition can be found.

While it is syntactically legal, you should not use leading underscores in identifiers you create. Identifiers beginning with an underscore can cause conflicts with the names of system routines or variables and produce errors. As a result, programs containing names beginning with leading underscores are not guaranteed to be portable. Use of two sequential underscore characters (__) in an identifier is reserved for C++ implementations and standard libraries.

One stylistic convention adopted by many C programmers is to precede all identifiers with an abbreviation of the identifier's data type. For example, all integer identifiers would begin with an "i," floats would begin with an "f," null-terminated strings would begin with "sz," pointer variables would begin with a "p," and so on. With this naming convention, you can easily look at a piece of code and see not only which identifiers are being used, but also their data type. This makes it easier to learn how a particular section of code operates and to do line-by-line source debugging. The programs throughout this book use both variable naming conventions since many of the programs you encounter in real life will use one format or another.

The following are examples of identifiers:

```
i
itotal
frange1
szfirst_name
lfrequency
imax
iMax
iMAX
NULL
EOF
```

See if you can determine why the following identifiers are illegal:

```
1st_year
#social_security
Not_Done!
```

The first identifier is illegal because it begins with a decimal number. The second begins with a # symbol, and the last ends with an illegal character.

Take a look at the following identifiers. Are they legal or not?

```
O
OO
OOO
_____
```

Actually, all four identifiers are legal. The first three use the uppercase letter "O." Since each has a different number of O's, they are all unique. The fourth identifier is composed of five underscore (_) characters. Is it meaningful? Definitely not. Is it legal? Yes. While these identifiers meet the letter of the law, they greatly miss its spirit. The point is that all identifiers, functions, constants, and variables should have meaningful names.

Since uppercase and lowercase letters are considered distinct characters, each of the following identifiers is unique:

```
MAX_RATIO
max_ratio
Max_Ratio
```

The C compiler's case sensitivity can create tremendous headaches for the novice C programmer. For example, trying to reference the printf( ) function when it was typed **PRINTF( )** will invoke "unknown identifier" complaints from the compiler. In Pascal, however, a writeln is a WRITELN is a WriteLn.

With experience you would probably detect the preceding printf( ) error, but can you see what's wrong with this next statement?

```
printf("%D",integer_value);
```

Assuming that *integer_value* was defined properly, you might think that nothing was wrong. Remember, however, that C is case sensitive—the %D print format has never been defined; only %d has.

For more advanced applications, some linkers may further restrict the number and type of characters for globally visible symbols. Also, the linker, unlike the compiler, may not distinguish between uppercase and lowercase letters. By default, the Visual C/C++ LINK sees all public and external symbols, such as *MYVARIABLE, MyVariable,* and *myvariable,* as the same. You can, however, make LINK case sensitive by using the /NOI option. This would then force LINK to see the preceding three example variables as unique. Use your PWB help utility for additional information on how to use this switch.

One last word on identifiers: an identifier cannot have the same spelling and case as a keyword of the language. The next section lists C and C++ keywords.

Keywords

Keywords are predefined identifiers that have special meanings to the C/C++ compiler. You can use them only as defined. Remember, the name of a program identifier cannot have the same spelling and case as a C/C++ keyword. The C/C++ language keywords are listed in Table 6-1.

_asm	_fastcall	public	signed
_except	new	unsigned	void
_virtual_inheritance	typedef	using directive	do
throw	class	default	_leave
case	goto	_int8	struct
_finally	register	sizeof	auto
operator	using declaration	volatile	explicit
typeid	uuid	double	mutable
const	delete	long	true
if	_int16	switch	catch
reinterpret_cast	static	template	float
return	wmain	_based	private
_uuidof	dynamic_cast	extern	typename
dllexport	main	naked	const_cast
_int32	__multiple _inheritance	try	inline
static_cast	this	_cdecl	_inline
while	bool	for	short
else	false	protected	virtual
enum	namespace	union	dllimport
_single_inheritance	_try	continue	_int64
thread	char	_declspec	_stdcall
break	friend	int	xalloc

Table 6-1.   *C/C++ Keywords (Those with Leading Underscores Are Microsoft-Specific)*

You cannot redefine keywords. However, you can specify text to be substituted for keywords before compilation by using C preprocessor directives.

Standard C and C++ Data Types

All programs deal with some kind of information that you can usually represent by using one of the eight basic C and C++ types: text or char, integer values or int, floating-point values or float, double floating-point values or double (long double), enumerated or enum, valueless or void, pointers, and bool. Following is an explanation of the types:

- *Text* (data type *char*) is made up of single characters, such as a, Z, ?, 3; and strings, such as "There is more to life than increasing its speed." (Usually, 8 bits, or 1 byte per character, with the range of 0 to 255.)

- *Integer values* are those numbers you learned to count with (1, 2, 7, –45, and 1,345). (Usually, 16 bits wide, 2 bytes, or 1 word, with the range of –32,768 to 32,767. Under Windows 95 and Windows NT, integers are now 32 bits wide with a range from –2147483648 to 2147483647.)

- *Floating-point values* are numbers that have a fractional portion, such as pi (3.14159), and exponents (7.563^{1021}). These are also known as real numbers. (Usually, 32 bits, 4 bytes, or 2 words, with the range of +/– 3.4E–38 to 3.4E+38.)

- *Double floating-point values* have an extended range (usually, 64 bits, 8 bytes, or 4 words, with the range of 1.7E–308 to 1.7E+308). Long double floating-point values are even more precise (usually, 80 bytes, or 5 words, with the range of +/– 1.18E–4932 to 1.18E+4932).

- *Enumerated* data types allow for user-defined types.

- The type *void* is used to signify values that occupy zero bits and have no value. (This type can also be used for the creation of generic pointers, as discussed in Chapter 10.)

- The *pointer* data type doesn't hold information in the normal sense of the other data types; instead, each pointer contains the address of the memory location holding the actual data. (This is also discussed in Chapter 10.)

- And, the new *bool* data type, which can be assigned the two constants, true, and false.

Characters

Every language uses a set of characters to construct meaningful statements. For instance, all books written in English use combinations of 26 letters of the alphabet, the ten digits, and the punctuation marks. Similarly, C and C++ programs are written using a set of characters, consisting of the 26 lowercase letters of the alphabet:

abcdefghijklmnopqrstuvwxyz

the 26 uppercase letters of the alphabet:

ABCDEFGHIJKLMNOPQRSTUVWXYZ

the ten digits:

0 1 2 3 4 5 6 7 8 9

and the following symbols:

+ - * / =, . _ : ; ? \ " ' ~ | ! # % $ & ( ) [ ] { } ^ @

C and C++ also use the blank space, sometimes referred to as white space. Combinations of symbols, with no blank space between them, are also valid C and C++ characters. In fact, the following is a mixture of valid C and C++ symbols:

++ -- == && | | << >> >= <= += -= *= /= ?: :: /* */ //

The following C program illustrates how to declare and use char data types:

```c
/*
 *   char.c
 *   A C program demonstrating the char data type and showing
 *   how a char variable can be interpreted as an integer.
 *   Copyright (c) Chris H. Pappas and William H. Murray, 1997
 */

#include <stdio.h>
#include <ctype.h>

int main( )
{
  char csinglechar, cuppercase, clowercase;

  printf("\nPlease enter a single character: ");
  scanf("%c",&csinglechar);

  cuppercase = toupper(csinglechar);
  clowercase = tolower(csinglechar);

  printf("The UPPERcase character \'%c\' has a decimal ASCII"
         " value of %d\n",cuppercase,cuppercase);
  printf("The ASCII value represented in hexadecimal"
         " is %X\n",cuppercase);

  printf("If you add sixteen you will get \'%c\'\n",
```

```
                    (cuppercase+16));
        printf("The calculated ASCII value in hexadecimal"
                " is %X\n",(cuppercase+16));
        printf("The LOWERcase character \'%c\' has a decimal ASCII"
                " value of %d\n",clowercase,clowercase);

        return(0);
}
```

The output from the program looks like this:

```
Please enter a single character: d
The UPPERcase character 'D' has a decimal ASCII value of 68
The ASCII value represented in hexadecimal is 44
If you add sixteen you will get 'T'
The calculated ASCII value in hexadecimal is 54
The LOWERcase character 'd' has a decimal ASCII value of 100
```

The %X format control instructs the compiler to interpret the value as an uppercase hexadecimal number.

Three Integers

Microsoft Visual C/C++ supports three types of integers. Along with the standard type int, the compiler supports short int and long int. These are most often abbreviated to just short and long. While the C language is not hardware dependent (syntax, etc.), data types used by the C language are. Thus, the actual sizes of short, int, and long depend upon the implementation. Across all C compilers, the only guarantee is that a variable of type short will not be larger than one of type long. Microsoft Visual C/C++ allocates 2 bytes for both short and int. (Under Windows 95 and Windows NT, integers are now 32 bits.) The type long occupies 4 bytes of storage.

Unsigned Modifier

All C and C++ compilers allow you to declare certain types to be unsigned. Currently, you can apply the unsigned modifier to four types: char, short int, int, and long int. (See Table 6-2 for a summary of storage and range for the fundamental C/C++ data types.) When one of these data types is modified to be unsigned, you can think of the range of values it holds as representing the numbers displayed on a car odometer. An automobile odometer starts at 000..., increases to a maximum of 999..., and then recycles back to 000.... It also displays only positive whole numbers. In a similar way, an unsigned data type can hold only positive values in the range of zero to the maximum number that can be represented.

For example, suppose you are designing a new data type called *my_octal* and have decided that *my_octal* variables can hold only 3 bits. You have also decided that the data type *my_octal* is signed by default. Since a variable of type *my_octal* can only contain the bit patterns 000 through 111 (or zero to 7 decimal), and you want to represent both positive and negative values, you have a problem. You can't have both positive and negative numbers in the range zero to 7 because you need one of the three bits to represent the sign of the number. Therefore, *my_octal*'s range is a subset. When the most significant bit is zero, the value is positive. When the most significant bit is 1, the value is negative. This gives a *my_octal* variable the range of –4 to +3.

Type Name	Bytes	Other Names	Range of Values
int	*	signed, signed int	System dependent
unsigned int	*	unsigned	System dependent
__int8	1	char, signed char	–128 to 127
__int16	2	short, short int, signed short int	–32,768 to 32,767
__int32	4	signed, signed int	–2,147,483,648 to 2,147,483,647
__int64	8	none	–9,223,372,036,854,775,808 to 9,223,372,036,854,775,807
char	1	signed char	–128 to 127
unsigned char	1	none	0 to 255
short	2	short int, signed short int	–32,768 to 32,767
unsigned short	2	unsigned short int	0 to 65,535
long	4	long int, signed long int	–2,147,483,648 to 2,147,483,647
unsigned long	4	unsigned long int	0 to 4,294,967,295
enum	*	none	Same as int
float	4	none	3.4E +/–38 (7 digits)
double	8	none	1.7E +/–308 (15 digits)
long double	10	none	1.2E +/–4932 (19 digits)

Table 6-2. *ANSI C/C++ Standard Data Types and Sizes*

However, applying the unsigned data type modifier to a *my_octal* variable would yield a range of zero to 7, since the most significant bit can be combined with the lower 2 bits to represent a broader range of positive values instead of identifying the sign of the number. This simple analogy holds true for any of the valid C data types defined to be of type unsigned.

The long double data type (80-bit, 10-byte precision) is mapped directly to double (64-bit, 8-byte precision) in Windows NT and Windows 95. Signed and unsigned are modifiers that can be used with any integral type. The char type is signed by default, but you can specify /J to make it unsigned by default. The int and unsigned int types have the size of the system word. This is 2 bytes (the same as short and unsigned short) in MS-DOS and 16-bit versions of Windows, and 4 bytes in 32-bit operating systems. However, portable code should not depend on the size of int. Microsoft C/C++ also features support for sized integer types. Table 6-3 lists the valid data type modifiers in all of the various legal and abbreviated combinations.

Floating Point

Visual C/C++ uses the three floating-point types float, double, and long double. While the ANSI C standard does not specifically define the values and storage that are to be allocated for each of these types, the standard did require each type to hold a

Type Specifier	Equivalent
signed char	char
signed int	signed, int
signed short int	short, signed short
signed long int	long, signed long
unsigned char	none
unsigned int	unsigned
unsigned short int	unsigned short
unsigned long int	unsigned long
float	none
long double	none

Table 6-3. *Valid Data Type Modifier Abbreviations*

minimum of any value in the range 1E–37 to 1E+37. As you saw in Table 6-2, the Microsoft Visual C/C++ environment has greatly expanded upon this minimum requirement. Historically, most C compilers have always had the types float and double. The ANSI C committee added the third type, long double. Here are some examples of floating-point numbers:

```
float altitude = 47000;
double joules;
long double budget_deficit;
```

You can use the third type, long double, on any computer, even those that have only two types of floating-point numbers. However, if the computer does not have a specific data type of long double, then the data item will have the same size and storage capacity as a double.

The following C++ program illustrates how to declare and use floating-point variables:

```
//
//   float.cpp
//   A C++ program demonstrating using the float data type.
//   Copyright (c) Chris H. Pappas and William H. Murray, 1997
//

#include <iostream.h>
#include <iomanip.h>

int main( )
{
  long loriginal_flags=cin.flags( );
  float fvalue;

  cout << "Please enter a float value to be formatted: ";
  cin >> fvalue;

  cout << "Standard Formatting:   " << fvalue << "\n";
  cout.setf(ios::scientific);
  cout << "Scientific Formatting: " << fvalue << "\n";

  cout.setf(ios::fixed);
  cout << "Fixed Formatting:      " << setprecision
       << fvalue;
```

```
    cout.flags(loriginal_flags);

    return(0);
}
```

The output looks like this:

```
Please enter a float value to be formatted: 1234.5678
Standard Formatting:    1234.57
Scientific Formatting: 1.234568e+003
Fixed Formatting:       0x004010191234.57
```

Notice the different value printed depending on the print format specification standard, scientific or fixed.

Enumerated

When an enumerated variable is defined, it is associated with a set of named integer constants called the *enumeration set*. (These are discussed in Chapter 13.) The variable can contain any one of the constants at any time, and the constants can be referred to by name. For example, the following definition creates the enumerated type *air_supply*; the enumerated constants EMPTY, USEABLE, and FULL; and the enumerated variable *instructor_tank*:

```
enum air_supply { EMPTY,
                  USEABLE,
                  FULL=5 } instructor_tank;
```

All the constants and variables are type int, and each constant is automatically provided a default initial value unless another value is specified. In the preceding example, the constant name EMPTY has the integer value zero by default since it is the first in the list and was not specifically overridden. The value of USEABLE is 1 since it occurs immediately after a constant with the value of zero. The constant FULL was specifically initialized to the value 5, and if another constant were included in the list after FULL, the new constant would have the integer value of 6.

Having created *air_supply*, you can later define another variable, *student_tank*, as follows:

```
enum air_supply student_tank;
```

After this statement it is legal to say

```
instructor_tank = FULL;
student_tank    = EMPTY;
```

This places the value 5 into the variable *instructor_tank* and the value of zero into the variable *student_tank*.

> **NOTE:** *When defining additional enumerated variables in C++, it is not necessary to repeat the* enum *keyword. However, both syntaxes are accepted by the C++ compiler.*

One common mistake is to think that air_supply is a variable. It is a "type" of data that can be used later to create additional enumerated variables like *instructor_tank* or *student_tank.*

Since the name *instructor_tank* is an enumerated variable of type air_supply, *instructor_tank* can be used on the left of an assignment operator and can receive a value. This occurred when the enumerated constant FULL was explicitly assigned to it. EMPTY, USEABLE, and FULL are names of constants; they are not variables and their values cannot be changed.

Tests can be performed on the variables in conjunction with the constants. The following is a complete C program that uses the preceding definitions:

```
/*
 *    enum.c
 *    A C program demonstrating the use of enumeration variables
 *    Copyright (c) Chris H. Pappas and William H. Murray, 1997
 */

#include <stdio.h>
#include <stdlib.h>

int main( )
{
   enum air_supply { EMPTY,
                     USEABLE,
                     FULL=5 }  instructor_tank;
   enum air_supply student_tank;
```

```
instructor_tank = FULL;
student_tank = EMPTY;

printf("The value of instructor_tank is %d\n",instructor_tank);
if (student_tank < USEABLE) {
  printf("Refill this tank.\n");
  printf("Class is cancelled.\n");
  exit(1);
}
if (instructor_tank >= student_tank)
  printf("Proceed with lesson\n");
else
  printf("Class is cancelled!\n");

return(0);
}
```

In C, an enum type is equivalent to the type int. This technically allows a program to assign integer values directly to enumerated variables. C++ enforces a stronger type check and does not allow this mixed-mode operation. The output from the program looks like this:

```
The value of instructor_tank is 5
Refill this tank.
Class is cancelled.
```

And, the New C++ Type—bool

This keyword is an integral type. A variable of this type can have values true and false. All conditional expressions now return a value of type bool. For example, myvar! = 0 now returns true or false depending on the value of *myvar*.

The values true and false have the following relationship:

!false == true

!true == false

Look at the following statement:

```
if (myexpression)
  statement1;
```

If *myexpression* evaluates to true, statement1 is always executed; if *myexpression* evaluates to false, statement1 is never executed. An important fundamental to keep in mind when writing test expressions is this: Both C and C++ view *any* non-zero (!0) value as true, and *any* expression evaluating to zero (0) as false.

 NOTE: When a postfix or prefix ++ operator is applied to a variable of type bool, the variable is set to true. The postfix or prefix -- operator cannot be applied to a variable of this type. Also, the bool type participates in integral promotions. An r-value of type bool can be converted to an r-value of type int, with false becoming zero and true becoming one.

Access Modifiers

The const and volatile modifiers are new to C and C++. They were added by the ANSI C standard to help identify which variables will never change (const) and which can change unexpectedly (volatile).

const Modifier

At certain times you will need to use a value that does not change throughout the program. Such a quantity is called a *constant*. For example, if a program deals with the area and circumference of a circle, the constant value pi=3.14159 would be used frequently. In a financial program, an interest rate might be a constant. In such cases, you can improve the readability of the program by giving the constant a descriptive name.

Using descriptive names can also help prevent errors. Suppose that a constant value (not a constant variable) is used at many points throughout the program. A typographical error might result in the wrong value being typed at one or more of these points. However, if the constant is given a name, a typographical error would then be detected by the compiler because the incorrectly spelled identifier would probably not have been declared.

Suppose you are writing a program that repeatedly uses the value pi. It might seem as though a *variable* called *pi* should be declared with an initial value of 3.14159. However, the program should not be able to change the value of a constant. For instance, if you inadvertently wrote "pi" to the left of an equal sign, the value of pi would be changed, causing all subsequent calculations to be in error. C and C++ provide mechanisms that prevent such an error from occurring: you can establish constants, the values of which cannot be changed.

In C and C++, you declare a constant by writing "const" before the keyword (such as int, float, or double) in the declaration. For example:

```
const int iMIN=1,iSALE_PERCENTAGE=25;
const float fbase_change=32.157;
int irow_index=1,itotal=100,iobject;
double ddistance=0,dvelocity;
```

Because a constant cannot be changed, it must be initialized in its declaration. The integer constants iMIN and iSALE_PERCENTAGE are declared with values 1 and 25, respectively; the constant *fbase_change* is of type float and has been initialized to 32.157. In addition, the integer (nonconstant) variables *irow_index, itotal,* and *iobject* have been declared. Initial values of 1 and 100 have been established for *irow_index* and *itotal,* respectively. Finally, *ddistance* and *dvelocity* have been declared to be (nonconstant) variables of type double. An initial value of zero has been set up for *ddistance.*

Constants and variables are used in the same way in a program. The only difference is that the initial values assigned to the constants cannot be changed. That is, the constants are not *lvalues*; they cannot appear to the left of an equal sign. (Expressions that refer to memory locations are called *lvalue expressions.* Expressions referring to modifiable locations are *modifiable lvalues.* One example of a modifiable *lvalue* expression is a variable name declared without the const specifier.)

Normally, the assignment operation assigns the value of the right-hand operand to the storage location named by the left-hand operand. Therefore, the left-hand operand of an assignment operation (or the single operand of a unary assignment expression) must be an expression that refers to a modifiable memory location.

#define Constants

C and C++ provide another method for establishing constants: the #define compiler directive. Let's look at an example. Suppose that at the beginning of a program you have the statement:

```
#define SALES_TEAM 10
```

The form of this statement is #define followed by two strings of characters separated by blanks. When the program is compiled, there are several passes made through it. The first step is accomplished by the *compiler preprocessor,* which does such things as carry out the #include and #define directives. When the preprocessor encounters the #define directive, it replaces every occurrence of SALES_TEAM in the source file(s) with the number 10.

In general, when the preprocessor encounters a #define directive, it replaces every occurrence of the first string of characters, "SALES_TEAM", in the program with the second string of characters, "10". Additionally, no value can be assigned to SALES_TEAM because it has never been declared to be a variable. As a result of the syntax, SALES_TEAM has all the attributes of a constant. Note that the #define statement is *not* terminated by a semicolon. If a semicolon followed the value 10, then every occurrence of SALES_TEAM would be replaced with "10;". The directive's action is to replace the first string with *everything* in the second string.

All of the programs that have been discussed so far are short and would usually be stored in a single file. If a statement such as the #define for SALES_TEAM appeared at the beginning of the file, the substitution of "10" for "SALES_TEAM" would take place throughout the program. (Later we discuss breaking a program down into many subprograms, with each subprogram being broken down into separate files.) Under these circumstances, the compiler directive would be effective only for the single file in which it is written.

The preceding discussion explored two methods for defining constants—the keyword const and the #define compiler directive. In many programs, the action of each of these two methods is essentially the same. On the other hand, the use of the modifier keyword const results in a "variable" whose value cannot be changed. Later in this chapter, in "Storage Classes," you will see how variables can be declared in such a way that they exist only over certain regions of a program. The same can be said for constants declared with the keyword const. Thus, the const declaration is somewhat more versatile than the #define directive. Also, the #define directive is found in standard C and is therefore already familiar to C programmers.

volatile Modifier

The volatile keyword signifies that a variable can unexpectedly change because of events outside the control of the program. For example, the following definition indicates that the variable *event_time* can have its value changed without the knowledge of the program:

```
volatile int event_time;
```

A definition like this is needed, for example, if *event_time* is updated by hardware that maintains the current clock time. The program that contains the variable *event_time* could be interrupted by the timekeeping hardware and the variable *event_time* changed.

A data object should be declared volatile if it is a memory-mapped device register or a data object shared by separate processes, as would be the case in a multitasking operating environment.

const and volatile Used Together

You can use the const and volatile modifiers with any other data types (for example, char and float) and also with each other. The following definition specifies that the program does not intend to change the value in the variable *constant_event_time*:

```
const volatile constant_event_time;
```

However, the compiler is also instructed, because of the volatile modifier, to make no assumptions about the variable's value from one moment to the next. Therefore, two things happen. First, an error message will be issued by the compiler for any line of source code that attempts to change the value of the variable *constant_event_time*. Second, the compiler will not remove the variable *constant_event_time* from inside loops since an external process can also be updating the variable while the program is executing.

pascal, cdecl, near, far, and huge Modifiers

The first two modifiers, pascal and cdecl, are used most frequently in advanced applications. Microsoft Visual C/C++ allows you to write programs that can easily call other routines written in different languages. The opposite of this also holds true. For example, you can write a Pascal program that calls a C++ routine. When you mix languages this way, you have to take two very important issues into consideration: identifier names and the way parameters are passed.

When Microsoft Visual C/C++ compiles your program, it places all of the program's global identifiers (functions and variables) into the resulting object code file for linking purposes. By default, the compiler saves those identifiers using the same case in which they were defined (uppercase, lowercase, or mixed). Additionally, the compiler appends an underscore (_) to the front of the identifier. Since Microsoft Visual C/C++'s integrated linking (by default) is case sensitive, any external identifiers you declare in your program are also assumed to be in the same form with a prepended underscore and the same spelling and case as defined.

pascal

The Pascal language uses a different calling sequence than C and C++. Pascal (along with FORTRAN) passes function arguments from left to right and does not allow variable-length argument lists. In Pascal, it is also the called function's responsibility to remove the arguments from the stack, rather than having the invoking function do so when control returns from the invoked function.

A C and C++ program can generate this calling sequence in one of two ways. First, it can use the compile-time switch /Gz, which makes the Pascal calling sequence the default for all enclosed calls and function definitions. Second, the C program can override the default C calling sequence explicitly by using the pascal keyword in the function definition.

As mentioned earlier, when C generates a function call, by default it appends an underscore to the function name and declares the function as external. It also preserves the casing of the name. However, when the pascal keyword is used, the underscore is not prepended and the identifier (function or variable) is converted to all uppercase.

The following code segment demonstrates how to use the pascal keyword on a function. (The same keyword can be used to ensure FORTRAN code compatibility.)

```
float pascal pfcalculate(int iscore, int iweight)
{
     .
     .
     .
}
```

Of course, variables can also be given a Pascal convention, as seen in this next example:

```
#define TABLESIZE 30

float pascal pfcalculate(int iscore, int iweight)
{
     .
     .
     .
}

float pascal pfscore_table[TABLESIZE];

int main( )
{
   int iscore 95, iweight = 10;

   pfscore_table[0] = pfcalculate(iscore,iweight);

   return(0);
}
```

In this example, *pfscore_table* has been globally defined with the pascal modifier. Function main( ) also shows how to make an external reference to a pascal function type. Since both functions, main( ) and pfcalculate( ), are in the same source file, the function pfcalculate( ) is global to main( ).

cdecl

If the /Gz compile-time switch was used to compile your C or C++ program, all function and variable references were generated matching the Pascal calling convention. However, there may be occasions when you want to guarantee that certain identifiers you are using in your program remain case sensitive and keep the underscore at the front. This is most often the case for identifiers being used in another C file.

To maintain this C compatibility (preserving the case and having a leading underscore prepended), you can use the cdecl keyword. When the cdecl keyword is used in front of a function, it also affects how the parameters are passed.

Note that all C and C++ functions prototyped in the header files of Microsoft Visual C/C++—for example, STDIO.H—are of type cdecl. This ensures that you can link with the library routines, even when you are compiling using the /Gz option. The following example was compiled using the /Gz option and shows how you would rewrite the previous example to maintain C compatibility:

```c
#define TABLESIZE 30

float cdecl cfcalculate(int iscore, int iweight)
{
    .
    .
    .
}

float cdecl cfscore_table[TABLESIZE];

int main( )
{
    int iscore 95, iweight = 10;

    cfscore_table[0] = cfcalculate(iscore,iweight);

    return(0);
}
```

near, far, and huge

 NOTE: *These old-style C/C++ keywords are only mentioned here in case you run across them in an older text or program. They are 16-bit C/C++ compiler specific and no longer needed by today's state-of-the-art 32-bit C/C++ compilers.*

However, this is an appropriate time to caution you. C and C++ are continuing to evolve, even as you read this text. Therefore, any time you peruse other C/C++ literature, beware: there are Historic C, C, ANSI C, Historic C++, C++, ANSI C++, and the flavor-of-the-month language out there! Case in point: the old-style keywords near, far, and huge.

You use the three modifiers near, far, and huge to affect the action of the indirection operator (*); in other words, they modify pointer sizes to data objects. A near pointer is only 2 bytes long, a far pointer is 4 bytes long, and a huge pointer is also 4 bytes long. The difference between the far pointer and the huge pointer is that the latter has to deal with the form of the address.

Data Type Conversions

In the programs so far, the variables and numbers used in any particular statement were all of the same type—for example, int or float. You can write statements that perform operations involving variables of different types. These operations are called *mixed-mode operations*. In contrast to some other programming languages, C and C++ perform automatic conversions from one type to another. As you progress through the book, additional types will be introduced, and mixing of those types will be discussed.

Data of different types is stored differently in memory. Suppose that the number 10 is being stored. Its representation will depend upon its type. That is, the pattern of zeros and ones in memory will be different when 10 is stored as an integer than when it is stored as a floating-point number.

Suppose that the following operation is executed, where both *fresult* and *fvalue* are of type float, and the variable *ivalue* is of type int:

```
fresult = fvalue * ivalue;
```

The statement is therefore a mixed-mode operation. When the statement is executed, the value of *ivalue* will be converted into a floating-point number before the multiplication takes place. The compiler recognizes that a mixed-mode operation is occurring, and therefore generates code to perform the following operations. The integer value assigned to *ivalue* is read from memory. This value is then converted to the corresponding floating-point value, which is multiplied by the real value assigned to *fvalue*, and the resulting floating-point value is assigned to *fresult*. In other words, the compiler performs the conversion automatically. Note that the value assigned to *ivalue* is unchanged by this process and remains of type int.

You have seen that in mixed-mode operations involving a value of type int and another value of type float, the value of type int is converted into a value of type float for calculation. This is done without changing the stored integral value during the conversion process. Now let's consider mixed-mode operations between two different types of variables.

Actually, before doing this, you need to know that there is in fact a *hierarchy of conversions*, in that the object of lower priority is temporarily converted to the type of higher priority for the performance of the calculation. The hierarchy of conversions takes the following structure, from highest priority to lowest: double, float, long, int, and short.

For example, the type double has a higher priority than the type int. When a type is converted to one that has more significant digits, the value of the number and its accuracy are unchanged.

Look at what happens when a conversion from type float to type int takes place. Suppose that the variables *ivalue1* and *ivalue2* have been defined to be of type int, while *fvalue* and *fresult* have been defined to be of type float. Consider the following sequence of statements:

```
ivalue1 = 3;
ivalue2 = 4;
fvalue = 7.0;
fresult = fvalue + ivalue1/ivalue2;
```

The statement *ivalue1/ivalue2* is *not* a mixed-mode operation; instead, it represents the division of two integers, and its result is zero since the fractional part (0.75, in this case) is *discarded* when integer division is performed. Therefore, the value stored in *fresult* is 7.0.

What if *ivalue2* had been defined to be of type float? In this case *fresult* would have been assigned the floating-point value 7.75, since the statement *ivalue1/ivalue2* would be a mixed-mode operation. Under these circumstances, the value of *ivalue1* is temporarily converted to the floating-point value 3.0, and the result of the division is 0.75. When that is added to *fvalue*, the result is 7.75.

It is important to know that the type of the value to the left of the assignment statement determines the type of the result of the operation. For example, suppose that *fx* and *fy* have been declared to be of type float and *iresult* has been declared to be of type int. Consider the following statements:

```
fx = 7.0;
fy = 2.0;
iresult = 4.0 + fx/fy
```

The result of executing the statement *fx/fy* is 3.5; when this is added to 4.0, the floating-point value generated is 7.5. However, this value cannot be assigned to *iresult* because *iresult* is of type int. The number 7.5 is therefore converted into an integer. When this is done, the fraction part is truncated. The resulting whole number is converted from a floating-point representation to an integer representation, and the value assigned to *iresult* is the integer number 7.

Explicit Type Conversions Using the Cast Operator

You have seen that the C and C++ compiler automatically changes the format of a variable in mixed-mode operations using different data types. However, there are circumstances where, although automatic conversion is *not* performed, type conversion would be desirable. For those occasions, you must specifically designate that a change of type is to be made. These explicit specifications also clarify to other programmers the statements involved. The C language provides several procedures that allow you to designate that type conversion must occur.

One of these procedures is called the *cast operator*. Whenever you want to temporarily change the format of a variable, you simply precede the variable's identifier with the parenthesized type you want it converted to. For example, if *ivalue1* and *ivalue2* were defined to be of type int and *fvalue* and *fresult* have been defined to be of type float, the following three statements would perform the same operation:

```
fresult = fvalue + (float)ivalue1/ivalue2;
fresult = fvalue + ivalue1/(float)ivalue2;
fresult = fvalue + (float)ivalue1/(float)ivalue2;
```

All three statements perform a floating-point conversion and division of the variables *ivalue1* and *ivalue2*. Because of the usual rules of mixed-mode arithmetic discussed earlier, if either variable is cast to type float, a floating-point division occurs. The third statement explicitly highlights the operation to be performed.

Storage Classes

Visual C/C++ supports four storage-class specifiers. They are auto, register, static, and extern.

The storage class precedes the variable's declaration and instructs the compiler how the variable should be stored. Items declared with the auto or register specifier have local lifetimes; items declared with the static or extern specifier have global lifetimes.

The four storage-class specifiers affect the visibility of a variable or function, as well as its storage class. *Visibility* (sometimes defined as *scope*) refers to that portion of the source program in which the variable or function can be referenced by name. An item with a global lifetime exists throughout the execution of the source program.

The placement of a variable or a function declaration within a source file also affects storage class and visibility. Declarations outside all function definitions are said to appear at the *external level,* while declarations within function definitions appear at the *internal level.*

The exact meaning of each storage-class specifier depends on two factors: whether the declaration appears at the external or internal level and whether the item being declared is a variable or a function.

Variable Declarations at the External Level

Variable declarations at the external level may only use the static or extern storage class, not auto or register. They are either definitions of variables or references to variables defined elsewhere. An external variable declaration that also initializes the variable (implicitly or explicitly) is a defining declaration:

```
static int ivalue1;        // implicit 0 by default
static int ivalue1 = 10   // explicit

int ivalue2 = 20;          // explicit
```

Once a variable is defined at the external level, it is visible throughout the rest of the source file in which it appears. The variable is not visible prior to its definition in the same source file. Also, it is not visible in other source files of the program unless a referencing declaration makes it visible, as described shortly.

You can define a variable at the external level only once within a source file. If you give the static storage-class specifier, you can define another variable with the same name and the static storage-class specifier in a different source file. Since each static definition is visible only within its own source file, no conflict occurs.

The extern storage-class specifier declares a reference to a variable defined elsewhere. You can use an external declaration to make a definition in another source file visible or to make a variable visible above its definition in the same source file. The variable is visible throughout the remainder of the source file in which the declared reference occurs.

For an external reference to be valid, the variable it refers to must be defined once, and only once, at the external level. The definition can be in any of the source files that form the program. The following C++ program demonstrates the use of the extern keyword:

```
//
//      Source File A - incomplete file do not compile.
//
#include <iostream.h>

extern int ivalue;                  // makes ivalue visible
                                    // above its declaration

int main( )
{
  ivalue++;                         // uses the above extern
                                    // reference
```

```
   cout << ivalue << "\n";             // prints 11
   function_a( );

   return(0);
}

int ivalue = 10;                       // actual definition of
                                       // ivalue

void function_a(void)
{
   ivalue++;                           // references ivalue
   cout << ivalue << "\n";             // prints 12
   function_b( );
}

----------------------------------------

//
//      Source File B
//

#include <iostream.h>

extern int ivalue;                     // references ivalue
                                       // declared in Source A

void function_b(void)
{
   ivalue++;
   cout <<("%d\n", ivalue);            // prints 13
}
```

Variable Declarations at the Internal Level

You can use any of the four storage-class specifiers for variable declarations at the internal level. (The default is auto.) The auto storage-class specifier declares a variable with a local lifetime. It is visible only in the block in which it is declared and can include initializers.

The register storage-class specifier tells the compiler to give the variable storage in a register, if possible. This specifier speeds access time and reduces code size. It has the same visibility as an *auto* variable. If no registers are available when the compiler encounters a register declaration, the variable is given the auto storage class and stored in memory.

ANSI C does not allow for taking the address of a register object. However, this restriction does not apply to C++. Applying the address operator (&) to a C++ register variable forces the compiler to store the object in memory, since the compiler must put the object in a location for which an address can be represented.

A variable declared at the internal level with the static storage-class specifier has a global lifetime but is visible only within the block in which it is declared. Unlike auto variables, static variables keep their values when the block is exited. You can initialize a static variable with a constant expression. It is initialized to zero by default.

A variable declared with the extern storage-class specifier is a reference to a variable with the same name defined at the external level in any of the source files of the program. The internal extern declaration is used to make the external-level variable definition visible within the block. The next program demonstrates these concepts:

```
int ivalue1=1; // incomplete file do not compile.

void main( )
{ // references the ivalue1 defined above
    extern int ivalue1;

  // default initialization of 0, ivalue2 only visible
  // in main( )
    static int ivalue2;

  // stored in a register (if available), initialized
  // to 0
    register int rvalue = 0;

  // default auto storage class, int_value3 initialized
  // to 0
    int int_value3 = 0;

  // values printed are 1, 0, 0, 0:
    cout << ivalue1 << rvalue \
        <<ivalue2 << int_value3;
    function_a( );
}

void function_a(void)
  // stores the address of the global variable ivalue1
    static int *pivalue1= &ivalue1;
```

```
   // creates a new local variable ivalue1 making the
   // global ivalue1 unreachable
      int ivalue1 = 32;

   // new local variable ivalue2
   // only visible within function_a
      static int ivalue2 = 2;

      ivalue2 += 2;

   // the values printed are 32, 4, and 1:
      cout << ivalue1 << ivalue2 \
      << *pivalue1);
   }
```

Since *ivalue1* is redefined in function_a( ), access to the global *ivalue1* is denied. However, by using the data pointer *pivalue1* (discussed in Chapter 10), the address of the global *ivalue1* was used to print the value stored there.

Variable Scope Review

To review, there are four rules for variable visibility, also called *scope rules*. The four scopes for a variable are the block, function, file, and program. A variable declared within a block or function is known only within the block or function. A variable declared external to a function is known within the file in which it appears, from the point of its appearance to the end of the file. A variable declared as external in one source file and declared as external in other files has program scope.

Function Declarations at the External Level

When declaring a function at the external or internal level, you can use either the static or the extern storage-class specifier. Functions, unlike variables, always have a global lifetime. The visibility rules for functions vary slightly from the rules for variables.

Functions declared to be static are visible only within the source file in which they are defined. Functions in the same source file can call the static function, but functions in *other* source files cannot. Also, you can declare another static function with the same name in a different source file without conflict.

Functions declared as external are visible throughout *all* source files that make up the program (unless you later redeclare such a function as static). Any function can call an external function. Function declarations that omit the storage-class specifier are external by default.

Operators

C has many operators not found in other languages. These include bitwise operators, increment and decrement operators, conditional operators, the comma operator, and assignment and compound assignment operators.

Bitwise Operators

Bitwise operators treat variables as combinations of bits rather than as numbers. They are useful in accessing the individual bits in memory, such as the screen memory for a graphics display. Bitwise operators can operate only on integral data types, not on floating-point numbers. Three bitwise operators act just like the logical operators, but on each bit in an integer. These are AND (&), OR (|), and XOR (^). An additional operator is the one's complement (~), which simply inverts each bit.

AND

The bitwise AND operation compares two bits; if both bits are a 1, the result is a 1, as shown here:

Bit 0	Bit 1	Result
0	0	0
0	1	0
1	0	0
1	1	1

Note that this is different from binary addition, where the comparison of two 1 bits would result in a sum flag set to zero and the carry flag set to 1. Very often the AND operation is used to select out, or *mask*, certain bit positions.

OR

The bitwise OR operation compares two bits and generates a 1 result if either or both bits are a 1, as shown here:

Bit 0	Bit 1	Result
0	0	0
0	1	1
1	0	1
1	1	1

The OR operation is useful for setting specified bit positions.

XOR

The EXCLUSIVE OR operation compares two bits and returns a result of 1 when and only when the two bits are complementary, as shown here:

Bit 0	Bit 1	Result
0	0	0
0	1	1
1	0	1
1	1	0

This logical operation can be very useful when it is necessary to complement specified bit positions, as in the case of computer graphics applications.

Following is an example of using these operators with the hexadecimal and octal representation of constants. The bit values are shown for comparison.

```
0xF1       &    0x35          yields 0x31 (hexadecimal)
0361       &    0065          yields 061 (octal)
11110011   &    00110101      yields 00110001 (bitwise)

0xF1       |    0x35          yields 0xF5 (hexadecimal)
0361       |    0065          yields 0365 (octal)
11110011   |    00110101      yields 11110111 (bitwise)

0xF1       ^    0x35          yields 0xC4 (hexadecimal)
0361       ^    0065          yields 0304 (octal)
11110011   ^    00110101      yields 00000000 11000110 (bitwise)

~0xF1                         yields 0xFF0E (hexadecimal)
~0361                         yields 0177416 (octal)
~11110011                     yields 11111111 00001100 (bitwise)
```

Left Shift and Right Shift

C incorporates two shift operators, the left shift (<<) and the right shift (>>). The left shift moves the bits to the left and sets the rightmost (least significant) bit to zero. The leftmost (most significant) bit shifted out is thrown away.

In terms of unsigned integers, shifting the number one position to the left and filling the LSB with a zero doubles the number's value. The following C++ code segment demonstrates how this would be coded:

```
unsigned int value1 = 65;
value1 <<= 1;
cout << value1;
```

If you were to examine *value1*'s lower byte, you would see the following bit changes performed.

```
<< 0100 0001 ( 65 decimal)
-------------------------
   1000 0010 (130 decimal)
```

The right shift operator moves bits to the right. The lower-order bits shifted out are thrown away. Halving an unsigned integer is as simple as shifting the bits one position to the right, filling the MSB position with a zero. A C-coded example would look very similar to the preceding example except for the compound operator assignment statement (discussed later in the chapter) and the output statement:

```
unsigned int value1 = 10;
value1 >>= 1;
printf("%d",value1);
```

Examining just the lower byte of the variable *value1* would reveal the following bit changes:

```
>> 0000 1010 (10 decimal)
-------------------------
   0000 0101 ( 5 decimal)
```

ncrement and Decrement

Adding 1 to or subtracting 1 from a number is so common in programs that C has a special set of operators to do this. They are the *increment* (++) and *decrement* (- -) *operators*. The two characters must be placed next to each other without any white space. They can be applied only to variables, not to constants. Instead of coding as follows:

```
value1 + 1;
```

you can write:

```
value1++;
```

or

```
++value1;
```

When these two operators are the sole operators in an expression, you will not have to worry about the difference between the different syntaxes. A for loop very often uses this type of increment for the loop control variable:

```
sum = 0;
for(i = 1; i <= 20; i++)
    sum = sum + i;
```

A decrement loop would be coded as

```
sum = 0;
for(i = 20; i >= 1; i--)
    sum = sum + i;
```

If you use these operators in complex expressions, you have to consider *when* the increment or decrement actually takes place.

The postfix increment, for example *i*++, uses the value of the variable in the expression first and then increments its value. However, the prefix increment—for example, ++*I*—increments the value of the variable first and then uses the value in the expression. Assume the following data declarations:

```
int i=3,j,k=0;
```

See if you can figure out what happens in each of the following statements. For simplicity, for each statement assume the original initialized values of the variables:

```
k = ++i;          // i = 4, k = 4
k = i++;          // i = 4, k = 3
k = --i;          // i = 2, k = 2
k = i--;          // i = 2, k = 3
i = j = k--;      // i = 0, j = 0, k = -1
```

While the subtleties of these two different operations may currently elude you, they are included in the C language because of specific situations that cannot be eloquently handled in any other way. In Chapter 10 you will look at a program that uses array indexes that need to be manipulated by using the initially confusing prefix syntax.

Arithmetic Operators

The C language naturally incorporates the standard set of arithmetic operators for addition (+), subtraction (–), multiplication (*), division (/), and modulus (%). The first four are straightforward and need no amplification. However, an example of the modulus operator will help you understand its usage and syntax:

```
int a=3,b=8,c=0,d;

d = b % a;                 // returns 2
d = a % b;                 // returns 3

d = b % c;                 // returns an error message
```

The modulus operator returns the remainder of integer division. The last assignment statement attempts to divide 8 by zero, resulting in an error message.

Assignment Operator

The assignment operator in C is different than the assignment statement in other languages. Assignment is performed by an assignment operator rather than an assignment statement. Like other C operators, the result of an assignment operator is a value that is assigned. An expression with an assignment operator can be used in a large expression such as this:

8 * (value2 = 5);

Here, *value2* is first assigned the value 5. This is multiplied by the 8, with *value1* receiving a final value of 40.

Overuse of the assignment operator can rapidly lead to unmanageable expressions. There are two places in which this feature is normally applied. First, it can be used to set several variables to a particular value, as in

```
value1 = value2 = value3 = 0;
```

The second use is most often seen in the condition of a while loop, such as

```
while ((c = getchar( )) != EOF) {
  .
  .
  .
}
```

This assigns the value that getchar( ) returned to *c* and then tests the value against EOF. If it is EOF, the loop is not executed. The parentheses are necessary because the assignment operator has a lower precedence than the nonequality operator. Otherwise, the line would be interpreted as

```
c = (getchar( ) != EOF)
```

The variable *c* would be assigned a value of 1 (TRUE) each time getchar( ) returned EOF.

Compound Assignment Operators

The C language also incorporates an enhancement to the assignment statement used by other languages. This additional set of assignment operators allows for a more concise way of expressing certain computations. The following code segment shows the standard assignment syntax applicable in many high-level languages:

```
irow_index = irow_index + irow_increment;
ddepth = ddepth - d1_fathom;
fcalculate_tax = fcalculate_tax * 1.07;
fyards = fyards / ifeet_convert;
```

C's compound assignment statements would look like this:

```
irow_index += irow_increment;
ddepth -= d1_fathom;
fcalculate_tax *= 1.07;
fyards /= ifeet_convert;
```

If you look closely at these two code segments, you will quickly see the required syntax. Using a C compound assignment operator requires you to remove the redundant variable reference from the right-hand side of the assignment operator and place the operation to be performed immediately before the =. The bottom of Table 6-4 lists all of the compound assignment operators. Other parts of this table are discussed in the section "Understanding Operator Precedence Levels" later in this chapter.

Symbol	Name or Meaning	Associates from
+	Post-increment	Left to right
--	Post-decrement	
( )	Function call	
[ ]	Array element	
->	Pointer to structure member	
.	Structure or union member	
+	Pre-increment	Right to left
--	Pre-decrement	
!	Logical NOT	
~	Bitwise NOT	
−	Unary minus	
+	Unary plus	
&	Address	
*	Indirection	
sizeof	Size in bytes	
new	Allocate program memory	
delete	Deallocate program memory	
(type)	type cast [for example, (int) i]	
.*	Pointer to member (objects)	Left to right
->*	Pointer to member (pointers)	
*	Multiply	Left to right
/	Divide	
%	Remainder	

Table 6-4. *C/C++ Operator Precedence Levels (from Highest to Lowest)*

Symbol	Name or Meaning	Associates from
+	Add	Left to right
−	Subtract	
<<	Left shift	Left to right
>>	Right shift	
<	Less than	Left to right
<=	Less than or equal to	
>	Greater than	
>=	Greater than or equal to	
==	Equal	Left to right
!=	Not equal	
&	Bitwise AND	Left to right
^	Bitwise exclusive OR	Left to right
|	Bitwise OR	Left to right
&&	Logical AND	Left to right
||	Logical OR	Left to right
? :	Conditional	Right to left
=	Assignment	Right to left
*=, /=, %=, +=, -=, <<=, >>=, &=, ^=, |=	Compound assignment	
,	Comma	Left to right

Table 6-4. *C/C++ Operator Precedence Levels (from Highest to Lowest) (continued)*

Relational and Logical Operators

All relational operators are used to establish a relationship between the values of the operands. They always produce a value of !0 if the relationship evaluates to TRUE or a 0 value if the relationship evaluates to FALSE. Following is a list of the C and C++ relational operators:

Operator	Meaning
==	Equality (not assignment)
!=	Not equal
>	Greater than
<	Greater than or equal
<=	Less than or equal

The logical operators AND (&&), OR (| |), and NOT (!) produce a TRUE (!0) or FALSE (zero) based on the logical relationship of their arguments. The simplest way to remember how the logical AND && works is to say that an ANDed expression will only return a TRUE (!0) when both arguments are TRUE (!0). The logical OR | | operation in turn will only return a FALSE (zero) when both arguments are FALSE (zero). The logical NOT ! simply inverts the value. Following is a list of the C and C++ logical operators:

Operator	Meaning
!	NOT
&&	AND
			OR

Have some fun with the following C program as you test the various combinations of relational and logical operators. See if you can predict the results ahead of time.

```c
/*
 *   oprs.c
 *   A C program demonstrating some of the subtleties of
 *   logical and relational operators.
 *   Copyright (c) Chris H. Pappas and William H. Murray, 1997
 */

#include <stdio.h>

int main( )
{
  float foperand1, foperand2;

  printf("\nEnter foperand1 and foperand2: " );
  scanf("%f%f",&foperand1,&foperand2);
```

```
  printf("\n  foperand1  > foperand2 is %d",
            (foperand1  > foperand2));
  printf("\n  foperand1  < foperand2 is %d",
            (foperand1  < foperand2));
  printf("\n  foperand1 >= foperand2 is %d",
            (foperand1 >= foperand2));
  printf("\n  foperand1 <= foperand2 is %d",
            (foperand1 <= foperand2));
  printf("\n  foperand1 == foperand2 is %d",
            (foperand1 == foperand2));
  printf("\n  foperand1 != foperand2 is %d",
            (foperand1 != foperand2));
  printf("\n  foperand1 && foperand1 is %d",
            (foperand1 && foperand2));
  printf("\n  foperand1 || foperand2 is %d",
            (foperand1 || foperand2));

  return(0);
}
```

You may be surprised at some of the results obtained for some of the logical comparisons. Remember, there is a very strict comparison that occurs for both data types float and double when values of these types are compared with zero—a number that is very slightly different from another number is still not equal. Also, a number that is just slightly above or below zero is still TRUE (!0).

The C++ equivalent of the program just examined follows:

```
//
//  oprs.cpp
//  A C++ program demonstrating some of the subtleties of
//  logical and relational operators.
//  Copyright (c) Chris H. Pappas and William H. Murray, 1997
//

#include <iostream.h>

int main( )
{
  float foperand1, foperand2;
```

```
cout << "\nEnter foperand1 and foperand2: ";
cin >> foperand1 >> foperand2;
cout << "\n";
cout << "  foperand1  > foperand2 is "
      << (foperand1  > foperand2) << "\n";
cout << "  foperand1  < foperand2 is "
      << (foperand1  < foperand2) << "\n";
cout << "  foperand1 >= foperand2 is "
      << (foperand1 >= foperand2) << "\n";
cout << "  foperand1 <= foperand2 is "
      << (foperand1 <= foperand2) << "\n";
cout << "  foperand1 == foperand2 is "
      << (foperand1 == foperand2) << "\n";
cout << "  foperand1 != foperand2 is "
      << (foperand1 != foperand2) << "\n";
cout << "  foperand1 && foperand1 is "
      << (foperand1 && foperand2) << "\n";
cout << "  foperand1 || foperand2 is "
      << (foperand1 || foperand2) << "\n";

return(0);
}
```

Conditional Operator

You can use the conditional operator (?:) in normal coding, but its main use is for creating macros. The operator has the syntax

condition ? true_expression : false-expression

If the condition is TRUE, the value of the conditional expression is *true-expression*. Otherwise, it is the value of *false-expression*. For example, look at the following statement:

```
if('A' <= c && c <= 'Z')
  printf("%c",'a' + c - 'A');
else
  printf("%c",c);
```

You could rewrite the statement using the conditional operator:

```
printf("%c",('A' <= c && c <= 'Z') ? ('a' + c - 'A') : c );
```

Both statements will make certain that the character printed, "c," is always lowercase.

Comma Operator

The comma operator (,) evaluates two expressions where the syntax allows only one. The value of the comma operator is the value of the right-hand expression. The format for the expression is

left-expression, right-expression

One place where the comma operator commonly appears is in a for loop, where more than one variable is being iterated. For example:

```
for(min=0,max=length-1; min < max; min++,max--) {
    .
    .
    .
}
```

Understanding Operator Precedence Levels

The order of evaluation of an expression in C is determined by the compiler. This normally does not alter the value of the expression, unless you have written one with side effects. Side effects are those operations that change the value of a variable while yielding a value that is used in the expression, as seen with the increment and decrement operators. The other operators that have side effects are the assignment and compound assignment operators.

Calls to functions that change values of external variables also are subject to side effects. For example:

```
inum1 = 3;
ianswer = (inum1 = 4) + inum1;
```

This could be evaluated in one of two ways: either *inum1* is assigned 4 and *ianswer* is assigned 8 (4+4); or the value of 3 is retrieved from *inum1* and 4 is then assigned to *inum1*, with the result being assigned a 7.

There are, however, four operators for which the order of evaluation is guaranteed to be left to right: logical AND (&&), logical OR (| |), the comma operator (,), and the conditional operator (?:). Because of this default order of evaluation you can specify a typical test as follows:

```
while((c=getchar( )) != EOF) && (C!='\n'))
```

The second part of the logical AND (&&) is performed after the character value is assigned to *c*.

Table 6-4 lists all of the C and C++ operators from highest precedence to lowest and describes how each operator is associated (left to right or right to left). All operators between lines have the same precedence level. Throughout the book you will be introduced to the various operators and how their precedence level affects their performance.

Standard C and C++ Libraries

Certain calculations are routinely performed in many programs and are written by almost all programmers. Taking the square root of a number is an example of such a calculation. Mathematical procedures for calculating square roots make use of combinations of the basic arithmetic operations of addition, subtraction, multiplication, and division.

It would be a waste of effort if every programmer had to design and code a routine to calculate the square root and then to incorporate that routine into the program. C and C++ resolve difficulties like this by providing you with *libraries* of functions that perform particular common calculations. With the libraries, you need only a single statement to invoke such a function.

This section discusses functions that are commonly provided with the C and C++ compiler. These library functions are usually not provided in source form but in compiled form. When linking is performed, the code for the library functions is combined with the compiled programmer's code to form the complete program.

Library functions not only perform mathematical operations, they also deal with many other commonly encountered operations. For example, there are library functions that deal with reading and writing disk files, managing memory, input/output, and a variety of other operations. Library functions are not part of standard C or C++, but virtually every system provides certain library functions.

Most library functions are designed to use information contained in particular files that are supplied with the system. These files, therefore, must be included when the library functions are used and are provided with the Visual C/C++ compiler. They usually have the extension .H and are called *header files.* Table 6-5 lists the header files supplied with Microsoft Visual C++.

Header	Size	Header	Size
ACCCTRL.H	8,711	CUSTCNTL.H	8,537
ACLAPI.H	14,090	CUSTOMAW.H	3,368
ACTIVSCP.H	45,596	D3D.H	18,414
ALPHAOPS.H	43,059	D3DCAPS.H	13,527
ASPTLB.H	17,564	D3DRM.H	5,488
ASSERT.H	1,469	D3DRMDEF.H	14,133
ATALKWSH.H	4,608	D3DRMOBJ.H	32,372
BASETYPS.H	8,965	D3DRMWIN.H	1,180
CDERR.H	2,197	D3DTYPES.H	31,957
CGUID.H	3,497	DAOGETRW.H	5,143
COLORDLG.H	1,434	DBDAOERR.H	69,776
COMCAT.H	32,382	DBDAOID.H	11,933
COMDEF.H	39,062	DBDAOINT.H	43,043
COMIP.H	22,023	DBT.H	10,633
COMMCTRL.H	131,448	DDE.H	5,072
COMMDLG.H	28,166	DDEML.H	17,868
COMPOBJ.H	435	DDRAW.H	102,313
COMUTIL.H	43,037	DIGITALV.H	37,699
CONIO.H	3,183	DIRECT.H	3,595
CPL.H	8,282	DISPATCH.H	437
CPLEXT.H	2,158	DISPDIB.H	11,161
CRTDBG.H	13,860	DLCAPI.H	33,975
CTL3D.H	2,673	DLGS.H	5,692
CTYPE.H	12,848	DOCOBJ.H	51,721

Table 6-5. *Header Files Shipped with Visual C++*

Header	Size	Header	Size
DOS.H	4,605	IMM.H	20,961
DPLAY.H	10,913	INETSDK.H	1,892
DRIVINIT.H	34	INITGUID.H	1,442
DSOUND.H	13,356	INITOID.H	1,467
DVOBJ.H	424	INTSHCUT.H	15,073
EH.H	2,144	IO.H	7,986
ERRNO.H	2,641	IOMANIP.H	4,408
ERROR.H	14,337	IOS.H	9,101
EXCHEXT.H	30,413	IOSTREAM.H	2,373
EXCHFORM.H	1,796	ISGUIDS.H	747
EXCPT.H	3,960	ISO646.H	419
EXDISP.H	10,024	ISTREAM.H	6,626
EXDISPID.H	1,518	LARGEINT.H	5,279
FCNTL.H	2,292	LIMITS.H	4,133
FLOAT.H	11,052	LM.H	1,284
FPIEEE.H	5,260	LMACCESS.H	40,810
FSTREAM.H	4,619	LMALERT.H	3,738
FTSIFACE.H	6,789	LMAPIBUF.H	1,321
HLIFACE.H	1,879	LMAT.H	3,576
HLINK.H	69,266	LMAUDIT.H	10,910
HTTPEXT.H	7,775	LMBROWSR.H	5,967
HTTPFILT.H	12,861	LMCHDEV.H	5,439
IDF.H	12,538	LMCONFIG.H	1,698
IDISPIDS.H	430	LMCONS.H	7,239
IMAGEHLP.H	23,452	LMERR.H	36,393
IME.H	6,939	LMERRLOG.H	38,479
IMESSAGE.H	8,229	LMMSG.H	2,125

Table 6-5.   *Header Files Shipped with Visual C++ (continued)*

PROGRAMMING
FOUNDATIONS

Header	Size	Header	Size
LMREMUTL.H	2,921	MAPIVAL.H	90,055
LMREPL.H	6,726	MAPIWIN.H	15,665
LMSERVER.H	47,741	MAPIWZ.H	1,977
LMSHARE.H	10,475	MAPIX.H	28,494
LMSNAME.H	3,065	MATH.H	20,528
LMSTATS.H	5,134	MBCTYPE.H	4,712
LMSVC.H	13,334	MBSTRING.H	7,570
LMUSE.H	3,641	MCIAVI.H	2,989
LMUSEFLG.H	676	MCX.H	3,915
LMWKSTA.H	16,742	MEMORY.H	2,660
LOADPERF.H	1,407	MGMTAPI.H	5,210
LOCALE.H	3,308	MIDLES.H	5,962
LSAPI.H	11,774	MINMAX.H	451
LZEXPAND.H	1,679	MMREG.H	69,235
MALLOC.H	4,429	MMSYSTEM.H	154,496
MAPI.H	11,857	MONIKER.H	435
MAPICODE.H	10,528	MSACM.H	58,508
MAPIDBG.H	24,876	MSACMDLG.H	1,029
MAPIDEFS.H	103,616	MSCONF.H	13,545
MAPIFORM.H	28,081	MSFS.H	16,926
MAPIGUID.H	11,650	MSPAB.H	2,143
MAPIHOOK.H	2,649	MSPST.H	4,977
MAPINLS.H	6,893	MSSTKPPG.H	1,191
MAPIOID.H	2,759	MSWSOCK.H	4,189
MAPISPI.H	47,359	MTX.H	19,513
MAPITAGS.H	68,440	MTXATTR.H	1,522
MAPIUTIL.H	30,573	MTXSPM.H	26,216

Table 6-5. *Header Files Shipped with Visual C++ (continued)*

Header	Size	Header	Size
NB30.H	12,693	PENWIN.H	106,402
NDDEAPI.H	14,642	PLAN32.H	915
NDDESEC.H	3,146	POPPACK.H	1,023
NEW.H	2,509	PROCESS.H	9,450
NSPAPI.H	18,996	PRSHT.H	12,580
NTSDEXTS.H	1,502	PSHPACK1.H	911
OAIDL.H	197,254	PSHPACK2.H	911
OBJBASE.H	30,028	PSHPACK4.H	911
OBJERROR.H	301	PSHPACK8.H	911
OBJIDL.H	330,903	RAS.H	32,269
OBJSAFE.H	7,808	RASDLG.H	6,445
OCIDL.H	244,528	RASERROR.H	18,219
ODBCINST.H	15,315	RASSAPI.H	10,573
OLE.H	25,650	RASSHOST.H	4,620
OLE2.H	12,682	RECGUIDS.H	567
OLE2VER.H	664	RECONCIL.H	5,560
OLEAUTO.H	33,100	REGSTR.H	60,127
OLECTL.H	20,424	RICHEDIT.H	29,848
OLECTLID.H	824	RICHOLE.H	6,473
OLEDLG.H	74,489	RPC.H	1,983
OLEIDL.H	159,627	RPCDCE.H	42,018
OLENLS.H	22,637	RPCDCEP.H	9,678
OSTREAM.H	4,908	RPCNDR.H	75,799
PBT.H	1,409	RPCNSI.H	14,654
PCRT32.H	1,534	RPCNSIP.H	1,176
PDH.H	16,235	RPCNTERR.H	1,569
PDHMSG.H	8,303	RPCPROXY.H	18,105

Table 6-5. *Header Files Shipped with Visual C++ (continued)*

Header	Size	Header	Size
SCODE.H	214	STDLIB.H	19,150
SCRNSAVE.H	8,622	STL.H	6,704
SEARCH.H	2,559	STORAGE.H	435
SEHMAP.H	557	STREAMB.H	5,419
SERVPROV.H	5,953	STRING.H	9,170
SETJMP.H	8,092	STRSTREA.H	3,074
SETJMPEX.H	956	SVCGUID.H	16,113
SETUPAPI.H	102,225	SVRAPI.H	47,005
SHARE.H	828	TAPI.H	150,246
SHELLAPI.H	16,824	TCHAR.H	27,828
SHLGUID.H	4,747	TIME.H	7,494
SHLOBJ.H	94,740	TLHELP32.H	6,068
SIGNAL.H	2,833	TNEF.H	14,111
SMPAB.H	1,233	TSPI.H	41,575
SMPMS.H	1,892	TYPEINFO.H	2,074
SMPXP.H	3,778	UNKNWN.H	9,289
SNMP.H	16,987	URLHLINK.H	89
SPORDER.H	1,944	URLMON.H	83,404
SQL.H	29,810	USE_ANSI.H	812
SQLEXT.H	76,694	USEOLDIO.H	1,028
SQLTYPES.H	6,621	VARARGS.H	4,675
SQLUCODE.H	22,825	VARIANT.H	435
STDARG.H	4,730	VCR.H	20,052
STDDEF.H	2,458	VDMDBG.H	13,476
STDEXCPT.H	1,935	VER.H	113
STDIO.H	13,087	VFW.H	139,508
STDIOSTR.H	2,082	WCHAR.H	24,960

Table 6-5. *Header Files Shipped with Visual C++ (continued)*

PROGRAMMING
FOUNDATIONS

Header	Size	Header	Size
WCTYPE.H	7,037	WINVER.H	9,504
WDBGEXTS.H	13,287	WINWLX.H	21,983
WFEXT.H	6,531	WOWNT16.H	4,380
WINBASE.H	154,540	WOWNT32.H	9,744
WINCON.H	14,592	WPAPI.H	2,731
WINCRYPT.H	13,176	WPGUID.H	800
WINDEF.H	6,760	WPOBJ.H	2,038
WINDOWS.H	4,903	WPSPI.H	8,411
WINDOWSX.H	73,255	WS2ATM.H	16,643
WINERROR.H	203,050	WS2SPI.H	18,485
WINGDI.H	147,629	WS2TCPIP.H	2,611
WININET.H	78,807	WSHISOTP.H	3,355
WINIOCTL.H	30,511	WSIPX.H	1,941
WINNETWK.H	22,739	WSNETBS.H	2,257
WINNLS.H	39,651	WSNWLINK.H	9,315
WINNLS32.H	2,125	WSVNS.H	1,250
WINNT.H	179,078	WSVV.H	1,590
WINPERF.H	28,279	WTYPES.H	29,754
WINREG.H	14,324	XCMC.H	14,014
WINRESRC.H	53,424	XCMCEXT.H	2,726
WINSOCK.H	33,611	XCMCMSX2.H	1,039
WINSOCK2.H	93,959	XCMCMSXT.H	1,816
WINSPOOL.H	52,635	XLOCINFO.H	3,052
WINSVC.H	19,076	YMATH.H	1,616
WINTRUST.H	11,053	YVALS.H	2,111
WINUSER.H	192,575	ZMOUSE.H	7,305

Table 6-5. *Header Fles Shipped with Visual C++ (continued)*

In general, different header files are required by different library functions. The header files' function needs will be listed in the description for that function. For example, the sqrt( ) function needs the declarations found in the MATH.H header file. Your *Microsoft Visual C/C++ Run-Time Library Reference* lists all of the library functions and their associated header files.

The following list briefly summarizes the library categories provided by the Visual C/C++ compiler:

Classification routines
Conversion routines
Directory control routines
Diagnostic routines
Graphics routines
Input/output routines
Interface routines (DOS, 8086, BIOS)
Manipulation routines
Math routines
Memory allocation routines
Process control routines
Standard routines
Text window display routines
Time and date routines

Check your reference manual for a detailed explanation of the individual functions provided by each library.

After reading this chapter, you should understand C's basic data types and operators, so it's time to move on to the topic of logic control. Chapter 7 introduces you to C's decision, selection, and iteration control statements.

Visual
C++ 5

Chapter 7

Program Control

In order to begin writing simple C/C++ programs, you will need a few more tools. This chapter discusses C/C++'s control statements. Many of these control statements are similar to other high-level language controls, such as if, if-else, and switch statements and for, while, and do-while loops. However, there are several new control statements unique to C/C++, such as the ? (conditional), break, and continue statements.

The problem with these *new* controls is that they typically have no equivalent in the traditional older high-level languages, such as FORTRAN, COBOL, and Pascal. Therefore, beginner C/C++ programmers leave them out of their problem solutions. That is unfortunate for two reasons. First, it means you are not taking advantage of the coding efficiencies provided by these new controls. Second, it flags you immediately as a beginner.

Conditional Controls

The C/C++ language supports four basic conditional statements: the if, the if-else, the conditional ?, and the switch. Before a discussion of the individual conditional statements, however, one general rule needs to be highlighted.

You can use most of the conditional statements to selectively execute either a single line of code or multiple lines of related code (called a *block*). Whenever a conditional statement is associated with only one line of executable code, braces ({}) are *not* required around the executable statement. However, if the conditional statement is associated with multiple executable statements, braces are required to relate the block of executable statements with the conditional test. For this reason, switch statements are required to have an opening and a closing brace.

if

You use the if statement to conditionally execute a segment of code. The simplest form of the if statement is

```
if (expression)
   true_action;
```

Notice that the expression must be enclosed in parentheses. To execute an if statement, the expression must evaluate to either TRUE or FALSE. If *expression* is TRUE, *true_action* will be performed and execution will continue on to the next statement following the action. However, if *expression* evaluates to FALSE, *true_action* will *not* be executed, and the statement following *action* will be executed. For example, the following code segment will print the message "Have a great day!" whenever the variable *ioutside_temp* is greater than or equal to 72:

```
if(ioutside_temp >= 72)
  printf("Have a great day!");
```

The syntax for an if statement associated with a block of executable statements looks like this:

if (*expression*) {
 true_action1;
 true_action2;
 true_action3;
 true_action4;
}

The syntax requires that all of the associated statements be enclosed by a pair of braces ({}) and that each statement within the block must also end with a semicolon (;). Here is an example of a compound if statement:

```
/*
 *    if.c
 *    A C program demonstrating an if statement
 *    Copyright (c) Chris H. Pappas and William H. Murray, 1997
 *
 */

#include <stdio.h>

int main( )
{
    int inum_As, inum_Bs, inum_Cs;
    float fGPA;

    printf("\nEnter number of courses receiving a grade of A: ");
    scanf("%d",&inum_As);
    printf("\nEnter number of courses receiving a grade of B: ");
    scanf("%d",&inum_Bs);
    printf("\nEnter number of courses receiving a grade of C: ");
    scanf("%d",&inum_Cs);
    fGPA = (inum_As * 4 + inum_Bs * 3 + inum_Cs * 2)/
           (float) (inum_As + inum_Bs + inum_Cs);
```

```
printf("\nYour overall GPA is: %5.2f\n",fGPA);
if(fGPA >= 3.5) {
  printf("\nC O N G R A T U L A T I O N S !\n");
  printf("You are on the President's list.");
}
return(0);
}
```

In this example, if *fGPA* is greater than or equal to 3.5, a congratulatory message is added to the calculated *fGPA*. Regardless of whether the if block was entered, the calculated *fGPA* is printed.

if-else

The if-else statement was invented to allow a program to take two separate actions based on the validity of a particular expression. The simplest syntax for an if-else statement looks like this:

if (*expression*)
  true_action;

else
  false_action;

In this case, if *expression* evaluates to TRUE, *true_action* will be taken; otherwise, when *expression* evaluates to FALSE, *false_action* will be executed. Here is a coded example:

```
if(ckeypressed == UP)
  iy_pixel_coord++;

else
  iy_pixel_coord--;
```

This example takes care of either incrementing or decrementing the current horizontal coordinate location based on the current value stored in the character variable *ckeypressed*.

Of course, either *true_action, false_action,* or both could be compound statements, or blocks, requiring braces. The syntax for these three combinations is straightforward:

```
if (expression) {
  true_action1;
  true_action2;
  true_action3;
}
else
  false_action;
```

```
if (expression)
  true_action;
else {
  false_action1;
  false_action2;
  false_action3;
}
```

```
if (expression) {
  true_action1;
  true_action2;
  true_action3;
}
else {
  false_action1;
  false_action2;
  false_action3;
}
```

Just remember, whenever a block action is being taken, you do not follow the closing brace (}) with a semicolon.

The following C program uses an if-else statement with the if part being a compound block:

```
/*
 *   cmpif.c
 *   A C program demonstrating the use of a compound
 *   if-else statement.
 *   Copyright (c) Chris H. Pappas and William H. Murray, 1997
 */
```

PROGRAMMING
FOUNDATIONS

```c
#include <stdio.h>

int main( )
{
  char c;
  int ihow_many,i,imore;

  imore=1;

  while(imore == 1) {
    printf("Please enter the product name: ");
    if(scanf("%c",&c) != EOF) {
      while(c != '\n') {
        printf("%c",c);
        scanf("%c",&c);
      }
      printf("s purchased? ");
      scanf("%d",&ihow_many);
      scanf("%c",&c);

      for(i = 1;i <= ihow_many; i++)
        printf("*");
      printf("\n");
    }
    else
      imore=0;
  }
  return(0);
}
```

The program prompts the user for a product name, and if the user does not enter a
^Z (EOF), the program inputs the product name character by character, echo printing
the information to the next line. The "s purchased" string is appended to the product,
requesting the number of items sold. Finally, a for loop prints out the appropriate
number of asterisks (*). Had the user entered a ^Z, the if portion of the if-else
statement would have been ignored and program execution would have picked up
with the else setting the *imore* flag to zero, thereby terminating the program.

Nested if-elses

When you are nesting if statements, care must be taken to ensure that you know which else action will be matched up with which if. Look at an example and see if you can figure out what will happen:

```
if(iout_side_temp < 50)
if(iout_side_temp < 30) printf("Wear the down jacket!");
else printf("Parka will do.");
```

The listing was purposely misaligned to avoid giving you any visual clues as to which statement went with which if. The question becomes, what happens if *iout_side_temp* is 55? Does the "Parka will do." message get printed? The answer is no. In this example, the else action is associated with the second if expression. This is because C matches each else with the first unmatched if.

To make debugging as simple as possible under such circumstances, the C compiler has been written to associate each else with the closest if that does not already have an else associated with it.

Of course, proper indentation will always help clarify the situation:

```
if(iout_side_temp < 50)
  if(iout_side_temp < 30) printf("Wear the down jacket!");
  else printf("Parka will do.");
```

The same logic can also be represented by the alternate listing that follows:

```
if(iout_side_temp < 50)
  if(iout_side_temp < 30)
    printf("Wear the down jacket!");
  else
    printf("Parka will do.");
```

Each particular application you write will benefit most by one of the two styles, as long as you are consistent throughout the source code.

See if you can figure out this next example:

```
if(test1_expression)
  if(test2_expression)
    test2_true_action;
else
  test1_false_action;
```

You may be thinking this is just another example of what has already been discussed. That's true, but what if you really did want *test1_false_action* to be associated with *test1* and not *test2*? The examples so far have all associated the else action with the second, or closest, if. (By the way, many a programmer has spent needless time debugging programs of this nature. As in the preceding example, they're indented to work the way you are logically thinking. Unfortunately, the compiler doesn't care about your "pretty printing.")

Correcting this situation requires the use of braces:

```
if(test1_expression) {
  if(test2_expression)
    test2_true_action;
  }
else
  test1_false_action;
```

The problem is solved by making *test2_expression* and its associated *test2_true_action* a block associated with a TRUE evaluation of *test1_expression*. This makes it clear that *test1_false_action* will be associated with the else clause of *test1_expression*.

if-else-if

The if-else-if statement combination is often used to perform multiple successive comparisons. Its general form looks like this:

if(*expression1*)
  test1_true_action;

else if(*expression2*)
  test2_true_action;

else if(*expression3*)
  test3_true_action;

Of course, each action could be a compound block requiring its own set of braces (with the closing brace *not* followed by a semicolon). This type of logical control flow evaluates each expression until it finds one that is TRUE. When this occurs, all remaining test conditions are bypassed. In the preceding example, if none of the expressions evaluated to TRUE, no action would be taken.

Look at this next example and see if you can guess the result:

```
if(expression1)
  test1_true_action;

else if(expression2)
  test2_true_action;

else if(expression3)
  test3_true_action;

else
  default_action;
```

Unlike the previous example, this if-else-if statement combination will always perform some action. If none of the if expressions evaluate to TRUE, the else *default_action* will be executed. For example, the following program checks the value assigned to *econvert_to* to decide which type of conversion to perform. If the requested *econvert_to* is not one of the ones provided, the code segment prints an appropriate message.

```
if(econvert_to == YARDS)
  fconverted_value = length / 3;

else if(econvert_to == INCHES)
  fconverted_value = length * 12;

else if(econvert_to == CENTIMETERS)
  fconverted_value = length * 12 * 2.54;

else if(econvert_to == METERS)
  fconverted_value = (length * 12 * 2.54)/100;

else
  printf("No conversion required");
```

The ?: Conditional Operator

The conditional statement ? provides a quick way to write a test condition. Associated actions are performed depending on whether *test_expression* evaluates to TRUE or FALSE. The operator can be used to replace an equivalent if-else statement. The syntax for a conditional statement is

test_expression ? true_action : false_action;

The ? operator is also sometimes referred to as the ternary operator because it requires three operands. Examine this statement:

```
if(fvalue >= 0.0)
   fvalue = fvalue;
else
   fvalue = -fvalue;
```

You can rewrite the statement using the conditional operator:

```
fvalue=(fvalue >= 0.0) ? fvalue : -fvalue;
```

Both statements yield the absolute value of *fvalue*. The precedence of the conditional operator is less than that of any of the other operators used in the expression; therefore, no parentheses are required in the example. Nevertheless, parentheses are frequently used to enhance readability.

The following C++ program uses the ? operator to cleverly format the program's output:

```
//
//   condit.cpp
//   A C++ program using the CONDITIONAL OPERATOR
//   Copyright (c) Chris H. Pappas and William H. Murray, 1997
//

#include <math.h>                            // for abs macro def.
#include <iostream.h>

int main( )
{
   float fbalance, fpayment;
```

```
cout << "Enter your loan balance: ";
cin  >> fbalance;

cout << "\nEnter your loan payment amount: ";
cin  >> fpayment;

cout << "\n\nYou have ";
cout << ((fpayment > fbalance) ? "overpaid by $" : "paid $");
cout << ((fpayment > fbalance) ? abs(fbalance - fpayment)) :
                                 fpayment);
cout << " on your loan of $" << fbalance << ".";

return(0);
}
```

The program uses the first conditional statement inside a cout statement to decide which string—"overpaid by $" or "paid $"—is to be printed. The following conditional statement calculates and prints the appropriate dollar value.

switch-case

You will often want to test a variable or an expression against several values. You could use nested if-else-if statements to do this, or you could use a switch statement. Be very careful, though; unlike many other high-level language selection statements such as Pascal's case statement, the C switch statement has a few peculiarities. The syntax for a switch statement is

```
switch (integral_expression) {
 case constant1:
   statements1;
   break;
 case constant2:
   statements2;
   break;
   .
   .
   .
 case constantn:
   statementsn;
   break;
 default: statements;
}
```

The redundant statement you need to pay particular attention to is the break statement. If this example had been coded in Pascal and *constant1* equaled *integral_expression, statements1* would have been executed, with program execution picking up with the next statement at the end of the case statement (below the closing brace).

In C the situation is quite different. In the preceding syntax, if the break statement had been removed from constant1's section of code, a match similar to the one used in the preceding paragraph would have left *statements2* as the next statement to be executed. It is the break statement that causes the remaining portion of the switch statements to be skipped. Let's look at a few examples.

Examine the following if-else-if code segment:

```
if(emove == SMALL_CHANGE_UP)
  fycoord =    5;

else if(emove == SMALL_CHANGE_DOWN)
  fycoord =   -5;

else if(emove == LARGE_CHANGE_UP)
  fycoord =   10;

else
  fycoord = -10;
```

You can rewrite this code using a switch statement:

```
switch(emove) {
  case  SMALL_CHANGE_UP:
    fycoord =    5;
    break;
  case  SMALL_CHANGE_DOWN:
    fycoord =   -5;
    break;
  case  LARGE_CHANGE_UP:
    fycoord =   10;
    break;
  default:
    fycoord = -10;
}
```

In this example, the value of *emove* is consecutively compared to each case value looking for a match. When one is found, fycoord is assigned the appropriate value.

Then the break statement is executed, skipping over the remainder of the switch statements. However, if no match is found, the default assignment is performed (fycoord = -10). Since this is the last option in the switch statement, there is no need to include a break. A switch default is optional.

Proper placement of the break statement within a switch statement can be very useful. Look at the following example:

```
/*
 *    switch.c
 *    A C program demonstrating the
 *    drop-through capabilities of the switch statement.
 *    Copyright (c) Chris H. Pappas and William H. Murray, 1997
 */

int main( )
{
  char c='a';
  int ivowelct=0, iconstantct=0;

  switch(c) {
    case 'a':
    case 'A':
    case 'e':
    case 'E':
    case 'i':
    case 'I':
    case 'o':
    case 'O':
    case 'u':
    case 'U': ivowelct++;
              break;
    default : iconstantct++;
  }
  return(0);
}
```

This program actually illustrates two characteristics of the switch statement: the enumeration of several test values that all execute the same code section and the drop-through characteristic.

Several other high-level languages have their own form of selection (the case statement in Pascal and the select statement in PL/I), which allows for several test values, all producing the same result, to be included on the same selection line. C, however, requires a separate case for each. But notice in this example how the same effect has been created by not inserting a break statement until all possible vowels have been checked. Should C contain a constant, all of the vowel case tests will be checked and skipped until the default statement is reached.

The next example shows a C program that uses a switch statement to invoke the appropriate function:

```c
/*
 *    fnswth.c
 *    A C program demonstrating the switch statement
 *    Copyright (c) Chris H. Pappas and William H. Murray, 1997
 */

#include <stdio.h>

#define QUIT 0
#define BLANK ' '

double fadd(float fx,float fy);
double fsub(float fx,float fy);
double fmul(float fx,float fy);
double fdiv(float fx,float fy);

int main( )
{
  float fx,fy;
  char cblank, coperator = BLANK;

  while (coperator != QUIT) {
    printf("\nPlease enter an expression a operator b: ");
    scanf("%f%c%c%f", &fx, &cblank, &coperator, &fy);

    switch (coperator) {
      case '+': printf("answer = %8.2f\n", fadd(fx,fy));
              break;
      case '-': printf("answer = %8.2f\n", fsub(fx,fy));
              break;
      case '*': printf("answer = %8.2f\n", fmul(fx,fy));
              break;
      case '/': printf("answer = %8.2f\n", fdiv(fx,fy));
              break;
      case 'x': coperator = QUIT;
              break;
      default : printf("\nOperator not implemented");
```

```
      }
    }
  return(0);
}

double fadd(float fx,float fy)
  {return(fx + fy);}

double fsub(float fx,float fy)
  {return(fx - fy);}

double fmul(float fx,float fy)
  {return(fx * fy);}

double fdiv(float fx,float fy)
  {return(fx / fy);}
```

While the use of functions in this example is a bit advanced (functions are discussed in Chapter 8), the use of the switch statement is very effective. After the user has entered an expression such as 10 + 10 or 23 * 15, the *coperator* is compared in the body of the switch statement to determine which function to invoke. Of particular interest are the last set of statements, where the *coperator* equals *x*, and the default statement.

If the user enters an expression with an *x* operator, the *coperator* variable is assigned a QUIT value, and the break statement is executed, skipping over the default printf( ) statement. However, if the user enters an unrecognized operator—for example, %—only the default statement is executed, printing the message that the *coperator* has not been implemented.

The following C++ program illustrates the similarity in syntax between a C switch statement and its C++ counterpart:

```
//
//  calndr.cpp
//  A C++ program using a switch statement
//  to print a yearly calendar.
//  Copyright (c) Chris H. Pappas and William H. Murray, 1997
//

#include <iostream.h>

int main( )
```

```
{
  int jan_1_start_day,num_days_per_month,
      month,date,leap_year_flag;

  cout << "Please enter January 1's starting day;\n";
  cout << "\nA 0 indicates January 1 is on a Monday,";
  cout << "\nA 1 indicates January 1 is on a Tuesday, etc: ";
  cin >> jan_1_start_day;
  cout << "\nEnter the year you want the calendar generated: ";
  cin >> leap_year_flag;
  cout << "\n\n The calendar for the year " << leap_year_flag;

  leap_year_flag=leap_year_flag % 4;
  cout.width(20);

  for (month = 1;month <= 12;month++) {
    switch(month) {
      case 1:
        cout << "\n\n\n" << " January" << "\n";
        num_days_per_month = 31;
        break;
      case 2:
        cout << "\n\n\n" << " February" << "\n";
        num_days_per_month = leap_year_flag ? 28 : 29;
        break;
      case 3:
        cout << "\n\n\n" << "  March " << "\n";
        num_days_per_month = 31;
        break;
      case 4:
        cout << "\n\n\n" << "  April " << "\n";
        num_days_per_month = 30;
        break;
      case 5:
        cout << "\n\n\n" << "   May  " << "\n";
        num_days_per_month = 31;
        break;
      case 6:
        cout << "\n\n\n" << "  June  " << "\n";
        num_days_per_month = 30;
        break;
      case 7:
```

```
      cout << "\n\n\n" << "   July   " << "\n";
      num_days_per_month = 31;
      break;
  case 8:
      cout << "\n\n\n" << " August " << "\n";
      num_days_per_month = 31;
      break;
  case 9:
      cout << "\n\n\n" << "September" << "\n";
      num_days_per_month = 30;
      break;
  case 10:
      cout << "\n\n\n" << " October " << "\n";
      num_days_per_month = 31;
      break;
  case 11:
      cout << "\n\n\n" << "November " << "\n";
      num_days_per_month = 30;
      break;
  case 12:
      cout << "\n\n\n" << "December " << "\n";
      num_days_per_month = 31;
      break;
}

cout.width(0);
cout << "\nSun  Mon  Tue  Wed  Thu  Fri  Sat\n";
cout << "---  ---  ---  ---  ---  ---  ---\n";

for ( date = 1; date <= 1 + jan_1_start_day * 5; date++ )
  cout <<  " ";

for ( date = 1; date <= num_days_per_month; date++ ) {
  cout.width(2);
  cout << date;
  cout.width(0);
  if ( ( date + jan_1_start_day ) % 7 > 0 )
    cout <<  "   ";
  else
    cout <<  "\n ";
}
```

```
    jan_1_start_day=(jan_1_start_day + num_days_per_month) % 7;
  }
  return(0);
}
```

The program begins by asking the user to enter an integer code representing the day of the week on which January 1 occurs (zero for Monday, 1 for Tuesday, and so on). The second prompt asks for the year for the calendar. The program can now print the calendar heading, and use the year entered to generate a *leap_year_flag*. Using the modulus operator (%) with a value of 4 generates a remainder of zero whenever it is leap year and a nonzero value whenever it is not a leap year.

Next, a 12-iteration loop is entered, printing the current month's name and assigning *num_days_per_month* the correct number of days for that particular month. All of this is accomplished by using a switch statement to test the current *month* integer value.

Outside the switch statement, after the month's name has been printed, day-of-the-week headings are printed, and an appropriate number of blank columns is skipped, depending on when the first day of the month was.

The last for loop actually generates and prints the dates for each month. The last statement in the program prepares the day_code for the next month to be printed.

Combining if-else-if and switch

The following example program uses an enumerated type (enum) to perform the requested length conversions:

```
/*
 *   ifelsw.c
 *   A C program demonstrating the if-else-if statement
 *   used in a meaningful way with several switch statements.
 *   Copyright (c) Chris H. Pappas and William H. Murray, 1997
 */


typedef enum conversion_type {YARDS, INCHES, CENTIMETERS, \
                              METERS} C_TYPE;

#include <stdio.h>

int main( )
{
  int iuser_response;
  C_TYPE C_Tconversion;
```

```
int ilength=30;
float fmeasurement;

printf("\nPlease enter the measurement to be converted : ");
scanf("%f",&fmeasurement);

printf("\nPlease enter :            \
        \n\t\t 0 for YARDS        \
        \n\t\t 1 for INCHES       \
        \n\t\t 2 for CENTIMETERS \
        \n\t\t 3 for METERS       \
        \n\n\t\tYour response -->> ");

scanf("%d",&iuser_response);

switch(iuser_response) {
  case 0  :  C_Tconversion = YARDS;
             break;
  case 1  :  C_Tconversion = INCHES;
             break;
  case 2  :  C_Tconversion = CENTIMETERS;
             break;
  default :  C_Tconversion = METERS;
}


if(C_Tconversion == YARDS)
  fmeasurement = ilength / 3;

else if(C_Tconversion == INCHES)
  fmeasurement = ilength * 12;

else if(C_Tconversion == CENTIMETERS)
  fmeasurement = ilength * 12 * 2.54;

else if(C_Tconversion == METERS)
  fmeasurement = (ilength * 12 * 2.54)/100;

else
  printf("No conversion required");
```

```
switch(C_Tconversion) {
   case YARDS        : printf("\n\t\t  %4.2f yards",
                                fmeasurement);
                       break;
   case INCHES       : printf("\n\t\t  %4.2f inches",
                                fmeasurement);
                       break;
   case CENTIMETERS  : printf("\n\t\t  %4.2f centimeters",
                                fmeasurement);
                       break;
   default           : printf("\n\t\t  %4.2f meters",
                                fmeasurement);
   }

   return(0);
}
```

The example program uses an enumerated type to perform the specified length conversion. In standard C, enumerated types exist only within the code itself (for reasons of readability) and cannot be input or output directly. The program uses the first switch statement to convert the input code to its appropriate *C_Tconversion* type. The nested if-else-if statements perform the proper conversion. The last switch statement prints the converted value with its appropriate "literal" type. Of course, the nested if-else-if statements could have been implemented by using a switch statement. (A further discussion of enumerated types can be found in Chapter 12.)

Loop Controls

The C language includes the standard set of repetition control statements; for loops, while loops, and do-while loops (called repeat-until loops in several other high-level languages). You may be surprised, however, by the ways a program can leave a repetition loop. C provides four methods for altering the repetitions in a loop. All repetition loops can naturally terminate based on the expressed test condition. In C, however, a repetition loop can also terminate because of an anticipated error condition by using either a break or exit statement. Repetition loops can also have their logic control flow altered by a break statement or a continue statement.

The basic difference between a for loop and a while or do-while loop has to do with the "known" number of repetitions. Typically, for loops are used whenever there is a definite, predefined, required number of repetitions, and while and do-while loops are reserved for an "unknown" number of repetitions.

for

The syntax for a for loop is

for(*initialization_exp; test_exp; increment_exp*)
  statement;

When the for loop statement is encountered, the *initialization_exp* is executed first. This is done at the start of the loop, and it is never executed again. Usually this statement involves the initialization of the loop control variable. Following this, *test_exp*, which is called the *loop terminating condition*, is tested. Whenever *test_exp* evaluates to TRUE, the statement or statements within the loop are executed. If the loop was entered, then after all of the statements within the loop are executed, *increment_exp* is executed. However, if *test_exp* evaluates to FALSE, the statement or statements within the loop are ignored, along with *increment_exp*, and execution continues with the statement following the end of the loop. The indentation scheme applied to for loops with several statements to be repeated looks like this:

for(*initialization_exp; test_exp; increment_exp*) {
  statement_a;
  statement_b;
  statement_c;
  statement_n;
}

When several statements need to be executed, a pair of braces is required to tie their execution to the loop control structure. Let's examine a few examples of for loops.

The following example sums up the first five integers. It assumes that *isum* and *ivalue* have been predefined as integers:

```
isum = 0;
for(ivalue=1; ivalue <= 5; ivalue++)
  isum += ivalue;
```

After *isum* has been initialized to zero, the for loop is encountered. First, *ivalue* is initialized to 1 (this is done only once); second, *ivalue*'s value is checked against the loop terminating condition, <= 5. Since this is TRUE, a 1 is added to *isum*. Once the statement is executed, the loop control variable (*ivalue*) is incremented by 1. This process continues four more times until *ivalue* is incremented to 6 and the loop terminates.

PROGRAMMING FOUNDATIONS

In C++, the same code segment could be written as follows. See if you can detect the subtle difference:

```
for(int ivalue=1; ivalue <= 5; ivalue++)
   isum += ivalue;
```

C++ allows the loop control variable to be declared and initialized within the for loop. This brings up a very sensitive issue among structured programmers: the proper placement of variable declarations. In C++, you can declare variables right before the statement that actually uses them. In the preceding example, since *ivalue* is used only to generate an *isum*, with *isum* having a larger scope than *ivalue*, the local declaration for *ivalue* is harmless. However, look at the following code segment:

```
int isum = 0;
for(int ivalue=1; ivalue <= 5; ivalue++)
   isum += ivalue;
```

This would obscure the visual "desk check" of the variable *isum* because it was not declared below the function head. For the sake of structured design and debugging, it is best to localize all variable declarations. It is the rare code segment that can justify the usefulness of moving a variable declaration to a nonstandard place, in sacrifice of easily read, easily checked, and easily modified code.

The value used to increment for loop control variables does not always have to be 1 or ++. The following example sums all the odd numbers up to 9:

```
iodd_sum = 0;
for(iodd_value=1; iodd_value <= 9; iodd_value+=2);
   iodd_sum += iodd_value;
```

In this example, the loop control variable *iodd_value* is initialized to 1 and is incremented by 2.

Of course, for loops don't always have to go from a smaller value to a larger one. The following example uses a for loop to read into an array of characters and then print the character string backward:

```
//
//  forlp.cpp
//  A C++ program that uses a for loop to input a character array
//  Copyright (c) Chris H. Pappas and William H. Murray, 1997
//
```

```
#include <stdio.h>

#define CARRAY_SIZE 10

int main( )
{
  int ioffset;
  char carray[CARRAY_SIZE];

  for(ioffset = 0; ioffset < CARRAY_SIZE; ioffset++)
    carray[ioffset] = getchar( );
  for(ioffset = CARRAY_SIZE - 1; ioffset >= 0; ioffset--)
    putchar(carray[ioffset]);

  return(0);
}
```

In this example, the first for loop initialized *ioffset* to zero (necessary since all array indexes are offsets from the starting address of the first array element), and while there is room in *carray*, reads characters in one at a time. The second for loop initializes the loop control variable *ioffset* to the offset of the last element in the array and, while *ioffset* contains a valid offset, prints the characters in reverse order. This process could be used to parse an infix expression that was being converted to prefix notation.

When you combine for loops, as in the next example, take care to include the appropriate braces to make certain the statements execute properly:

```
/*
 *    nslop1.c
 *    A C program demonstrating
 *    the need for caution when nesting for loops.
 *    Copyright (c) Chris H. Pappas and William H. Murray, 1997
 */

#include <stdio.h>

int main( )
{
  int iouter_val, iinner_val;

  for(iouter_val = 1; iouter_val <= 4; iouter_val++) {
    printf("\n%3d --",iouter_val);
```

```c
    for(iinner_val = 1; iinner_val <= 5; iinner_val++ )
      printf("%3d",iouter_val * iinner_val);
  }

  return(0);
}
```

The output produced by this program looks like this:

```
1 --  1  2  3  4  5
2 --  2  4  6  8 10
3 --  3  6  9 12 15
4 --  4  8 12 16 20
```

However, suppose the outer for loop had been written without the braces, like this:

```c
/*
 *   nslop2.c
 *   A C program demonstrating what happens when you nest
 *   for loops without the logically required braces {}.
 *   Copyright (c) Chris H. Pappas and William H. Murray, 1997
 */

#include <stdio.h>

int main( )
{
  int iouter_val, iinner_val;

 for(iouter_val = 1; iouter_val <= 4; iouter_val++)
   printf("\n%3d --",iouter_val);
   for(iinner_val = 1; iinner_val <= 5; iinner_val++ )
     printf("%3d",iouter_val * iinner_val);

  return(0);
}
```

The output would have looked quite different:

```
1 --
2 --
3 --
4 --   5 10 15 20 25
```

Without the braces surrounding the first for loop, only the first printf( ) statement is associated with the loop. Once the printf( ) statement is executed four times, the second for loop is entered. The inner loop uses the last value stored in *iouter_val*, or 5, to generate the values printed by its printf( ) statement.

The need to include or not include braces can be a tricky matter at best that needs to be approached with some thought to readability. Look at the next two examples and see if you can figure out if they would produce the same output.

Here is the first example:

```c
/*
 *    lpdmo1.c
 *    Another C program demonstrating the need
 *    for caution when nesting for loops.
 *    Copyright (c) Chris H. Pappas and William H. Murray, 1997
 */

#include <stdio.h>

int main( )
{
  int iouter_val, iinner_val;

  for(iouter_val = 1; iouter_val <= 4; iouter_val++) {
    for(iinner_val = 1; iinner_val <= 5; iinner_val++ )
      printf("%d ",iouter_val * iinner_val);
  }

  return(0);
}
```

Compare the preceding program with the following example:

```c
/*
 *    lpdmo2.c
```

```
    A comparison C program demonstrating the need
*    for caution when nesting for loops.
*    Copyright (c) Chris H. Pappas and William H. Murray, 1997
*/

 #include <stdio.h>

int main( )
{
  int iouter_val, iinner_val;

  for(iouter_val = 1; iouter_val <= 4; iouter_val++)
    for(iinner_val = 1; iinner_val <= 5; iinner_val++ )
      printf("%d ",iouter_val * iinner_val);

  return(0);
}
```

Both programs produce the identical output:

```
1 2 3 4 5 2 4 6 8 10 3 6 9 12 15 4 8 12 16 20
```

In these last two examples, the only statement associated with the outer for loop is the inner for loop. The inner for loop is considered a single statement. This would still be the case even if the inner for loop had multiple statements to execute. Since braces are needed only around code blocks or multiple statements, the outer for loop does not need braces to execute the program properly.

while

Just like the for loop, the C while loop is a *pretest loop*. This means that the program evaluates *test_exp* before entering the statement or statements within the body of the loop. Because of this, pretest loops may be executed from zero to many times. The syntax for a C while loop is

while(*test_exp*)
  statement;

For while loops with several statements, braces are needed:

while(*test_exp*) {
 statement1;
 statement2;
 statement3;
 statementn;
}

Usually, while loop control structures are used whenever an indefinite number of repetitions is expected. The following C program uses a while loop to control the number of times *ivalue* is shifted to the right. The program prints the binary representation of a signed integer.

```c
/*
*   while.c
*   A C program using a pretest while loop with flag
*   Copyright (c) Chris H. Pappas and William H. Murray, 1997
*/


#include <stdio.h>

#define WORD 16
#define ONE_BYTE 8

int main( )
{
  int ivalue = 256, ibit_position=1;
  unsigned int umask = 1;

  printf("The following value %d,\n",ivalue);
  printf("in binary form looks like: ");

  while(ibit_position <= WORD) {
    if((ivalue >> (WORD - ibit_position)) & umask) /*shift each*/
      printf("1");                                 /*bit to 0th*/
    else                                           /*position &*/
      printf("0");                                 /*compare to*/
    if(ibit_position == ONE_BYTE)                  /*umask     */
      printf(" ");
```

```
        ibit_position++;
    }

    return(0);
}
```

The program begins by defining two constants, *WORD* and *ONE_BYTE,* that can be easily modified for different architectures. *WORD* will be used as a flag to determine when the while loop will terminate. Within the while loop, *ivalue* is shifted, compared to *umask,* and printed from most significant bit to least. This allows the algorithm to use a simple printf( ) statement to output the results.

The next C program prompts the user for an input filename and an output filename. The program then uses a while loop to read in and echo print the input file of unknown size.

```c
/*
 *    dowhil.c
 *    A C program using a while loop to echo print a file
 *    The program demonstrates additional file I/O techniques
 *    Copyright (c) Chris H. Pappas and William H. Murray, 1997
 */

#include <stdio.h>
#include <process.h>

#define sz_TERMINATOR 1         /* sz, null-string designator */
#define MAX_CHARS 30

int main( )
{
  int c;
  FILE *ifile, *ofile;
  char sziDOS_file_name[MAX_CHARS + sz_TERMINATOR],
       szoDOS_file_name[MAX_CHARS + sz_TERMINATOR];

  fputs("Enter the input file's name: ",stdout);
  gets(sziDOS_file_name);

  if((ifile=fopen(sziDOS_file_name,"r")) == NULL) {
    printf("\nFile: %s cannot be opened",sziDOS_file_name);
```

```
      exit(1);
  }

  fputs("Enter the output file's name: ",stdout);
  gets(szoDOS_file_name);
  if((ofile=fopen(szoDOS_file_name,"w")) == NULL) {
    printf("\nFile: %s cannot be opened",szoDOS_file_name);
    exit(2);
  }
  while(!feof(ifile)) {
    c=fgetc(ifile);
    fputc(c,ofile);
  }

  return(0);
}
```

In this example, the while loop contains two executable statements, so the brace pair is required. The program also illustrates the use of several file I/O statements like fgetc( ) and fputc( ), along with feof( ) (discussed in Chapter 11).

do-while

The do-while loop differs from both the for and while loops in that it is a *post-test loop*. In other words, the loop is always entered at least once, with the loop condition being tested at the end of the first iteration. In contrast, for loops and while loops may execute from zero to many times, depending on the loop control variable. Since do-while loops always execute at least one time, they are best used whenever there is no doubt you want the particular loop entered. For example, if your program needs to present a menu to the user, even if all the user wants to do is immediately quit the program, he or she needs to see the menu to know which key terminates the application.

The syntax for a do-while loop is

do
 action;
while(*test_condition*);

Braces are required for do-while statements that have compound actions:

```
do {
  action1;
  action2;
  action3;
  actionn;
} while(test_condition);
```

The following C++ program uses a do-while loop to calculate some statistics for a user-entered sentence:

```
//
//  dowhile.cpp
//  A C++ program demonstrating the usefulness of a
//  do-while loop to process user-defined sentence.
//  Copyright (c) Chris H. Pappas and William H. Murray, 1997
//

#include <iostream.h>

#define LENGTH 80
#define NULL_TERM 1


int main( )
{
  char cSentence[LENGTH + NULL_TERM];
  int iNumChars = 0, iNumWords = 1;

  do {
    cout << "Please enter your sentence : ";
    cin.getline(cSentence,LENGTH);
  } while (cSentence[0] == '\0');

  while (cSentence[iNumChars] != '\0') {
    if (cSentence[iNumChars] == ' ')
      iNumWords++;
    iNumChars++;
  }
```

```
cout << "You entered " << iNumChars << " characters\n";
cout << "You entered " << iNumWords << " words";

return (0);
}
```

The do-while loop in this program repeats the prompt and input statements for the user-requested sentence until the user enters at least one character. Simply pressing the ENTER key causes the getline( ) function to store the null character in the first array element position, repeating the loop. Once the user enters the sentence, the program jumps out of the do-while loop printing the calculated statistics.

break

The C break statement can be used to exit a loop before the test condition becomes FALSE. The break statement is similar in many ways to a goto statement, only the point jumped to is not known directly. When breaking out of a loop, program execution continues with the next statement following the loop itself. Look at a very simple example:

```
/*
 *   break.c
 *   A C program demonstrating the use of the break statement.
 *   Copyright (c) Chris H. Pappas and William H. Murray, 1997
 */

int main( )
{
  int itimes = 1, isum = 0;

  while(itimes < 10){
    isum += isum + itimes;
    if(isum > 20)
      break;
    itimes++;
  }

  return(0);
}
```

Debugger Trace

Use the integrated debugger to trace through the program. Trace the variables *isum* and *itimes*. Pay particular attention to which statements are executed after *isum* reaches the value 21.

What you should have noticed is that when *isum* reached the value 21, the break statement was executed. This caused the increment of *itimes* to be jumped over, *itimes++*, with program execution continuing on the line of code below the loop. In this example, the next statement executed was the return.

continue

There is a subtle difference between the C break statement and the C continue statement. As you have already seen from the last example program, break causes the loop to terminate execution altogether. In contrast, the continue statement causes all of the statements following the continue statement to be ignored but does *not* circumvent incrementing the loop control variable or the loop control test condition. In other words, if the loop control variable still satisfies the loop test condition, the loop will continue to iterate.

The following program demonstrates this concept, using a number guessing game:

```c
/*
 *    contnu.c
 *    A C program demonstrating the use of the continue
 *    statement.
 *    Copyright (c) Chris H. Pappas and William H. Murray, 1997
 */

#include <stdio.h>

#define TRUE 1
#define FALSE 0

int main( )
{
  int ilucky_number=77,
      iinput_val,
      inumber_of_tries=0,
      iam_lucky=FALSE;

  while(!iam_lucky){
    printf("Please enter your lucky guess: ");
    scanf("%d",&iinput_val);
```

```
      inumber_of_tries++;
      if(iinput_val == ilucky_number)
        iam_lucky=TRUE;
      else
        continue;
      printf("It only took you %d tries to get lucky!",
        inumber_of_tries);
    }

  return(0);
}
```

Debugger Trace

Enter the preceding program and trace the variables *iinput_val, inumber_of_tries*, and *iam_lucky*. Pay particular attention to which statements are executed after *iinput_val* is compared to *ilucky_number*.

   The program uses a while loop to prompt the user for a value, increments the *inumber_of_tries* for each guess entered, and then determines the appropriate action to take based on the success of the match. If no match was found, the else statement is executed. This is the continue statement. Whenever the continue statement is executed, the printf( ) statement is ignored. Note, however, that the loop continues to execute. When *iinput_val* matches *ilucky_number*, the *iam_lucky* flag is set to TRUE and the continue statement is ignored, allowing the printf( ) statement to execute.

Combining break and continue

The break and continue statements can be combined to solve some interesting program problems. Look at the following C++ example:

```
//
//   bracntg.cpp
//   A C++ program demonstrating the usefulness of combining
//   the break and continue statements.
//   Copyright (c) Chris H. Pappas and William H. Murray, 1997
//

#include <stdio.h>
#include <iostream.h>
#include <ctype.h>

#define NEWLINE '\n'
```

```
int main( )
{
  int c;

  while((c=getchar( )) != EOF)
  {
    if(isascii(c) == 0) {
      cout << "Not an ASCII character; ";
      cout << "not going to continue/n";
      break;
    }

    if(ispunct(c) || isspace(c)) {
      putchar(NEWLINE);
      continue;
    }

    if(isprint(c) == 0) {
      c = getchar( );
      continue;
    }

    putchar(c);
  }

  return(0);
}
```

Before seeing how the program functions, take a look at the input to the program:

```
word control ^B exclamation! apostrophe' period.
^Z
```

Also examine the output produced:

```
word
control
```

```
B
exclamation

apostrophe

period
```

The program continues to read character input until the EOF character ^Z is typed. It then examines the input, removing any nonprintable characters, and places each "word" on its own line. It accomplishes all of this by using some very interesting functions defined in CTYPE.H, including isascii( ), ispunct( ), isspace( ), and isprint( ). Each of the functions is passed a character parameter and returns either a zero or some other value indicating the result of the comparison.

The function isascii( ) indicates whether the character passed falls into the acceptable ASCII value range, ispunct( ) indicates whether the character is a punctuation mark, isspace( ) indicates whether the character is a space, and function isprint( ) reports whether the character parameter is a printable character.

Using these functions, the program determines whether to continue the program at all and, if it is to continue, what it should do with each of the characters input.

The first test within the while loop evaluates whether the file is even in readable form. For example, the input data could have been saved in binary format, rendering the program useless. If this is the case, the associated if statements are executed, printing a warning message and breaking out of the while loop permanently.

If all is well, the second if statement is encountered; it checks whether the character input is either a punctuation mark or a blank space. If either of these conditions is TRUE, the associated if statements are executed. This causes a blank line to be skipped in the output and executes the continue statement. The continue statement efficiently jumps over the remaining test condition and output statement but does not terminate the loop. It merely indicates that the character's form has been diagnosed properly and that it is time to obtain a new character.

If the file is in an acceptable format and the character input is not punctuation or a blank, the third if statement asks whether the character is printable or not. This test takes care of any control codes. Notice that the example input to the program included a control ^B. Since ^B is not printable, this if statement immediately obtains a new character and then executes a continue statement. In like manner, this continue statement indicates that the character in question has been diagnosed, the proper action has been taken, and it is time to get another character. The continue statement also causes the putchar( ) statement to be ignored while *not* terminating the while loop.

exit( )

Under certain circumstances, it is proper for a program to terminate long before all of the statements in the program have been examined and/or executed. For these specific circumstances, C incorporates the exit( ) library function. The function exit( ) expects one integer argument, called a *status value*. The UNIX and MS-DOS operating systems interpret a status value of zero as signaling a normal program termination, while any nonzero status values signify different kinds of errors.

The particular status value passed to exit( ) can be used by the process that invoked the program to take some action. For example, if the program were invoked from the command line and the status value indicated some type of error, the operating system might display a message. In addition to terminating the program, exit( ) writes all output waiting to be written and closes all open files.

The following C++ program averages a list of up to 30 grades. The program will exit if the user requests to average more than *SIZE* number of integers.

```cpp
//
//   exit1.cpp
//   A C++ program demonstrating the use of the exit function
//   Copyright (c) Chris H. Pappas and William H. Murray, 1997
//

#include <iostream.h>
#include <process.h>

#define LIMIT 30

int main( )
{
  int irow,irequested_qty,iscores[LIMIT];
  float fsum=0,imax_score=0,imin_score=100,faverage;

  cout << "\nEnter the number of scores to be averaged: ";
  cin >>  irequested_qty;
  if(irequested_qty > LIMIT) {
    cout << "\nYou can only enter up to " << LIMIT << \
            " scores" << " to be averaged.\n";
    cout << "\n        >>> Program was exited. <<<\n";
    exit(1);
  }

  for(irow = 0; irow < irequested_qty; irow++) {
    cout << "\nPlease enter a grade " << irow+1 << ":   ";
```

```
    cin >> iscores[irow];
  }

  for(irow = 0; irow < irequested_qty; irow++)
    fsum = fsum + iscores[irow];

  faverage = fsum/(float)irequested_qty;

  for(irow = 0; irow < irequested_qty; irow++) {
    if(iscores[irow] > imax_score)
      imax_score = iscores[irow];
    if(iscores[irow] < imin_score)
      imin_score = iscores[irow];
  }

  cout << "\nThe maximum grade is " << imax_score;
  cout << "\nThe minimum grade is " << imin_score;
  cout << "\nThe average grade is " << faverage;

  return(0);
}
```

The program begins by including the PROCESS.H header file. Either PROCESS.H or STDLIB.H can be included to prototype the function exit( ). The constant *LIMIT* is declared to be 30 and is used to dimension the array of integers, *iscores*. After the remaining variables are declared, the program prompts the user for the number of *iscores* to be entered. For this program, the user's response is to be typed next to the prompt.

The program inputs the requested value into the variable *irequested_qty* and uses this for the if comparison. When the user wants to average more numbers than will fit in *iscores*, the two warning messages are printed and then the exit( ) statement is executed. This terminates the program altogether.

See if you can detect the two subtle differences between the preceding program and the one that follows:

```
//
//  exit2.cpp
//  A C++ program demonstrating the use of the exit function
//  in relation to the difference between the process.h
//  and stdlib.h header files.
```

```cpp
//   Copyright (c) Chris H. Pappas and William H. Murray, 1997
//

#include <iostream.h>
#include <stdlib.h>

#define LIMIT 30

int main( )
{
  int irow,irequested_qty,iscores[LIMIT];
  float fsum=0,imax_score=0,imin_score=100,faverage;

  cout << "\nEnter the number of scores to be averaged: ";
  cin >>  irequested_qty;
  if(irequested_qty > LIMIT) {
    cout << "\nYou can only enter up to " << LIMIT << \
            " scores" << " to be faveraged.\n";
    cout << "\n         >>> Program was exited. <<<\n";
    exit(EXIT_FAILURE);
  }

  for(irow = 0; irow < irequested_qty; irow++) {
    cout << "\nPlease enter a grade " << irow+1 << ":   ";
    cin >> iscores[irow];
  }

  for(irow = 0; irow < irequested_qty; irow++)
    fsum = fsum + iscores[irow];

  faverage = fsum/(float)irequested_qty;

  for(irow = 0; irow < irequested_qty; irow++) {
    if(iscores[irow] > imax_score)
      imax_score = iscores[irow];
    if(iscores[irow] < imin_score)
      imin_score = iscores[irow];
  }
```

```
   cout << "\nThe maximum grade is " << imax_score;
   cout << "\nThe minimum grade is " << imin_score;
   cout << "\nThe average grade is " << faverage;

   return(EXIT_SUCCESS);
}
```

By the inclusion of the STDLIB.H header file instead of PROCESS.H, two additional definitions became visible: EXIT_SUCCESS (which returns a value of zero) and EXIT_FAILURE (which returns an unsuccessful value). This program used the EXIT_FAILURE definition for a more readable parameter to the function exit( ).

atexit( )

Whenever a program invokes the exit( ) function or performs a normal program termination, it can also call any registered "exit functions" posted with atexit( ). The following C program demonstrates this capability:

```
/*
 *    atexit.c
 *    A C program demonstrating the relationship between the
 *    function atexit and the order in which the functions
 *    declared are executed.
 *    Copyright (c) Chris H. Pappas and William H. Murray, 1997
 */

#include <stdio.h>
#include <stdlib.h>

void atexit_fn1(void);
void atexit_fn2(void);
void atexit_fn3(void);

int main( )
{

   atexit(atexit_fn1);
   atexit(atexit_fn2);
   atexit(atexit_fn3);
```

```
    printf("Atexit program entered.\n");
    printf("Atexit program exited.\n\n");
    printf(">>>>>>>>>>> <<<<<<<<<<<\n\n");

    return(0);
}

void atexit_fn1(void)
{
  printf("atexit_fn1 entered.\n");
}

void atexit_fn2(void)
{
  printf("atexit_fn2 entered.\n");
}

void atexit_fn3(void)
{
  printf("atexit_fn3 entered.\n");
}
```

The output from the program looks like this:

```
Atexit program entered.
Atexit program exited.

>>>>>>>>>>> <<<<<<<<<<<

atexit_fn3 entered.
atexit_fn2 entered.
atexit_fn1 entered.
```

The atexit( ) function uses the name of a function as its only parameter and registers the specified function as an exit function. Whenever the program terminates normally, as in the preceding example, or invokes the exit( ) function, all atexit( ) declared functions are executed.

Technically, each time the atexit( ) statement is encountered in the source code, the specified function is added to a list of functions to execute when the program terminates. When the program terminates, any functions that have been passed to atexit( ) are executed, with the *last* function added being the *first* one executed. This explains why the *atexit_fn3* output statement was printed before the similar statement in *atexit_fn1*. atexit( ) functions are normally used as cleanup routines for dynamically allocated objects. Since one object (B) can be built upon another (A), atexit( ) functions execute in reverse order. This would delete object B before deleting object A.

Chapter 8

Writing and Using Functions

215

Functions form the cornerstone of C and C++ programming. This chapter introduces you to the concept of a function and how it is prototyped under the latest ANSI C standard. Using many example programs, you will examine the different types of functions and how arguments are passed. You will also learn how to use the standard C/C++ variables *argc* and *argv* to pass command-line arguments to the main( ) function. Additionally, the chapter explores several unique features available in C++.

Functions are the main building blocks of C and C++ programs. By separating and coding parts of your program in separate modules, called *functions*, your program can take on a modular appearance. Modular programming allows a program to be separated into workable parts that contribute to a final program form. For example, one function might be used to capture input data, another to print information, and yet another to write data to the disk. As a matter of fact, all C and C++ programming is done within a function. The one function every C or C++ program has is main( ).

If you have programmed in other languages, you will find that C functions are similar to programming modules in other languages. For example, Pascal uses functions and procedures, while FORTRAN uses just functions. The proper development of C and C++ functions determines, to a great extent, the efficiency, readability, and portability of your program code.

Many programming examples have been included in this chapter with the intent of showing you how to create and implement a wide range of functions. Many of the example programs also use built-in C and C++ library functions that give your program extended power.

What is Function Prototyping?

When the ANSI C standard was implemented for C, it was the C functions that underwent the greatest change. The ANSI C standard for functions is based upon the function prototype that has already been extensively used in C++.

At this point, the world of C programming is in transition. As you read magazine articles and books that use C code, you will see many forms used to describe C functions. These may or may not conform to the new ANSI C standard, as programmers attempt to bring themselves in line with this standard. The Visual C/C++ compiler uses the ANSI C standard for functions but will also compile the earlier forms. The C programs in this book conform to the ANSI C standard. An attempt has been made to pattern C++ programs after the ANSI C standard for C since one has not yet been set for C++.

The Syntax for Prototypes

If you are not familiar with writing C functions, you probably have a few questions. What does a function look like? Where do functions go in a program? How are functions declared? What constitutes a function? Where is type checking performed?

Under the ANSI C standard, all functions must be prototyped. The prototyping can take place in the C or C++ program itself or in a header file. For the programs in this book, most function prototyping is contained within the program itself. Function declarations begin with the C and C++ function prototype. The function prototype is simple, and it is usually included at the start of program code to notify the compiler of the type and number of arguments that a function will use. Prototyping enforces stronger type checking than was previously possible when C standards were less strongly enforced.

Although other prototyping style variations are legal, this book recommends the function prototype form that is a replication of the function's declaration line, with the addition of a semicolon at the end, whenever possible. For example:

return_type function_name(argument_type optional_argument_name [,...]);

The function can be of type void, int, float, and so on. The *return_type* gives this specification. The *function_name( )* is any meaningful name you choose to describe the function. If any information is passed to the function, an *argument_type* followed by an *optional_argument_name* should also be given. Argument types can also be of type void, int, float, and so on. You can pass many values to a function by repeating the argument type and name separated by a comma. It is also correct to list just the argument type, but that prototype form is used specifically for library routine prototypes.

The function itself is actually an encapsulated piece of C or C++ program code that usually follows the main( ) function definition. A function can take the following form:

return_type function_name(argument_types and names)
{
.
.
(data declarations and body of function)
.
.
 return( );
}

Notice that the first line of the actual function is identical to the prototype that is listed at the beginning of a program, with one important exception: it does *not* end with a semicolon. A function prototype and function used in a program are shown in the following C example:

```
/*
 *   proto.c
 *   A C program to illustrate function prototyping.
 *   Function adds two integers
```

```
*     and returns an integer result.
*     Copyright (c) Chris H. Pappas and William H. Murray, 1997
*/

#include <stdio.h>

int iadder(int ix,int iy);              /* function prototype  */

int main( )
{
  int ia=23;
  int ib=13;
  int ic;

  ic=iadder(ia,ib);
  printf("The sum is: %d\n", ic);

  return (0);
}

int iadder(int ix,int iy)              /* function declaration */
{
  int iz;

  iz=ix+iy;
  return(iz);                          /* function return      */
}
```

The function is called iadder( ). The prototype states that the function will accept two integer arguments and return an integer type. Actually, the ANSI C standard suggests that all functions be prototyped in a separate header file. This, as you might guess, is how header files are associated with their appropriate C libraries. For simple programs, as already mentioned, including the function prototype within the body of the program is acceptable.

The same function written for C++ takes on an almost identical appearance:

```
//  proto.cpp
//  C++ program to illustrate function prototyping.
//  Function adds two integers
//  and returns an integer result.
//  Copyright (c) Chris H. Pappas and William H. Murray, 1997
//

#include <iostream.h>

int iadder(int ix,int iy);                // function prototype
```

```
int main( )
{
  int ia=23;
  int ib=13;
  int ic;

  ic=iadder(ia,ib);
  cout << "The sum is: " << ic << endl;

  return (0);
}

int iadder(int ix,int iy)              // function declaration
{
  int iz;

  iz=ix+iy;
  return(iz);                          // function return
}
```

Ways to Pass Actual Arguments

In the previous two examples, arguments have been *passed by value* to the functions. When variables are passed by value, a copy of the variable's actual contents is passed to the function. Since a copy of the variable is passed, the variable in the calling function itself is not altered. Calling a function by value is the most popular means of passing information to a function, and it is the default method in C and C++. The major restriction to the call-by-value method is that the function typically returns only one value.

When you use a *call-by-reference,* the address of the argument, rather than the actual value, is passed to the function. This approach also requires less program memory than a call-by-value. When you use call-by-reference, the variables in the calling function can be altered. Another advantage to a call-by-reference is that more than one value can be returned by the function.

The next example uses the iadder( ) function from the previous section. The arguments are now passed by a call-by-reference. In C, you accomplish a call-by-reference by using a pointer as an argument, as shown here. This same method can be used with C++.

```
/*
 *   cbref.c
 *   A C program to illustrate call-by-reference.
 *   Copyright (c) Chris H. Pappas and William H. Murray, 1997
```

```
*/

#include <stdio.h>

int iadder(int *pix,int *piy);

int main( )
{
  int ia=23;
  int ib=13;
  int ic;

  ic=iadder(&ia,&ib);
  printf("The sum is: %d\n", ic);

  return (0);
}

int iadder(int *pix,int *piy)
{
  int iz;

  iz=*pix+*piy;
  return(iz);
}
```

As you have learned, in C you can use variables and pointers as arguments in function declarations. C++ uses variables and pointers as arguments in function declarations and adds a third type, called a *reference type*. The reference type specifies a location but does not require a dereferencing operator. Many advanced C++ programs use this syntax to simplify the use of pointer variables within called subroutines. Examine the following syntax carefully and compare it with the previous example:

```
//
//  refrnc.cpp
//  C++ program to illustrate an equivalent
//  call-by-reference, using the C++ reference type.
//  Copyright (c) Chris H. Pappas and William H. Murray, 1997
//

#include <iostream.h>

int iadder(int &rix,int &riy);
```

```
int main( )
{
  int ia=23;
  int ib=13;
  int ic;

  ic=iadder(ia,ib);
  cout << "The sum is: " << ic << endl;

  return (0);
}

int iadder(int &rix,int &riy)
{
  int iz;

  iz=rix+riy;
  return(iz);
}
```

When you examined the listing, did you notice the lack of pointers in the C++ program code? The reference types in this example are rix and riy. In C++, references to references, references to bit-fields, arrays of references, and pointers to references are not allowed. Regardless of whether you use call-by-reference or a reference type, C++ always uses the address of the argument.

Storage Classes

Storage classes can be affixed to data type declarations, as you saw earlier in Chapter 6. A variable might, for example, be declared as

static float *fyourvariable;*

Functions can also use extern and static storage class types. A function is declared with an extern storage class when it has been defined in another file, external to the present program. A function can be declared static when external access, apart from the present program, is not permitted.

Identifier Visibility Rules

The *scope* of a variable, when used in a function, refers to the variable's range of effects. The scope rules are similar for C and C++ variables used with functions. Variables can have a local, file, or class scope. (Class scope is discussed in Chapter 16.)

You may use a *local variable* completely within a function definition. Its scope is then limited to the function itself. The variable is said to be accessible, or visible, within the function only and has a local scope.

Variables with a *file scope* are declared outside of individual functions or classes. These variables have visibility or accessibility throughout the file in which they are declared and are global in range.

A variable may be used with a file scope and later within a function definition with a *local scope*. When this is done, the local scope takes precedence over the file scope. C++ offers a new programming feature called the *scope resolution operator* (::). When the C++ resolution operator is used, a variable with local scope is changed to one with file scope. In this situation, the variable would possess the value of the "global" variable. The syntax for referencing the global variable is

::yourvariable

Scope rules allow unique programming errors. Various scope rule errors are discussed at the end of this chapter.

Recursion

Recursion occurs in a program when a function calls itself. Initially, this might seem like an endless loop, but it is not. Both C and C++ support recursion. Recursive algorithms allow for creative, readable, and terse problem solutions. For example, the next program uses recursion to generate the factorial of a number. The *factorial* of a number is defined as the number multiplied by all successively lower integers. For example:

8 * 7 * 6 * 5 * 4 * 3 * 2 * 1
= 40320

Care must be taken when choosing data types since the product increases very rapidly. The factorial of 15 is 1307674368000.

```
/*
 *   factr.c
 *   A C program illustrating recursive function calls.
 *   Calculation of the factorial of a number.
 *   Example:   7! = 7 x 6 x 5 x 4 x 3 x 2 x 1 = 5040
 *   Copyright (c) Chris H. Pappas and William H. Murray, 1997
 */

#include <stdio.h>

double dfactorial(double danswer);
```

```
int main( )
{
  double dnumber=15.0;
  double dresult;

  dresult=dfactorial(dnumber);

  printf("The factorial of %15.0lf is: %15.0lf\n",
         dnumber,dresult);

  return (0);
}

double dfactorial(double danswer)
{
  if (danswer <= 1.0)
    return(1.0);
  else
    return(danswer*dfactorial(danswer-1.0));
}
```

PROGRAMMING
FOUNDATIONS

Recursion occurs because the function, dfactorial( ), has a call to itself within the function. Notice, too, that the printf( ) function uses a new format code for printing a double value: %...lf. Here the "l" is a modifier to the "f" and specifies a double instead of a float.

Function Arguments

In this section you learn about passing function arguments to a function. These arguments go by many different names. Some programmers call them arguments, while others refer to them as parameters or dummy variables.

Function arguments are optional. Some functions you design may receive no arguments, while others may receive many. Function argument types can be mixed; that is, you can use any of the standard data types as a function argument. Many of the following examples illustrate passing various data types to functions. Furthermore, these programs employ functions from the various C and C++ libraries. Additional details on these library functions and their prototypes can be found in the Visual C/C++ reference manuals.

Actual Versus Formal Parameters

Each function definition contains an argument list called the *formal argument list.* Items in the list are optional, so the actual list may be empty or it may contain any combination of data types, such as integer, float, and character.

When the function is called by the program, an argument list is also passed to the function. This is called the *actual argument list.* Generally, when writing ANSI C code, there is a 1:1 match between the formal and actual argument lists, although in reality no strong enforcement is used.

Examine the following coded C example:

```
printf("This is hexadecimal %x and octal %o",ians);
```

In this case, only one argument is being passed to printf( ), although two are expected. When fewer arguments are supplied, the missing arguments are initialized to meaningless values. C++ overcomes this problem, to a degree, by permitting a default value to be supplied with the formal argument list. When an argument is missing in the actual argument list, the default argument is automatically substituted. For example, in C++, the function prototype might appear as

int *iyourfunction(int it,float fu=4.2,int iv=10)*

Here, if either *fu* or *iv* is not specified in the call to the function iyourfunction( ), the values shown (4.2 or 10) will be used. C++ requires that all formal arguments using default values be listed at the end of the formal argument list. In other words, iyourfunction(10) and iyourfunction(10,15.2) are valid. If *fu* is not supplied, *iv* cannot be supplied either.

void Parameters

In ANSI C, void should be used to explicitly state the absence of function arguments. In C++, the use of void is not yet required but should be considered wise. The following program has a simple function named voutput( ) that receives no arguments and does not return a value. The main( ) function calls the function voutput( ). When the voutput( ) function is finished, control is returned to the main( ) function. This is one of the simplest types of functions you can write.

```
/*
 *    fvoid.c
 *    A C program that will print a message with a function.
 *    Function uses a type void argument and sqrt function
 *    from the standard C library.
 *    Copyright (c) Chris H. Pappas and William H. Murray, 1997
 */

#include <stdio.h>
#include <math.h>
```

```
void voutput(void);

int main( )
{
  printf("This program will find the square root. \n\n");
  voutput( );

  return (0);
}

void voutput(void)
{
  double dt=12345.0;
  double du;

  du=sqrt(dt);
  printf("The square root of %lf is %lf  \n",dt,du);
}
```

If you study the example, you will notice that the voutput( ) function calls a C library function named sqrt( ). The prototype for the sqrt( ) library function is contained in MATH.H. It accepts a double as an argument and returns the square root as a double value.

char Parameters

Character information can also be passed to a function. In the next example, a single character is intercepted from the keyboard, in the function main( ), and passed to the function voutput( ). The getch( ) function reads the character. There are other functions that are closely related to getch( ) in the standard C library: getc( ), getchar( ), and getche( ). These functions can also be used in C++, but in many cases a better choice will probably be cin. Additional details for using getch( ) are contained in your Visual C/C++ reference manuals and are available as online help. The getch( ) function intercepts a character from the standard input device (keyboard) and returns a character value, without echo to the screen, as shown here:

```
/*
 *   fchar.c
 *   C program will accept a character from keyboard,
 *   pass it to a function and print a message using
 *   the character.
 *   Copyright (c) Chris H. Pappas and William H. Murray, 1997
 */
```

```c
#include <stdio.h>

void voutput(char c);

int main( )
{
  char cyourchar;

  printf("Enter one character from the keyboard. \n");
  cyourchar=getch( );
  voutput(cyourchar);

  return (0);
}

void voutput(char c)
{
  int j;

  for(j=0;j<16;j++)
    printf("The character typed is %c  \n",c);
}
```

From the listing you will notice that a single character is passed to the function. The function then prints a message and the character 16 times. The %c in the printf( ) function specifies that a single character is to be printed.

int Parameters

In the next example, a single integer will be read from the keyboard with C's scanf( ) function. That integer will be passed to the function vside( ). The vside( ) function uses the supplied length to calculate and print the area of a square and the volume and the surface area of a cube.

```c
/*
 *    fint.c
 *    C program will calculate values given a length.
 *    Function uses a type int argument, accepts length
 *    from keyboard with scanf function.
 *    Copyright (c) Chris H. Pappas and William H. Murray, 1997
 */


#include <stdio.h>

void vside(int is);
```

```
int main( )
{
  int iyourlength;

  printf("Enter the length, as an integer,\n");
  printf("from the keyboard. \n");
  scanf("%d",&iyourlength);
  vside(iyourlength);

  return (0);
}

void vside(int is)
{
  int iarea,ivolume,isarea;

  iarea=is*is;
  ivolume=is*is*is;
  isarea=6*iarea;

  printf("The length of a side is %d  \n\n",is);
  printf("A square would have an area of %d \n",iarea);
  printf("A cube would have a volume of %d \n",ivolume);
  printf("The surface area of the cube is %d \n",isarea);
}
```

Notice that *is* and all calculated values are integers. What would happen if *is* represented the radius of a circle and sphere to the calculated types?

float Parameters

Floats are just as easy to pass as arguments to a function as are integer values. In the following C example, two floating-point values are passed to a function called vhypotenuse( ). scanf( ) is used to intercept both float values from the keyboard.

```
/*
 *   ffloat.c
 *   C program will find hypotenuse of a right triangle.
 *   Function uses a type float argument and accepts
 *   input from the keyboard with the scanf function.
 *   Copyright (c) Chris H. Pappas and William H. Murray, 1997
 */

#include <stdio.h>
#include <math.h>
```

```
void vhypotenuse(float fx,float fy);

int main( )
{
  float fxlen,fylen;

  printf("Enter the base of the right triangle. \n");
  scanf("%f",&fxlen);
  printf("Enter the height of the right triangle. \n");
  scanf("%f",&fylen);
  vhypotenuse(fxlen,fylen);

  return (0);
}

void vhypotenuse(float ft,float fu)
{
  double dresult;
  dresult=hypot((double) ft,(double) fu);
  printf("The hypotenuse of the right triangle is %g \n",
         dresult);
}
```

Notice that both arguments received by vhypotenuse( ) are cast to doubles when used by the hypot( ) function from MATH.H. All MATH.H functions accept and return double types. You can also display the contents of your MATH.H header file for additional details.

double Parameters

The double type is a very precise float value. All MATH.H functions accept and return double types. The next program accepts two double values from the keyboard. The function named vpower( ) will raise the first number to the power specified by the second number. Since both values are of type double, you can calculate $45.7^{5.2}$ and find that it equals 428118741.757.

```
/*
 *    fdoubl.c
 *    C program will raise a number to a power.
 *    Function uses a type double argument and the pow function.
 *    Copyright (c) Chris H. Pappas and William H. Murray, 1997
 */

#include <stdio.h>
#include <math.h>
```

```
void vpower(double dt,double du);

int main( )
{
  double dtnum,dunum;

  printf("Enter the base number. \n");
  scanf("%lf",&dtnum);
  printf("Enter the power. \n");
  scanf("%lf",&dunum);
  vpower(dtnum,dunum);

  return (0);
}

void vpower(double dt,double du)
{
  double danswer;

  danswer=pow(dt,du);
  printf("The result is %lf \n",danswer);
}
```

This function uses the library function pow( ) to raise one number to a power, prototyped in MATH.H.

Array Parameters

In the following example, the contents of an array are passed to a function as a call-by-reference. In this case the address of the first array element is passed via a pointer.

```
/*
 *   fpntr.c
 *   C program will call a function with an array.
 *   Function uses a pointer to pass array information.
 *   Copyright (c) Chris H. Pappas and William H. Murray, 1997
 */

#include <stdio.h>

void voutput(int *pinums);

int main( )
{
  int iyourarray[7]={2,7,15,32,45,3,1};
```

```
    printf("Send array information to function. \n");
    voutput(iyourarray);

    return (0);
}

void voutput(int *pinums)
{
    int t;

    for(t=0;t<7;t++)
        printf("The result is %d \n",pinums[t]);
}
```

Notice that when the function is called, only the name *iyourarray* is specified. In Chapter 9 you will learn more details concerning arrays. In this example, by specifying the name of the array, you are providing the address of the first element in the array. Since *iyourarray* is an array of integers, it is possible to pass the array by specifying a pointer of the element type.

It is also permissible to pass the address information by using an unsized array. The next example shows how you can do this in C++. (The same approach can be used in C.) The information in *iyourarray* is transferred by passing the address of the first element.

```
//
//  farray.cpp
//  C++ program will call a function with an array.
//  Function passes array information, and calculates
//  the average of the numbers.
//  Copyright (c) Chris H. Pappas and William H. Murray, 1997
//

#include <iostream.h>

void avg(float fnums[]);

int main( )
{
    float iyourarray[8]={12.3,25.7,82.1,6.0,7.01,
                         0.25,4.2,6.28};

    cout << "Send information to averaging function. \n";
    avg(iyourarray);

    return (0);
```

```
}

void avg(float fnums[])
{
  int iv;
  float fsum=0.0;
  float faverage;

  for(iv=0;iv<8;iv++) {
    fsum+=fnums[iv];
    cout << "number " << iv+1 << " is " << fnums[iv] << endl;
  }
  faverage=fsum/iv;
  cout << "\nThe average is " << faverage << endl;
}
```

The average is determined by summing each of the terms together and dividing by the total number of terms. The cout stream is used to format the output to the screen.

Function Return Types

The following sections provide an example for each of the important return types for functions possible in C and C++ programming. Function types specify the type of value returned by the function. None of the examples in the last section returned information from the function and thus were of type void.

void Return Type

Since void was used in all of the previous examples, the example for this section is a little more involved. As you have learned, C and C++ permit numeric information to be formatted in hexadecimal, decimal, and octal—but not binary. Specifying data in a binary format is useful for doing binary arithmetic or developing bit masks. The function vbinary( ) will convert a decimal number entered from the keyboard to a binary representation on the screen. The binary digits are not packed together as a single binary number but are stored individually in an array. Thus, to examine the binary number, the contents of the array must be printed out.

```
/*
 *   voidf.c
 *   C program illustrates the void function type.
 *   Program will print the binary equivalent of a number.
 *   Copyright (c) Chris H. Pappas and William H. Murray, 1997
 */
```

```
#include <stdio.h>

void vbinary(int ivalue);

int main( )
{
  int ivalue;

  printf("Enter a number (base 10) for conversion to binary.\n");
  scanf("%d",&ivalue);
  vbinary(ivalue);

  return (0);
}

void vbinary(int idata)
{
  int t=0;
  int iyourarray[50];

  while (idata !=0) {
    iyourarray[t]=(idata % 2);
    idata/=2;
    t++;
  }

  t--;
  for(;t>=0;t--)
    printf("%1d",iyourarray[t]);
  printf("\n");
}
```

The conversion process from higher-order to lower-order bases is a rather simple mathematical algorithm. For example, base 10 numbers can be converted to another base by dividing the number by the new base a successive number of times. If conversion is from base 10 to base 2, a 2 is repeatedly divided into the base 10 number. This produces a quotient and a remainder. The quotient becomes the dividend for each subsequent division. The remainder becomes a digit in the converted number. In the case of binary conversion, the remainder is either a 1 or a zero.

In the function vbinary( ), a while loop is used to perform the arithmetic as long as *idata* has not reached zero. The modulus operator determines the remainder and saves the bit in the array. Division is then performed on *idata*, saving only the integer result. This process is repeated until the quotient (also *data* in this case) is reduced to zero.

The individual array bits, which form the binary result, must be unloaded from the array in reverse order. You can observe this in the program listing. Study the for loop used in the function. Can you think of a way to perform this conversion and save the binary representation in a variable instead of an array?

char Return Type

In this section, you will see an example that is a minor variation of an earlier example. The C function clowercase( ) accepts a character argument and returns the same character type. For this example, an uppercase letter received from the keyboard is passed to the function. The function uses the library function tolower( ) (from the standard library and prototyped in CTYPE.H) to convert the character to a lowercase letter. Related to functions tolower( ), include toascii( ), and toupper( ).

```c
/*
 *    charf.c
 *    C program illustrates the character function type.
 *    Function receives uppercase character and
 *    converts it to lowercase.
 *    Copyright (c) Chris H. Pappas and William H. Murray, 1997
 */


#include <stdio.h>
#include <ctype.h>

char clowercase(char c);

int main( )
{
  char clowchar,chichar;

  printf("Enter an uppercase character.\n");
  chichar=getchar( );
  clowchar=clowercase(chichar);
  printf("%c\n",clowchar);

  return (0);
}

char clowercase(char c)
{
  return(tolower(c));
}
```

PROGRAMMING
FOUNDATIONS

bool Return Type

The following example program demonstrates the use of the new bool data type by defining two functions, is_upper( ) and is_lower( ), that return this new ANSI C++ type:

```cpp
/*
 * bool.cpp
 * C++ program illustrating the use
 * of the new ANSI C++ type bool
 * Copyright (c) Chris H. Pappas and William H. Murray, 1997
 */

#include <iostream.h>

bool is_upper(int cTestChar);
bool is_lower(int CTestChar);

int main( )
{
  int   cTestChar = 'T';
  bool bIsUppercase, bIsLowercase;

  bIsUppercase = is_upper(cTestChar);
  bIsLowercase = is_lower(cTestChar);

  cout << "The letter %s upper case."
       << bIsUppercase ? "is" : "isn't";
  cout << "The letter %s lower case."
       << bIsLowercase ? "is" : "isn't";

  return(0);
}

bool is_upper(int ch)
{
  return ( ch >= 'A' && ch <= 'Z' );
}

bool is_lower(int ch)
{
  return ( ch >= 'a' && ch <= 'z' );
}
```

Notice the use of the conditional operator ?: to reduce each printf( ) statement to a single line each, instead of the more verbose if-else alternative.

int Return Type

The following function accepts and returns integers. The function icube( ) accepts a number generated in main( ) (0, 2, 4, 6, 8, 10, etc.), cubes the number, and returns the integer value to main( ). The original number and its cube are printed to the screen.

```
/*
*    intf.c
*    C program illustrates the integer function type.
*    Function receives integers, one at a time, and
*    returns the cube of each, one at a time.
*    Copyright (c) Chris H. Pappas and William H. Murray, 1997
*/

#include <stdio.h>

int icube(int ivalue);

int main( )
{
  int k,inumbercube;

  for (k=0;k<20;k+=2) {
    inumbercube=icube(k);
    printf("The cube of the number %d is %d \n",
           k,inumbercube);
  }

  return (0);
}

int icube(int ivalue)
{
  return (ivalue*ivalue*ivalue);
}
```

long Return Type

The following example is a C++ program that accepts an integer value as an argument and returns a type long. The long type, used by Visual C/C++ and other popular compilers, is not recognized as a standard ANSI C type. The function will raise the number 2 to an integer power.

```cpp
//
//  longf.cpp
//  C++ program illustrates the long integer function type.
//  Function receives integers, one at a time, and
//  returns 2 raised to that integer power.
//  Copyright (c) Chris H. Pappas and William H. Murray, 1997
//

#include <iostream.h>

long lpower(int ivalue);

int main( )
{
  int k;
  long lanswer;

  for (k=0;k<31;k++) {
    lanswer=lpower(k);
    cout << "2 raised to the " << k << " power is "
         << lanswer << endl;
  }

  return (0);
}

long lpower(int ivalue)
{
  int t;
  long lseed=1;

  for (t=0;t<ivalue;t++)
    lseed*=2;
  return (lseed);
}
```

The function simply multiplies the original number by the number of times it is to be raised to the specified power. For example, if you wanted to raise 2 to the 6th power (2^6), the program will perform the following multiplication:

$2 * 2 * 2 * 2 * 2 * 2 = 64$

Can you think of a function described in MATH.H that could achieve the same results? See Table 8-1 for some ideas.

double _cabs(struct _complex);	double _hypot(double, double);
double _j0(double);	double _j1(double);
double _jn(int, double);	double _y0(double);
double _y1(double);	double _yn(int, double);
double acos(double);	double asin(double);
double atan(double);	double atan2(double, double);
double atof(const char *);	double cabs(struct _complex);
double ceil(double);	double cos(double);
double cosh(double);	double exp(double);
double fabs(double);	double floor(double);
double fmod(double, double);	double frexp(double, int *);
double hypot(double, double);	double j0(double);
double j1(double);	double jn(int, double);
double ldexp(double, int);	double log(double);
double log10(double);	double modf(double, double *);
double pow(double, double);	double sin(double);
double sinh(double);	double sqrt(double);

Table 8-1.   *Macro and Function Prototypes Provided by MATH.H*

double tan(double);	double tanh(double);
double y0(double);	double y1(double);
double yn(int, double);	float acosf(float);
float asinf(float);	float atan2f(float,float);
float atanf(float);	float ceilf(float);
float cosf(float);	float coshf(float);
float expf(float);	float fabsf(float);
float floorf(float);	float fmodf(float,float);
float hypotf(float,float);	float log10f(float);
float logf(float);	float modff(float,float *);
float powf(float,float);	float sinf(float);
float sinhf(float);	float sqrtf(float);
float tanf(float);	float tanhf(float);
int_matherrl(struct _exceptionl *);	int_matherr(struct _exception *);
int abs(int);	int matherr(struct _exception *);
long labs(long);	long double _atold(const char *);
long double _cabsl(struct _complexl);	long double _hypotl(long double, long double);
long double _j0l(long double);	long double _j1l(long double);
long double _jnl(int, long double);	long double _y0l(long double);
long double _y1l(long double);	long double _ynl(int, long double);
long double acosl(long double);	long double asinl(long double);
long double atan2l(long double, long double);	long double atanl(long double);
long double ceill(long double);	long double coshl(long double);

Table 8-1. *Macro and Function Prototypes Provided by MATH.H (continued)*

long double cosl(long double);	long double expl(long double);
long double fabsl(long double);	long double floorl(long double);
long double fmodl(long double, long double);	long double frexpl(long double, int *);
long double ldexpl(long double, int);	long double log10l(long double);
long double logl(long double);	long double modfl(long double, long double *);
long double powl(long double, long double);	long double sinhl(long double);
long double sinl(long double);	long double sqrtl(long double);
long double tanhl(long double);	long double tanl(long double);

Table 8-1. *Macro and Function Prototypes Provided by MATH.H* (continued)

float Return Type

In the next example, a float array argument will be passed to a function and a float will be returned. This C++ example will find the product of all the elements in an array.

```
//
//   floatf.cpp
//   C++ program illustrates the float function type.
//   Function receives an array of floats and returns
//   their product as a float.
//   Copyright (c) Chris H. Pappas and William H. Murray, 1997
//

#include <iostream.h>

float fproduct(float farray[]);

int main( )
```

```
{
   float fmyarray[7]={4.3,1.8,6.12,3.19,0.01234,0.1,9876.2};
   float fmultiplied;

   fmultiplied=fproduct(fmyarray);
   cout << "The product of all array entries is: "
        << fmultiplied << endl;

   return (0);
}

float fproduct(float farray[])
{
   int i;
   float fpartial;

   fpartial=farray[0];
   for (i=1;i<7;i++)
     fpartial*=farray[i];
   return (fpartial);
}
```

Since the elements are multiplied together, the first element of the array must be loaded into *fpartial* before the for loop is entered. Observe that the loop in the function fproduct( ) starts at 1 instead of the normal zero value.

double Return Type

The following C example accepts and returns a double type. The function dtrigcosine( ) will convert an angle, expressed in degrees, to its cosine value.

```
/*
 *    double.c
 *    C program illustrates the double function type.
 *    Function receives integers from 0 to 90, one at a
 *    time, and returns the cosine of each, one at a time.
 *    Copyright (c) Chris H. Pappas and William H. Murray, 1997
 */

#include <stdio.h>
#include <math.h>
```

```
const double dPi=3.14159265359;

double dtrigcosine(double dangle);

int main( )
{
  int j;
  double dcosine;

  for (j=0;j<91;j++) {
    dcosine=dtrigcosine((double) j);
    printf("The cosine of %d degrees is %19.18lf \n",
            j,dcosine);
  }

  return (0);
}

double dtrigcosine(double dangle)
{
  double dpartial;
  dpartial=cos((dPi/180.0)*dangle);
  return (dpartial);
}
```

Notice that the cos( ) function described in MATH.H is used by dtrigcosine( ) for obtaining the answer. Angles must be converted from degrees to radians for all trigonometric functions. Recall that pi radians equals 180 degrees.

Command-Line Arguments

C and C++ share the ability to accept command-line arguments. *Command-line arguments* are those entered along with the program name when called from the operating system's command line. This gives you the ability to pass arguments directly to your program without additional program prompts. For example, a program might pass four arguments from the command line:

```
YOURPROGRAM  Sneakers, ThinkingDog, Tango, BigDog
```

In this example, four values are passed from the command line to YOURPROGRAM. Actually, it is main( ) that is given specific information. One argument received by main( ), *argc,* is an integer giving the number of command-line terms plus 1. The program title is counted as the first term passed from the command line since DOS 3.0. The second argument is a pointer to an array of string pointers called *argv.* All arguments are strings of characters, so *argv* is of type char *[*argc*]. Since all programs have a name, *argc* is always one greater than the number of command-line arguments. In the following examples, you will learn different techniques for retrieving various data types from the command line. The argument names *argc* and *argv* are the commonly agreed upon variable names used in all C/C++ programs.

Alphanumeric

Arguments are passed from the command line as strings of characters, and thus they are the easiest to work with. In the next example, the C program expects that the user will enter several names on the command line. To ensure that the user does enter several names, if *argc* isn't greater than 2, the user will be returned to the command line with a reminder to try again.

```
/*
 *    sargv.c
 *    C program illustrates how to read string data
 *    into the program with a command-line argument.
 *    Copyright (c) Chris H. Pappas and William H. Murray, 1997
 */

#include <stdio.h>
#include <process.h>

int main(int argc,char *argv[])
{
  int t;

  if(argc<2) {
    printf("Enter several names on the command line\n");
    printf("when executing this program!\n");
    printf("Please try again.\n");
    exit(0);
  }

  for (t=1; t<argc; t++)
    printf("Entry #%d is %s\n",t,argv[t]);

  return (0);
}
```

This program is completely contained in main( ) and does not use additional functions. The names entered on the command line are printed to the screen in the same order. If numeric values are entered on the command line, they will be interpreted as an ASCII string of individual characters and must be printed as such.

Integral

In many programs, it is desirable to enter integer numbers on the command line; perhaps in a program that would find the average of a student's test scores. In such a case, the ASCII character information must be converted to an integer value. The C++ example in this section will accept a single integer number on the command line. Since the number is actually a character string, it will be converted to an integer with the atoi( ) library function. The command-line value, *ivalue*, is passed to a function used earlier, called vbinary( ). The function will convert the number in *ivalue* to a string of binary digits and print them to the screen. When control is returned to main( ), the *ivalue* will be printed in octal and hexadecimal formats.

```
//
//   iargv.cpp
//   C++ program illustrates how to read an integer
//   into the program with a command-line argument.
//   Copyright (c) Chris H. Pappas and William H. Murray, 1997
//

#include <iostream.h>
#include <stdlib.h>
#include <process.h>

void vbinary(int idigits);

int main(int argc, char *argv[])
{
  int ivalue;

  if(argc!=2) {
    cout << "Enter a decimal number on the command line.\n";
    cout << "It will be converted to binary, octal and\n";
    cout << "hexadecimal.\n";
    exit(1);
  }

  ivalue=atoi(argv[1]);
  vbinary(ivalue);
```

```
   cout << "The octal value is: " << oct
        << ivalue << endl;
   cout << "The hexadecimal value is: "
        << hex << ivalue << endl;

   return (0);
}

void vbinary(int idigits)
{
  int t=0;
  int iyourarray[50];

  while (idigits != 0) {
    iyourarray[t]=(idigits % 2);
    idigits/=2;
    t++;
  }

  t--;
  cout << "The binary value is: ";
  for(;t>=0;t--)
    cout << dec << iyourarray[t];
    cout << endl;
}
```

Of particular interest is the formatting of the various numbers. You learned earlier that the binary number is saved in the array and printed one digit at a time, using decimal formatting, by unloading the array *iyourarray* in reverse order:

```
cout << dec << myarray[i];
```

To print the number in octal format, the statement is

```
cout << "The octal value is: "
     << oct << ivalue << endl;
```

It is also possible to print the hexadecimal equivalent by substituting hex for oct, as shown here:

```
cout << "The hexadecimal value is: "
     << hex << ivalue << endl;
```

Without additional formatting, the hexadecimal values a, b, c, d, e, and f are printed in lowercase. You'll learn many formatting techniques for C++ in Chapters 11 and 12, including how to print those characters in uppercase.

Real

Once you have learned how to intercept integers from the command line, floats will not present any additional problems. The following C example will allow several angles to be entered on the command line. The cosine of the angles will be extracted and printed to the screen. Since the angles are of type float, they can take on values such as 12.0, 45.78, 0.12345, or 15.

```
/*
 *    fargv.c
 *    C program illustrates how to read float data types
 *    into the program with a command-line argument.
 *    Copyright (c) Chris H. Pappas and William H. Murray, 1997
 */

#include <stdio.h>
#include <math.h>
#include <process.h>

const double dPi=3.14159265359;

int main(int argc, char *argv[])
{
  int t;
  double ddegree;

  if(argc<2) {
    printf("Type several angles on the command line.\n");
    printf("Program will calculate and print\n");
    printf("the cosine of the angles entered.\n");
    exit(1);
  }
```

```
for (t=1; t<argc; t++) {
  ddegree=(double) atof(argv[t]);
  printf("The cosine of %f is %15.14lf\n",
         ddegree,cos((dPi/180.0)*ddegree));
}

return (0);
}
```

The atof( ) function converts the command-line string argument to a float type. The program uses the cos( ) function within the printf( ) function to retrieve the cosine information.

Functions in C Versus C++

C++ provides you with the ability to use several special features when writing functions. The ability to write inline functions is one such advantage. The code for an inline function is reproduced at the spot where the function is called in the main program. Since the compiler places the code at the point of the function call, execution time is saved when using short, frequently called functions.

C++ also permits function overloading. *Overloading* permits several function prototypes to be given the same function name. The numerous prototypes are then recognized by their type and argument list, not just by their name. Overloading is very useful when a function is required to work with different data types.

When Is a Function a Macro?

You can think of the inline keyword as a directive or, better yet, a suggestion to the C++ compiler to insert the function inline. The compiler may ignore this suggestion for any of several reasons. For example, the function might be too long. Inline functions are used primarily to save time when short functions are called many times within a program.

```
//
//   inline.cpp
//   C++ program illustrates the use of an inline function.
//   Inline functions work best on short functions that are
//   used repeatedly. This example calculates the square
//   of an integer.
//   Copyright (c) Chris H. Pappas and William H. Murray, 1997
```

```
//

#include <iostream.h>

inline long squareit(int iValue) {return iValue * iValue;}

int main( )
{
  int iValue = 5;

  cout << squareit(iValue)
       << endl;

 return (0);
}
```

Here the function squareit( ) is declared inline, which returns the square of the formal integer argument *iValue*. When the function main( ) calls function squareit( ), the compiler substitutes the function call with the expression *iValue * iValue*. In other words, the compiler replaces the function call with the function's statement and also replaces the function's parameters with the function's arguments.

One advantage of inline functions versus macros is error checking. Invoking a macro with the wrong data type goes unchecked by the compiler. However, since an inline function has a prototype, the compiler performs type matching between the formal argument type(s) in the prototype and the actual argument(s) in the function call.

Prototyping Multiple Functions with the Same Name

The following example illustrates function overloading. Notice that two functions with the same name are prototyped within the same scope. The correct function will be selected based on the arguments provided. A function call to adder( ) will process integer or float data correctly.

```
//
//   ovrlod.cpp
//   C++ program illustrates function overloading.
//   Overloaded function receives an array of integers or
```

```
//   floats and returns either an integer or float product.
//   Copyright (c) Chris H. Pappas and William H. Murray, 1997
//

#include <iostream.h>

int adder(int iarray[]);
float adder(float farray[]);

int main( )
{
  int iarray[7]={5,1,6,20,15,0,12};
  float farray[7]={3.3,5.2,0.05,1.49,3.12345,31.0,2.007};
  int isum;
  float fsum;

  isum=adder(iarray);
  fsum=adder(farray);
  cout << "The sum of the integer numbers is: "
       << isum << endl;
  cout << "The sum of the float numbers is: "
       << fsum << endl;

  return (0);
}

int adder(int iarray[])
{
  int i;
  int ipartial;

  ipartial=iarray[0];
  for (i=1;i<7;i++)
    ipartial+=iarray[i];
  return (ipartial);
}

float adder(float farray[])
{
  int i;
  float fpartial;
```

```
    fpartial=farray[0];
    for (i=1;i<7;i++)
      fpartial+=farray[i];
    return (fpartial);
}
```

There are a few programming snags to function overloading that must be avoided. For example, if a function differs only in the function type and not in the arguments, the function cannot be overloaded. Also, the following attempt at overloading is not permitted:

int *yourfunction*(int *number*)
int *yourfunction*(int &*value*)   //not allowed

This syntax is not allowed because each prototype would accept the same type of arguments. Despite these limitations, overloading is a very important topic in C++ and is fully explored starting with Chapter 14.

Functions with Varying-Length Formal Argument Lists

You use the ellipsis when the number of arguments is not known. As such, they can be specified within the function's formal argument statement. For example:

void *yourfunction*(int *t*,float *u*,...);

This syntax tells the C compiler that other arguments may or may not follow *t* and *u*, which are required. Naturally, type checking is suspended with the ellipsis.

The following C program demonstrates how to use the ellipsis. You may want to delay an in-depth study of the algorithm, however, until you have a thorough understanding of C string pointer types (see Chapter 10).

```
/*
 *   elip.c
 *   A C program demonstrating the use of ... and its support
 *   macros va_arg, va_start, and va_end
 *   Copyright (c) Chris H. Pappas and William H. Murray, 1997
 */

#include <stdio.h>
```

```
#include <stdarg.h>
#include <string.h>

void vsmallest(char *szmessage, ...);

int main( )
{
  vsmallest("Print %d integers, %d %d %d",10,4,1);

  return(0);
}

void vsmallest(char *szmessage, ...)
{
  int inumber_of_percent_ds=0;
  va_list type_for_ellipsis;
  int ipercent_d_format = 'd';
  char *pchar;
  pchar=strchr(szmessage,ipercent_d_format);

  while(*++pchar != '\0') {
    pchar++;
    pchar=strchr(pchar,ipercent_d_format);
    inumber_of_percent_ds++;
  }
  printf("print %d integers,",inumber_of_percent_ds);

  va_start(type_for_ellipsis,szmessage);

  while(inumber_of_percent_ds--)
    printf(" %d",va_arg(type_for_ellipsis,int));

  va_end(type_for_ellipsis);
}
```

The function vsmallest( ) has been prototyped to expect two arguments, a string pointer, and an argument of type ..., or a varying-length argument list. Naturally, functions using a varying-length argument list are not omniscient. Something within the argument list must give the function enough information to process the varying part. In ELIP.C, this information comes from the string argument.

In a very crude approach, vsmallest( ) attempts to mimic the printf( ) function. The subroutine scans the *szmessage* format string to see how many %ds it finds. It then uses this information to make a calculated fetching and printing of the information in the variable argument. While this sounds straightforward, the algorithm requires a sophisticated sequence of events.

The strchr( ) function returns the address of the location containing the "d" in %d. The first %d can be ignored since this is required by the output message. The while loop continues processing the remainder of the *szmessage* string looking for the variable number of %ds and counting them (*inumber_of_percent_ds*). With this accomplished, the beginning of the output message is printed.

The va_start( ) macro sets the *type_for_ellipsis* pointer to the beginning of the variable argument list. The va_arg( ) support macro retrieves the next argument in the variable list. The macro uses its second parameter to know what data type to retrieve; for the example program, this is type int. The function vsmallest( ) terminates with a call to va_end( ). The last of the three standard C ellipsis support macros, va_end( ), resets the pointer to null.

Things Not to Do with Functions

If variables are used with different scope levels, you may run into completely unexpected programming results, called *side effects*. For example, you have learned that it is possible to use a variable of the same name with both file and local scopes. The scope rules state that the variable with a local scope (called a *local variable*) will take precedence over the variable with a file scope (called a *global variable*). That all seems easy enough, but let's now consider some problem areas you might encounter in programming that are not so obvious.

Attempting to Access Out of Scope Identifiers

In the following example, four variables are given a local scope within the function main( ). Copies of the variables *il* and *im* are passed to the function iproduct( ). This does not violate scope rules. However, when the iproduct( ) function attempts to use the variable *in*, it cannot find the variable. Why? Because the scope of the variable was local to main( ) only.

```
/*
 *   scopep.c
 *   C program to illustrate problems with scope rules.
 *   Function is supposed to form a product of three numbers.
 *   Compiler signals problems since variable n isn't known
 *   to the function multiplier.
 *   Copyright (c) Chris H. Pappas and William H. Murray, 1997
 */

#include <stdio.h>
```

```
int iproduct(int iw,int ix);

int main( )
{
   int il=3;
   int im=7;
   int in=10;
   int io;

   io=iproduct(il,im);
   printf("The product of the numbers is: %d\n", io);

   return (0);
}

int iproduct(int iw,int ix)
{
   int iy;

   iy=iw*ix*in;
   return(iy);
}
```

The C compiler issues a warning and an error message. It reports first a warning that the *in* variable is never used within the function, and then the error message that *in* has never been declared in the function iproduct( ). One way around this problem is to give *in* a file scope.

External Versus Internal Identifier Access

In this example, the variable *in* is given a file scope. Making *in* global to the whole file allows both main( ) and iproduct( ) to use it. Also note that both main( ) and iproduct( ) can change the value of the variable. It is good programming practice not to allow functions to change global program variables if they are created to be truly portable.

```
/*
*    fscope.c
*    C program to illustrate problems with scope rules.
*    Function is supposed to form a product of three numbers.
*    Previous problem is solved, c variable is given file
```

```
*     SCOPE.
*     Copyright (c) Chris H. Pappas and William H. Murray, 1997
*/

#include <stdio.h>

int iproduct(int iw,int ix);

int in=10;

int main( )
{
  int il=3;
  int im=7;
  int io;

  io=iproduct(il,im);
  printf("The product is: %d\n", io);

  return (0);
}

int iproduct(int iw,int ix)
{
  int iy;

  iy=iw*ix*in;
  return(iy);
}
```

This program will compile correctly and print the product 210 to the screen.

Internal Versus External Identifier Access

The scope rules state that a variable with both file and local scope will use the local variable value over the global value. Here is a small program that illustrates this point:

```
/*
*     lscope.c
*     C program to illustrate problems with scope rules.
*     Function forms a product of three numbers, but which
```

```
*    three?   Two are passed as function arguments.  The
*    variable c has both a file and local scope.
*    Copyright (c) Chris H. Pappas and William H. Murray, 1997
*/

#include <stdio.h>

int iproduct(int iw,int ix);

int in=10;

int main( )
{
   int il=3;
   int im=7;
   int io;

   io=iproduct(il,im);
   printf("The product of the numbers is: %d\n", io);

   return (0);
}

int iproduct(int iw,int ix)
{
   int iy;
   int in=2;

   iy=iw*ix*in;
   return(iy);
}
```

In this example, the variable *in* has both file and local scope. When *in* is used within the function iproduct( ), the local scope takes precedence and the product of 3 * 7 * 2 = 42 is returned.

It's Legal, But Don't Ever Do It!

In the following C++ example, everything works fine up to the point of printing the information to the screen. The cout statement prints the values for *il* and *im* correctly. When selecting the *in* value, it chooses the global variable with file scope. The program reports that the product of 3 * 7 * 10 = 42 is clearly a mistake. You know that in this case the iproduct( ) function used the local value of *in*.

```cpp
//
//   scopep.cpp
//   C++ program to illustrate problems with scope rules.
//   Function forms a product of three numbers. The n
//   variable is of local scope and used by function
//   product. However, main function reports that
//   the n value used is 10. What is wrong here?
//   Copyright (c) Chris H. Pappas and William H. Murray, 1997
//

#include <iostream.h>

int iproduct(int iw,int ix);

int in=10;

int main( )
{
  int il=3;
  int im=7;
  int io;

  io=iproduct(il,im);
  cout << "The product of " << il <<" * " << im
       << " * " << in << " is: " << io << endl;

  return (0);
}

int iproduct(int iw,int ix)
{
  int iy;
  int in=2;

  iy=iw*ix*in;
  return(iy);
}
```

PROGRAMMING
FOUNDATIONS

If you actually wanted to form the product with the global value of *in*, how could this conflict be resolved? C++ would permit you to use the scope resolution operator mentioned earlier in the chapter, as shown here:

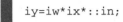

```
iy=iw*ix*::in;
```

Overriding Internal Precedence

In this example, the scope resolution operator (::) is used to avoid conflicts between a variable with both file and local scope. The last program reported an incorrect product since the local value was used in the calculation. Notice in the following listing that the iproduct( ) function uses the scope resolution operator.

```cpp
//
//   gscope.cpp
//   C++ program to illustrate problems with scope rules,
//   and how to use the scope resolution operator.
//   Function product uses resolution operator to "override"
//   local scope and utilize variable with file scope.
//   Copyright (c) Chris H. Pappas and William H. Murray, 1997
//

#include <iostream.h>

int iproduct(int iw,int ix);

int in=10;

int main( )
{
  int il=3;
  int im=7;
  int io;

  io=iproduct(il,im);
  cout << "The product of " << il <<" * " << im
       << " * " << in << " is: " << io;

  return (0);
}

int iproduct(int iw,int ix)
```

```
{
  int iy;
  int in=2;

  iy=iw*ix*(::in);
  return(iy);
}
```

The scope resolution operator need not be enclosed in parentheses—they were used for emphasis in this example. Now, the value of the global variable, with file scope, will be used in the calculation. When the results are printed to the screen, you will see that 3 * 7 * 10 = 210.

The scope resolution operator is very important in C++. Additional examples illustrating the resolution operator are given starting with Chapter 16.

PROGRAMMING FOUNDATIONS

The
Complete
Reference

Visual
C++ 5

Chapter 9

Arrays

In C and C++, the topics of arrays, pointers, and strings are all related. In this chapter you learn how to define and use arrays. Many C/C++ books combine the topics of arrays and pointers into one discussion. This is unfortunate because there are many uses for arrays in C and C++ that are not dependent on a detailed understanding of pointers. Also, since there is a great deal of material to cover about arrays in general, it is best not to confuse the topic with a discussion of pointers. Pointers, however, allow you to fully comprehend just how an array is processed. Chapter 10 examines the topic of pointers and completes this chapter's discussion of arrays.

What Are Arrays?

Think of *arrays* as variables containing several homogeneous data types. Each individual data item can be accessed by using a subscript, or index, in the variable. In the C and C++ language, an array is not a standard data type; instead, it is an aggregate type made up of any other types of data. It is possible to have an array of anything: characters, integers, floats, doubles, arrays, pointers, structures, and so on. The concept of arrays and their use is basically the same in both C and C++.

Array Properties

There are four basic properties to an array:

- The individual data items in the array are called *elements*.
- All elements must be of the same data type.
- All elements are stored contiguously in the computer's memory, and the subscript (or index) of the first element is zero.
- The name of the array is a constant value that represents the address of the first element in the array.

Since all elements of an array are assumed to be the same size, arrays cannot be defined by using mixed data types. Without this assumption, it would be very difficult to determine where any given element was stored. Since the elements are all the same size, which helps determine how to locate a given element, it follows that the elements are stored contiguously in the computer's memory (with the lowest address corresponding to the first element, the highest address to the last element). This means that there is no filler space between elements and that they are physically adjacent in the computer.

It is possible to have arrays within arrays—that is, multidimensional arrays. Actually, if an array element is a structure (which will be covered in Chapter 13), then mixed data types can exist in the array by existing inside the structure member.

The name of an array represents a constant value that cannot change during the execution of the program. For this reason, arrays can never be used as *lvalues*. *lvalues* represent storage locations that can have their contents altered by the program; they frequently appear to the left of assignment statements. If array names were legal *lvalues*, your program could change their contents. The effect would be to change the starting address of the array itself. This may seem like a small thing, but some forms of expressions that might appear valid on the surface are not allowed. All programmers eventually learn these subtleties, but it helps if you understand why these differences exist.

Array Declarations

The following are examples of array declarations:

```
int  iarray[12];  /* an array of twelve integers    */
char carray[20];  /* an array of twenty characters  */
```

As is true with all data declarations, an array's declaration begins with its data type, followed by a valid array name and a pair of matching square brackets enclosing a constant expression. The constant expression defines the size of the array. It is illegal to use a variable name inside the square brackets. For this reason it is not possible to avoid specifying the array size until the program executes. The expression must reduce to a constant value so that the compiler knows exactly how much storage space to reserve for the array.

It is best to use defined constants to specify the size of the array:

```
#define iARRAY_MAX 20
#define fARRAY_MAX 15

int iarray[iARRAY_MAX];
float farray[fARRAY_MAX];
```

Use of defined constants guarantees that subsequent references to the array will not exceed the defined array size. For example, it is very common to use a for loop to access array elements:

```
#include <stdio.h>

#define iARRAY_MAX 20
```

```
int iarray[iARRAY_MAX];

main( )
{
  int i;
  for(i = 0; i < iARRAY_MAX; i++) {
    .


    .


    .

  }
  return(0);
}
```

Initializing Arrays

There are three techniques for initializing arrays:

- By default when they are created. This applies only to global and static arrays.
- Explicitly when they are created, by supplying constant initializing data.
- During program execution when you assign or copy data into the array.

You can only use constant data to initialize an array when it is created. If the array elements must receive their values from variables, you must initialize the array by writing explicit statements as part of the program code.

Default Initialization

The ANSI C standard specifies that arrays are either global (defined outside of main( ) and any other function) or static automatic (static, but defined after any opening brace), and will always be initialized to binary zero if no other initialization data is supplied. C initializes numeric arrays to zero. Pointer arrays are initialized to null. You can run the following program to make certain that a compiler meets this standard:

```
/*
 *    initar.c
 *    A C program verifying array initialization
 *    Copyright (c) Chris H. Pappas and William H. Murray, 1997
 */

#include <stdio.h>
```

```
#define iGLOBAL_ARRAY_SIZE 10
#define iSTATIC_ARRAY_SIZE 20

int iglobal_array[iGLOBAL_ARRAY_SIZE];              /*a global array*/

main( )
{
  static int istatic_array[iSTATIC_ARRAY_SIZE]; /*a static array*/
  printf("iglobal_array[0]: %d\n",iglobal_array[0]);
  printf("istatic_array[0]: %d\n",istatic_array[0]);

  return(0);
}
```

When the program is run, you should see zeros printed verifying that both array types are automatically initialized. This program also highlights another very important point: that the first subscript for all arrays in C is zero. Unlike other languages, there is no way to make a C program think that the first subscript is 1. If you are wondering why, remember that one of C's strengths is its close link to assembly language. In assembly language, the first element in a table is always at the zeroth offset.

Explicit Initialization

Just as you can define and initialize variables of type int, char, float, double, and so on, you can also initialize arrays. The ANSI C standard lets you supply initialization values for any array, global or otherwise, defined anywhere in a program. The following code segment illustrates how to define and initialize four arrays:

```
int iarray[3] = {-1,0,1};
static float fpercent[4] = {1.141579,0.75,55E0,-.33E1};
static int idecimal[3] = {0,1,2,3,4,5,6,7,8,9};
char cvowels[] = {'A','a','E','e','I','i','O','o','U','u'};
```

The first line of code declares the *iarray* array to be three integers and provides the values of the elements in curly braces, separated by commas. As usual, a semicolon ends the statement. The effect of this is that after the compiled program loads into the memory of the computer, the reserved space for the *iarray* array will already contain the initial values, so they won't need assignments when the program executes. It is important to realize that this is more than just a convenience—it happens at a different time. If the program goes on to change the values of *iarray* array, they stay changed.

Many compilers permit you to initialize arrays only if they are global or static, as in the second line of code. This statement initializes the array *fpercent* when the entire program loads.

The third line of code illustrates putting the wrong count in the array declaration. Many compilers consider this an error, while others reserve enough space to hold whichever is greater—the number of values you ask for or the number of values you provide. This example will draw complaints from the Visual C/C++ compiler by way of an error message indicating too many initializers. In the opposite case, when you ask for more space than you provide values for, the values go into the beginning of the array and the extra elements become zeros. This also means that you do not need to count the values when you provide all of them. If the count is empty, as in the fourth line of code, the number of values determines the size of the array.

Unsized Initialization

You can provide the size of the array or the list of actual array values. It usually doesn't matter for most compilers, as long as you provide at least one of them. For example, a program will frequently want to define its own set of error messages. This can be done two ways. Here is the first method:

```
char szInput_Error[37] = "Please enter a value between 0 - 9:\n";
char szDevice_Error[16] = "Disk not ready\n";
char szMonitor_Error[32] = "Program needs a color monitor.\n";
char szWarning[44]="This operation will erase the active file!\n";
```

This method requires you to count the number of characters in the string, remembering to add 1 to the count for the unseen null-string terminator \0. This can become a very tedious approach at best, straining the eyes as you count the number of characters, and very error prone. The second method allows C to automatically dimension the arrays through the use of unsized arrays, as shown here:

```
char szInput_Error[] = "Please enter a value between 0 - 9:\n";
char szDevice_Error[] = "Disk not ready\n";
char szMonitor_Error[] = "Program needs a color monitor.\n";
char szWarning[] = "This operation will erase the active file!\n";
```

When an array initialization statement is encountered and the array size is not specified, the compiler automatically creates an array big enough to hold all of the specified data.

There are a few major pitfalls that await the inexperienced programmer when initializing arrays. For example, an array with an empty size declaration and no list of values has a null length. If there are any data declarations after the array, then the name of the null array refers to the same address, and storing values in the null array puts them in addresses allocated to other variables.

Unsized array initializations are not restricted to one-dimensional arrays. For multidimensional arrays, you must specify all but the leftmost dimension for C to properly index the array. With this approach you can build tables of varying lengths, with the compiler automatically allocating enough storage.

Accessing Array Elements

A variable declaration usually reserves one or more cells in internal memory and, through a lookup table, associates a name with the cell or cells that you can use to access the cells. For example, the following definition reserves only one integer-sized cell in internal memory and associates the name *ivideo_tapes* with that cell. See the top of Figure 9-1.

```
int ivideo_tapes;
```

On the other hand, the next definition reserves seven contiguous cells in internal memory and associates the name *ivideo_library* with the seven cells. See the bottom of Figure 9-1.

```
int ivideo_library[7];
```

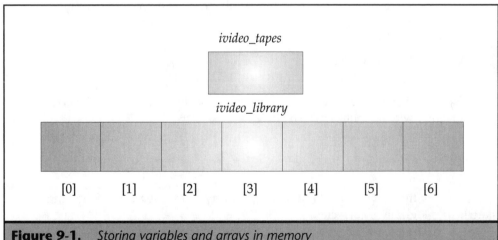

Figure 9-1. *Storing variables and arrays in memory*

PROGRAMMING FOUNDATIONS

Since all array elements must be of the same data type, each of the seven cells in the array *ivideo_library* can hold one integer.

Consider the difference between accessing the single cell associated with the variable *ivideo_tapes* and the seven cells associated with the array *ivideo_library*. To access the cell associated with the variable *ivideo_tapes*, you simply use the name *ivideo_tapes*. For the array *ivideo_library*, you must specify an *index* to indicate exactly which cell among the seven you wish to access. The following statements designate the first cell, the second cell, the third cell, and so on, up to the last cell of the array:

```
ivideo_library[0];
ivideo_library[1];
ivideo_library[2];
ivideo_library[3];
               .

               .

               .

ivideo_library[6];
```

When accessing an array element, the integer enclosed in the square brackets is the index, which indicates the *offset*, or the distance between the cell to be accessed and the first cell.

One of the principal mistakes novice programmers make has to do with the index value used to reference an array's first element. The first element is not at index position [1]; instead, it is [0] since there is zero distance between the first element and itself. The third cell has an index value of 2 because its distance from the first cell is 2.

When working with arrays, you can use the square brackets in two quite different ways. When you are defining an array, the number of cells is specified in square brackets:

```
int ivideo_library[7];
```

However, when you are accessing a specific array element, you use the array's name together with an index enclosed in square brackets:

```
ivideo_library[3];
```

Assuming the previous declaration for the array *ivideo_library*, the following statement is logically incorrect:

```
ivideo_library[7] = 53219;
```

It is not a legal reference to a cell under the name *ivideo_library*. The statement attempts to reference a cell that is a distance of 7 from the first cell, that is, the eighth cell. Because there are only seven cells, this is an error. It is up to you to ensure that index expressions remain within the array's bounds.

Examine the following declarations:

```
#define iDAYS_OF_WEEK 7

int ivideo_library[iDAYS_OF_WEEK];
int iweekend = 1;
int iweekday = 2;
```

Take a look at what happens with this set of executable statements:

```
ivideo_library[2];
ivideo_library[iweekday];
ivideo_library[iweekend + iweekday];
ivideo_library[iweekday - iweekend];
ivideo_library[iweekend - iweekday];
```

The first two statements both reference the third element of the array. The first statement accomplishes this with a constant value expression, while the second statement uses a variable. The last three statements demonstrate that you can use expressions as subscripts, as long as they evaluate to a valid integer index. Statement three has an index value of 3 and references the fourth element of the array. The fourth statement, with an index value of 1, accesses the second element of the array. The last statement is illegal because the index value -1 is invalid.

It is also possible to access any element in an array without knowing how big each element is. For example, suppose you want to access the third element in *ivideo_library*, an array of integers. Remember from Chapter 6 that different systems allocate different size cells to the same data type. On one computer system, an integer might occupy 2 bytes of storage, whereas on another system, an integer might occupy 8 bytes of storage. On either system, you can access the third element as *ivideo_library[2]*. The index value indicates the number of elements to move, regardless of the number of bits allocated.

This offset addressing holds true for other array types. On one system, integer variables might require twice as many bits of storage as does a char type; on another system, integer variables might require four times as many bits as do character variables. Yet to access the fourth element in either an array of integers or an array of characters, you would use an index value of 3.

Calculating Array Dimensions

You have already learned that the sizeof( ) operator returns the physical size, in bytes, of the data object to which it is applied. You can use it with any type of data object except bit-fields. A frequent use of sizeof( ) is to determine the physical size of a variable when the size of the variable's data type can vary from machine to machine. You have already seen how an integer can be either 2 or 4 bytes, depending on the machine being used. If an additional amount of memory to hold seven integers will be requested from the operating system, some way is needed to determine whether 14 bytes (7x2 bytes/integer) or 28 bytes (7x4 bytes/integer) are needed. The following program automatically takes this into consideration (and prints a value of 28 for systems allocating 4 bytes per integer cell):

```
/*
 *   sizeof.c
 *   A C program applying sizeof( ) to determine an array's size
 *   Copyright (c) Chris H. Pappas and William H. Murray, 1997
 */

#include <stdio.h>

#define iDAYS_OF_WEEK 7

main( )
{
  int ivideo_library[iDAYS_OF_WEEK]={1,2,3,4,5,6,7};

  printf("There are %d number of bytes in the array"
    " ivideo_library.\n",(int)sizeof(ivideo_library));

  return(0);
}
```

This concept becomes essential when the program must be portable and independent of any particular hardware. If you are wondering why there is an int type cast on the result returned by sizeof( ), in the ANSI C standard, sizeof( ) does not return an int type. Instead, sizeof( ) returns a data type, size_t, that is large enough to hold the return value. The ANSI C standard added this to C because on certain computers an integer is not big enough to represent the size of all data items. In the example, casting the return value to an integer allows it to match the %d conversion character of the printf( ) function. Otherwise, if the returned value had been larger than an integer, the printf( ) function would not have worked properly.

By changing *iarray*'s data type in the following program, you can explore how
various data types are stored internally:

```
/*
 *   array.c
 *   A C program illustrating contiguous array storage
 *   Copyright (c) Chris H. Pappas and William H. Murray, 1997
 */

#include <stdio.h>

#define iDAYS 7

main( )
{
  int index, iarray[iDAYS];

  printf("sizeof(int) is %d\n\n", (int)sizeof(int));

  for(index = 0; index < iDAYS; index++)
    printf("&iarray[%d] = %X\n", index,
           &iarray[index]);

  return(0);
}
```

If the program is run on a machine with a word length of 2 bytes, the output will
look similar to the following:

```
sizeof(int) is 4

&iarray[0] = 64FDDC
&iarray[1] = 64FDE0
&iarray[2] = 64FDE4
&iarray[3] = 64FDE8
&iarray[4] = 64FDEC
&iarray[5] = 64FDF0
&iarray[6] = 64FDF4
```

Notice how the & (address) operator can be applied to any variable, including an
array element. An array element can be treated like any other variable; its value can

form an expression, it can be assigned a value, and it can be passed as an argument (or parameter) to a function. In this example you can see how the array elements' addresses are exactly 2 bytes apart. You will see the importance of this contiguous storage when you use arrays in conjunction with pointer variables.

The following C++ listing is similar in structure to the program just discussed:

```
//
//  array.cpp
//  A C++ program illustrating contiguous array storage
//  Copyright (c) Chris H. Pappas and William H. Murray, 1997
//

#include <iostream.h>

#define iMAX 10

main( )
{
  int index, iarray[iMAX];

  cout << "sizeof(int) is " << (int)sizeof(int) << "\n\n";

  for(index = 0; index < iMAX; index++)
    cout << "&iarray[" << index << "] = " << index
         << &iarray[index] << endl;

  return(0);
}
```

Array Index Out of Bounds

There is a popular saying that states, "You don't get something for nothing." This holds true with array types. The "something" you get is faster executing code at the expense of the "nothing," which is zero boundary checking. Remember, since C and C++ were designed to replace assembly language code, error checking was left out of the compiler to keep the code lean. Without any compiler error checking, you must be very careful when dealing with array boundaries. For example, the following program elicits no complaints from the compiler, yet it can change the contents of other variables or even crash the program by writing beyond the array's boundary:

```
/*
 *    norun.c
 *    Do NOT run this C program
 *    Copyright (c) Chris H. Pappas and William H. Murray, 1997
 */


#include <stdio.h>

#define iMAX 10
#define iOUT_OF_RANGE 50

main( )
{
  int inot_enough_room[iMAX], index;

  for(index=0; index < iOUT_OF_RANGE; index++)
    inot_enough_room[index]=index;

  return(0);
}
```

Output and Input of Strings

While C and C++ do supply the data type char, they do not have a data type for character strings. Instead, the programmer must represent a string as an array of characters. The array uses one cell for each character in the string, with the final cell holding the null character \0.

The next example shows how you can represent the three major types of transportation as a character string. The array *szmode1* is initialized character by character using the assignment operator, the array *szmode2* is initialized using the function scanf( ), and the array *szmode3* is initialized in the following definition.

```
/*
 *    string.c
 *    This C program demonstrates the use of strings
 *    Copyright (c) Chris H. Pappas and William H. Murray, 1997
 */
```

PROGRAMMING
FOUNDATIONS

```
#include <stdio.h>

main( )
{
    char            szmode1[4],          /* car    */
                    szmode2[6];          /* plane */
    static char szmode3[5] = "ship";     /* ship   */

    szmode1[0] = 'c';
    szmode1[1] = 'a';
    szmode1[2] = 'r';
    szmode1[3] = '\0';

    printf("\n\n\tPlease enter the mode --> plane ");
    scanf("%s",szmode2);

    printf("%s\n",szmode1);
    printf("%s\n",szmode2);
    printf("%s\n",szmode3);

    return(0);
}
```

The next definitions show how C treats character strings as arrays of characters:

```
char    szmode1[4],              /* car    */
        szmode2[6];              /* plane */
static char szmode3[5] = "ship"; /* ship   */
```

Even though the *szmode1* "car" has three characters, the array *szmode1* has four cells—one cell for each letter in the mode "car" and one for the null character. Remember, \0 counts as one character. Similarly, the mode "plane" has five characters ("ship" has four) but requires six storage cells (five for *szmode3*), including the null character. Remember, you could also have initialized the *szmode3[5]* array of characters by using braces:

```
static char szmode3[5] = {'s','h','i','p','\0'};
```

When you use double quotes to list the initial values of the character array, the system will automatically add the null terminator \0. Also, remember that the same line could have been written like this:

```
static char szmode3[] = "ship";
```

This uses an unsized array. Of course, you could have chosen the tedious approach to initializing an array of characters that was done with *szmode1.* A more common approach is to use the scanf( ) function to read the string directly into the array as was done with *szmode2.* The scanf( ) function uses a %s conversion specification. This causes the function to skip white space (blanks, tabs, and carriage returns) and then to read into the character array *szmode2* all characters up to the next white space. The system will then automatically add a null terminator. Remember, the array's dimension must be large enough to hold the string along with a null terminator. Look at this statement one more time:

```
scanf("%s",szmode2);
```

Are you bothered by the fact that *szmode2* was not preceded by the address operator &? While it is true that scanf( ) was written to expect the address of a variable, as it turns out, an array's name, unlike simple variable names, is an address expression—the address of the first element in the array.

When you use the printf( ) function in conjunction with a %s, the function is expecting the corresponding argument to be the address of some character string. The string is printed up to but not including the null character.

The following listing illustrates these principles by using an equivalent C++ algorithm:

```
//
//  string.cpp
//  This C++ program demonstrates the use of strings
//  Copyright (c) Chris H. Pappas and William H. Murray, 1997
//

#include <iostream.h>

main( )
{
```

```
char        szmode1[4],                 // car
            szmode2[6];                 // plane
static char szmode3[5] = "ship";        // ship

szmode1[0] = 'c';
szmode1[1] = 'a';
szmode1[2] = 'r';
szmode1[3] = '\0';

cout << "\n\n\tPlease enter the mode --> plane ";
cin >> szmode2;

cout << szmode1 << "\n";
cout << szmode2 << "\n";
cout << szmode3 << "\n";

return(0);
}
```

The output from the program looks like this:

```
car
plane
ship
```

Multidimensional Arrays

The term *dimension* represents the number of indexes used to reference a particular element in an array. All of the arrays discussed so far have been one-dimensional and require only one index to access an element. By looking at an array's declaration, you can tell how many dimensions it has. If there is only one set of brackets ([ ]), the array is one-dimensional; two sets of brackets ([ ][ ]) indicate a two-dimensional array; and so on. Arrays of more than one dimension are called *multidimensional arrays*. For real-world modeling, the working maximum number of dimensions is usually three.

The following declarations set up a two-dimensional array that is initialized while the program executes:

```
/*
 *   2daray.c
 *   A C program demonstrating the use of a two-dimensional array
```

```
*    Copyright (c) Chris H. Pappas and William H. Murray, 1997
*/

#include <stdio.h>

#define iROWS 4
#define iCOLUMNS 5

main( )
{
  int irow;
  int icolumn;
  int istatus[iROWS][iCOLUMNS];
  int iadd;
  int imultiple;

  for(irow=0; irow < iROWS; irow++)
    for(icolumn=0; icolumn < iCOLUMNS; icolumn++) {
      iadd = iCOLUMNS - icolumn;
      imultiple = irow;
      istatus[irow][icolumn] = (irow+1) *
        icolumn + iadd * imultiple;
    }

  for(irow=0; irow<iROWS; irow++) {
    printf("CURRENT ROW: %d\n",irow);
    printf("RELATIVE DISTANCE FROM BASE:\n");
    for(icolumn=0; icolumn<iCOLUMNS; icolumn++)
      printf(" %d ",istatus[irow][icolumn]);
    printf("\n\n");
  }

  return(0);
}
```

The program uses two for loops to calculate and initialize each of the array
elements to its respective "offset from the first element." The created array has four
rows (*iROWS*) and five columns (*iCOLUMNS*) per row, for a total of 20 integer
elements. Multidimensional arrays are stored in linear fashion in the computer's
memory. Elements in multidimensional arrays are grouped from the rightmost index
inward. In the preceding example, row 1, column 1 would be element three of the

storage array. Although the calculation of the offset appears a little tricky, note how easily each array element itself is referenced:

```
istatus[irow][icolumn] = . . .
```

The output from the program looks like this:

```
CURRENT ROW: 0
RELATIVE DISTANCE FROM BASE:
 0  1  2  3  4

CURRENT ROW: 1
RELATIVE DISTANCE FROM BASE:
 5  6  7  8  9

CURRENT ROW: 2
RELATIVE DISTANCE FROM BASE:
 10  11  12  13  14

CURRENT ROW: 3
RELATIVE DISTANCE FROM BASE:
 15  16  17  18  19
```

Multidimensional arrays can also be initialized in the same way as one-dimensional arrays. For example, the following program defines a two-dimensional array *dpowers* and initializes the array when it is defined. The function pow( ) returns the value of *x* raised to the *y* power:

```
/*
 *    2dadbl.c
 *    A C program using a 2-dimensional array of doubles
 *    Copyright (c) Chris H. Pappas and William H. Murray, 1997
 */

#include <stdio.h>
#include <math.h>

#define iBASES 6
#define iEXPONENTS 3
#define iBASE 0
#define iRAISED_TO 1
```

```
#define iRESULT 2

main( )
{
  double dpowers[iBASES][iEXPONENTS]={
    1.1, 1, 0,
    2.2, 2, 0,
    3.3, 3, 0,
    4.4, 4, 0,
    5.5, 5, 0,
    6.6, 6, 0
  };

  int irow_index;

  for(irow_index=0; irow_index < iBASES; irow_index++)
    dpowers[irow_index][iRESULT] =
      pow(dpowers[irow_index][iBASE],
      dpowers[irow_index][iRAISED_TO]);

  for(irow_index=0; irow_index < iBASES; irow_index++) {
    printf("    %d\n",(int)dpowers[irow_index][iRAISED_TO]);
    printf(" %2.1f = %.2f\n\n",dpowers[irow_index][iBASE],
                               dpowers[irow_index][iRESULT]);
  }

  return(0);
}
```

The array *dpowers* was declared to be of type double because the function pow( )
expects two double variables and returns a double. Of course, you must take care
when initializing two-dimensional arrays; you must make certain you know which
dimension is increasing the fastest. Remember, this is always the rightmost dimension.

The output from the program looks like this:

```
1
1.1 = 1.10

   2
2.2 = 4.84
```

PROGRAMMING
FOUNDATIONS

```
    3
3.3 = 35.94

    4
4.4 = 374.81

    5
5.5 = 5032.84

    6
6.6 = 82653.95
```

Arrays as Function Arguments

Just like other variables, arrays can be passed from one function to another. Because arrays as function arguments can be discussed in full only after an introduction to pointers, this chapter begins the topic and Chapter 10 expands upon this base.

Passing Arrays to C Functions

Consider a function isum( ) that computes the sum of the array elements *inumeric_values[0], inumeric_values[1],..., numeric_values[n]*. Two parameters are required—an array parameter called *iarray_address_received* to hold a copy of the array's address and a parameter called *imax_size* to hold the index of the last item in the array to be summed. Assuming that the array is an array of integers and that the index is also of type int, the parameters in isum( ) can be described as

```
int isum(int iarray_address_received[], int imax_size)
```

The parameter declaration for the array includes square brackets to signal the function isum( ) that *iarray_address_received* is an array name and not the name of an ordinary parameter. Note that the number of cells is not enclosed in the square brackets. Of course, the simple parameter *imax_size* is declared as previously described. Invoking the function is as simple as this:

```
isum(inumeric_values,iactual_index);
```

Passing the array *inumeric_values* is a simple process of entering its name as the argument. When passing an array's name to a function, you are actually passing the *address* of the array's first element. Look at the following expression:

```
inumeric_values
is really shorthand for
&inumeric_values[0]
```

Technically, you can invoke the function isum( ) with either of the following two valid statements:

```
isum(inumeric_values,iactual_index);
itotal = isum(&inumeric_values[0],iactual_index);
```

In either case, within the function isum( ) you can access every cell in the array.

When a function is going to process an array, the calling function includes the name of the array in the function's argument list. This means that the function receives and carries out its processing on the actual elements of the array, not on a local copy as in single-value variables where functions pass only their values.

By default, all arrays are passed call-by-variable or call-by-reference. This prevents the frequent "stack overruns heap" error message many Pascal programmers encounter if they have forgotten to include the var modifier for formal array argument declarations. In contrast, the Pascal language passes all array arguments call-by-value. A call-by-value forces the compiler to duplicate the array's contents. For large arrays, this is time consuming and wastes memory.

When a function is to receive an array name as an argument, there are two ways to declare the argument locally: as an array or as a pointer. Which one you use depends on how the function processes the set of values. If the function steps through the elements with an index, the declaration should be an array with square brackets following the name. The size can be empty since the declaration does not reserve space for the entire array, just for the address where it begins. Having seen the array declaration at the beginning of the function, the compiler then permits brackets with an index to appear after the array name anywhere in the function.

The following example declares an array of five elements, and after printing its values, calls in a function to determine what the smallest value in the array is. To do this, it passes the array name and its size to the function iminimum( ), which declares them as an array called *iarray[]* and an integer called *isize*. The function then passes through the array, comparing each element against the smallest value it has seen so far, and every time it encounters a smaller value, it stores that new value in the variable *icurrent_minimum*. At the end, it returns the smallest value it has seen for the main( ) to print.

```c
/*
 *    pasary.c
 *    A C program using arrays as parameters
 *    Copyright (c) Chris H. Pappas and William H. Murray, 1997
 */

#include <stdio.h>

#define iMAX 10
#define iUPPER_LIMIT 100

main( )
{
  int iarray[iMAX] = {3,7,2,1,5,6,8,9,0,4};
  int i, ismallest;
  int iminimum(int iarray[],int imax);

  printf("The original list looks like: ");
  for(i = 0; i < iMAX; i++)
    printf("%d ",iarray[i]);
  ismallest = iminimum(iarray,iMAX);
  printf("\nThe smallest value is: %d: \n",ismallest);

  return(0);
}

int iminimum(int iarray[], int imax)
{
  int i, icurrent_minimum;

  icurrent_minimum = iUPPER_LIMIT;
  for(i = 0; i < imax; i++)
    if (iarray[i] < icurrent_minimum)
      icurrent_minimum = iarray[i];
  return(icurrent_minimum);
}
```

Passing Arrays to C++ Functions

The following C++ program format is very similar to the C programs examined so far.
The program demonstrates how to declare and pass an array argument.

```
//
//   fncary.cpp
//   A C++ program demonstrating how to use arrays with
//   functions
//   Copyright (c) Chris H. Pappas and William H. Murray, 1997
//

#include <iostream.h>

#define iSIZE 5
void vadd_1(int iarray[]);

main( )
{
  int iarray[iSIZE]={0,1,2,3,4};
  int i;

  cout << "iarray before calling add_1:\n\n";
  for(i=0; i < iSIZE; i++)
    cout << "  " << iarray[i];

  vadd_1(iarray);

  cout << "\n\niarray after calling add_1:\n\n";
  for(i=0; i < iSIZE; i++)
    cout << "  " << iarray[i];

  return(0);
}

void vadd_1(int iarray[])
{
  int i;

  for(i=0; i < iSIZE; i++)
    iarray[i]++;
}
```

The output from the program looks like this:

```
iarray before calling add_1:

  0  1  2  3  4

iarray after calling add_1:

  1  2  3  4  5
```

Here is a question you should be able to answer. What do the values in the
output tell you about the array argument? Is the array passed call-by-value or
call-by-reference? The function vadd_1( ) simply adds 1 to each array element. Since
this incremented change is reflected back in main( ) *iarray,* it would appear that the
parameter was passed call-by-reference. Previous discussions about what an array
name really is indicate that this is true. Remember, array names are addresses to the
first array cell.

The following C++ program incorporates many of the array features discussed so
far, including multidimensional array initialization, referencing, and arguments:

```
//
//   2daray.cpp
//   A C++ program that demonstrates how to define, pass,
//   and walk through the different dimensions of an array
//   Copyright (c) Chris H. Pappas and William H. Murray, 1997
//

#include <iostream.h>

void vdisplay_results(char carray[][3][4]);

char cglobal_cube[5][4][5]= {
                {
                  {'P','L','A','N','E'},
                  {'Z','E','R','O',' '},
                  {' ',' ',' ',' ',' '},
                  {'R','O','W',' ','3'},
                },
                {
                  {'P','L','A','N','E'},
                  {'O','N','E',' ',' '},
                  {'R','O','W',' ','2'}
                },
```

```
              {
                {'P','L','A','N','E'},
                {'T','W','O',' ',' '}
              },
              {
                {'P','L','A','N','E'},
                {'T','H','R','E','E'},
                {'R','O','W',' ','2'},
                {'R','O','W',' ','3'}
              },
              {
                {'P','L','A','N','E'},
                {'F','O','U','R',' '},
                {'r','o','w',' ','2'},
                {'a','b','c','d','e'}
              }
};

int imatrix[4][3]={ {1},{2},{3},{4} };

main( )
{
  int irow_index, icolumn_index;
  char clocal_cube[2][3][4];

  cout << "sizeof clocal_cube          = "<< sizeof(clocal_cube)
                                      << "\n";
  cout << "sizeof clocal_cube[0]       = "<< sizeof(clocal_cube[0])
                                      << "\n";
  cout << "sizeof clocal_cube[0][0]    = "<<
          sizeof(clocal_cube[0][0])       << "\n";
  cout << "sizeof clocal_cube[0][0][0]= "<<
          sizeof(clocal_cube[0][0][0])  << "\n";

  vdisplay_results(clocal_cube);

  cout << "cglobal_cube[0][1][2] is     = "
       << cglobal_cube[0][1][2] << "\n";
  cout << "cglobal_cube[1][0][2] is     = "
       << cglobal_cube[1][0][2] << "\n";

  cout << "\nprint part of the cglobal_cube's plane 0\n";
```

```
    for(irow_index=0; irow_index < 4; irow_index++) {
      for(icolumn_index=0; icolumn_index < 5; icolumn_index++)
        cout << cglobal_cube[0][irow_index][icolumn_index];
      cout << "\n";
    }

    cout << "\nprint part of the cglobal_cube's plane 4\n";
    for(irow_index=0; irow_index < 4; irow_index++) {
      for(icolumn_index=0; icolumn_index < 5; icolumn_index++)
        cout << cglobal_cube[4][irow_index][icolumn_index];
      cout << "\n";
    }

    cout << "\nprint all of imatrix\n";
    for(irow_index=0; irow_index < 4; irow_index++) {
      for(icolumn_index=0; icolumn_index < 3; icolumn_index++)
        cout << imatrix[irow_index][icolumn_index];
      cout << "\n";
    }

    return (0);
}

void vdisplay_results(char carray[][3][4])
{
cout << " sizeof carray         =" << sizeof(carray) << "\n";
cout << " sizeof carray[0]      =" << sizeof(carray[0]) << "\n";
cout << " sizeof cglobal_cube   =" << sizeof(cglobal_cube) << "\n";
cout << " sizeof cglobal_cube[0]=" << sizeof(cglobal_cube[0])
                                     << "\n";
}
```

Notice first how *cglobal_cube* is defined and initialized. Braces are used to group the characters together so that they have a form similar to the dimensions of the array. This helps in visualizing the form of the array. The braces are not required in this case since you are not leaving any gaps in the array with the initializing data. If you were initializing only a portion of any dimension, various sets of the inner braces would be required to designate which initializing values should apply to which part of the array. The easiest way to visualize the three-dimensional array is to imagine five layers, each having a two-dimensional, four-row by five-column array (see Figure 9-2).

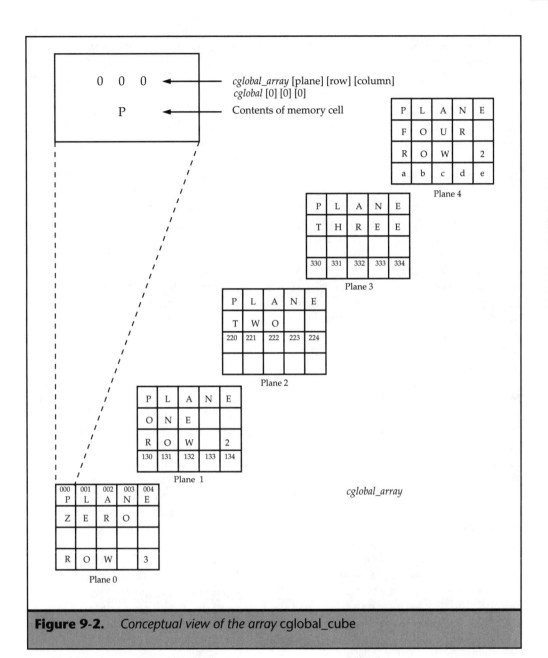

Figure 9-2. *Conceptual view of the array* cglobal_cube

The first four lines of the program output show the size of the *clocal_cube* array, various dimensions, and an individual element. The output illustrates how the total size of the multidimensional array is the product of all the dimensions times the size of the array data type, that is, 2 * 3 * 4 * *sizeof(char)*, or 24.

Observe how the array element *clocal_cube[0]* is in itself an array that contains a two-dimensional array of [3][4], thereby giving *clocal_cube[0]* the size of 12. The size of *clocal_cube[0][0]* is 4, which is the number of elements in the final dimension since each element has a size of 1, as the *sizeof(clocal_cube[0][0][0])* shows.

To fully understand multidimensional arrays, it is very important to realize that *clocal_cube[0]* is both an array name and a pointer constant. Because the program did not subscript the last dimension, the expression does not have the same type as the data type of each fundamental array element. Because *clocal_cube[0]* does not refer to an individual element, but rather to another array, it does not have the type of char. Since *clocal_cube[0]* has the type of pointer constant, it is not a legal *lvalue* and cannot appear to the left of an assignment operator in an assignment expression.

Something very interesting happens when you use an array name in a function argument list, as was done when the function vdisplay_results( ) was invoked with *clocal_cube*. While inside the function, if you perform a sizeof( ) operation against the formal parameter that represents the array name, you do not correctly compute the actual size of *carray*. What the function sees is only a copy of the address of the first element in the array. Therefore, the function sizeof( ) will return the size of the address, not the item to which it refers.

The sizeof( ) *carray[0]* in function vdisplay_results( ) is 12 because it was declared in the function that the formal parameter was an array whose last two dimensions were [3] and [4]. You could not have used any values when you declared the size of these last two dimensions because the function prototype defined them to be [3] and [4]. Without a prototype, the compiler would not be able to detect the difference in the way the array was dimensioned. This would let you redefine the way in which you viewed the array's organization. The function vdisplay_results( ) also outputs the size of the global *cglobal_cube*. This points out that while a function may have access to global data directly, it has access only to the address of an array that is passed to a function as an argument.

With regard to the main( ) function, the next two statements demonstrate how to reference specific elements in *cglobal_cube* when they are executed. *cglobal_cube[0][1][2]* references the zeroth layer, second row, third column, or "R." *cglobal_cube[1][0][2]* references the second layer, row zero, third column, or "A."

The next block of code in main( ) contains two nested for loops demonstrating that the arrays are stored in plane-row-column order. As already seen, the rightmost subscript (column) of the array varies the fastest when you view the array in a linear fashion. The first for loop pair hardwires the output to the zeroth layer and selects a row, with the inner loop traversing each column in *cglobal_cube*. The program continues by duplicating the same loop structures but printing only the fifth layer (plane [4]), of the *cglobal_cube*.

The last for loop pair displays the elements of *imatrix* in the form of a rectangle, similar to the way many people visualize a two-dimensional array.

The output from the program looks like this:

```
sizeof clocal_cube          = 24
sizeof clocal_cube[0]       = 12
sizeof clocal_cube[0][0]    = 4
sizeof clocal_cube[0][0][0] = 1
sizeof carray               = 4
sizeof carray[0]            = 12
sizeof cglobal_cube         = 100
sizeof cglobal_cube[0]      = 20
cglobal_cube[0][1][2] is    = R
cglobal_cube[1][0][2] is    = A

print part of the cglobal_cube's plane 0
PLANE
ZERO

ROW 3

print part of the cglobal_cube's plane 4
PLANE
FOUR
row 2
abcde

print all of imatrix
100
200
300
400
```

Does the output catch your attention? Look at the initialization of *imatrix*. Because each inner set of braces corresponds to one row of the array and enough values were not supplied inside the inner braces, the system padded the remaining elements with zeros. Remember, C and C++ automatically initialize all undefined static automatic numeric array elements to zero.

String Functions and Character Arrays

Because of the way string data types are handled, many of the functions that use character arrays as function arguments were not discussed. Specifically, these functions are gets( ), puts( ), fgets( ), fputs( ), sprintf( ), strcpy( ), strcat( ), strncmp( ), and strlen( ). Understanding how these functions operate will be much easier now that you are familiar with the concepts of character arrays and null-terminated strings. One of the easiest ways to explain these functions is to show a few program examples.

gets( ), puts( ), fgets( ), fputs( ), and sprintf( )

The following example program demonstrates how you can use gets( ), puts( ), fgets( ), fputs( ), and sprintf( ) to format I/O:

```c
/*
 *   strio.c
 *   A C program using several string I/O functions
 *   Copyright (c) Chris H. Pappas and William H. Murray, 1997
 */

#include <stdio.h>

#define iSIZE 20

main( )
{
  char sztest_array[iSIZE];

  fputs("Please enter the first string  : ",stdout);
  gets(sztest_array);
  fputs("The first string entered is    : ",stdout);
  puts(sztest_array);

  fputs("Please enter the second string : ",stdout);
  fgets(sztest_array,iSIZE,stdin);
  fputs("The second string entered is   : ",stdout);
  fputs(sztest_array,stdout);

  sprintf(sztest_array,"This was %s a test","just");
  fputs("sprintf( ) created             : ",stdout);
  fputs(sztest_array,stdout);

  return(0);
}
```

Here is the output from the first run of the program:

```
Please enter the first string  : string one
The first string entered is    : string one
Please enter the second string : string two
The second string entered is   : string two
sprintf( ) created             : This was just a test
```

Since the strings that were entered were less than the size of *sztest_array,* the program works fine. However, when you enter a string longer than *sztest_array,* something similar to the following can occur when the program is run:

```
Please enter the first string  : one two three four five
The first string entered is    : one two three four five
Please enter the second string : six seven eight nine ten
The second string entered is   : six seven eight ninsprintf( ) created
  : This was just a testPlease enter the first string  : The
first string entered is    :e ten
The second string entered is   :
```

Take care when running the program. The gets( ) function receives characters from standard input (stdin, the keyboard by default for most computers) and places them into the array whose name is passed to the function. When you press the ENTER key to terminate the string, a newline character is transmitted. When the gets( ) function receives this newline character, it changes it into a null character, thereby ensuring that the character array contains a string. No checking occurs to ensure that the array is big enough to hold all the characters entered.

The puts( ) function echoes to the terminal just what was entered with gets( ). It also adds a newline character on the end of the string in the place where the null character appeared. The null character, remember, was automatically inserted into the string by the gets( ) function. Therefore, strings that are properly entered with gets( ) can be displayed with puts( ).

When you use the fgets( ) function, you can guarantee a maximum number of input characters. This function stops reading the designated file stream when *one fewer* character is read than the second argument specifies. Since *sztest_array size* is 20, only 19 characters will be read by fgets( ) from stdin. A null character is automatically placed into the string in the last position, and if a newline were entered from the keyboard, it would be retained in the string. (It would appear before the null debug example.) The fgets( ) function does not eliminate the newline character like gets( ) did; it merely adds the null character at the end so that a valid string is stored. In much the same way as gets( ) and puts( ) are symmetrical, so too are fgets( ) and fputs( ). fgets( ) does not eliminate the newline, nor does fputs( ) add one.

To understand how important the newline character is to these functions, look closely at the second run output given. Notice the phrase "sprintf( ) created..."; it follows immediately after the numbers six, seven, eight, and nine that had just been entered. The second input string actually had five more characters than the fgets( ) function read in (one fewer than *iSIZE* of 19 characters). The others were left in the input buffer. Also dropped was the newline that terminated the input from the keyboard. (It is left in the input stream because it occurs after the 19th character.) Therefore, no newline character was stored in the string. Since fputs( ) does not add 1 back, the next fputs( ) output begins on the line where the previous output ended. Reliance was on the newline character read by fgets( ) and printed by fputs( ) to help control the display formatting.

The function sprintf( ) stands for "string printf( )." It uses a control string with conversion characters in exactly the same way that printf( ) does. The additional feature is that sprintf( ) places the resulting formatted data in a string rather than immediately sending the result to standard output. This can be beneficial if the exact same output must be created twice—for example, when the same string must be output to both the display monitor and the printer.

To review:

- gets( ) converts newline to a null.

- puts( ) converts null to a newline.

- fgets( ) retains newline and appends a null.

- fputs( ) drops the null and does not add a newline; instead, it uses the retained newline (if one was entered).

strcpy( ), strcat( ), strncmp( ), and strlen( )

All of the functions discussed in this section are predefined in the STRING.H header file. When using these functions, make certain to include the header file in your program. Remember, all of the string functions prototyped in STRING.H expect null-terminated string parameters. The following program demonstrates how to use the strcpy( ) function:

```
/*
 *    strcpy.c
 *    A C program using the strcpy function
 *    Copyright (c) Chris H. Pappas and William H. Murray, 1997
```

```
*/

#include <stdio.h>
#include <string.h>

#define iSIZE 20

main( )
{
  char szsource_string[iSIZE]="Initialized String!",
       szdestination_string[iSIZE];

  strcpy(szdestination_string,"String Constant");
  printf("%s\n",szdestination_string);

  strcpy(szdestination_string,szsource_string);
  printf("%s\n",szdestination_string);

  return(0);
}
```

The function strcpy( ) copies the contents of one string, *szsource_string*, into a second string, *szdestination_string*. The preceding program initializes *szsource_string* with the message, "Initialized String!". The first strcpy( ) function call actually copies "String Constant" into the *szdestination_string*, while the second call to the strcpy( ) function copies *szsource_string* into the *szdestination_string* variable. The program outputs this message:

```
String Constant
Initialized String!
```

The following example is an equivalent C++ program.

```
//
//   strcpy.cpp
//   A C++ program using the strcpy function
//   Copyright (c) Chris H. Pappas and William H. Murray, 1997
//

#include <iostream.h>
```

```
#include <string.h>

#define iSIZE 20

main( )
{
  char szsource_string[iSIZE]="Initialized String!",
       szdestination_string[iSIZE];

  strcpy(szdestination_string,"String Constant");
  cout << "\n" << szdestination_string;

  strcpy(szdestination_string,szsource_string);
  cout << "\n" << szdestination_string;

  return(0);
}
```

The strcat( ) function appends two separate strings. Both strings must be null
terminated and the result itself is null terminated. The following program builds on
your understanding of the strcpy( ) function and introduces strcat( ):

```
/*
 *    strcat.c
 *    A C program demonstrating how to use the strcat function
 *    Copyright (c) Chris H. Pappas and William H. Murray, 1997
 */

#include <stdio.h>
#include <string.h>

#define iSTRING_SIZE 35

main( )
{
  char szgreeting[] = "Good morning",
       szname[] =" Carolyn, ",
       szmessage[iSTRING_SIZE];

  strcpy(szmessage,szgreeting);
  strcat(szmessage,szname);
```

```
strcat(szmessage,"how are you?");
printf("%s\n",szmessage);

return(0);
}
```

In this example, both *szgreeting* and *szname* are initialized, while *szmessage* is not. The first thing the program does is to use the function strcpy( ) to copy the *szgreeting* into *szmessage*. Next, the strcat( ) function is used to concatenate *szname* (" Carolyn, ") to "Good morning", which is stored in *szmessage*. The last strcat( ) function call demonstrates how a string constant can be concatenated to a string. Here, "how are you?" is concatenated to the now current contents of *szmessage* ("Good morning Carolyn, "). The program outputs the following:

```
Good morning Carolyn, how are you?
```

The next program demonstrates how to use strncmp( ) to decide if two strings are identical:

```
/*
 *    strncmp.c
 *    A C program that uses strncmp to compare two strings with
 *    the aid of the strlen function
 *    Copyright (c) Chris H. Pappas and William H. Murray, 1997
 */

#include <stdio.h>
#include <string.h>

main( )
{
  char szstringA[]="Adam", szstringB[]="Abel";
  int istringA_length,iresult=0;

  istringA_length=strlen(szstringA);
  if (strlen(szstringB) >= strlen(szstringA))
    iresult = strncmp(szstringA,szstringB,istringA_length);
  printf("The string %s found", iresult == 0 ? "was" : "wasn't");

  return(0);
}
```

The strlen( ) function is very useful; it returns the number of characters, not including the null terminator, in the string pointed to. In the preceding program it is used in two different forms just to give you additional exposure to its use. The first call to the function assigns the length of *szstringA* to the variable *istringA_length.* The second invocation of the function is actually encountered within the if condition. Remember, all test conditions must evaluate to a TRUE (not 0 or !0) or FALSE (0). The if test takes the results returned from the two calls to strlen( ) and then asks the relational question >=. If the length of *szstringB* is >= to that of *szstringA,* the strncmp( ) function is invoked.

Why is the program using a >= test instead of an = =? To know the answer, you need a further explanation of how strncmp( ) works. The function strncmp( ) compares two strings, starting with the first character in each string. If both strings are identical, the function returns a value of zero; if not, strncmp( ) will return a value less than zero if *szstringA* is less than *szstringB,* or a value greater than zero when *szstringA* is greater than *szstringB.* The relational test >= was used in case you wanted to modify the code to include a report of equality, greater than, or less than for the compared strings.

The program terminates by using the value returned by *iresult,* along with the conditional operator (?:), to determine which string message is printed. For this example, the program output is

```
The string wasn't found
```

Before moving on to the next chapter, remind yourself that two of the most frequent causes for irregular program behavior are exceeding array boundaries and forgetting that character arrays, used as strings, must end with \0, a null-string terminator. Both errors can sit dormant for months until that one user enters a response one character too long.

The Complete Reference

Visual
C++ 5

Chapter 10

Using Pointers

nless you have taken a formal course in data structures, you have probably never encountered pointer variables. Pointer variables take the normally invisible memory address of a variable and bring it into the foreground. This can make for extremely efficient algorithms and definitely adds some complexity to your coding. It's similar to the difference between an automobile with an automatic transmission (or static variables—see following definition) versus a manual transmission (or dynamic variables). So, while you have the ability to select just the right gear at the right time, you also need to know how to clutch! And if you remember back to the first time you attempted to drive a stick shift, you know there were a few bumps and grinds until you perfected your skill.

In C/C++, the topics of pointers, arrays, and strings are closely related. Consequently, you can consider this chapter to be an extension of Chapter 9. Learning about pointers—what they are and how to use them—can be a challenging experience to the novice programmer. However, by mastering the concept of pointers, you will be able to author extremely efficient, powerful, and flexible C/C++ applications.

It is very common practice for most introductory-level programs to use only the class of variables known as static. *Static variables*, in this sense, are variables declared in the variable declaration block of the source code. While the program is executing, the application can neither obtain more of these variables nor deallocate storage for a variable. In addition, you have no way of knowing the address in memory for each variable or constant. Accessing an actual cell is a straightforward process—you simply use the variable's name. For example, in C/C++, if you want to increment the int variable *idecade* by 10, you access *idecade* by name:

```
idecade += 10;
```

Pointer Variables

Another, often more convenient and efficient way to access a variable is through a second variable that holds the address of the variable you want to access. Chapter 8 introduced the concept of pointer variables, which are covered in more detail in this chapter. For example, suppose you have an int variable called *imemorycell_contents* and another variable called *pimemorycell_address* (admittedly verbose, but highly symbolic) that can hold the *address* of a variable of type int. In C/C++, you have already seen that preceding a variable with the & address operator returns the address of the variable instead of its contents. Therefore, the syntax for assigning the address of a variable to another variable of the type that holds addresses should not surprise you:

pimemorycell_address = &imemorycell_contents;

A variable that holds an address, such as *pimemorycell_address*, is called a *pointer variable*, or simply a *pointer*. Figure 10-1 illustrates this relationship. The variable *imemorycell_contents* has been placed in memory at address 7751. After the preceding

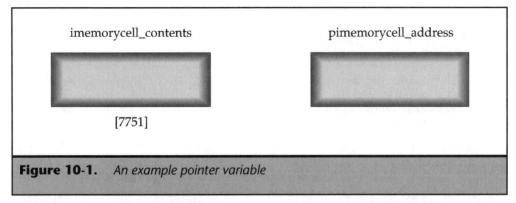

Figure 10-1. *An example pointer variable*

statement is executed, the address of *imemorycell_contents* will be assigned to the pointer variable *pimemorycell_address*. This relationship is expressed in English by saying that *pimemorycell_address* points to *imemorycell_contents*. Figure 10-2 illustrates this relationship. The arrow is drawn from the cell that stores the address to the cell whose address is stored.

Accessing the contents of the cell whose address is stored in *pimemorycell_address* is as simple as preceding the pointer variable with an asterisk: **pimemorycell_address*. What you have done is to *dereference* the pointer *pimemorycell_address*. For example, if you execute the following two statements, the value of the cell named *imemorycell_contents* will be 20 (see Figure 10-3).

> *pimemorycell_address = &imemorycell_contents;*
> **pimemorycell_address = 20;*

You can think of the * as a directive to follow the arrow (see Figure 10-3) to find the cell referenced. Notice that if *pimemorycell_address* holds the address of *imemorycell_contents*, then both of the following statements will have the same effect; that is, both will store the value of 20 in *imemorycell_contents*:

> *imemorycell_contents = 20;*
> **pimemorycell_address = 20;*

Declaring Pointers

C/C++, like any other language, requires a definition for each variable. To define a pointer variable *pimemorycell_address* that can hold the address of an int variable, you write

```
int *pimemorycell_address;
```

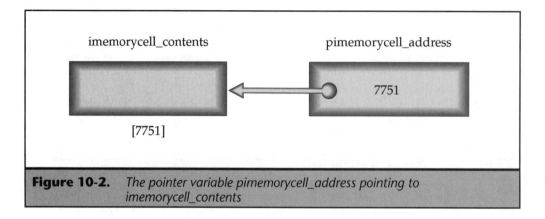

Figure 10-2.   *The pointer variable pimemorycell_address pointing to imemorycell_contents*

Actually, there are two separate parts to this declaration. The data type of *pimemorycell_address* is

```
int *
```

and the identifier for the variable is

```
pimemorycell_address
```

The asterisk following int means "pointer to." That is, the following data type is a pointer variable that can hold an address to an int:

```
int *
```

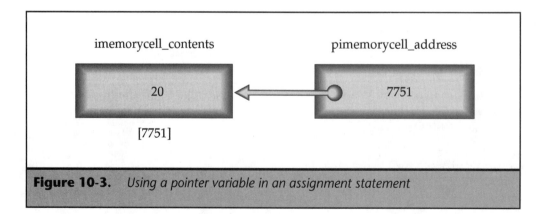

Figure 10-3.   *Using a pointer variable in an assignment statement*

This is a very important concept to remember. In C/C++, unlike many other languages, a pointer variable holds the address of a *particular* data type.

Let's look at an example:

```
char *pcaddress;
int *piaddress;
```

The data type of *pcaddress* is distinctly different from the data type of the pointer variable *piaddress*. Run-time errors and compile-time warnings may occur in a program that defines a pointer to one data type and then uses it to point to some other data type. It would be poor programming practice to define a pointer in one way and then use it in some other way. For example, look at the following code segment:

```
int *pi;
float real_value = 98.26;
pi = &real_value;
```

Here *pi* is defined to be of type int *, meaning it can hold the address of a memory cell of type int. The third statement attempts to assign *pi* the address, *&real_value*, of a declared float variable.

Using Pointer Variables

The following code segment exchanges the contents of the variables *iresult_a* and *iresult_b* but uses the address and dereferencing operators to do so:

```
int iresult_a = 15, iresult_b = 37, itemporary;
int *piresult;

piresult = &iresult_a;
itemporary = *piresult;
*piresult = iresult_b;
iresult_b = itemporary;
```

The first line of the program contains standard definitions and initializations. The statement allocates three cells to hold a single integer, gives each cell a name, and initializes two of them (see Figure 10-4). For discussion purposes, assume that the cell named *iresult_a* is located at address 5328, the cell named *iresult_b* is located at address 7916, and the cell named *itemporary* is located at address 2385.

The second statement in the program defines *piresult* to be a pointer to an int data type. The statement allocates the cell and gives it a name (placed at address 1920).

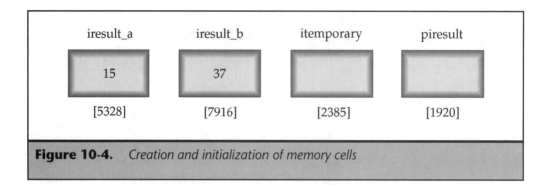

Figure 10-4. *Creation and initialization of memory cells*

Remember, when the * is combined with the data type (in this case, int), the variable contains the *address* of a cell of the same data type. Because *piresult* has not been initialized, it does not point to any particular int variable. If your program were to try to use *piresult*, the compiler would not give you any warning and would try to use the variable's garbage contents to point with. The fourth statement assigns *piresult* the address of *iresult_a* (see Figure 10-5).

The next statement in the program uses the expression **piresult* to access the contents of the cell to which *piresult* points—*iresult_a*:

```
itemporary = *piresult;
```

Therefore, the integer value 15 is stored in the variable *itemporary* (see Figure 10-6). If you left off the * in front of *piresult*, the assignment statement would illegally store the contents of *piresult*—the address 5328—in the cell named *itemporary*, but *itemporary*

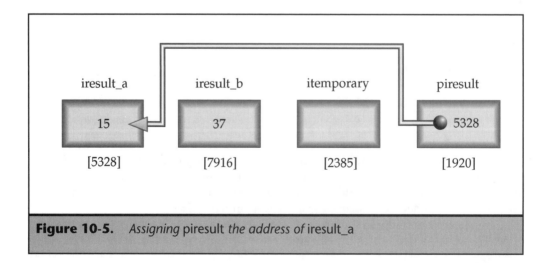

Figure 10-5. *Assigning* piresult *the address of* iresult_a

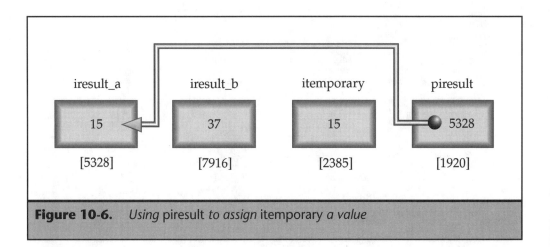

Figure 10-6. *Using* piresult *to assign* itemporary *a value*

PROGRAMMING
FOUNDATIONS

is supposed to hold an integer, not an address. This can be a very annoying bug to locate since many compilers will not issue any warnings/errors. (The Visual C/C++ compiler issues the warning "different levels of indirection.")

To make matters worse, most pointers are near, meaning they occupy 2 bytes, the same data size as a PC-based integer. The fifth statement in the program copies the contents of the variable *iresult_b* into the cell pointed to by the address stored in *piresult* (see Figure 10-7).

```
piresult = iresult_b;
```

The last statement in the program simply copies the contents of one integer variable, *itemporary,* into another integer variable, *iresult_b* (see Figure 10-8). Make certain you understand the difference between what is being referenced when a

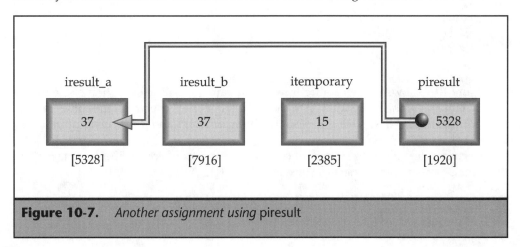

Figure 10-7. *Another assignment using* piresult

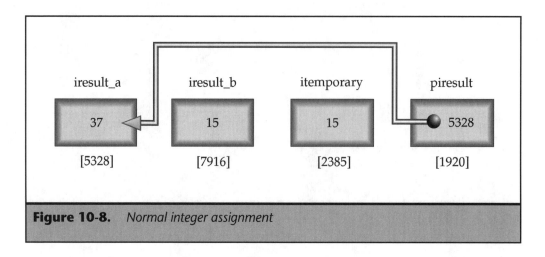

Figure 10-8. *Normal integer assignment*

pointer variable is preceded (**piresult*) and when it is not preceded (*piresult*) by the dereference operator *. For this example, the first syntax is a pointer to a cell that can contain an integer value. The second syntax references the cell that holds the address to another cell that can hold an integer.

The following short program illustrates how to manipulate the addresses in pointer variables. Unlike the previous example, which swapped the program's data within the variables, this program swaps the addresses to where the data resides:

```
char cswitch1 = 'S', cswitch2 = 'T';
char *pcswitch1, *pcswitch2, *pctemporary;

pcswitch1   = &cswitch1;
pcswitch2   = &cswitch2;
pctemporary = pcswitch1;
pcswitch1   = pcswitch2;
pcswitch2   = pctemporary;
printf( "%c%c", *pcswitch1, *pcswitch2);
```

Figure 10-9 shows the cell configuration and values after the execution of the first four statements of the program. When the fifth statement is executed, the contents of *pcswitch1* are copied into *pctemporary* so that both *pcswitch1* and *pctemporary* point to *cswitch1* (see Figure 10-10).

Executing the following statement copies the contents of *pcswitch2* into *pcswitch1* so that both pointers point to *cswitch2* (see Figure 10-11).

```
pcswitch1 = pcswitch2;
```

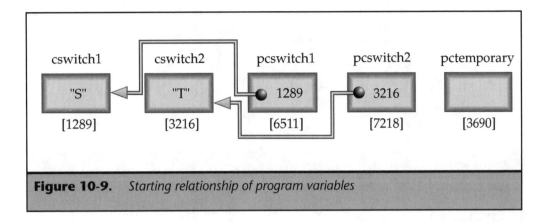

Figure 10-9.   *Starting relationship of program variables*

Notice that if the code had not preserved the address to *cswitch1* in a temporary location, *pctemporary*, there would be no pointer access to *cswitch1*. The next-to-last statement copies the address stored in *pitemporary* into *pcswitch2* (see Figure 10-12). When the printf statement is executed, since the value of **pcswitch1* is "T" and the value of **pcswitch2* is "S", you will see

TS

Notice how the actual values stored in the variables *cswitch1* and *cswitch2* haven't changed from their original initializations. However, since you have swapped the contents of their respective pointers, **pcswitch1* and **pcswitch2*, it *appears* that their order has been reversed. This is an important concept to grasp. Depending on the size of a data object, moving a pointer to the object can be much more efficient than copying the entire contents of the object.

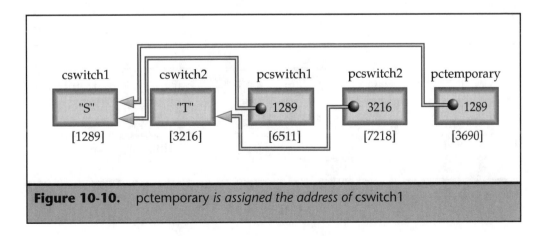

Figure 10-10.   pctemporary *is assigned the address of* cswitch1

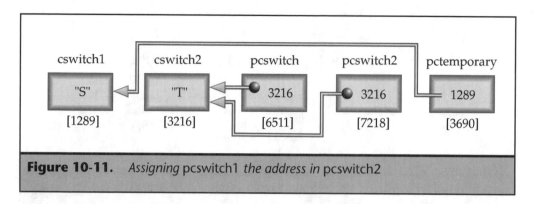

Figure 10-11.   *Assigning* pcswitch1 *the address in* pcswitch2

Initializing Pointers

Pointer variables can be initialized in their definitions, just like many other variables in C/C++. For example, the following two statements allocate storage for the two cells *iresult* and *piresult*:

```
int iresult;
int *piresult = &iresult;
```

The variable *iresult* is an ordinary integer variable, and *piresult* is a pointer to an integer. Additionally, the code initializes the pointer variable *piresult* to the address of *iresult*. Be careful: the syntax is somewhat misleading; you are *not* initializing *piresult* (which would have to be an integer value) but *piresult* (which must be an address to an integer). The second statement in the preceding listing can be translated into the following two equivalent statements:

```
int *piresult;
piresult = &iresult;
```

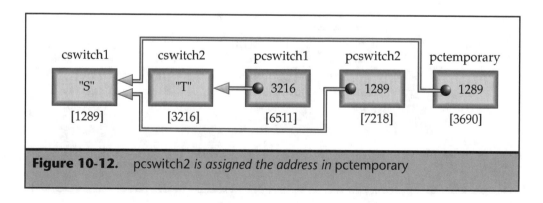

Figure 10-12.   pcswitch2 *is assigned the address in* pctemporary

The following code segment shows how to declare a string pointer and then initialize it:

```
/*
 *   psz.c
 *   A C program that initializes a string pointer and
 *   then prints the palindrome backwards then forwards
 *   Copyright (c) Chris H. Pappas and William H. Murray, 1997
 */

#include <stdio.h>
#include <string.h>

void main( )
{
  char *pszpalindrome="MADAM I'M ADAM";
  int I;

  for (i=strlen(pszpalindrome)-1; i >= 0; I--)
    printf("%c",pszpalindrome[i]);
    printf("%s",pszpalindrome);
}
```

Technically, the C/C++ compiler stores the address of the first character of the string "MADAM I'M ADAM" in the variable *pszpalindrome.* While the program is running, it can use *pszpalindrome* like any other string. This is because all C/C++ compilers create a *string table,* which is used internally by the compiler to store the string constants a program is using.

The strlen( ) function prototyped in STRING.H calculates the length of a string. The function expects a pointer to a null-terminated string and counts all of the characters up to, but not including, the null character itself. The index variable *i* is initialized to one less than the value returned by strlen( ) since the for loop treats the string *psz* like an array of characters. The palindrome has 14 letters. If *psz* is treated as an array of characters, each element is indexed from 0 to 13. This example program highlights the somewhat confusing relationship between pointers to character strings and arrays of characters. However, if you remember that an array's name is actually the address of the first element, you should understand why the compiler issues no complaints.

What Not to Do with the Address Operator

You cannot use the address operator on every C/C++ expression. The following examples demonstrate those situations where the & address operator cannot be applied:

```
/*
   not with CONSTANTS
*/

pivariable = &48;


/*
   not with expressions involving operators such as + and /
   given the definition int iresult = 5;
*/

pivariable = &(iresult + 15);


/*
   not preceding register variables
   given the definition register register1;
*/

pivariable = &register1;
```

The first statement tries to illegally obtain the address of a hardwired constant value. Since the 48 has no memory cell associated with it, the statement is meaningless.

The second assignment statement attempts to return the address of the expression *iresult* + 15. Since the expression itself is actually a stack manipulation process, there is no address associated with the expression.

Normally, the last example honors the programmer's request to define *register1* as a register rather than as a storage cell in internal memory. Therefore, no memory cell address could be returned and stored. Microsoft Visual C/C++ gives the variable memory, not register storage.

Pointers to Arrays

As mentioned, pointers and arrays are closely related topics. Remember from Chapter 9 that an array's name is a constant whose value represents the address of the array's first element. For this reason, the value of an array's name cannot be changed by an assignment statement or by any other statement. Given the following data declarations, the array's name, *ftemperatures,* is a constant whose value is the address of the first element of the array of 20 floats:

```
#define IMAXREADINGS 20

float ftemperatures[IMAXREADINGS];
float *pftemp;
```

The following statement assigns the address of the first element of the array to the pointer variable *pftemp*:

```
pftemp = ftemperatures;
```

An equivalent statement looks like this:

```
pftemp = &ftemperatures[0];
```

However, if *pftemp* holds the address of a float, the following statements are illegal:

```
ftemperatures = pftemp;
&ftemperatures[0] = pftemp;
```

These statements attempt to assign a value to the constant *ftemperatures* or its equivalent *&ftemperatures[0]*, which makes about as much sense as

```
10 = pftemp;
```

Pointers to Pointers

In C/C++, it is possible to define pointer variables that point to other pointer variables, which in turn point to the data, such as an integer. Figure 10-13 illustrates this relationship; *ppi* is a pointer variable that points to another pointer variable whose contents can be used to point to 10.

You may be wondering why this is necessary. The arrival of Windows and the Windows NT programming environment signals the development of multitasking operating environments designed to maximize the use of memory. To compact the use of memory, the operating system has to be able to move objects in memory. If your program points directly to the physical memory cell where the object is stored and the operating system moves it, disaster will strike. Instead of pointing directly to a data

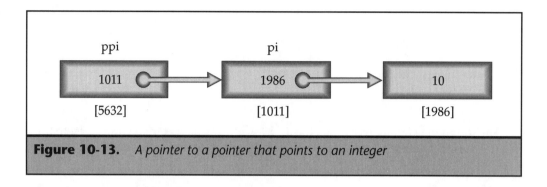

Figure 10-13. *A pointer to a pointer that points to an integer*

object, your application points to a memory cell address that will not change while your program is running (for example, let's call this a *virtual_address*), and the *virtual_address* memory cell holds the *current_physical_address* of the data object. Now, whenever the operating environment wants to move the data object, all the operating system has to do is update the *current_physical_address* pointed to by the *virtual_address*. As far as your application is concerned, it still uses the unchanged address of the *virtual_address* to point to the updated address of the *current_physical_address*.

To define a pointer to a pointer in C/C++, you simply increase the number of asterisks preceding the identifier:

```
int **ppi;
```

In this example, the variable *ppi* is defined to be a pointer to a pointer that points to an int data type. *ppi*'s data type is

```
int **
```

Each asterisk is read "pointer to." The number of pointers that must be followed to access the data item or, equivalently, the number of asterisks that must be attached to the variable to reference the value to which it points, is called the *level of indirection* of the pointer variable. A pointer's level of indirection determines how much dereferencing must be done to access the data type given in the definition. Figure 10-14 illustrates several variables with different levels of indirection.

The first four lines of code in Figure 10-14 define four variables: the integer variable *ivalue*, the *pi* pointer variable that points to an integer (one level of indirection), the *ppi* variable that points to a pointer that points to an integer (two levels of indirection), and *pppi*, illustrating that this process can be extended beyond two levels of indirection. The fifth line of code is

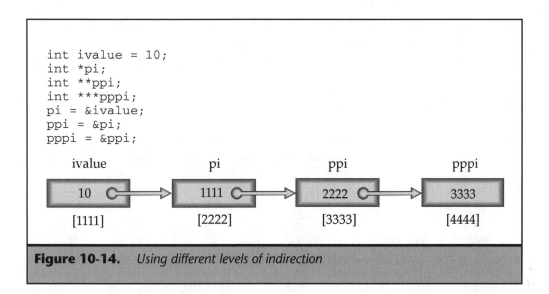

```
int ivalue = 10;
int *pi;
int **ppi;
int ***pppi;
pi = &ivalue;
ppi = &pi;
pppi = &ppi;
```

Figure 10-14. *Using different levels of indirection*

```
pi = &ivalue
```

This is an assignment statement that uses the address operator. The expression assigns the address of *&ivalue* to *pi*. Therefore, *pi*'s contents contain 1111. Notice that there is only one arrow from *pi* to *ivalue*. This indicates that *ivalue*, or 10, can be accessed by dereferencing *pi* just once. The next statement, along with its accompanying picture, illustrates double indirection:

```
ppi = &pi;
```

Because *ppi*'s data type is int **, to access an integer you need to dereference the variable twice. After the preceding assignment statement, *ppi* holds the address (not the contents) of *pi*, so *ppi* points to *pi*, which in turn points to *ivalue*. Notice that you must follow two arrows to get from *ppi* to *ivalue*.

The last statement demonstrates three levels of indirection:

```
pppi = &ppi;
```

It also assigns the address (not the contents) of *ppi* to *pppi*. Notice that the accompanying illustration shows that three arrows are now necessary to reference *ivalue*.

To review, *pppi* is assigned the address of a pointer variable that indirectly points to an integer, as in the preceding statement. However, ****pppi* (the cell pointed to) can only be assigned an integer value, not an address, since ****pppi* is an integer:

```
***pppi = 10;
```

C/C++ allows pointers to be initialized like any other variable. For example, *pppi* could have been defined and initialized using the following single statement:

```
int ***pppi = &ppi;
```

Pointers to Strings

A string constant such as "File not ready" is actually stored as an array of characters with a null terminator added as the last character (see Figure 10-15). Because a char pointer can hold the address of a character, it is possible to define and initialize it. For example:

```
char *psz = "File not ready";
```

This statement defines the char pointer *psz* and initializes it to the address of the first character in the string (see Figure 10-16). Additionally, the storage is allocated for the string itself. The same statement could have been written as follows:

```
char *psz;
psz = "File not ready";
```

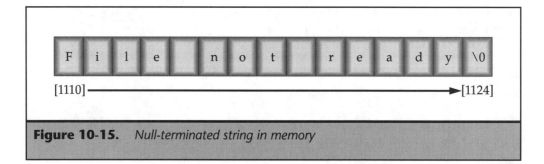

| F | i | l | e | | n | o | t | | r | e | a | d | y | \0 |

[1110] ————————————————————————————►[1124]

Figure 10-15. *Null-terminated string in memory*

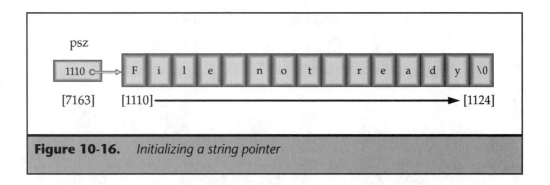

Figure 10-16. *Initializing a string pointer*

Again, care must be taken to realize that *psz* was assigned the address, not **psz*, which points to the "F." The second example given helps to clarify this by using two separate statements to define and initialize the pointer variable.

The following example highlights a common misconception when dealing with pointers to strings and pointers to arrays of characters:

```
char *psz = "File not ready";
char pszarray[] = "Drive not ready";
```

The main difference between these two statements is that the value of *psz* can be changed (since it is a pointer variable), but the value of *pszarray* cannot be changed (since it is a pointer constant). Along the same line of thinking, the following assignment statement is illegal:

```
/* NOT LEGAL */
char pszarray[16];
pszarray = "Drive not ready";
```

While the syntax looks similar to the correct code in the preceding example, the assignment statement attempts to copy the *address* of the first cell of the storage for the string "Drive not ready" into *pszarray*. Because *pszarray* is a pointer constant, not a pointer variable, an error results.

The following input statement is incorrect because the pointer *psz* has not been initialized:

```
/* NOT LEGAL */
char *psz;
cin >> psz;
```

Correcting the problem is as simple as reserving storage for and initializing the pointer variable *psz*:

```
char sztring[10];
char *psz = sztring;
cin.get(psz,10);
```

Since the value of *sztring* is the address of the first cell of the array, the second statement in the code not only allocates storage for the pointer variable, but it also initializes it to the address of the first cell of the array *sztring*. At this point, the cin.get statement is satisfied since it is passed the valid address of the character array storage.

Pointer Arithmetic

If you are familiar with assembly language programming, then you are already comfortable with using actual physical addresses to reference information stored in tables. For those of you who are only used to using subscript indexing into arrays, believe it or not, you have been effectively using the same assembly language equivalent. The only difference is that in the latter case you were allowing the compiler to manipulate the addresses for you.

Remember that one of C/C++'s strengths are their closeness to the hardware. In C/C++, you can actually manipulate pointer variables. Many of the example programs seen so far have demonstrated how one pointer variable's address, or address contents, can be assigned to another pointer variable of the same data type. C/C++ allows you to perform only two arithmetic operations on a pointer address— namely, addition and subtraction. Let's look at two different pointer variable types and perform some simple pointer arithmetic:

```
//
//   ptarth.cpp
//   A C++ program demonstrating pointer arithmetic
//   Copyright (c) Chris H. Pappas and William H. Murray, 1997
//

#include <iostream.h>

void main( )
{

  int *pi;
  float *pf;
```

```
int an_integer;
float a_real;

pi = &an_integer;
pf = &a_real;

pi++;
pf++;

}
```

Let's also assume that an integer is 2 bytes and a float is 4 bytes (for 16-bit C/C++ environments). Also, *an_integer* is stored at memory cell address 2000, and *a_real* is stored at memory cell address 4000. When the last two lines of the program are executed, *pi* will contain the address 2002 and *pf* will contain the address 4004. But wait a minute—didn't you think that the increment operator ++ incremented by 1? This is true for character variables but not always for pointer variables.

In Chapter 6, you were introduced to the concept of operator overloading. Increment (++) and decrement (- -) are examples of this C/C++ construct. For the immediate example, since *pi* was defined to point to integers (which for the system in this example are 2 bytes), when the increment operation is invoked, it checks the variable's type and then chooses an appropriate increment value. For integers, this value is 2; for floats, the value is 4 (on the example system). This same principle holds true for whatever data type the pointer is pointing to. Should the pointer variable point to a structure of 20 bytes, the increment or decrement operator would add or subtract 20 from the current pointer's address.

You can also modify a pointer's address by using integer addition and subtraction, not just the ++ and - - operators. For example, moving four float values over from the one currently pointed to can be accomplished with the following statement:

```
pf = pf + 4;
```

Look at the following program carefully and see if you can predict the results. Does the program move the float pointer *pf* one number over?

```
//
//   sizept.cpp
//   A C++ program using sizeof and pointer arithmetic
//   Copyright (c) Chris H. Pappas and William H. Murray, 1997
//
```

```
#include <iostream.h>
#include <stddef.h>

void main( )
{
  float fvalues[] = {15.38,12.34,91.88,11.11,22.22};
  float *pf;
  size_t fwidth;

  pf = &fvalues[0];

  fwidth = sizeof(float);

  pf = pf + fwidth;

}
```

Try using the integrated debugger to single-step through the program. Use the Trace window to keep an eye on the variables *pf* and *fwidth*.

Assume that the debugger has assigned *pf* the address of *fvalues* and that *pf* contains an FFCA. The variable *fwidth* is assigned the sizeof(float) that returns a 4. When you executed the final statement in the program, what happened? The variable *pf* changed to FFDA, not FFDE. Why? You forgot that pointer arithmetic takes into consideration the size of the object pointed to (4 x (4-byte floats) = 16). The program actually moves the *pf* pointer over four float values to 22.22.

Actually, you were intentionally misled by the naming of the variable *fwidth*. To make logical sense, the program should have been written as

```
//
//   ptsize.cpp
//   The same C++ program using meaningful variable names
//   Copyright (c) Chris H. Pappas and William H. Murray, 1997
//

#include <iostream.h>

void main( )
{
  float fvalues[] = {15.38,12.34,91.88,11.11,22.22};
  float *pf;
  int inumber_of_elements_to_skip;
```

```
  pf = fvalues;

  inumber_of_elements_to_skip = 1;

  pf = pf + inumber_of_elements_to_skip;

}
```

Pointer Arithmetic and Arrays

The following two programs index into a ten-character array. Both programs read in ten characters and then print out the same ten characters in reverse order. The first program uses the more conventional high-level language approach of indexing with subscripts. The second program is identical except that the array elements are referenced by address, using pointer arithmetic. Here is the first program:

```c
/*
 *    arysub.c
 *    A C program using normal array subscripting
 *    Copyright (c) Chris H. Pappas and William H. Murray, 1997
 */

#include <stdio.h>

#define ISIZE 10

void main( )
{
  char string10[ISIZE];
  int I;

  for(i = 0; i < ISIZE; I++)
    string10[i]=getchar( );

  for(i = ISIZE-1; i >= 0; I--)
    putchar(string10[i]);
}
```

Here is the second example:

```
/*
 *    aryptr.c
 *    A C program using pointer arithmetic to access elements
 *    Copyright (c) Chris H. Pappas and William H. Murray, 1997
 */

#include <stdio.h>

#define ISIZE 10

void main( )
{
  char string10[ISIZE];
  char *pc;
  int icount;

  pc=string10;

  for(icount = 0; icount < ISIZE; icount++) {
    *pc=getchar( );
    pc++;
  }

  pc=string10 + (ISIZE - 1);

  for(icount = 0; icount < ISIZE; icount++) {
    putchar(*pc);
    pc--;
  }
}
```

Since the first example is straightforward, the discussion will center on the second program, which uses pointer arithmetic. *pc* has been defined to be of type char *, which means it is a pointer to a character. Because each cell in the array *string10* holds a character, *pc* is suitable for pointing to each. The following statement stores the address of the first cell of *string10* in the variable *pc*:

```
pc=string10;
```

The for loop reads *ISIZE* characters and stores them in the array *string10*. The following statement uses the dereference operator * to ensure that the target, the left-hand side of this assignment (another example of an *lvalue*), will be the cell to which *pc* points, not *pc* (which itself contains just an address).

```
*pc=getchar( );
```

The idea is to store a character in each cell of *string10*, not to store it in *pc*.

To start printing the array backward, the program first initializes the *pc* to the last element in the array:

```
pc=string10 + (ISIZE - 1);
```

By adding 9 (*ISIZE - 1*) to the initial address of *string10*, *pc* points to the *tenth* element. Remember, these are offsets. The first element in the array is at offset zero. Within the for loop, *pc* is decremented to move backward through the array elements. Make certain you use the integrated debugger to trace through this example if you are unsure of how *pc* is modified.

Problems with the Operators ++ and - -

Just as a reminder, the following two statements do *not* perform the same cell reference:

```
*pc++=getchar( );
*++pc=getchar( );
```

The first statement assigns the character returned by getchar( ) to the *current* cell pointed to by *pc* and then increments *pc*. The second statement increments the address in *pc* first and then assigns the character returned by the function to the cell pointed to by the updated address. Later in this chapter you will use these two different types of pointer assignments to reference the elements of *argv*.

Using const with Pointers

Just when you think you are getting the hang of it, C/C++ throws you a subtle potential curveball. Look at the following two pointer variable declarations and see if you can detect the subtle differences:

```
const MYTYPE *pmytype_1;
MYTYPE * const pmytype_2 = &mytype;
```

The first pointer declaration defines *pmytype_1* as a pointer variable that may be assigned any address to a memory location of type *MYTYPE*. The second declaration defines *pmytype_2*, as a pointer constant to *mytype*. Was that enough of a hint?

OK, let's try that one more time. The identifier *pmytype_1* is a pointer variable. Variables can be assigned *any* value appropriate to their defined type—in this case, *pmytype_1* can be assigned any address to a previously defined location of type *MYTYPE*. Well then, you might ask, what does the const keyword do in the declaration? What that const tells the compiler is this: While *pmytype_1* may be assigned any address to a memory cell of type *MYTYPE*, when you use *pmytype_1* to actually point to a memory location, what you point to cannot be changed. The following sample statements highlight these subtleties:

```
pmytype_1 = &mytype1; // legal
pmytype_1 = &mytype2; // legal
*pmytype_1 = (MYTYPE)some_legal_value; // illegal attempting to
change contents
```

Now, compare *pmytype_1* with *pmytype_2*, which is declared as a pointer constant. In other words, *pmytype_2* can hold the address to a memory location of type *MYTYPE*. However, it is a locked address. Therefore, *pmytype_2* must be initialized to hold a valid address when the pointer constant is declared (= *&mytype;*). On the other hand, the contents of the memory location pointed to by *pmytype_2* are not locked. Look at the following statements, which highlight these subtleties:

```
pmytype_2 = &mytype_n; // illegal, attempting to change locked
pointer address
*pmytype_2 = (MYTYPE) some_legal_value_1; // legal to change
memory contents
*pmytype_2 = (MYTYPE) some_legal_value_n; // legal to change
memory contents
```

Now, of the two uses for the const keyword with pointer declarations, which do you think is closest to an array declaration? Answer: the second use of const, as in *pmytype_2*'s declaration. Remember, the name of an array is a locked address to the array's first element:

```
int iarray[ SIZE ];
```

For this reason, the compiler views the identifier *iarray* as if you had actually declared it as:

```
int * const iarray = &array[0];
```

Comparing Pointers

You have already seen examples demonstrating the effect of incrementing and decrementing pointers using the ++ and - - operators and the effect of adding an integer to a pointer. There are other operations that may be performed on pointers. These include

- Subtracting an integer from a pointer
- Subtracting two pointers (usually pointing to the same object)
- Comparing pointers using a relational operator such as <=, =, or >=

Since (pointer – integer) subtraction is so similar to (pointer + integer) addition (these have already been discussed by example), it should be no surprise that the resultant pointer value points to a storage location for integer elements before the original pointer.

Subtracting two pointers yields a constant value that is the number of array elements between the two pointers. This assumes that both pointers are of the same type and initially point into the same array. Subtracting pointers that are not of the same type or that initially point to different arrays will yield unpredictable results.

 NOTE: *No matter which pointer arithmetic operation you choose, there is no check to see if the pointer value calculated is outside the defined boundaries of the array.*

Pointers of like type (that is, pointers that reference the same kind of data, like int and float) can also be compared to each other. The resulting TRUE (!0) or FALSE (0) can either be tested or assigned to an integer, just like the result of any logical expression. Comparing two pointers tests whether they are equal, not equal, greater than, or less than each other. One pointer is less than another pointer if the first pointer refers to an array element with a lower number subscript. (Remember that pointers and subscripts are virtually identical.) This operation also assumes that the pointers reference the same array.

Finally, pointers can be compared to zero, the null value. In this case, only the test for equal or not equal is valid since testing for negative pointers makes no sense. The null value in a pointer means that the pointer has no value, or does not point to anything. Null, or zero, is the only numeric value that can be directly assigned into a pointer without a type cast.

It should be noted that pointer conversions are performed on pointer operands. This means that any pointer may be compared to a constant expression evaluating to zero and any pointer may be compared to a pointer of type void *. (In this last case, the pointer is first converted to void *.)

Pointer Portability

The examples in this section have represented addresses as integers. This may suggest to you that a C/C++ pointer is of type int. It is not. A pointer holds the address of a particular type of variable, but a pointer itself is not one of the primitive data types int, float, and the like. A particular C/C++ system may allow a pointer to be copied into an int variable and an int variable to be copied into a pointer; however, C/C++ does not guarantee that pointers can be stored in int variables. To guarantee code portability, the practice should be avoided.

Also, not all arithmetic operations on pointers are allowed. For example, it is illegal to add two pointers, to multiply two pointers, or to divide one pointer by another.

Using sizeof with Pointers under 16-Bit DOS Environments

NOTE: *The following section describes old, outdated keywords. These pointer size modifiers are no longer needed under the newer 32-bit C/C++ compilers and operating systems. Under a 32-bit operating system and C/C++ compiler, all addresses are a full 32 bits (equivalent to the _ _far and _ _huge modifiers described next). However, as many readers already know, you often encounter code, for purposes of reference or modification, that is written in Historic C/C++, ANSI C/C++, and so forth. For this reason the discussion of these old-style keywords is presented here.*

The actual size of a pointer variable depends on one of two things: the size of the memory model you have chosen for the application or the use of the nonportable, implementation-specific _ _near, _ _far, and _ _huge keywords.

The 80486 to 8088 microprocessors use a *segmented addressing* scheme that breaks an address into two pieces: a segment and an offset. Many local post offices have several walls of post office boxes, with each box having its own unique number. Segment:offset addressing is similar to this design. To get to your post office box, you first need to know which bank of boxes, or wall, yours is on (the *segment*), and then the actual box number (the *offset*).

When you know that all of your application's code and data will fit within a single 64K of memory, you choose the small memory model. Applying this to the post office box metaphor, this means that all of your code and data will be in the same location, or wall (segment), with the application's code and data having a unique box number (offset) on the wall.

For those applications where this compactness is not feasible, possibly because of the size and the amount of data that must be stored and referenced, you would choose a large memory model. Using the analogy, this could mean that all of your application's code would be located on one wall, while all the data would be on a completely separate wall.

When an application shares the same memory segment for code and data, calculating an object's memory location merely involves finding out the object's offset within the segment. This is a very simple calculation.

When an application has separate segments for code and data, calculating an object's location is a bit more complicated. First, the code or data's segment must be calculated, and then its offset within the respective segment. Naturally, this requires more processor time.

C++ also allows you to override the default pointer size for a specific variable by using the keywords _ _near, _ _far, and _ _huge. Note, however, that by including these in your application, you make your code less portable since the keywords produce different results on different compilers. The _ _near keyword forces an offset-only pointer when the pointers would normally default to segment:offset. The _ _far keyword forces a segment:offset pointer when the pointers would normally default to offset-only. The _ _huge keyword also forces a segment:offset pointer that has been normalized. The _ _near keyword is generally used to increase execution speed, while the _ _far keyword forces a pointer to do the right thing regardless of the memory model chosen.

For many applications, you can simply ignore this problem and allow the compiler to choose a default memory model. But eventually you will run into problems with this approach—for example, when you try to address an absolute location (some piece of hardware, perhaps, or a special area in memory) outside your program's segment area.

On the other hand, you may be wondering why you can't just use the largest memory model available for your application. You can, but you pay a price in efficiency. If all of your data is in one segment, the pointer is the size of the offset. However, if your data and code range all over memory, your pointer is the size of the segment *and* the offset, and both must be calculated every time you change the pointer. The following program uses the function sizeof( ) to print out the smallest pointer size and largest pointer size available.

This C++ program prints the default pointer sizes, their _ _far sizes, and their _ _near sizes. The program also uses the *stringize* preprocessor directive (#) with the A_POINTER argument, so the name as well as the size of the pointer will be printed.

```
//
//  strize.cpp
//  A C++ program illustrating the sizeof(pointers) and
//  the program is only valid under 16-bit C/C++ environments.
//  Copyright (c) Chris H. Pappas and William H. Murray, 1997
//

#include <stdio.h>

#define PRINT_SIZEOF(A_POINTER) \
  printf("sizeof\t("#A_POINTER")\t= %d\n", \
  sizeof(A_POINTER))

void main( )
{
  char *reg_pc;
  long double *reg_pldbl;
  char _ _far *far_pc;
  long double _ _far *far_pldbl;
  char _ _near *near_pc;
  long double _ _near *near_pldbl;

  PRINT_SIZEOF(reg_pc);
  PRINT_SIZEOF(reg_pldbl);
  PRINT_SIZEOF(far_pc);
  PRINT_SIZEOF(far_pldbl);
  PRINT_SIZEOF(near_pc);
  PRINT_SIZEOF(near_pldbl);
}
```

The output from the program looks like this:

```
sizeof    (reg_pc)      = 2
sizeof    (reg_pldbl)   = 2
sizeof    (far_pc)      = 4
sizeof    (far_pldbl)   = 4
sizeof    (near_pc)     = 2
sizeof    (near_pldbl)  = 2
```

Pointers to Functions

All the examples so far have shown you how various items of data can be referenced by a pointer. As it turns out, you can also access *portions of code* by using a pointer to a function. Pointers to functions serve the same purpose as do pointers to data; that is, they allow the function to be referenced indirectly, just as a pointer to a data item allows the data item to be referenced indirectly.

A pointer to a function can have a number of important uses. For example, consider the qsort( ) function. The qsort( ) function has as one of its parameters a pointer to a function. The referenced function contains the necessary comparison that is to be performed between the array elements being sorted. qsort( ) has been written to require a function pointer because the comparison process between two elements can be a complex process beyond the scope of a single control flag. It is not possible to pass a function by value, that is, pass the code itself. C/C++, however, does support passing a pointer to the code, or a pointer to the function.

The concept of function pointers is frequently illustrated by using the qsort( ) function supplied with the compiler. Unfortunately, in many cases, the function pointer is declared to be of a type that points to other built-in functions. The following C and C++ programs demonstrate how to define a pointer to a function and how to "roll your own" function to be passed to the STDLIB.H function qsort( ). Here is the C program:

```c
/*
 *    fncptr.c
 *    A C program illustrating how to declare your own
 *    function and function pointer to be used with qsort( )
 *    Copyright (c) Chris H. Pappas and William H. Murray, 1997
 */

#include <stdio.h>
#include <stdlib.h>

#define IMAXVALUES 10

int icompare_funct(const void *iresult_a, const void *iresult_b);
int (*ifunct_ptr)(const void *, const void *);

void main( )
{
  int i;
  int iarray[IMAXVALUES]={0,5,3,2,8,7,9,1,4,6};

  ifunct_ptr=icompare_funct;
```

```
  qsort(iarray,IMAXVALUES,sizeof(int),ifunct_ptr);
  for(i = 0; i < IMAXVALUES; i++)
    printf("%d ",iarray[i]);
}

int icompare_funct(const void *iresult_a, const void *iresult_b)
{
  return((*(int *)iresult_a) - (*(int *) iresult_b));
}
```

The function icompare_funct( ) (which will be called the *reference function*) was prototyped to match the requirements for the fourth parameter to the function qsort( ) (which will be called the *invoking function*).

To digress slightly, the fourth parameter to the function qsort( ) must be a function pointer. This reference function must be passed two const void * parameters and it must return a type int. (Note: Remember that the position of the const keyword, in the formal parameter list, *locks* the data pointed to, not the address used to point. This means that even if you write your compare routine so that it *does not* sort properly, it can in *no way* destroy the contents of your array!) This is because qsort( ) uses the reference function for the sort comparison algorithm. Now that you understand the prototype of the reference function icompare_funct( ), take a minute to study the body of the reference function.

If the reference function returns a value < 0, then the reference function's first parameter value is less than the second parameter's value. A return value of zero indicates parameter value equality, with a return value > 0 indicating that the second parameter's value was greater than the first's. All of this is accomplished by the single statement in icompare_funct( ):

```
  return((*(int *)iresult_a) - (*(int *) iresult_b));
```

Since both of the pointers were passed as type void *, they were cast to their appropriate pointer type int * and then dereferenced (*). The result of the subtraction of the two values pointed to returns an appropriate value to satisfy qsort( )'s comparison criterion.

While the prototype requirements for icompare_funct( ) are interesting, the meat of the program begins with the pointer function declaration below the icompare_funct( ) function prototype:

```
  int icompare_funct(const void *iresult_a, const void *iresult_b);
  int (*ifunct_ptr)(const void *, const void *);
```

A function's type is determined by its return value and argument list signature. A pointer to icompare_funct( ) must specify the same signature and return type. You might therefore think the following statement would accomplish this:

```
int *ifunct_ptr(const void *, const void *);
```

That is almost correct. The problem is that the compiler interprets the statement as the definition of a function ifunct_ptr( ) taking two arguments and returning a pointer of type int *. The dereference operator unfortunately is associated with the type specifier, not ifunct_ptr( ). Parentheses are necessary to associate the dereference operator with ifunct_ptr( ).

The corrected statement declares ifunct_ptr( ) to be a pointer to a function taking two arguments and with a return type int—that is, a pointer of the same type required by the fourth parameter to qsort( ).

In the body of main( ), the only thing left to do is to initialize ifunct_ptr( ) to the address of the function icompare_funct( ). The parameters to qsort( ) are the address to the base or zeroth element of the table to be sorted (*iarray*), the number of entries in the table (*IMAXVALUES*), the size of each table element (sizeof(int)), and a function pointer to the comparison function (ifunct_ptr( )).

The C++ equivalent follows:

```
//
//   qsort.cpp
//   A C program illustrating how to declare your own
//   function and function pointer to be used with qsort( )
//   Copyright (c) Chris H. Pappas and William H. Murray, 1997
//

#include <iostream.h>
#include <stdlib.h>

#define IMAXVALUES 10

int icompare_funct(const void *iresult_a, const void *iresult_b);
int (*ifunct_ptr)(const void *,const void *);

void main( )
{
  int i;
  int iarray[IMAXVALUES]={0,5,3,2,8,7,9,1,4,6};

  ifunct_ptr=icompare_funct;
```

PROGRAMMING
FOUNDATIONS

```
   qsort(iarray,IMAXVALUES,sizeof(int),ifunct_ptr);
   for(i = 0; i < IMAXVALUES; i++)
     cout <<[{|"|}]" << iarray[i];
}

int icompare_funct(const void *iresult_a, const void *iresult_b)
{
   return((*(int *)iresult_a) - (*(int *)iresult_b));
}
```

Learning to understand the syntax of a function pointer can be challenging. Let's look at just a few examples. Here is the first one:

```
int *(*(*ifunct_ptr)(int))[5];
float (*(*ffunct_ptr)(int,int))(float);
typedef double (*(*(*dfunct_ptr)( ))[5])( );
  dfunct_ptr A_dfunct_ptr;
(*(*function_ary_ptrs( ))[5])( );
```

The first statement defines ifunct_ptr( ) to be a function pointer to a function that is passed an integer argument and returns a pointer to an array of five int pointers.

The second statement defines ffunct_ptr( ) to be a function pointer to a function that takes two integer arguments and returns a pointer to a function taking a float argument and returning a float.

By using the typedef declaration, you can avoid the unnecessary repetition of complicated declarations. The typedef declaration (discussed in greater detail in Chapter 13) is read as follows: dfunct_ptr( ) is defined as a pointer to a function that is passed nothing and returns a pointer to an array of five pointers that point to functions that are passed nothing and returns a double.

The last statement is a function declaration, not a variable declaration. The statement defines function_ary_ptrs( ) to be a function taking no arguments and returning a pointer to an array of five pointers that point to functions taking no arguments and returning integers. The outer functions return the default C and C++ type int.

The good news is that you will rarely encounter complicated declarations and definitions like these. However, by making certain you understand these declarations, you will be able to confidently parse the everyday variety.

Dynamic Memory

When a C/C++ program is compiled, the computer's memory is broken down into four zones that contain the program's code, all global data, the stack, and the heap. The *heap* is an area of free memory (sometimes referred to as the *free store*) that is manipulated by using the dynamic allocation functions malloc( ) and free( ).

When malloc( ) is invoked, it allocates a contiguous block of storage for the object specified and then returns a pointer to the start of the block. The function free( ) returns previously allocated memory to the heap, permitting that portion of memory to be reallocated.

The argument passed to malloc( ) is an integer that represents the number of bytes of storage that is needed. If the storage is available, malloc( ) will return a void *, which can be cast into whatever type pointer is desired. The concept of *void pointers* was introduced in the ANSI C standard and means a pointer of unknown type, or a generic pointer. A void pointer cannot itself be used to reference anything (since it doesn't point to any specific type of data), but it can contain a pointer of any other type. Therefore, any pointer can be converted into a void pointer and back without any loss of information.

The following code segment allocates enough storage for 300 float values:

```
float *pf;
int inum_floats = 300;

pf = (float *) malloc(inum_floats * sizeof(float));
```

The malloc( ) function has been instructed to obtain enough storage for 300 * the current size of a float. The cast operator (float *) is used to return a float pointer type. Each block of storage requested is entirely separate and distinct from all other blocks of storage. Absolutely no assumption can be made about where the blocks are located. Blocks are typically "tagged" with some sort of information that allows the operating system to manage the location and size of the block. When the block is no longer needed, it can be returned to the operating system by using the following statement:

```
free((void *) pf);
```

Just as in C, C++ allocates available memory in two ways. When variables are declared, they are created on the stack by pushing the stack pointer down. When these variables go out of scope (for instance, when a local variable is no longer needed), the space for that variable is freed automatically by moving the stack pointer up. The size of stack-allocated memory must always be known at compilation.

Your application may also have to use variables with an unknown size at compilation. Under these circumstances, you must allocate the memory yourself, on the free store. The free store can be thought of as occupying the bottom of the program's memory space and growing *upward,* while the stack occupies the top and grows *downward.*

Your C and C++ programs can allocate and release free store memory at any point. It is important to realize that free store-allocated memory variables are not subject to scoping rules, as other variables are. These variables never go out of scope, so once you allocate memory on the heap, you are responsible for freeing it. If you continue to allocate free store space without freeing it, your program could eventually crash.

Most C compilers use the library functions malloc( ) and free( ), just discussed, to provide dynamic memory allocation, but in C++ these capabilities were considered so important they were made a part of the core language. C++ uses new and delete to allocate and free free store memory. The argument to new is an expression that returns the number of bytes to be allocated; the value returned is a pointer to the beginning of this memory block. The argument to delete is the starting address of the memory block to be freed. The following two programs illustrate the similarities and differences between a C and C++ application using dynamic memory allocation. Here is the C example:

```
/*
 *   malloc.c
 *   A simple C program using malloc( ), free( )
 *   Copyright (c) Chris H. Pappas and William H. Murray, 1997
 */

#include <stdio.h>
#include <stdlib.h>

#define ISIZE 512

void main( )
{
  int * pimemory_buffer;
  pimemory_buffer=malloc(ISIZE * sizeof(int));
  if(pimemory_buffer == NULL)
    printf("Insufficient memory\n");
  else
    printf("Memory allocated\n");
  free(pimemory_buffer);
}
```

The first point of interest in the program begins with the second #include statement that brings in the STDLIB.H header file, containing the definitions for both functions, malloc( ) and free( ). After the program defines the int * pointer variable *pimemory_buffer*, the malloc( ) function is invoked to return the address to a memory block that is ISIZE * sizeof(int) big. A robust algorithm will always check for the success or failure of the memory allocation, and it explains the purpose behind the if-else statement. The function malloc( ) returns a null whenever not enough memory is available to allocate the block. This simple program ends by returning the allocated memory to the free store by using the function free( ) and passing it the beginning address of the allocated block.

The C++ program does not look significantly different:

```
//
//  newdel.cpp
//  A simple C++ program using new and delete
//  Copyright (c) Chris H. Pappas and William H. Murray, 1997
//

#include <iostream.h>
// #include <stdlib.h> not needed for malloc( ), free( )

#define NULL 0
#define ISIZE 512

void main( )
{
  int *pimemory_buffer;

  pimemory_buffer=new int[ISIZE];
  if(pimemory_buffer == NULL)
    cout << "Insufficient memory\n";
  else
    cout << "Memory allocated\n";
  delete(pimemory_buffer);
}
```

The only major difference between the two programs is the syntax used with the function free( ) and the operator new. Whereas the function free( ) requires the sizeof operator to ensure proper memory allocation, the operator new has been written to automatically perform the sizeof( ) function on the declared data type it is passed. Both programs will allocate 512 2-byte blocks of consecutive memory (on systems that allocate 2 bytes per integer).

Using void Pointers

Now that you have a detailed understanding of the nature of pointer variables, you can begin to appreciate the need for the pointer type void. To review, the concept of a pointer is that it is a variable that contains the address of another variable. If you always knew how big a pointer was, you wouldn't have to determine the pointer type at compile time. You would therefore also be able to pass an address of any type to a function. The function could then cast the address to a pointer of the proper type (based on some other piece of information) and perform operations on the result. This process would enable you to create functions that operate on a number of different data types.

That is precisely the reason C++ introduced the void pointer type. When void is applied to a pointer, its meaning is different from its use to describe function argument lists and return values (which mean "nothing"). A void pointer means a pointer to any type of data. The following C++ program demonstrates this use of void pointers:

```
//
//   voidpt.cpp
//   A C++ program using void pointers
//   Copyright (c) Chris H. Pappas and William H. Murray, 1997
//

#include <iostream.h>
#define ISTRING_MAX 50

void voutput(void *pobject, char cflag);

void main( )
{
  int *pi;
  char *psz;
  float *pf;
  char cresponse,cnewline;

  cout << "Please enter the dynamic data type\n";
  cout << "    you would like to create.\n\n";
  cout << "Use (s)tring, (i)nt, or (f)loat ";
  cin >> cresponse;
    cin.get(cnewline);
      switch(cresponse) {
        case 's':
          psz=new char[ISTRING_MAX];
          cout << "\nPlease enter a string: ";
```

```
              cin.get(psz,ISTRING_MAX);
              voutput(psz,cresponse);
              break;
            case 'i':
              pi=new int;
              cout << "\nPlease enter an integer: ";
              cin >> *pi;
              voutput(pi,cresponse);
              break;
            case 'f':
              pf=new float;
              cout << "\nPlease enter a float: ";
              cin >> *pf; voutput(pf,cresponse);
              break;
            default:
              cout << "\n\n  Object type not implemented!";
      }
}
void voutput(void *pobject, char cflag)
{
  switch(cflag) {
    case 's':
      cout << "\nThe string read in:  " << (char *) pobject;
      delete pobject;
      break;
    case 'i':
      cout << "\nThe integer read in: "
           << *((int *) pobject);
      delete pobject;
      break;
    case 'f':
      cout << "\nThe float value read in: "
           << *((float *) pobject);
      delete pobject;
      break;
    }
}
```

The first statement of interest in the program is the voutput( ) function prototype. Notice that the function's first formal parameter, pobject, is of type void *, or a generic pointer. Moving down to the data declarations, you will find three pointer variable types: int *, char *, and float *. These will eventually be assigned valid pointer addresses to their respective memory cell types.

The action in the program begins with a prompt asking the user to enter the data type he or she would like to dynamically create. You may be wondering why the two separate input statements are used to handle the user's response. The first cin statement reads in the single-character response but leaves the \n linefeed hanging around. The second input statement, cin.get(cnewline), remedies this situation.

The switch statement takes the user's response and invokes the appropriate prompt and pointer initialization. The pointer initialization takes one of three forms:

```
psz=new char;
pi=new int;
pf=new float;
```

The following statement is used to input the character string, and in this example it limits the length of the string to ISTRING_MAX (50) characters.

```
cin.get(psz,ISTRING_MAX);
```

Since the cin.get( ) input statement expects a string pointer as its first parameter, there is no need to dereference the variable when the voutput( ) function is invoked:

```
voutput(psz,cresponse);
```

Things get a little quieter if the user wants to input an integer or a float. The last two case options are the same except for the prompt and the reference variable's type.

Notice how the three invocations of the function voutput( ) have different pointer types:

```
voutput(psz,cresponse);
voutput(pi,cresponse);
voutput(pf,cresponse);
```

Function voutput( ) accepts these parameters only because the matching formal parameter's type is void *. Remember, in order to use these pointers, you must first cast them to their appropriate pointer type. When using a string pointer with cout, you must first cast the pointer to type char *.

Just as creating integer and float dynamic variables was similar, printing their values is also similar. The only difference between the last two case statements is the string and the cast operator used.

While it is true that all dynamic variables pass into bit oblivion whenever a program terminates, each of the case options takes care of explicitly deleting the pointer variable. When and where your program creates and deletes dynamic storage is application dependent.

Pointers and Arrays—a Closer Look

The following sections include many example programs that deal with the topic of arrays and how they relate to pointers.

Strings (Arrays of Type char)

Many string operations in C/C++ are generally performed by using pointers and pointer arithmetic to reference character array elements. This is because character arrays or strings tend to be accessed in a strictly sequential manner. Remember, all strings in C/C++ are terminated by a null (\0). The following C++ program is a modification of a program used earlier in this chapter to print palindromes and illustrates the use of pointers with character arrays:

```
//
//   chrary.cpp
//   A C++ program that prints a character array backwards
//   using a character pointer and the decrement operator
//   Copyright (c) Chris H. Pappas and William H. Murray, 1997
//

#include <iostream.h>
#include <string.h>

void main( )
{
  char pszpalindrome[]="POOR DAN IN A DROOP";
  char *pc;

  pc=pszpalindrome+(strlen(pszpalindrome)-1);
  do {
    cout << *pc ;
    pc--;
  } while (pc >= pszpalindrome);
}
```

After the program declares and initializes the *pszpalindrome* palindrome, it creates a *pc* of type char *. Remember that the name of an array is in itself an address variable.

PROGRAMMING FOUNDATIONS

The body of the program begins by setting the *pc* to the address of the last character in the array. This requires a call to the function strlen( ), which calculates the length of the character array.

NOTE: *The strlen( ) function counts just the number of characters, excluding the null terminator \0.*

You were probably thinking that was the reason for subtracting the 1 from the function's returned value. This is not exactly true; the program has to take into consideration the fact that the first array character's address is at offset zero. Therefore, you want to increment the pointer variable's offset address to one less than the number of valid characters.

Once the pointer for the last valid array character has been calculated, the do-while loop is entered. The loop simply uses the pointer variable to point to the memory location of the character to be printed and prints it. It then calculates the next character's memory location and compares this value with the starting address of *pszpalindrome*. As long as the calculated value is >=, the loop iterates.

Arrays of Pointers

In C and C++, you are not restricted to making simple arrays and simple pointers. You can combine the two into a very useful construct—arrays of pointers. An *array of pointers* is an array whose elements are pointers to other objects. Those objects can themselves be pointers. This means you can have an array of pointers that point to other pointers.

The concept of an array of pointers to pointers is used extensively in the *argc* and *argv* command-line arguments for main( ) you were introduced to in Chapter 8. The following program finds the largest or smallest value entered on the command line. Command-line arguments can include numbers only, or they may be prefaced by a command selecting a choice for the smallest value entered (-s,-S) or the largest (-l,-L).

```
//
//   argcgv.cpp
//   A C++ program using an array of pointers to process
//   the command-line arguments argc, argv
//   Copyright (c) Chris H. Pappas and William H. Murray, 1997
//

#include <iostream.h>
#include <process.h>      // exit( )
#include <stdlib.h>       // atoi( )
```

```
#define IFIND_LARGEST 1
#define IFIND_SMALLEST 0

int main(int argc,char *argv[])
{
  char *psz;
  int ihow_many;
  int iwhich_extreme=0;
  int irange_boundary=32767;

  if(argc < 2) {
    cout << "\nYou need to enter an -S,-s,-L,-l"
         << " and at least one integer value";
    exit(1);
  }

  while(--argc > 0 && (*++argv)[0] == '-') {
    for(psz=argv[0]+1; *psz != '\0'; psz++) {
      switch(*psz) {
        case 's':
        case 'S':
          iwhich_extreme=IFIND_SMALLEST;
          irange_boundary=32767;
          break;
        case 'l':
        case 'L':
          iwhich_extreme=IFIND_LARGEST;
          irange_boundary=0;
          break;
        default:
          cout << "unknown argument "<< *psz << endl;
          exit(1);
      }
    }
  }

  if(argc==0) {
    cout << "Please enter at least one number\n";
    exit(1);
  }

  ihow_many=argc;
```

```
while(argc--) {
  int present_value;
  present_value=atoi(*(argv++));
  if(iwhich_extreme==IFIND_LARGEST && present_value >
     irange_boundary)
    irange_boundary=present_value;
  if(iwhich_extreme==IFIND_SMALLEST && present_value <
     irange_boundary)
    irange_boundary=present_value;
}

cout << "The ";
cout << ((iwhich_extreme) ? "largest" : "smallest");
cout << " of the " << ihow_many << " value(s) input is " <<
        irange_boundary << endl;

return(0);
}
```

Before looking at the source code, take a moment to familiarize yourself with the possible command combinations that can be used to invoke the program. The following list illustrates the possible command combinations:

```
10argcgv
10argcgv 98
10argcgv 98 21
10argcgv -s 98
10argcgv -S 98 21
10argcgv -l 14
10argcgv -L 14 67
```

Looking at the main( ) program, you will see the formal parameters *argc* and *argv* that you were introduced to in Chapter 8. To review, *argc* is an integer value containing the number of separate items, or arguments, that appeared on the command line. The variable *argv* refers to an array of pointers to character strings.

NOTE: *argv is not a constant. It is a variable whose value can be altered, a key point to remember when viewing how* argv *is used next. The first element of the array,* argv[0], *is a pointer to a string of characters that contains the program name.*

Moving down the code to the first if statement, you find a test to determine if the value of *argc* is less than 2. If this test evaluates to TRUE, it means that the user has typed just the name of the program *extreme* without any switches. Since this action would indicate that the user does not know the switch and value options, the program will prompt the user at this point with the valid options and then exit( ).

The while loop test condition evaluates from left to right, beginning with the decrement of *argc*. If *argc* is still greater than zero, the right side of the logical expression will be examined.

The right side of the logical expression first increments the array pointer *argv* past the first pointer entry (++*argv*), skipping the program's name, so that it now points to the second array entry. Once the pointer has been incremented, it is then used to point (*++*argv*) to the zeroth offset ((*++*argv*)[0]) of the first character of the string pointed to. Obtaining this character, if it is a - symbol, the program diagnoses that the second program command was a possible switch—for example, -s or -L.

The for loop initialization begins by taking the current pointer address of *argv*, which was just incremented in the line above to point to the second pointer in the array. Since *argv*'s second element is a pointer to a character string, the pointer can be subscripted (*argv*[0]). The complete expression, *argv*[0]+1, points to the second character of the second string pointed to by the current address stored in *argv*. This second character is the one past the command switch symbol -. Once the program calculates this character's address, it stores it in the variable *psz*. The for loop repeats while the character pointed to by *psz* is not the null terminator \0.

The program continues by analyzing the switch to see if the user wants to obtain the smallest or largest of the values entered. Based on the switch, the appropriate constant is assigned to the *iwhich_extreme*. Each case statement also takes care of initializing the variable *irange_boundary* to an appropriate value for the comparisons that follow. Should the user enter an unrecognized switch—for example, -d—the default case will take care of printing an appropriate message.

The second if statement now checks to see if *argc* has been decremented to zero. An appropriate message is printed if the switches have been examined on the command line and there are no values left to process. If so, the program terminates with an exit code of decimal 1.

A successful skipping of this if test means there are now values from the command line that need to be examined. Since the program will now decrement *argc*, the variable *ihow_many* is assigned *argc*'s current value.

The while loop continues while there are at least two values to compare. The while loop needs to be entered only if there is more than one value to be compared, since the cout statement following the while loop is capable of handling a command line with a single value.

The function atoi( ) converts each of the remaining arguments into an integer and stores the result in the variable *present_value*. Remember, *argv*++ needed to be incremented first so that it points to the first value to be compared. Also, the while loop test condition had already decremented the pointer to make certain the loop wasn't entered with only a single command value.

The last two if statements take care of updating the variable *irange_boundary* based on the user's desire to find either the smallest or largest of all values entered. Finally, the results of the program are printed by using an interesting combination of string literals and the conditional operator.

More on Pointers to Pointers

The next program demonstrates the use of pointer variables that point to other pointers. It is included at this point in the chapter instead of in the section describing pointers to pointers because the program uses dynamic memory allocation. You may want to refer back to the general discussion of pointers to pointers before looking at the program.

```
/*
 *   dblptr.c
 *   A C program using pointer variables with double
 *   indirection
 *   Copyright (c) Chris H. Pappas and William H. Murray, 1997
 */

#include <stdio.h>
#include <stdlib.h>

#define IMAXELEMENTS 3

void voutput(int **ppiresult_a, int **ppiresult_b,
             int **ppiresult_c);
void vassign(int *pivirtual_array[],int *pinewblock);

void main( )
{
  int **ppiresult_a, **ppiresult_b, **ppiresult_c;
  int *pivirtual_array[IMAXELEMENTS];
  int *pinewblock, *pioldblock;

  ppiresult_a=&pivirtual_array[0];
  ppiresult_b=&pivirtual_array[1];
  ppiresult_c=&pivirtual_array[2];

  pinewblock=(int *)malloc(IMAXELEMENTS * sizeof(int));
  pioldblock=pinewblock;
```

```
    vassign(pivirtual_array,pinewblock);

    **ppiresult_a=7;
    **ppiresult_b=10;
    **ppiresult_c=15;

    voutput(ppiresult_a,ppiresult_b,ppiresult_c);

    pinewblock=(int *)malloc(IMAXELEMENTS * sizeof(int));

    *pinewblock=**ppiresult_a;
    *(pinewblock+1)=**ppiresult_b;
    *(pinewblock+2)=**ppiresult_c;

    free(pioldblock);

    vassign(pivirtual_array,pinewblock);

    voutput(ppiresult_a,ppiresult_b,ppiresult_c);
}

void vassign(int *pivirtual_array[],int *pinewblock)
{
  pivirtual_array[0]=pinewblock;
  pivirtual_array[1]=pinewblock+1;
  pivirtual_array[2]=pinewblock+2;
}

void voutput(int **ppiresult_a, int **ppiresult_b, int
**ppiresult_c)
{
  printf("%d\n",**ppiresult_a);
  printf("%d\n",**ppiresult_b);
  printf("%d\n",**ppiresult_c);
}
```

The program is designed so that it highlights the concept of a pointer variable (*ppiresult_a*, *ppiresult_b*, and *ppiresult_c*), pointing to a constant address (*&pivirtual_array[0]*, *&pivirtual_array[1]*, and *&pivirtual_array[2]*), whose pointer address contents can dynamically change.

Look at the data declarations in main( ). *ppiresult_a, ppiresult_b,* and *ppiresult_c* have been defined as pointers to pointers that point to integers. Let's take this slowly, looking at the various syntax combinations:

```
ppiresult_a
*ppiresult_a
**ppiresult_a
```

The first syntax references the address stored in the pointer variable *ppiresult_a.* The second syntax references the pointer address pointed to by the address in *ppiresult_a.* The last syntax references the integer that is pointed to by the pointer address pointed to by *ppiresult_a.* Make certain you do not proceed any further until you understand these three different references.

The three variables *ppiresult_a, ppiresult_b,* and *ppiresult_c* have all been defined as pointers to pointers that point to integers int **. The variable *pivirtual_array* has been defined to be an array of integer pointers int *, of size IMAXELEMENTS. The last two variables, *pinewblock* and *pioldblock,* are similar to the variable *pivitrual_array,* except they are single variables that point to integers int *. Figure 10-17 shows what these six variables look like after their storage has been allocated and, in particular, after *ppiresult_a, ppiresult_b,* and *ppiresult_c* have been assigned the address of their respective elements in the *pivirtual_array.*

It is this array that is going to hold the addresses of the dynamically changing memory cell addresses. Something similar actually happens in a true multitasking environment. Your program thinks it has the actual physical address of a variable stored in memory, when what it really has is a fixed address to an array of pointers that in turn point to the current physical address of the data item in memory. When the multitasking environment needs to conserve memory by moving your data objects, it simply moves their storage locations and updates the array of pointers. The variables in your program, however, are still pointing to the same physical address, albeit not the physical address of the data but of the array of pointers.

To understand how this operates, pay particular attention to the fact that the physical addresses stored in the pointer variables *ppiresult_a, ppiresult_b,* and *ppiresult_c* never change once they are assigned.

Figure 10-18 illustrates what has happened to the variables after the dynamic array *pinewblock* has been allocated and *pioldblock* has been initialized to the same address of the new array. Most important, notice how the physical addresses of *pinewblock's* individual elements have been assigned to their respective counterparts in *pivirtual_array.*

The pointer assignments were all accomplished by the vassign( ) function. vassign( ) was passed the *pivirtual_array* (call-by-value) and the address of the recently allocated dynamic memory block in the variable *pinewblock.* The function takes care of assigning the addresses of the dynamically allocated memory cells to each element of the

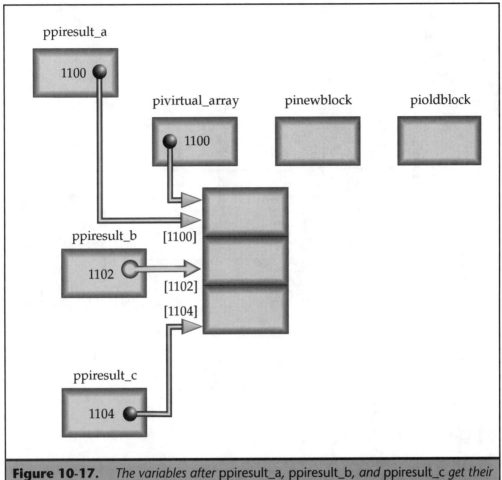

Figure 10-17. *The variables after* ppiresult_a, ppiresult_b, *and* ppiresult_c *get their initial addresses*

pivirtual_array. Since the array was passed call-by-value, the changes are effective in the main( ).

At this point, if you were to use the debugger to print out *ppiresult_a,* you would see ACC8 (the address of *pivirtual_array*'s first element), and **ppiresult_a* would print 1630 (or the contents of the address pointed to). You would encounter a similar dump for the other two pointer variables, *ppiresult_b* and *ppiresult_c.*

Figure 10-19 shows the assignment of three integer values to the physical memory locations. Notice the syntax to accomplish this:

```
**ppiresult_a=7;
**ppiresult_b=10;
**ppiresult_c=15;
```

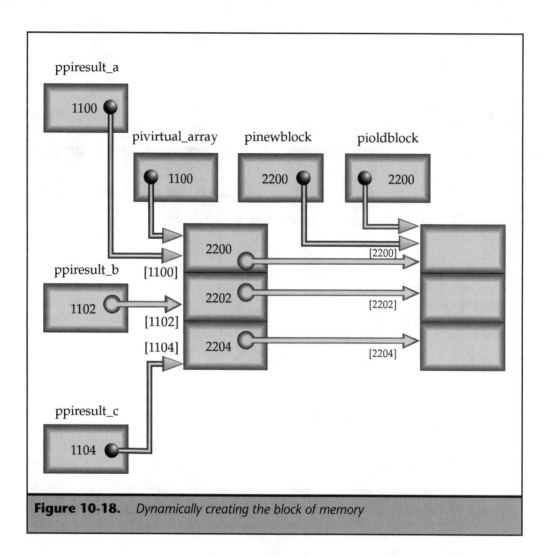

Figure 10-18. *Dynamically creating the block of memory*

At this point, the program prints out the values 7, 10, and 15 by calling the function voutput( ). Notice that the function has been defined as receiving three int ** variables. Notice that the actual parameter list does *not* need to precede the variables with the double indirection operator ** since that is their type by declaration.

As shown in Figure 10-20, the situation has become very interesting. A new block of dynamic memory has been allocated with the malloc( ) function, with its new physical memory address stored in the pointer variable *pinewblock*. *pioldblock* still points to the previously allocated block of dynamic memory. Using the incomplete analogy to a multitasking environment, the figure would illustrate the operating system's desire to physically move the data objects' memory locations.

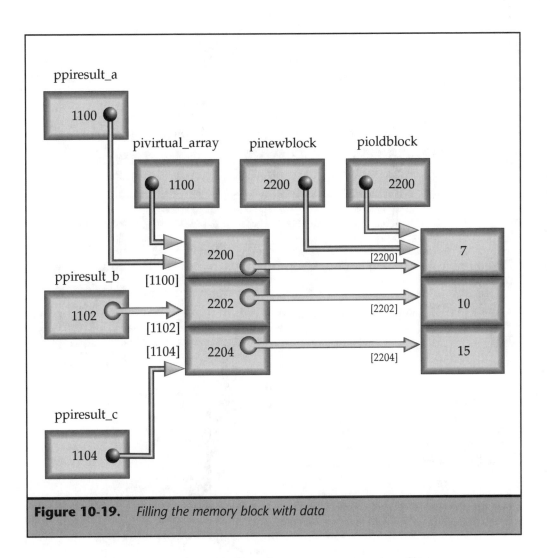

Figure 10-19. *Filling the memory block with data*

Figure 10-20 also shows that the data objects themselves were copied into the new memory locations. The program accomplished this with the following three lines of code:

```
*pinewblock=**ppiresult_a;
*(pinewblock+1)=**ppiresult_b;
*(pinewblock+2)=**ppiresult_c;
```

Since the pointer variable *pinewblock* holds the address to the first element of the dynamic block, its address is dereferenced (*), pointing to the memory cell itself, and

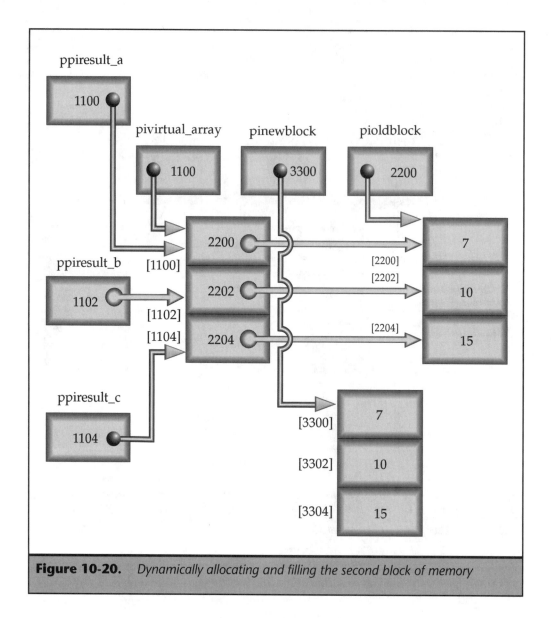

Figure 10-20. *Dynamically allocating and filling the second block of memory*

the 7 is stored there. Using a little pointer arithmetic, the other two memory cells are accessed by incrementing the pointer. The parentheses were necessary so that the pointer address was incremented *before* the dereference operator * was applied.

Figure 10-21 shows what happens when the function free( ) is called and the function vassign( ) is called to link the new physical address of the dynamically allocated memory block to the *pivirtual_array* pointer address elements.

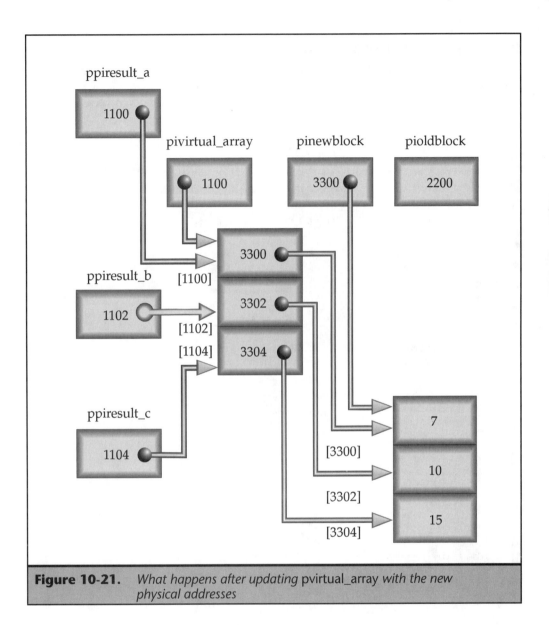

Figure 10-21. *What happens after updating* pvirtual_array *with the new physical addresses*

The most important fact to notice in this last figure is that the actual physical address of the three pointer variables *ppiresult_a*, *ppiresult_b*, and *ppiresult_c* has not changed. Therefore, when the program prints the values pointed to **ppiresult_a* and so on, you still see the values 7, 10, and 15, even though their *physical* location in memory has changed.

Arrays of String Pointers

One of the easiest ways to keep track of an array of strings is to define an array of pointers to strings. This is much simpler than defining a two-dimensional array of characters. The following program uses an array of string pointers to keep track of three function error messages:

```c
/*
 *    aofptr.c
 *    A C program that demonstrates how to define and use
 *    arrays of pointers.
 *    Copyright Chris H. Pappas and William H. Murray, 1997
 */

#include <ctype.h>
#include <stdio.h>

#define INUMBER_OF_ERRORS 3

char *pszarray[INUMBER_OF_ERRORS] =
          {
             "\nFile not available.\n",
             "\nNot an alpha character.\n",
             "\nValue not between 1 and 10.\n"
          };

FILE *fopen_a_file(char *psz);
char cget_a_char(void);
int iget_an_integer(void);

FILE *pfa_file;

void main( )
{
  char cvalue;
  int ivalue;

  fopen_a_file("input.dat");
  cvalue = cget_a_char( );
  ivalue = iget_an_integer( );

}
```

```
FILE *fopen_a_file(char *psz)
{
  const ifopen_a_file_error = 0;

  pfa_file = fopen(psz,"r");
  if(!pfa_file)
    printf("%s",pszarray[ifopen_a_file_error]);
  return(pfa_file);
}

char cget_a_char(void)
{
  char cvalue;
  const icget_a_char_error = 1;

  printf("\nEnter a character: ");
  scanf("%c",&cvalue);
  if(!isalpha(cvalue))
    printf("%s",pszarray[icget_a_char_error]);
  return(cvalue);
}

int iget_an_integer(void)
{
  int ivalue;
  const iiget_an_integer = 2;
  printf("\nEnter an integer between 1 and 10: ");
  scanf("%d",&ivalue);
  if( (ivalue < 1) || (ivalue > 10) )
    printf("%s",pszarray[iiget_an_integer]);
  return(ivalue);
}
```

The *pszarray* is initialized outside all function declarations. This gives it a global lifetime. For large programs, an array of this nature could be saved in a separate source file dedicated to maintaining all error message control. Notice that each function, fopen_a_file( ), cget_a_char( ), and iget_an_integer( ), takes care of defining its own constant index into the array. This combination of an error message array and unique function index makes for a very modular solution to error exception handling. If a project requires the creation of a new function, the new piece of code selects a vacant index value and adds one error condition to *pszarray*. The efficiency of this approach allows each code segment to quickly update the entire application to its peculiar I/O requirements without having to worry about an elaborate error detection/alert mechanism.

The C++ Reference Type

C++ provides a form of call-by-reference that is even easier to use than pointers. First, let's examine the use of reference variables in C++. As with C, C++ enables you to declare regular variables or pointer variables. In the first case, memory is actually allocated for the data object; in the second case, a memory location is set aside to hold an address for an object that will be allocated at another time. C++ has a third kind of declaration, the reference type. Like a pointer variable, a *reference variable* refers to another variable location, but like a regular variable, it requires no special dereferencing operators. The syntax for a reference variable is straightforward:

```
int iresult_a=5;
int& riresult_a=iresult_a; // valid
int& riresult_b;           // invalid: uninitialized
```

This example sets up the reference variable *riresult_a* and assigns it to the existing variable *iresult_a*. At this point, the referenced location has two names associated with it—*iresult_a* and *riresult_a.* Because both variables point to the same location in memory, they are, in fact, the same variable. Any assignment made to *riresult_a* is reflected through *iresult_a;* the inverse is also true, and changes to *iresult_a* occur through any access to *riresult_a.* Therefore, with the reference data type, you can create what is sometimes referred to as an *alias* for a variable.

The reference type has a restriction that serves to distinguish it from pointer variables, which, after all, do something very similar. The value of the reference type must be set at declaration, and it cannot be changed during the run of the program. After you initialize this type in the declaration, it always refers to the same memory location. Therefore, any assignments you make to a reference variable change only the data in memory, not the address of the variable itself. In other words, you can think of a reference variable as a pointer to a constant location.

For example, using the preceding declarations, the following statement doubles the contents of *iresult_a* by multiplying 5 * 2:

```
riresult_a *= 2;
```

The next statement assigns *icopy_value* (assuming it is of type int) a copy of the value associated with *riresult_a*:

```
icopy_value = riresult_a;
```

The next statement is also legal when using reference types:

int *piresult_a = &riresult_a;

This statement assigns the address of *riresult_a* to the int * variable *piresult_a*.

The primary use of a reference type is as an argument or a return type of a function, especially when applied to user-defined class types (see Chapter 15).

Functions Returning Addresses

When you return an address from a function using either a pointer variable or a reference type, you are giving the user a memory address. The user can read the value at the address, and if you haven't declared the pointer type to be const, the user can always write the value. By returning an address, you are giving the user permission to read and, for non-const pointer types, write to private data. This is a significant design decision. See if you can anticipate what will happen in this next program:

```
//
//  refvar.cpp
//  A C++ program showing what NOT to do with address
//  variables
//  Copyright (c) Chris H. Pappas and William H. Murray, 1997
//

#include <iostream.h>

int *ifirst_function(void);
int *isecond_function(void);

void main( )
{
  int *pi=ifirst_function( );
  isecond_function( );
  cout << "Correct value? " << *pi;
}

int *ifirst_function(void)
{
```

```
    int ilocal_to_first=11;
    return &ilocal_to_first;
}
int *isecond_function(void)
{
    int ilocal_to_second=44;
    return &ilocal_to_second;
}
```

Using the Integrated Debugger

To examine the operation of this C++ code while it is actually working, you can use the integrated debugger. Use the Trace window to keep an eye on the variable *pi*.

What has happened? When the ifirst_function( ) is called, local space is allocated on the stack for the variable *ilocal_to_first*, and the value 11 is stored in it. At this point the ifirst_function( ) returns the address of this *local* variable (very bad news). The second statement in the main program invokes the isecond_function( ). isecond_function( ) in turn allocates local space for *ilocal_to_second* and assigns it a value of 44. So how does the printf statement print a value of 44 when it was passed the address of *ilocal_to_first* when ifirst_function( ) was invoked?

What happened was this. When the address of the *itemporary* local variable *ilocal_to_first* was assigned to *pi* by ifirst_function( ), the address to the *itemporary* location was retained even after *ilocal_to_first* went out of scope. When b was invoked, it also needed local storage. Since *ilocal_to_first* was gone, *ilocal_to_second* was given the same storage location as its predecessor. With *pi* hanging onto this same busy memory cell, you can see why printing the value it now points to yields a 44. Extreme care must be taken not to return the addresses of local variables.

When Should You Use Reference Types?

To review, there are four main reasons for using C++ reference types:

- They lend themselves to more readable code by allowing you to ignore details of how a parameter is passed.

- They put the responsibility for argument passing on the programmer who writes the functions, not on the individual who uses them.

- They are a necessary counterpart to operator overloading.
- They are also used with passing classes to functions so constructors and destructors are not called.

These concepts are described in greater detail in Chapter 16.

Chapter 11

Complete I/O in C

Many commonly used high-level languages have restrictive input and output mechanisms. As a result, programmers generate convoluted algorithms to perform sophisticated data retrieval and display. This is not the case with C, which has a very complete I/O (input/output) function library, although historically I/O was not even part of the C language itself. However, if you have used only simple I/O statements like Pascal's readln and writeln statements, you're in for a surprise. This chapter discusses the more than 20 different ways to perform I/O in C.

The standard C library I/O routines allow you to read and write data to files and devices. However, the C language itself does not include any predefined file structures. C treats all data as a sequence of bytes. There are three basic types of I/O functions: stream, console and port, and low-level.

All of the stream I/O functions treat a data file or data items as a stream of individual characters. By selecting the appropriate stream function, your application can process data in any size or format required, from single characters to large, complicated data structures.

Technically, when a program opens a file for I/O using the stream functions, the opened file is associated with a structure of type FILE (predefined in STDIO.H) that contains basic information about the file. Once the stream is opened, a pointer to the file structure is returned. The file pointer, sometimes called the *stream pointer* or the *stream,* is used to refer to the file for all subsequent I/O.

All stream I/O functions provide buffered, formatted, or unformatted input and output. A *buffered stream* provides an intermediate storage location for all information that is input from the stream and output that is being sent to the stream.

Since disk I/O is such a time-consuming operation, stream buffering streamlines the application. Instead of inputting stream data one character at a time or one structure's worth at a time, stream I/O functions access data a block at a time. As the application needs to process the input, it merely accesses the buffer, a much less time-consuming process. When the buffer is empty, another disk block access is made.

The reverse situation holds true for *stream output.* Instead of all data being physically output at the time the output statement is executed, all output data is put into the buffer. When the buffer is full, the data is written to the disk.

Most high-level languages have a problem with buffered I/O that you need to take into consideration. For example, if your program has executed several output statements that do not fill the output buffer, causing it to dump to the disk, that information is lost when your program terminates.

The solution usually involves making a call to an appropriate function to flush the buffer. Unlike other high-level languages, C solves this problem with buffered I/O by automatically flushing the buffer's contents whenever the program terminates. Of course, a well-written application should not rely on these automatic features but should always explicitly detail every action the program is to take. One additional note: when you use stream I/O, if the application terminates abnormally, the output buffers may not be flushed, resulting in loss of data.

Similar in function are the *console and port I/O routines,* which can be seen as an extension of the stream routines. They allow you to read or write to a terminal (console) or an input/output port (such as a printer port). The port I/O functions simply read and write data in bytes. Console I/O functions provide several additional options. For example, you can detect whether a character has been typed at the console and whether or not the characters entered are echoed to the screen as they are read.

The last type of input and output is called *low-level I/O*. None of the low-level I/O functions perform any buffering and formatting; instead, they invoke the operating system's input and output capabilities directly. These routines let you access files and peripheral devices at a more basic level than the stream functions. Files opened in this mode return a *file handle*. This handle is an integer value that is used to refer to the file in subsequent operations.

In general, it is very bad practice to mix stream I/O functions with low-level routines. Since stream functions are buffered and low-level functions are not, attempting to access the same file or device by two different methods leads to confusion and eventual loss of data in the buffers. Therefore, either stream or low-level functions should be used exclusively on a given file.

Stream Functions

To use the stream functions, your application must include the file STDIO.H. This file contains definitions for constants, types, and structures used in the stream functions and contains function prototypes and macro definitions for the stream routines.

Many of the constants predefined in STDIO.H can be useful in your application. For example, *EOF* is defined to be the value returned by input functions at end-of-file, and *NULL* is the null pointer. Also, *FILE* defines the structure used to maintain information about a stream, and *BUFSIZ* defines the default size, in bytes, of the stream buffers.

Opening Streams

You can use one of three functions to open a stream before input and output can be performed on the stream: fopen( ), fdopen( ), or freopen( ). The file mode and form are set at the time the stream is opened. The stream file can be opened for reading, writing, or both and can be opened in either text or binary mode.

All three functions return a file pointer, which is used to refer to the stream. For example, if your program contains the following line, you can use the file pointer variable *pfinfile* to refer to the stream:

```
pfinfile = fopen("input.dat","r");
```

When your application begins execution, five streams are automatically opened. These streams are the standard input (stdin), standard output (stdout), standard error (stderr), standard printer (stdprn), and standard auxiliary (stdaux).

By default, the standard input, standard output, and standard error refer to the user's console. This means that whenever a program expects input from the standard input, it receives that input from the console. Likewise, a program that writes to the standard output prints its data to the console. Any error messages that are generated by the library routines are sent to the standard error stream, meaning that error messages appear on the user's console. The standard auxiliary and standard print streams usually refer to an auxiliary port and a printer, respectively.

You can use the five file pointers in any function that requires a stream pointer as an argument. Some functions, such as getchar( ) and putchar( ), are designed to use stdin or stdout automatically. Since the pointers stdin, stdout, stderr, stdprn, and stdaux are constants, not variables, do not try to reassign them to a new stream pointer value.

Input and Output Redirection

Modern operating systems consider the keyboard and video display as files. This is reasonable since the system can read from the keyboard just as it can read from a disk or tape file. Similarly, the system can write to the video display just as it can write to a disk or tape file.

Suppose your application reads from the keyboard and outputs to the video display. Now suppose you want the input to come from a file called SAMPLE.DAT. You can use the same application if you tell the system to replace input from the keyboard, considered now as a file, with input from another file, namely the file SAMPLE.DAT. The process of changing the standard input or standard output is called *input redirection* or *output redirection.*

Input and output redirection in MS-DOS are effortless. You use < to redirect the input and > to redirect the output. Suppose the executable version of your application is called REDIRECT. The following system-level command will run the program REDIRECT and use the file SAMPLE.DAT as input instead of the keyboard:

```
redirect < sample.dat
```

The next statement will redirect both the input (SAMPLE.DAT) and the output (SAMPLE.BAK):

```
redirect < sample.dat > sample.bak
```

This last example will redirect the output (SAMPLE.BAK) only:

```
redirect > sample.bak
```

Note, however, that the standard error file STDERR cannot be redirected.

There are two techniques for managing the association between a standard filename and a physical file or device: redirection and piping. *Piping* is the technique of directly connecting the standard output of one program to the standard input of another. The control and invocation of redirection and piping normally occur outside the program, which is exactly the intent since the program itself need not care where the data is really coming from or going to.

The way to connect the standard output from one program to the standard input of another program is to pipe them together by using the vertical bar symbol, |. Therefore, to connect the standard output of the program PROCESS1 to the standard input of the program PROCESS2, you would type

```
process1 | process2
```

The operating system handles all the details of physically getting the output from PROCESS1 to the input of PROCESS2.

Altering the Stream Buffer

All files opened using the stream functions (stdin( ), stdout( ), and stdprn( )) are buffered by default except for the preopened streams stderr and stdaux. The two streams stderr and stdaux are unbuffered by default unless they are used in either the printf( ) or scanf( ) family of functions. In this case, they are assigned a temporary buffer. You can buffer stderr and stdaux with setbuf( ) or setvbuf( ). The stdin, stdout, and stdprn streams are flushed automatically whenever they are full.

You can use the two functions setbuf( ) and setvbuf( ) to make a buffered stream unbuffered, or you can use them to associate a buffer with an unbuffered stream. Note that buffers allocated by the system are not accessible to the user, but buffers allocated with the functions setbuf( ) and setvbuf( ) are named by the user and can be manipulated as if they were variables. These user-defined stream buffers are very useful for checking input and output before any system-generated error conditions.

You can define a buffer to be of any size; if you use the function setbuf( ), the size is set by the constant *BUFSIZ* defined in STDIO.H. The syntax for setbuf( ) looks like this:

void setbuf(FILE *stream, char *buffer);

The following example program uses setbuf( ) and *BUFSIZ* to define and attach a buffer to stderr. A buffered stderr gives an application greater control over error-exception handling. Using the integrated debugger, single-step the application exactly as you see it.

```
/*
 *   setbf.c
 *   A C program demonstrating how to define and attach
 *   a buffer to the unbuffered stderr.
 *   Copyright (c) Chris H. Pappas and William H. Murray, 1997
 */

#include <stdio.h>
char cmyoutputbuffer[BUFSIZ];

void main(void)
{
   /* associate a buffer with the unbuffered output stream */
   setbuf(stderr, cmyoutputbuffer); /* line to comment out */

   /* insert into the output stream buffer */
   fputs("Sample output inserted into the\n",stderr);
   fputs("output stream buffer.\n",stderr);

   /* dump the output stream buffer */
   fflush(stderr);
}
```

Try running the program a second time with the setbuf( ) statement commented out. This will prevent the program from associating a buffer with stderr. When you ran the program, did you see the difference? Without a buffered stderr, the integrated debugger outputs each fputs( ) statement as soon as the line is executed.

The next application uses the function setvbuf( ). The syntax for setvbuf( ) looks like this:

int setvbuf(FILE *stream, char *buffer, int *buftype*, size_t *bufsize*);

Here, the program determines the size of the buffer instead of using *BUFSIZ* defined in STDIO.H:

```
/*
 *   setvbuf.c
 *   A C program demonstrating how to use setvbuf( )
 *   Copyright (c) Chris H. Pappas and William H. Murray, 1997
```

```
*/

#include <stdio.h>
#define MYBUFSIZ 512

void main(void)
{
    char ichar, cmybuffer[MYBUFSIZ];
    FILE *pfinfile, *pfoutfile;

    pfinfile = fopen("sample.in", "r");
    pfoutfile = fopen("sample.out", "w");

    if (setvbuf(pfinfile, cmybuffer, _IOFBF, MYBUFSIZ) != 0)
        printf("pfinfile buffer allocation error\n");
    else
        printf("pfinfile buffer created\n");

    if (setvbuf(pfoutfile, NULL, _IOLBF, 132) != 0)
        printf("pfoutfile buffer allocation error\n");
    else
        printf("pfoutfile buffer created\n");

    while(fscanf(pfinfile,"%c",&ichar) != EOF)
        fprintf(pfoutfile,"%c",ichar);

    fclose(pfinfile);
    fclose(pfoutfile);
}
```

The program creates a user-accessible buffer pointed to by *pfinfile* and a malloc( )-allocated buffer pointed to by *pfoutfile*. This last buffer is defined as *buftype,* _IOLBF, or line buffered. Other options defined in STDIO.H include _IOFBF, for fully buffered, and _IONBF, for no buffer.

Remember, both setbuf( ) and setvbuf( ) cause the user-defined *buffer* to be used for I/O buffering, instead of an automatically allocated buffer. With setbuf( ), if the *buffer* argument is set to null, I/O will be unbuffered. Otherwise, it will be fully buffered.

With setvbuf( ), if the *buffer* argument is null, a buffer will be allocated using malloc( ). The setvbuf( ) *buffer* will use the *bufsize* argument as the amount allocated and automatically free the memory on close.

Closing Streams

The two functions fclose( ) and fcloseall( ) close a stream or streams, respectively. The fclose( ) function closes a single file, while fcloseall( ) closes all open streams except stdin, stdout, stderr, stdprn, and stdaux. However, if your program does not explicitly close a stream, the stream is automatically closed when the application terminates. Since the number of streams that can be open at a given time is limited, it is a good practice to close a stream when you are finished with it.

Low-Level Input and Output in C

Table 11-1 lists the most commonly used low-level input and output functions used by an application.

Low-level input and output calls do not buffer or format data. Files opened by low-level calls are referenced by a file handle (an integer value used by the operating system to refer to the file). You use the open( ) function to open files. You can use the sopen( ) macro to open a file with file-sharing attributes.

Low-level functions are different from their stream counterparts because they do not require the inclusion of the STDIO.H header file. However, some common constants that are predefined in STDIO.H, such as *EOF* and *NULL*, may be useful. Declarations for the low-level functions are given in the IO.H header file.

This second disk-file I/O system was originally created under the UNIX operating system. Because the ANSI C standard committee has elected not to standardize this low-level, UNIX-like, unbuffered I/O system, it cannot be recommended for future use. Instead, the standardized buffered I/O system described throughout this chapter is recommended for all new projects.

Function	Definition
close( )	Closes a disk file
lseek( )	Seeks to the specified byte in a file
open( )	Opens a disk file
read( )	Reads a buffer of data
unlink( )	Removes a file from the directory
write( )	Writes a buffer of data

Table 11-1. *Commonly Used Low-Level Input and Output Functions*

Character Input and Output

There are certain character input and output functions defined in the ANSI C standard that are supplied with all C compilers. These functions provide standard input and output and are considered to be high-level routines (as opposed to low-level routines, which access the machine hardware more directly). I/O in C is implemented through vendor-supplied functions rather than keywords defined as part of the language.

Using getc( ), putc( ), fgetc( ), and fputc( )

The most basic of all I/O functions are those that input and output one character. The getc( ) function inputs one character from a specified file stream, like this:

```
int ic;
ic = getc(stdin);
```

The input character is passed back in the name of the function getc( ) and then assigns the returned value to *ic*. By the way, if you are wondering why *ic* isn't of type char, it is because the function getc( ) has been prototyped to return an int type. This is necessary because of the possible system-dependent size of the end-of-file marker, which might not fit in a single char byte size.

Function getc( ) converts the integer into an unsigned character. This use of an unsigned character preserved as an integer guarantees that the ASCII values above 127 are not represented as negative values. Therefore, negative values can be used to represent unusual situations like errors and the end of the input file. For example, the end-of-file has traditionally been represented by -1, although the ANSI C standard states only that the constant *EOF* represent some negative value.

Because an integer value is returned by getc( ), the data item that inputs the value from getc( ) must also be defined as an integer. While it may seem odd to be using an integer in a character function, the C language actually makes very little distinction between characters and integers. If a character is provided when an integer is needed, the character will be converted to an integer.

The complement to the getc( ) function is putc( ). The putc( ) function outputs one character to the file stream represented by the specified file pointer. To send the same character that was just input to the standard output, use the following statement:

```
putc(ic,stdout);
```

The getc( ) function is normally buffered, which means that when a request for a character is made by the application, control is not returned to the program until a carriage return is entered into the standard input file stream. All the characters entered before the carriage return are held in a buffer and delivered to the program one at a time. The application invokes the getc( ) function repeatedly until the buffer has been exhausted. After the carriage return has been sent to the program by getc( ), the next request for a character results in more characters accumulating in the buffer until a carriage return is again entered. This means that you cannot use the getc( ) function for one-key input techniques that do not require pressing the carriage return.

One final note: getc( ) and putc( ) are actually implemented as macros rather than as true functions. The functions fgetc( ) and fputc( ) are identical to their macro getc( ) and putc( ) counterparts.

Using getchar( ), putchar( ), fgetchar( ), and fputchar( )

The two macros getchar( ) and putchar( ) are actually specific implementations of the getc( ) and putc( ) macros, respectively. They are always associated with standard input (stdin) and standard output (stdout). The only way to use them on other file streams is to redirect either standard input or standard output from within the program.

The same two coded examples used earlier could be rewritten by using these two functions:

```
int ic;
ic = getchar( );
```

and

```
putchar(ic);
```

Like getc( ) and putc( ), getchar( ) and putchar( ) are implemented as macros. The function putchar( ) has been written to return an *EOF* value whenever an error condition occurs. The following code can be used to check for an *output* error condition. Because of the check for *EOF* on output, it tends to be a bit confusing, although it is technically correct.

```
if(putchar(ic) == EOF)
   printf("An error has occurred writing to stdout");
```

Both fgetchar( ) and fputchar( ) are the function equivalents of their macro getchar( ) and putchar( ) counterparts.

Using getch( ) and putch( )

Both getch( ) and putch( ) are true functions, but they do not fall under the ANSI C standard because they are low-level functions that interface closely with the hardware. For PC's, these functions do not use buffering, which means that they immediately input a character typed at the keyboard. They can be redirected, however, so they are not associated exclusively with the keyboard.

You can use the functions getch( ) and putch( ) exactly like getchar( ) and putchar( ). Usually, a program running on a PC will use getch( ) to trap keystrokes ignored by getchar( )—for example, PGUP, PGDN, HOME, and END. The function getchar( ) sees a character entered from the keyboard as soon as the key is pressed; a carriage return is not needed to send the character to the program. This ability allows the function getch( ) to provide a one-key technique that is not available with getc( ) or getchar( ).

On a PC, the function getch( ) operates very differently from getc( ) and getchar( ). This is partly due to the fact that the PC can easily determine when an individual key on the keyboard has been pressed. Other systems, such as the DEC and VAX C, do not allow the hardware to trap individual keystrokes. These systems typically echo the input character and require the pressing of a carriage return, with the carriage return character not seen by the program unless no other characters have been entered. Under such circumstances, the carriage return returns a null character or a decimal zero. Additionally, the function keys are not available, and if they are pressed, they produce unreliable results.

String Input and Output

In many applications, it is more natural to handle input and output in larger pieces than characters. For example, a file of boat salesmen may contain one record per line, with each record consisting of four fields: salesman's name, base pay, commission, and number of boats sold, with white space separating the fields. It would be very tedious to use character I/O.

Using gets( ), puts( ), fgets( ), and fputs( )

Because of the organization of the file, it would be better to treat each record as a single character string and read or write it as a unit. The function fgets( ), which reads whole strings rather than single characters, is suited to this task. In addition to the function fgets( ) and its inverse fputs( ), there are also the macro counterparts gets( ) and puts( ).

The function fgets( ) expects three arguments: the address of an array in which to store the character string, the maximum number of characters to store, and a pointer to a file to read. The function will read characters into the array until the number of characters read in is one less than the size specified, all of the characters up to and including the next newline character have been read, or the end-of-file is reached, whichever comes first.

If fgets( ) reads in a newline, the newline will be stored in the array. If at least one character was read, the function will automatically append the null string terminator \0. Suppose the file SALESMAN.DAT looks like this:

```
Pat Pharr 32767 0.15 30
Beth Mollen 35000 0.12 23
Gary Kohut 40000 0.15 40
```

Assuming a maximum record length of 40 characters including the newline, the following program will read the records from the file and write them to the standard output:

```c
/*
 *    fgets.c
 *    A C program that demonstrates how to read
 *    in whole records using fgets and prints
 *    them out to stdout using fputs.
 *    Copyright (c) Chris H. Pappas and William H. Murray, 1997
 */

#include <stdio.h>

#define INULL_CHAR 1
#define IMAX_REC_SIZE 40

void main( )
{
  FILE *pfinfile;
  char crecord[IMAX_REC_SIZE + INULL_CHAR];

  pfinfile=fopen("a:\\salesman.dat", "r");
  while(fgets(crecord,IMAX_REC_SIZE +INULL_CHAR,pfinfile) != NULL)
    fputs(crecord,stdout);
  fclose(pfinfile);
}
```

Because the maximum record size is 40, you must reserve 41 cells in the array; the extra cell is to hold the null terminator \0. The program does not generate its own newline when it prints each record to the terminal but relies instead on the newline read into the character array by fgets( ). The function fputs( ) writes the contents of the character array, *crecord,* to the file specified by the file pointer, stdout.

If your program happens to be accessing a file on a disk drive other than the one where the compiler is residing, it may be necessary to include a path in your filename. Notice this description in the preceding program; the double backslashes (\\) are necessary syntactically to indicate a subdirectory. Remember that a single \ usually signals that an escape or line continuation follows.

While the functions gets( ) and fgets( ) are very similar in usage, the functions puts( ) and fputs( ) operate differently. The function fputs( ) writes to a file and expects two arguments: the address of a null-terminated character string and a pointer to a file; fputs( ) simply copies the string to the specified file. It does not add a newline to the end of the string.

The macro puts( ), however, does not require a pointer to a file since the output automatically goes to stdout, and it automatically adds a newline character to the end of the output string. An excellent example of how these functions differ can be found in Chapter 9 in the section "String Functions and Character Arrays."

Integer Input and Output

For certain types of applications, it may be necessary to read and write stream (or buffered) integer information. The C language incorporates two functions for this purpose: getw( ) and putw( ).

Using getw( ) and putw( )

The complementary functions getw( ) and putw( ) are very similar to the functions getc( ) and putc( ) except that they input and output integer data instead of character data to a file. You should use both getw( ) and putw( ) only on files that are opened in binary mode. The following program opens a binary file, writes ten integers to it, closes the file, and then reopens the file for input and echo print:

```
/*
 *   badfil.c
 *   A C program that uses the functions getw and putw on
 *   a file created in binary mode.
 *   Copyright (c) Chris H. Pappas and William H. Murray, 1997
 */

#include <stdio.h>
#include <stdlib.h>

#define ISIZE 10

void main( )
{
```

```
FILE *pfi;
int ivalue,ivalues[ISIZE],i;

pfi = fopen("a:\\integer.dat", "wb");
if(pfi == NULL) {
  printf("File could not be opened");
  exit(1);
}

for(i = 0; i < ISIZE; i++) {
  ivalues[i]=i+1;
  putw(ivalues[i],pfi);
}

fclose(pfi);

pfi=fopen("a:\\integer.dat", "r+b");
if(pfi == NULL) {
  printf("File could not be re-opened");
  exit(1);
}

  while(!feof(pfi)) {
    ivalue = getw(pfi);
    printf("%3d",ivalue);
  }
}
```

Look at the output from this program and see if you can figure out what went wrong:

```
1  2  3  4  5  6  7  8  9 10 -1
```

Because the integer value read in by the last loop may have a value equal to *EOF,* the program uses the function feof( ) to check for the end-of-file marker. However, the function does not perform a look-ahead operation as do some other high-level language end-of-file functions. In C, an actual read of the end-of-file value must be performed in order to flag the condition.

To correct this situation, the program needs to be rewritten using what is called a *priming read statement*:

```c
/*
 *    geputw.c
 *    A C program that uses the functions getw and putw on
 *    a file created in binary mode.
 *    Copyright (c) Chris H. Pappas and William H. Murray, 1997
 */

#include <stdio.h>

#define ISIZE 10

void main( )
{
  FILE *pfi;
  int ivalue,ivalues[ISIZE],i;
  pfi = fopen("a:\\integer.dat", "w+b");
  if(pfi == NULL) {
    printf("File could not be opened");
    exit(1);
  }

  for(i = 0; i < ISIZE; i++) {
    ivalues[i]=i+1;
    putw(ivalues[i],pfi);
  }

  fclose(pfi);

  pfi=fopen("a:\\integer.dat", "rb");
  if(pfi == NULL) {
    printf("File could not be re-opened");
    exit(1);
  }

  ivalue = getw(pfi);
  while(!feof(pfi)) {
    printf("%3d",ivalue);
    ivalue=getw(pfi);
  }
}
```

Before the program enters the final while loop, the priming read is performed to check to see if the file is empty. If it is not, a valid integer value is stored in *ivalue*. If the file is empty, however, the function feof( ) will acknowledge this, preventing the while loop from executing.

Also notice that the priming read necessitated a rearrangement of the statements within the while loop. If the loop is entered, then *ivalue* contains a valid integer. Had the statements within the loop remained the same as the original program, an immediate second getw( ) function call would be performed. This would overwrite the first integer value. Because of the priming read, the first statement within the while loop must be an output statement. This is next followed by a call to getw( ) to get another value.

Suppose the while loop has been entered nine times. At the end of the ninth iteration, the integer numbers 1 through 8 have been echo printed and *ivalue* has been assigned a 9. The next iteration of the loop prints the 9 and inputs the 10. Since 10 is not *EOF*, the loop iterates, causing the 10 to be echo printed and *EOF* to be read. At this point, the while loop terminates because the function feof( ) sees the end-of-file condition.

These two simple example programs should highlight the need to take care when writing code that is based on the function feof( ). This is a peculiarly frustrating programming task since each high-level language tends to treat the end-of-file condition in a different way. Some languages read a piece of data and at the same time look ahead to see the end-of-file; others, like C, do not.

Formatting Output

C's rich assortment of output formatting controls makes it easy to create a neatly printed graph, report, or table. The two main functions that accomplish this formatted output are printf( ) and the file equivalent form, fprintf( ). These functions can use any of the format specifiers shown in Table 11-2. The format specification uses the following form:

```
%[flags] [width] [.precision] [{h | l | L}]type
```

The field of the specification is a character or a number that gives a format option. The simplest form can be just a percent sign and a type; for example, %f. *%type* is used to determine if the argument is to be interpreted as a character, a string, or a number. *flags* are used to control the printing of signs, blanks, decimal points, radix of output, and so on. *width* refers to the minimum number of characters to print. *precision* refers to the maximum number of characters that are printed for the output. *h | l | L* are optional prefixes for giving the argument size.

TYPE FIELD:

Character	Type	Format of Output
c	int or wint_t	printf—means a single-byte character.
		wprintf—means a wide character.
C	int or wint_t	printf—means a wide character.
		wprintf—means a single-byte character.
d	int	Signed decimal integer.
e	double	Signed number of the form [-]d.ddd e [sign]dddd.
		Here d is a single decimal digit, ddd is one or more decimal digits, dddd is exactly four decimal digits, and the sign is a + or -.
E	double	Same as e, except "E" is in front of the exponent.
f	double	Signed number of the form [-]ddd.ddd. Here ddd is one or more decimal digits. The number of digits after the decimal point depends upon the precision.
g	double	Signed number in f or e format. The most compact format is used. No trailing zeros. No decimal point if no digits follow it.
G	double	Same as g format, except "E" is in front of the exponent.
i	int	Signed decimal integer.
n	Pointer to integer	The number of characters written to the stream or buffer.
		Address of buffer given as integer argument.
o	int	Unsigned octal integer.
p	Pointer to void	Address (given by argument) is printed.
s	String	printf—gives a single-byte-character string.
		wprintf—gives a wide-character string.
		(print to NULL or max precision)

Table 11-2. *Format Specifiers for printf( ) and fprintf( ) Functions*

TYPE FIELD:

Character	Type	Format of Output
S	String	printf—gives a wide-character string.
		wprintf—gives a single-byte-character string.
		(print to NULL or max precision)
u	int	Unsigned decimal integer.
x	int	Unsigned hexadecimal integer (lowercase letters used).
X	int	Unsigned hexadecimal integer (uppercase letters used).

FLAG FIELD:

Flag	Meaning
-	Left-align the result (right alignment is the default).
+	Use a leading sign (+ or -) if number is a signed type (sign used with negative number only is the default).
0	When width has 0 prefix, zeros will be added until the minimum width is reached (no padding is the default).
blank (' ')	Output is prefixed with a blank. If positive and signed, the blank will be ignored (no appearing blank is the default).
#	Prefixes nonzero output value with 0, 0x, or 0X (no appearing blank is the default).
.	For e, E, or f formats, a # makes the output value contain a decimal point in all cases (point appears only if digits follow is the default).

Table 11-2. *Format Specifiers for printf( ) and fprintf( ) Functions* (continued)

Using printf( ) and fprintf( )

The following example program defines four variable types: character, array-of-characters, integer, and real. It then demonstrates how to use the appropriate format controls on each variable. The source code has been heavily commented and output line numbering has been included to make associating the output generated with the statement that created it as simple as possible:

```
/*
*    printf.c
*    A C program demonstrating advanced conversions and
*    formatting
*    Copyright (c) Chris H. Pappas and William H. Murray, 1997
*/

#include <stdio.h>

void main( )
{
  char    c         =   'A',
          psz1[]    =   "In making a living today many no ",
          psz2[]    =   "longer leave any room for life.";
  int     iln       =   0,
          ivalue    =   1234;
  double dPi         =   3.14159265;

  /*            conversions           */

  /* print the c                      */
  printf("\n[%2d] %c",++iln,c);

  /* print the ASCII code for c       */
  printf("\n[%2d] %d",++iln,c);

  /* print character with ASCII 90    */
  printf("\n[%2d] %c",++iln,90);

  /* print ivalue as octal value      */
  printf("\n[%2d] %o",++iln,ivalue);

  /* print lower-case hexadecimal     */
  printf("\n[%2d] %x",++iln,ivalue);

  /* print upper-case hexadecimal     */
  printf("\n[%2d] %X",++iln,ivalue);


  /* conversions and format options   */
```

```
/* minimum width 1               */
printf("\n[%2d] %c",++iln,c);

/* minimum width 5, right-justify */
printf("\n[%2d] %5c",++iln,c);

/* minimum width 5, left-justify  */
printf("\n[%2d] %-5c",++iln,c);

/* 33 non-null, automatically     */
printf("\n[%d] %s",++iln,psz1);

/* 31 non-null, automatically     */
printf("\n[%d] %s",++iln,psz2);

/* minimum 5 overridden, auto 33  */
printf("\n[%d] %5s",++iln,psz1);

/* minimum width 38, right-justify */
printf("\n[%d] %38s",++iln,psz1);

/* minimum width 38, left-justify */
printf("\n[%d] %-38s",++iln,psz2);

/* default ivalue width, 4        */
printf("\n[%d] %d",++iln,ivalue);

/* printf ivalue with + sign      */
printf("\n[%d] %+d",++iln,ivalue);

/* minimum 3 overridden, auto 4   */
printf("\n[%d] %3d",++iln,ivalue);

/* minimum width 10, right-justify */
printf("\n[%d] %10d",++iln,ivalue);

/* minimum width 10, left-justify  */
printf("\n[%d] %-d",++iln,ivalue);

/* right justify with leading 0's  */
printf("\n[%d] %010d",++iln,ivalue);
```

```
/* using default number of digits  */
printf("\n[%d] %f",++iln,dPi);

/* minimum width 20, right-justify */
printf("\n[%d] %20f",++iln,dPi);

/* right-justify with leading 0's  */
printf("\n[%d] %020f",++iln,dPi);

/* minimum width 20, left-justify  */
printf("\n[%d] %-20f",++iln,dPi);

/* no longer available since R1.2  */
/* left-justify with trailing 0's  */


/* additional formatting precision */

/* minimum width 19, print all 17  */
printf("\n[%d] %19.19s",++iln,psz1);

/* prints first 2 chars            */
printf("\n[%d] %.2s",++iln,psz1);

/* prints 2 chars, right-justify   */
printf("\n[%d] %19.2s",++iln,psz1);

/* prints 2 chars, left-justify    */
printf("\n[%d] %-19.2s",++iln,psz1);

/* using printf arguments          */
printf("\n[%d] %*.*s",++iln,19,6,psz1);

/* width 10, 8 to right of '.'     */
printf("\n[%d] %10.8f",++iln,dPi);

/* width 20, 2 to right-justify    */
printf("\n[%d] %20.2f",++iln,dPi);

/* 4 decimal places, left-justify  */
printf("\n[%d] %-20.4f",++iln,dPi);
```

```
   /* 4 decimal places, right-justify */
   printf("\n[%d] %20.4f",++iln,dPi);

   /* width 20, scientific notation    */
   printf("\n[%d] %20.2e",++iln,dPi);
}
```

The output generated by the program looks like this:

```
[ 1] A
[ 2] 65
[ 3] Z
[ 4] 2322
[ 5] 4d2
[ 6] 4D2
[ 7] A
[ 8]        A
[ 9] A
[10] In making a living today many no
[11] longer leave any room for life.
[12] In making a living today many no
[13]        In making a living today many no
[14] longer leave any room for life.
[15] 1234
[16] +1234
[17] 1234
[18]          1234
[19] 1234
[20] 0000001234
[21] 3.141593
[22]              3.141593
[23] 0000000000003.141593
[24] 3.141593
[25] In making a living
[26] In
[27]                    In
[28] In
[29]              In mak
[30] 3.14159265
[31]                3.14
[32] 3.1416
```

```
[33]                3.1416
[34]            3.14e+000
```

You can neatly format your application's output by studying the preceding example and selecting those combinations that apply to your program's data types.

Using fseek( ), ftell( ), and rewind( )

You can use the functions fseek( ), ftell( ), and rewind( ) to determine or change the location of the file position marker. The function fseek( ) resets the file position marker, in the file pointed to by *pf*, to the number of *ibytes* from the beginning of the file (*ifrom* = 0), from the current location of the file position marker (*ifrom* = 1), or from the end of the file (*ifrom* = 2). C has predefined three constants that can also be used in place of the variable *ifrom*: *SEEK_SET* (offset from beginning-of-file), *SEEK_CUR* (current file marker position), and *SEEK_END* (offset from the end-of-file). The function fseek( ) will return zero if the seek is successful and *EOF* otherwise. The general syntax for the function fseek( ) looks like this:

fseek(*pf,ibytes,ifrom*);

The function ftell( ) returns the current location of the file position marker in the file pointed to by *pf*. This location is indicated by an offset, measured in bytes, from the beginning of the file. The syntax for the function ftell( ) looks like this:

long_variable=ftell(*pf*);

The value returned by ftell( ) can be used in a subsequent call to fseek( ).

The function rewind( ) simply resets the file position marker in the file pointed to by *pf* to the beginning of the file. The syntax for the function rewind( ) looks like this:

rewind(*pf*);

The following C program illustrates the functions fseek( ), ftell( ), and rewind( ):

```
/*
 *    fseek.c
 *    A C program demonstrating the use of fseek,
 *    ftell, and rewind.
 *    Copyright (c) Chris H. Pappas and William H. Murray, 1997
```

```
*/

#include <stdio.h>

void main( )
{
  FILE *pf;
  char c;
  long llocation;

  pf=fopen("test.dat","r+t");

  c=fgetc(pf);
  putchar(c);

  c=fgetc(pf);
  putchar(c);

  llocation=ftell(pf);

  c=fgetc(pf);
  putchar(c);

  fseek(pf,llocation,0);

  c=fgetc(pf);
  putchar(c);

  fseek(pf,llocation,0);
  fputc('E',pf);

  fseek(pf,llocation,0);

  c=fgetc(pf);
  putchar(c);

  rewind(pf);

  c=fgetc(pf);
  putchar(c);
}
```

The variable *llocation* has been defined to be of type long. This is because C supports files larger than 64K. The input file TEST.DAT contains the string "ABCD". After the program opens the file, the first call to fgetc( ) gets the letter "A" and then prints it to the video display. The next statement pair inputs the letter "B" and prints it.

When the function ftell( ) is invoked, *llocation* is set equal to the file position marker's current location. This is measured as an offset, in bytes, from the beginning of the file. Since the letter "B" has already been processed, *llocation* contains a 2. This means that the file position marker is pointing to the third character, which is 2 bytes over from the first letter, "A".

Another I/O pair of statements now reads the letter "C" and prints it to the video display. After the program executes this last statement pair, the file position marker is 3 offset bytes from the beginning of the file, pointing to the fourth character, "D".

At this point in the program, the function fseek( ) is invoked. It is instructed to move *llocation* offset bytes (or 2 offset bytes) from the beginning of the file (since the third parameter to the function fseek( ) is a zero, as defined earlier). This repositions the file position marker to the third character in the file. The variable *c* is again assigned the letter "C", and it is printed a second time.

The second time the function fseek( ) is invoked, it uses parameters identical to the first invocation. The function fseek( ) moves the pointer to the third character, "C" (2 offset bytes into the file). However, the statement that follows doesn't input the "C" a third time, but instead writes over it with a new letter, "E". Since the file position marker has now moved past this new "E", to verify that the letter was indeed placed in the file, the function fseek( ) is invoked still another time.

The nest statement pair inputs the new "E" and prints it to the video display. With this accomplished, the program invokes the function rewind( ), which moves the *pf* back to the beginning of the file. When the function fgetc( ) is then invoked, it returns the letter "A" and prints it to the file. The output from the program looks like this:

```
ABCCEA
```

You can use the same principles illustrated in this simple character example to create a random-access file of records. Suppose you have the following information recorded for a file of individuals: social security number, name, and address. Suppose also that you are allowing 11 characters for the social security number, in the form ddd-dd-dddd, with the name and address being given an additional 60 characters (or bytes). So far, each record would be 11 + 60 bytes long, or 71 bytes.

All of the possible contiguous record locations on a random-access disk file may not be full; the personnel record needs to contain a flag indicating whether or not that disk record location has been used. This requires adding one more byte to the personnel record, bringing the total for one person's record to 72 bytes, plus 2 additional bytes to represent the record number, for a grand total record byte count of 74 bytes. One record could look like the following:

1 U111-22-3333Linda Lossannie, 521 Alan Street, Anywhere, USA

Record 1 in the file would occupy bytes zero through 73; record 2 would occupy bytes 74 through 147; record 3, 148 through 221; and so on. If you use the record number in conjunction with the fseek( ) function, any record location can be located on the disk. For example, to find the beginning of record 2, use the following statements:

```
loffset=(iwhich_record - 1) * sizeof(stA_PERSON);
fseek(pfi,loffset,0);
```

Once the file position marker has been moved to the beginning of the selected record, the information at that location can either be read or written by using various I/O functions such as fread( ) and fwrite( ).

With the exception of the comment block delimiter symbols /* and */ and the header STDIO.H, the program just discussed would work the same in C++. Just substitute the symbol // for both /* and */ and change STDIO.H to IOSTREAM.H.

Using the Integrated Debugger

Try entering this next program and printing out the value stored in the variable *stcurrent_person.irecordnum* after you have asked to search for the 25th record:

```
/*
*    rndacs.c
*    A C random access file program using fseek, fread,
*    and fwrite.
*    Copyright (c) Chris H. Pappas and William H. Murray, 1997
*/

#include <stdio.h>
#include <string.h>

#define iFIRST 1
#define iLAST 50
#define iSS_SIZE 11
#define iDATA_SIZE 60
#define cVACANT 'V'
#define cUSED 'U'

typedef struct strecord {
  int  irecordnum;
  char cavailable;                /* V free, U used */
```

```
    char csoc_sec_num[iSS_SIZE];
    char cdata[iDATA_SIZE];
} stA_PERSON;

void main( )
{
  FILE *pfi;
  stA_PERSON stcurrent_person;
  int i,iwhich_record;
  long int loffset;

  pfi=fopen("A:\\sample.fil","r+");

  for(i = iFIRST; i <= iLAST; i++) {
    stcurrent_person.cavailable=cVACANT;
    stcurrent_person.irecordnum=i;
    fwrite(&stcurrent_person,sizeof(stA_PERSON),1,pfi);
  }

  printf("Please enter the record you would like to find.");
  printf("\nYour response must be between 1 and 50: ");
  scanf("%d",&iwhich_record);

  loffset=(iwhich_record - 1) * sizeof(stA_PERSON);
  fseek(pfi,loffset,0);
  fread(&stcurrent_person,sizeof(stA_PERSON),1,pfi);

  fclose(pfi);
}
```

The typedef has defined *stA_PERSON* as a structure that has a 2-byte *irecordnum*, a 1-byte *cavailable* character code, an 11-byte character array to hold a *csoc_sec_num* number, and a 60-byte *cdata* field. This brings the total structure's size to 2 + 1 + 11 + 60, or 74 bytes.

Once the program has opened the file in read-and-update text mode, it creates and stores 50 records, each with its own unique *irecordnum* and all initialized to *cVACANT*. The fwrite( ) statement wants the address of the structure to output, the size in bytes of what it is outputting, how many to output, and which file to send it to. With this accomplished, the program next asks the user which record he or she would like to search for.

Finding the record is accomplished in two steps. First, an offset address from the beginning of the file must be calculated. For example, record 1 is stored in bytes zero to 73, record 2 is stored in bytes 74 to 148, and so on. By subtracting 1 from the record number entered by the user, the program multiplies this value by the number of bytes occupied by each structure and calculates the *loffset*. For example, finding record 2 is accomplished with the following calculation: (2-1) x 74. This gives the second record a starting byte offset of 74. Using this calculated value, the fseek( ) function is then invoked and moves the file position marker *loffset* bytes into the file.

As you are tracing through the program asking to view records 1 through 10, all seems fine. However, when you ask to view the 11th record, what happens? You get garbage. The reason for this is that the program opened the file in text mode. Records 1 through 9 are all exactly 74 bytes, but records 10 and up take 75 bytes. Therefore, the 10th record starts at the appropriate *loffset* calculation, but it goes 1 byte further into the file. Therefore, the 11th record is at the address arrived at by using the following modified calculation:

```
loffset=((iwhich_record - 1) * sizeof(stA_PERSON)) + 1;
```

However, this calculation won't work with the first nine records. The solution is to open the file in binary mode:

```
pfi=fopen("A:\\sample.fil","r+b");
```

In character mode, the program tries to interpret any two-digit number as two single characters, increasing records with two-digit *record_number*s by 1 byte. In binary mode, the integer *record_number* is interpreted properly. Exercise care when deciding how to open a file for I/O.

Formatting Input

Formatted input can be obtained for a C program by using the very versatile functions scanf( ) and fscanf( ). The main difference between the two functions is that the latter requires that you specifically designate the input file from which the data is to be obtained. Table 11-3 lists all of the possible control string codes that can be used with the functions scanf( ), fscanf( ), and sscanf( ).

Using scanf( ), fscanf( ), and sscanf( )

You can use all three input functions, scanf( ), fscanf( ), and sscanf( ), for extremely sophisticated data input. For example, look at the following statement:

```
scanf("%2d%5s%4f",&ivalue,psz,&fvalue);
```

Code	Interpretation	Example Input	Receiving Address Parameter Type
c	A character	W	char
s	A string	William	char
d	int	23	int
hd	short	-99	short
ld	long	123456	long
o	octal	1727	int
ho	short octal	1727	short
lo	long octal	1727	long
x	hexadecimal	2b5	int
hx	short hexadecimal	2b5	short
lx	long hexadecimal	2b5	long
e	float as float	3.14159e+03	float
f	Same as e		
le	float as double	3.14159e+03	double
lf	Same as le		
[A-Za-z]	String with only chars	Test string	char
[0-9]	String with only digits	09823145	char

Table 11-1. *Control Codes for scanf( ) and sscanf( )*

The statement inputs only a two-digit integer, a five-character string, and a real number that occupies a maximum of four spaces (2.97, 12.5, and so on). See if you can even begin to imagine what this next statement does:

```
scanf("%*[ \t\n]\"%[^A-Za-z]%[^\"]\"",ps1,ps2);
```

The statement begins by reading and *not* storing any white space. This is accomplished with the following format specification: "%*[\t\n]". The * symbol instructs the function to obtain the specified data but not to save it in any variable.

As long as only a space, tab, or newline is on the input line, scanf( ) will keep reading until it encounters a double quote ("). This is accomplished by the \" format specification, which says the input must match the designated symbol. However, the double quote is not input.

Once scanf( ) has found the double quote, it is instructed to input all characters that are digits into *ps1*. The %[^A-Za-z] format specification accomplishes this with the caret (^) modifier, which says to input anything not an uppercase letter "A" through "Z" or lowercase letter "a" through "z". Had the caret been omitted, the string would have contained only alphabetic characters. It is the hyphen between the two symbols "A" and "Z" and "a" and "z" that indicates the entire range is to be considered.

The next format specification, %[^\"], instructs the input function to read all remaining characters up to but not including a double quote into *ps2*. The last format specification, \", indicates that the string must match and end with a double quote. You can use the same types of input conversion control with the functions fscanf( ) and sscanf( ). The only difference between the two functions scanf( ) and fscanf( ) is that the latter requires that an input file be specified. The function sscanf( ) is identical to scanf( ) except that the data is read from an array rather than a file.

The next example shows how you can use sscanf( ) to convert a string (of digits) to an integer. If *ivalue* is of type int and *psz* is an array of type char that holds a string of digits, then the following statement will convert the string *psz* into type int and store it in the variable *ivalue*:

```
sscanf(psz,"%d",&ivalue);
```

Very often, the functions gets( ) and sscanf( ) are used in combination, since the function gets( ) reads in an entire line of input and the function sscanf( ) goes into a string and interprets it according to the format specifications.

One problem often encountered with scanf( ) occurs when programmers try to use it in conjunction with various other character input functions such as getc( ), getch( ), getchar( ), gets( ), and so on. The typical scenario goes like this: scanf( ) is used to input various data types that would otherwise require conversion from characters to something else. Then the programmer tries to use a character input function such as getch( ) and finds that getch( ) does not work as expected. The problem occurs because scanf( ) sometimes does not read all the data that is waiting to be read, and the waiting data can fool other functions (including scanf( )) into thinking that input has already been entered. To be safe, if you use b in a program, don't also use other input functions in the same program.

Chapter 12 introduces you to the basics of C++ I/O. Chapters 13 through 17 explain the concepts necessary to do advanced C++ I/O, and Chapter 18 completes the subject of I/O in C++.

The Complete Reference

Visual
C++ 5

Chapter 12

An Introduction to I/O in C++

While it is technically true that C++ is a superset of the C language, this does not mean that by simply taking a C statement and translating it into a C++ equivalent form, you have written a C++ program! In many cases C++ has a better way of solving a programming problem. Often the C++ equivalent of a C program streamlines the way your program inputs and outputs data. However, this is not always true. This chapter introduces you to C++ I/O.

The topic of advanced C++ input and output is continued in Chapter 18. The division of the topic is necessary because of the diverse I/O capabilities available to C++ programmers. Chapters 16 to 19 teach the fundamentals of object-oriented programming. Once you understand how objects are created, it will be much easier to understand advanced object-oriented C++ I/O. Chapter 17 picks up with C++'s ability to effortlessly manipulate objects.

Streamlining I/O with C++

The software supplied with the Microsoft Visual C++ compiler includes a standard library that contains functions commonly used by the C++ community. The standard I/O library for C, described by the header file STDIO.H, is still available in C++. However, C++ introduces its own header file, called IOSTREAM.H, which implements its own collection of I/O functions.

The C++ stream I/O is described as a set of classes in IOSTREAM.H. These classes overload the "put to" and "get from" operators, << and >>. To better understand why the stream library in C++ is more convenient than its C counterpart, let's first review how C handles input and output.

First, recall that C has no built-in input or output statements; functions such as printf( ) are part of the standard library but not part of the language itself. Similarly, C++ has no built-in I/O facilities. The absence of built-in I/O gives you greater flexibility to produce the most efficient user interface for the data pattern of the application at hand.

The problem with the C solution to input and output lies with its implementation of these I/O functions. There is little consistency among them in terms of return values and parameter sequences. Because of this, programmers tend to rely on the formatted I/O functions printf( ), scanf( ), and so on—especially when the objects being manipulated are numbers or other noncharacter values. These formatted I/O functions are convenient and, for the most part, share a consistent interface, but they are also big and unwieldy because they must manipulate many kinds of values.

In C++, the class provides modular solutions to your data manipulation needs. The standard C++ library provides three I/O classes as an alternative to C's general-purpose I/O functions. These classes contain definitions for the same pair of operators—>> and <<—that are optimized for all kinds of data. (See Chapter 17 for a discussion of classes.)

cin, cout, and cerr

The C++ stream counterparts to stdin, stdout, and stderr, prototyped in STDIO.H, are cin, cout, and cerr, which are prototyped in IOSTREAM.H. These three streams are opened automatically when your program begins execution and become the interface between the program and the user. The cin stream is associated with the terminal keyboard. The cout and cerr streams are associated with the video display.

The >> Extraction and << Insertion Operators

Input and output in C++ have been significantly enhanced and streamlined by the stream library operators >> ("get from" or *extraction*) and << ("put to" or *insertion*). One of the major enhancements that C++ added to C was operator overloading. Operator overloading allows the compiler to determine which like-named function or operator is to be executed based on the associated variables' data types. The extraction and insertion operators are good examples of this new C++ capability. Each operator has been overloaded so it can handle all of the standard C++ data types, including classes. The following two code segments illustrate the greater ease of use for basic I/O operations in C++. First, take a quick look at a C output statement using printf( ):

```
printf("Integer value: %d, Float value: %f",ivalue,fvalue);
```

Here is the C++ equivalent:

```
cout << "Integer value: " << ivalue << ", Float value: "
     << fvalue;
```

A careful examination of the C++ equivalent will reveal how the insertion operator has been overloaded to handle the three separate data types: string, integer, and float. If you are like many C programmers, you are not going to miss having to hunt down the % symbol needed for your printf( ) and scanf( ) format specifications. As a result of operator overloading, the insertion operator will examine the data type you have passed to it and determine an appropriate format.

An identical situation exists with the extraction operator, which performs data input. Look at the following C example and its equivalent C++ counterpart:

```
/* C code */
scanf("%d%f%c",&ivalue,&fvalue,&c);

// C++ code
cin >> ivalue >> fvalue >> c;
```

No longer is it necessary to precede your input variables with the & address operator. In C++, the extraction operator takes care of calculating the storage variable's address, storage requirements, and formatting.

Having looked at two examples of the C++ operators << and >>, you might be slightly confused as to why they are named the way they are. The simplest way to remember which operator performs output and which performs input is to think of these two operators as they relate to the stream I/O files. When you want to input information, you extract it (>>) from the input stream, cin, and put the information into a variable—for example, *ivalue*. To output information, you take a copy of the information from the variable *fvalue* and insert it (<<) into the output stream, cout.

As a direct result of operator overloading, C++ will allow a program to expand upon the insertion and extraction operators. The following code segment illustrates how the insertion operator can be overloaded to print the new type *stclient*:

```
ostream& operator << (ostream& osout, stclient staclient)
{
  osout << " " << staclient.pszname;
  osout << " " << staclient.pszaddress;
  osout << " " << staclient.pszphone;
}
```

Assuming the structure variable *staclient* has been initialized, printing the information becomes a simple one-line statement:

```
cout << staclient;
```

Last but not least, the insertion and extraction operators have an additional advantage—their final code size. The general-purpose I/O functions printf( ) and scanf( ) carry along code segments into the final executable version of a program that are often unused. In C, even if you are dealing only with integer data, you still pull along all of the conversion code for the additional standard data types. In contrast, the C++ compiler incorporates only those routines actually needed.

The following program demonstrates how to use the input, or extraction, operator >> to read different types of data:

```
//
//  insrt1.cpp
//  A C++ program demonstrating how to use the
//  extraction >> operator to input a char,
//  integer, float, double, and string.
//  Copyright (c) Chris H. Pappas and William H. Murray, 1997
```

```
//

#include <iostream.h>

#define INUMCHARS 45
#define INULL_CHAR 1

void main(void)
{
  char canswer;
  int ivalue;
  float fvalue;
  double dvalue;
  char pszname[INUMCHARS + INULL_CHAR];

  cout << "This program allows you to enter various data types.";
  cout << "Would you like to try it? "<< "\n\n";
  cout << "Please type a Y for yes and an N for no: ";

  cin  >> canswer;

  if(canswer == 'Y') {

    cout << "\n" << "Enter an integer value: ";
    cin >> ivalue;
    cout << "\n\n";

    cout << "Enter a float value: ";
    cin >> fvalue;
    cout << "\n\n";

    cout << "Enter a double value: ";
    cin >> dvalue;
    cout << "\n\n";

    cout << "Enter your first name: ";
    cin >> pszname;
    cout << "\n\n";
  }

}
```

In this example, the insertion operator << is used in its simplest form to output literal string prompts. Notice that the program uses four different data types and yet each input statement, cin >>, looks identical except for the variable's name. For those of you who are fast typists but are tired of trying to find the infrequently used %, ", and & symbols (required by scanf( )), you can give your fingers and eyes a rest. The C++ extraction operator makes code entry much simpler and less error prone.

Because of the rapid evolutionary development of C++, you have to be careful when using C or C++ code found in older manuscripts. For example, if you had run the previous program under a C++ compiler, Release 1.2, the program execution would look like the following example:

```
This program allows you to enter various data types
Would you like to try it?

Please type a Y for yes and an N for no: Y

Enter an integer value:
                        10
```

This is because the C++ Release 1.2 input stream is processing the newline character you entered after typing the letter "Y". The extraction operator >> reads up to but does not get rid of the newline. The following program solves this problem by adding an additional input statement:

```cpp
//
//   insrt2.cpp
//   A C++ program demonstrating how to use the
//   extraction >> operator to input a char,
//   integer, float, double, and string.
//   Copyright (c) Chris H. Pappas and William H. Murray, 1997
//

#include <iostream.h>

#define INUMCHARS 45
#define INULL_CHAR 1

void main(void)
{
  char canswer,cAnewline;
  int ivalue;
  float fvalue;
```

```
  double dvalue;
  char pszname[INUMCHARS + INULL_CHAR];

  cout << "This program allows you to enter various data types.";
  cout << "Would you like to try it? << "\n\n";
  cout << "Please type a Y for yes and an N for no: ";

  cin  >> canswer;
  cin.get(cAnewline);

  if(canswer == 'Y') {

    cout << "\n" << "Enter an integer value: ";
    cin >> ivalue;
    cout << "\n\n";

    cout << "Enter a float value: ";
    cin >> fvalue;
    cout << "\n\n";

    cout << "Enter a double value: ";
    cin >> dvalue;
    cout << "\n\n";

    cout << "Enter your first name: ";
    cin >> pszname;
    cout << "\n\n";
  }

}
```

Did you notice the change? After *canswer* is read in, the program executes

```
cin.get(cAnewline);
```

This processes the newline character so that when the program runs, it now looks like this:

```
This program allows you to enter various data types
Would you like to try it?
```

```
Please type a Y for yes and an N for no:

Enter an integer value: 10
```

Both algorithms work properly since the introduction of C++ Release 2.0. However, it is worth mentioning that you must take care when modeling your code from older texts. Mixing what is known as historic C and C++ with current compilers can cause you to spend many hours trying to figure out why your I/O doesn't perform as expected.

This next example demonstrates how to use the output, or insertion, operator <<
in its various forms:

```cpp
//
//  extrct.cpp
//  A C++ program demonstrating how to use the
//  insertion << operator to input a char,
//  integer, float, double, and string.
//  Copyright (c) Chris H. Pappas and William H. Murray, 1997
//

#include <iostream.h>

void main(void)
{
  char c='A';
  int ivalue=10;
  float fvalue=45.67;
  double dvalue=2.3e32;
  char fact[]="For all have...";

  cout << "Once upon a time there were ";
  cout << ivalue << " people."<< endl;
  cout << "Some of them earned " << fvalue;
  cout << " dollars per hour." << "\n";
  cout << "While others earned " << dvalue << " per year!";
  cout << "\n\n" << "But you know what they say: ";
  cout << fact << "\n\n";
  cout << "So, none of them get an ";
  cout << c;
  cout << "!";
}
```

The output from the program looks like this:

```
Once upon a time there were 10 people.
Some of them earned 45.67 dollars per hour.
While others earned 2.3e+32 per year!

But you know what they say: "For all have..."

So, none of them get an A!
```

When comparing the C++ source code with the output from the program, one thing you should immediately notice is that the insertion operator << does not automatically generate a newline. You still have complete control over when this occurs by including the newline symbol \n or endl when necessary.

endl is very useful for outputting data in an interactive program because it not only inserts a newline into the stream but also flushes the output buffer. You can also use flush; however, this does not insert a newline. Notice too that the placement of the newline symbol can be included after its own << insertion operator or as part of a literal string, as is contrasted in the second and fourth << statements in the program.

Also notice that while the insertion operator very nicely handles the formatting of integers and floats, it isn't very helpful with doubles. Another interesting facet of the insertion operator has to do with C++ Release 1.2 character information. Look at the following line of code:

```
cout << c;
```

This would have given you the following output in Release 1.2:

```
So, none of them get an 65!
```

This is because the character is translated into its ASCII equivalent. The Release 1.2 solution is to use the put( ) function for outputting character data. This would require you to rewrite the statement in the following form:

```
cout.put(c);
```

Try running this next example:

```
//
//   string.cpp
//   A C++ program demonstrating what happens when you use
//   the extraction operator >> with string data.
//   Copyright (c) Chris H. Pappas and William H. Murray, 1997
//

#include <iostream.h>

#define INUMCHARS 45
#define INULL_CHARACTER 1

void main(void)
{
  char pszname[INUMCHARS + INULL_CHARACTER];

  cout << "Please enter your first and last name: ";
  cin >> pszname;
  cout << "\n\nThank you, " << pszname;

}
```

A sample execution of the program looks like this:

```
Please enter your first and last name: Kirsten Tuttle

Thank you, Kirsten
```

There is one more fact you need to know when inputting string information. The extraction operator >> is written to stop reading in information as soon as it encounters white space. *White space* can be a blank, tab, or newline. Therefore, when *pszname* is printed, only the first name entered is output. You can solve this problem by rewriting the program and using the cin.get( ) function:

```
//
//   cinget.cpp
```

```
//  A C++ program demonstrating what happens when you use
//  the extraction operator >> with cin.get( ) to process an
//  entire string.
//  Copyright (c) Chris H. Pappas and William H. Murray, 1997
//

#include <iostream.h>

#define INUMCHARS 45
#define INULL_CHARACTER 1

void main(void)
{
  char pszname[INUMCHARS + INULL_CHARACTER];

  cout << "Please enter your first and last name: ";
  cin.get(pszname,INUMCHARS);
  cout << "\n\nThank you, " << pszname;
}
```

The output from the program now looks like this:

```
Please enter your first and last name: Kirsten Tuttle

Thank you, Kirsten Tuttle
```

The cin.get( ) function has two additional parameters. Only one of these, the number of characters to input, was used in the previous example. The function cin.get( ) will read everything, including white space, until the maximum number of characters specified has been read in, or up to the next newline, whichever comes first. The optional third parameter, not shown, identifies a terminating symbol. For example, the following line would read into *pszname INUMCHARS* characters, all of the characters up to but not including a * symbol, or a newline, whichever comes first:

```
cin.get(pszname,INUMCHARS,'*');
```

From STREAM.H to IOSTREAM.H

One of the most exciting enhancements to the compiler is the new C++ I/O library, referred to as the iostream library. By not including input/output facilities within the C++ language itself, but rather implementing them in C++ and providing them as a component of a C++ standard library, I/O can evolve as needed. This new iostream library replaces the earlier version of the I/O library referred to as the Release 1.2 stream library.

At its lowest level, C++ interprets a file as a sequence, or *stream,* of bytes. At this level, the concept of a data type is missing. One component of the I/O library is involved in the transfer of these bytes. From the user's perspective, however, a file is composed of a series of intermixed alphanumerics, numeric values, or possibly, class objects. A second component of the I/O library takes care of the interface between these two viewpoints. The iostream library predefines a set of operations for handling reading and writing of the built-in data types. The library also provides for user-definable extensions to handle class types.

Basic input operations are supported by the istream class and basic output via the ostream class. Bidirectional I/O is supported via the iostream class, which is derived from both istream and ostream. There are four stream objects predefined for the user:

cin	An istream class object linked to standard input.
cout	An ostream class object linked to standard output.
cerr	An unbuffered output ostream class object linked to standard error.
clog	A buffered output ostream class object linked to standard error.

Any program using the iostream library must include the header file IOSTREAM.H. Since IOSTREAM.H treats STREAM.H as an alias, programs written using STREAM.H may or may not need alterations, depending on the particular structures used.

You can also use the new I/O library to perform input and output operations on files. You can tie a file to your program by defining an instance of one of the following three class types:

fstream	Derived from iostream and links a file to your application for both input and output.
ifstream	Derived from istream and links a file to your application for input only.
ofstream	Derived from ostream and links a file to your application for output only.

Operators and Member Functions

The extraction operator and the << insertion operator have been modified to accept arguments of any of the built-in data types, including char *. They can also be extended to accept class argument types.

Probably the first upgrade incompatibility you will experience when converting a C++ program using the older I/O library will be the demised cout << form extension. Under the new release, each iostream library class object maintains a *format state* that controls the details of formatting operations, such as the conversion base for integral numeric notation or the precision of a floating-point value.

You can manipulate the format state flags by using the setf( ) and unsetf( ) functions. The setf( ) member function sets a specified format state flag. There are two overloaded instances:

```
setf(long);
setf(long,long);
```

The first argument can be either a format bit *flag* or a format bit *field*. Table 12-1 lists the format flags you can use with the setf(long) instance (using just the format flag).

Flag	Meaning
ios::showbase	Displays numeric constants in a format that can be read by the C++ compiler.
ios::showpoint	Shows floating-point values with a decimal point and trailing zeros.
ios::dec	Formats numeric values using base 10 (decimal) default radix.
ios::oct	Formats numeric values using base 8 (octal).
ios::hex	Formats numeric values using base 16 (hexadecimal).
ios::fixed	Shows floating-point numbers with fixed format.
ios::scientific	Shows floating-point numbers with scientific format.
ios::showpos	Displays plus signs (+) in front of positive values.
ios::skipws	Skips white space on input.
ios::left	Left-aligns all values (pad on the right with the specified fill character).

Table 12-1. *Format Flags*

Flag	Meaning
ios::right	Right-aligns all values (pad on the left with the specified fill character—default alignment).
ios::internal	Adds fill characters after any leading sign or base indication, but before the value.
ios::uppercase	Displays uppercase "A" through "F" for hexadecimal values and "E" for scientific values.
ios::unitbuf	Causes ostream::osfx to flush the stream after each insertion (default, cerr is buffered).
ios::stdio	Causes ostream::osfx to flush stdout and stderr after each insertion.

Table 12-1. *Format Flags (continued)*

The following table lists some of the format bit fields you can use with the setf(long,long) instance (using a format flag and format bit field).

Bit Field	Meaning	Flags
ios::basefield	Integral base	ios::hex
		ios::oct
		ios::dec
ios::floatfield	Floating-point	ios::fixed
		ios::scientific

There are certain predefined defaults. For example, integers are written and read in decimal notation. You can change the base to octal, hexadecimal, or back to decimal. By default, a floating-point value is output with six digits of precision. You can modify this by using the precision member function. The following C++ program uses these new member functions:

```
//
//  advio.cpp
//  A C++ program demonstrating advanced conversions and
//  formatting member functions since Release 2.0. The program
//  will also demonstrate how to convert each of the older
//  Release 1.2 form statements.
```

```
//   Copyright (c) Chris H. Pappas and William H. Murray, 1995

//

#include <string.h>
#include <strstrea.h>

#define INULL_TERMINATOR 1

void row (void);
main( )
{
  char    c         =    'A',
          psz1[]    =    "In making a living today many no ",
          psz2[]    =    "longer leave any room for life.";
  int     iln       =    0,
          ivalue    =    1234;
  double dPi         =    3.14159265;

  // new declarations needed for Release 2.0
  char psz_padstring5[5+INULL_TERMINATOR],
  psz_padstring38[38+INULL_TERMINATOR];

  // conversions

  // print the c
  // R1.2 cout << form("\n[%2d] %c",++iln,c);
  // Notice that << has been overloaded to output char
  row( ); // [ 1]
  cout << c;

  // print the ASCII code for c
  // R1.2  form("\n[%2d] %d",++iln,c);
  row( ); // [ 2]
  cout << (int)c;

  // print character with ASCII 90
  // R1.2  form("\n[%2d] %c",++iln,90);
  row( ); // [ 3]
  cout << (char)90;

  // print ivalue as octal value
  // R1.2  form("\n[%2d] %o",++iln,ivalue);
```

PROGRAMMING
FOUNDATIONS

```
row( ); // [ 4]
cout << oct << ivalue;

// print lowercase hexadecimal
// R1.2  form("\n[%2d] %x",++ln,ivalue);
row( ); // [ 5]
cout << hex << ivalue;

// print uppercase hexadecimal
// R1.2  form("\n[%2d] %X",++ln,ivalue);
row( ); // [ 6]
cout.setf(ios::uppercase);
cout << hex << ivalue;
cout.unsetf(ios::uppercase);    // turn uppercase off
cout << dec;                    // return to decimal base

// conversions and format options

// minimum width 1
// R1.2  form("\n[%2d] %c",++ln,c);
row( ); // [ 7]
cout << c;

// minimum width 5, right-justify
// R1.2  form("\n[%2d] %5c",++ln,c);
row( ); // [ 8]
ostrstream(psz_padstring5,sizeof(psz_padstring5))
<< "    " << c << ends;
cout << psz_padstring5;

// minimum width 5, left-justify
// R1.2  form("\n[%2d] %-5c",++ln,c);
row( ); // [ 9]
ostrstream(psz_padstring5,sizeof(psz_padstring5))
<< c << "    " << ends;

cout << psz_padstring5;

// 33 automatically
// R1.2  form("\n[%d] %s",++ln,psz1);
row( ); // [10]
cout << psz1;
```

```
// 31 automatically
// R1.2  form("\n[%d] %s",++ln,psz2);
row( ); // [11]
cout << psz2;

// minimum 5 overriden, auto
// R1.2  form("\n[%d] %5s",++ln,psz1);
// notice that the width of 5 cannot be overridden!
row( ); // [12]
cout.write(psz1,5);

// minimum width 38, right-justify
// R1.2  form("\n[%d] %38s",++ln,psz1);
// notice how the width of 38 ends with garbage data
row( ); // [13]
cout.write(psz1,38);

// the following is the correct approach
cout << "\n\nCorrected approach:\n";
ostrstream(psz_padstring38,sizeof(psz_padstring38))
<< "        "
  << psz1 << ends;
row( ); // [14]
cout << psz_padstring38;

// minimum width 38, left-justify
// R1.2  form("\n[%d] %-38s",++ln,psz2);
ostrstream(psz_padstring38,sizeof(psz_padstring38))
  << psz2 << "        " << ends;
row( ); // [15]
cout << psz_padstring38;

// default ivalue width
// R1.2  form("\n[%d] %d",++ln,ivalue);
row( ); // [16]

cout << ivalue;

// printf ivalue with + sign
// R1.2  form("\n[%d] %+d",++ln,ivalue);
row( ); // [17]
cout.setf(ios::showpos);      // don't want row number with +
```

```
        cout << ivalue;
        cout.unsetf(ios::showpos);

        // minimum 3 overridden, auto
        // R1.2  form("\n[%d] %3d",++ln,ivalue);
        row( ); // [18]
        cout.width(3); // don't want row number padded to width of 3
        cout << ivalue;

        // minimum width 10, right-justify
        // R1.2  form("\n[%d] %10d",++ln,ivalue);
        row( ); // [19]
        cout.width(10);    // only in effect for first value printed
        cout << ivalue;

        // minimum width 10, left-justify
        // R1.2  form("\n[%d] %-d",++ln,ivalue);
        row( ); // [20]
        cout.width(10);
        cout.setf(ios::left);
        cout << ivalue;
        cout.unsetf(ios::left);

        // right-justify with leading 0's
        // R1.2  form("\n[%d] %010d",++ln,ivalue);
        row( ); // [21]
        cout.width(10);
        cout.fill('0');
        cout << ivalue;
        cout.fill(' ');

        // using default number of digits
        // R1.2  form("\n[%d] %f",++ln,dPi);
        row( ); // [22]
        cout << dPi;

        // minimum width 20, right-justify
        // R1.2  form("\n[%d] %20f",++ln,dPi);
        row( ); // [23]
        cout.width(20);
        cout << dPi;

        // right-justify with leading 0's
        // R1.2  form("\n[%d] %020f",++ln,dPi);
```

```
row( ); // [24]
cout.width(20);
cout.fill('0');
cout << dPi;
cout.fill(' ');

// minimum width 20, left-justify
// R1.2  form("\n[%d] %-20f",++ln,dPi);
row( ); // [25]
cout.width(20);
cout.setf(ios::left);
cout << dPi;

// left-justify with trailing 0's
// R1.2  form("\n[%d] %-020f",++ln,dPi);
row( ); // [26]
cout.width(20);
cout.fill('0');
cout << dPi;
cout.unsetf(ios::left);
cout.fill(' ');

// additional formatting precision

// minimum width 19, print all 17
// R1.2  form("\n[%d] %19.19s",++ln,psz1);
row( ); // [27]
cout << psz1;

// prints first 2 chars
// R1.2  form("\n[%d] %.2s",++ln,psz1);
row( ); // [28]
cout.write(psz1,2);

// prints 2 chars, right-justify
// R1.2  form("\n[%d] %19.2s",++ln,psz1);
row( ); // [29]
cout << "                  "; cout.write(psz1,2);

// prints 2 chars, left-justify
// R1.2  form("\n[%d] %-19.2s",++ln,psz1);
row( ); // [30]
cout.write(psz1,2);
```

```
  // using printf arguments
  // R1.2  form("\n[%d] %*.*s",++ln,19,6,psz1);
  row( ); // [31]
  cout << "                   "; cout.write(psz1,6);

  // width 10, 8 to right of '.'
  // R1.2  form("\n[%d] %10.8f",++ln,dPi);
  row( ); // [32]
  cout.precision(9);
  cout << dPi;

  // width 20, 2 to right-justify
  // R1.2  form("\n[%d] %20.2f",++ln,dPi);
  row( ); // [33]
  cout.width(20);
  cout.precision(2);
  cout << dPi;

  // 4 decimal places, left-justify
  // R1.2  form("\n[%d] %-20.4f",++ln,dPi);
  row( ); // [34]
  cout.precision(4);
  cout << dPi;

  // 4 decimal places, right-justify
  // R1.2  form("\n[%d] %20.4f",++ln,dPi);
  row( ); // [35]
  cout.width(20);
  cout << dPi;

  // width 20, scientific notation
  // R1.2  form("\n[%d] %20.2e",++ln,dPi);
  row( ); // [36] cout.setf(ios::scientific); cout.width(20);
  cout << dPi; cout.unsetf(ios::scientific);

  return(0);
}

void row (void)
{
  static int ln=0;
  cout << "\n[";
  cout.width(2);
  cout << ++ln << "] ";
}
```

You can use the output from the program to help write advanced output statements of your own:

```
[ 1]  A
[ 2]  65
[ 3]  Z
[ 4]  2322
[ 5]  4d2
[ 6]  4d2
[ 7]  A
[ 8]      A
[ 9]  A
[10]  In making a living today many no
[11]  longer leave any room for life.
[12]  In ma
[13]  In making a living today many no A

Corrected approach:

[14]        In making a living today many no
[15]  longer leave any room for life.
[16]  1234
[17]  +1234
[18]  1234
[19]        1234
[20]  1234
[21]  0000001234
[22]  3.14159
[23]                3.14159
[24]  00000000000003.14159
[25]  3.14159
[26]  3.141590000000000000
[27]  In making a living today many no
[28]  In
[29]                    In
[30]  In
[31]                In mak
[32]  3.14159265
[33]                    3.1
[34]  3.142
[35]                3.142
[36]  3.142
```

The following section highlights those output statements used in the preceding program that need special clarification. One point needs to be made: IOSTREAM.H is automatically included by STRSTREAM.H. The latter file is needed to perform string output formatting. If your application needs to output numeric data or simple character and string output, you will need to include only IOSTREAM.H.

C++ Character Output

In the new I/O library (since Release 2.0), the insertion operator << has been overloaded to handle character data. With the earlier release, the following statement would have output the ASCII value of *c*:

```
cout << c;
```

In the current I/O library, the letter itself is output. For those programs needing the ASCII value, a case is required:

```
cout << (int)C;
```

C++ Base Conversions

There are two approaches to outputting a value using a different base:

```
cout << hex << ivalue;
```

and

```
cout.setf(ios::hex,ios::basefield);
cout << ivalue;
```

Both approaches cause the base to be permanently changed from the statement forward (not always the effect you want). Each value output will now be formatted as a hexadecimal value. Returning to some other base is accomplished with the unsetf( ) function:

```
cout.unsetf(ios::hex,ios::basefield);
```

If you are interested in uppercase hexadecimal output, use the following statement:

```
cout.setf(ios::uppercase);
```

When it is no longer needed, you will have to turn off this option:

```
cout.unsetf(ios::uppercase);
```

C++ String Formatting

Printing an entire string is easy in C++. However, string formatting has changed because the Release 1.2 cout << form is no longer available. One approach to string formatting is to declare an array of characters and then select the desired output format, printing the string buffer:

```
pszpadstring38[38+INULL_TERMINATOR];
.
.
.
ostrstream(pszpadstring38,sizeof(pszpadstring38))
    << "      "   << psz1;
```

The ostrstream( ) member function is part of STRSTREAM.H and has three parameters: a pointer to an array of characters, the size of the array, and the information to be inserted. This statement appends leading blanks to right-justify *psz1*. Portions of the string can be output using the write form of cout:

```
cout.write(psz1,5);
```

This statement will output the first five characters of *psz1*.

C++ Numeric Formatting

You can easily format numeric data with right or left justification, varying precisions, varying formats (floating-point or scientific), leading or trailing fill patterns, and signs. There are certain defaults. For example, the default for justification is right and for floating-point precision is six. The following code segment outputs *dPi* left-justified in a field width of 20, with trailing zeros:

```
cout.width(20);
cout.setf(ios::left);
cout.fill('0');
cout << dPi;
```

Had the following statement been included, *dPi* would have been printed with a precision of two:

```
cout.precision(2);
```

With many of the output flags such as left justification, selecting uppercase hexadecimal output, base changes, and many others, it is necessary to unset these flags when they are no longer needed. The following statement turns left justification off:

```
cout.unsetf(ios::left);
```

Selecting scientific format is a matter of flipping the correct bit flag:

```
cout.setf(ios::scientific);
```

You can print values with a leading + sign by setting the *showpos* flag:

```
cout.setf(ios::showpos);
```

There are many minor details of the current I/O library functions that will initially cause some confusion. This has to do with the fact that certain operations, once executed, make a permanent change until turned off, while others take effect only for the next output statement. For example, an output width change, as in cout.width(20);, affects only the next value printed. That is why the function row( ) has to repeatedly change the width to get the output row numbers formatted within two spaces, as in [1]. However, other formatting operations like base changes, uppercase, precision, and floating-point/scientific remain active until specifically turned off.

C++ File Input and Output

All of the examples so far have used the predefined streams cin and cout. It is possible that your program will need to create its own streams for I/O. If an application needs to create a file for input or output, it must include the FSTREAM.H header file (FSTREAM.H includes IOSTREAM.H). The classes ifstream and ofstream are derived from istream and ostream and inherit the extraction and insertion operations, respectively. The following C++ program demonstrates how to declare a file for reading and writing using ifstream and ofstream, respectively:

```
//
//   fstrm.cpp
```

```
//   A C++ program demonstrating how to declare an
//   ifstream and ofstream for file input and output.
//   Copyright (c) Chris H. Pappas and William H. Murray, 1997
//

#include <fstream.h>

int main(void)
{
  char c;

  ifstream ifsin("a:\\text.in",ios::in);
  if( !ifsin )
    cerr << "\nUnable to open 'text.in' for input.";

  ofstream ofsout("a:\\text.out",ios::out);
  if( !ofsout )
    cerr << "\nUnable to open 'text.out' for output.";

  while( ofsout && ifsin.get(c) )
    ofsout.put(c);

  ifsin.close( );

  ofsout.close( );

  return(0);
}
```

The program declares *ifsin* to be of class ifstream and is associated with the file
TEXT.IN stored in the A drive. It is always a good idea for any program dealing with
files to verify the existence or creation of the specified file in the designated mode.
By using the handle to the file *ifsin,* a simple if test can be generated to check the
condition of the file. A similar process is applied to *ofsout,* with the exception that
the file is derived from the ostream class.

The while loop continues inputting and outputting single characters while the *ifsin*
exists and the character read in is not *EOF.* The program terminates by closing the two
files. Closing an output file can be essential to dumping all internally buffered data.

There may be circumstances when a program will want to delay a file specification
or when an application may want to associate several file streams with the same file
descriptor. The following code segment demonstrates this concept:

PROGRAMMING
FOUNDATIONS

```
ifstream ifsin;
.
.
.
ifsin.open("week1.in");
.
.
.
ifsin.close( );
ifsin.open("week2.in");
.
.
.
ifsin.close( );
```

Whenever an application wishes to modify the way in which a file is opened or used, it can apply a second argument to the file stream constructors. For example:

```
ofstream ofsout("week1.out",ios::app|ios::noreplace);
```

This statement declares *ofsout* and attempts to append it to the file named WEEK1.OUT. Because ios::noreplace is specified, the file will not be created if WEEK1.OUT doesn't already exist. The ios::app parameter appends all writes to an existing file. The following table lists the second argument flags to the file stream constructors that can be logically ORed together:

Mode Bit	Action
ios::in	Opens for reading
ios::out	Opens for writing
ios::ate	Seeks to *EOF* after file is created
ios::app	All writes added to end of file
ios::trunc	If file already exists, truncates
ios::nocreate	Unsuccessful open if file does not exist
ios::noreplace	Unsuccessful open if file does exist
ios::binary	Opens file in binary mode (default text)

An fstream class object can also be used to open a file for both input and output. For example, the following definition opens the file UPDATE.DAT in both input and append mode:

```
fstream io("update.dat",ios::in|ios::app);
```

You can reposition all iostream class types by using either the seekg( ) or seekp( ) member function, which can move to an absolute address within the file or move a byte offset from a particular position. Both seekg( ) (sets or reads the get pointer's position) and seekp( ) (sets or reads the put pointer's position) can take one or two arguments. When used with one parameter, the iostream is repositioned to the specified pointer position. When it is used with two parameters, a relative position is calculated. The following listing highlights these differences, assuming the preceding declaration for *io*:

```
streampos current_position = io.tellp( );
io << obj1 << obj2 << obj3;
io.seekp(current_position);
io.seekp(sizeof(MY_OBJ),ios::cur);
io << objnewobj2;
```

The pointer *current_position* is first derived from streampos and initialized to the current position of the put-file pointer by the function tellp( ). With this information stored, three objects are written to *io*. Using seekp( ), the put-file pointer is repositioned to the beginning of the file. The second seekp( ) statement uses the sizeof( ) operator to calculate the number of bytes necessary to move one object's width into the file. This effectively skips over *obj1*'s position, permitting an *objnewobj2* to be written.

If a second argument is passed to seekg( ) or seekp( ), it defines the direction to move: ios::beg (from the beginning), ios::cur (from the current position), and ios::end (from the end of the file). For example, this line will move into the get_file pointer file 5 bytes from the current position:

```
io.seekg(5,ios::cur);
```

The next line will move the get_file pointer 7 bytes backward from the end of the file:

```
io.seekg(-7,ios::end);
```

C++ File Condition States

Associated with every stream is an error state. When an error occurs, bits are set in the state according to the general category of the error. By convention, inserters ignore attempts to insert things into an ostream with error bits set, and such attempts do not change the stream's state. The iostream library object contains a set of predefined condition flags, which monitor the ongoing state of the stream. The following table lists the six member functions that can be invoked:

Member Function	Action
eof( )	Returns a nonzero value on end-of-file
fail( )	Returns a nonzero value if an operation failed
bad( )	Returns a nonzero value if an error occurred
good( )	Returns a nonzero value if no state bits are set
rdstate( )	Returns the current stream state
clear( )	Sets the stream state (int=0)

You can use these member functions in various algorithms to solve unique I/O conditions and to make the code more readable:

```
ifstream pfsinfile("sample.dat",ios::in);
if(pfsinfile.eof( ))

  pfsinfile.clear( ); // sets the state of pfsinfile to 0

if(pfsinfile.fail( ))
  cerr << ">>> sample.dat creation error <<<";

if(pfsinfile.good( ))
  cin >> my_object;

if(!pfsinfile) // shortcut
  cout << ">>> sample.dat creation error <<<";
```

This chapter has served as an introduction to C++ I/O concepts. To really understand various formatting capabilities, you'll need to learn about C++ classes and various overloading techniques. Chapters 16 and 17 teach object-oriented programming concepts. With this information, you'll be introduced to additional C++ I/O techniques in Chapter 18.

The Complete Reference

Visual C++ 5

Chapter 13

Structures, Unions, and
Miscellaneous Items

This chapter investigates several advanced C and C++ types, such as structures, unions, and bit-fields, along with other miscellaneous topics. You will learn how to create and use structures in programs. The chapter also covers how to pass structure information to functions, use pointers with structures, create and use unions in programs, and use other important features, such as typedef and enumerated types (enum).

The bulk of the chapter concentrates on two important features common to C and C++: the structure and the union. The C or C++ structure is conceptually an array or vector of closely related items. Unlike an array or vector, however, a structure permits the contained items to be of assorted data types.

The structure is very important to C and C++. Structures serve as the flagship of a more advanced C++ type, called the *class*. If you become comfortable with structures, it will be much easier for you to understand C++ classes. This is because C++ classes share, and expand upon, many of the features of a structure. Chapters 16 and 18 are devoted to the C++ class.

Unions are another advanced type. Unions allow you to store different data types at the same place in your system's memory. These advanced data types serve as the foundation of most spreadsheet and database programs.

In the section that follows, you will learn how to build simple structures, create arrays of structures, pass structures and arrays of structures to functions, and access structure elements with pointers.

Structures

The notion of a data structure is a very familiar idea in everyday life. A card file containing friends' addresses, telephone numbers, and so on, is a structure of related items. A file of favorite CDs or LP records is a structure. A computer's directory listing is a structure. These are examples that use a structure, but what is a structure? Literally, a *structure* can be thought of as a group of variables, which can be of different types, held together in a single unit. The single unit is the structure.

Structures: Syntax and Rules

A structure is formed in C or C++ by using the keyword struct, followed by an optional tag field, and then a list of members within the structure. The optional tag field is used to create other variables of the particular structure's type. The syntax for a structure with the optional tag field looks like this:

```
struct tag_field {
    member_type member1;
    member_type member2;
```

member_type member3;

    .

    .

    .

member_type member n;
};

A semicolon terminates the structure definition because it is actually a C and C++ statement. Several of the example programs in this chapter use a structure similar to the following:

```
struct stboat {
  char sztype [iSTRING15 + iNULL_CHAR];
  char szmodel[iSTRING15 + iNULL_CHAR];
  char sztitle[iSTRING20 + iNULL_CHAR];
  int iyear;
  long int lmotor_hours;
  float fsaleprice;
};
```

The structure is created with the keyword struct followed by the tag field or type for the structure. In this example, *stboat* is the tag field for the structure.

This structure declaration contains several members; *sztype, szmodel,* and *sztitle* are null-terminated strings of the specified length. These strings are followed by an integer, *iyear,* a long integer, *lmotor_hours,* and a float, *fsaleprice.* The structure will be used to save sales information for a boat.

So far, all that has been defined is a new hypothetical structure type called *stboat.* However, no variable has been associated with the structure at this point. In a program, you can associate a variable with a structure by using a statement similar to the following:

```
struct stboat stused_boat;
```

The statement defines *stused_boat* to be of the type struct *stboat.* Notice that the declaration required the use of the structure's tag field. If this statement is contained within a function, then the structure, named *stused_boat,* is local in scope to that function. If the statement is contained outside of all program functions, the structure will be global in scope. It is also possible to declare a structure variable using this syntax:

```
struct stboat {
  char sztype [iSTRING15 + iNULL_CHAR];
  char szmodel[iSTRING15 + iNULL_CHAR];
  char sztitle[iSTRING20 + iNULL_CHAR];
  int iyear;
  long int lmotor_hours;
  float fsaleprice;
} stused_boat;
```

Here, the variable declaration is sandwiched between the structure's closing brace (}) and the required semicolon (;). In both examples, *stused_boat* is declared as structure type *stboat*. Actually, when only one variable is associated with a structure type, the tag field can be eliminated, so it would also be possible to write

```
struct {
   char sztype [iSTRING15 + iNULL_CHAR];
   char szmodel[iSTRING15 + iNULL_CHAR];
   char sztitle[iSTRING20 + iNULL_CHAR];
   int iyear;
   long int lmotor_hours;
   float fsaleprice;
} stused_boat;
```

Notice that this structure declaration does not include a tag field and creates what is called an *anonymous structure type*. While the statement does define a single variable, *stused_boat*, there is no way the application can create another variable of the same type somewhere else in the application. Without the structure's tag field, there is no syntactically legal way to refer to the new type. However, it is possible to associate several variables with the same structure type, without specifying a tag field, as shown in the following listing:

```
struct {
   char sztype [iSTRING15 + iNULL_CHAR];
   char szmodel[iSTRING15 + iNULL_CHAR];
   char sztitle[iSTRING20 + iNULL_CHAR];
   int iyear;
   long int lmotor_hours;
   float fsaleprice;
} stboat1,stboat2,stboat3;
```

The compiler allocates all necessary memory for the structure members, as it does for any other variable. To decide if your structure declarations need a tag field, ask yourself the following questions: "Will I need to create other variables of this structure type somewhere else in the program?" and "Will I be passing the structure type to functions?". If the answer to either of these questions is yes, you need a tag field.

C++ Structures: Additional Syntax and Rule Extensions

C++, in many cases, can be described as a superset of C. In general, this means that what works in C should work in C++.

NOTE: Using C design philosophies in a C++ program often ignores C++'s streamlining enhancements.

The structure declaration syntax styles just described all work with both the C and C++ compilers. However, C++ has one additional method for declaring variables of a particular structure type. This exclusive C++ shorthand notation eliminates the need to repeat the keyword struct. The following example highlights this subtle difference:

```
/* legal C and C++ structure declaration syntax */
struct stboat stused_boat;

// exclusive C++ structure declaration syntax
stboat stused_boat;
```

Accessing Structure Members

Individual members can be referenced within a structure by using the *dot* or *member operator* (.). The syntax is

stname.*mname*

Here, *stname* is the variable associated with the structure type and *mname* is the name of any member variable in the structure.

In C, for example, information can be placed in the *szmodel* member with a statement such as,

```
gets(stused_boat.szmodel);
```

Here, *stused_boat* is the name associated with the structure and *szmodel* is a member variable of the structure. In a similar manner, you can use a printf( ) function to print information for a structure member:

```
printf("%ld",stused_boat.lmotor_hours);
```

The syntax for accessing structure members is basically the same in C++:

cin >> stused_boat.sztype;

This statement will read the make of the *stused_boat* into the character array, while the next statement will print the *stused_boat* selling price to the screen:

```
cout << stused_boat.fsaleprice;
```

Structure members are handled like any other C or C++ variable with the exception that the dot operator must always be used with them.

Constructing a Simple Structure

In the following example, you will see a structure similar to the *stboat* structure given earlier in this chapter. Examine the listing to see if you understand how the various structure elements are accessed by the program:

```
/*
 *   struct.c
 *   C program illustrates how to construct a structure.
 *   Program stores data about your boat in a C structure.
 *   Copyright (c) Chris H. Pappas and William H. Murray, 1997
 */

#include <stdio.h>

#define iSTRING15 15
#define iSTRING20 20
#define iNULL_CHAR 1

struct stboat {
  char sztype [iSTRING15 + iNULL_CHAR];
  char szmodel[iSTRING15 + iNULL_CHAR];
```

```
    char sztitle[iSTRING20 + iNULL_CHAR];
    int iyear;
    long int lmotor_hours;
    float fsaleprice;
} stused_boat;

int main(void)
{
  printf("\nPlease enter the make of the boat: ");
  gets(stused_boat.sztype);

  printf("\nPlease enter the model of the boat: ");
  gets(stused_boat.szmodel);

  printf("\nPlease enter the title number for the boat: ");
  gets(stused_boat.sztitle);

  printf("\nPlease enter the model year for the boat: ");
  scanf("%d",&stused_boat.iyear);

  printf("\nPlease enter the current hours on ");
  printf("the motor for the boat: ");
  scanf("%ld",&stused_boat.lmotor_hours);

  printf("\nPlease enter the purchase price of the boat: ");
  scanf("%f",&stused_boat.fsaleprice);

  printf("\n\n\n");
  printf("A %d %s %s with title number #%s\n",
     stused_boat.iyear,stused_boat.sztype,
     stused_boat.szmodel,stused_boat.sztitle);
  printf("currently has %ld motor hours",
     stused_boat.lmotor_hours);
  printf(" and was purchased for $%8.2f\n",
     stused_boat.fsaleprice);

  return (0);
}
```

The output from the preceding example shows how information can be manipulated with a structure:

```
A 1952 Chris Craft with title number #CC1011771018C
currently has 34187 motor hours and was purchased for $68132.98
```

You might notice, at this point, that *stused_boat* has a global file scope since it was declared outside of any function.

Passing Structures to Functions

It is often necessary to pass structure information to functions. When a structure is passed to a function, the information is passed call-by-value. Since only a copy of the information is being passed in, it is impossible for the function to alter the contents of the original structure. You can pass a structure to a function by using the following syntax:

fname(*stvariable*);

If *stused_boat* was made local in scope to main( ), if you move its declaration inside the function, it could be passed to a function named vprint_data( ) with the statement

```
vprint_data(stused_boat);
```

The vprint_data( ) prototype must declare the structure type it is about to receive, as you might suspect:

```
/* legal C and C++ structure declaration syntax */
void vprint_data(struct stboat stany_boat);

// exclusive C++ structure declaration syntax
void vprint_data(stboat stany_boat);
```

Passing entire copies of structures to functions is not always the most efficient way of programming. Where time is a factor, the use of pointers might be a better choice. If saving memory is a consideration, the malloc( ) function for dynamically allocating structure memory in C when using linked lists is often used instead of statically allocated memory. You'll see how this is done in the next chapter.

The next example shows how to pass a complete structure to a function. Notice that it is a simple modification of the last example. The next four example programs use the same basic approach. Each program modifies only that portion of the algorithm necessary to explain the current subject. This approach will allow you to easily view the code and syntax changes necessary to implement a particular language feature.

Study the listing and see how the structure, *stused_boat*, is passed to the function vprint_data( ).

```c
/*
 *    passst.c
 *    C program shows how to pass a structure to a function.
 *    Copyright (c) Chris H. Pappas and William H. Murray, 1997
 */

#include <stdio.h>

#define iSTRING15 15
#define iSTRING20 20
#define iNULL_CHAR 1

struct stboat {
  char sztype [iSTRING15 + iNULL_CHAR];
  char szmodel[iSTRING15 + iNULL_CHAR];
  char sztitle[iSTRING20 + iNULL_CHAR];
  int iyear;
  long int lmotor_hours;
  float fsaleprice;
};

void vprint_data(struct stboat stany_boat);

int main(void)
{
  struct stboat stused_boat;

  printf("\nPlease enter the make of the boat: ");
  gets(stused_boat.sztype);

  printf("\nPlease enter the model of the boat: ");
  gets(stused_boat.szmodel);

  printf("\nPlease enter the title number for the boat: ");
  gets(stused_boat.sztitle);

  printf("\nPlease enter the model year for the boat: ");
  scanf("%d",&stused_boat.iyear);
```

```
    printf("\nPlease enter the current hours on ");
    printf("the motor for the boat: ");
    scanf("%ld",&stused_boat.lmotor_hours);

    printf("\nPlease enter the purchase price of the boat: ");
    scanf("%f",&stused_boat.fsaleprice);

    vprint_data(stused_boat);

    return (0);
}

void vprint_data(struct stboat stany_boat)
{
  printf("\n\n");
  printf("A %d %s %s with title number #%s\n",stany_boat.iyear,
      stany_boat.sztype,stany_boat.szmodel,stany_boat.sztitle);
  printf("currently has %ld motor hours",stany_boat.lmotor_hours);
  printf(" and was purchased for $%8.2f",
        stany_boat.fsaleprice);
}
```

In this example, an entire structure was passed by value to the function. The calling procedure simply invokes the function by passing the structure variable, *stused_boat.* Notice that the structure's tag field, *stboat,* was needed in the vprint_data( ) function prototype and declaration. As you will see later in this chapter, it is also possible to pass individual structure members by value to a function. The output from this program is similar to the previous example.

Constructing an Array of Structures

A structure can be thought of as similar to a single card from a card file. The real power in using structures comes about when a collection of structures, called an *array of structures,* is used. An array of structures is similar to a whole card file containing a great number of individual cards. If you maintain an array of structures, a database of information can be manipulated for a wide range of items.

This array of structures might include information on all of the boats at a local marina. It would be practical for a boat dealer to maintain such a file and be able to pull out of a database all boats on the lot selling for less than $45,000 or all boats with a minimum of one stateroom. Study the following example and note how the code has been changed from earlier examples:

```
/*
 *    stcary.c
 *    C program uses an array of structures.
 *    This example creates a "used boat inventory" for
 *    Nineveh Boat Sales.
 *    Copyright (c) Chris H. Pappas and William H. Murray, 1997
 */

#include <stdio.h>

#define iSTRING15 15
#define iSTRING20 20
#define iNULL_CHAR 1
#define iMAX_BOATS 50

struct stboat {
  char sztype [iSTRING15 + iNULL_CHAR];
  char szmodel[iSTRING15 + iNULL_CHAR];
  char sztitle[iSTRING20 + iNULL_CHAR];
  char szcomment[80];
  int iyear;
  long int lmotor_hours;
  float fretail;
  float fwholesale;
};

int main(void)
{
  int i,iinstock;
  struct stboat astNineveh[iMAX_BOATS];

  printf("How many boats in inventory? ");
  scanf("%d",&iinstock);

  for (i=0; i<iinstock; i++) {

    flushall( );      /* flush keyboard buffer */
    printf("\nPlease enter the make of the boat: ");
    gets(astNineveh[i].sztype);

    printf("\nPlease enter the model of the boat: ");
    gets(astNineveh[i].szmodel);
```

```
      printf("\nPlease enter the title number for the boat: ");
      gets(astNineveh[i].sztitle);

      printf("\nPlease enter a one line comment about the boat: ");
      gets(astNineveh[i].szcomment);

      printf("\nPlease enter the model year for the boat: ");
      scanf("%d",&astNineveh[i].iyear);

      printf("\nPlease enter the current hours on ");
      printf("the motor for the boat: ");
      scanf("%ld",&astNineveh[i].lmotor_hours);

      printf("\nPlease enter the retail price of the boat :");
      scanf("%f",&astNineveh[i].fretail);

      printf("\nPlease enter the wholesale price of the boat :");
      scanf("%f",&astNineveh[i].fwholesale);
    }

  printf("\n\n\n");

  for (i=0; i<iinstock; i++) {
    printf("A %d %s %s beauty with %ld low hours.\n",
           astNineveh[i].iyear,astNineveh[i].sztype,
           astNineveh[i].szmodel,astNineveh[i].lmotor_hours);
    printf("%s\n",astNineveh[i].szcomment);
    printf(
       "Grab the deal by asking your Nineveh salesperson for");
    printf(" #%s ONLY! $%8.2f.\n",astNineveh[i].sztitle,
           astNineveh[i].fretail);
    printf("\n\n");
  }

  return (0);
}
```

Here, Nineveh Boat Sales has an array of structures set up to hold information about the boats in the marina.

The variable *astNineveh[iMAX_BOATS]* associated with the structure, struct stboat, is actually an array. In this case, *iMAX_BOATS* sets the maximum array size to 50. This simply means that data on 50 boats can be maintained in the array of structures. It will be necessary to know which of the boats in the file you wish to view. The first array element is zero. Therefore, information on the first boat in the array of structures can be accessed with a statement such as

```
gets(astNineveh[0].sztitle);
```

As you study the program, notice that the array elements are accessed with the help of a loop. In this manner, element members are obtained with code, such as

```
gets(astNineveh[i].sztitle);
```

The flushall( ) statement inside the for loop is necessary to remove the newline left in the input stream from the previous scanf( ) statements (the one before the loop is entered and the last scanf( ) statement within the loop). Without the call to flushall( ), the gets( ) statement would be skipped over. Remember, gets( ) reads everything up to and including the newline. Both scanf( ) statements leave the newline in the input stream. Without the call to flushall( ), the gets( ) statement would simply grab the newline from the input stream and move on to the next executable statement.

The previous program's output serves to illustrate the small stock of boats on hand at Nineveh Boat Sales. It also shows how structure information can be rearranged in output statements:

```
A 1957 Chris Craft Dayliner 124876 low hours.
A great riding boat owned by a salesperson.
Grab the deal by asking your Nineveh salesperson for
#BS12345BFD ONLY! $36234.00.

A 1988 Starcraft Weekender a beauty with 27657 low hours.
Runs and looks great. Owned by successful painter.
Grab the deal by asking your Nineveh salesperson for
#BG7774545AFD ONLY! $18533.99.

A 1991 Scarab a wower with 1000 low hours.
A cheap means of transportation. Owned by grandfather.
Grab the deal by asking your Nineveh salesperson for
#156AFG4476 ONLY! $56999.99.
```

When you are working with arrays of structures, be aware of the memory limitations of the system you are programming on—statically allocated memory for arrays of structures can require large amounts of system memory.

Using Pointers to Structures

In the following example, an array of structures is created in a similar manner to the last program. The *arrow operator* is used in this example to access individual structure members. The arrow operator can be used *only* when a pointer to a structure has been created.

```c
/*
 *  ptrstc.c
 *  C program uses pointers to an array of structures.
 *  The Nineveh boat inventory example is used again.
 *  Copyright (c) Chris H. Pappas and William H. Murray, 1997
 */

#include <stdio.h>

#define iSTRING15 15
#define iSTRING20 20
#define iNULL_CHAR 1
#define iMAX_BOATS 50

struct stboat {
  char sztype [iSTRING15 + iNULL_CHAR];
  char szmodel[iSTRING15 + iNULL_CHAR];
  char sztitle[iSTRING20 + iNULL_CHAR];
  char szcomment[80];
  int iyear;
  long int lmotor_hours;
  float fretail;
  float fwholesale;
};

int main(void)
{
  int i,iinstock;
  struct stboat astNineveh[iMAX_BOATS],*pastNineveh;
  pastNineveh=&astNineveh[0];

  printf("How many boats in inventory? ");
  scanf("%d",&iinstock);


    for (i=0; i<iinstock; i++) {
```

```
        flushall( );      /*  flush keyboard buffer */
        printf("\nPlease enter the make of the boat: ");
        gets(pastNineveh->sztype);

        printf("\nPlease enter the model of the boat: ");
        gets(pastNineveh->szmodel);

        printf("\nPlease enter the title number for the boat: ");
        gets(pastNineveh->sztitle);

        printf(
          "\nPlease enter a one line comment about the boat: ");
        gets(pastNineveh->szcomment);

        printf("\nPlease enter the model year for the boat: ");
        scanf("%d",&pastNineveh->iyear);

        printf("\nPlease enter the current hours on ");
        printf("the motor for the boat: ");
        scanf("%ld",&pastNineveh->lmotor_hours);

        printf("\nPlease enter the retail price of the boat: ");
        scanf("%f",&pastNineveh->fretail);

        printf(
            "\nPlease enter the wholesale price of the boat: ");
        scanf("%f",&pastNineveh->fwholesale);

        pastNineveh++;
    }

pastNineveh=&astNineveh[0];
printf("\n\n\n");

for (i=0; i<iinstock; i++) {
   printf("A %d %s %s beauty with %ld low hours.\n",
            pastNineveh->iyear,pastNineveh->sztype,
            pastNineveh->szmodel,pastNineveh->lmotor_hours);
   printf("%s\n",pastNineveh->szcomment);
   printf(
     "Grab the deal by asking your Nineveh salesperson for:");
   printf("\n#%s ONLY! $%8.2f.\n",pastNineveh->sztitle,
```

```
            pastNineveh->fretail);
            printf("\n\n");
            pastNineveh++;
    }

    return (0);
}
```

The array variable, *astNineveh[iMAX_BOATS]*, and the pointer, *pastNineveh*, are associated with the structure by using the following statement:

```
struct stboat astNineveh[iMAX_BOATS],*pastNineveh;
```

The address of the array, *astNineveh*, is copied into the pointer variable, *pastNineveh*, with the following code:

```
pastNineveh=&astNineveh[0];
```

While it is syntactically legal to reference array elements with the syntax that follows, it is not the preferred method:

```
gets((*pastNineveh).sztype);
```

Because of operator precedence, the extra parentheses are necessary to prevent the dot (.) member operator from binding before the pointer, *pastNineveh, is dereferenced. It is better to use the arrow operator, which makes the overall operation much cleaner:

```
gets(pastNineveh->sztype);
```

While this is not a complex example, it does illustrate the use of the arrow operator. The example also prepares you for the real advantage in using pointers—passing an array of structures to a function.

Passing an Array of Structures to a Function

You learned earlier in the chapter that passing a pointer to a structure could have a speed advantage over simply passing a copy of a structure to a function. This fact becomes more evident when a program makes heavy use of structures. The next program shows how an array of structures can be accessed by a function with the use of a pointer:

```
/*
 *   psastc.c
 *   C program shows how a function can access an array
 *   of structures with the use of a pointer.
 *   The Nineveh boat inventory is used again!
 *   Copyright (c) Chris H. Pappas and William H. Murray, 1997
 */

#include <stdio.h>

#define iSTRING15 15
#define iSTRING20 20
#define iNULL_CHAR 1
#define iMAX_BOATS 50

int iinstock;

struct stboat {
  char sztype [iSTRING15 + iNULL_CHAR];
  char szmodel[iSTRING15 + iNULL_CHAR];
  char sztitle[iSTRING20 + iNULL_CHAR];
  char szcomment[80];
  int iyear;
  long int lmotor_hours;
  float fretail;
  float fwholesale;
};

void vprint_data(struct stboat *stany_boatptr);

int main(void)
{
  int i;
  struct stboat  astNineveh[iMAX_BOATS],*pastNineveh;
  pastNineveh=&astNineveh[0];

  printf("How many boats in inventory?\n");
  scanf("%d",&iinstock);
```

```
for (i=0; i<iinstock; i++) {

  flushall( );      /*  flush keyboard buffer */
  printf("\nPlease enter the make of the boat: ");
  gets(pastNineveh->sztype);

  printf("\nPlease enter the model of the boat: ");
  gets(pastNineveh->szmodel);

  printf("\nPlease enter the title number for the boat: ");
  gets(pastNineveh->sztitle);

  printf("\nPlease enter a one line comment about the boat: ");
  gets(pastNineveh->szcomment);

  printf("\nPlease enter the model year for the boat: ");
  scanf("%d",&pastNineveh->iyear);

  printf("\nPlease enter the current hours on ");
  printf("the motor for the boat: ");
  scanf("%ld",&pastNineveh->lmotor_hours);

  printf("\nPlease enter the retail price of the boat: ");
  scanf("%f",&pastNineveh->fretail);

  printf("\nPlease enter the wholesale price of the boat: ");
  scanf("%f",&pastNineveh->fwholesale);

  pastNineveh++;
}

pastNineveh=&astNineveh[0];

vprint_data(pastNineveh);

return (0);
}

void vprint_data(struct stboat *stany_boatptr)
{
  int i;
  printf("\n\n\n");
```

```
  for (i=0; i<iinstock; i++) {
    printf("A %d %s %s beauty with %ld low hours.\n",
            stany_boatptr->iyear,stany_boatptr->sztype,
            stany_boatptr->szmodel,stany_boatptr->lmotor_hours);
    printf("%s\n",stany_boatptr->szcomment);
    printf(
        "Grab the deal by asking your Nineveh salesperson for");
    printf(" #%s ONLY! $%8.2f.\n",stany_boatptr->sztitle,
            stany_boatptr->fretail);
    printf("\n\n");
    stany_boatptr++;
  }
}
```

The first indication that this program will operate differently from the last program comes from the vprint_data( ) function prototype:

```
void vprint_data(struct stboat *stany_boatptr);
```

This function expects to receive a pointer to the structure mentioned. In the function, main( ), the array *astNineveh[iMAX_BOATS]*, and the pointer *pastNineveh are associated with the structure with the following code:

```
struct stboat astNineveh[iMAX_BOATS],*pastNineveh;
```

Once the information has been collected for Nineveh Boat Sales, it is passed to the vprint_data( ) function by passing the pointer:

```
vprint_data(pastNineveh);
```

One major advantage of passing an array of structures to a function using pointers is that the array is now passed call-by-variable or call-by-reference. This means that the function can now access the original array structure, not just a copy. With this calling convention, any change made to the array of structures within the function is global in scope. The output from this program is the same as for the previous examples.

Structure Use in C++

The following C++ program is similar to the previous C program. In terms of syntax, both languages can handle structures in an identical manner. However, the example program takes advantage of C++'s shorthand structure syntax:

```cpp
//
//   struct.cpp
//   C++ program shows the use of pointers when
//   accessing structure information from a function.
//   Note:  Comment line terminates with a period (.)
//   Copyright (c) Chris H. Pappas and William H. Murray, 1997
//

#include <iostream.h>

#define iSTRING15 15
#define iSTRING20 20
#define iNULL_CHAR 1
#define iMAX_BOATS 50

int iinstock;

struct stboat {
  char sztype [iSTRING15 + iNULL_CHAR];
  char szmodel[iSTRING15 + iNULL_CHAR];
  char sztitle[iSTRING20 + iNULL_CHAR];
  char szcomment[80];
  int iyear;
  long int lmotor_hours;
  float fretail;
  float fwholesale;
};

void vprint_data(stboat *stany_boatptr);

int main(void)
{
  int i;
  char newline;
  stboat astNineveh[iMAX_BOATS],*pastNineveh;
  pastNineveh=&astNineveh[0];
```

```
  cout << "How many boats in inventory? ";
  cin >> iinstock;

  for (i=0; i<iinstock; i++) {
    cout << "\nPlease enter the make of the boat: ";
    cin >> pastNineveh->sztype;

    cout << "\nPlease enter the model of the boat: ";
    cin >> pastNineveh->szmodel;

    cout << "\nPlease enter the title number for the boat: ";
    cin >> pastNineveh->sztitle;

    cout << "\nPlease enter the model year for the boat: ";
    cin >> pastNineveh->iyear;

    cout << "\nPlease enter the current hours on "
         << "the motor for the boat: ";
    cin >> pastNineveh->lmotor_hours;

    cout << "\nPlease enter the retail price of the boat: ";
    cin >> pastNineveh->fretail;

    cout << "\nPlease enter the wholesale price of the boat: ";
    cin >> pastNineveh->fwholesale;

    cout << "\nPlease enter a one line comment about the boat: ";
    cin.get(newline);   // process carriage return
    cin.get(pastNineveh->szcomment,80,'.');
    cin.get(newline);   // process carriage return

    pastNineveh++;
  }

  pastNineveh=&astNineveh[0];
  vprint_data(pastNineveh);

  return (0);
}

void vprint_data(stboat *stany_boatptr)
{
```

```
int i;
cout << "\n\n\n";
for (i=0; i<iinstock; i++) {
  cout << "A " << stany_boatptr->iyear << " "
       << stany_boatptr->sztype << " "
       << stany_boatptr->szmodel << " beauty with "
       << stany_boatptr->lmotor_hours << " low hours.\n";
  cout << stany_boatptr->szcomment << endl;
  cout << "Grab the deal by asking your Nineveh "
       << "salesperson for #";
  cout << stany_boatptr->sztitle << "ONLY! $"
       << stany_boatptr->fretail << "\n\n";
  stany_boatptr++;
}
}
```

One of the real differences between the C++ and C programs is how stream I/O is handled. Usually, simple C++ cout and cin streams can be used to replace the standard C printf( ) and gets( ) functions. For example:

```
cout << "\nPlease enter the wholesale price of the boat: ";
cin >> pastNineveh->fwholesale;
```

One of the program statements requests that the user enter a comment about each boat. The C++ input statement needed to read in the comment line uses a different approach for I/O. Recall that cin will read character information until the first white space. In this case, a space between words in a comment serves as white space. If cin were used, only the first word from the comment line would be saved in the *szcomment* member of the structure. Instead, a variation of cin is used so that a whole line of text can be entered:

```
cout << "\nPlease enter a one line comment about the boat: ";
cin.get(newline);   // process carriage return
cin.get(pastNineveh->szcomment,80,'.');
cin.get(newline);   // process carriage return
```

First, cin.get(newline) is used in a manner similar to the flushall( ) function of earlier C programs. In a buffered keyboard system, it is often necessary to strip the newline character from the input buffer. There are, of course, other ways to accomplish this, but they are not more eloquent. The statement cin.get(newline) receives the newline character and saves it in *newline*. The variable *newline* is just a collector for the information and is not actually used by the program. The comment line is accepted with the following code:

```
cin.get(pastNineveh->szcomment,80,'.');
```

Here, cin.get( ) uses a pointer to the structure member, followed by the maximum length of the *szcomment*, 80, followed by a termination character (.). In this case, the comment line will be terminated when (n-1) or 80-1 characters are entered or a period is typed (the nth space is reserved for the null-string terminator, \0). The period is not saved as part of the comment, so the period is added back when the comment is printed. Locate the code that performs this action.

Additional Manipulations with Structures

There are a few points regarding structures that the previous examples have not illustrated. For example, it is also possible to pass individual structure members to a function. Another property allows the nesting of structures.

Passing Structure Members to a Function

Passing individual structure members is an easy and efficient means of limiting access to structure information within a function. For example, a function might be used to print a list of wholesale boat prices available on the lot. In that case, only the *fwholesale* price, which is a member of the structure, would be passed to the function. If this is the case, the call to the function would take the form

```
vprint_price(astNineveh.fwholesale);
```

In this case, vprint_price( ) is the function name and *astNineveh.fwholesale* is the structure name and member.

Nesting Structures Within Structures

Structure declarations can be nested. That is, one structure contains a member or members that are structure types. Consider that the following structure could be included in yet another structure:

```
struct strepair {
    int ioilchange;
    int iplugs;
    int iairfilter;
    int ibarnacle_cleaning;
};
```

In the main structure, the strepair structure could be included as follows:

```
struct stboat {
  char sztype [iSTRING15 + iNULL_CHAR];
  char szmodel[iSTRING15 + iNULL_CHAR];
  char sztitle[iSTRING20 + iNULL_CHAR];
  char szcomment[80];
  struct strepair strepair_record;
  int iyear;
  long int lmotor_hours;
  float fretail;
  float fwholesale;
} astNineveh[iMAX_BOATS];
```

If a particular member from strepair_record is desired, it can be reached by using the following code:

```
printf("%d\n",astNineveh[0].strepair_record.ibarnacle_cleaning);
```

Structures and Bit-Fields

Both C and C++ give you the ability to access individual bits within a larger data type, such as a byte. This is useful, for example, in altering data masks used for system information and graphics. The capability to access bits is built around the C and C++ structure.

For example, it might be desirable to alter the keyboard status register in a computer. The keyboard status register in a computer contains the following information:

register bits

Keyboard Status: 76543210
Port(417h)

where

bit 0 = RIGHT SHIFT depressed (1)
bit 1 = LEFT SHIFT depressed (1)
bit 2 = CTRL depressed (1)
bit 3 = ALT depressed (1)
bit 4 = SCROLL LOCK active (1)
bit 5 = NUM LOCK active (1)
bit 6 = CAPS LOCK active (1)
bit 7 = INS active (1)

In order to access and control this data, a structure could be constructed that uses the following form:

```
struct stkeybits {
  unsigned char
    ucrshift  : 1,        /* lsb */
    uclshift  : 1,
    ucctrl    : 1,
    ucalt     : 1,
    ucscroll  : 1,
    ucnumlock : 1,
    uccaplock : 1,
    ucinsert  : 1;        /* msb */
} stkey_register;
```

The bits are specified in the structure starting with the least significant bit (lsb) and progressing toward the most significant bit (msb). It is feasible to specify more than one bit by just typing the quantity (in place of the 1). Only integer data types can be used for bit-fields.

The members of the bit-field structure are accessed in the normal fashion.

Unions

A *union* is another data type that can be used in many distinctive ways. A specific union, for example, could be construed as an integer in one operation and a float or double in another operation. Unions have an appearance similar to structures. However, they are very dissimilar. Like a structure, a union can contain a group of many data types. In a union, however, those data types all share the same location in memory! Thus, a union can contain information on only one data type at a time. Many other high-level languages refer to this capability as a "variant record."

Unions: Syntax and Rules

A union is constructed by using the keyword union and the syntax that follows:

```
union tag_field {
  type field1;
  type field2;
  type field3;
       .
       .
       .
  type fieldn;
};
```

A semicolon is used for termination because the structure definition is actually a C and C++ statement.

Notice the declaration syntax similarities between structures and unions in the following example declaration:

```
union unmany_types {
   char c;
   int ivalue;
   float fvalue;
   double dvalue;
} unmy_union
```

The union is defined with the keyword union followed by the optional tag field, *unmany_types*. The union's optional tag field operates exactly the way its structure counterpart does. This union contains several members: a character, integer, float, and double. The union will allow *unmany_types* to save information on any one data type at a time.

The variable associated with the union is *unmy_union*. If this statement is contained in a function, the union is local in scope to that function. If the statement is contained outside of all functions, the union will be global in scope.

As with structures, it is also possible to associate several variables with the same union. Also like a structure, members of a union are referenced by using the dot (.) operator. The syntax is simply

unname.*mname*

In this case, *unname* is the variable associated with the union type and *mname* is the name of any member of the union.

Constructing a Simple Union

In order to illustrate some concepts about unions, the following C++ program creates a union of the type just discussed. The purpose of this example is to show that a union can contain the definitions for many data types but can hold the value for only one type at a time.

```
//
//   unions.cpp
//   C++ program demonstrates the use of a union.
//   A union is created with several data types.
//   Copyright (c) Chris H. Pappas and William H. Murray, 1997
//
```

```
#include <iostream.h>

union unmany_types {
  char c;
  int ivalue;
  double fvalue;
  double dvalue;
} unmy_union;

int main(void)
{
  // valid I/O

  unmy_union.c='b';
  cout << unmy_union.c << "\n";

  unmy_union.ivalue=1990;
  cout << unmy_union.ivalue << "\n";

  unmy_union.fvalue=19.90;
  cout << unmy_union.fvalue << "\n";

  unmy_union.dvalue=987654.32E+13;
  cout << unmy_union.dvalue << "\n";

  // invalid I/O

  cout << unmy_union.c << "\n";
  cout << unmy_union.ivalue << "\n";
  cout << unmy_union.fvalue << "\n";
  cout << unmy_union.dvalue << "\n";

  // union size
  cout << "The size of this union is: "
       << sizeof(unmany_types) << " bytes." << "\n";

  return (0);
}
```

The first part of this program simply loads and unloads information from the union. The program works because the union is called upon to store only one data type at a time. In the second part of the program, however, an attempt is made to output each data type from the union. The only valid value is the double, since it was the last value loaded in the previous portion of code.

```
b
1990
19.9
9.876543e+18
ÿ
-154494568
-2.05461e+033
9.87654e+018
The size of this union is: 8 bytes.
```

Unions set aside storage room for the largest data type contained in the union. All other data types in the union share part, or all, of this memory location.

By using the integrated debugger, you can get an idea of what is happening with storage within a union.

Miscellaneous Items

There are two additional topics that should be mentioned at this point: typedef declarations and enumerated types using enum. Both typedef and enum have the capability to clarify program code when used appropriately.

Using typedef

New data types can be associated with existing data types by using typedef. In a mathematically intense program, for example, it might be necessary to use the data type fixed, whole, real, or complex. These new types can be associated with standard C types with typedef. In the next program, two novel data types are created:

```
/*
 *   typedf.c
 *   C program shows the use of typedef.
 *   Two new types are created, "whole" and "real",
 *   which can be used in place of "int" and "double".
 *   Copyright (c) Chris H. Pappas and William H. Murray, 1997
 */

#include <stdio.h>

typedef int whole;
typedef double real;
```

```
int main(void)
{
  whole wvalue=123;
  real  rvalue=5.6789;

  printf("The whole number is %d.\n",wvalue);
  printf("The real number is %f.\n",rvalue);
  return (0);
}
```

Be aware that using too many newly created types can have a reverse effect on program readability and clarity. Use typedef carefully.

You can use a typedef declaration to simplify declarations. Look at the next two coded examples and see if you can detect the subtle code difference introduced by the typedef keyword:

```
struct stboat {
  char sztype [iSTRING15 + iNULL_CHAR];
  char szmodel[iSTRING15 + iNULL_CHAR];
  char sztitle[iSTRING20 + iNULL_CHAR];
  int iyear;
  long int lmotor_hours;
  float fsaleprice;
} stused_boat;
typedef struct {
  char sztype [iSTRING15 + iNULL_CHAR];
  char szmodel[iSTRING15 + iNULL_CHAR];
  char sztitle[iSTRING20 + iNULL_CHAR];
  int iyear;
  long int lmotor_hours;
  float fsaleprice;
} STBOAT;
```

Three major changes have taken place:

- The optional tag field has been deleted. (However, when using typedef you can still use a tag field, although it is redundant in meaning.)

- The tag field, *stboat*, has now become the new type STBOAT and is placed where structure variables have been defined traditionally.

- There now is no variable declaration for *stused_boat*.

The advantage of typedefs lies in their usage. For the remainder of the application, the program can now define variables of the type STBOAT using the simpler syntax

STBOAT STused_boat;

The use of uppercase letters is not syntactically required by the compiler; however, it does illustrate an important coding convention. With all of the possible sources for an identifier's declaration, C programmers have settled on using uppercase to indicate the definition of a new type, constant, enumerated value, and macro, usually defined in a header file. The visual contrast between lowercase keywords and uppercase user-defined identifiers makes for more easily understood code since all uppercase usually means, "Look for this declaration in another file."

Using enum

The enumerated data type, enum, exists for one reason only: to make your code more readable. In other computer languages, this data type is referred to as a user-defined type. The general syntax for enumerated declarations looks like this:

enum *op_tag_field* { *val1,. . .valn* } *op_var_dec* ;

As you may have already guessed, the optional tag field operates exactly as it does in structure declarations. If you leave the tag field off, you must list the variable or variables after the closing brace. Including the tag field allows your application to declare other variables of the tag type. When declaring additional variables of the tag type in C++, it is not necessary to repeat the keyword enum.

Enumerated data types allow you to associate a set of easily understood human symbols—for example, Monday, Tuesday, Wednesday, and so on—with an integral data type. They also help you create self-documenting code. For example, instead of having a loop that goes from 0 to 4, it can now read from Monday to Friday:

```
enum eweekdays { Monday, Tuesday, Wednesday, Thursday, Friday };

/* C enum variable declaration   */
enum eweekdays ewToday;

/* Same declaration in C++        */
eweekdays ewToday;

/* Not using the enumerated type */
```

```
for(i = 0; i <= 4; i++)
    .
    .
    .
/* Using the enumerated type    */
for(ewToday = Monday; ewToday <= Friday; ewToday++)
```

C compilers, historically speaking, have seen no difference between the data types int and enum. This meant that a program could assign an integer value to an enumerated type. In C++ the two types generate a warning message from the compiler without an explicit type cast:

```
/* legal in C not C++ */
ewToday = 1;

/* correcting the problem in C++ */
ewToday = (eweekdays)1;
```

The use of enum is popular in programming when information can be represented by a list of integer values such as the number of months in a year or the number of days in a week. This type of list lends itself to enumeration.

The following example contains a list of the number of months in a year. These are in an enumeration list with a tag name *emonths*. The variable associated with the list is *emcompleted*. Enumerated lists will always start with zero unless forced to a different integer value. In this case, January is the first month of the year.

```
/*
 *    enum.c
 *    C program shows the use of enum types.
 *    Program calculates elapsed months in year, and
 *    remaining months using enum type.
 *    Copyright (c) Chris H. Pappas and William H. Murray, 1997
 */

#include <stdio.h>

enum emonths {
  January=1,
  February,
  March,
```

```
   April,
   May,
   June,
   July,
   August,
   September,
   October,
   November,
   December
} emcompleted;

int main(void)
{
   int ipresent_month;
   int isum,idiff;

   printf("\nPlease enter the present month (1 to 12): ");
   scanf("%d",&ipresent_month);

   emcompleted = December;
   isum = ipresent_month;
   idiff = (int)emcompleted - ipresent_month;

    printf("\n%d month(s) past, %d months to go.\n",isum,idiff);

   return (0);
}
```

The enumerated list is actually a list of integer values, from 1 to 12, in this program. Since the names are equivalent to consecutive integer values, integer arithmetic can be performed with them. The enumerated variable *emcompleted*, when set equal to December, is actually set to 12.

This short program will just perform some simple arithmetic and report the result to the screen:

```
Please enter the current month (1 to 12): 4
4 month(s) past, 8 months to go.
```

The next chapter completes the coverage of standard C and C++ programming features. After completing Chapter 14, you will be ready to investigate the fundamentals of C/C++ libraries, which are presented in Chapter 15.

Chapter 14

Advanced Programming Topics

This chapter deals with advanced programming concepts common to both C and C++. Many of the topics discussed, such as type compatibility and macros, will illustrate those areas of the language where caution must be used when designing an algorithm. Other topics discussed, such as compiler-supplied macros and conditional preprocessor statements, will help you create more streamlined applications. The chapter ends by examining the concepts and syntax necessary to create dynamic linked lists.

Once you have completed Chapters 5 through 15, you will have enough knowledge of C and C++ to make a jump to the world of object-oriented programming. The topic occupies the bulk of the remainder of this book.

Type Compatibility

You have learned that C is not a strongly typed language. C++ is only slightly more strongly typed (for example, enumerated types). You have also learned how C can perform automatic type conversions and explicit type conversions using the cast operator. The following section highlights the sometimes confusing way the compiler interprets compatible types.

ANSI C Definition for Type Compatibility

The ANSI C committee is chiefly responsible for the discussion of and solution for compatible types. Many of the committee's recommendations added features to C that made the language more readily maintained, such as function prototyping. The committee tried to define a set of rules or coded syntax that nailed down the language's automatic behind-the-scenes behavior.

The ANSI C committee decided that for two types to be compatible, they either must be the same type, or must be pointers, functions, or arrays with certain properties as described in the following sections.

What Is an Identical Type?

The term *composite type* is associated with the subject of compatibility. The composite type is the common type that is produced by two compatible types. Any two types that are the same are compatible and their composite type is the same type.

Two arithmetic types are identical if they are the same type. Abbreviated declarations for the same type are also identical. In the following example, both *shivalue1* and *shivalue2* are identical types:

```
short shivalue1;
short int shivalue2;
```

Similarly, the type int is the same as signed int in this next example:

```
int sivalue1;
signed int sivalue2;
```

However, the types int, short, and unsigned are all different. When dealing with character data, the types char, signed char, and unsigned char are always different.

The ANSI C committee stated that any type preceded by an access modifier generates incompatible types. For example, the next two declarations are not compatible types:

```
int ivalue1;
const int ivalue2;
```

In this next set of declarations, see if you can guess which types are compatible:

```
char *pc1, * pc2;
struct {int ix, iy;} stanonymous_coord1, stanonymous_coord2;
struct stxy {int ix, iy;} stanycoords;
typedef struct stxy STXY;
STXY stmorecoords;
```

Both *pc1* and *pc2* are compatible character pointers since the additional space between the * symbol and *pc2* in the declaration is superfluous.

You are probably not surprised that the compiler sees *stanonymous_coord1* and *stanonymous_coord2* as the same type. However, the compiler does not see *stanycoords* as being the identical type to the previous pair of variables. Even though all three variables seem to have the same two integer fields, *stanonymous_coord1* and *stanonymous_coord2* are of an anonymous structure type, while *stanycoords* is of tag type, *stxy*.

Because of the typedef declaration, the compiler does see *struct stxy* as being the identical type to *STXY*. For this reason *stanycoords* is identical to *stmorecoords*.

It is important to remember that the compiler sees typedef declarations as being synonymous for types, not totally new types. The following code segment defines a new type called MYFLOAT that is the same type as float:

```
typedef float MYFLOAT;
```

Enumerated Types

The ANSI C committee initially stated that each enumerated type be compatible with the implementation-specific integral type; this is not the case with C++. In C++, enumeration types are not compatible with integral types. In both C and C++, no two enumerated type definitions in the same source file are compatible. This rule is analogous to the tagged and untagged (anonymous) structures. This explains why *ebflag1* and *ebflag2* are compatible types, while *eflag1* is not a compatible type:

```
enum boolean {0,1} ebflag1;
enum {0,1} eflag1;
enum boolean ebflag2;
```

Array Types

If two arrays have compatible array elements, the arrays are considered compatible. If only one array specifies a size, or neither does, the types are still compatible. However, if both arrays specify a size, both sizes must be identical for the arrays to be compatible. See if you can find all of the compatible arrays in the following declarations:

```
int imax20[20];
const int cimax20[20];
int imax10[10];
int iundefined[];
```

The undimensioned integer array *iundefined* is compatible with both *imax20* and *imax10*. However, this last pair is incompatible because they use different array bounds. The arrays *imax20* (element type int) and *cimax20* (element type const int) are incompatible because their elements are not compatible. If either array specifies an array bound, the composite type of the compatible arrays has that size also. Using the previous code segment, the composite type of *iundefined* and *imax20* is *int[20]*.

Function Types

There are three conditions that must be met in order for two prototyped functions to be considered compatible. The two functions must have the same return types and number of parameters, and the corresponding parameters must be compatible types. However, parameter names do not have to agree.

Structure and Union Types

Each new structure or union type a program declares introduces a new type that is not the same as, nor compatible with, any other type in the same source file. For this reason, the variables *stanonymous1*, *stanonymous2*, and *stfloat1* in the following code segment are all different.

However, a reference to a type specifier that is a structure, union, or enumerated type is the same type. You use the tag field to associate the reference with the type declaration. For this reason, the tag field can be thought of as the name of the type. This rule explains why *stfloat1* and *stfloat2* are compatible types.

```
struct {float fvalue1, fvalue2;} stanonymous1;
struct {float fvalue1, fvalue2;} stanonymous2;
struct sttwofloats {float fvalue1, fvalue2} stfloat1;
struct sttwofloats stfloat2;
```

Pointer Types

Two pointer types are considered compatible if they both point to compatible types. The composite type of the two compatible pointers is the same as the pointed-to composite type.

Multiple Source File Compatibility

The compiler views each declaration of a structure, union, or enumerated type as being a new noncompatible type. This might raise the question, "What happens when you want to reference these types across files within the same program?"

Multiple structure, union, and enumerated declarations are compatible across source files if they declare the same members, in the same order, with compatible member types. However, with enumerated types, the enumeration constants do not have to be declared in the same order, although each constant must have the same enumeration value.

Macros

In Chapter 6 you learned how to use the #define preprocessor to declare symbolic constants. You can use the same preprocessor to define macros. A *macro* is a piece of code that can look and act just like a function.

The advantage of a properly written macro is in its execution speed. A macro is expanded (replaced by its #define definition) during preprocessing, creating *inline*

PROGRAMMING
FOUNDATIONS

code. For this reason, macros do not have the overhead normally associated with function calls. However, each substitution lengthens the overall code size.

Conversely, function definitions expand only once no matter how many times they are called. The trade-off between execution speed and overall code size can help you decide which way to write a particular routine.

There are other subtle differences between macros and functions that are based on when the code is expanded. These differences fall into three categories:

■ In C, a function name evaluates to the address of where to find the subroutine. Because macros sit inline and can be expanded many times, there is no one address associated with a macro. For this reason, a macro cannot be used in a context requiring a function pointer. Also, you can declare pointers to functions, but you cannot declare a pointer to a macro.

■ The compiler sees a function declaration differently from a #define macro. Because of this, the compiler does not do any type checking on macros. The result is that the compiler will not flag you if you pass the wrong number or wrong type of arguments to a macro.

■ Because macros are expanded before the program is actually compiled, some macros treat arguments incorrectly when the macro evaluates an argument more than once.

Defining Macros

Macros are defined the same way you define symbolic constants. The only difference is that the *substitution_string* usually contains more than a single value:

```
#define search_string substitution_string
```

The following example uses the preprocessor statement to define both a symbolic constant and a macro to highlight the similarities.

```
/* #define symbolic constant */
#define iMAX_ROWS 100

/* #define macro              */
#define NL putchar('\n')
```

The *NL* macro causes the preprocessor to search through the source code looking for every occurrence of *NL* and substituting it with putchar('\n'). Notice that the macro did not end with a semicolon. The reason for this has to do with how you invoke a macro in your source code:

```
int main(void)
{
        .
        .
        .
    NL;
```

The compiler requires that the macro call end with a semicolon if the *substitution_string* of the macro ends with a semicolon:

```
#define NL putchar('\n');
```

After the macro expansion had taken place, the compiler would see this code:

```
int main(void)
{
        .
        .
        .
    putchar('\n');;
```

Macros and Parameters

Both C and C++ support macros that take arguments. These macros must be defined with parameters, which serve a purpose similar to that of a function's parameters. The parameters act as placeholders for the actual arguments. The following example demonstrates how to define and use a parameterized macro:

```
/* macro definition */
#define READ_RESPONSE(c) scanf("%c",(&c))
#define MULTIPLY(x,y) ((x)*(y))

int main(void)
{
  char cresponse;
  int a = 10, b = 20;
      .
      .
      .
  READ_RESPONSE(cresponse); /* macro expansions */
```

```
printf("%d",MULTIPLY(a,b));
```

In this example *x*, *y*, and *c* serve as placeholders for *a*, *b*, and *cresponse*, respectively. The two macros, READ_RESPONSE and MULTIPLY, demonstrate the different ways you can invoke macros in your program. For example, MULTIPLY is substituted within a printf( ) statement, while READ_RESPONSE is standalone.

Problems with Macro Expansions

Macros operate purely by substituting one set of characters, or tokens, with another. The actual parsing of the declaration, expression, or statement invoking the macro occurs after the macro expansion process. This can lead to some surprising results if care is not taken. For example, the following macro definition appears to be perfectly legal:

```
#define SQUAREIT(x) x * x
```

If the statement is invoked with a value of 5, as in:

```
iresult = SQUAREIT(5);
```

the compiler sees the following statement:

```
iresult = 5 * 5;
```

On the surface everything still looks okay. However, the same macro invoked with this next statement:

```
iresult = SQUAREIT(x + 1);
```

is seen by the compiler as:

```
iresult = x + (1 * x) + 1;
```

instead of:

```
iresult = (x + 1) * (x + 1);
```

As a general rule, it is safest to always parenthesize each parameter appearing in the body of the macro, as seen in the previous READ_RESPONSE and MULTIPLY macro definitions. And under those circumstances where the macro expansion may appear in a cast expression, for example:

```
dresult = (double)SQUAREIT(x + 1);
```

it is best to parameterize the entire body of the macro:

```
#define SQUAREIT(x) ((x) * (x))
```

Most of the time the compiler is insensitive to additional spacing within standard C and C++ statements. This is not the case with macro definitions. Look closely at this next example and see if you can detect the error:

```
/* incorrect macro definition */
#define BAD_MACRO (ans) scanf("%d",(&ans))
```

Remember that the #define preprocessor searches for the *search_string* and substitutes it with the *substitution_string*. These two strings are delineated by one or more blanks. The previous definition, when expanded, will appear to the compiler as:

```
(ans) scanf("%d",(&ans));
```

This creates an illegal statement. The problem has to do with the space between the macro name BAD_MACRO and *(ans)*. That extra space made the parameter list part of the *substitution_string* instead of its proper place in the *search_string*. To fix the BAD_MACRO definition, remove the extra space:

```
#define BAD_MACRO(ans) scanf("%d",(&ans))
```

To see if you really understand the hidden problems that you can encounter when using macros, see if you can determine what the following statement evaluates to:

```
int x = 5;
iresult = SQUAREIT(x++);
```

The situation gets worse when using certain C and C++ operators like increment, ++, and decrement, --. The result of this expression may be 30, instead of the expected

25, because various compilers may evaluate the expression in several different ways. For example, the macro could be expanded syntactically to read:

```
/* iresult = x * x; */
iresult = 5 * 5;
```

or

```
/* iresult = x * (x+1); */
iresult = 5 * 6;
```

Creating and Using Your Own Macros

Macros can include other macros in their definitions. This feature can be used to streamline your source code. For example, look at the following progressive macro definitions:

```
#define NL putchar('\n')
#define TAB putchar('\t')
#define FORMAT1 NL, NL, TAB
#define FORMAT2 NL, TAB, TAB
#define BEGIN_PROMPT FORMAT1, printf("Want to begin?"); \
                              printf("\nType 1 for yes, 0 for no")
#define READ_RESPONSE FORMAT2,scanf("%d",(&c))
#define FORMAT_PRINT(ccontrol,ivalue,fvalue) \
          printf("\n%c\t%d\t%8.2f",(ccontrol),(ivalue),(fvalue))
```

Now, instead of seeing all of the code defined in the macro, your program code takes on the following appearance:

```
int main(void)
{
  char cresponse;
  int ivalue = 23;
  float fvalue = 56.78;

    .

    .

    .

  BEGIN_PROMPT;
  READ_RESPONSE(cresponse);
  FORMAT_PRINT(cresponse,ivalue,fvalue);
```

Remember, however, that you trade off automatic compiler type checking for source code readability, along with possible side effects generated by invoking the statement's syntax.

Macros Shipped with the Compiler

The ANSI C committee has recommended that all C compilers define five special macros that take no arguments. Each macro name begins and ends with two underscore characters as listed in Table 14-1.

Predefined macros are invoked the same way user-defined macros are invoked. For example, print your program's name, date, and current line number to the screen with the following statement:

```
printf("%s | %s | Line number: %d",__FILE__,__DATE__,__LINE__);
```

Advanced Preprocessor Statements

There are actually 12 standard preprocessor statements, sometimes referred to as *directives*, shown in the following listing.

```
#define
#else
#elif
#endif
#error
#if
#ifdef
#ifndef
#include
#line
#pragma
#undef
```

You are already familiar with two of them, #include, and #define.

Recall that the preprocessor processes a source file before the compiler translates the program into object code. By carefully selecting the correct directives, you can create more efficient header files, solve unique programming problems, and prevent combined files from crashing in on your declarations.

The following sections explain the unique function of each of the ten new preprocessor directives not previously discussed. Some of the examples will use the code found in STDIO.H to illustrate the construction of header files.

Macro Name	Meaning
__LINE__	A decimal integer constant representing the line number of the current source program line
__FILE__	A string constant representing the name of the current source file
__DATE__	A string constant representing the calendar date of the translation in the form "Mmm dd yyyy"
__TIMESTAMP__	A string constant representing the date and time of the last modification of the source file, in the form "Ddd Mmm hh:mm:ss yyyy"
__STDC__	Represents a decimal 1 if the compiler is ANSI C compatible

Table 14-1. *Predefined Macros*

#ifdef and #endif Directives

The #ifdef and #endif directives are two of several conditional preprocessor statements. They can be used to selectively include certain statements in your program. The #endif directive is used with all of the conditional preprocessor statements to signify the end of the conditional block. For example, if the name LARGE_CLASSES has been previously defined, the following code segment will define a new name called MAX_SEATS:

```
#ifdef LARGE_CLASSES
#define MAX_SEATS 100
#endif
```

Whenever a C++ program uses standard C functions, use the #ifdef directive to modify the function declarations so that they have the required extern "C" linkage, which inhibits the encoding of the function name. This usually calls for the following pair of directive code segments to encapsulate the translated code:

```
/*  used in GRAPH.H  */

#ifdef __cplusplus
extern "C" {          /* allow use with C++ */
```

```
#endif

/* translation units */

#ifdef __cplusplus
}
#endif
```

#undef Directive

The #undef directive tells the preprocessor to cancel any previous definition of the specified identifier. This next example combines your understanding of #ifdef with the use of #undef, to change the dimension of MAX_SEATS:

```
#ifdef LARGE_CLASSES
#undef MAX_SEATS 30
#define MAX_SEATS 100
#endif
```

The compiler will not complain if you try to undefine a name not previously defined. Notice that once a name has been undefined, it may be given a completely new definition with another #define directive.

#ifndef Directive

Undoubtedly, you are beginning to understand how the conditional directives operate. The #ifndef preprocessor checks to see if the specified identifier does not exist, and then performs some action. The code segment that follows is taken directly from STDIO.H:

```
#ifndef _SIZE_T_DEFINED
typedef unsigned int size_t;
#define _SIZE_T_DEFINED
#endif
```

In this case the conditionally executed statements include both a typedef and #define preprocessor. This code takes care of defining the type size_t, specified by the ANSI C committee as the return type for the operator sizeof( ). Make sure that you read the section titled "Proper Use of Header Files" to understand what types of statements can be placed in header files.

#if Directive

The #if preprocessor also recognizes the term *defined*.

```
#if defined(LARGE_CLASSES) && !defined (PRIVATE_LESSONS)
#define MAX_SEATS 30
#endif
```

The code shows how the #if directive, together with the defined construct, accomplishes what would otherwise require an #ifndef nested in an #ifdef:

```
#ifdef LARGE_CLASSES
#ifndef PRIVATE_LESSONS
#define MAX_SEATS 30
#endif
```

The two examples produce the same result, but the first is more immediately discerned. Both #ifdef and b directives are restricted to a single test expression. However, the #if combined with defined allows compound expressions.

#else Directive

The #else directive has the expected use. Suppose a program is going to be run on a VAX computer and a PC operating under DOS. The VAX may allocate 4 bytes, or 32 bits, to the type integer, while the PC may allocate only 2 bytes, or 16 bits. The following code segment uses the #else directive to make certain that an integer is seen the same on both systems:

```
#ifdef VAX_SYSTEM
#define INTEGER short int
#else
#define INTEGER int
#endif
```

Of course, the program will have to take care of defining the identifier VAX_SYSTEM when you run it on the VAX. As you can readily see, combinations of preprocessor directives make for interesting solutions.

NOTE: *This type of directive played a major role in the development of Windows applications that were to be source code compatible among Windows 3.x, Windows 95, and Windows NT. Windows 3.1 applications were 16-bit, while Windows 95 and NT applications were essentially 32-bit.*

#elif Directive

The #elif directive is an abbreviation for "else if" and provides an alternate approach to nested #if statements. The following code segment checks to see which class size is defined and uniquely defines the BILL macro:

```
#if defined (LARGE_CLASSES)
     #define BILL printf("\nCost per student $100.00.\n")
  #elif defined (PRIVATE_LESSONS)
     #define BILL printf("\nYour tuition is $1000.00.\n")
    #else
     #define BILL printf("\nCost per student $150.00.\n")
#endif
```

Notice that the preprocessors don't have to start in column 1. The ability to indent preprocessor statements for readability is only one of the many useful recommendations made by the ANSI C committee and adopted by Visual C++.

#line Directive

The #line directive overrides the compiler's automatic line numbering. You can use it to help in debugging your program. Suppose that you have just merged a 50-line routine into a file of over 400 statements. All you care about are any errors that could be generated within the merged code.

Normally, the compiler starts line numbering from the beginning of the file. If your routine had an error, the compiler would print a message with a line number of, say, 289. From your merged files' point of view, where is that?

However, if you include a #line directive in the beginning of your freshly merged subroutine, the compiler would give you a line error number relative to the beginning of the function:

```
#line 1
int imy_mergefunction(void)
{
    .
    .
    .
}
```

#error Directive

The #error directive instructs the compiler to generate a user-defined error message.
It can be used to extend the compiler's own error-detection and message capabilities.
After the compiler encounters an #error directive, it scans the rest of the program for
syntax errors but does not produce an object file. For example:

```
#if !defined( _CHAR_UNSIGNED )
#error /J option required.
#endif
```

This code prints a warning message if _CHAR_UNSIGNED is undefined.

#pragma Directive

The #pragma directive gives the compiler implementation-specific instructions.
The Visual C++ compiler supports the pragmas shown in the following list:

```
alloc_text
auto_inline
check_pointer
check_stack
code_seg
comment
data_seg
function
hdrstop
init_seg
inline_depth
inline_recursion
intrinsic
linesize
```

```
loop_opt
message
native_caller
optimize
pack
pagesize
skip
subtitle
title
warning
```

Conditional Compilation

Preprocessor statements aren't always found in header files. Preprocessor directives can be used in a program's source code to generate efficient compilations. Look at this next code segment and see if you can detect the subtle difference (hint: executable code size):

```
/* compiled if statement */
if(DEBUG_ON) {
  printf("Entering Example Function");
  printf("First argument passed has a value of %d",ifirst_arg);
}

/* comparison statement   */
#if defined(DEBUG_ON)
  printf("Entering Example Function");
  printf("First argument passed has a value of %d",ifirst_arg);
#endif
```

The first if statement is always compiled. This means that the debugging information is perpetually reflected in the executable size of your program. But what if you don't want to ship a product with your intermediate development cycle code? The solution is to conditionally compile these types of statements.

The second portion of the code demonstrates how to selectively compile code with the #if-defined directive. To debug your program, you simply define DEBUG_ON. This makes the nested #if...#endif statements visible to the compiler. However, when you are ready to ship the final product, you remove the DEBUG_ON definition. This makes the statements invisible to the compiler, reducing the size of the executable file.

Try the following simple test to prove to yourself how invisible the #if...#endif directives make the printf( ) statement pair. Copy the previous code segment into a simple C program that does nothing else. Include all necessary overhead (#include, main( ), {, and so on). Do not define DEBUG_ON. Make certain that when you compile the program, there are no error messages. Now, remove the #include <stdio.h> statement from the program and recompile.

At this point the compiler stops at the first printf( ) statement nested within the if...printf( ) block statement. The message printed is "Function 'printf' should have a prototype." You would expect this since the printf( ) statement within the if is always visible to the compiler. Now, simply remove or comment out the if...printf( ) block statement and recompile.

The compiler does not complain about the printf( ) statements nested within the #if...#endif preprocessors. It never saw them. They would only become visible to the compilation phase of the compiler if DEBUG_ON is defined. You can use this selective visibility for more than executable statements. Look at this next code streamlining option:

```
#if defined(DEBUG_ON)
  /****************************************/
  /* The following code segment performs  */
  /* a sophisticated enough solution step  */
  /* to require a comment and debug output */
  /****************************************/
  printf("    debug code goes here        ");
#endif
```

This example not only has a conditional output debug statement, but it also provides room for an explanatory comment. The little extra time it takes to write conditionally compiled code has its trade-off in easily debugged code and small executable code size.

Preprocessor Operators

There are three operators that are only available to preprocessor directives. These are the *stringize*, #, *concatenation*, ##, and *charizing*, #@, operators.

Stringize Operator

Placing a single # in front of a macro parameter causes the compiler to insert the name of the argument instead of its value. This has the overall effect of converting the argument name into a string. The operator is necessary because parameters are not replaced if they occur inside string literals that are explicitly coded in a macro. The following example demonstrates the syntax for the stringize operator:

```
#define STRINGIZE(ivalue) printf(#ivalue " is: %d",ivalue)
    .
    .
    .
int ivalue = 2;
  STRINGIZE(ivalue);
```

The output from the macro will appear as:

```
ivalue is: 2
```

Concatenation Operator

The concatenation operator is useful when building variable and macro names
dynamically. The operator concatenates the items, removing any white space on either
side, forming a new token. When ## is used in a macro, it is processed after the macro
parameters are substituted and before the macro is examined for any additional macro
processing. For example, the following code shows how to create preprocessed
variable names:

```
#define IVALUE_NAMES(icurrent_number) ivalue ## icurrent_number;
    .
    .
    .
int IVALUE_NAMES(1);
```

The compiler sees the previous listing as the following declaration:

```
int ivalue1;
```

Notice that the preprocessor removed the blanks so that the compiler didn't
see *ivalue1* as *ivalue 1*. The operator can be combined with other preprocessor
directives to form complex definitions. The following example uses the concatenation
operator to generate a macro name, which causes the preprocessor to invoke the
appropriate macro:

```
#define MACRO1 printf("MACRO1 invoked.")
#define MACRO2 printf("MACRO2 invoked.")
```

```
#define MAKE_MACRO(n) MACRO ## n
    .
    .
    .
MAKE_MACRO(1);
```

The output from the example will appear as:

```
MACRO1 invoked.
```

#@ Charizing Operator

The charizing preprocessor precedes formal parameters in a macro definition. This causes the actual argument to be treated as a single character with single quotation marks around it. For example:

```
#define CHARIZEIT(cvalue) #@cvalue
    .
    .
    .
cletter = CHARIZEIT(z);
```

The compiler sees the previous code as:

```
cletter = 'z';
```

Proper Use of Header Files

Since header files are made up of syntactically correct C and C++ ASCII text, and are included in other files at the point of the #include directive, many beginning programmers misuse them. Sometimes they are incorrectly used to define entire functions, or collections of functions. While this approach does not invoke any complaints from the compiler, it is a logical misuse of the structure.

Header files are used to define and share common declarations with several source files. They provide a centralized location for the declaration of all external variables, function prototypes, class definitions, and inline functions. Files that must declare a variable, function, or class include header files.

This provides two safeguards. First, all files are guaranteed to contain the same declarations. Second, should a declaration require updating, only one change to the header file need be made. The possibility of failing to update the declaration in a particular file is removed. Header files are frequently made up of:

- const declarations
- enumerated types
- function prototypes
- preprocessor directives
- references to externs
- structure definitions
- typedefs

Caution should be exercised when designing header files. The declarations provided should logically belong together. A header file takes time to compile. If it is too large or filled with too many disparate elements, programmers will be reluctant to incur the compile-time cost of including them.

A second consideration is that a header file should never contain a nonstatic definition. If two files in the same program include a header file with an external definition, most link editors will reject the program because of multiple defined symbols. Because constant values are often required in header files, the default linkage of a const identifier is static. For this reason constants can be defined inside header files.

Making Header Files More Efficient

The compiling of header files is made more efficient by using combinations of preprocessor directives. The best way to learn how to construct an efficient header file is to look at an example:

```
#ifndef _INC_IOSTREAM
#define _INC_IOSTREAM

#if !defined(_INC_DEFS )
#include <_defs.h>
#endif

#if !defined(_INC_MEM )
#include <mem.h>     // to get memcpy and NULL
#endif

#endif  /* !_INC_IOSTREAM */
```

Before looking at the individual statements in the example, you need to know that pass one of the compiler builds a symbol table. One of the entry types in a symbol table is the *mangled* names of header files. Mangling is something that the compiler does to distinguish one symbol from another. The C compiler prepends an underscore to these symbols.

The easiest way to control the compiled visibility of a header file is to surround the code within the header file with a tri-statement combination in the form:

```
#ifndef _INC_MYHEADER
#define _INC_MYHEADER    /* begin _INC_MYHEADER visibility */
       .

       .

       .

#endif /* end of conditional _INC_MYHEADER visibility */
```

This is exactly what was done with the previous coded example where _INC_IOSTREAM was substituted for _INC_MYHEADER. The first time the compiler includes this header file, _INC_IOSTREAM is undefined. The code segment is included, making all of the nested statements visible. From this point forward, any additional #include <iostream.h> statements found in any of the other files used to create the executable, bypass the nested code.

Precompiled Header Files

Writing efficient header files is one method of speeding up the compiling of a program. Another technique is to use precompile header files. Precompilation is most useful for compiling a stable body of code for use with another body of code that is under development.

Creating Precompiled Headers

When working in the development environment, the compiler is set, by default, to automatically use precompiled header files. To create such files, use the Project menu and select the Settings menu item. Click the mouse on the C/C++ tab and select Precompiled Headers in the Category box. You will then be able to set the Create precompiled header file (.PCH) option from this folder.

A similar action can be achieved from the command line. The compiler's command-line option, /Yc, instructs the compiler to create a precompiled header (.PCH) file. The syntax looks like:

```
/Yc[yourfile]
```

No space is allowed between /Yc and [yourfile]. The /Yc switch causes the compiler to compile the entire source file, including any and all header files. The precompiled file is saved with the *yourfile* name of the source file and a .PCH extension.

> *NOTE:* *Precompiled header files are often quite large. When developing multiple projects, keep an eye on how many of these files you are willing to store on your hard disk.*

Using Precompiled Headers

You must follow a certain procedure to create a project that uses precompiled headers. The use of such headers in a project makefile has certain restrictions. First, there can only be one precompiled header *yourfile*.PCH file for each source language in the project (C and/or C++).

Second, all files for a given language must use the identical precompiled header. Additionally, each source file must include the same set of include files, in the same order, up to the include file that you specify. The same path must be specified with the include file in each source file.

The following section lists the steps necessary to insure that a project uses precompiled headers:

1. Start by creating a normal project, making sure that you add at least one source file to the project file list. You can specify the source file from which the .PCH file will be generated by selecting this file in the list of files visible in the FileView window.

2. Next, choose the appropriate compiler options from the Project menu by selecting the Settings menu item and then the C/C++ tab.

At this point, select the Precompiled Headers option in the Category box. Make sure the Automatic use of precompiled headers option is selected.

LIMITS.H and FLOAT.H

The ANSI C committee requires that all C compilers document the system-dependent ranges of integer and floating-point types in order to help you write portable code. Table 14-2 contains a listing of the ANSI C-required integral definitions found in the LIMITS.H header file. Table 14-3 shows the ANSI C-required floating-point definitions.

Program code can use these ranges to make certain that data will fit in the specified data type. For example, a VAX integer may be 4 bytes, while an older DOS-based integer is only 2. To solve this problem, the following code might be used:

Defined Type	Size	Description
#define CHAR_BIT	8	number of bits in a char
#define CHAR_MAX	SCHAR_MAX	maximum char value
#define CHAR_MIN	SCHAR_MIN	minimum char value
#define INT_MAX	2147483647	maximum (signed) int value
#define INT_MIN	(-2147483647 – 1)	minimum (signed) int value
#define LONG_MAX	2147483647L	maximum (signed) long value
#define LONG_MIN	(-2147483647L – 1)	minimum (signed) long value
#define SCHAR_MAX	127	maximum signed char value
#define SCHAR_MIN	(-128)	minimum signed char value
#define SHRT_MAX	32767	maximum (signed) short value
#define SHRT_MIN	(-32768)	minimum (signed) short value
#define UCHAR_MAX	0xff	maximum unsigned char value
#define UINT_MAX	0xffffffff	maximum unsigned int value
#define ULONG_MAX	0xffffffffUL	maximum unsigned long value
#define USHRT_MAX	0xffff	maximum unsigned short value

Table 14-2.   *Values Defined in LIMITS.H (ANSI C)*

```
if (PROGRAM_NEEDED_MAX > INT_MAX)
  pvoid = new llong_storage;
else
  pvoid = new iinteger_storage;
```

Handling Errors—perror( )

One of the many interesting functions prototyped in STDIO.H is a function called
perror( ). The function prints to the stderr stream the system error message for the last
library routine called that generated an error. It does this by using errno and
_sys_errlist prototyped in STDLIB.H. The _sys_errlist value is an array of error
message strings. The errno value is an index into the message string array and is
automatically set to the index for the error generated. The number of entries in the
array is determined by another constant, _sys_nerr, also defined in STDLIB.H.

Definition	Value	Comment
#define FLT_RADIX	2	exponent radix
#define FLT_ROUNDS	1	addition rounding: near
smallest such that 1.0+FLT_EPSILON != 1.0 #define FLT_EPSILON	1.192092896e-07F	
smallest such that 1.0+DBL_EPSILON != 1.0 #define DBL_EPSILON	2.2204460492503131e-016	
smallest such that 1.0+LDBL_EPSILON != 1.0 #define LDBL_EPSILON	DBL_EPSILON	
#define FLT_DIG	6	number of decimal digits of precision
#define DBL_DIG	15	number of decimal digits of precision
#define LDBL_DIG	DBL_DIG	number of decimal digits of precision
#define FLT_MIN	1.175494351e-38F	min positive val
#define DBL_MIN	2.2250738585072014e-308	min positive val
#define LDBL_MIN	DBL_MIN	min pos val
#define FLT_MIN_EXP	(-125)	min binary exponent
#define DBL_MIN_EXP	(-1021)	min binary exponent
#define LDBL_MIN_EXP	DBL_MIN_EXP	min binary exponent
#define FLT_MIN_10_EXP	(-37)	min decimal exponent
#define DBL_MIN_10_EXP	(-307)	min decimal exponent
#define LDBL_MAX_10_EXP	DBL_MIN_10_EXP	max decimal exponent
#define FLT_MAX	3.402823466e+38F	max value
#define DBL_MAX	1.7976931348623158e+308	max value
#define LDBL_MAX	DBL_MAX	max value

Table 14-3. *Values Defined in FLOAT.H (ANSI C)*

Definition	Value	Comment
#define FLT_MAX_EXP	128	max binary exponent
#define DBL_MAX_EXP	1024	max binary exponent
#define LDBL_MAX_EXP	DBL_MAX_EXP	max binary exponent
#define FLT_MAX_10_EXP	38	max decimal exponent
#define DBL_MAX_10_EXP	308	max decimal exponent
#define LDBL_MAX_10_EXP	DBL_MAX_10_EXP	max decimal exponent

Table 14-3. *Values Defined in FLOAT.H (ANSI C) (continued)*

The function perror( ) has only one parameter, a character string. Normally the argument passed is a string representing the file or function that generated the error condition. The following example demonstrates the simplicity of the function:

```c
/*
 *  perror.c
 *  A C program demonstrating the function perror( )
 *  prototyped in stdio.h
 *  Copyright (c) Chris H. Pappas and William H. Murray, 1997
 */

#include <stdio.h>

void main(void)
{
   FILE *fpinfile;
   fpinfile = fopen("input.dat", "r");

   if (!fpinfile)
     perror("Could not open input.dat in file main( ) :");
}
```

The output from the program looks like:

```
Could not open input.dat in file main( ) : No such file or directory
```

Dynamic Memory Allocation—Linked Lists

Linked lists are often the best choice when trying to create memory-efficient algorithms. Previous programs involving arrays of structures (see Chapter 9 and 13, for example) have all included definitions for the total number of structures used. For example, MAX_BOATS might be set to 25. This means that the program can accept data for a maximum of 25 boats. If 70 or 100 boats are brought into the marina, the program itself will have to be altered and recompiled to accommodate the increased number. This is because the structure allocation is *static* (do not confuse this with the storage class modifier—static). Static used in this sense means a variable that is created by the compiler at compile time. These types of variables exist for their normal scope and the programmer cannot create more of them, or destroy any of them, while the program is executing. The disadvantage of static allocation should be immediately clear.

One way around the problem is to set the number of structures higher than needed. If MAX_BOATS is set to 10,000, not even Nineveh Boat Sales could have a marina that large. However, 10,000 means that you are requiring the computer to set aside more than 400 times more memory than before. This is not a wise or efficient way to program.

A better approach is to set aside memory *dynamically* as it is needed. With this approach, memory allocation for structures is requested as the inventory grows. Linked lists allow the use of dynamic memory allocation.

A *linked list* is a collection of structures. Each structure in the list contains an element or pointer that points to another structure in the list. This pointer serves as the link between structures. The concept is similar to an array but enables the list to grow dynamically. Figure 14-1 shows the simple linked list structure for the Nineveh Boat Sales Program.

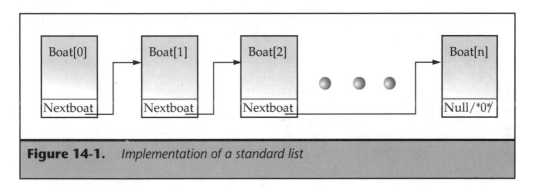

Figure 14-1. *Implementation of a standard list*

The linked list for this example includes a pointer to the next boat in the inventory:

```
struct stboat {
  char sztype[15];
  char szmodel[15];
  char sztitle[20];
  char szcomment[80];
  int iyear;
  long int lmotor_hours;
  float fretail;
  float fwholesale;
  struct stboat *nextboat;
} Nineveh, *firstboat,*currentboat;
```

The user-defined structure type *stboat* is technically known as a *self-referential* structure because it contains a field that holds an address to another structure just like itself. The pointer, *nextboat*, contains the address of the next related structure. This allows the pointer, **nextboat*, in the first structure to point to the second structure, and so on. This is the concept of a linked list of structures.

Considerations When Using Linked Lists

To allow your program to dynamically reflect the size of your data, you need a means for allocating memory as each new item is added to the list. In C, memory allocation is accomplished with the malloc( ) function while in C++ new( ) is used. In the next section below titled "A Simple Linked List," the complete program allocates memory for the first structure with the code:

```
firstboat=(struct stboat *) new (struct stboat);
```

The following code segment demonstrates how you can use a similar statement to achieve subsequent memory allocation for each additional structure. The while loop continues the entire process while there is valid data to be processed:

```
while (datain(&Nineveh) == 0) {
  currentboat->nextboat = (struct stboat *) new (struct stboat);
  if (currentboat->nextboat == NULL) return(1);
  currentboat=currentboat->nextboat;
  *currentboat=Nineveh;
}
```

To give you some experience with passing structures, the while loop begins by sending datain( ), the address of the *stboat* structure, &*Nineveh*. The function datain( ) takes care of filling the structure with valid data or returns a value of 1 if the user has entered the letter "Q" indicating that he or she wants to quit. If datain( ) does not return a 1, the pointer *currentboat->nextboat* is assigned the address of a dynamically allocated *stboat* structure. Notice that the address returned by new( ) was cast, *(struct stboat *)*, so that it matched the data type of the receiving variable. The if statement checks to see if the function call to new( ) was successful or not (new( ) returns a NULL if unsuccessful).

Since the logical use for *currentboat* is to keep track of the address of the last valid *stboat* structure in the list, the statement after the if updates *currentboat* to the address of the new end of the list, namely, *currentboat*'s new *nextboat* address.

The last statement in the loop takes care of copying the contents of the *stboat* structure *Nineveh* into the new dynamically allocated structure pointed to by **currentboat*. The last structure in the list will have its pointer set to NULL. Using NULL marks the end of a linked list. See if you can tell where this is done in the complete program that follows.

A Simple Linked List

The following program shows how to implement the Nineveh Boat Sales example using linked lists. Compare this program with the one in Chapter 13 under the section titled "Constructing an Array of Structures." The C example in Chapter 13 is similar except that it uses a static array implementation. Study the two listings and see which items are similar and which have changed.

```
//
//    C++ program is an example of a simple linked list.
//    Nineveh used boat inventory example is used again
//    Copyright (c) Chris H. Pappas and William H. Murray, 1997
//

#include <stdlib.h>
#include <iostream.h>

struct stboat {
  char sztype[15];
  char szmodel[15];
  char sztitle[20];
  char szcomment[80];
  int iyear;
  long int lmotor_hours;
  float fretail;
```

```
    float fwholesale;
    struct stboat *nextboat;
} Nineveh, *firstboat,*currentboat;

void boatlocation(struct stboat *node);
void output_data(struct stboat *boatptr);
int datain(struct stboat *Ninevehptr);

main( )
{
  firstboat=(struct stboat *) new (struct stboat);

  if (firstboat==NULL) exit(1);

  if (datain(&Nineveh) != 0) exit(1);

  *firstboat=Nineveh;
  currentboat=firstboat;

  while (datain(&Nineveh)==0) {
  currentboat->nextboat=
    (struct stboat *) new (struct stboat);
  if (currentboat->nextboat==NULL) return(1);
  currentboat=currentboat->nextboat;
  *currentboat=Nineveh;
  }

  currentboat->nextboat=NULL; // signal end of list

  boatlocation(firstboat);

  return (0);
}


void boatlocation(struct stboat *node)
{
  do {
    output_data(node);
  } while ((node=node->nextboat) != NULL);
}
```

```
void output_data(struct stboat *boatptr)
{
  cout << "\n\n\n";
  cout << "A " << boatptr->iyear << " "
    << boatptr->sztype << boatptr->szmodel << " "
    << "beauty with " << boatptr->lmotor_hours << " "
    << "low miles.\n";
  cout << boatptr->szcomment << ".\n";
  cout << "Grab the deal by asking your Nineveh salesperson for";
  cout << " #" << boatptr->sztitle << " ONLY! $"
    << boatptr->fretail << ".\n";
}

int datain(struct stboat *Ninevehptr)
{
  char newline;

  cout << "\n[Enter new boat information - a Q quits]\n\n";
  cout << "Enter the make of the boat.\n";
  cin >> Ninevehptr->sztype;

  if (*(Ninevehptr->sztype) == 'Q') return(1);

  cout << "Enter the model of the boat.\n";
  cin >> Ninevehptr->szmodel;

  cout << "Enter the title number for the boat.\n";
  cin >> Ninevehptr->sztitle;

  cout << "Enter the model year for the boat.\n";
  cin >> Ninevehptr->iyear;

  cout << "Enter the number of hours on the boat motor.\n";
  cin >> Ninevehptr->lmotor_hours;

  cout << "Enter the retail price of the boat.\n";
  cin >> Ninevehptr->fretail;

  cout << "Enter the wholesale price of the boat.\n";
  cin >> Ninevehptr->fwholesale;
```

```
cout << "Enter a one line comment about the boat.\n";
cin.get(newline);    // process carriage return
cin.get(Ninevehptr->szcomment,80,'.');

cin.get(newline);    // process carriage return
return(0);
}
```

Notice that the three functions are all passed pointers to a *stboat* structure:

```
int datain(struct stboat *Ninevehptr)
void boatlocation(struct stboat *node)
void output_data(struct stboat *boatptr)
```

The function boatlocation( ) checks the linked list for entries before calling the function output_data( ). It does this with a do...while loop that is terminated whenever *node* pointer is assigned a NULL address. This is only true when you have tried to go beyond the last *stboat* structure in the list. The output_data( ) function formats the output from each linked list structure.

NOTE: *As you test this application, don't forget to add a period (.) at the end of the comment regarding each boat. Failure to do this will cause the program to hang.*

In most high-level languages, linked lists provide the most efficient use of memory but are often the most difficult to debug. You will learn in Chapter 15 that the use of C/C++ libraries can improve efficiency even more.

Chapter 15

Power Programming: Tapping
Important C and C++ Libraries

Programmers rely heavily on functions built into C and C++ compiler libraries. These built-in functions save you from "reinventing the wheel" when you need a special routine. Both C and C++ offer extensive support for character, string, math, and time and date functions. Most library functions are portable from one computer to another and from one operating system to another. There are some functions, however, that are system or compiler dependent. Using these functions efficiently requires you to know where to locate the library functions and how to call them properly.

Many C and C++ functions have already been heavily used in earlier chapters. These include, for example, functions prototyped in the STDIO.H and IOSTREAM.H header files. It is difficult to do any serious programming without taking advantage of their power. This chapter does not repeat a study of their use; it concentrates on new functions that will enhance character, string, and math work.

Important C and C++ Header Files

If you do a directory listing of your Visual C++ INCLUDE subdirectory, the frequently used header files shown in Table 15-1 should be present.

There will be others, too, but these are the header files you will use repeatedly. Since these files are in ASCII format, you may want to print a copy of their contents for a reference. You will find that some header files are short while others are quite long. All contain function prototypes and many contain built-in macros.

Header File	Description
CONIO.H	Console and port I/O
CTYPE.H*	Character functions
IO.H	File handling and low-level I/O
MATH.H*	Math functions
STDIO.H	Stream routines for C
STDLIB.H*	Standard library routines
IOSTREAM.H	Stream routines for C++
STRING.H*	String functions
TIME.H*	Date and time utilities

Table 15-1. *Important Header Files for C and C++*

This chapter will illustrate a use for many popular functions prototyped in the header files marked with an asterisk in the preceding table. These include the system-independent functions prototyped in STDLIB.H, CTYPE.H, MATH.H, STRING.H, and TIME.H. Other functions contained in STDIO.H, IOSTREAM.H, and so on have already been used throughout the book.

Standard Library Functions (STDLIB.H)

The standard library macros and functions comprise a powerful group of items for data conversion, memory allocation, and other miscellaneous operations. The most frequently encountered macros and functions are shown in Table 15-2. The prototypes are found in STDLIB.H.

As you examine Table 15-2, notice that almost half of the functions shown perform a data conversion from one format to another.

You'll make use of many of these functions and macros as you develop your own C and C++ programs.

Performing Data Conversions

The first important group of functions described in STDLIB.H are the data converting functions. Their principal job is to convert data from one data type to another. For example, the atol( ) function converts string information to a long.

The syntax of each function is shown in the following list of function prototypes:

```
double atof(const char *s)
int atoi(const char *s)
long atol(const char *s)
char *ecvt (double value,int n,int *dec,int *sign)
char *fcvt(double value,int n,int *dec,int *sign)
char *gcvt(double value,int n,char *buf)
char *itoa(int value,char *s,int radix)
char *ltoa(long value,char *s,int radix)
double strtod(const char *s,char **endptr)
long strtol(const char *s,char **endptr,int radix)
unsigned long strtoul(const char *s,char **endptr,int radix)
char *ultoa(unsigned long value,char *s,int radix)
```

In these functions, *s points to a string, *value* is the number to be converted, *n* represents the number of digits in the string, and *dec* locates the decimal point relative to the start of the string. The variable *sign* represents the sign of the number, *buf* is a character buffer, *radix* represents the number base for the converted value, and *endptr* is usually null. If not a null value, the function sets it to the character that stops the scan.

Macro or Function	Description
_exit( )	Terminates a program
_lrotl( )	Rotates an unsigned long to the left
_lrotr( )	Rotates an unsigned long to the right
_rotl( )	Rotates an unsigned integer to the left
_rotr( )	Rotates an unsigned integer to the right
abort( )	Aborts program; terminates abnormally
abs( )	Absolute value of an integer
atexit( )	Registers termination function
atof( )	Converts a string to a float
atoi( )	Converts a string to an integer
atol( )	Converts a string to a long
bsearch( )	Binary search on an array
calloc( )	Allocates main memory
div( )	Divides integers
_ecvt( )	Converts a float to a string
exit( )	Terminates a program
_fcvt( )	Converts a float to a string
free( )	Frees memory
_gcvt( )	Converts a float to a string
getenv( )	Gets a string from the environment
_itoa( )	Converts an integer to a string
labs( )	Absolute value of a long
ldiv( )	Divides two long integers
_ltoa( )	Converts a long to a string
malloc( )	Allocates memory
_putenv( )	Puts a string in the environment
qsort( )	Performs a quick sort

Table 15-2. *Popular Standard Library Functions*

Macro or Function	Description
rand( )	Random number generator
realloc( )	Reallocates main memory
srand( )	Initializes random number generator
strtod( )	Converts a string to a double
strtol( )	Converts a string to a long
strtoul( )	Converts a string to an unsigned long
_swab( )	Swaps bytes from s1 to s2
system( )	Invokes DOS COMMAND.COM file
_ultoa( )	Converts an unsigned long to a string

Table 15-2.   *Popular Standard Library Functions* (continued)

The use of several of these functions is illustrated in the following programs.

Changing a Float to a String

The fcvt( ) function converts a float to a string. It is also possible to obtain information regarding the sign and location of the decimal point.

```
/*
 *   fcvt.c
 *   Demonstrating the use of the fcvt( ) function.
 *   Copyright (c) Chris H. Pappas and William H. Murray, 1997
 */

#include <stdio.h>
#include <stdlib.h>

main( )
{
  int dec_pt,sign;
  char *ch_buffer;
  int num_char=7;
```

```
ch_buffer = fcvt(-234.5678,num_char,&dec_pt,&sign);
printf("The buffer holds: %s\n",ch_buffer);
printf("The sign (+=0, -=1) is stored as a: %d\n",sign);
printf("The decimal place is %d characters from right\n",
       dec_pt);
return (0);
}
```

The output from this program is shown here:

```
The buffer holds: 2345678000
The sign (+=0, -=1) is stored as a: 1
The decimal place is 3 characters from right
```

Changing a String to a Long Integer

The strtol( ) function converts the specified string, in the given base, to its decimal equivalent. The following example shows a string of binary characters that will be converted to a decimal number:

```
/*
 *   strtol.c
 *   Demonstrating the use of the strtol( ) function.
 *   Copyright (c) Chris H. Pappas and William H. Murray, 1997
 */

#include <stdlib.h>
#include <stdio.h>

main( )
{
  char *s="101101",*endptr;
  long long_number;

  long_number=strtol(s,&endptr,2);
  printf("The binary value %s is equal to %ld decimal.\n",
          s,long_number);
  return (0);
}
```

In this example, "101101" is a string that represents several binary digits. The program produces the following results:

```
The binary value 101101 is equal to 45 decimal.
```

This is an interesting function since it allows a string of digits to be specified in one base and converted to another. This function would be a good place to start if you wanted to develop a general base change program.

Performing Searches and Sorts

The bsearch( ) function is used to perform a binary search of an array. The qsort( ) function performs a quick sort. The lfind( ) function can be used to perform a linear search for a key in an array of sequential records. The lsearch( ) function performs a linear search on a sorted or unsorted table. Examine the function syntax shown in the following list.

```
void *bsearch(const void *key,const void *base,
    size_t nelem,size_t width,int(*fcmp)(const void *,
    const void *))

void qsort(void *base,size_t nelem,size_t width,
    int(*fcmp)(const void *,const void *))

void *lfind(const void *key,const void *base,
    size_t *,size_t width,int(*fcmp)
    (const void *,const void *))

void *lsearch(const void *key, void *base,
    size_t *,size_t width,int(*fcmp)
    (const void *,const void *))
```

Here, *key* represents the search key, *base* is the array to search, *nelem* contains the number of elements in the array, *width* is the number of bytes for each table entry, *fcmp* is the comparison routine used, and *num* reports the number of records.

The next application shows the use of two of the search and sort functions just described.

Using qsort( ) to Sort a Group of Integers

In C and C++, as in any language, sorting data is very important. Visual C++ provides the qsort( ) function for sorting data. The following example is one application in which qsort( ) can be used.

```
/*
 *    qsort.c
 *    Demonstrating the use of the qsort( ) function.
 *    Copyright (c) Chris H. Pappas and William H. Murray, 1997
 */

#include <stdio.h>
#include <stdlib.h>

int int_comp(const void *i,const void *j);

int list[12]={95,53,71,86,11,28,34,53,10,11,74,-44};

main( )
{
  int i;

  qsort(list,12,sizeof(int),int_comp);

  printf("The array after qsort:\n");
  for(i=0;i<12;i++)
    printf("%d ",list[i]);
  return (0);
}

int int_comp(const void *i,const void *j)
{
  return ((*(int *)i)-(*(int *)j));
}
```

The original numbers, in the variable *list*, are signed integers. The qsort( ) function will arrange the original numbers in ascending order, leaving them in the variable *list*. Here, the original numbers are sorted in ascending order:

```
The array after qsort:

--44 10 11 11 28 34 53 53 71 74 86 95
```

Can qsort( ) be used with floats? Why not alter the previous program and see?

Finding an Integer in an Array of Integers

You use the bsearch( ) function to perform a search in an integer array. The search
value for this example is contained in *search_number*.

```c
/*
 *    bsearch.c
 *    Demonstrating the use of the bsearch( ) function.
 *    Copyright (c) Chris H. Pappas and William H. Murray, 1997
 */

#include <stdlib.h>
#include <stdio.h>

int int_comp(const void *i,const void *j);

int data_array[]={100,200,300,400,500,
                  600,700,800,900};

main( )
{
  int *search_result;
  int search_number=400;

  printf("Is 400 in the data_array? ");
  search_result=bsearch(&search_number,data_array,9,
                        sizeof(int),int_comp);
  if (search_result) printf("Yes!\n");
    else printf("No!\n");
  return (0);
}

int int_comp(const void *i,const void *j)
{
  return ((*(int *)i)-(*(int *)j));
}
```

This application sends a simple message to the screen regarding the outcome of
the search, as shown here:

```
Is 400 in the data_array? Yes!
```

You can also use this function to search for a string of characters in an array.

Miscellaneous Operations

There are several miscellaneous functions, listed in Table 15-3 and described in this section, that perform a variety of diverse operations. These operations include calculating the absolute value of an integer and bit rotations on an integer.

Function	Description
Abort or End:	
void abort(void)	Returns an exit code of 3
int atexit(atexit_t func)	Calls function prior to exit
void exit(int status)	Returns zero for normal exit
int system(const char * command)	Command is a DOS command
void_exit(int status)	Terminates with no action
Math:	
div_t div(int number,int denom)	Divides and returns quotient and remainder in div_t
int abs(int x)	Determines absolute value of x
long labs(long x)	Determines absolute value of x
ldiv_t ldiv(long numerator,long denominator)	Similar to div( ) with longs
int rand(void)	Calls random number generator
void srand(unsigned seed)	Seeds random number generator
Rotate:	
unsigned long_lrotl(unsigned long val,int count)	Rotates the long val to the left
unsigned long_llrotr(unsigned long val,int count)	Rotates the long val to the right
unsigned _rotl(unsigned val,int count)	Rotates the integer val to the left
unsigned _rotr(unsigned val,int count)	Rotates the integer val to the right
Miscellaneous:	
char * getenv(const char * name)	Gets environment string
int putenv(const char * name)	Puts environment string
void _swap(char * from, char * to,int nbytes)	Swaps the number of characters in nbytes

Table 15-3.   *Miscellaneous Functions*

Bit rotation functions give you the ability to perform operations that were once just in the realm of assembly language programmers.

Using the Random Number Generator

Visual C++ provides a random number function. The random number generator can be initialized or seeded with a call to srand( ). The seed function accepts an integer argument and starts the random number generator.

```
/*
 *    rand.c
 *    Demonstrating the use of the srand( ) and rand( ),
 *    random number functions.
 *    Copyright (c) Chris H. Pappas and William H. Murray, 1997
 */

#include <stdlib.h>
#include <stdio.h>

main( )
{
  int x;

  srand(3);

  for (x=0;x<8;x++)
    printf("Trial #%d, random number=%d\n",
           x,rand( ));
  return (0);
}
```

An example of random numbers generated by rand( ) is shown here:

```
Trial #0, random number=48
Trial #1, random number=7196
Trial #2, random number=9294
Trial #3, random number=9091
Trial #4, random number=7031
Trial #5, random number=23577
Trial #6, random number=17702
Trial #7, random number=23503
```

Random number generators are important in programming for statistical work and for applications that rely on the generation of random patterns. It is important that the numbers produced be unbiased, that is, that all numbers have an equal probability of appearing.

Rotating Data Bits

C and C++ provide a means of rotating the individual bits of integers and longs to the right and to the left. In the next example, two rotations in each direction are performed:

```
/*
 *   rotate.c
 *   Demonstrating the use of the _rotl( ) and _rotr( )
 *   bit rotate functions.
 *   Copyright (c) Chris H. Pappas and William H. Murray, 1997
 */

#include <stdio.h>
#include <stdlib.h>

main( )
{
 unsigned int val = 0x2345;

 printf("rotate bits of %X to the left 2 bits and get %X\n",
        val,_rotl(val,2));
 printf("rotate bits of %X to the right 2 bits and get %X\n",
        val,_rotr(val,2));
}
```

Here are the results:

```
rotate bits of 2345 to the left 2 bits and get 8D14
rotate bits of 2345 to the right 2 bits and get 400008D1
```

Note that the original numbers are in hexadecimal format.

The use of the bit rotation functions and the use of logical operators such as and, or, xor, and so on, give C and C++ the ability to manipulate data bit by bit.

The Character Functions (CTYPE.H)

Characters are defined in most languages as single-byte values. Chinese is one case where 2 bytes are needed. The character macros and functions in C and C++, prototyped or contained in CTYPE.H, take integer arguments but utilize only the lower byte of the integer value. Automatic type conversion usually permits character arguments to also be passed to the macros or functions. The macros and functions shown in Table 15-4 are available.

These macros and functions allow characters to be tested for various conditions or to be converted between lowercase and uppercase.

Checking for Alphanumeric, Alpha, and ASCII Values

The macros shown in Table 15-5 allow ASCII-coded integer values to be checked with the use of a lookup table.

Macro	Description
isalnum( )	Checks for alphanumeric character
isalpha( )	Checks for alpha character
isascii( )	Checks for ASCII character
iscntrl( )	Checks for control character
isdigit( )	Checks for decimal digit (0–9)
isgraph( )	Checks for printable character (no space)
islower( )	Checks for lowercase character
isprint( )	Checks for printable character
ispunct( )	Checks for punctuation character
isspace( )	Checks for white space character
isupper( )	Checks for uppercase character
isxdigit( )	Checks for hexadecimal digit
toascii( )	Translates character to ASCII equivalent
tolower( )	Translates character to lowercase
toupper( )	Translates character to uppercase

Table 15-4. *Character Macros Available in C and C++*

Macro	Description
int isalnum(ch)	Checks for alphanumeric values A–Z, a–z, and 0–9; ch0 is integer
int isalpha(ch)	Checks for alpha values A–Z and a–z; ch0 is integer
int isascii(ch)	Checks for ASCII values 0–127 (0–7Fh); ch0 is integer

Table 15-5. *Three Important Macros*

The following program checks the ASCII integer values from zero to 127 and reports which of the preceding three functions produce a TRUE condition for each case:

```c
/*
 *   alpha.c
 *   Demonstrating the use of the isalnum( ), isalpha( ),
 *   and isascii( ) library functions.
 *   Copyright (c) Chris H. Pappas and William H. Murray, 1997
 */

#include <stdio.h>
#include <ctype.h>

main( )
{
  int ch;
  for (ch=0;ch<=127;ch++) {
    printf("The ASCII digit %d is an:\n",ch);
    printf("%s",isalnum(ch) ? "  alpha-numeric char\n" : "");
    printf("%s",isalpha(ch) ? "  alpha char\n" : "");
    printf("%s",isascii(ch) ? "  ascii char\n" : "");
    printf("\n");
  }
  return (0);
}
```

A portion of the information sent to the screen is shown here:

```
The ASCII digit 0 is an:
  ascii char

The ASCII digit 1 is an:
  ascii char

        .

        .

        .

The ASCII digit 48 is an:
  alpha-numeric char
  ascii char

The ASCII digit 49 is an:
  alpha-numeric char
  ascii char

        .

        .

        .

The ASCII digit 65 is an:
  alpha-numeric char
  alpha char
  ascii char

The ASCII digit 66 is an:
  alpha-numeric char
  alpha char
  ascii char
```

These functions are very useful in checking the contents of string characters.

Checking for Control, White Space, and Punctuation

The routines shown in Table 15-6 are implemented as both macros and functions.

These routines allow ASCII-coded integer values to be checked via a lookup table. A zero is returned for FALSE and a nonzero for TRUE. A valid ASCII character set is assumed. The value *ch* is an integer.

Routine	Description
int iscntrl(ch)	Checks for control character
int isdigit(ch)	Checks for digit 0–9
int isgraph(ch)	Checks for printable characters (no space)
int islower(ch)	Checks for lowercase a–z
int isprint(ch)	Checks for printable character
int ispunct(ch)	Checks for punctuation
int isspace(ch)	Checks for white space
int isupper(ch)	Checks for uppercase A–Z
int isxdigit(ch)	Checks for hexadecimal value 0–9, a–f, or A–F

Table 15-6.   *Routines Implemented as Both Macros and Functions*

The next application checks the ASCII integer values from zero to 127 and reports which of the preceding nine functions give a TRUE condition for each value:

```
/*
 *   contrl.c
 *   Demonstrating several character functions such as
 *   isprint( ), isupper( ), iscntrl( ), etc.
 *   Copyright (c) Chris H. Pappas and William H. Murray, 1997
 */

#include <stdio.h>
#include <ctype.h>

main( )
{
  int ch;
  for (ch=0;ch<=127;ch++) {
    printf("The ASCII digit %d is a(n):\n",ch);
    printf("%s",isprint(ch)  ? "  printable char\n" : "");
    printf("%s",islower(ch)  ? "  lowercase char\n" : "");
    printf("%s",isupper(ch)  ? "  uppercase char\n" : "");
    printf("%s",ispunct(ch)  ? "  punctuation char\n" : "");
```

```
      printf("%s",isspace(ch)  ? "  space char\n" : "");
      printf("%s",isdigit(ch)  ? "  char digit\n" : "");
      printf("%s",isgraph(ch)  ? "  graphics char\n" : "");
      printf("%s",iscntrl(ch)  ? "  control char\n" : "");
      printf("%s",isxdigit(ch) ? "  hexadecimal char\n" : "");
      printf("\n");
   }
   return (0);
}
```

A portion of the information sent to the screen is shown here:

```
The ASCII digit 0 is a(n):
  control char

The ASCII digit 1 is a(n):
  control char

            .

            .

            .

The ASCII digit 32 is a(n):
  printable char
  space char

The ASCII digit 33 is a(n):
  printable char
  punctuation char
  graphics char

The ASCII digit 34 is a(n):
  printable char
  punctuation char
  graphics char

            .

            .

            .

The ASCII digit 65 is a(n):
  printable char
  uppercase char
  graphics char
  hexadecimal char
```

```
The ASCII digit 66 is a(n):
  printable char
  uppercase char
  graphics char
  hexadecimal char
```

Conversions to ASCII, Lowercase, and Uppercase

The macros and functions shown in Table 15-7 allow ASCII-coded integer values to be translated.

The macro toascii( ) converts *ch* to ASCII by retaining only the lower 7 bits. The functions tolower( ) and toupper( ) convert the character value to the format specified. The macros _tolower( ) and _toupper( ) return identical results when supplied proper ASCII values. A valid ASCII character set is assumed. The value *ch* is an integer.

The next example shows how the macro toascii( ) converts integer information to correct ASCII values:

```c
/*
 *   ascii.c
 *   Demonstrating the use of the toascii( ) function.
 *   Copyright (c) Chris H. Pappas and William H. Murray, 1997
 */

#include <stdio.h>
#include <ctype.h>

int ch;

main( )
{
  for(ch=0;ch<=512;ch++) {
    printf("The ASCII value for %d is %d\n",
          ch,toascii(ch));
  }
  return (0);
}
```

Macro	Description
int toascii(ch)	Translates to ASCII character
int tolower(ch)	Translates *ch* to lowercase if uppercase
int _tolower(ch)	Translates *ch* to lowercase
int toupper(ch)	Translates *ch* to uppercase if lowercase
int _toupper(ch)	Translates *ch* to uppercase

Table 15-7.   *Functions Used to Translate ASCII-Coded Integer Values*

Here is a partial list of the information sent to the screen:

```
The ASCII value for 0 is 0
The ASCII value for 1 is 1
The ASCII value for 2 is 2
                .
                .
                .
The ASCII value for 128 is 0
The ASCII value for 129 is 1
The ASCII value for 130 is 2
                .
                .
                .
The ASCII value for 256 is 0
The ASCII value for 257 is 1
The ASCII value for 258 is 2
                .
                .
                .
The ASCII value for 384 is 0
The ASCII value for 385 is 1
The ASCII value for 386 is 2
```

PROGRAMMING
FOUNDATIONS

The String Functions (STRING.H)

Strings in C and C++ are usually considered one-dimensional character arrays terminated with a null character. The string functions, prototyped in STRING.H, typically use pointer arguments and return pointer or integer values. You can study the syntax of each command in the next section or, in more detail, from the Help facility provided with the Visual C++ compiler. Additionally, buffer-manipulation functions such as memccpy( ) and memset( ) are also prototyped in STRING.H. The functions shown in Table 15-8 are the most popular ones in this group.

Function	Description
memccpy( )	Copies from source to destination
memchr( )	Searches buffer for first *ch*
memcmp( )	Compares *n* characters in buf1 and bufs
memcpy( )	Copies *n* characters from source to destination
memicmp( )	Same as memcmp( ), except case sensitive
memmove( )	Moves one buffer to another
memset( )	Copies *ch* into *n* character positions in buf
strcat( )	Appends a string to another string
strchr( )	Locates first occurrence of a *ch* in a string
strcmp( )	Compares two strings
strcmpi( )	Compares two strings (case insensitive)
strcoll( )	Compares two strings (local specific)
strcpy( )	Copies a string to another string
strcspn( )	Locates first occurrence of a character in a string from a given character set
strdup( )	Replicates the string
strerror( )	System-error message saved
stricmp( )	Same as strcmpi( )

Table 15-8. *Popular String Functions*

Function	Description
strlen( )	Length of string
strlwr( )	String converted to lowercase
strncat( )	Characters of string appended
strncmp( )	Characters of two strings compared
strncpy( )	Characters of a string copied to another
strnicmp( )	Characters of two strings compared (case insensitive)
strnset( )	String characters set to a given character
strpbrk( )	First occurrence of a character from one string in another string
strrchr( )	Last occurrence of a character in a string
strrev( )	Reverses characters in a string
strset( )	All characters in a string set to given character
strspn( )	Locates first substring from a given character set in a string
strstr( )	Locates one string in another string
strtok( )	Locates tokens within a string
strupr( )	Converts a string to uppercase
strxfrm( )	Transforms local-specific string

Table 15-8. *Popular String Functions* (continued)

The memory and string functions provide flexible programming power to C and C++ programmers.

Working with Memory Functions

The memory functions, discussed in the previous section, are accessed with the following syntax.

void *memccpy(void *dest,void *source,int *ch*,unsigned *count*)

void *memchr(void *buf,int *ch*,unsigned *count*)

int memcmp(void *buf1,void *buf2,unsigned *count*)

void *memcpy(void *dest,void *source,unsigned *count*)

int memicmp(void *buf1,void *buf2,unsigned *count*)

void *memmove(void *dest,void *source,unsigned *count*)

void *memset(void *dest,int *ch*,unsigned *count*)

Here, *buf, *buf1, *buf2, *dest, and *source are pointers to the appropriate string buffer. The integer *ch* points to a character value. The unsigned *count* holds the character count for the function.

The next section includes a number of examples that show the use of many of these functions.

Find a Character in a String

In this example, the buffer is searched for the occurrence of the lowercase character "f," using the memchr( ) function:

```
/*
 *    memchr.c
 *    Demonstrating the use of the memchr( ) function.
 *    Finding a character in a buffer.
 *    Copyright (c) Chris H. Pappas and William H. Murray, 1997
 */

#include <string.h>
#include <stdio.h>

char buf[35];
char *ptr;

main( )
{
  strcpy(buf,"This is a fine day for a search." );
  ptr=(char *)memchr(buf,'f',35);
  if (ptr != NULL)
    printf("character found at location: %d\n",
```

```
            ptr-buf+1);
  else
    printf("character not found.\n");
  return (0);
}
```

For this example, if a lowercase "f" is in the string, the memchr( ) function will report the "character found at location: 11."

Compare Characters in Strings

This example highlights the memicmp( ) function. This function compares two strings contained in *buf1* and *buf2*. This function is insensitive to the case of the string characters.

```
/*
 *   memcmp.c
 *   Demonstrating the use of the memicmp( ) function
 *   to compare two string buffers.
 *   Copyright (c) Chris H. Pappas and William H. Murray, 1997
 */

#include <stdio.h>
#include <string.h>

char buf1[40],
     buf2[40];

main( )
{
  strcpy(buf1,"Well, are they identical or not?");
  strcpy(buf2,"Well, are they identicle or not?");
  /* 0 - identical strings except for case */
  /* x - any integer, means not identical */

  printf("%d\n",memicmp(buf1,buf2,40));
  /* returns a nonzero value */
  return (0);
}
```

If it weren't for the fact that "identical" (or is it "identicle"?) was spelled incorrectly in the second string, both strings would have been the same. A nonzero value, -1, is returned by memicmp( ) for this example.

Loading the Buffer with memset( )

Often it is necessary to load or clear a buffer with a predefined character. In those cases you might consider using the memset( ) function, shown here:

```
/*
 *   memset.c
 *   Demonstrating the use of the memset( ) function
 *   to set the contents of a string buffer.
 *   Copyright (c) Chris H. Pappas and William H. Murray, 1997
 */

#include <stdio.h>
#include <string.h>

char buf[20];

main( )
{
  printf("The contents of buf: %s",memset(buf,'+',15));
  buf[15] = '\0';
  return (0);
}
```

In this example, the buffer is loaded with 15 + characters and a null character. The program will print 15 + characters to the screen.

Working with String Functions

The prototypes for using several string manipulating functions contained in STRING.H are shown in Table 15-9.

Here, *s is a pointer to a string, while *s1 and *s2 are pointers to two strings. Usually *s1 points to the string to be manipulated and *s2 points to the string doing the manipulation. *ch* is a character value.

Function	Description
int strcmp(const char * s1, const char * s2)	Compares 2 strings
size_t strcspn(const char * s1, const char * s2)	Finds a substring in a string
char * strcpy(char * s1, const char * s2)	Copies a string
char * strerror(int errnum)	ANSI-supplied number
char * _strerror(char * s)	User-supplied message
size_t strlen(const char * s)	Null-terminated string
char * strlwr(char * s)	String to lowercase
char * strncat(char * s1, const char * s2, size_t n)	Appends *n* char s2 to s1
int strncmp(const char * s1, char * s2, size_t n)	Compares first *n* characters of two strings
int strnicmp(const char * s1, const char * s2, size_t n)	Compares first *n* characters of two strings (case insensitive)
char * strncpy(char * s1, const char * s2, size_t n)	Copies *n* characters of s2 to s1
char * strnset(char * s, int ch, size_t n)	Sets first *n* characters of string to char setting
char * strpbrk(const char * s1, const char * s2)	Locates character from const s2 in s1
char * strrchr(const char * s, int ch)	Locates last occurrence of *ch* in string
char * strrev(char * s)	Converts string to reverse
char * strset(char * s, int ch)	String to be set with *ch*
size_t strspn(const char * s1, const char * s2)	Searches s1 with char set in s2
char * strstr(const char * s1, const char * s2)	Searches s1 with s2
char * strtok(char * s1, char * s2)	Finds token in s1; s1 contains token(s), s2 contains the delimiters
char * strupr(char * s)	Converts string to uppercase

Table 15-9.   *String Manipulating Functions*

Comparing the Contents of Two Strings

The following program uses the strcmp( ) function and reports how one string compares to another.

```c
/*
 *   strcmp.c
 *   Demonstrating the use of the strcmp( ) function
 *   to compare two strings.
 *   Copyright (c) Chris H. Pappas and William H. Murray, 1997
 */

#include <stdio.h>
#include <string.h>

char s1[45] = "A group of characters makes a good string.";
char s2[45] = "A group of characters makes a good string?";
int answer;

main( )
{
  answer = strcmp(s1,s2);
  if (answer>0) printf("s1 is greater than s2");
    else if (answer==0) printf("s1 is equal to s2");
      else printf("s1 is less than s2");
  return (0);
}
```

Can you predict which of the preceding strings would be greater? Can you do it without running the program? The answer is that s1 is less than s2.

Searching for Several Characters in a String

The next program searches a string for the first occurrence of one or more characters:

```c
/*
 *   strspn.c
 *   Demonstrating the use of the strcspn( ) function to find
 *   the occurrence of one of a group of characters.
 *   Copyright (c) Chris H. Pappas and William H. Murray, 1997
 */
```

```
#include <stdio.h>
#include <string.h>

char s1[35];
int answer;

main( )
{
  strcpy(s1,"We are looking for great strings." );
  answer=strcspn(s1,"abc");
  printf("The first a,b,c appeared at position %d\n",
         answer+1);
  return (0);
}
```

This program will report the position of the first occurrence of an "a", a "b", or a "c." A 1 is added to the answer since the first character is at index position zero. This program reports an "a" at position 4.

The First Occurrence of a Single Character in a String

Have you ever wanted to check a sentence for the occurrence of a particular character? You might consider using the strchr( ) function. The following application looks for the first blank or space character in the string.

```
/*
 *    strchr.c
 *    Demonstrating the use of the strchr( ) function to
 *    locate the first occurrence of a character in a string.
 *    Copyright (c) Chris H. Pappas and William H. Murray, 1997
 */

#include <stdio.h>
#include <string.h>

char s1[20] = "What is a friend?";
char *answer;

main( )
{
```

```
    answer=strchr(s1,' ');
    printf("After the first blank: %s\n",answer);
    return (0);
}
```

What is your prediction on the outcome after execution? Run the program and see.

Finding the Length of a String

The strlen( ) function reports the length of any given string. Here is a simple example:

```
/*
 *    strlen.c
 *    Demonstrating the use of the strlen( ) function to
 *    determine the length of a string.
 *    Copyright (c) Chris H. Pappas and William H. Murray, 1997
 */

#include <stdio.h>
#include <string.h>

char *s1="String length is measured in characters!";

main( )
{
    printf("The string length is %d",strlen(s1));
    return (0);
}
```

In this example, the strlen( ) function reports on the total number of characters contained in the string. In this example, there are 40 characters.

Locating One String in Another String

The strstr( ) function searches a given string within a group (a string) of characters, as shown here:

```
/*
 *    strstr.c
 *    Demonstrating the use of the strstr( ) function to
 *    locate a string within a string.
```

```
*    Copyright (c) Chris H. Pappas and William H. Murray, 1997
*/

#include <stdio.h>
#include <string.h>

main( )
{
  char *s1="There is always something you miss.";
  char *s2="way";

  printf("%s\n",strstr(s1,s2));
  return (0);
}
```

This program sends the remainder of the string to the printf( ) function after the first occurrence of "way." The string printed to the screen is "ways something you miss."

Converting Characters to Uppercase

A handy function to have in a case-sensitive language is one that can convert the characters in a string to another case. The strupr( ) function converts lowercase characters to uppercase, as shown here:

```
/*
*    strupr.c
*    Demonstrating the use of the strupr( ) function to
*    convert lowercase letters to uppercase.
*    Copyright (c) Chris H. Pappas and William H. Murray, 1997
*/

#include <stdio.h>
#include <string.h>

char *s1="Uppercase characters are easier to read.";
char *s2;

main( )
{
  s2=strupr(s1);
```

```
    printf("The results: %s",s2);
    return (0);
}
```

This program converts each lowercase character to uppercase. Note that only lowercase letters will be changed.

The Math Functions (MATH.H)

The functions prototyped in the MATH.H header file permit a great variety of mathematical, algebraic, and trigonometric operations.

The math functions are relatively easy to use and to understand for those familiar with algebraic and trigonometric concepts. The most popular math functions are shown in Table 15-10.

 NOTE: Functions accept and return double values except where noted. Functions ending in "l" accept and return long double values.

Many of these functions were demonstrated in earlier chapters. When using trigonometric functions, remember that angle arguments are always specified in radians.

Programmers desiring complex number arithmetic must resort to using struct complex and the _cabs( ) function described in MATH.H. Following is the only structure available for complex arithmetic in Visual C++:

```
struct complex {double x,double y}
```

This structure is used by the _cabs( ) function. The _cabs( ) function returns the absolute value of a complex number.

Building a Table of Trigonometric Values

Since math functions have already been used extensively in this book, the only example for this section involves an application that will generate a table of sine, cosine, and tangent values for the angles from zero to 45 degrees.

Function	Description
abs( )	Returns absolute value of integer argument
acos( ), acosl( )	Arc cosine
asin( ), asinl( )	Arc sine
atan( ), atanl( )	Arc tangent
atan2( ), atan2l( )	Arc tangent of two numbers
ceil( ), ceill( )	Greatest integer
cos( ), cosl( )	Cosine
cosh( ), coshl( )	Hyberbolic cosine
exp( ), expl( )	Exponential value
fabs( ), fabsl( )	Absolute value
floor( ), floorl( )	Smallest value
fmod( ), fmodl( )	Modulus operator
frexp( ), frexpl( )	Split mantissa and exponent
hypot( ), hypotl( )	Hypotenuse
labs( )	Returns absolute value of long argument
ldexp( ), ldexpl( )	x times 2 to the exp power
log( ), logl( )	Natural log
log10( ), log10l( )	Common log
modf( ), modfl( )	Mantissa and exponent
pow( ), powl( )	x to y power
pow10( ), pow10l( )	x raised by power of 10
sin( ), sinl( )	Sine
sinh( ), sinhl( )	Hyperbolic sine
sqrt( ), sqrtl( )	Square root
tan( ), tanl( )	Tangent
tanh( ), tanhl( )	Hyperbolic tangent

Table 15-10. *Popular Math Functions*

This application also takes advantage of the special C++ formatting abilities. Study the following listing to determine how the output will be sent to the screen:

```cpp
//
//   math.cpp
//   A program that demonstrates the use of several
//   math functions.
//   Copyright (c) Chris H. Pappas and William H. Murray, 1997
//

#include <iostream.h>
#include <iomanip.h>
#include <math.h>

#define PI 3.14159265359

main( )
{
  int i;
  double x,y,z,ang;

  for (i=0;i<=45;i++) {
    ang=PI*i/180;   // convert degrees to radians
    x=sin(ang);
    y=cos(ang);
    z=tan(ang);
    // formatting output columns
    cout << setiosflags(ios::left) << setw(8)
         << setiosflags(ios::fixed) << setprecision(6);
    // data to print
    cout << i << "\t" << x << "\t" <<
            y << "\t" << z << "\n";
  }
  return (0);
}
```

This application uses the sin( ), cos( ), and tan( ) functions to produce a formatted trigonometric table. The angles are stepped from zero to 45 degrees and are converted to radians before being sent to each function. This particular C++ formatting is discussed in more detail in Chapter 18.

Following is a partial output from this application:

```
0  0.000000  1.000000  0.000000
1  0.017452  0.999848  0.017455
2  0.034899  0.999391  0.034921
.      .       .          .

.      .       .          .

.      .       .          .

28  0.469472  0.882948  0.531709
29  0.484810  0.874620  0.554309
30  0.500000  0.866025  0.577350
31  0.515038  0.857167  0.600861
32  0.529919  0.848048  0.624869
.      .       .          .

.      .       .          .

.      .       .          .

43  0.681998  0.731354  0.932515
44  0.694658  0.719340  0.965689
45  0.707107  0.707107  1.000000
```

The Time Functions (TIME.H)

Table 15-11 shows some of the time and date functions found in TIME.H.

Names	Description
asctime( )	Converts date and time to an ASCII string and uses tm structure
ctime( )	Converts date and time to a string
difftime( )	Calculates the difference between two times
gmtime( )	Converts date and time to GMT using tm structure
localtime( )	Converts date and time to tm structure
strftime( )	Allows formatting of date and time data for output
time( )	Obtains current time (system)
tzset( )	Sets time variables for environment variable TZ

Table 15-11. *Time and Date Functions*

These functions offer a variety of ways to obtain time and/or date formats for programs. A discussion of the syntax for each function is included in the next section.

Time and Date Structures and Syntax

Many of the date and time functions described in the previous section use the tm structure defined in TIME.H. This structure is shown here:

```
struct tm   {
  int   tm_sec;
  int   tm_min;
  int   tm_hour;
  int   tm_mday;
  int   tm_mon;
  int   tm_year;
  int   tm_wday;
  int   tm_yday;
  int   tm_isdst;
};
```

The syntax for calling each date and time function differs according to the function's ability. The syntax and parameters for each function are shown in Table 15-12.

The TZ environment string uses the following syntax:

TZ = zzz[+/-]d[d]{lll}

Here, zzz represents a three-character string with the local time zone—for example, "EST" for Eastern Standard Time. The [+/]d[d] argument contains an adjustment for the local time zone's difference from GMT. Positive numbers are a westward adjustment, while negative numbers are an eastward adjustment. For example, a five (5) would be used for EST. The last argument, {lll}, represents the local time zone's daylight savings time—for example, EDT for Eastern Daylight Savings Time.

Several of these functions are used in example programs in the next section.

Function	Description
char * asctime(const struct tm * tblock)	Converts the structure into a 26-character string
	For example: Sun June 1, 10:18:20 1997\n\0
char * ctime(const time_t * time)	Converts a time value, pointed to by * time into a 26-char string (see asctime( ))
double difftime(time_t time2, time_t time1)	Calculates the difference between time2 and time1 and returns a double
struct tm * gmtime(const time_t * timer)	Accepts address of a value returned by the function time( ) and returns a pointer to the structure with GMT information
struct tm * localtime(const time_t * timer)	Accepts address of a value returned by the function time( ) and returns a pointer to the structure with local time information
size_t strftime (char * s, size_t maxsize, const char * fmt, const struct tm * t)	Formats date and time information for output. s points to the string information, maxsize is maximum string length, fmt represents the format, and t points to a structure of type tm. The formatting options include:
	%a Abbreviate weekday name
	%A Full weekday name
	%b Abbreviate month name
	%B Full month name
	%c Date and time information
	%d Day of month (01 to 31)
	%H Hour (00 to 23)

Table 15-12.   *Time and Date Function Parameters*

Function	Description
	%I Hour (00 to 12)
	%j Day of year (001 to 366)
	%m Month (01 to 12)
	%M Minutes (00 to 59)
	%p AM or PM
	%S Seconds (0 to 59)
	%U Week number (00 to 51), Sunday is first day
	%w Weekday (0 to 6)
	%W Week number (00 to 51), Monday is first day
	%x Date
	%X Time
	%y Year, without century (00 to 99)
	%Y Year, with century
	%Z Time zone name
	%% Character %
time_t time(time_t * timer)	Returns the time in seconds since 00:00:00 GMT, January 1, 1970
void _tzset (void)	Sets the global variables daylight, timezone0, and tzname0 based on the environment string

Table 15-12. *Time and Date Function Parameters* (continued)

Working with the localtime( ) and asctime( ) Functions

Many times it is necessary to obtain the time and date in a programming application. The next program returns these values by using the localtime( ) and asctime( ) functions:

```
/*
 *   asctim.c
 *   Demonstrating the use of the localtime( ) and asctime( )
 *   functions.
 *   Copyright (c) Chris H. Pappas and William H. Murray, 1997
 */

#include <time.h>
#include <stdio.h>

struct tm *date_time;
time_t timer;

main( )
{
  time(&timer);
  date_time=localtime(&timer);

  printf("The present date and time is: %s\n",
  asctime(date_time));
  return (0);
}
```

This program formats the time and date information in the manner shown here:

```
The present date and time is: Sat May 31 13:16:20 1997
```

Working with the gmtime( ) and asctime( ) Functions

There are other functions that you can also use to return time and date information. The next program is similar to the last example, except that the gmtime( ) function is used.

```
/*
 *   cmtime.c
 *   Demonstrating the use of the gmtime( ) and asctime( )
 *   functions.
 *   Copyright (c) Chris H. Pappas and William H. Murray, 1997
 */
```

```
#include <time.h>
#include <stdio.h>

main( )
{
  struct tm *date_time;
  time_t timer;

  time(&timer);
  date_time=gmtime(&timer);

  printf("%.19s\n",asctime(date_time));
  return (0);
}
```

The following date and time information was returned by this program:

```
Sat May 31 14:13:25
```

Working with the strftime( ) Function

The strftime( ) function provides the greatest formatting flexibility of all the date and time functions. The following program illustrates several formatting options.

```
/*
 *    strtm.c
 *    Demonstrating the use of the strftime( ) function.
 *    Copyright (c) Chris H. Pappas and William H. Murray, 1997
 */

#include <time.h>
#include <stdio.h>

main( )
{
  struct tm *date_time;
  time_t timer;
  char str[80];
```

```
    time(&timer);
    date_time=localtime(&timer);
    strftime(str,80,"It is %X on %A, %x",
             date_time);
    printf("%s\n",str);
    return (0);
}
```

Here is a sample of the output for this program:

```
It is 17:18:45 on Saturday, 05/31/97
```

You may find that the strftime( ) function is not portable from one system to another. Use it with caution if portability is a consideration.

Working with the ctime( ) Function

The following C++ program illustrates how to make a call to the ctime( ) function. This program shows how easy it is to obtain date and time information from the system.

```
//
//   ctime.cpp
//   Demonstrating the use of the ctime( ) function.
//   Copyright (c) Chris H. Pappas and William H. Murray, 1997
//

#include <time.h>
#include <iostream.h>

time_t longtime;

main( )
{
  time(&longtime);
  cout << "The time and date are " <<
          ctime(&longtime) << "\n";
  return (0);
}
```

The output, sent to the screen, would appear in the following format:

```
The time and date are Sat May 31 14:23:27 1997
```

Creating a Time Delay Routine

Usually it is desirable for programs to execute as quickly as possible. However, there are times when slowing down information makes it easier for the user to view and understand. The time_delay( ) function in the following application delays program execution. The delay variable is in seconds. For this example, there is a two-second delay between each line of output to the screen.

```c
/*
 *    tdelay.c
 *    A C program that demonstrates how to create a delay
 *    function for slowing program output.
 *    Copyright (c) Chris H. Pappas and William H. Murray, 1997
 */

#include <stdio.h>
#include <time.h>

void time_delay(int);

main( )
{
  int i;

  for (i=0;i<25;i++) {
    time_delay(2);
    printf("The count is %d\n",i);
  }
  return (0);
}

void time_delay(int t)
{
  long initial,final;
  long ltime;

  initial=time(&ltime);
  final=initial+t;
```

```
    while (time(&ltime) < final);
    return;
}
```

What other uses might the time_delay( ) function have? One case might be where the computer is connected to an external data sensing device, such as a thermocouple or strain gauge. The function could be used to take readings every minute, hour, or day.

What's Coming

The next chapter begins a new section of this book dealing with object-oriented programming. You'll find that many of the library functions discussed in this chapter can be extended to object-oriented programming techniques.

Part III

Foundations for Object-Oriented Programming in C++

Chapter 16

An Introduction to
Object-Oriented
Programming

There is *great* news to be found in this chapter! But first, here is a question for you: Do you need to buy a new computer, with a special state-of-the-art microprocessor, to run object-oriented programs? Of course, the answer is NO. Now take a moment to think about just what that means. In file type terms, it means that a *.EXE is a *.EXE is a *.EXE. In other words, no matter if the source file was interpreted (as in the case of the BASIC language), compiled (as in assembly language, Pascal, FORTRAN, C, and C++), or compiled *and* interpreted (as in Java), once the translator generated the final executable form, they all ran on the same microprocessor.

This is fantastic news for you! Regardless of the source syntax, all of the program's instructions are translated down to simple adds, subtracts, compares, jumps, loops, and so on—native to the microprocessor's machine language. If you know assembly language, you already know just how close a language can be to the actual microprocessor's native tongue. As a language becomes more "high-level," you simply force the interpreter or compiler to do more work in getting your English-like statements down to something the computer understands. And, in the case of *all* object-oriented languages, even more work is required.

Notice, however, what is doing all that work: the translator. Notice something else: since you do not buy a new computer to run object-oriented programs, object-oriented languages are inherently incapable of providing any more raw horsepower than, say, assembly language! Please stop for a moment to fully appreciate this last statement.

So what is different about object-oriented languages such as C++? In a word, packaging. Here is a simple analogy. For the purpose of argument, imagine a program that declares and uses 100 integer variables. Messy, yes, but structurally possible. Now, imagine that you are in an intro computer course and your instructor begins teaching you the topic of Arrays. Ah, you say, what a logical and syntactical way to clean up this mess of 100 separate, standalone integer variables! But notice, the rewritten array version did not give your program any more horsepower, just streamlined logical and syntactical efficiency. In a similar sense, that is all that object-oriented programming does.

Object-oriented programming languages streamline and repackage concepts you, as a programmer, already know! What *are* new are those language constructs unique to C and C++, not found in other programming languages, that are the foundational building blocks to C++'s object-oriented capabilities. For example, C's keyword static is a non-object-oriented language feature. However, static can be used in object-oriented programs. If you are new to object-oriented design and syntax, your problem will not be learning how to repackage what you already know— such as how to write a function (called a *member function* or *method* in OOP terminology), but instead, how to incorporate C and C++'s *new* constructs in conjunction with the repackaging.

Here is one more fundamental concept you need to get clear on. You do not need to use object-oriented syntax to write a Windows application, and you can use object-oriented syntax to write DOS applications! Object-oriented syntax is a separate issue from what a program needs structurally to run under a multitasking operating system like Windows, or under the now fading command-line MS-DOS mode. Beginning OOPS and Windows programmers often view the two requirements as one entity.

Adding even more confusion to the mix are the product-specific recombinations of this packaging of "standard Windows syntax" used by companies such as Microsoft and Borland International. Using all of the objects given to you to create a Windows application can be an overwhelming experience at first. To avoid this, Microsoft, for example, has preselected "standard" Windows objects and repackaged the already repackaged horsepower.

Microsoft calls this double repackaging *MFC (Microsoft Foundation Class Library)*. Borland International calls their recombination *OWL (Object Windows Library)*. And guess what? While the "standard" Windows objects these repackaged products are based on are compatible, the double recombinations are not! So, when you buy either MFC or OWL, realize that you are diverting from pure form. The good news, at least from Microsoft's point of view, is that MFC has the market dominance.

With all of this information under your belt, sit back and relax. In this chapter you will see how what you already know as a programmer are really the underpinnings to object-oriented horsepower. What stands between you now and what you will easily understand after having read this chapter is terminology. Many of the procedural language fundamentals you already know simply have new names in an object-oriented world. For example, in this chapter you will learn how the C++ class type (an actual object-definition syntax/concept) is an outgrowth of the C struct type (a regular procedural language record-definition syntax/concept)!

There Is Nothing New Under the Sun

Advertisers know that a product will sell better if the word "new" appears somewhere on the product's label. If, however, the saying "There is nothing new under the sun" is applied to programming, the conclusion would have to be that object-oriented programming is not a new programming concept at all. Scott Guthery states that "object-oriented programming has been around since subroutines were invented in the 1940s" ("Are the Emperor's New Clothes Object Oriented?," *Dr. Dobb's Journal*, December 1989). The article continues by suggesting that objects, the foundation of object-oriented programming, have appeared in earlier languages, such as FORTRAN II.

Considering these statements, why are we only hearing about object-oriented programming in the closing decade of the 1900s? Why is it being touted as the newest programming technique of the century? It seems that the bottom line is packaging. OOP concepts may have been available in 1940, but we certainly didn't have them packaged in a usable container.

Early programmers, growing up with the BASIC language, often wrote large programs without the use of structured programming concepts. Pages and pages of programming code were tied together with one- or two-letter variables that had a global scope. goto statements abounded. The code was a nightmare to read, understand, and debug. Adding new features to such a program was like unlocking Pandora's box. To say the least, the code was very difficult to maintain.

In the 1960s, structured programming concepts were introduced suggesting the use of meaningful variable names, global and local variable scope, and a procedure-oriented top-down programming approach. Applying these concepts made code easier to read, understand, and debug. Program maintenance was improved because the program could now be studied and altered one procedure at a time. Programming languages such as Ada, C, and Pascal encourage a structured approach to programming problems.

Bjarne Stroustrup is considered the father of C++; he developed the language at Bell Labs in the early 1980s. He may well be the father of object-oriented programming as we know it in the C++ language. Jeff Duntemann stated that "Object-oriented programming is structured Structured Programming. It's the second derivative of software development, the Grand Unifying Theory of program structure" ("Dodging Steamships," *Dr. Dobb's Journal,* July 1989). Indeed, what you'll see as we go along is that object-oriented programming, using C++, builds upon foundations established earlier in the C language. Even though C++ is the foundational language for object-oriented programming, it is still possible to write unstructured code or procedure-oriented code. The choice is yours.

There might not be anything new under the sun if Scott Guthery's statements are taken to mean "programming concepts," but this chapter introduces you to the most elegant packaging method for a programming concept you have ever seen. At last, we truly have the tools, with languages such as C++, to enter the golden age of object-oriented programming.

Traditional Structured Programming

The earlier chapters of this book were devoted to teaching traditional procedure-oriented structured programming techniques for solving C and C++ problems. These chapters introduced you to fundamental C and C++ syntax in a familiar programming environment. (If you have been programming in a language such as Pascal for any length of time, you have probably been using a structured procedure approach in solving programming problems. A procedural approach is common among all structured languages including C, C++, Pascal, and PL/I.) You have seen that a procedure-oriented C or C++ program is structured in such a way that there is typically a main function and possibly one or more functions (subroutines) that are called from the main function. This is a top-down approach. The main function is typically short, shifting the work to the remaining functions in the program. Program execution flows from the top of the main function and terminates at the bottom of the same function.

In this approach, code and data are separate. Procedures define what is to happen to data, but the two never become one. You'll see that this changes in object-oriented programming. The procedural approach suffers from several disadvantages, chiefly program maintenance. When additions or deletions must be made to the program code, such as in a database program, often the entire program must be reworked to include the new routines. This approach takes enormous amounts of time in both development and debugging. A better approach toward program maintenance is needed.

Object-Oriented Programming

Object-oriented programs (OOPs) function differently from the traditional procedural approach. They require a new programming strategy that is often difficult for traditional procedure-oriented programmers to grasp. In this and the next three chapters you will be introduced to the concepts that make up object-oriented programming in C++. If you have already written or examined program code for Microsoft Windows 3.*x*, Windows 95, or Windows NT, you have had a taste of one of the concepts used in object-oriented programming—that a program consists of a group of objects that are often related. With C++, you form objects by using the new class data type. A class provides a set of values (data) and the operations (methods or member functions) that act on those values. You can then manipulate the resulting objects by using messages.

It is the message component of object-oriented languages that is also common to Windows and Presentation Manager programs. In object-oriented programming, objects hold not only the data (member data) but the methods (member functions) for working on that data. The two items have been combined into one working concept. Simply put, objects contain data and the methods for working on that data.

There are three distinct advantages offered to the programmer by object-oriented programming. The first is program maintenance. Programs are easier to read and understand, and object-oriented programming controls program complexity by allowing only the necessary details to be viewed by the programmer. The second advantage is program alteration (adding or deleting features). You can often make additions and deletions to programs, such as in a database program, by simply adding or deleting objects. New objects can inherit everything from a parent object, and they only need to add or delete items that differ. The third advantage is that you can use objects numerous times. You can save well-designed objects in a toolkit of useful routines that you can easily insert into new code, with few or no changes to that code.

In the earlier chapters of this book, you discovered that you could convert many C programs to C++, and vice versa, by making simple program alterations. For example, printf is switched to cout for I/O streams. This is an easy switch because the conversion is from and to a procedural programming structure. However, object-oriented programming is exclusively in the C++ realm because C does not provide the vital link—the abstract data type class. It is therefore more difficult to convert a procedure-oriented program to object-oriented form. Programs have to be reworked, with traditional functions being replaced with objects. In some cases, it turns out to be easier to discard the old program and create an object-oriented program from the ground up. This can be considered a distinct disadvantage.

C++ and Object-Oriented Programming

Object-oriented programming concepts cross language boundaries. Microsoft Quick Pascal, for example, was one of the first languages to allow the use of objects. What does C++ have that makes it a suitable language for developing object-oriented programs? The answer is, as previously mentioned, the class data type. It is C++'s class type, built upon C's struct type, that gives the language the ability to build objects. Also, C++ brings several additional features to object-oriented programming not included in other languages that simply make use of objects. C++'s advantages include strong typing, operator overloading, and less emphasis on the preprocessor. It is true that you can do object-oriented programming with other products and in other languages, but with C++ the benefits are outstanding. This is a language that was designed, not retrofitted, for object-oriented programming.

In the next section of this chapter, you will learn some object-oriented terminology. These terms and definitions will help you form a solid understanding of this programming technique. Be prepared; the new terminology will be your biggest hurdle as you enter the world of object-oriented programming.

Object-Oriented Terminology

Much of the terminology of object-oriented programming is language independent; that is, it is not associated with a specific language such as Pascal or C++. Therefore, many of the following definitions apply to the various implementations of object-oriented languages. Chapter 17 discusses terms that are more C++ specific.

Object-oriented programming is a programming technique that allows you to view concepts as a variety of objects. By using objects, you can represent the tasks that are to be performed, their interaction, and any given conditions that must be observed. A data structure often forms the basis of an object; thus, in C or C++, the struct type can form an elementary object. Communicating with objects can be done through the use of messages, as mentioned earlier. Using messages is similar to calling a function in a procedure-oriented program. When an object receives a message, methods contained within the object respond. *Methods* are similar to the functions of procedure-oriented programming. However, methods are part of an object.

The C++ class is an extension of the C and C++ struct type and forms the required abstract data type for object-oriented programming. The class can contain closely related items that share attributes. Stated more formally, an object is simply an instance of a class. In Figure 16-1, the Lincoln automobile class is illustrated.

Assume that the Lincoln automobile class is described in the program's code. This class might include a description of items that are common to all Lincolns and data concerning maintenance intervals. At run-time, three additional objects of the Lincoln class can be created. They could include the Lincoln Town Car, the Lincoln Mark VII,

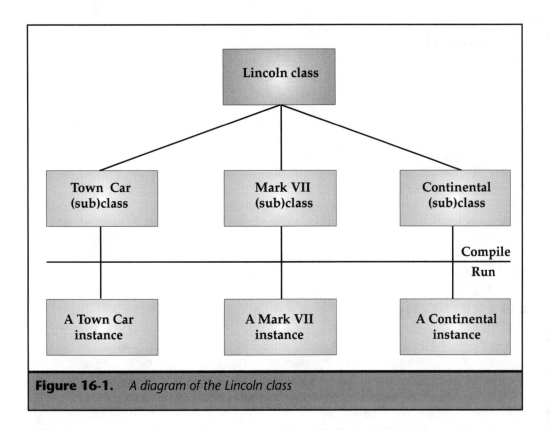

Figure 16-1. *A diagram of the Lincoln class*

and the Lincoln Continental. The additional objects might include details of features and data common to each individual model. For example, a Mark VII is an object that describes a particular type of Lincoln automobile. It is an instance of the Lincoln class.

If a message is sent to the instance of the Lincoln class (similar to a call to a function) with instructions to dynamically adjust the air suspension on all four wheels during a sharp turn, that message could be utilized only by the Continental (at least in 1992 models) object of the class. Only the Lincoln Continental had an active air suspension in the 1992 model.

Ultimately, there should emerge class libraries containing many object types. You could use instances of those object types to piece together program code. You will see interesting examples of this when Windows class libraries are described in Chapters 22 and 23.

Before you examine these terms in closer detail, it is a good idea to become familiar with several additional concepts that relate to C++ and object-oriented programming, as described in the next few sections.

Encapsulation

Encapsulation refers to the way each object combines its member data and member functions (methods) into a single structure. Figure 16-2 illustrates how you can combine data fields and methods to build an object.

Typically, an object's description is part of a C++ class and includes a description of the object's internal structure, how the object relates with other objects, and some form of protection that isolates the functional details of the object from outside the class. The C++ class structure does all of this.

In a C++ class, you control functional details of the object by using private, public, and/or protected descriptors. In object-oriented programming, the *public* section is typically used for the interface information (methods) that makes the class reusable across applications. If data or methods are contained in the public section, they are available outside the class. The *private* section of a class limits the availability of data or methods to the class itself. A *protected* section containing data or methods is limited to the class and any derived subclasses.

Class Hierarchy

The C++ class actually serves as a template or pattern for creating objects. The objects formed from the class description are *instances* of the class. It is possible to develop a *class hierarchy* where there is a parent class and several child classes. In C++, the basis for doing this revolves around *derived classes*. Parent classes represent more

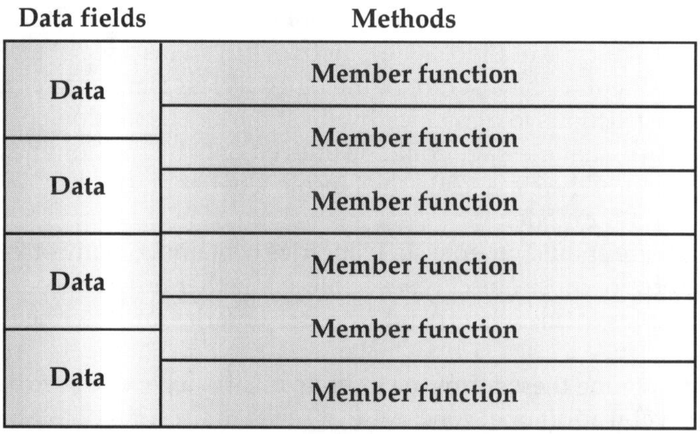

Figure 16-2.   *Data fields and methods combined to build an object*

generalized tasks, while derived child classes are given specific tasks to perform. For example, the Lincoln class discussed earlier might contain data and methods common to the entire Lincoln line, such as engines, instrumentation, batteries, braking ability, and handling. Child classes derived from the parent, such as Town Car, Mark VII, and Continental, could contain items specific to the class. For example, the 1992 Continental was the only car in the line with an active suspension system.

Inheritance

Inheritance in object-oriented programming allows a class to inherit properties from a class of objects. The parent class serves as a pattern for the derived class and can be altered in several ways. (In the next chapter you will learn that member functions can be overloaded, new member functions can be added, and member access privileges can be changed.) If an object inherits its attributes from a single parent, it is called *single inheritance*. If an object inherits its attributes from multiple parents, it is called *multiple inheritance*. Inheritance is an important concept since it allows reuse of a class definition without requiring major code changes. Inheritance encourages the reuse of code since child classes are extensions of parent classes.

Polymorphism

Another important object-oriented concept that relates to the class hierarchy is that common messages can be sent to the parent class objects and all derived subclass objects. In formal terms, this is called *polymorphism.*

Polymorphism allows each subclass object to respond to the message format in a manner appropriate to its definition. Imagine a class hierarchy for gathering data. The parent class might be responsible for gathering the name, social security number, occupation, and number of years of employment for an individual. You could then use child classes to decide what additional information would be added based on occupation. In one case a supervisory position might include yearly salary, while in another case a sales position might include an hourly rate and commission information. Thus, the parent class gathers general information common to all child classes while the child classes gather additional information relating to specific job descriptions. Polymorphism allows a common data-gathering message to be sent to each class. Both the parent and child classes respond in an appropriate manner to the message. Polymorphism encourages extendability of existing code.

Virtual Functions

Polymorphism gives objects the ability to respond to messages from routines when the object's exact type is not known. In C++, this ability is a result of *late binding*. With late binding, the addresses are determined dynamically at run-time, rather than statically at compile time, as in traditional compiled languages. This static (fixed) method is often called *early binding*. Function names are replaced with memory addresses. You accomplish late binding by using *virtual functions,* which are defined in the parent class when subsequent derived classes will overload the function by redefining the function's implementation. When you use virtual functions, messages are passed as a pointer that points to the object instead of directly to the object.

Virtual functions utilize a table for address information. The table is initialized at run-time by using a constructor. A constructor is invoked whenever an object of its class is created. The job of the constructor here is to link the virtual function with the table of address information. During the compile operation, the address of the virtual function is not known; rather, it is given the position in the table (determined at run-time) of addresses that will contain the address for the function.

A First Look at the C++ Class

It has already been stated that the C++ class type is an extension of C's struct type. In this section, you learn how you can use the struct type in C++ to form a primitive class, complete with data and members. Next, you examine the formal syntax for defining a class and see several simple examples of its implementation. The section discusses the differences between a primitive struct class type and an actual C++ class and presents several simple examples to illustrate class concepts. (Chapter 17 is devoted to a detailed analysis of the C++ class as it applies to object-oriented programming.)

A Structure as a Primitive Class

Chapter 13 discussed structures for C and C++. In many respects, the structure in C++ is an elementary form of a class. You use the keyword struct to define a structure. Examine the following code:

```
//
//   sqroot.cpp
//   C++ program using the keyword "struct" to illustrate a
//   primitive form of class. Here several member functions
//   are defined within the structure.
//   Copyright (c) Chris H. Pappas and William H. Murray, 1997
//

#include <iostream.h>
#include <math.h>

struct math_operations {
  double data_value;

    void set_value(double ang) {data_value=ang;}
    double get_square(void) {double answer;
```

```
                           answer=data_value*data_value;
                           return (answer);}
  double get_square_root(void)  {double answer;
                                 answer=sqrt(data_value);
                                 return (answer);}
} math;

main( )
{
  // set numeric value to 35.63
  math.set_value(35.63);

  cout << "The square of the number is: "
       << math.get_square( ) << endl;
  cout << "The square root of the number is: "
       << math.get_square_root( ) << endl;
  return (0);
}
```

The first thing to notice in this code is that the structure definition contains member data and functions. While you are used to seeing data declarations as part of a structure, this is probably the first time you have seen member functions defined within the structure definition. There was no mention of member functions in the discussion of the struct type in Chapter 13 because they are exclusive to C++. These member functions can act upon the data contained in the structure (or class) itself.

Recall that a class can contain member data and functions. By default, in a struct declaration in C++, member data and functions are public. (A *public* section is one in which the data and functions are available outside the structure.) Here is the output sent to the screen when the program is executed:

```
sdi15.1
```

In this example, the structure definition contains a single data value:

```
double data_value;
```

Next, three member functions are defined. Actually, the code for each function is contained within the structure:

```
void set_value(double ang) {data_value=ang;}
double get_square(void) {double answer;
                         answer=data_value*data_value;
                         return (answer);}
double get_square_root(void) {double answer;
                              answer=sqrt(data_value);
                              return (answer);}
```

The first member function is responsible for initializing the variable, *data_value*. The remaining two member functions return the square and square root of *data_value*. Notice that the member functions are not passed a value; *data_value* is available to them as members of the structure. Both member functions return a double.

The program's main( ) function sets the value of *data_value* to 35.63 with a call to the member function, set_value( ):

```
math.set_value(35.63);
```

Notice that the name *math* has been associated with the structure math_operations. The remaining two member functions return values to the cout stream:

```
cout << "The square of the number is: "
     << math.get_square( ) << endl;
cout << "The square root of the number is: "
     << math.get_square_root( ) << endl;
```

This example contains a structure with member data and functions. The functions are contained within the structure definition. You won't find an example simpler than this one.

In the next program, the struct keyword is still used to develop a primitive class, but this time the member functions are written outside the structure. This is the way you will most commonly see structures and classes defined.

This example contains a structure definition with one data member, *data_value,* and seven member functions. The member functions return information for various trigonometric values.

```
//
//   16TSTRUC.CPP
//   C++ program using the keyword "struct" to illustrate a
//   primitive form of class. This program uses a structure
//   to obtain trigonometric values for an angle.
//   Copyright (c) Chris H. Pappas and William H. Murray, 1997
//

#include <iostream.h>
#include <math.h>

const double DEG_TO_RAD=0.0174532925;

struct degree {
  double data_value;

  void set_value(double);
  double get_sine(void);
  double get_cosine(void);
  double get_tangent(void);
  double get_secant(void);
  double get_cosecant(void);
  double get_cotangent(void);
} deg;

void degree::set_value(double ang)
{
  data_value=ang;
}

double degree::get_sine(void)
{
  double answer;

  answer=sin(DEG_TO_RAD*data_value);
  return (answer);
}
```

```
double degree::get_cosine(void)
{
  double answer;

  answer=cos(DEG_TO_RAD*data_value);
  return (answer);
}

double degree::get_tangent(void)
{
  double answer;

  answer=tan(DEG_TO_RAD*data_value);
  return (answer);
}

double degree::get_secant(void)
{
  double answer;

  answer=1.0/sin(DEG_TO_RAD*data_value);
  return (answer);
}

double degree::get_cosecant(void)
{
  double answer;

  answer=1.0/cos(DEG_TO_RAD*data_value);
  return (answer);
}

double degree::get_cotangent(void)
{
  double answer;

  answer=1.0/tan(DEG_TO_RAD*data_value);
  return (answer);
}

main( )
{
```

```
// set angle to 25.0 degrees
deg.set_value(25.0);

cout << "The sine of the angle is: "
     << deg.get_sine( ) << endl;
cout << "The cosine of the angle is: "
     << deg.get_cosine( ) << endl;
cout << "The tangent of the angle is: "
     << deg.get_tangent( ) << endl;
cout << "The secant of the angle is: "
     << deg.get_secant( ) << endl;
cout << "The cosecant of the angle is: "
     << deg.get_cosecant( ) << endl;
cout << "The cotangent of the angle is: "
     << deg.get_cotangent( ) << endl;
return (0);
}
```

Notice that the structure definition contains the prototypes for the member functions. The variable, *deg*, is associated with the degree structure type.

```
struct degree {
  double data_value;

  void set_value(double);
  double get_sine(void);
  double get_cosine(void);
  double get_tangent(void);
  double get_secant(void);
  double get_cosecant(void);
  double get_cotangent(void);
} deg;
```

Immediately after the structure is defined, the various member functions are developed and listed. The member functions are associated with the structure or class by means of the scope operator (::). Other than the use of the scope operator, the member functions take on the appearance of normal functions.

Examine the first part of the main( ) function:

```
// set angle to 25.0 degrees
deg.set_data(25.0);
```

Here the value 25.0 is being passed as an argument to the set_value( ) function. Observe the syntax for this operation. The set_value( ) function itself is very simple:

```
void degree::set_value(double ang)
{
  data_value=ang;
}
```

The function accepts the argument and assigns the value to the class variable, *data_value*. This is one way of initializing class variables. From this point forward, in the class, *data_value* is accessible by each of the six member functions. The job of the member functions is to calculate the sine, cosine, tangent, secant, cosecant, and cotangent of the given angle. The respective values are printed to the screen from the main( ) function with statements similar to the following:

```
cout << "The sine of the angle is: "
     << deg.get_sine( ) << endl;
```

You can use the dot notation commonly used for structures to access the member functions. Pointer variables can also be assigned to a structure or class, in which case the arrow operator is used. You will see examples of this in Chapter 17.

The Syntax and Rules for C++ Classes

The definition of a C++ class begins with the keyword class. The class name (tag type) immediately follows the keyword. The framework of the class is very similar to the struct type definition you have already seen.

```
class type {
  type var1
  type var2
  type var3

     .

     .

     .
public:
  member function 1
  member function 2
  member function 3
```

```
member function 4
     .
     .
     .
} name associated with class type;
```

Member variables immediately follow the class declaration. These variables are, by default, private to the class and can be accessed only by the member functions that follow. Member functions typically follow a public declaration. This allows access to the member functions from calling routines external to the class. All class member functions have access to public, private, and protected parts of a class.

The following is an example of a class that is used in the next programming example:

```
class degree {
  double data_value;

public:
  void set_value(double);
  double get_sine(void);
  double get_cosine(void);
  double get_tangent(void);
  double get_secant(void);
  double get_cosecant(void);
  double get_cotangent(void);
} deg;
```

This class has a type (tag name) degree. A private variable, *data_value*, will share degree values among the various member functions. Seven functions make up the function members of the class. They are set_value( ), get_sine( ), get_cosine( ), get_tangent( ), get_secant( ), get_cosecant( ), and get_cotangent( ). The name that is associated with this class type is *deg*. Unlike this example, the association of a variable name with the class name is most frequently made in the main( ) function.

Does this class definition look familiar? It is basically the structure definition from the previous example converted to a true class.

A Simple C++ Class

In a C++ class, the visibility of class members is by default private. That is, member variables are accessible only to member functions of the class. If the member functions are to have visibility beyond the class, you must explicitly specify that visibility.

The conversion of the last program's structure to a true C++ class is simple and straightforward. First, the struct keyword is replaced by the class keyword. Second, the member functions that are to have public visibility are separated from the private variable of the class with the use of a public declaration. Examine the complete program:

```cpp
//
//  tclass.cpp
//  C++ program illustrates a simple but true class and
//  introduces the concept of private and public.
//  This program uses a class to obtain the trigonometric
//  value for a given angle.
//  Copyright (c) Chris H. Pappas and William H. Murray, 1997
//

#include <iostream.h>
#include <math.h>

const double DEG_TO_RAD=0.0174532925;

class degree {
  double data_value;

public:
  void set_value(double);
  double get_sine(void);
  double get_cosine(void);
  double get_tangent(void);
  double get_secant(void);
  double get_cosecant(void);
  double get_cotangent(void);
} deg;

void degree::set_value(double ang)
{
  data_value=ang;
}

double degree::get_sine(void)
{
  double answer;

  answer=sin(DEG_TO_RAD*data_value);
```

```
    return (answer);
}

double degree::get_cosine(void)
{
  double answer;

  answer=cos(DEG_TO_RAD*data_value);
  return (answer);
}

double degree::get_tangent(void)
{
  double answer;

  answer=tan(DEG_TO_RAD*data_value);
  return (answer);
}

double degree::get_secant(void)
{
  double answer;

  answer=1.0/sin(DEG_TO_RAD*data_value);
  return (answer);
}

double degree::get_cosecant(void)
{
  double answer;

  answer=1.0/cos(DEG_TO_RAD*data_value);
  return (answer);
}

double degree::get_cotangent(void)
{
  double answer;

  answer=1.0/tan(DEG_TO_RAD*data_value);
  return (answer);
}
```

```
main( )
{
  // set angle to 25.0 degrees
  deg.set_value(25.0);

  cout << "The sine of the angle is: "
       << deg.get_sine( ) << endl;
  cout << "The cosine of the angle is: "
       << deg.get_cosine( ) << endl;
  cout << "The tangent of the angle is: "
       << deg.get_tangent( ) << endl;
  cout << "The secant of the angle is: "
       << deg.get_secant( ) << endl;
  cout << "The cosecant of the angle is: "
       << deg.get_cosecant( ) << endl;
  cout << "The cotangent of the angle is: "
       << deg.get_cotangent( ) << endl;
  return (0);
}
```

In this example, the body of the program remains the same. The structure definition has been converted to a true, but elementary, class definition with private and public parts.

Note that the variable, *data_value*, is private to the class (by default) and as a result is accessible only by the member functions of the class. The member functions themselves have been declared public in visibility and are accessible from outside the class. Each class member, however, whether public or private, has access to all other class members, public or private.

Here is the output from the program:

sdi15.2

Again, class member functions are usually defined immediately after the class has been defined and before the main( ) function of the program. Nonmember class functions are still defined after the function main( ) and are prototyped in the normal fashion. The next chapter looks at the details of C++ classes more closely.

The
Complete
Reference

Visual
C++ 5

Chapter 17

C++ Classes

A primitive C++ class can be created by using the struct keyword, as you learned in the previous chapter. You also learned how to create several elementary C++ classes by using the class keyword. Both types of examples illustrated the simple fact that classes can contain member data and member functions that act on that data. In this chapter, you will learn more details about C++ classes—nesting of classes and structures, the use of constructors and destructors, overloading member functions, friend functions, operator overloading, derived classes, virtual functions, and other miscellaneous topics. These class structures create objects that form the foundation of object-oriented programs.

The programming flexibility offered to the C++ programmer is, to a large degree, a result of the various data types discussed in earlier chapters. The C++ class gives you another advantage: the benefits of a structure along with the ability to limit access to specific data to functions that are also members of the class. As a result, classes are one of the greatest contributions made by C++ to programming. The added features of the class, over earlier structures, include the ability to initialize and protect sensitive functions and data.

Consider, for example, the increase in programming power you have gained with each new data type. Vectors or one-dimensional arrays allow a group of like data types to be held together. Next, structures allow related items of different data types to be combined in a group. Finally, the C++ class concept takes you one step further with abstract data types. A class allows you to implement a member data type and associate member functions with the data. Using classes gives you the storage concept associated with a structure along with the member functions to operate on the member variables.

Special Class Features

The syntax for correctly creating an elementary C++ class was illustrated in the previous chapter. However, classes have extended capabilities that go far beyond this simple syntax. This section is devoted to exploring these capabilities with an eye toward object-oriented programming. In Chapter 19, class objects will be woven into more complicated object-oriented programs.

A Simple Class

In this section we'll present a short review of a simple class based on the definitions from Chapter 16. Remember that a class starts with the keyword class followed by a class name (tag). In the following example, the class tag name is car. If the class contains member variables, they are defined at the start of the class. Their declaration type is private, by default. This example defines three member variables: *mileage, tire_pressure*, and *speed*. Class member functions follow the member variable list. Typically, the member functions are declared public. A private declaration limits the member variables to member functions within the class. This is often referred to as *data hiding.* A public declaration makes the member functions available outside of the class:

```
class car {
  int    mileage;
  int    tire_pressure;
  float speed;

public:
  int maintenance(int);
  int wear_record(int);
  int air_resistance(float);
} mycar;
```

Notice that three member functions are prototyped within the class definition. They are maintenance( ), wear_record( ), and air_resistance( ). All three return an int type. Typically, however, the contents of the member functions are defined outside the class definition—usually, immediately after the class itself.

Let's continue the study of classes with a look at additional class features.

Nesting Classes

In Chapter 13 you learned that structures can be nested. This also turns out to be true for C++ classes. When using nested classes, you must take care not to make the resulting declaration more complicated than necessary. The following examples illustrate the nesting concept.

Nesting Structures Within a Class

The next listing is a simple example of how two structures can be nested within a class definition. Using nesting in this fashion is both common and practical. You can also use the class keyword in this manner.

```
//
// wages.cpp
// C++ program illustrates the use of nesting concepts
// in classes. This program calculates the wages for
// the named employee.
// Copyright (c) Chris H. Pappas and William H. Murray, 1997
//

#include <iostream.h>
```

```cpp
char newline;

class employee {
  struct emp_name {
    char firstname[20];
    char middlename[20];
    char lastname[20];
  } name;
  struct emp_hours {
    double hours;
    double base_sal;
    double overtime_sal;
  } hours;

public:
  void emp_input(void);
  void emp_output(void);
};

void employee::emp_input( )
{
  cout << "Enter first name of employee: ";
  cin >> name.firstname;
  cin.get(newline);    // flush carriage return
  cout << "Enter middle name of employee: ";
  cin >> name.middlename;
  cin.get(newline);
  cout << "Enter last name of employee:  ";
  cin >> name.lastname;
  cin.get(newline);

  cout << "Enter total hours worked:  ";
  cin >> hours.hours;
  cout << "Enter hourly wage (base rate):    ";
  cin >> hours.base_sal;
  cout << "Enter overtime wage (overtime rate): ";
  cin >> hours.overtime_sal;
  cout << "\n\n";
}
```

```
void employee::emp_output( )
{
  cout << name.firstname << " " << name.middlename
       << " " << name.lastname << endl;
  if (hours.hours <= 40)
    cout << "Base Pay:  $"
         << hours.hours * hours.base_sal << endl;
    else {
      cout << "Base Pay:  $"
           << 40 * hours.base_sal << endl;
      cout << "Overtime Pay: $"
           << (hours.hours-40) * hours.overtime_sal
           << endl;
    }
}

main( )
{
  employee acme_corp;      // associate acme_corp with class

  acme_corp.emp_input( );
  acme_corp.emp_output( );
  return (0);
}
```

FOUNDATIONS FOR
OBJECT-ORIENTED
PROGRAMMING IN C++

In the next example, two classes are nested within the employee class definition. As you can see, the use of nesting can be quite straightforward.

```
class employee {
  class emp_name {
    char firstname[20];
    char middlename[20];
    char lastname[20];
  } name;
  class emp_hours {
    double hours;
    double base_salary;
    double overtime_sal;
  } hours;
```

```
public:
  void emp_input(void);
  void emp_output(void);
};
```

The employee class includes two nested classes, emp_name and emp_hours. The nested classes, while part of the private section of the employee class, are actually available outside the class. In other words, the visibility of the nested classes is the same as if they were defined outside the employee class. The individual member variables, for this example, are accessed through the member functions (public, by default), emp_input( ) and emp_output( ).

The member functions, emp_input( ) and emp_output( ), are of type void and do not accept arguments. The emp_input( ) function prompts the user for employee data that will be passed to the nested structures (classes). The data collected includes the employee's full name, the total hours worked, the regular pay rate, and the overtime pay rate. Output is generated when the emp_output( ) function is called. The employee's name, base pay, and overtime pay will be printed to the screen:

```
Enter first name of employee: Peter
Enter middle name of employee: Harry
Enter last name of employee: Jones
Enter total hours worked: 52
Enter hourly wage (base rate): 7.50
Enter overtime wage (overtime rate): 10.00

Peter Harry Jones
Base Pay:   $300.00
Overtime Pay: $120.00
```

The main( ) function in this program is fairly short. This is because most of the work is being done by the member functions of the class:

```
employee acme_corp;     // associate acme_corp with class

acme_corp.emp_input( );
acme_corp.emp_output( );
```

The variable *acme_corp*, representing the Acme Computer Corporation, is associated with the employee class. To request a member function, the dot operator is used. Next, acme_corp.emp_input( ) is called to collect the employee information, and then acme_corp.emp_output( ) is used to calculate and print the payroll results.

An Alternate Nesting Form

There is an alternate way to perform nesting. The following form of nesting is also considered acceptable syntax:

```
class cars {
  int mileage;
public:
  void trip(int t);
  int speed(float s);
};

class contents {
  int count;
public:
  cars mileage;
  void rating(void);
{
```

Here, cars becomes nested within the contents class. Nested classes, whether inside or outside, have the same scope.

Working with Constructors and Destructors

A *constructor* is a class member function. Constructors are useful for initializing class variables or allocating memory storage. The constructor always has the same name as the class it is defined within. Constructors have additional versatility: they can accept arguments and be overloaded. A constructor is executed automatically when an object of the class type is created. *Free store objects* are objects created with the new operator and serve to allocate memory for the objects created. Constructors are generated by Microsoft's Visual C++ compiler if they are not explicitly defined.

A *destructor* is a class member function typically used to return memory allocated from free store memory. The destructor, like the constructor, has the same name as the class it is defined in, preceded by the tilde character (~). Destructors are the complement to their constructor counterparts. A destructor is automatically called when the delete operator is applied to a class pointer or when a program passes beyond the scope of a class object. Destructors, unlike their constructor counterparts, cannot accept an argument and may not be overloaded. Destructors are also generated by Microsoft's Visual C++ compiler if they are not explicitly defined.

FOUNDATIONS FOR OBJECT-ORIENTED PROGRAMMING IN C++

A Simple Constructor and Destructor

The following listing represents the first example involving the use of constructors and destructors. Here a constructor and destructor are used to signal the start and end of a coin conversion example. This program illustrates that constructors and destructors are called automatically:

```cpp
//
//   coins.cpp
//   C++ program illustrates the use of constructors and
//   destructors in a simple program.
//   This program converts cents into appropriate coins:
//   (quarters, dimes, nickels, and pennies).
//   Copyright (c) Chris H. Pappas and William H. Murray, 1997
//

#include <iostream.h>

const int QUARTER=25;
const int DIME=10;
const int NICKEL=5;

class coins {
  int number;

public:
  coins( ) {cout << "Begin Conversion!\n";}      // constructor
  ~coins( ) {cout << "\nFinished Conversion!";}  // destructor
  void get_cents(int);
  int quarter_conversion(void);
  int dime_conversion(int);
  int nickel_conversion(int);
};

void coins::get_cents(int cents)
{
  number=cents;
  cout << number << " cents, converts to:"
       << endl;
}

int coins::quarter_conversion( )
{
```

```
    cout << number/QUARTER << " quarter(s), ";
    return(number%QUARTER);
}

int coins::dime_conversion(int d)
{
    cout << d/DIME << " dime(s), ";
    return(d%DIME);
}

int coins::nickel_conversion(int n)
{
    cout << n/NICKEL << " nickel(s), and ";
    return(n%NICKEL);
}

main( )
{
    int c,d,n,p;

    cout << "Enter the cash, in cents, to convert: ";
    cin >> c;

    // associate cash_in_cents with coins class.
    coins cash_in_cents;

    cash_in_cents.get_cents(c);
    d=cash_in_cents.quarter_conversion( );
    n=cash_in_cents.dime_conversion(d);
    p=cash_in_cents.nickel_conversion(n);
    cout << p << " penny(ies).";
    return (0);
}
```

FOUNDATIONS FOR
OBJECT-ORIENTED
PROGRAMMING IN C++

This program uses four member functions. The first function passes the number of pennies to the private class variable *number*. The remaining three functions convert cash, given in cents, to the equivalent cash in quarters, dimes, nickels, and pennies. Notice in particular the placement of the constructor and destructor in the class definition. The constructor and destructor function descriptions contain nothing more than a message that will be printed to the screen. Constructors are not specifically called by a program. Their appearance on the screen is your key that the constructor and destructor were automatically called when the object was created and destroyed.

```
class coins {
  int number;

public:
  coins( ) {cout << "Begin Conversion!\n";}      // constructor
  ~coins( ) {cout << "\nFinished Conversion!";}  // destructor
  void get_cents(int);
  int quarter_conversion(void);
  int dime_conversion(int);
  int nickel_conversion(int);
};
```

Here is an example of the output from this program:

```
Enter the cash, in cents, to convert: 159
Begin Conversion!
159 cents, converts to:
6 quarter(s), 0 dime(s), 1 nickel(s), and 4 penny(ies).
Finished Conversion!
```

In this example, the function definition is actually included within the constructor and destructor. When the function definition is included with member functions, it is said to be *implicitly defined*. Member functions can be defined in the typical manner or declared explicitly as inline functions.

You can expand this example to include dollars and half-dollars.

Initializing Member Variables with Constructors

Another practical use for constructors is for initialization of private class variables. In the previous examples, class variables were set by utilizing separate member functions. In the next example, the original class of the previous program is modified slightly to eliminate the need for user input. In this case, the variable *number* will be initialized to 431 pennies.

```
class coins {
  int number;

public:
  coins( ) {number=431;}                         // constructor
  ~coins( ) {cout << "\nFinished Conversion!";}  // destructor
```

```
   int quarter_conversion(void);
   int dime_conversion(int);
   int nickel_conversion(int);
};
```

The route to class variables is always through class member functions. Remember that the constructor is considered a member function.

Creating and Deleting Free Store Memory

Perhaps the most significant reason for using a constructor is in utilizing free store memory. In the next example, a constructor is used to allocate memory for the *string1* pointer with the new operator. A destructor is also used to release the allocated memory back to the system, when the object is destroyed. This is accomplished with the use of the delete operator.

```
class string_operation {
  char *string1;
  int  string_len;

public:
  string_operation(char *) {string1=new char[string_len];}
  ~string_operation( ) {delete string1;}
  void input_data(char *);
  void output_data(char *);
};
```

The memory allocated by new to the pointer *string1* can only be deallocated with a subsequent call to delete. For this reason, you will usually see memory allocated to pointers in constructors and deallocated in destructors. This also ensures that if the variable assigned to the class passes out of its scope, the allocated memory will be returned to the system. These operations make memory allocation dynamic and are most useful in programs that utilize linked lists.

The memory used by data types, such as int and float, is automatically restored to the system.

Overloading Class Member Functions

Class member functions can be overloaded just like ordinary C++ functions. *Overloading* functions means that more than one function can have the same function name in the current scope. It becomes the compiler's responsibility to select the correct function based upon the number and type of arguments used during the function call.

The first example in this section illustrates the overloading of a class function named number( ). This overloaded function will return the absolute value of an integer or double with the use of the math functions abs( ), which accepts and returns integer values, and fabs( ), which accepts and returns double values. With an overloaded function, the argument types determine which member function will actually be used.

```cpp
//
//   abso1.cpp
//   C++ program illustrates member function overloading.
//   Program determines the absolute value of an integer
//   and a double.
//   Copyright (c) Chris H. Pappas and William H. Murray, 1997
//

#include <iostream.h>
#include <math.h>
#include <stdlib.h>

class absolute_value {
public:
  int number(int);
  double number(double);
};

int absolute_value::number(int test_data)
{
  int answer;

  answer=abs(test_data);
  return (answer);
}

double absolute_value::number(double test_data)
{
  double answer;

  answer=fabs(test_data);
  return (answer);
}

main( )
{
```

```
    absolute_value neg_number;

    cout << "The absolute value is "
         << neg_number.number(-583) << endl;
    cout << "The absolute value is "
         << neg_number.number(-583.1749) << endl;
    return (0);
}
```

Notice that the dot operator is used in conjunction with the member function name to pass a negative integer and negative double values. The program selects the proper member function based upon the type (integer or double) of argument passed along with the function name. The positive value returned by each function is printed to the screen:

```
the absolute value is 583
the absolute value is 583.1749
```

In another example, angle information is passed to member functions in one of two formats—a double or a string. With member function overloading, it is possible to process both types.

```
//
//  overld.cpp
//  C++ program illustrates overloading two class member
//  functions. The program allows an angle to be entered
//  in decimal or deg/min/sec format. One member function
//  accepts data as a double, the other as a string. The
//  program returns the sine, cosine, and tangent.
//  Copyright (c) Chris H. Pappas and William H. Murray, 1997
//

#include <iostream.h>
#include <math.h>
#include <string.h>

const double DEG_TO_RAD=0.0174532925;
```

```cpp
class trigonometric {
  double angle;
  double answer_sine;
  double answer_cosine;
  double answer_tangent;

public:
  void trig_calc(double);
  void trig_calc(char *);
};

void trigonometric::trig_calc(double degrees)
{
  angle=degrees;
  answer_sine=sin(angle * DEG_TO_RAD);
  answer_cosine=cos(angle * DEG_TO_RAD);
  answer_tangent=tan(angle * DEG_TO_RAD);
  cout << "\nFor an angle of " << angle
       << " degrees." << endl;
  cout << "The sine is " << answer_sine << endl;
  cout << "The cosine is " << answer_cosine << endl;
  cout << "The tangent is " << answer_tangent << endl;
}

void trigonometric::trig_calc(char *dat)
{
  char *deg,*min,*sec;

  deg=strtok(dat,"d");
  min=strtok(0,"m");
  sec=strtok(0,"s");
  angle=atof(deg)+((atof(min))/60.0)+((atof(sec))/360.0);
  answer_sine=sin(angle * DEG_TO_RAD);
  answer_cosine=cos(angle * DEG_TO_RAD);
  answer_tangent=tan(angle * DEG_TO_RAD);
  cout << "\nFor an angle of " << angle
       << " degrees." << endl;
  cout << "The sine is " << answer_sine << endl;
  cout << "The cosine is " << answer_cosine << endl;
  cout << "The tangent is " << answer_tangent << endl;
}
```

```
main( )
{
  trigonometric data;

  data.trig_calc(75.0);
  data.trig_calc("35° 75m 20s");
  data.trig_calc(145.72);
  data.trig_calc("65° 45m 30s");
  return (0);
}
```

This program makes use of a very powerful built-in function, strtok( ), prototyped in STRING.H. The syntax for using strtok( ) is straightforward:

```
char *strtok(string1,string2);    //locates token in string1
char *string1;                    //string that has token(s)
const char *string2;              //string with delimiter chars
```

The strtok( ) function will scan the first string, *string1,* looking for a series of character tokens. For this example, the tokens representing degrees, minutes, and seconds are used. The actual length of the tokens can vary. The second string, *string2,* contains a set of delimiters. Spaces, commas, or other special characters can be used for delimiters. The tokens in *string1* are separated by the delimiters in *string2.* Because of this, all of the tokens in *string1* can be retrieved with a series of calls to the strtok( ) function. strtok( ) alters *string1* by inserting a null character after each token is retrieved. The function returns a pointer to the first token the first time it is called. Subsequent calls return a pointer to the next token, and so on. When there are no more tokens in the string, a null pointer is returned.

This example permits angle readings formatted as decimal values, or in degrees, minutes, and seconds of arc. For the latter case, strtok( ) uses the symbol (d) to find the first token. For minutes, a minute symbol (m) will pull out the token containing the number of minutes. Finally, the (s) symbol is used to retrieve seconds.

This program produces the following formatted output:

```
For an angle of 75 degrees.
The sine is 0.965926
The cosine is 0.258819
The tangent is 3.732051
```

```
For an angle of 36.305556 degrees.
The sine is 0.592091
The cosine is 0.805871
The tangent is 0.734722

For an angle of 145.72 degrees.
The sine is 0.563238
The cosine is -0.826295
The tangent is -0.681642

For an angle of 65.833333 degrees.
The sine is 0.912358
The cosine is 0.409392
The tangent is 2.228568
```

Class member function overloading gives programs and programmers flexibility when dealing with different data formats. If you are not into math or engineering programs, can you think of any applications that interest you where this feature might be helpful? Consider this possibility: if you are the cook in your household, you could develop an application that modifies recipes. You could write a program that would accept data as a decimal value or in mixed units. For example, the program might allow you to enter "1 pint 1.75 cups" or "1 pint 1 cup 2 tbs".

Friend Functions

Another important feature of classes is their ability to hide data. Recall that member data is private by default in classes—that is, sharable only with member functions of the class. It is almost ironic, then, that there exists a category of functions specifically designed to override this feature. Functions of this type, called *friend functions,* allow the sharing of private class information with nonmember functions. Friend functions, not defined in the class itself, can share the same class resources as member functions.

Friend functions offer the advantage that they are external to the class definition, as shown here:

```
//
//   secs.cpp
//   C++ program illustrates the use of friend functions.
//   Program will collect a string of date and time
//   information from system. Time information will
//   be processed and converted into seconds.
```

```
//  Copyright (c) Chris H. Pappas and William H. Murray, 1997
//

#include <iostream.h>
#include <time.h>     // for tm & time_t structure
#include <string.h>   // for strtok function prototype
#include <stdlib.h>   // for atol function prototype

class time_class {
  long secs;
  friend char * present_time(time_class);   //friend
public:
  time_class(char *);
};

time_class::time_class(char *tm)
{
  char *hours,*minutes,*seconds;

  // data returned in the following string format:
  // (day month date hours:minutes:seconds year)
  // Thus, need to skip over three tokens, ie.
  // skip day, month and date
  hours=strtok(tm," ");
  hours=strtok(0," ");
  hours=strtok(0," ");

  // collect time information from string
  hours=strtok(0,":");
  minutes=strtok(0,":");
  seconds=strtok(0," ");

  // convert data to long type and accumulate seconds.
  secs=atol(hours)*3600;
  secs+=atol(minutes)*60;
  secs+=atol(seconds);
}

char * present_time(time_class);   // prototype

main( )
```

FOUNDATIONS FOR
OBJECT-ORIENTED
PROGRAMMING IN C++

```
{
    // get the string of time & date information
    struct tm *ptr;
    time_t ltime;
    ltime=time(NULL);
    ptr=localtime(&ltime);

    time_class tz(asctime(ptr));

    cout << "The date/time string information: "
         << asctime(ptr) << endl;
    cout << "The time converted to seconds: "
         << present_time(tz) << endl;
    return (0);
}

char * present_time(time_class tz)
{
    char *ctbuf;
    ctbuf=new char[40];
    long int seconds_total;

    seconds_total=tz.secs;
    ltoa(seconds_total,ctbuf,10);
    return (ctbuf);
}
```

Notice in the class definition the use of the keyword friend along with the description of the present_time( ) function. When you examine the program listing, you will notice that this function, external to the class, appears after the main( ) function description. In other words, it is written as a traditional C++ function, external to member functions of the defined class.

This program has a number of additional interesting features. In the function main( ), the system's time is obtained with the use of *time_t* and its associated structure *tm*. In this program, *ltime* is the name of the variable associated with *time_t*. Local time is initialized and retrieved into the pointer, *ptr*, with the next two lines of code. By using asctime(ptr), the pointer will point to an ASCII string of date and time information.

```
struct tm *ptr;
time_t ltime;
ltime=time(NULL);
ptr=localtime(&ltime);

time_class tz(asctime(ptr));
```

The date and time string is formatted in this manner:

day month date hours:minutes:seconds year \n \0

For example:

```
Mon Nov 24 13:12:21 1997
```

There is a more detailed discussion of built-in functions, including those prototyped in *time.h*, in Chapter 15.

The string information that is retrieved is sent to the class by associating *tz* with the class time_class:

```
time_class tz(asctime(ptr));
```

A constructor, time_class(char *), is used to define the code required to convert the string information into integer data. This is accomplished by using the strtok( ) function. The date/time information is returned in a rather strange format. To process this information, strtok( ) must use a space as the delimiter in order to skip over the day, month, and date information in the string. In this program the variable *hours* initially serves as a junk collector for unwanted tokens. The next delimiter is a colon (:), which is used in collecting both hour and minute tokens from the string. Finally, the number of seconds can be retrieved by reading the string until another space is encountered. The string information is then converted to a long type and converted to the appropriate number of seconds. The variable *secs* is private to the class but accessible to the friend function.

The friend function takes the number of accumulated seconds, *tz.seconds*, and converts it back to a character string. The memory for storing the string is allocated with the new operator. This newly created string is a result of using the friend function.

The program prints two pieces of information:

```
The date/time string information: Wed Jun 11 09:31:14 1997

The time converted to seconds: 34274
```

First, cout sends the string produced by asctime( ) to the screen. This information is obtainable from time_t( ) and is available to the main( ) function. Second, the system time is printed by passing *present_time* to the cout stream.

While friend functions offer some interesting programming possibilities when programming with C++ classes, they should be used with caution.

The this Pointer

The keyword this is used to identify a self-referential pointer that is implicitly declared in C++, as follows:

```
class_name *this;    //class_name is class type.
```

The this pointer is used to point to the object for which the member function is invoked. Here is an example, used in a class definition:

```
class class_name {
  char chr;

public:
  void begin_conv(char k) {chr=k;}
  char conv_chr(void) {return (this -> chr);}
};
```

In this case, the pointer this is used to access the private class variable member 20*chr*.

There are additional uses for the this pointer. You can use it to include a link on a doubly linked list or when writing constructors and destructors involving memory allocations. Examine the following example:

```
class class_name {
  int x,y,z;
  char chr;

public:
  class_name(size) {this=new(size);}
  ~class_name(void) {delete(this);}
};
```

Operator Overloading

You have already learned in this chapter that it is possible to overload member functions in a class. In this section, you will learn that it is also possible to overload C++ operators. In C++, new definitions can be applied to such familiar operators as +, -, *, and / in a given class.

The concept of operator overloading is common in numerous programming languages, even if it is not specifically implemented. For example, all compiled languages make it possible to add two integers, two floats, or two doubles (or their equivalent types) with the + operator. This is the essence of operator overloading— using the same operator on different data types. In C++ it is possible to extend this simple concept even further. In most compiled languages it is not possible, for example, to take a complex number, matrix, or character string and add them together with the + operator.

These operations are valid in all programming languages:

```
3 + 8
3.3 + 7.2
```

These operations are typically not valid operations:

```
(4 - j4) + (5 + j10)
(15d 20m 45s) + (53d 57m 40s)
"combine " + "strings"
```

If the last three operations were possible with the + operator, the workload of the programmer would be greatly reduced when designing new applications. The good news is that in C++, the + operator can be overloaded and the previous three operations can be made valid. Many additional operators can also be overloaded. Operator overloading is used extensively in C++. You will find examples throughout the various Microsoft C++ libraries.

Overloading Operators and Function Calls

In C++, the operators shown in Table 17-1 can be overloaded.

+	-	*0	/	=	<	>	+=	-=
*0=	/=	<<	>>	>>=	<<=	==	!=	<=
>=	++	--	%	&	^^	!	|	~
&=	^=	|=	&&	||	%=	[]	()	new
delete								

Table 17-1. *Operators That Can be Overloaded in C++*

The main restrictions are that the syntax and precedence of the operator must remain unchanged from its originally defined meaning. Another important point is that operator overloading is valid only within the scope of the class in which overloading occurs.

Overloading Syntax

In order to overload an operator, the operator keyword is followed by the operator itself:

type operator *opr(param list)*

For example:

```
angle_value operator +(angle_argument);
```

Here, angle_value is the name of the class type, followed by the operator keyword, then the operator itself (+) and a parameter to be passed to the overloaded operator.

Within the scope of a properly defined class, several angles specified in degrees/minutes/seconds could be directly added together:

```
angle_value angle1("37d 15m 56s");
angle_value angle2("10d 44m 44s");
angle_value angle3("75d 17m 59s");
angle_value angle4("130d 32m 54s");
angle_value sum_of_angles;

sum_of_angles=angle1+angle2+angle3+angle4;
```

In this example, the symbol for degrees is (d), for minutes (m), and for seconds (s).
The carry information from seconds-to-minutes and from minutes-to-hours must
be handled properly. A carry occurs in both cases when the total number of seconds or
minutes exceeds 59. This doesn't have anything to do with operator overloading
directly, but the program must take this fact into account if a correct total is to be
produced, as shown here:

```
//
//   opover.cpp
//   C++ program illustrates operator overloading.
//   Program will overload the "+" operator so that
//   several angles, in the format degrees minutes seconds,
//   can be added directly.
//   Copyright (c) Chris H. Pappas and William H. Murray, 1997
//

#include <strstream.h>
#include <stdlib.h>
#include <string.h>

class angle_value {
  int degrees,minutes,seconds;

  public:
  angle_value( ) {degrees=0,
                  minutes=0,
                  seconds=0;}  // constructor
  angle_value(char *);
  angle_value operator +(angle_value);
  char * info_display(void);
};

angle_value::angle_value(char *angle_sum)
{
  degrees=atoi(strtok(angle_sum,"d"));
  minutes=atoi(strtok(0,"m"));
  seconds=atoi(strtok(0,"s"));
}

angle_value angle_value::operator+(angle_value angle_sum)
{
  angle_value ang;
```

```
  ang.seconds=(seconds+angle_sum.seconds)%60;
  ang.minutes=((seconds+angle_sum.seconds)/60+
               minutes+angle_sum.minutes)%60;
  ang.degrees=((seconds+angle_sum.seconds)/60+
               minutes+angle_sum.minutes)/60;
  ang.degrees+=degrees+angle_sum.degrees;
  return ang;
}

char * angle_value::info_display( )
{
  char *ang[40];
  // strstream.h required for incore formatting
  ostrstream(*ang,sizeof(ang)) << degrees << "d "
                               << minutes << "m "
                               << seconds << "s"
                               << ends;
  return *ang;
}

main( )
{
  angle_value angle1("37d 15m 56s");
  angle_value angle2("10d 44m 44s");
  angle_value angle3("75d 17m 59s");
  angle_value angle4("130d 32m 54s");
  angle_value sum_of_angles;

  sum_of_angles=angle1+angle2+angle3+angle4;
  cout << "the sum of the angles is "
       << sum_of_angles.info_display( ) << endl;
  return (0);
}
```

The following portion of code shows how the mixed units are added together. Here the + operator is to be overloaded:

```
angle_value angle_value::operator+(angle_value angle_sum)
{
  angle_value ang;
  ang.seconds=(seconds+angle_sum.seconds)%60;
```

```
ang.minutes=((seconds+angle_sum.seconds)/60+
           minutes+angle_sum.minutes)%60;
ang.degrees=((seconds+angle_sum.seconds)/60+
           minutes+angle_sum.minutes)/60;
ang.degrees+=degrees+angle_sum.degrees;
return ang;
}
```

The divide and modulus operations are performed on the sums to ensure correct carry information.

Further details of the program's operation are omitted since you have seen most of the functions and modules in earlier examples. However, it is important to remember that when you overload operators, proper operator syntax and precedence must be maintained.

The output from this program shows the sum of the four angles to be as follows:

```
the sum of the angles is 253d 51m 33s
```

Is this answer correct?

Derived Classes

A derived class can be considered an extension or inheritance of an existing class. The original class is known as a *base* or *parent class* and the derived class as a *subclass* or *child class*. As such, a derived class provides a simple means for expanding or customizing the capabilities of a parent class, without the need for re-creating the parent class itself. With a parent class in place, a common interface is possible to one or more of the derived classes.

Any C++ class can serve as a parent class, and any derived class will reflect its description. The derived class can add additional features to those of the parent class. For example, the derived class can modify access privileges, add new members, or overload existing ones. When a derived class overloads a function declared in the parent class, it is said to be a *virtual member function*. You will see that virtual member functions are very important to the concept of object-oriented programming.

Derived Class Syntax

You describe a derived class by using the following syntax:

```
class derived-class-type :(public/private/protected) . . .
     parent-class-type { . . . .};
```

For example, in creating a derived class, you might write:

```
class retirement:public consumer { . . . .};
```

In this case, the derived class tag is retirement. The parent class has public visibility, and its tag is consumer.

A third visibility specifier is often used with derived classes—protected. A protected specifier is the same as a private specifier with the added feature that class member functions and friends of derived classes are given access to the class.

Working with Derived Classes

The following example is used to illustrate the concept of a derived class. The parent class collects and reports information on a consumer's name, address, city, state, and ZIP code. Two similar child classes are derived. One derived child class maintains information on a consumer's accumulated airline mileage, while the second reports information on a consumer's accumulated rental car mileage. Both derived child classes inherit information from the parent class. Study the listing and see what you can discern about these derived classes.

```cpp
//
//   dercls.cpp
//   C++ program illustrates derived classes.
//   The parent class contains name, street, city,
//   state, and zip information. Derived classes add
//   either airline or rental car mileage information
//   to parent class information.
//   Copyright (c) Chris H. Pappas and William H. Murray, 1997
//

#include <iostream.h>
#include <string.h>

char newline;
```

```
class consumer {
  char name[60],
       street[60],
       city[20],
       state[15],
       zip[10];
public:
  void data_output(void);
  void data_input(void);
};

void consumer::data_output( )
{
  cout << "Name: " << name << endl;
  cout << "Street: " << street << endl;
  cout << "City: " << city << endl;
  cout << "State: " << state << endl;
  cout << "Zip: " << zip << endl;
}

void consumer::data_input( )
{
  cout << "Enter The Consumer's Full Name: ";
  cin.get(name,59,'\n');
  cin.get(newline);       //flush carriage return
  cout << "Enter The Street Address: ";
  cin.get(street,59,'\n');
  cin.get(newline);
  cout << "Enter The City: ";
  cin.get(city,19,'\n');
  cin.get(newline);
  cout << "Enter The State: ";
  cin.get(state,14,'\n');
  cin.get(newline);
  cout << "Enter The Five Digit Zip Code: ";
  cin.get(zip,9,'\n');
  cin.get(newline);
}

class airline:public consumer {
  char airline_type[20];
  float acc_air_miles;
```

FOUNDATIONS FOR
OBJECT-ORIENTED
PROGRAMMING IN C++

```cpp
public:
  void airline_consumer( );
  void disp_air_mileage( );
};

void airline::airline_consumer( )
{
  data_input( );
  cout << "Enter Airline Type: ";
  cin.get(airline_type,19,'\n');
  cin.get(newline);
  cout << "Enter Accumulated Air Mileage: ";
  cin >> acc_air_miles;
  cin.get(newline);        //flush carriage return
}

void airline::disp_air_mileage( )
{
  data_output( );

  cout << "Airline Type: " << airline_type
       << endl;
  cout << "Accumulated Air Mileage: "
       << acc_air_miles << endl;
}

class rental_car:public consumer {
  char rental_car_type[20];
  float acc_road_miles;
public:
  void rental_car_consumer( );
  void disp_road_mileage( );
};

void rental_car::rental_car_consumer( )
{
  data_input( );
  cout << "Enter Rental_car Type: ";
  cin.get(rental_car_type,19,'\n');
  cin.get(newline);        //flush carriage return
  cout << "Enter Accumulated Road Mileage: ";
  cin >> acc_road_miles;
```

```
      cin.get(newline);
   }

   void rental_car::disp_road_mileage( )
   {
      data_output( );

      cout << "Rental Car Type: "
           << rental_car_type << endl;
      cout << "Accumulated Mileage: "
           << acc_road_miles << endl;
   }

   main( )
   {
      //associate variable names with classes
      airline jetaway;
      rental_car varooom;

      //get airline information
      cout << "\n--Airline Consumer--\n";
      jetaway.airline_consumer( );

      //get rental_car information
      cout << "\n--Rental Car Consumer--\n";
      varooom.rental_car_consumer( );

      //now display all consumer information
      cout << "\n--Airline Consumer--\n";
      jetaway.disp_air_mileage( );
      cout << "\n--Rental Car Consumer--\n";
      varooom.disp_road_mileage( );

      return (0);
   }
```

In this example, the parent class is of type consumer. The private part of this class accepts consumer information for name, address, city, state, and ZIP code. The public part describes two functions, data_output( ) and data_input( ). You have seen functions similar to these to gather class information in earlier programs. The first derived child class is airline.

```
class airline:public consumer {
  char airline_type[20];
  float acc_air_miles;
public:
  void airline_consumer(void);
  void disp_air_mileage(void);
};
```

This derived child class contains two functions, airline_consumer( ) and disp_air_mileage( ). The first function, airline_consumer( ), uses the parent class to obtain name, address, city, state, and ZIP code, and *attaches* the airline type and accumulated mileage.

```
void airline::airline_consumer( )
{
  data_input( );
  cout << "Enter Airline Type: ";
  cin.get(airline_type,19,'\n');
  cin.get(newline);
  cout << "Enter Accumulated Air Mileage: ";
  cin >> acc_air_miles;
  cin.get(newline);       //flush carriage return
}
```

Do you understand how the derived class is being used? A call to the function data_input( ) is a call to a member function that is part of the parent class. The remainder of the derived class is involved with obtaining the additional airline type and accumulated mileage.

The information on accumulated air mileage can be displayed for a consumer in a similar manner. The parent class function, data_output( ), prints the information gathered by the parent class (name, address, and so on), while disp_air_mileage( ) attaches the derived child class's information (airline type and mileage) to the output. The process is repeated for the rental car consumer.

Thus, one parent class serves as the data-gathering base for two derived child classes, each obtaining its own specific information.

The following is a sample output from the program:

```
--Airline Consumer--
Name: Peter J. Smith
Street: 401 West Summit Avenue
City: Middletown
```

```
State: Delaware
Zip: 19804
Airline Type: US AIR
Accumulated Air Mileage: 55321.0

--Rental Car Consumer--
Name: Harry Z. Beener
Street: 511 West Pacific Road
City: Longtown
State: New York
Zip: 25888
Rental Car Type: Audi
Accumulated Road Mileage: 33446.5
```

Experiment with this program by entering your own database of information. You might also consider adding additional member functions to the consumer class.

Now that you have learned about the class structure, you'll look at complete I/O in C++ in the next chapter.

Chapter 18

Complete I/O in C++

In Chapter 12 you were introduced to the iostream objects cin and cout, along with the *put to* (insertion) operator, <<; and the *get from* (extraction) operator, >>. In this chapter you will learn about the classes behind C++ I/O streams.

This chapter also introduces several additional topics of concern when writing C++ code, such as how to use C library functions in a C++ program.

Using enum Types in C++

You will find that user-defined enumerated types behave differently in C++ than their C counterparts. For example, C enum types are compatible with the type int. This means they can be cross-assigned with no complaints from the compiler. However, in C++ the two types are incompatible.

Another difference between C and C++ enumerated types involves the syntax shorthand when you define C++ enum variables. The following example program highlights the enumerated type differences between the two languages:

```
//
//   enum.cpp
//   C++ program demonstrates how to use enumerated types and
//   how C++ enumerated types differ from C enumerated types
//   Copyright (c) Chris H. Pappas and William H. Murray, 1997
//

#include <iostream.h>

typedef enum boolean { FALSE, TRUE };

void main(void)
{
// enum boolean bflag = 0; legal C, but illegal C++ statement
    boolean bcontinue, bflag = FALSE;

    bcontinue = (boolean)1;

    bflag = bcontinue;
}
```

This code starts by defining the enumerated type *boolean,* which is a standard type in several other high-level languages. Because of the ordering of the definition—FALSE, then TRUE—the compiler assigns a zero to FALSE and a 1 to TRUE. This is perfect for their logical use in a program.

The statement, commented-out in the main( ) program, represents a legal C statement. Remember, when you define enumerated variables in C, such as *bflag*, you must use the enum keyword with the enumerated type's tag field—in this case, *boolean*. Since C enum types are compatible with int types, it is also legal to initialize a variable with an integer value. This statement would not get past the C++ compiler. The second statement in main( ) shows the legal C++ counterpart.

The final two statements in the program show how to use enumerated types. Notice that in C++, an explicit cast *(boolean)*, is needed to convert the 1 to a *boolean* compatible type.

As you may recall, user-defined types cannot be directly input from or output to a file. Either they must go through a conversion routine or you can custom overload the >> and << operators, as discussed in Chapter 12.

Reference Variables

The reference variable is a C++ feature that you will grow to appreciate more and more. This is because it simplifies the syntax and readability of the more confusing pointer notation. Remember that by using pointer parameters, a program could pass something to a function either call-by-reference or call-by-variable, which enables the function to change the item passed. In contrast, call-by-value sends a copy of the variable's contents to the function. Any change to the variable in this case is a local change not reflected in the calling routine.

In the next example, the program passes an *stStudent* structure to a function, using the three possible calling methods: call-by-value, call-by-reference with pointer notation, and call-by-reference using the simpler C++ reference type. If the program were sending the entire array to the subroutine, by default, the array parameter would be passed call-by-reference. However, single structures within the array, by default, are passed call-by-value.

```
//
//   refvar.cpp
//   C++ program demonstrating how the C++ reference type
//   eliminates the more confusing pointer notation.
//   The program also demonstrates how to pass a single
//   array element, call by value, variable, and reference.
//   Copyright (c) Chris H. Pappas and William H. Murray, 1997
//

#include <iostream.h>

struct stStudent {
  char    pszName[66],
```

```cpp
            pszAddress[66],
            pszCity[26],
            pszState[3],
            pszPhone[13];
  int     icourses;
  float   GPA;
};

void vByValueCall     (stStudent    stAStudent);
void vByVariableCall  (stStudent *pstAStudent);
void vByReferenceCall (stStudent &rstAStudent);

void main(void)
{
  stStudent astLargeClass[100];

  astLargeClass[0].icourses = 10;

  vByValueCall     ( astLargeClass[0]);
  cout << astLargeClass[0].icourses << "\n"; // icourses still 10

  vByVariableCall  (&astLargeClass[0]);
  cout << astLargeClass[0].icourses << "\n"; // icourses = 20

  vByReferenceCall ( astLargeClass[0]);
  cout << astLargeClass[0].icourses << "\n"; // icourses = 30
}

void vByValueCall(stStudent    stAStudent)
{
  stAStudent.icourses += 10;    // normal structure syntax
}

void vByVariableCall(stStudent *pstAStudent)
{
  pstAStudent->icourses += 10;  // pointer syntax
}

void vByReferenceCall(stStudent &rstAStudent)
{
  rstAStudent.icourses += 10;   // simplified reference syntax
}
```

Notice that the following portion of code has spliced together each function's prototype, along with its matching invoking statement:

```
void vByValueCall      (stStudent   stAStudent);
     vByValueCall      ( astLargeClass[0]   );

void vByVariableCall   (stStudent *pstAStudent);
     vByVariableCall   (&astLargeClass[0]   );

void vByReferenceCall  (stStudent &rstAStudent);
     vByReferenceCall  ( astLargeClass[0]   );
```

One immediate advantage of this style is the simpler syntax needed to send a reference variable, *astLargeClass[0]* (the last statement), over the equivalent pointer syntax, *&astLargeClass[0]*. At this point the difference may appear small. However, as your algorithms become more complicated, this simpler syntax can avoid unnecessary precedence-level conflicts with other operators such as the pointer *dereference operator* (*) and the period *member operator* (.), which qualifies structure fields.

The next three statements were pulled out of the program's respective functions to show the syntax for using the structure within each function:

```
stAStudent.icourses   += 10;   // normal structure syntax
pstAStudent->icourses += 10;   // pointer syntax
rstAStudent.icourses  += 10;   // simplified reference syntax
```

The last two statements make a permanent change to the passed *stStudent* structure because the structure was passed call-by-reference (variable). Notice that the last statement did not require the pointer operator.

The difference between the first and third statements is dramatic. Although they look identical, the first statement references only a copy of the *stStudent* structure. In this case, when *stAStudent.icourses* is incremented, it is done only to the function's local copy. Exiting the function returns the structure to bit-oblivion, along with the incremented value. This explains why the program outputs 10, 20, 30, instead of 20, 30, 40.

Default Arguments

A function can be prototyped in C++ by using default arguments. This means that if the invoking statement omits certain fields, predefined default values will be supplied by the function. Default argument definitions cannot be spread throughout a function's prototype; they must be the last formal parameters defined. The following example program demonstrates how to define and use such a function:

```
//
//  defrag.cpp
//  C++ program demonstrates how to prototype functions
//  with default arguments. Default arguments must always
//  be the last formal parameters defined.
//  Copyright (c) Chris H. Pappas and William H. Murray, 1997
//

#include <iostream.h>

void fdefault_argument(char ccode='Q', int ivalue=0,
                       double fvalue=0);

void main(void)
{
  fdefault_argument('A',2,12.34);
  fdefault_argument( );

}

void fdefault_argument(char ccode, int ivalue, double fvalue)
{
  if(ccode == 'Q')
    cout << "\n\nUsing default values only.";
    cout << "\nivalue = " << ivalue;
    cout << "\nfvalue = " << fvalue;
}
```

Notice that in this program, all three formal parameter types have been given default values. The function fdefault( ) checks the *ccode* value to switch on or off an appropriate message. The output from the program is straightforward:

```
ivalue = 2
fvalue = 12.34

Using default values only.
ivalue = 0
fvalue = 0
```

Careful function prototyping, using default argument assignments, can be an important approach to avoiding unwanted side effects. This is one means of guaranteeing that dynamically allocated variables will not have garbage values if the user did not supply any. Another way to initialize dynamically allocated memory is with the function memset( ).

The memset( ) Function

The memset( ) function can be used to initialize a dynamically allocated byte, or bytes, to a specific character. The prototype for memset( ) looks like this:

void *memset(void *dest, int *cchar*, size_t *count*);

Once the memset( ) function is called, *dest* points to *count* bytes of memory initialized to the character *cchar*. The following example program demonstrates a dynamic structure declaration:

```
//
//   memset.cpp
//   C++ program demonstrating the function memset( ),
//   which can initialize dynamically allocated memory.
//   Copyright (c) Chris H. Pappas and William H. Murray, 1997
//

#include <iostream.h>
#include <memory.h>

struct keybits {
  unsigned char rshift, lshift,  ctrl,   alt,
                scroll, numlock, caplock, insert;
};

void main(void)
{
  keybits *pstkinitialized;

  pstkinitialized = new keybits;
  memset(pstkinitialized, 0, sizeof(keybits));
}
```

Because of the memset( ) function, the dynamically allocated structure pointed to by *pstkinitialized* contains all zeros. The call to the function memset( ) also used the

sizeof( ) operator instead of hardwiring the statement to a "magic number." The use of
sizeof( ) allows the algorithm to automatically adjust to the size of any object passed to
it. Also, remember that C++ does not require the struct keyword to precede a structure
tag field (*keybits*) when defining structure variables, as is the case with *pstkinitialized*.

Formatting Output

The next example continues the development of C++-formatted output initially
introduced in Chapter 12. The first program demonstrates how to print a table of
factorials using long doubles with the default right justification:

```
//
//   fact1.cpp
//   A C++ program that prints a table of
//   factorials for the numbers from 1 to 25.
//   Program uses the long double type.
//   Formatting includes precision, width, and fixed,
//   with default of right justification when printing.
//   Copyright (c) Chris H. Pappas and William H. Murray, 1997
//

#include <iostream.h>
#include <iomanip.h>

main( )
{
  long double number,factorial;

  number=1.0;
  factorial=1.0;

  cout.precision(0);            // no decimal place
  cout.setf(ios::fixed);        // use fixed format

  for(int i=0;i<25;i++) {
    factorial*=number;
    number=number+1.0;
    cout.width(30);             // width of 30 characters
    cout << factorial << endl;
  }

  return (0);
}
```

The precision( ), width( ), and setf( ) class members functions were repeated in the loop. The output from the program takes on the following form:

```
                              1
                              2
                              6
                             24
                            120
                            720
                           5040
                          40320
                         362880
                        3628800
                       39916800
                      479001600
                     6227020800
                    87178291200
                  1307674368000
                 20922789888000
                355687428096000
               6402373705728000
             121645100408832000
            2432902008176640000
           51090942171709440000
         1124000727777607680000
        25852016738884976640000
       620448401733239439360000
    15511210043330985984000000
```

The next program/output pair demonstrates how to vary output column width and override the default right justification:

```
//
//   fact2.cpp
//   A C++ program that prints a table of
//   factorials for the numbers from 1 to 15.
//   Program uses the long double type.
//   Formatting includes precision, width, alignment,
//   and format of large numbers.
//   Copyright (c) Chris H. Pappas and William H. Murray, 1997
//
```

```
#include <iostream.h>
#include <iomanip.h>

main( )
{
  long double number,factorial;

  number=1.0;
  factorial=1.0;

  cout.precision(0);            // no decimal point
  cout.setf(ios::left);         // left justify numbers
  cout.setf(ios::fixed);        // use fixed format

  for(int i=0;i<25;i++) {
    factorial*=number;
    number=number+1.0;
    cout.width(30);             // width of 30 characters
    cout << factorial << endl;
  }

  return (0);
}
```

The left-justified output takes on the following form:

```
1
2
6
24
120
720
5040
40320
362880
3628800
39916800
479001600
6227020800
87178291200
1307674368000
```

```
20922789888000
355687428096000
6402373705728000
121645100408832000
2432902008176640000
51090942171709440000
1124000727777607680000
25852016738884976640000
620448401733239439360000
15511210043330985984000000
```

The next example prints out a table of numbers, their squares, and their square roots. The program demonstrates how easy it is to align columns, pad with blanks, fill spaces with zeros, and control numeric precision in C++.

```cpp
//
//   sqrt.cpp
//   A C++ program that prints a table of
//   numbers, squares, and square roots for the
//   numbers from 1 to 15. Program uses the type
//   double. Formatting aligns columns, pads blank
//   spaces with '0' character, and controls
//   precision of answer.
//   Copyright (c) Chris H. Pappas and William H. Murray, 1997
//

#include <iostream.h>
#include <iomanip.h>
#include <math.h>

main( )
{
  double number,square,sqroot;

  cout << "num\t" << "square\t\t" << "square root\n";
  cout << "_____\n";

  number=1.0;
  cout.setf(ios::fixed);           // use fixed format

  for(int i=1;i<16;i++) {
```

```
        square=number*number;        // find square
        sqroot=sqrt(number);         // find square root

        cout.fill('0');              // fill blanks with zeros
        cout.width(2);               // column 2 characters wide
        cout.precision(0);           // no decimal place
        cout << number << "\t";

        cout.width(6);               // column 6 characters wide
        cout.precision(1);           // print 1 decimal place
        cout << square << "\t\t";

        cout.width(8);               // column 8 characters wide
        cout.precision(6);           // print 6 decimal places
        cout << sqroot << endl;

        number+=1.0;
    }
    return (0);
}
```

The formatted output takes on the following form:

num	square	square root
01	0001.0	1.000000
02	0004.0	1.414214
03	0009.0	1.732051
04	0016.0	2.000000
05	0025.0	2.236068
06	0036.0	2.449490
07	0049.0	2.645751
08	0064.0	2.828427
09	0081.0	3.000000
10	0100.0	3.162278
11	0121.0	3.316625
12	0144.0	3.464102
13	0169.0	3.605551
14	0196.0	3.741657
15	0225.0	3.872983

I/O Options

In Chapter 16 you were introduced to the concepts and syntax for object-oriented classes, constructors, destructors, member functions, and operators. This understanding is required for a deeper understanding of C++ I/O.

C++, like C, does not have any built-in I/O routines. Instead, all C++ compilers come bundled with object-oriented iostream classes. These standard I/O class objects have a cross-compiler syntax consistency because they were developed by the authors of the C++ language. If you are trying to write a C++ application that is portable to other C++ compilers, you will want to use these iostream classes. The Visual C++ compiler provides the following five ways to perform C++ I/O:

- **ANSI C buffered I/O** C also supports buffered functions such as fread( ) and fwrite( ). These STDIO.H library functions perform their own buffering before calling the direct I/O base routines.

- **C console and port I/O** C provides additional I/O routines that have no C++ equivalent, such as _getch( ), _ungetch( ), and _kbhit( ). All non-Windows applications can use these functions, which give you direct access to the hardware.

- **Microsoft Foundation Class library** The Microsoft CFile class found in the Foundation Class library provides C++ and especially Windows applications with objects for disk I/O. Using this library of routines guarantees that your application will be portable and easy to maintain.

- **Microsoft iostream class library** The iostream class library provides C++ programs with object-oriented I/O. You can use them in place of functions such as scanf( ), printf( ), fscanf( ), and fprintf( ). However, while these iostream classes are not required by C++ programs, many of the character-mode objects, such as cin, cout, cerr, and clog, are incompatible with the Windows graphical user interface.

- **Unbuffered C library I/O** The C compiler provides unbuffered I/O through functions such as _read( ) and _write( ). These functions are very popular with C programmers because of their efficiency and the ease with which they can be customized.

The iostream Class List

All of the I/O objects defined in the iostream class library share the same abstract stream base class, called ios, with the exception of the stream buffer classes. These derived classes fall into four broad categories, as listed in Table 18-1.

Figure 18-1 illustrates the interrelationship between these ios stream classes.

Input Stream Classes

istream	Used for general-purpose input or as a parent class for other derived input classes
ifstream	Used for file input
istream_withassign	Used for cin input
istrstream	Used for string input

Output Stream Classes

ostream	Used for general-purpose output or as a parent class for other derived output streams
ofstream	Used for file output
ofstream_withassign	Used for cout, cerr, and clog
ostrstream	Used for string output

Input/Output Stream Classes

iostream	Used for general-purpose input and output, or as a parent class for other derived I/O streams
fstream	File I/O stream class
strstream	String I/O stream class
stdiostream	Standard I/O stream class

Stream Buffer Classes

streambuf	Used as a parent class for derived objects
filebuf	Disk file stream buffer class
strstreambuf	Stream buffer class for strings
stdiobuf	Stream buffer class for standard file I/O

Table 18-1.   *The Four ios Class Categories*

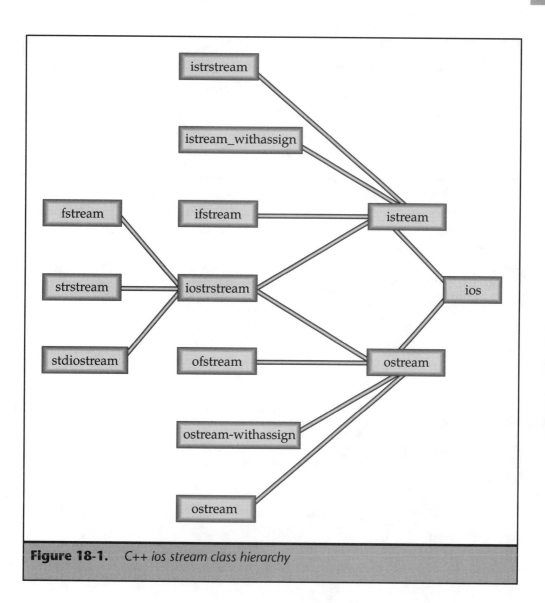

Figure 18-1. *C++ ios stream class hierarchy*

All ios-derived iostream classes use a streambuf class object for the actual I/O processing. The iostream class library uses the three derived buffer classes with streams as shown in Table 18-2.

Recall that all derived classes usually expand upon their inherited parent class definitions. This is why it is possible to use an operator or member function for a derived class that doesn't directly appear to be in the derived class' definition.

Buffered Class	Description
filebuf	Provides buffered disk file I/O.
strstreambuf	Provides an in-memory array of bytes to hold the stream data.
stdiobuf	Provides buffered disk I/O with all buffering done by the standard I/O system.

Table 18-2. *Buffered Classes*

Often, because of this fact, you will have to research back to the root or parent class definition. Since C++ derives so many of its classes from the ios class, a portion of ios.h follows. You will be able to use this as an easy reference for understanding any class derived from ios.

```
#ifndef EOF
#define EOF (-1)
#endif

class streambuf;
class ostream;

class ios {

public:
    enum io_state {  goodbit    = 0x00,
                     eofbit     = 0x01,
                     failbit    = 0x02,
                     badbit     = 0x04 };

    enum open_mode { in         = 0x01,
                     out        = 0x02,
                     ate        = 0x04,
                     app        = 0x08,
                     trunc      = 0x10,
                     nocreate   = 0x20,
                     noreplace  = 0x40,
                     binary     = 0x80 }; // not in latest spec.
```

```
enum seek_dir { beg=0, cur=1, end=2 };

enum {  skipws      = 0x0001,
        left        = 0x0002,
        right       = 0x0004,
        internal    = 0x0008,
        dec         = 0x0010,
        oct         = 0x0020,
        hex         = 0x0040,
        showbase    = 0x0080,
        showpoint   = 0x0100,
        uppercase   = 0x0200,
        showpos     = 0x0400,
        scientific  = 0x0800,
        fixed       = 0x1000,
        unitbuf     = 0x2000,
        stdio       = 0x4000
                              };

static const long basefield;   // dec | oct | hex
static const long adjustfield; // left | right | internal
static const long floatfield;  // scientific | fixed

ios(streambuf*);               // differs from ANSI
virtual ~ios( );

inline long flags( ) const;
inline long flags(long _l);

inline long setf(long _f,long _m);
inline long setf(long _l);
inline long unsetf(long _l);

inline int width( ) const;
inline int width(int _i);
inline ostream* tie(ostream* _os);
inline ostream* tie( ) const;

inline char fill( ) const;
inline char fill(char _c);
```

```
      inline int precision(int _i);
      inline int precision( ) const;

      inline int rdstate( ) const;
      inline void clear(int _i = 0);

//    NOTE: inline operator void*( ) const;
      operator void *( ) const { if(state&(badbit|failbit) ) \
                                  return 0; return (void *)this; }
      inline int operator!( ) const;

      inline int  good( ) const;
      inline int  eof( ) const;
      inline int  fail( ) const;
      inline int  bad( ) const;
```

The programs in the following sections use a derived class based on some parent class. Some of the example program code uses derived class member functions, while other statements use inherited characteristics. These examples will help you understand the many advantages of derived classes and of inherited characteristics. While these concepts may appear difficult or frustrating at first, you'll quickly appreciate how you can inherit functionality from a predefined class simply by defining a derived class based on the predefined one.

Input Stream Classes

The ifstream class used in the next example program is derived from fstreambase and istream. It provides input operations on a filebuf. The program concentrates on text stream input.

```
//
// ifstrm.cpp
// C++ program demonstrating how to use ifstream class,
// derived from the istream class.
// Copyright (c) Chris H. Pappas and William H. Murray, 1997
//
// Valid member functions for ifstream include:
//        ifstream::open        ifstream::rdbuf
//
// Valid member functions for istream include:
//        istream::gcount       istream::get
```

```
//          istream::getline    istream::ignore
//          istream::istream    istream::peek
//          istream::putback    istream::read
//          istream::seekg      istream::tellg

#include <fstream.h>
#define iCOLUMNS 80

void main(void)
{
  char cOneLine[iCOLUMNS];

  ifstream ifMyInputStream("IFSTRM.CPP",ios::in);
  while(ifMyInputStream) {
    ifMyInputStream.getline(cOneLine,iCOLUMNS);
    cout << '\n' << cOneLine;
  }
  ifMyInputStream.close( );
}
```

The ifstream constructor is used first to create an ifstream object and connect it to an open file descriptor, *ifMyInputStream*. The syntax uses the name of a file, including a path if necessary ("IFSTRM.CPP"), along with one or more open modes (for example, ios::in | ios::nocreate | ios::binary). The default is text input. The optional ios::nocreate parameter tests for the file's existence. The *ifMyInputStream* file descriptor's integer value can be used in logical tests such as if and while statements and the value is automatically set to zero on *EOF*.

The getline( ) member function inherited from the iostream class allows a program to read whole lines of text up to a terminating null character. Function getline( ) has three formal parameters: a *char **, the number of characters to input—including the null character—and an optional delimiter (default = '\n').

cOneLine meets the first parameter requirement since char array names are technically pointers to characters. The number of characters to be input matches the array's definition, or *iCOLUMNS*. No optional delimiter was defined. However, if you knew your input lines were delimited by a special character—for example, '*'—you could have written the getline( ) statement like this:

```
ifMyInputStream.getline(cOneLine,iCOLUMNS,'*');
```

The example program continues by printing the string and then manually closes the file ifMyInputStream.close( ).

Output Stream Classes

All ofstream classes are derived from fstreambase and ostream and allow a program to perform formatted and unformatted output to a streambuf. The output from this program is used later in this chapter in the section entitled "Binary Files" to contrast text output with binary output.

The following example uses the ofstream constructor, which is very similar to its ifstream counterpart, described earlier. It expects the name of the output file, "MYOSTRM.OUT," and the open mode, ios::out.

```cpp
//
// ostrm.cpp
// C++ program demonstrating how to use the ofstream class
// derived from the ostream class.
// Copyright (c) Chris H. Pappas and William H. Murray, 1997

// Valid ofstream member functions include:
//          ofstream::open      ofstream::rdbuf

// Valid ostream member functions include:
//          ostream::flush      ostream::ostream
//          ostream::put        ostream::seekp
//          ostream::tellp      ostream::write

#include <fstream.h>
#include <string.h>
#define iSTRING_MAX 40

void main(void)
{
  int i=0;
  long ltellp;
  char pszString[iSTRING_MAX] = "Sample test string\n";

  // file opened in the default text mode
  ofstream ofMyOutputStream("MYOSTRM.OUT",ios::out);

  // write string out character by character
  // notice that '\n' IS translated into 2 characters
```

```
while(pszString[i] != '\0') {
  ofMyOutputStream.put(pszString[i]);
  ltellp = ofMyOutputStream.tellp( );
  cout << "\ntellp value: " << ltellp;
  i++;
}


// write entire string out with write member function

ltellp = ofMyOutputStream.tellp( );
cout << "\ntellp's value before writing 2nd string: "
     << ltellp;
ofMyOutputStream.write(pszString,strlen(pszString));
ltellp = ofMyOutputStream.tellp( );
cout << "\ntellp's updated value: " << ltellp;

ofMyOutputStream.close( );

}
```

The first while loop prints out the *pszString* character by character with the put( ) member function. After each character is output, the variable *ltellp* is assigned the current put pointer's position as returned by the call to the tellp( ) member function. It is important that you stop at this point to take a look at the output generated by the program, shown at the end of this section.

The string variable *pszString* is initialized with 19 characters plus a '\0' null terminator, bringing the count to a total of 20. However, although the program output generates a *tellp* count of 1..20, the 20th character isn't the '\0' null terminator. This is because in text mode, the *pszString*'s '\n' is translated into a 2-byte output, one for the carriage return (19th character) and the second for the linefeed (20th character). The null terminator is not output.

The last portion of the program calculates the output pointer's position before and after using the write( ) member function to print *pszString* as a whole string. Notice that the *tellp* values printed show that the function write( ) also translates the single null terminator into a two-character output. If the character translation had not occurred, *tellp*'s last value would be 39 (assuming put( ) left the first count at 20, not 19). The abbreviated output from the program looks like this:

```
tellp value: 1
tellp value: 2
tellp value: 3

      .

      .

      .

tellp value: 17
tellp value: 18
tellp value: 20
tellp's value before writing 2nd string: 20
tellp's updated value: 40
```

Fortunately, istream-derived class member functions such as get( ) and read( ) automatically convert the 2-byte output back to a single '\n'. The program highlights the need for caution when dealing with file I/O. If the file created by this program were used later on as an input file, opened in binary mode, a disaster would occur because binary files do not use such translation; file positions and contents would be incorrect.

Buffered Stream Classes

The streambuf class is the foundation for C++ stream I/O. This general class defines all of the basic operations that can be performed with character-oriented buffers. The streambuf class is also used to derive file buffers (filebuf class) and the istream and ostream classes that contain pointers to streambuf objects.

Any derived classes based on the ios class inherit a pointer to a streambuf. The filebuf class, as seen in Figure 18-2, is derived from streambuf and specializes the parent class to handle files.

The following example begins by defining two filebuf handles, *fbMyInputBuf* and *fbMyOutputBuf*, using the open( ) member function to create each text file. Assuming there were no file-creation errors, each handle is then associated with an appropriate istream (input) and ostream (output) object. With both files opened, the while loop performs a simple echo print from the input stream is.get( ) to the output stream

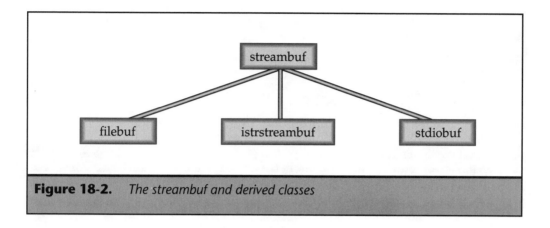

Figure 18-2. *The streambuf and derived classes*

os.put( ), counting the number of linefeeds, '\n'. The overloaded close( ) member
function manually closes each file.

```
//
//   filebuf.cpp
//   C++ program demonstrating how to use filebuf class.
//   Copyright (c) Chris H. Pappas and William H. Murray, 1997
//
//   Valid member functions include:
//          filebuf::attach      filebuf::close
//          filebuf::fd          filebuf::~filebuf
//          filebuf::filebuf     filebuf::is_open
//          filebuf::open        filebuf::overflow
//          filebuf::seekoff     filebuf::setbuf
//          filebuf::sync        filebuf::underflow
//

#include <fstream.h>
#include <fcntl.h>
#include <process.h> // exit prototype
```

```
void main(void)
{
  char ch;
  int iLineCount=0;
  filebuf fbMyInputBuf, fbMyOutputBuf;

  fbMyInputBuf.open("c:\\FILBUF.CPP",_O_WRONLY | _O_TEXT);
  if(fbMyInputBuf.is_open( ) == 0) {
    cerr << "Can't open input file";
    exit (1);
  }

  istream is(&fbMyInputBuf);

  fbMyOutputBuf.open("c:\\output.dat",_O_WRONLY | _O_TEXT);
  if(fbMyOutputBuf.is_open( ) == 0) {
    cerr << "Can't open output file";
    exit (2);
  }

  ostream os(&fbMyOutputBuf);

  while(is) {
    is.get(ch);
    os.put(ch);
    iLineCount += (ch == '\n');
  }

  fbMyInputBuf.close( );
  fbMyOutputBuf.close( );

  cout << "You had " << iLineCount << " lines in your file";
}
```

String Stream Class

The streambuf class can be used to extend the capabilities of the iostream class. Figure 18-1, shown earlier, illustrated the relationship between the ios and derived classes. It is the ios class that provides the derived classes with the programming interface and formatting features. However, it is the streambuf public members and virtual functions that do all the work. All derived ios classes make calls to these routines.

All buffered streambuf objects manage a fixed memory buffer called a *reserve area*. This reserve area can be divided into a get area for input and a put area for output. If your application requires, the get and put areas may overlap. Your program can use protected member functions to access and manipulate the two separate get and put pointers for character I/O. Each application determines the behavior of the buffers and pointers based on the program's implementation of the derived class.

There are two constructors for streambuf objects. Their syntax looks like this:

streambuf::streambuf( );
streambuf::streambuf(char* pr, int nLength);

The first constructor is used indirectly by all streambuf derived classes. It sets all the internal pointers of the streambuf object to null. The second constructor creates a streambuf object that is attached to an existing character array. The following program demonstrates how to declare a string strstreambuf object derived from the streambuf base class. Once the *stbMyStreamBuf* object is created, the program outputs a single character using the sputc( ) member function and then reads the character back in with the sgetc( ) member function.

```
//
//   strbuf.cpp
//   C++ program demonstrating how to use the streambuf class.
//   Copyright (c) Chris H. Pappas and William H. Murray, 1997
//

#include <strstrea.h>
#define iMYBUFFSIZE 1024

 void main(void)
{
  char c;

  strstreambuf stbMyStreamBuf(iMYBUFFSIZE);
  stbMyStreamBuf.sputc('A');  // output single character to buffer
  c = stbMyStreamBuf.sgetc( );
  cout << c;
}
```

There are two separate pointers for streambuf-based objects, a *put to* and a *get from*. Each is manipulated independently of the other. The reason the sgetc( ) member function retrieves the 'A' is to return the contents of the buffer at the location to which the get pointer points. sputc( ) moves the put pointer but does not move the get pointer and does not return a character from the buffer.

Table 18-3 gives the names and explanations for all streambuf public members and highlights which functions manipulate the put and get pointers.

Table 18-4 gives the names and explanations for all streambuf virtual functions.

Public Member	Meaning
sgetc	Returns the character pointed to by the get pointer. However, sgetc does not move the pointer.
sgetn	Gets a series of characters from the streambuf buffer.
sputc	Puts a character in the put area and moves the put pointer.
sputn	Puts a sequence of characters into the streambuf buffer and then moves the put pointer.
snextc	Moves the get pointer and returns the next character.
sbumpc	Returns the current character and then moves the get pointer.
stossc	Advances the get pointer one position. However, stossc does not return a character.
sputbackc	Attempts to move the get pointer back one position. Character put back must match one from previous get.
out_waiting	Reports the number of characters in the put area.
in_avail	Reports the number of characters in the get area.
dbp	Outputs streambuf buffer statistics and pointer values.

Table 18-3. *Members of streambuf*

Virtual Function	Meaning
seekoff	Seeks to the specified offset
seekpos	Seeks to the specified position
overflow	Clears out the put area
underflow	Fills the get area if necessary
pbackfail	Extends the sputbackc( ) function
setbuf	Tries to attach a reserve area to the streambuf
sync	Clears out the put and get area

Table 18-4. *Virtual Functions of streambuf*

Table 18-5 gives the names and explanations for all streambuf protected members. As you can readily see, the streambuf class comes equipped with every function a program could possibly need for manipulating a stream buffer. Since the streambuf class is used to derive file buffers (filebuf class) and istream and ostream classes, they all inherit streambuf characteristics.

Binary Files

Most of the example programs presented so far have used standard text files, or streams, as they are more appropriately called. This is not surprising since streams were originally designed for text, and text, therefore, is their default I/O mode.

Standard text files, or streams, contain a sequence of characters including carriage returns and linefeeds. In text mode, there is no requirement that individual characters remain unaltered as they are written to or read from a file. This can cause problems for certain types of applications. For example, the ASCII value for the newline character is a decimal 10. However, it could also be written as an 8-bit, hexadecimal 0A. In both C and C++ programs, it is considered to be the single character constant '\n'.

Protected Member	Meaning
allocate	Allocates a buffer by calling doalloc
doallocate	Allocates a reserve area (virtual function)
base	Returns a pointer to the beginning of the reserve area
ebuf	Returns a pointer to the end of the reserve area
blen	Returns the size of the reserve area
pbase	Returns a pointer to the beginning of the put area
pptr	Returns the put pointer
gptr	Returns the get pointer
eback	Returns the lower bound of the get area
epptr	Returns a pointer to the end of the put area
egptr	Returns a pointer to the end of the get area
setp	Sets all the put area pointers
setg	Sets all the get area pointers
pbump	Increments/decrements the put pointer
gbump	Increments/decrements the get pointer
setb	Sets up the reserve area
unbuffered	Sets or tests the streambuf0 buffer state variable

Table 18-5. *Protected Members of streambuf*

Under MS-DOS-compatible operations, the newline character is physically represented as a character pair—carriage return (decimal 13)/linefeed (decimal 10). Normally, this isn't a problem since the program automatically maps the two-character sequence into the single newline character on input, reversing the sequence on output. The problem is that a newline character occupies 1 byte, while the CR/LF pair occupies 2 bytes of storage.

Binary files, or streams, contain a sequence of bytes with a one-to-one correspondence to the sequence found in the external device (disk, tape, or terminal). In a binary file, no character translations will occur. For this reason, the number of bytes read or written will be the same as that found in the external device.

When an application is developed that needs to read an executable file, the file should be read as a binary file. Likewise, binary files should be used when reading or writing pure data files, like databases. This guarantees that no alteration of the data occurs except those changes performed explicitly by the application.

The following program is identical to OSTRM.CPP, described earlier in this chapter, except that the output file mode has been changed from text to ios::binary:

```
//
// binary.cpp
// This program is a modification of OSTRM.CPP and
// demonstrates binary file output.
// Copyright (c) Chris H. Pappas and William H. Murray, 1997
// Valid ofstream member functions include:
//          ofstream::open      ofstream::rdbuf
// Valid ostream member functions include:
//          ostream::flush      ostream::ostream
//          ostream::put        ostream::seekp
//          ostream::tellp      ostream::write

#include <fstream.h>
#include <string.h>
#define iSTRING_MAX 40

void main(void)
{
  int i=0;
  long ltellp;
  char pszString[iSTRING_MAX] = "Sample test string\n";
  // file opened in binary mode!
  ofstream ofMyOutputStream("MYOSTRM.OUT",ios::out | ios::binary);

  // write string out character by character
  // notice that '\n' is NOT translated into 2 characters!
  while(pszString[i] != '\0') {
    ofMyOutputStream.put(pszString[i]);
    ltellp = ofMyOutputStream.tellp( );
    cout << "\ntellp value: " << ltellp;
    i++;
  }

  // write entire string out with write member function
  ltellp = ofMyOutputStream.tellp( );
  cout << "\ntellp's value before writing 2nd string: " << ltellp;
  ofMyOutputStream.write(pszString,strlen(pszString));
  ltellp = ofMyOutputStream.tellp( );
```

```
cout << "\ntellp's updated value: " << ltellp;

ofMyOutputStream.close( );

}
```

The abbreviated output, seen in the following listing, illustrates the one-to-one relationship between a file and the data's internal representation:

```
tellp value: 1
tellp value: 2
tellp value: 3
        .
        .
        .
tellp value: 17
tellp value: 18
tellp value: 19
tellp's value before writing 2nd string: 19
tellp's updated value: 38
```

The string *pszString*, which has 19 characters plus a '\0' null string terminator, is output exactly as stored, without the appended '\0' null terminator. This explains why tellp( ) reports a multiple of 19 at the completion of each string's output.

Combining C and C++ Code

In previous discussions (see Chapter 6), you have seen how the extern keyword specifies that a variable or function has external linkage. This means that the variable or function referenced is defined in some other source file or later on in the same file.

In C and C++, the extern keyword can be used with a string. The string indicates that another language's linkage conventions are being used for the identifier(s) being defined. For C++ programs, the default string is "C++."

In C++, functions are overloaded by default. This causes the C++ compiler to assign a new name to each function. You can prevent the compiler from assigning a new name to each function by preceding the function definition with extern "C." This is necessary so that C functions and data can be accessed by C++ code. Naturally, this is only done for one of a set of functions with the same name. Without this override, the linker would find more than one global function with the same name. Currently,

"C" is the only other language specifier supported by Visual C++. The syntax for using extern "C" looks like this:

extern "C" *freturn_type fname(param_type(s) param(s))*

The following listing demonstrates how extern "C" is used with a single-function prototype:

```
extern "C" int fprintf(FILE *stream, char *format, ...);
```

To modify a group of function prototypes, a set of braces, {}, is needed:

```
nd-2extern "C"
  {
    .
    .
    .
  }
```

The next code segment modifies the getc( ) and putc( ) function prototypes:

```
extern "C"
  {
    int getc(FILE *stream);
    int putc(int c, FILE *stream);
  }
```

The following example program demonstrates how to use extern "C":

```
//
//  clink.cpp
//  C++ program demonstrating how to link C++ code
//  to C library functions.
//  Copyright (c) Chris H. Pappas and William H. Murray, 1997
//

#include <iostream.h>
#include <string.h>
#include <stdlib.h>
```

```
#define iMAX 9

extern "C" int imycompare(const void *pi1, const void *pi2);

void main(void)
{
  int iarray[iMAX] = { 1, 9, 2, 8, 3, 7, 4, 6, 5};

  for(int i = 0; i < iMAX; i++)
    cout << iarray[i] << " ";

  qsort(iarray,iMAX,sizeof(int),imycompare);

  for(i = 0; i < iMAX; i++)
    cout << iarray[i] << " ";
}

extern "C" int imycompare(const void *pi1, const void *pi2)
{
  return( *(int *)pi1 - *(int *)pi2);
}
```

All the Visual C++ include files use extern "C." This makes it possible for a C++ program to use the C run-time library functions. Rather than repeat extern "C" for every definition in these header files, the following conditional statement pair surrounds all C header file definitions:

```
// 3-statements found at the beginning of header file.

#ifdef __cplusplus
extern "C" {
#endif


// 3-statements found at the end of the header file.

#ifdef __cplusplus
}
#endif
```

When compiling a C++ program, the compiler automatically defines the __cplusplus name. This in turn makes the extern "C" { statement and the closing brace, }, visible only when needed.

Designing Unique Manipulators

The concept of stream manipulators was introduced in Chapter 12. Manipulators are used with the insertion, <<, and extraction, >>, operators, exactly as if they represented data for output or variables to receive input. As the name implies, however, manipulators can carry out arbitrary operations on the input and output streams.

Several of the example programs used the built-in manipulators dec, hex, oct, setw, and setprecision. Now you will learn how to write your own custom manipulators. To gradually build your understanding of the syntax necessary to create your own manipulators, the example programs begin with the simplest type of manipulator, one with no parameters, and then moves on to ones with parameters.

Manipulators Without Parameters

A custom manipulator can be created any time to repeatedly insert the same character sequence into the output stream. For example, maybe your particular application needs to flag the user to an important piece of data. You even want to beep the speaker to get the user's attention just in case he or she isn't looking directly at the monitor. Without custom manipulators, your output statements would look like this:

```
cout << '\a' << "\n\n\t\tImportant data: "
     << fcritical_mass << endl;
```

Every time you wanted to grab the user's attention, you would repeat the bell prompt, '\a', and the "...Important data: " string. An easier approach is to define a manipulator, called *beep*, that automatically substitutes the desired sequence. The *beep* manipulator also makes the statement easier to read:

```
cout << beep << fcritical_mass << endl;
```

The following program demonstrates how to define and use the beep( ) function:

```
//
//  beep.cpp
//  C++ program demonstrates how to create your own
//  non-parameterized manipulator.
```

FOUNDATIONS FOR OBJECT-ORIENTED PROGRAMMING IN C++

```
//  Copyright (c) Chris H. Pappas and William H. Murray, 1997
//

#include <iostream.h>

ostream& beep(ostream& os) {
   return os << '\a' << "\n\n\t\t\tImportant data: ";
}

void main(void)
{
 double fcritical_mass = 12459876.12;

 cout << beep << fcritical_mass;
}
```

The globally defined beep( ) function uses an ostream& formal parameter and returns the same ostream&. *Beep* works because it is automatically connected to the stream's << operator. The stream's insertion operator, <<, is overloaded to accept this kind of function with the following inline function:

```
Inline ostream& ostream::operator<<(ostream& (*f)(ostream&)) {
   (*f)(*this);
   return *this;
}
```

The inline function associates the << operator with the custom manipulator by accepting a pointer to a function passed an ostream& type and that returns the same. This is exactly how beep( ) is prototyped. Now when << is used with beep( ), the compiler dereferences the overloaded operator, finding where function beep( ) sits, and then executes it. The overloaded operator returns a reference to the original ostream. Because of this, you can combine manipulators, strings, and other data with the << operators.

Manipulators with One Parameter

The iostream class library, prototyped in IOMANIP.H, defines a special set of macros for creating parameterized macros. The simplest parameterized macro you can write accepts either one int or long parameter.

The following listing shows a prototype for such a manipulator, *fc*. The example program demonstrates the syntax necessary to create a single-parameter custom manipulator:

```
//
//   manip1.cpp
//   C++ program demonstrating how to create and use
//   one-parameter custom manipulators.
//   Copyright (c) Chris H. Pappas and William H. Murray, 1997
//

#include <iostream.h>
#include <iomanip.h>
#include <string.h>
#define iSCREEN_WIDTH 80


ostream& fc(ostream& os, int istring_width)
{
  os << '\n';
  for(int i=0; i < ((iSCREEN_WIDTH - istring_width)/2); i++)
  os << ' ';
  return(os);
}


OMANIP(int) center(int istring_width)
{
  return OMANIP(int) (fc, istring_width);
}


void main(void)
{
  char *psz = "This is auto-centered text!";
  cout << center(strlen(psz)) << psz;
}
```

FOUNDATIONS FOR OBJECT-ORIENTED PROGRAMMING IN C++

The *center* custom-parameterized manipulator accepts a single value, *strlen(psz)*, representing the length of a string. IOMANIP.H defines a macro, OMANIP(int), and expands into the class __OMANIP_int. The definition for this class includes a constructor and an overloaded ostream insertion operator. When function center( ) is inserted into the stream, it calls the constructor that creates and returns an __OMANIP_int object. The object's constructor then calls the fc( ) function.

Manipulators with Multiple Parameters

The next example should be familiar. Actually, it is the same code (SQRT.CPP) seen earlier in the chapter to demonstrate how to format numeric output. However, the program has been rewritten using a two-parameter custom manipulator to format the data.

The first modification to the program involves a simple structure definition to hold the format manipulator's actual parameter values:

```
struct stwidth_precision {
  int iwidth;
  int iprecision;
};
```

When you create manipulators that take arguments other than int or long, you must use the IOMANIPdeclare macro. This macro declares the classes for your new data type. The definition for the *format* manipulator begins with the OMANIP macro:

```
OMANIP(stwidth_precision) format(int iwidth, int iprecision)
{
  stwidth_precision stWidth_Precision;
  stWidth_Precision.iwidth = iwidth;
  stWidth_Precision.iprecision = iprecision;
  return OMANIP (stwidth_precision)(ff, stWidth_Precision);
}
```

In this example, the custom manipulator is passed two integer arguments, *iwidth* and *iprecision*. The first value defines the number of spaces to be used by *format*, and the second value specifies the number of decimal places. Once *format* has initialized the stWidth_Precision structure, it calls the constructor, which creates and returns an __OMANIP object. The object's constructor then calls the ff( ) function, which sets the specified parameters:

```
static ostream& ff(ostream& os, stwidth_precision
                   stWidth_Precision)
{
  os.width(stWidth_Precision.iwidth);
  os.precision(stWidth_Precision.iprecision);
  os.setf(ios::fixed);
  return os;
}
```

The complete program follows. All of the code replaced by the call to *format* has been left in the listing for comparison. Notice how the *format* custom manipulator streamlines each output statement.

```
//
//   manip2.cpp
//   This C++ program is the same as sqrt.cpp, except
//   for the fact that it uses custom parameterized
//   manipulators to format the output.
//   A C++ program that prints a table of
//   numbers, squares, and square roots for the
//   numbers from 1 to 15. Program uses the type
//   double. Formatting aligns columns, pads blank
//   spaces with '0' character, and controls
//   precision of answer.
//   Copyright (c) Chris H. Pappas and William H. Murray, 1997
//

#include <iostream.h>
#include <iomanip.h>
#include <math.h>

struct stwidth_precision {
  int iwidth;
  int iprecision;
};

IOMANIPdeclare(stwidth_precision);

static ostream& ff(ostream& os, stwidth_precision
                   stWidth_Precision)
{
  os.width(stWidth_Precision.iwidth);
  os.precision(stWidth_Precision.iprecision);
  os.setf(ios::fixed);
  return os;
}

OMANIP(stwidth_precision) format(int iwidth, int iprecision)
{
  stwidth_precision stWidth_Precision;
  stWidth_Precision.iwidth = iwidth;
  stWidth_Precision.iprecision = iprecision;
```

```
      return OMANIP (stwidth_precision) (ff, stWidth_Precision);
}

main( )
{
  double number,square,sqroot;

  cout << "num\t" << "square\t\t" << "square root\n";
  cout << "_____\n";

  number=1.0;

//cout.setf(ios::fixed);          // use fixed format
  for(int i=1;i<16;i++) {
    square=number*number;          // find square
    sqroot=sqrt(number);           // find square root

    cout.fill('0');                // fill blanks with zeros
//  cout.width(2);                 // column 2 characters wide
//  cout.precision(0);             // no decimal place
    cout << format(2,0) << number << "\t";

//  cout.width(6);                 // column 6 characters wide
//  cout.precision(1);             // print 1 decimal place
    cout << format(6,1) << square << "\t\t";

//  cout.width(8);                 // column 8 characters wide
//  cout.precision(6);             // print 6 decimal places
    cout << format(8,6) << sqroot << endl;

    number+=1.0;
  }
  return (0);
}
```

With the discussion of advanced C++ object-oriented I/O completed, you are ready to tackle object-oriented design philosophies. Chapter 19 explains how important good class design is to a successful object-oriented problem solution.

The Complete Reference

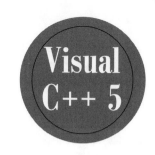
Visual C++ 5

Chapter 19

Working in an Object-Oriented Environment

While C++ may be the language of choice among object-oriented programmers, other languages are available. Every object-oriented language shares several common features. In his book *Object-Oriented Software Construction* (Prentice Hall), Bertrand Meyer suggests that there are seven features standard to true object-oriented programs as a whole:

- Object-based modularization
- Abstract data types
- Memory management (automatic)
- Classes
- Inheritance
- Polymorphism
- Inheritance (multiple)

From your study of C++ classes in Chapter 17, you have learned that Visual C++ provides these features to the object-oriented programmer. In fact, you might conclude that to do true object-oriented programming, you must work in a language, such as C++, that is itself object oriented. There are valid arguments against this notion, as you will see later in this book. For example, programs written for Microsoft's Windows contain many of the seven previously mentioned features, even though they can be written in C.

An Object-Oriented Stack

In Chapter 16, you were introduced to many object-oriented concepts. For example, you learned that the C++ class, an abstract data type, provides the encapsulation of data structures and the operations on those structures (member functions). As such, the C++ class serves as the mechanism for forming objects. The following simple example of object creation with a C++ class demonstrates the implementation of an object-oriented stack.

The traditional FILO (first-in, last-out) manner is used for the stack operations in this example. The stack class provides six member functions: clear( ), top( ), empty( ), full( ), push( ), and pop( ). Examine the following listing and observe how these member functions are implemented:

```
//
// stack.cpp
// C++ program illustrates object-oriented programming
// with a classical stack operation using a string of
// characters.
// Copyright (c) Chris H. Pappas and William H. Murray, 1997
```

```
//

#include <iostream.h>
#include <string.h>

#define maxlen 80

class stack {
  char str1[maxlen];
  int  first;

public:
  void clear(void);
  char top(void);
  int  empty(void);
  int  full(void);
  void push(char chr);
  char pop(void);
};

void stack::clear(void)
{
  first=0;
}

char stack::top(void)
{
  return (str1[first]);
}

int stack::empty(void)
{
  return (first==0);
}

int stack::full(void)
{
  return (first==maxlen-1);
}
```

```
void stack::push(char chr)
{
   str1[++first]=chr;
}

char stack::pop(void)
{
   return (str1[first--]);
}

main( )
{
   stack mystack;
   char str[11]="0123456789";

   // clear the stack
   mystack.clear( );

   // load the string, char-by-char, on the stack
   cout << "\nLoad character data on stack" << endl;
   for(int i=0; (int) i<strlen(str);i++) {
      if (!mystack.full( ))
         mystack.push(str[i]);
         cout << str[i] << endl;
   }

   // unload the stack, char-by-char
   cout << "\nUnload character data from stack" << endl;
   while (!mystack.empty( ))
      cout << mystack.pop( ) << endl;

   return (0);
}
```

In this program, characters from a string are pushed, one character at a time, onto the stack. Next, the stack is unloaded one character at a time. Loading and unloading are done from the stack top, so the first character information loaded on the stack is pushed down most deeply in the stack.

Notice in the following listing that the character for the number zero was pushed onto the stack first. It should be no surprise that it is the last character popped off the stack.

```
Load character data on stack
0
1
2
3
4
5
6
7
8
9

Unload character data from stack
9
8
7
6
5
4
3
2
1
0
```

This example lacks many of the more advanced object-oriented concepts such as memory management, inheritance, and polymorphism. However, the example is a complete object-oriented program. The power of object-oriented thinking is more apparent as more and more of Meyer's seven points are actually implemented.

An Object-Oriented Linked List in C++

In Chapter 14, a linked-list program was developed in C++ using a traditional procedural programming approach. When using the traditional approach, you learned that the linked-list program is difficult to alter and maintain. In this chapter, a linked-list program using objects is developed that will allow you to create a list of employee information. It will also be possible to add and delete employees from the list. To limit the size of the linked-list program, no user interface will be used for gathering employee data. Data for the linked list has been hardwired in the main( ) function. Examples of how to make this program interactive and able to accept information from the keyboard have been shown in earlier chapters.

This program is slightly more difficult than the example in Chapter 14. You will find that it includes, in addition to linked-list concepts, all seven of the object-oriented concepts listed earlier.

Creating a Parent Class

Several child classes derived from a common parent class are used in this example. The parent class for this linked-list example is named *NNR*. "NNR" represents the Nineveh National Research Company, developers of computer-related books and software. The linked-list program is a database that will keep pertinent information and payroll data on company employees. The purpose of the parent class NNR is to gather information common to all subsequent derived child classes. For this example, that common information includes an employee's last name, first name, occupation title, social security number, and year hired at the company. The parent class NNR has three levels of isolation: public, protected, and private. The protected section of this class shows the structure for gathering data common to each derived child class. The public section (member functions) shows how that information will be intercepted from the function main( ).

```
// PARENT CLASS
class NNR {

friend class payroll_list;

protected:
  char lstname[20];
  char fstname[15];
  char job_title[30];
  char social_sec[12];
  double year_hired;
  NNR *pointer;
  NNR *next_link;

public:
  NNR(char *lname,char *fname,char *ss,
      char *job,double y_hired)
  {
    strcpy(lstname,lname);
    strcpy(fstname,fname);
    strcpy(social_sec,ss);
    strcpy(job_title,job);
    year_hired=y_hired;
    next_link=0;
```

```
    }
           .
           .
           .
           .
```

A friend class named payroll_list is used by the parent class and all derived child classes. When you study the full program listing in the section entitled "Examining the Complete Program" later in this chapter, notice that all derived child classes share this common variable, too. (Remember how the terms "private" and "public" relate to encapsulation concepts used by object-oriented programmers.)

A Derived Child Class

Four derived child classes are used in this program. Each of these is derived from the parent class NNR shown in the last section. This segment presents one child class, salespersons, which represents the points common to all four derived classes. A portion of this derived class is shown next. The derived child class satisfies the object-oriented concept of inheritance.

```
//SUB OR DERIVED CHILD CLASS
class salespersons:public NNR {

friend class payroll_list;

private:
  double disk_sales;
  double comm_rate;

public:
  salespersons(char *lname,char *fname,char *ss,
               char *job,double y_hired,
               double d_sales,double c_rate):
               NNR(lname,fname,ss,
               job,y_hired)
  {
    disk_sales=d_sales;
    comm_rate=c_rate;
  }
```

.
.
.
.

The salespersons child class gathers information and adds it to the information already gathered by the parent class. This in turn forms a data structure composed of last name, first name, social security number, year hired, the total sales, and the appropriate commission rate.

Here is the remainder of the child class description:

.
.
.
.

```
void fill_sales(double d_sales)
{
  disk_sales=d_sales;
}

void fill_comm_rate(double c_rate)
{
  comm_rate=c_rate;
}

void add_info( )
{
  pointer=this;
}

void send_info( )
{
  NNR::send_info( );
  cout << "\n Sales (disks): " << disk_sales;
  cout << "\n Commission Rate: " << comm_rate;
}

};
```

Instead of add_info( ) setting aside memory for each additional linked-list node by using the new free store operator, the program uses each object's this pointer. The *pointer* is being assigned the address of an NNR node.

Output information on a particular employee is constructed in a unique manner. In the case of the salespersons class, notice that send_info( ) makes a request to NNR's send_info( ) function. NNR's function prints the information common to each derived class; then the salespersons' send_info( ) function prints the information unique to the particular child class. For this example, this information includes the sales and the commission rate.

It would also have been possible to print the information about the salesperson completely from within the child class, but the method used allows another advantage of object-oriented programming to be illustrated, and that is the use of *virtual* functions.

Using a Friend Class

The friend class, payroll_list, contains the means for printing the linked list and for the insertion and deletion of employees from the list. Here is a small portion of this class:

```
//FRIEND CLASS
class payroll_list {

private:
  NNR *location;

public:
  payroll_list( )
  {
    location=0;
  }

  void print_payroll_list( );

  void insert_employee(NNR *node);

  void remove_employee_id(char *social_sec);

};
       .
       .
       .
       .
```

Notice that messages that are sent to the member functions print_payroll_list( ), insert_employee( ), and remove_employee_id( ) form the functional part of the linked-list program.

Consider the function print_payroll_list( ), which begins by assigning the pointer to the list to the pointer variable *present*. While the pointer *present* is not zero, it will continue to point to employees in the linked list, direct them to *send_info,* and update the pointer until all employees have been printed. The next section of code shows how this is achieved:

```
        .
        .
        .
        .
void payroll_list::print_payroll_list( )
{
   NNR *present=location;

   while(present!=0) {
     present->send_info( );
     present=present->next_link;
   }
}
        .
        .
        .
```

The fact that the variable *pointer* contains the memory address of nodes inserted via add_info( ) was discussed earlier. This value is used by insert_employee( ) to form the link with the linked list. The insertion technique inserts data alphabetically by an employee's last name. Thus, the linked list is always ordered alphabetically by last name.

A correct insertion is made by the program by comparing the last name of a new employee with those already in the list. When a name (*node->lstname*) already in the list is found that is greater than the *current_node->lstname,* the first while loop ends. This is a standard linked-list insert procedure that leaves the pointer variable, *previous_node,* pointing to the node behind where the new node is to be inserted and leaves *current_node* pointing to the node that will follow the insertion point for the new node.

Once the insertion point is determined, the program creates a new link or node by calling node->add_info( ). The *current_node* is linked to the new node's *next_link.* The last decision that must be made is whether or not the new node is to be placed as the front node in the list or between existing nodes. The program establishes this by examining the contents of the pointer variable *previous_node.* If the pointer variable is zero, it cannot be pointing to a valid previous node, so *location* is updated to the address of the new node. If *previous_node* contains a nonzero value, it is assumed to be pointing to a valid previous node. In this case, *previous_node->next_link* is assigned the address of the new node's address, or *node->pointer*.

```
        .
        .
        .
        .
void payroll_list::insert_employee(NNR *node)
{
  NNR *current_node=location;
  NNR *previous_node=0;

  while (current_node != 0 &&
         strcmp(current_node->lstname,node->lstname) < 0) {
    previous_node=current_node;
    current_node=current_node->next_link;
  }
  node->add_info( );
  node->pointer->next_link=current_node;
  if (previous_node==0)
    location=node->pointer;
  else
    previous_node->next_link=node->pointer;
}
        .
        .
        .
        .
```

Items can be removed from the linked list only by knowing the employee's social security number. This technique adds a level of protection against accidentally deleting an employee.

As you examine remove_employee_id( ), shown in the next listing, note that the structure used for examining the nodes in the linked list is almost identical to that of insert_employee( ). However, the first while loop leaves the *current_node* pointing to the node to be deleted, not the node after the one to be deleted.

```
        .
        .
        .
```

```
void payroll_list::remove_employee_id(char *social_sec)
{
  NNR *current_node=location;
  NNR *previous_node=0;

  while(current_node != 0 &&
        strcmp(current_node->social_sec,
        social_sec) != 0) {
    previous_node=current_node;
    current_node=current_node->next_link;
  }

  if(current_node != 0 && previous_node == 0) {
    location=current_node->next_link;
    delete current_node;
  }
  else if(current_node != 0 && previous_node != 0) {
    previous_node->next_link=current_node->next_link;
    delete current_node;
  }
}
```

The first compound if statement takes care of deleting a node in the front of the list. The program accomplishes this by examining the contents of *previous_node* to see if it contains a zero. If it does, then the front of the list, *location,* needs to be updated to the node following the one to be deleted. This is achieved with the following line:

```
current_node->next_link
```

The second if statement takes care of deleting a node between two existing nodes. This requires the node behind to be assigned the address of the node after the one being deleted.

```
previous_node->next_link=current_node->next_link.
```

Now that the important pieces of the program have been examined, the next section puts them together to form a complete program.

Examining the Complete Program

The following listing is the complete operational object-oriented linked-list program. The only thing it lacks is an interactive user interface. When the program is executed, it will add nine employees, with their different job titles, to the linked list and then print the list. Next, the program will delete two employees from the list. This is accomplished by supplying their social security numbers. The altered list is then printed. The main( ) function contains information on which employees are added and deleted.

```
//
//  nnr.cpp
//  C++ program illustrates object-oriented programming
//  with a linked list. This program keeps track of
//  employee data at Nineveh National Research (NNR).
//  Copyright (c) Chris H. Pappas and William H. Murray, 1997
//

#include <iostream.h>
#include <string.h>

// PARENT CLASS
class NNR {

friend class payroll_list;

protected:
  char lstname[20];
  char fstname[15];
  char job_title[30];
  char social_sec[12];
  double year_hired;
  NNR *pointer;
  NNR *next_link;

public:
  NNR(char *lname,char *fname,char *ss,
      char *job,double y_hired)
  {
    strcpy(lstname,lname);
    strcpy(fstname,fname);
    strcpy(social_sec,ss);
    strcpy(job_title,job);
```

```
    year_hired=y_hired;
    next_link=0;
}

NNR( )
{
    lstname[0]=NULL;
    fstname[0]=NULL;
    social_sec[0]=NULL;
    job_title[0]=NULL;
    year_hired=0;
    next_link=0;
}

void fill_lstname(char *l_name)
{
    strcpy(lstname,l_name);
}

void fill_fstname(char *f_name)
{
    strcpy(fstname,f_name);
}

void fill_social_sec(char *soc_sec)
{
    strcpy(social_sec,soc_sec);
}

void fill_job_title(char *o_name)
{
    strcpy(job_title,o_name);
}

void fill_year_hired(double y_hired)
{
    year_hired=y_hired;
}

virtual void add_info( ) {
}
virtual void send_info( )
```

```
   {
     cout << "\n\n" << lstname << ", " << fstname
       << "\n Social Security: #" << social_sec;
     cout << "\n Job Title: " << job_title;
     cout << "\n Year Hired: " << year_hired;
   }

};

//SUB OR DERIVED CHILD CLASS
class administration:public NNR {

friend class payroll_list;

private:
  double yearly_salary;

public:
  administration(char *lname,char *fname,char *ss,
                 char *job,double y_hired,
                 double y_salary):
                 NNR(lname,fname,ss,
                 job,y_hired)
  {
    yearly_salary=y_salary;
  }

  administration( ):NNR( )
  {
    yearly_salary=0.0;
  }

  void fill_yearly_salary(double salary)
  {
    yearly_salary=salary;
  }

  void add_info( )
  {
    pointer=this;
  }
```

```
  void send_info( )
  {
    NNR::send_info( );
    cout << "\n Yearly Salary: $" << yearly_salary;
  }

};


//SUB OR DERIVED CHILD CLASS
class salespersons:public NNR {

friend class payroll_list;

private:
  double disk_sales;
  double comm_rate;

public:
  salespersons(char *lname,char *fname,char *ss,
               char *job,double y_hired,
               double d_sales,double c_rate):
               NNR(lname,fname,ss,
               job,y_hired)
  {
    disk_sales=d_sales;
    comm_rate=c_rate;
  }

  salespersons( ):NNR( )
  {
    disk_sales=0.0;
    comm_rate=0;
  }

  void fill_sales(double d_sales)
  {
    disk_sales=d_sales;
  }
  void fill_comm_rate(int c_rate)
```

```
  {
    comm_rate=c_rate;
  }

  void add_info( )
  {
    pointer=this;
  }

  void send_info( )
  {
    NNR::send_info( );
    cout << "\n Sales (disks): " << disk_sales;
    cout << "\n Commission Rate: " << comm_rate;
  }

};


//SUB OR DERIVED CHILD CLASS
class technicians:public NNR {

friend class payroll_list;

private:
  double hourly_salary;

public:
  technicians(char *lname,char *fname,char *ss,char *job,
              double y_hired,double h_salary):
              NNR(lname,fname,ss,job,y_hired)
  {
    hourly_salary=h_salary;
  }

  technicians( ):NNR( )
  {
    hourly_salary=0.0;
  }

  void fill_hourly_salary(double h_salary)
```

```
  {
    hourly_salary=h_salary;
  }

  void add_info( )
  {
    pointer=this;
  }

  void send_info( )
  {
    NNR::send_info( );
    cout << "\n Hourly Salary: $" << hourly_salary;
  }

};


//SUB OR DERIVED CHILD CLASS
class supplies:public NNR {

friend class payroll_list;

private:
  double hourly_salary;

public:
  supplies(char *lname,char *fname,char *ss,char *job,
           double y_hired,double h_salary):
           NNR(lname,fname,ss,
           job,y_hired)
  {
    hourly_salary=h_salary;
  }

  supplies( ):NNR( )
  {
    hourly_salary=0.0;
  }

  void fill_hourly_salary(double h_salary)
  {
```

```
      hourly_salary=h_salary;
  }

  void add_info( )
  {
    pointer=this;
  }

  void send_info( )
  {
    NNR::send_info( );
    cout << "\n Hourly Salary: $" << hourly_salary;
  }

};


//FRIEND CLASS
class payroll_list {

private:
  NNR *location;

public:
  payroll_list( )
  {
    location=0;
  }

  void print_payroll_list( );

  void insert_employee(NNR *node);

  void remove_employee_id(char *social_sec);

};

void payroll_list::print_payroll_list( )
{
  NNR *present=location;
```

```
  while(present!=0) {
    present->send_info( );
    present=present->next_link;
  }
}


void payroll_list::insert_employee(NNR *node)
{
  NNR *current_node=location;
  NNR *previous_node=0;
  while (current_node != 0 &&
          strcmp(current_node->lstname,node->lstname) < 0) {
    previous_node=current_node;
    current_node=current_node->next_link;
  }
  node->add_info( );
  node->pointer->next_link=current_node;
  if (previous_node==0)
    location=node->pointer;
  else
    previous_node->next_link=node->pointer;
}


void payroll_list::remove_employee_id(char *social_sec)
{
  NNR *current_node=location;
  NNR *previous_node=0;

  while(current_node != 0 &&
      strcmp(current_node->social_sec,social_sec) != 0) {
    previous_node=current_node;
    current_node=current_node->next_link;
  }

  if(current_node != 0 && previous_node == 0) {
    location=current_node->next_link;
    // delete current_node; needed if new( ) used in add_info( )
  }
  else if(current_node != 0 && previous_node != 0) {
    previous_node->next_link=current_node->next_link;
    // delete current_node; needed if new( ) used in add_info( )
  }
```

```
}

main( )
{
  payroll_list workers;

  // static data to add to linked list
  salespersons salesperson1("Harddrive","Harriet","313-56-7884",
                          "Salesperson",1985,6.5,7.5);
  salespersons salesperson2("Flex","Frank","663-65-2312",
                          "Salesperson",1985,3.0,3.2);
  salespersons salesperson3("Ripoff","Randle","512-34-7612",
                          "Salesperson",1987,9.6,6.8);
  technicians techperson1("Align","Alice","174-43-6781",
                          "Technician",1989,12.55);
  technicians techperson2("Tightscrew","Tom","682-67-5312",
                          "Technician",1992,10.34);
  administration vice_president1("Stuckup","Stewart",
                          "238-18-1119","Vice President",
                          1980,40000.00);
  administration vice_president2("Learnedmore","Lawrence",
                          "987-99-9653","Vice President",
                          1984,45000.00);
  supplies supplyperson1("Allpart","Albert","443-89-3772",
                          "Supplies",1983,8.55);
  supplies supplyperson2("Ordermore","Ozel","111-44-5399",
                          "Supplies",1988,7.58);

  // add the nine workers to the linked list
  workers.insert_employee(&techperson1);
  workers.insert_employee(&vice_president1);
  workers.insert_employee(&salesperson1);
  workers.insert_employee(&supplyperson1);
  workers.insert_employee(&supplyperson2);
  workers.insert_employee(&salesperson2);
  workers.insert_employee(&techperson2);
  workers.insert_employee(&vice_president2);
  workers.insert_employee(&salesperson3);

  // print the linked list
  workers.print_payroll_list( );
```

```
// remove two workers from the linked list
workers.remove_employee_id("238-18-1119");
workers.remove_employee_id("512-34-7612");

cout << "\n\n**********************************";

// print the revised linked list
workers.print_payroll_list( );

return (0);
}
```

As you study the complete listing, see if you understand how employees are inserted and deleted from the list. If it is still a little confusing, go back and study each major section of code discussed in earlier sections.

Output from the Linked List

The linked-list program sends output to the monitor. The first section of the list contains the nine employee names that were used to create the original list. The last part of the list shows the list after two employees are deleted. Here is a sample output sent to the screen:

```
Align, Alice
  Social Security: #174-43-6781
  Job Title: Technician
  Year Hired: 1989
  Hourly Salary: $12.55

Allpart, Albert
  Social Security: #443-89-3772
  Job Title: Supplies
  Year Hired: 1983
  Hourly Salary: $8.55

Flex, Frank
  Social Security: #663-65-2312
  Job Title: Salesperson
  Year Hired: 1985
  Sales (disks): 3
  Commission Rate: 3
```

```
Harddrive, Harriet
 Social Security: #313-56-7884
 Job Title: Salesperson
 Year Hired: 1985
 Sales (disks): 6.5
 Commission Rate: 7

Learnedmore, Lawrence
 Social Security: #987-99-9653
 Job Title: Vice President
 Year Hired: 1984
 Yearly Salary: $45000

Ordermore, Ozel
 Social Security: #111-44-5399
 Job Title: Supplies
 Year Hired: 1988
 Hourly Salary: $7.58

Ripoff, Randle
 Social Security: #512-34-7612
 Job Title: Salesperson
 Year Hired: 1987
 Sales (disks): 9.6
 Commission Rate: 6

Stuckup, Stewart
 Social Security: #238-18-1119
 Job Title: Vice President
 Year Hired: 1980
 Yearly Salary: $40000

Tightscrew, Tom
 Social Security: #682-67-5312
 Job Title: Technician
 Year Hired: 1992
 Hourly Salary: $10.34


*********************************
```

```
Align, Alice
 Social Security: #174-43-6781
 Job Title: Technician
 Year Hired: 1989
 Hourly Salary: $12.55

Allpart, Albert
 Social Security: #443-89-3772
 Job Title: Supplies
 Year Hired: 1983
 Hourly Salary: $8.55

Flex, Frank
 Social Security: #663-65-2312
 Job Title: Salesperson
 Year Hired: 1985
 Sales (disks): 3
 Commission Rate: 3

Harddrive, Harriet
 Social Security: #313-56-7884
 Job Title: Salesperson
 Year Hired: 1985
 Sales (disks): 6.5
 Commission Rate: 7

Learnedmore, Lawrence
 Social Security: #987-99-9653
 Job Title: Vice President
 Year Hired: 1984
 Yearly Salary: $45000

Ordermore, Ozel
 Social Security: #111-44-5399
 Job Title: Supplies
 Year Hired: 1988
 Hourly Salary: $7.58
```

```
Tightscrew, Tom
 Social Security: #682-67-5312
 Job Title: Technician
 Year Hired: 1992
 Hourly Salary: $10.34
```

More Object-Oriented Programming

We're sure your interest in object-oriented has increased after working through this chapter. You will really be interested in the Windows applications developed in Chapters 20 through 26. These particular Windows applications make use of Microsoft's Foundation Class (MFC) library. This library contains the reusable classes that make programming under Windows 95 and NT much easier. As you study these chapters, you will see the concepts you have mastered in this chapter applied to the Windows environment.

Part IV

Windows Programming Foundations

The Complete Reference

Visual C++ 5

Chapter 20

Concepts and Tools for

Windows 95 and NT

Microsoft's main development language for 32-bit Windows applications is C or C++. While assembly language plays a major role in speed-sensitive situations, the majority of code in Windows itself is written in C or C++. Microsoft has provided all of the necessary tools with this version of the compiler for developing 32-bit Windows programs from within the C/C++ environment. This chapter will deal with the features that relate to a procedure-oriented approach to Windows application development.

The Windows applications created in the remaining chapters of this book are all designed with the development tools provided with the Microsoft C++ compiler. When installing your Microsoft Visual C++ compiler, make sure that the setup program includes all of the available tools for Windows.

This chapter is divided into three major sections. The first deals with the language, definitions, and terms used with Windows 95 and NT. This section also includes a discussion of the graphics-based environment. The second section is devoted to a discussion of those Windows items most frequently used by application developers. Here, Windows components such as borders, icons, bitmaps, and so on are examined. The third section includes a description of Windows resources and many of the C/C++ tools provided for building them. Windows resources include icons, cursors, bitmaps, menus, hot keys, dialog boxes, and fonts.

 NOTE: Throughout this and the remaining chapters of this book the term "Windows" will refer to both the Windows 95 and NT environments. If specific versions are important, the terms "Windows 95" or "Windows NT" will be used.

Windows Concepts

Windows applications can be developed using a procedure-oriented approach in either C or C++. Additionally, it is possible to use an object-oriented approach when programming in C++. All approaches bring together point-and-shoot control, pop-up menus, and the ability to run applications written especially for Windows. The purpose of this portion of the chapter is to introduce you to Windows concepts and vocabulary. The graphics user interface is the interface of the future, and both Windows 95 and NT give you the ability to develop that code now!

The Windows Environment

Windows is a graphics-based multitasking operating system. Programs developed for this environment (those written specifically for Windows) all have a consistent look and command structure. To the user, this makes learning each successive Windows application easier.

To help in the development of Windows applications, Windows provides numerous built-in functions that allow for the easy implementation of pop-up menus, scroll bars, dialog boxes, icons, and many other features that represent a user-friendly interface. You can take advantage of the extensive graphics programming language provided with Windows, and easily format and output text in a variety of fonts and pitches.

Windows permits the application's treatment of the video display, keyboard, mouse, printer, serial port, and system timers in a hardware-independent manner. Device or hardware independence allows the same application to run identically on a variety of computers with differing hardware configurations.

 NOTE: Those interested in the Java programming language should pay particular attention to this chapter. Many of the terms and concepts once relegated to C and C++ Windows development have found their way into many Java applications and applets.

The Advantages of Windows

There are numerous advantages to Windows users and programmers alike over the older DOS text-based environment. Windows provides several major programming capabilities that include a standardized graphics interface, a multitasking capability, an OOP approach in programming, memory control, hardware independence, and the use of dynamic link libraries (DLLs).

The Graphics User Interface

The most noticeable Windows feature is the standardized graphics user interface, which is also the most important one for the user. Windows 95 and NT are based on the same standardized interface. The consistent interface uses pictures, or icons, to represent disk drives, files, subdirectories, and many of the operating system commands and actions. Figure 20-1 shows a typical Windows application.

Under Windows, program names appear in caption bars. Many of the basic file manipulation functions are accessed through the program's menus by pointing and clicking with the mouse. Most Windows programs provide both a keyboard and a mouse interface. Although you can access most Windows functions with just the keyboard, the mouse is the preferred tool of most users.

A similar look and feel is common to all Windows applications. Once a user learns how to manipulate common Windows commands, each new application becomes easier to master. For example, a Microsoft Excel screen is shown in Figure 20-2 and a Microsoft Word screen is shown in Figure 20-3.

These screens illustrate the similarity between applications including common File and Edit options. Compare the options in both of these applications with the Paint application illustrated in Figure 20-1.

The consistent user interface provides advantages for the programmer, too. For example, you can tap into built-in Windows functions for constructing menus and dialog boxes. All menus have the same style keyboard and mouse interface because Windows, rather than the programmer, handles its implementation.

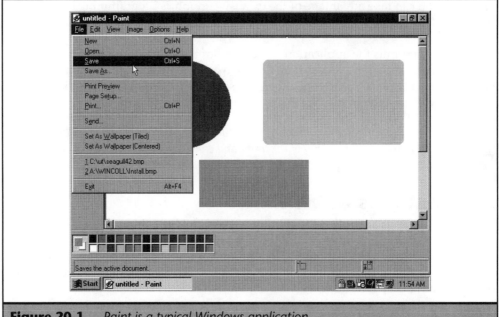

Figure 20-1. Paint is a typical Windows application

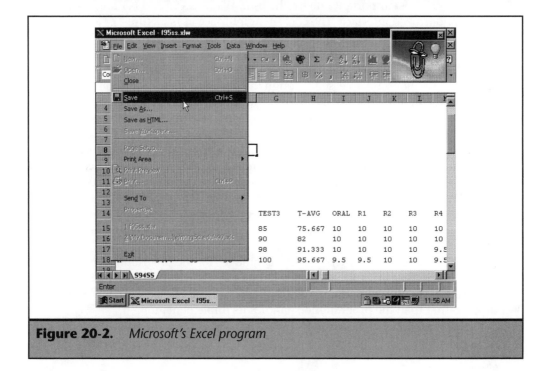

Figure 20-2. Microsoft's Excel program

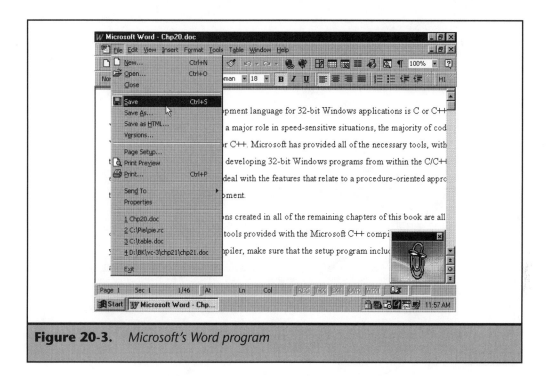

Figure 20-3. *Microsoft's Word program*

The Multitasking Environment

The Windows multitasking environment allows the user to have several applications, or several instances of the same application, running at the same time. The screen in Figure 20-4 shows two Windows applications running at the same time. Each application occupies a rectangular window on the screen. At any given time, the user can move the windows on the screen, switch between different applications, change the windows' sizes, and exchange information from window to window.

The example shown in Figure 4 is a group of two concurrently running processes—well, not really. In reality, only one application can be using the processor at any one time. The distinction between a task that is processing and one that is merely running is important. There is also a third state to consider. An application may be in the active state. An *active* application is one that is receiving the user's attention. Just as there can be only one application that is processing at any given instant, so too there can be only one active application at a time. However, there can be any number of concurrently running tasks. Partitioning of the microprocessor's processing time, called *time slicing*, is the responsibility of Windows. It is Windows that controls the sharing of the microprocessor by using a variety of techniques including queued input or messages.

Before multitasking was achieved under Windows 3.*x*, applications assumed they had exclusive control of all the computer's resources, including the input and output

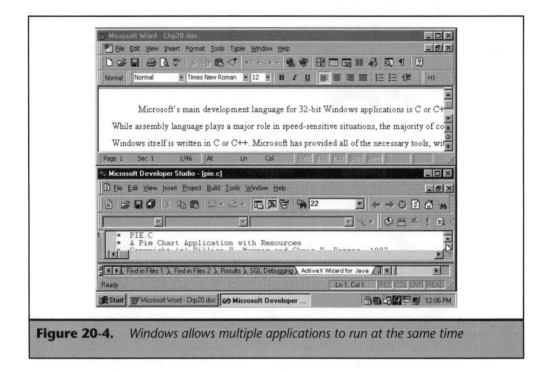

Figure 20-4. *Windows allows multiple applications to run at the same time*

devices, memory, the video display, and even the CPU itself. Under Windows, all of these resources must be shared. Thus, for example, memory management is controlled by Windows instead of by the application.

Advantages of Using a Queued Input

As you just learned, memory is a shared resource under Windows. However, so are most input devices such as the keyboard and mouse. Thus, when you develop a Windows program in C or C++, it is no longer possible to read directly from the keyboard with a getchar( ) function call or by using the C++ I/O stream. With Windows, an application does not make explicit calls to read from the keyboard or mouse. Rather, Windows receives all input from the keyboard, mouse, and timer in the system queue. It is the queue's responsibility to redirect the input to the appropriate program, since more than one application can be running. This redirection is achieved by copying the message from the system queue into the application's queue. At this point, when the application is ready to process the input, it reads from its queue and dispatches a message to the correct window.

Input is accessed with the use of a uniform format called an *input message*. All input messages specify the system time, state of the keyboard, scan code of any

depressed key, position of the mouse, and which mouse button has been pressed
(if any), as well as information specifying which device generated the message.

Keyboard, mouse, and timer messages all have identical formats and are processed
in a similar manner. Further, with each message, Windows provides a device-
independent virtual keycode that identifies the key, regardless of which keyboard it is
on; the device-dependent scan code generated by the keyboard; and the status of other
keys on the keyboard, including NUM LOCK, ALT, SHIFT, and CTRL.

The keyboard and mouse are a shared resource. One keyboard and one mouse
must supply all the input information for each program running under Windows.
Windows sends all keyboard input messages directly to the currently active window.
Mouse messages, on the other hand, are handled differently. They are sent to the
window that is physically underneath the mouse cursor.

Another shared resource is *timer messages,* which are similar to keyboard and
mouse messages. Windows allows a program to set a system timer so that one of its
windows receives a message at periodic intervals. This timer message goes directly
into the application's message queue. It is also possible for other messages to be
passed into an application's message queue as a result of the program's calling certain
Windows functions.

Windows Messages and OOPs

Windows has always employed a pseudo-OOPs (object-oriented programming)
environment. The message system under Windows is the underlying structure used to
disseminate information in the multitasking environment. From the application's
perspective, a message is a notification that some event of interest has occurred that
may or may not need a specific action. The user may initiate these events by clicking
or moving the mouse, changing the size of a window, or making a menu selection. The
events can also be initiated by the application itself. For example, a graphics-based
spreadsheet could finish a recalculation that results in the need to update a graphics
pie chart. In this situation, the application would send an "update window" message
to itself.

Windows itself can also generate messages, as in the case of the "close session"
message, in which Windows informs each application of the intent to shut down.

When thinking about the role of messages in Windows, consider the following
points. It is the message system that allows Windows to achieve its multitasking
capabilities. The message system makes it possible for Windows to share the processor
among different applications. Each time Windows sends a message to the application
program, it also grants processor time to the application. In reality, the only way an
application can get access to the microprocessor is when it receives a message. Second,
messages enable an application to respond to events in the environment. These events
can be generated by the application itself, by other concurrently running applications,
by the user, or by Windows. Each time an event occurs, Windows makes a note and
distributes an appropriate message to the interested applications.

Memory Management

One of the most important shared resources under Windows is system memory—at least when multitasking applications are involved. When more than one application is running at the same time, each application must cooperate to share memory in order not to exhaust the total resources of the system. Also, as new programs are started and old ones are terminated, memory can become fragmented. Windows is capable of consolidating free memory space by moving blocks of code and data in memory.

It is also possible to over-commit memory under Windows. For example, an application can contain more code than can actually fit into memory at one time. Windows can discard currently unused code from memory and later reload the code from the program's executable file.

Windows applications can share routines located in other executable files. The files that contain shareable routines are called *dynamic link libraries* (*DLLs*). Windows includes the mechanism to link the program with the DLL routines at run-time. Windows itself is comprised of a large set of DLLs. To facilitate all of this, Windows programs use a new format of executable file, called the New Executable format. These files include the information Windows needs to manage the code and data segments and to perform the dynamic linking.

Hardware Independence

Windows also provides hardware or device independence by freeing you from having to build programs that take into consideration every possible monitor, printer, and input device available for computers. For example, DOS applications had to be written to include drivers for every possible device. In order to make a DOS application capable of printing on any printer, the application designer had to furnish a different driver for each printer. This required many software companies to write essentially the same device driver over and over again—a LaserJet driver for Microsoft Word for DOS, one for Microsoft Works, and so on.

Under Windows, a device driver for each hardware device is written once. This device driver can be supplied by Microsoft, the application vendor, or the user. As you know, Microsoft includes a large variety of drivers with Windows.

It is hardware independence that makes programming a snap for the application developer. The application interacts with Windows rather than with any specific device. It doesn't need to know what printer is hooked up. The application instructs Windows to draw a filled rectangle, and Windows worries about how to accomplish it on the installed hardware. Likewise, each device driver works with every Windows application. Developers save time, and users do not have to worry about whether each new Windows application will support their hardware configuration.

You achieve hardware independence by specifying the minimum capabilities the hardware must have. These capabilities are the minimum specifications required to ensure that the appropriate routines will function correctly. Every routine, regardless of its complexity, is capable of breaking itself down into the minimal set of operations required for a given device. This is a very impressive feature. For example, not every plotter is capable of drawing a circle by itself. As an application developer, however, you can still use the routines for drawing a circle, even if the plotter has no specific circle capabilities. Since every plotter connected to Windows must be able to draw a line, Windows can break down the circle routine into a series of small lines.

Windows can specify a set of minimum capabilities to ensure that your application will receive only valid, predefined input. Windows has predefined the set of legal keystrokes allowed by applications. The valid keystrokes are very similar to those produced by the IBM-compatible keyboard. Should a manufacturer produce a keyboard that contains additional keys that do not exist in the Windows list of acceptable keys, the manufacturer would also have to supply additional software that would translate these illegal keystrokes into Windows' legal keystrokes. This predefined Windows-legal input covers all the input devices, including the mouse. Therefore, even if someone should develop a four-button mouse, you don't have to worry. The manufacturer would supply the software necessary to convert all mouse input to the Windows predefined possibilities of mouse-button clicks.

Dynamic Link Libraries

Dynamic link libraries provide much of Windows' functionality; they enhance the base operating system by providing a powerful and flexible graphics user interface. Dynamic link libraries contain predefined functions that are linked with an application program when it is loaded (dynamically), instead of when the executable file is generated (statically). Dynamic link libraries use the .DLL file extension.

Storing frequently used routines in libraries was not an invention of the Windows product. For example, the C/C++ language depends heavily on libraries to implement standard functions for different systems. The linker makes copies of run-time library functions, such as getchar( ) and printf( ), into a program's executable file. Libraries of functions save each programmer from having to re-create a new procedure for a common operation such as reading in a character or formatting output. Programmers can easily build their own libraries to include additional capabilities, such as changing a character font or justifying text. Making the function available as a general tool eliminates redundant design—a key feature in OOP.

Windows libraries are dynamically linked. In other words, the linker does not copy the library functions into the program's executable file. Instead, while the program is executing, it makes calls to the function in the library. Naturally, this conserves memory. No matter how many applications are running, there is only one copy of the library in RAM at a given time, and this library can be shared.

When a call is made to a Windows function, the C/C++ compiler must generate machine code for a far inter-segment call to the function located in a code segment in one of the Windows libraries. This presents a problem since, until the program is actually running inside Windows, the address of the Windows function is unknown. Doesn't this sound suspiciously similar to the concept of late binding, discussed in the OOP section of this book? The solution to this problem in Windows is called *delayed binding* or *dynamic linking*. Starting with Windows 3.0 and Microsoft C 6.0, the linker allows a program to have calls to functions that cannot be fully resolved at link time.

Only when the program is loaded into memory to be run are the far function calls resolved.

Special Windows import libraries are included with the C/C++ compiler; they are used to properly prepare a Windows program for dynamic linking. For example, the import library user32.dll is the import library that contains a record for each Windows function that your program can call. This record defines the Windows module that contains this function and, in many cases, an ordinal value that corresponds to the function in the module.

Windows applications typically make a call to the Windows PostMessage( ) function. When your application is linked at compile time, the linker finds the PostMessage( ) function listed in user32.lib. The linker obtains the ordinal number for the function and embeds this information in the application's executable file. When the application is run, Windows connects the call your application makes with the actual PostMessage( ) function.

The Windows Executable Format

An executable file format was developed for Windows and called the *New Executable format*. It includes a new-style header capable of holding information about DLL functions.

For example, DLL functions are included for the KERNEL, USER, and GDI modules. These libraries contain routines that help programs carry out various chores, such as sending and receiving messages. The library modules provide functions that can be called from the application program or from other library modules. To the module that contains the functions, the functions are known as *exports*. The New Executable format identifies these exported functions with a name and an ordinal number. Included in the New Executable format is an Entry Table section that indicates the address of each of these exported functions within the module.

From the perspective of the application program, the library functions that an application uses are known as *imports*. These imports use the various relocation tables and can identify the far calls that the application makes to an imported function. Almost all Windows programs contain at least one exported function. This window function is usually located in one of the library modules and is the one that receives window messages. It is important that the application indicate that this function is exported so Windows can properly allow the function to be called from an external module.

This new format also provides the additional information on each of the code and data segments in a program or library. Typically, code segments are flagged as moveable and discardable, while data segments are flagged as moveable. This allows Windows to move code and data segments in memory and even discard code segments if additional memory is needed. If Windows later decides it needs a discarded code segment, it can reload the code segment from the original executable file. Windows has another category called *load on call*. This defines a program or library code segment that will not be loaded into memory at all unless a function in the code segment is called from another code segment. Through this sophisticated memory-management scheme, Windows can simultaneously run several programs in a memory space that would normally be sufficient for only one program.

Originally, Windows depended on a module-definition file to specify the linker options just discussed. However, the linker that comes with Visual C++ now provides equivalent command-line options for most module-definition statements. Thus, a program designed for Windows 95 or NT does not usually require a module definition file to access these capabilities.

Windows Programming Concepts and Vocabulary

Windows programming is unique to most programmers. This is because Windows includes new programming concepts and its own vocabulary. These can be broken down into two major categories: the features of Windows that are visible to the user, such as menus, dialog boxes, icons, and so on; and the invisible features such as messages, function access, and so on. There is a standard vocabulary associated with Windows programming development designed to give application developers the ability to communicate effectively with one another. Thus, all Windows features have been given a name and an associated usage. In this section you will learn a variety of Windows terms that will give you the ability to confidently discuss and develop Windows applications.

The Windows Window

A Windows window appears to the user as a rectangular portion of the display device; its appearance is independent of the particular application at hand. To an application, however, the window is a rectangular area of the screen that is under the direct control of the application. The application has the ability to create and control everything about the main window, including its size and shape. When the user starts a program, a window is created. Each time the user clicks a window option, the application responds. Closing a window causes the application to terminate. Multiple windows convey to the user the multitasking capabilities of Windows. By partitioning the screen into different windows, the user can direct input to a specific application within the multitasking environment by using the keyboard or a mouse to select one of the concurrently running applications. Windows then intercepts the user's input and allocates any necessary resources (such as the microprocessor) as needed.

The Windows Layout

Features such as borders, control boxes, About boxes, and so on, are common to all Windows applications. It is this common interface that gives Windows a comforting predictability from one application to another. Figure 20-5 illustrates the fundamental components of a Windows 95 window.

The Border

A Windows window has a border surrounding it. The border is made up of lines that frame a window. To the novice, the border may appear only to delineate one application's screen viewport from another. Upon closer examination, however, a different conclusion will be drawn. For example, by positioning the mouse pointer over a border and holding down the left mouse button, the user can change the size of the active window.

The Title Bar

The name of the application program is displayed at the top of the window in the title bar. Title bars are located and centered at the top of each associated window. Title bars can be very useful in helping you remember which applications are currently running. The active application uses a different color in the title bar area than a nonactive application.

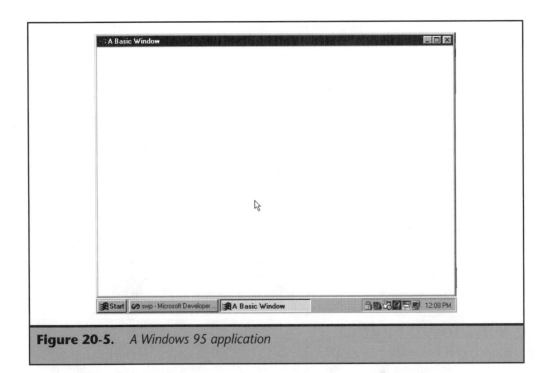

Figure 20-5.   *A Windows 95 application*

The Control Icon

A *control icon,* a small image in each window's upper-left corner, is used by each Windows application. Clicking the mouse pointer on the control icon (referred to as clicking the control icon) causes Windows to display the system menu.

The System Menu

The *system menu* is opened by clicking the mouse pointer on the control icon. It provides standard application options such as Restore, Move, Size, Minimize, Maximize, and Close.

The Minimize Icon

Each Windows 95 or NT application displays three iconic images in the upper-right corner of the window. The leftmost icon, a dash or underline symbol, is the *minimize icon.* It allows the application to be minimized.

The Maximize Icon

The *maximize icon* is in the middle of the three iconic images and appears as two very small windows. Use the maximize icon to make an application's window fill the entire screen. If this icon is selected, all other application windows will be covered.

The Vertical Scroll Bar

An application can show a *vertical scroll bar* if desired. The vertical scroll bar, located against the right-hand edge of the application's window, has opposite-pointing arrows at its extremes, a colored band, and a transparent window block. The latter is used to visually represent the orientation between the currently displayed contents and the overall document (the colored band). Use the vertical scroll bar to select which multiple pages of output you would like displayed. Clicking the mouse on either arrow typically shifts the display one line at a time. Clicking the mouse on the transparent window block, below the up arrow, and dragging it causes screen output to be quickly updated to any portion of the application's screen output. One of the best uses of the vertical scroll bar is for quickly moving through a multipage word processing document. Word processors such as Microsoft Word and WordPerfect take advantage of this feature.

The Horizontal Scroll Bar

It is also possible to display a *horizontal scroll bar.* The horizontal scroll bar, displayed at the bottom of each window, is similar in function to the vertical scroll bar. You use it to select which of multiple columns of information you would like displayed. Clicking the mouse on either arrow causes the screen image to be shifted one column at a time. Clicking the mouse on the transparent window block, to the right of the left-pointing arrow, and dragging it causes the screen output to be quickly updated to any horizontally shifted portion of the application's screen output. One of the best uses for the horizontal scroll bar is for quickly moving through the multiple columns of a spreadsheet application, where the number of columns of information cannot fit into one screen width. Microsoft Excel makes use of this feature.

The Menu Bar

An optional *menu bar* can also be displayed below the title bar. Use the menu bar for making menu and submenu selections. These selections are made by pointing and clicking the menu command or, alternately, by using a hot-key combination. Hot-key combinations often use the ALT key in conjunction with the underlined letter in a command, such as the "F" in the command File.

The Client Area

The *client area* usually occupies the largest portion of each window. This is the primary output area for the application. Managing the client area is the responsibility of the application program. Additionally, only the application can output to it.

The Windows Class

The basic components of a window help define the standard appearance of an application. There are also occasions when an application will create two windows with a similar appearance and behavior. Windows Paint is one such example. Paint allows the user to clip or copy a portion of a graphics image by running two instances (or copies) of Paint. Information is then copied from one instance to the other. Each instance of Paint looks and behaves like its counterpart. This requires each to create its own window with an identical appearance and functionality.

Windows created in this manner that look alike and behave in a similar fashion are said to be of the same window class. However, windows that you create can take on different characteristics. They may be different sizes, be placed in different areas of the display, have different display colors or different text in the caption bars, or use different mouse cursors.

Each window created must be based on a window class. With applications developed in C using traditional function calls, several window classes are registered by the Windows application during its initialization phase. Your application may register additional classes of its own. In order to allow several windows to be created and based on the same window class, Windows specifies some of a window's characteristics as parameters to the CreateWindow( ) function, while others are specified in a window class structure. Also, when you register a window class, the class becomes available to all programs running under Windows. For object-oriented applications using the Microsoft Foundation Classes, much of this registration work is already done through the use of predefined objects. In Chapter 21 you will learn how to write 32-bit Windows applications in C using traditional function calls. Chapters 22 and 23 are designed to teach you how to write similar object-oriented applications with the MFC library.

Windows of similar appearance and behavior can be grouped together into classes, thereby reducing the amount of information that needs to be maintained. Since each window class has its own shareable window class structure, there is no needless replication of the window class' parameters. Also, two windows of the same class use the same function and any of its associated subroutines. This feature saves time and storage because there is no code duplication.

OOPs and Windows

Traditional C programs take on the characteristics of object-oriented programs under Windows. Recall that in object-oriented programming, an object is an abstract data type that consists of a data structure and various functions that act on the data structure. Likewise, objects receive messages that can cause them to function differently.

A Windows graphics object, for example, is a collection of data that can be manipulated as a whole entity and that is presented to the user as part of the visual interface. In particular, a graphics object implies both the data and the presentation of data. Menus, title bars, control boxes, and scroll bars are examples of graphics objects. The next sections describe several new graphics objects that affect the user's view of an application.

Icons

An *icon* is a small graphics object used to remind the user of a particular operation, idea, or product. For example, a spreadsheet application when minimized could display a very small histogram icon to remind the user that the application is running. Double-clicking the mouse on the histogram would then cause Windows to bring the application to active status. Icons can be very powerful tools. They are good for gaining the user's attention, as in the case of an error warning, and also when presenting choices to the user. Windows provides several stock icons including a question mark, an exclamation point, an asterisk, an upturned palm icon, and so on. It is also possible to design your own device-independent color icons with the Microsoft C++ compiler's resource editor.

Cursors

Cursors are also Windows graphics symbols that are used to follow the movement of the pointing device. The graphics symbol is capable of changing shapes to indicate particular Windows actions. For example, the standard Windows arrow cursor changes to the small hourglass cursor to indicate a pause while a selected command is being executed. Windows provides several stock cursors: a diagonal arrow, a vertical arrow, an hourglass, a crosshair, an I-beam, and several others. You can also use the Microsoft C++ compiler's resource editor to create your own cursors.

Carets

Carets are symbols an application places in a window to show the user where input will be received. Carets are distinguished from other screen markers because they blink. Most of the time, mouse input is associated with a cursor and keyboard input with a caret. However, the mouse can move or change the input emphasis of a caret. To help clarify the difference between a cursor and a caret, Windows carets behave like the old DOS cursor. One of the carets provided for you automatically when entering a dialog box is the I-beam caret. Unlike in the cases of icons and cursors, an application must create its own carets using special functions. There are no stock carets.

Message Boxes

The *message box* is another common Windows graphics object. Message boxes are pop-up windows that contain a title, an icon, and a message. Figure 20-6 is the standard message box presented when terminating a Windows notepad session.

The application needs to supply the message title, the message itself, and instructions on which stock icon to use (if any). It must also indicate if a stock response is allowed (such as OK). Additional stock user responses include Yes/No, Yes/No/Cancel, OK/Cancel, and Retry/Cancel. Stock icons include IconHand, IconQuestion, IconExclamation, IconAsterisk, and so on.

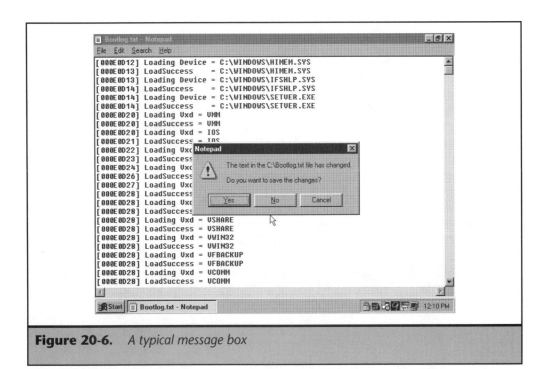

Figure 20-6.   *A typical message box*

Windows Dialog Boxes

A *dialog box* is similar to a message box in that it too is a pop-up window. Dialog boxes, however, are primarily used to receive input from the user rather than to just present output. A dialog box allows an application to receive information, one field at a time or one box's worth of information at a time, rather than a character at a time. Figure 20-7 shows a typical Windows dialog box. The graphic design of a dialog box is done automatically for you by Windows. The layout of a dialog box is normally done with the compiler's resource editor.

Fonts

A *font* is a graphics object or resource that defines a complete set of characters from one typeface. These characters are all of a certain size and style that can be manipulated to give text a variety of appearances. A *typeface* is a basic character design, defined by certain serifs and stroke widths. For instance, your application can use any of the different fonts provided with Windows including System, Courier, and Times Roman, or custom fonts that you define and include in the application program's executable file. By using built-in routines, Windows allows for the dynamic modification of a font, including boldface, italics, underline, and changes in size. Windows provides all of the necessary functions for displaying text anywhere within the client area. Additionally, because of Windows device independence, an

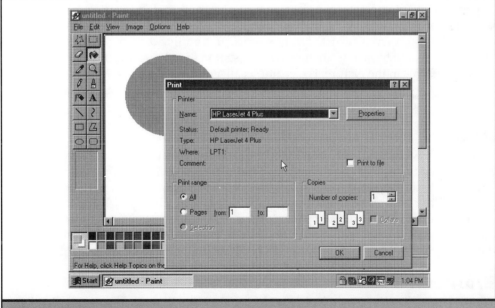

Figure 20-7.   *A typical dialog box for Windows*

application's output will have a consistent appearance from one output device to the next. TrueType font technology, first introduced with Windows 3.1, provides improved fonts for the screen and printer under both Windows 95 and NT.

Bitmaps

Bitmaps serve as a photographic image of the display (in pixels) and are stored in memory. Bitmaps are used whenever an application must display a graphics image quickly. Since bitmapped images are transferred directly from memory, they can be displayed more quickly than by executing the code necessary to re-create the image. There are two basic uses for bitmaps. First, they are used to draw pictures on the display. For example, Windows uses many small bitmaps for drawing arrows in scroll bars; displaying the check marks when selecting pop-up menu options; and drawing the system menu box, the size box, and many others. Bitmaps are also used for creating brushes. Brushes allow you to paint and fill objects on the screen.

There are two disadvantages to using bitmaps. First, depending on their size, they can occupy an unpredictably large portion of memory. For each pixel that is being displayed, there needs to be an equivalent representation in memory. Displaying the same bitmap on a color monitor versus a monochrome monitor would also require more memory. On a monochrome monitor, one bit can be used to define a pixel's being on or off. However, on a color monitor that can display 16 colors, each pixel would require 4 bits, or a nibble, to represent its characteristics. Also, as the resolution of the display device increases, so too does the memory requirement for the bitmap. Another disadvantage of bitmaps is that they contain only a static picture. For example, if an automobile is represented by a bitmap, there is no way to access the picture's various components, such as tires, hood, window, and so on. However, if the automobile had been constructed from a series of primitive drawing routines, an application would be able to change the data sent to these routines and modify individual items in the picture. For example, an application could modify the roof line and convert a sedan to a convertible. You can create or modify bitmaps with the compiler's resource editor.

Pens

When Windows draws a shape on the screen, it uses information on the current pen. *Pens* are used to draw lines and outline shapes. They have three basic characteristics: line width, style (dotted, dashed, solid), and color. Windows always has a pen for drawing black lines and one for drawing white lines available to each application. It is also possible to create your own pens. For example, you might want to create a thick, light gray line to outline a portion of the screen or a dot-dash-dot line for spreadsheet data analysis.

Brushes

Windows uses *brushes* to paint colors and fill areas with predefined patterns. Brushes have a minimum size of 8 x 8 pixels and, like pens, have three basic characteristics:

size, pattern, and color. With their 8 x 8-pixel minimum, brushes are said to have a pattern, not a style as pens do. The pattern may be a solid color, hatched, diagonal, or any other user-definable combination.

Windows Messages

With Windows, an application does not write directly to the screen, process any hardware interrupts, or output directly to the printer. Instead, the application uses the appropriate Windows functions, or waits for an appropriate message to be delivered. Applications development under Windows must now incorporate the processing of the application and the user's view of the application through Windows.

The Windows message system is the underlying structure used to disseminate information in a multitasking environment. From the application's viewpoint, a message is seen as a notification that some event of interest has occurred that may or may not need a specific response. These events may have been initiated on the part of the user, such as clicking or moving the mouse, changing the size of a window, or making a menu selection. However, the signaled event could also have been generated by the application itself.

The overall effect of this process is that your application must now be totally oriented toward the processing of messages. It must be capable of awakening, determining the appropriate action based on the type of message received, taking that action to completion, and returning to sleep.

Windows applications are significantly different from their older DOS counterparts. Windows provides an application program with access to hundreds of function calls directly or indirectly through foundation classes. These function calls are handled by several main modules including the KERNEL, GDI (graphics device interface), and USER modules. The KERNEL is responsible for memory management, loading and running an application, and scheduling. The GDI contains all of the routines to create and display graphics. The USER takes care of all other application requirements.

The next section takes a closer look at the message system by examining the format and sources of messages and looking at several common message types and the ways in which both Windows and your application process messages.

Message Format

Messages notify a program that an event of interest has occurred. Technically, a message is not just of interest to the application, but also to a specific window within that application. Therefore, every message is addressed to a window.

Only one message system exists under Windows—the system message queue. However, each program currently running under Windows also has its own program message queue. Each message in the system message queue must eventually be transferred by the USER module to a program's message queue. The program's message queue stores all messages for all windows in that program.

Four parameters are associated with all messages, regardless of their type: a window handle, a message type, two additional 32-bit parameters. The first parameter specified in a window message is the handle of the window to which the message is addressed.

NOTE: These are the parameters for 32-bit Windows 95 and NT applications. The parameters used for earlier 16-bit Windows 3.x applications differed.

Table 20-1 shows a list of data types frequently used with Win32 functions.

Handles are always used when writing Windows applications. Remember that a *handle* is a unique number that identifies many different types of objects, such as windows, controls, menus, icons, pens and brushes, memory allocation, output devices, and even window instances. Under Windows 95 and NT, each loaded copy of a program is called an *instance.*

Because Windows 95 and NT allow you to run more than one copy of the same application at the same time, the operating system needs to keep track of each of these instances. It does this by attaching a unique instance handle to each running copy of the application.

The instance handle is normally used as an index into an internally maintained table. By referencing a table element, rather than an actual memory address, Windows 95 and NT can dynamically rearrange all resources simply by inserting a new address into the resource's table position. For example, if Windows 95 and NT associate a

Data Type	Description
HANDLE	Defines a 32-bit unsigned integer that is used as a handle
HWND	Defines a 32-bit unsigned integer that is used as the handle to a window
HDC	Defines a handle to a device context
LONG	Specifies a 32-bit signed integer
LPSTR	Defines a 32-bit pointer
NULL	Specifies an integral zero value often used to trigger function default parameters or actions
UINT	Specifies a 32-bit unsigned integer
WCHAR	Specifies a 16-bit UNICODE character used to represent all of the symbols known for all of the world's written languages

Table 20-1. *Common Win32 Data Types*

particular application's resource with table lookup position 14, then no matter where Windows 95 or NT moves the resource in memory, table position 14 will contain the resource's current location.

Memory resources are conserved by Windows 95 and NT because of the way multiple instances of the same application are handled. Several multitasking environments load each duplicate instance of an application just as if each was an entirely new application.

The instance of an application has a very important role. It is the instance of an application that defines all of the objects necessary for the functioning of the application. This can include controls, menus, dialog boxes, and much more, along with new window classes.

The second parameter in a message is the *message type*. This is one of the identifiers specified in several header files unique to Windows. These header files can be pointed to with the use of WINDOWS.H. With Windows, each message type begins with a two-character mnemonic, followed by the underscore character and finally a descriptor. The most frequently encountered type of message in traditional C Windows applications is the window message. Windows messages include WM_CREATE, WM_PAINT, WM_CLOSE, WM_COPY, WM_PASTE, etc. Other message types include control window messages (BM_), edit control messages (EM_), and list box messages (LB_). An application can also create and register its own message type. This permits the use of private message types.

The last two parameters provide additional information necessary to interpret the message. The contents of these last two parameters will therefore vary depending on the message type. Examples of the types of information that would be passed include which key was just struck, the position of the mouse, the position of the vertical or horizontal scroll bar elevators, and the selected pop-up menu item.

Generating Messages

It is the message-passing concept that allows Windows to be multitasking. Thus, all messages must be processed by Windows. There are four basic sources for a message. An application can receive a message from the user, from Windows itself, from the application program itself, or from other applications.

User messages include keystroke information, mouse movements, point-and-click coordinates, any menu selections, the location of scroll bar elevators, and so on. The application program will devote a great deal of time to processing user messages. User-originated messages indicate that the person running the program wants to change the way the application is viewed.

A message is sent to an application whenever a state change is to take effect. An example of this would be when the user clicks an application's icon indicating that they want to make that application the active application. In this case, Windows tells the application that its main window is being opened, that its size and location are being modified, and so on. Depending on the current state of an application, Windows-originated messages can be processed or ignored.

In Chapter 21, you will learn how to write simple Windows applications in C. When you do this, you will see that the program is broken down into specific procedures, with each procedure processing a particular message type for a particular window. One procedure, for example, will deal with resizing the application's window. It is quite possible that the application may want to resize itself. In other words, the source of the message is the application itself.

Currently, most applications written for Windows do not take full advantage of the fourth type of message source, inter-task communication. However, this category will become increasingly important as more and more applications take advantage of this Windows integration capability. Microsoft's dynamic data exchange (DDE) protocol was the first to take advantage of this feature.

Responding to Messages

Traditional C procedure-oriented Windows applications have a procedure for processing each type of message they may encounter. Different windows can respond differently to messages of the same type. For example, one application may have created two windows that respond to a mouse-button click in two different ways. The first window could respond by changing the background color, while the second may respond by placing a crosshatch on a spreadsheet. It is because the same message can be interpreted differently by different windows that Windows addresses each message to a specific window within an application. Not only will the application have a different procedure to handle each message type, it will also need a procedure to handle each message type for each window. The window procedure groups together all the message type procedures for an application.

The Message Loop

A basic component of all Windows applications is the message-processing loop. The location of the message loop in procedure-oriented applications is easy to identify. In object-oriented code, it is processed in the CWinAPP foundation class.

Each C application performs the operation internally. C applications contain procedures to create and initialize windows, followed by the message-processing loop and finally some code required to close the application. The message loop is responsible for processing a message delivered by Windows to the main body of the program. Here, the program acknowledges the message and then requests Windows to send it to the appropriate window procedure for processing. When the message is received, the window procedure executes the desired action.

Two factors that can influence the sequence in which a message is processed are the message queue and the dispatching priority. Messages can be sent from one of two queues—either the system queue or the application's message queue. Messages, regardless of the source, are first placed in the system queue. When a given message reaches the front of the queue, it is sent to the appropriate application's message queue. This dual-mode action allows Windows to keep track of all messages and permits each application to concern itself with only those messages that pertain to it.

Messages are placed in the queues as you would expect: FIFO (first-in-first-out) order. These are called *synchronous* messages. Most Windows applications use this type of dispatching method. However, there are occasions when Windows will push a message to the end of the queue, thereby preventing it from being dispatched. Messages of this type are called *asynchronous* messages. Care must be taken when sending an asynchronous message that overrides the application's normal sequence of processing.

Several types of asynchronous messages exist, including paint, timer, and quit messages. A *timer* message, for example, causes a certain action to take effect at a specified time, regardless of the messages to be processed at that moment. A timer message has priority and will cause all other messages in the queue to be pushed farther from the queue front.

A few asynchronous messages can be sent to other applications. This is unique because the receiving application doesn't put the message into its queue. Rather, the received message directly calls the application's appropriate window procedure, where it is immediately executed.

How does Windows dispatch messages that are pending for several applications at the same time? Windows handles this problem in one of two ways. One method of message processing is called *dispatching priority*. Whenever Windows loads an application, it sets the application's priority to zero. Once the application is running, however, the application can change its priority. With everything else being equal, Windows will settle any message-dispatching contention by sending messages to the highest priority application.

One example of a high-priority program would be a data communications application. Tampering with an application's priority level is very uncommon. Windows has another method for dispatching messages to concurrent applications of the same priority level. Whenever Windows sees that a particular application has a backlog of unprocessed messages, it hangs onto the new message while continuing to dispatch other new messages to the other applications.

Accessing Windows Functions

As you have learned, Windows provides the application developer with hundreds of functions. Examples of these functions include DispatchMessage( ), PostMessage( ), RegisterWindowMessage( ), and SetActiveWindow( ). For C++ programmers using Foundation Classes, many of these functions are dispatched automatically.

Calling Convention for Functions

Function declarations under 16-bit Windows 3.*x* included the pascal modifier, which was more efficient under DOS. Windows 95 and NT do not use this modifier for 32-bit applications. As you have learned, the parameters to all Windows functions are passed via the system stack. The parameters for the function are pushed from the rightmost parameter to the leftmost parameter, in a normal C fashion. Upon return from the function, the calling procedure must adjust the stack pointer to a value equal to the number of bytes originally pushed onto the stack.

The Windows Header File: WINDOWS.H

The WINDOWS.H header file provides a path to over a thousand constant declarations, typedef declarations, and hundreds of function prototypes. One of the main reasons a Windows application takes longer to compile than a typical C or C++ program is the size of this file. The WINDOWS.H header file (and associated header files) is an integral part of all programs. Traditionally, WINDOWS.H is a required include file in all C Windows applications. When using the Foundation Class library in C++, the WINDOWS.H is included via the AFXWIN.H header file.

Usually, the #define statements found in WINDOWS.H or its associated files map a numeric constant with a text identifier. For example:

```
#define WM_CREATE 0x0001
```

In this case, the Visual C++ compiler will use the hexadecimal constant 0x0001 as a replacement for WM_CREATE during preprocessing.

Other #define statements may appear a bit unusual. For example:

```
#define NEAR near
#define VOID void
```

In Visual C++, both near and void are reserved words. Your applications should use the uppercase NEAR and VOID for one very good reason: if you port your application to another compiler, it will be much easier to change the #define statements within the header file than to change all of the occurrences of a particular identifier in your application.

The Components of a Windows Application

There are several important steps that are common in developing all Windows applications:

- Create the WinMain( ) and associated Windows functions in C or utilize foundation classes, such as CWinAPP, in C++.
- Create the menu, dialog box, and any additional resource descriptions and put them into a resource script file.
- (Optional) Use the appropriate resource editor in the Visual C++ compiler to create unique cursors, icons, and bitmaps.

■ (Optional) Use the appropriate resource editor in the Visual C++ compiler to create dialog boxes.

■ Compile and link all C/C++ language sources and resource files using a project file.

The actual creation of a Windows application requires the use of several new development tools. Before developing applications in C or C++, an understanding of these tools is needed. The next section briefly discusses the tools supplied with the Visual C++ compiler as they relate to creating a Windows application.

Visual C++ Windows Tools

The Visual C++ compiler contains several resource editors. The individual editors are available by selecting Insert | Resource from the compiler's main menu. These editors allow for the quick definition of icons, cursors, and bitmaps. They also provide a convenient method for creating your own unique fonts and make it easy to create dialog box descriptions for data entry.

Resources have the capability of turning ordinary Windows applications into truly exciting graphical presentations. When you develop icons, cursors, menus, bitmaps, and more for your application, the graphical flare makes your programs presentation quality in appearance. Resource files also let you add user-interactive components to your program such as menus, keyboard accelerators, and dialog boxes.

Graphics objects such as icons, cursors, carets, message boxes, dialog boxes, fonts, bitmaps, pens, and brushes are all examples of resources. A resource represents data that is included in an application's executable file. Technically speaking, however, it does not reside in a program's normal data segment. When Windows loads a program into memory for execution, it usually leaves all of the resources on the disk. Consider, as an example, when the user first requests to see an application's About box. Before Windows can display the About box, it must first access the disk to copy this information from the program's executable file into memory.

The resource compiler, RC.EXE, is a compiler for Windows resources. Many times a Windows application will use its own resources, such as dialog boxes, menus, and icons. Each one of these resources must be predefined in a file called a *resource file* or *resource script file*. These files are created with the resource editors previously mentioned. Resource script files can be compiled into resource files by the resource compiler. This information is then added to the application's final executable file. This method allows Windows to load and use the resources from the executable file.

The use of resources and additional compilers adds an extra layer of complexity to application development, but one that is easily incorporated with the project utility.

Project Files

Project files provide an efficient means of overseeing the compilation of resources and program code as well as keeping the executable version of an application up-to-date. They accomplish their incremental operation by keeping track of the dates and times of their source files.

Project files include information about the compile and link process for the particular program. Programmers often have the choice of changing libraries, hardware platforms, software platforms, and so on. Project files are created within the integrated C/C++ editing environment. In many cases, the default project file setup can be used with just minor adjustments for program titles and a file list to include in the build operation.

Project files also support incremental compiles and links. For example, consider a Windows application that simulates the flight of an arrow. During the development process you decide to create your own unique cursor instead of pointing with the standard arrow provided by Windows. You create a cursor that looks like an apple with an arrow through it. When the application is recompiled incrementally, the program only really needs to accommodate the changes in the cursor resource file, APPLE.CUR. The project utility will ensure that only the information about the new cursor is updated during recompilation, speeding up the overall operation.

Resources

Customizing a Windows application with your own icons, pointers, and bitmaps is easy when you use the resource editors provided with the C++ compiler. These editors give you a complete environment in which to develop graphical resources. The editors will also help you create menus and dialog boxes—the basic means of data entry in Windows. In this section you learn how to use these editors to create icons, cursors, menus, and dialog boxes. The editors can also help you manipulate individual bitmaps, keyboard accelerators, and strings. The cursor, menu, and dialog box created separately in this chapter will be assembled into a presentation-quality graphics program in Chapter 21.

Resource Editors

Each editor is included within the Visual C++ environment and is an integral part of the compiler. As such, each editor is a completely integrated resource development environment designed to run under Windows. You can start each editor by first selecting Insert | Resource.

Icons, Cursors, and Bitmaps

This section describes the general operation of three editors. A specific editor is capable of producing icons, cursors, or bitmaps. Although each is a separate editor, they share many common features. As an example of the use of these image editors, a custom icon and cursor will be created for an application in the next chapter. Icons and cursors are in reality small bitmaps. The resource editors for designing icons and cursors allow you to create device-independent bitmap images. The icons and cursors created with these editors are functionally device independent with respect to resolution.

This image-file format allows for the tailoring of a bitmap that has a consistent look on each particular display resolution. For example, one icon might consist of four definitions (called DIBs): one designed for monochrome displays, one for CGAs, one for EGAs, and one for VGAs. Whenever the application displays the icon, it simply refers to it by name; Windows then automatically selects the icon image best suited to the current display. Figure 20-8 shows the editor window during the construction of a custom icon.

Initially, a color palette appears at the bottom of the editor for selecting the drawing color. Associated with this palette is a color box that shows the currently selected value. You can also create custom colors. A group of editing tools is visible at the extreme right of the window.

A large editing area is provided for drawing the icons, cursors, or bitmaps. The area is initially divided into smaller cells with a 32 x 32 grid. The editor also provides a small View window to allow you to observe the graphics in true size.

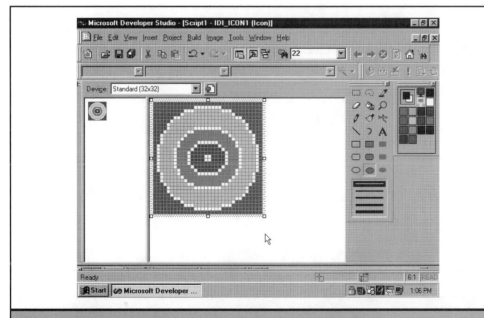

Figure 20-8. *A custom icon is created with the resource editor*

Designing a Custom Icon and Cursor

Creating your first icon or cursor is simple. First, click on the compiler's Insert menu and select Resource. Now select the proper resource type (Bitmap, Icon, Cursor) from the resources listed. This action clears the editing area of any previous design that is present and gives you a clean canvas.

After selecting the icon or cursor resource, you will need to pick a drawing tool from the toolbox or use the default drawing pen.

The editor can provide a broad spectrum of painting colors for icons and a selection of dithered colors for cursors. Click the color choice from the palette of colors shown. Now it is possible to draw the icon, cursor, or bitmap to your program's specification. You can also create custom colors. Be sure to save your final results by selecting the File menu and either the Save or Save As option.

Figure 20-9 shows the editor window with a completed cursor design. This cursor will be used in the graphics application created in Chapter 21. When looking at the completed icon or cursor designs, you will note that there are actually two renditions of the design. The larger one, within the editing area, allows your eyes to easily create an image. The smaller one, to the left, represents the actual size of the design as it will appear in the application's window.

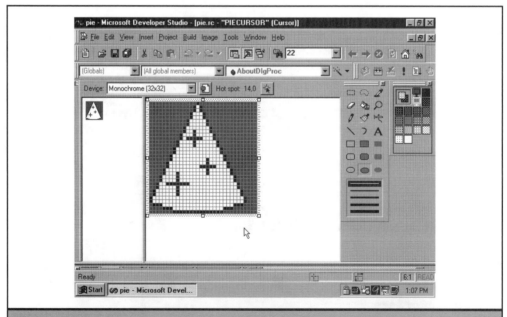

Figure 20-9.   *The resource editor during the creation of a unique cursor*

It takes a great deal of patience and practice to create a meaningful icon, cursor, or bitmap. This process often requires several trial-and-error attempts. Whenever you come up with a design that looks good, stop and save a copy of it. It is too easy to get your design to a point where you really like it, make one additional change, and ruin hours of work.

The first time you select the Save option from the File menu, the editor prompts you for a filename. If you are creating an icon, the file system will automatically append an .ICO file extension. The .CUR file extension is used for cursors. (Note that the file extension must be .ICO or .CUR, respectively.) If you are creating several possible designs, make certain you choose the Save As... option, not Save. Save overwrites your original file, but Save As... allows you to create multiple copies.

When you are creating cursors, you can select an optional hotspot. The hotspot button is located just above the drawing palette. The cursor hotspot is a point that will be used to return the current screen coordinates during the application's use. The hotspot on the pie wedge cursor is located at the tip of the pie wedge.

Once you have selected the HotSpot button, a very small set of crosshairs appears in the drawing box. Simply place the crosshairs on the pixel you want to select as the hotspot and click the mouse. The coordinates of the selected hotspot will be added to the display box's list of statistics. Only one hotspot per cursor is allowed.

Designing Menus

Menus are one of Windows' most important tools for creating interactive programs. Menus form the gateway for easy, consistent interfacing across applications. In their simplest form, menus allow the user to point-and-click selections that have been predefined. These selections include screen color choices, sizing options, and file operations. More advanced menu options allow the user to select dialog boxes from the menu list.

Dialog boxes permit data entry from the keyboard. They allow the user to enter string, integer, and even real number information for applications. However, before you can get to a dialog box, you typically must pass through a menu.

The menu created in this section is also used in the graphics application developed in the next chapter.

Menu Mechanics

The following sections describe what a menu is, what it looks like, how it is created, and the various menu options available to the programmer. Menus are very easy to create and implement in a program.

WHAT IS A MENU?   A *menu* is a list of items or names that represent options that an application can take. In some cases, the list of items in a menu can even be bitmap images. The user can select an option by using the mouse, the keyboard, or a hot key. Windows, in turn, responds by sending a message to the application stating which command was selected.

DESIGNING A MENU The resource editor lets you select a menu resource. The menu will then be designed in the resource editor. An alternative technique is to use the compiler's text editor to specify a menu resource.

The resource editor is capable of creating or reading menu descriptions contained in resource script files (.RC) or compiled resource files (.RES). Resource script files are simply uncompiled text files. If a header file is available describing constants used in a menu's description, these can be added at the start of the menu's description. For example, the constant IDM_ABOUT might be identified with 40 in a header file.

Figure 20-10 shows a menu (PieMenu) being developed in the resource editor.

Different styles and attributes for application menus can be included in this file. These styles and attributes include check marks to indicate the status of an item or define styles for an item's text (normal or grayed) and separator lines to divide menus (menu bar breaks), align menu items in column format, and assign a help attribute to a menu item.

MENUS AND THE RESOURCE COMPILER By following a set of simple rules, Windows will draw and manage menus for you. In so doing, Windows will produce consistent menus from one application to another. Menu resource information will be compiled by the resource compiler. The compiled file, a file with a .RES file extension, will be combined with your application at link time. At this time, the compiler and linker will create the final executable file (.EXE).

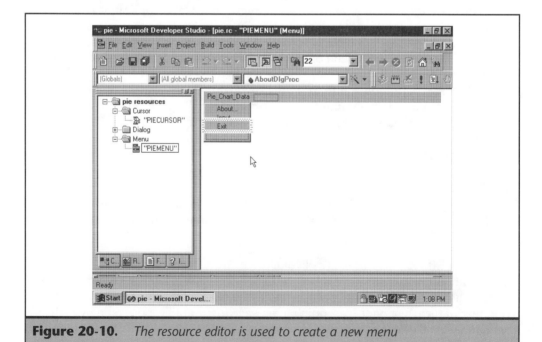

Figure 20-10. *The resource editor is used to create a new menu*

The structure of a simple menu is quite easy to understand. Here is a resource script file:

```
PIEMENU MENU DISCARDABLE
BEGIN
  POPUP "Pie_Chart_Data"
  BEGIN
    MENUITEM "About...",  IDM_ABOUT
    MENUITEM "Input...",  IDM_INPUT
    MENUITEM "Exit",      IDM_EXIT
  END
END
```

By studying this listing, you can identify a number of additional menu keywords such as MENU, POPUP, and MENUITEM. You can use brackets ({}) instead of the keywords BEGIN and END. It is also easy to identify the menu items that will appear in this menu: About Box..., Data Entry..., and Exit. The three dots following a menu selection indicate a dialog box to the user.

MENU KEYWORDS AND OPTIONS   The name of this program's menu definition is PIEMENU. The menu definition name is followed by the keyword MENU. This particular example describes the pop-up menu Pie_Chart_Data, which will appear on the menu bar. Pop-up menus are arranged from left to right on the menu bar. If a large number of pop-up items are used, an additional bar is provided automatically. Only one pop-up menu can be displayed at a time.

You can use an ampersand to produce an underscore under the character that follows the ampersand in the selection list. The ampersand allows the menu item to be selected from the keyboard. The simple menu in the example does not take advantage of this feature, but if the "A" in the About Box... choice had been preceded with an ampersand, that selection could have been made with a key combination of ALT-A. With the example menu, the item can be selected by positioning the mouse pointer on the item and clicking the left button. When a pop-up menu is selected, Windows pops the menu to the screen immediately under the selected item on the menu bar. Each MENUITEM describes one menu item or name, for example, "Data Entry...".

Identification numbers or constants from a header file appear to the right of the menu items. If numbers are present, they can be replaced with values identified in header files—for example, IDM_ABOUT 40, IDM_INPUT 50, and IDM_EXIT 70. IDM stands for the identification number of a menu item. This form of ID has become very popular but is not required. What is important, however, is that each menu item have a unique identification associated with it.

KEYBOARD ACCELERATORS   *Keyboard accelerators* are most often used by menu designers as a sort of "fast-key" combination for selecting menu items. For example, a menu may have 12 color items for selecting a background color. The user can point-and-click the menu for each color in the normal fashion, or with a keyboard accelerator simply hit a special key combination. If a keyboard accelerator is used, the function keys, for example, could be used for color selection without the menu popping up at all.

Dialog Box Data Entry

In the previous section, you learned that menus are considered as a means of simple data entry. This section investigates a more significant means of data entry—the dialog box. While data can be entered directly into the application's client area, dialog boxes are the preferred entry form for maintaining consistency across Windows programs.

Dialog boxes allow the user to check items in a window list, set buttons for various choices, directly enter strings and integers from the keyboard, and indirectly enter real numbers (floats). A special form of control can also be used in a dialog box. Combo boxes allow a combination of a single-line edit field and list boxes. The dialog box is the programmer's key to serious data entry in Windows programs. The dialog box is also the programmer's secret for ease of programming since Windows handles all necessary program overhead.

Dialog boxes can be called when selected as a choice from a menu and appear as a pop-up window to the user. To distinguish a dialog box choice from ordinary selections in a menu, three dots (an ellipsis) follow the dialog option name. In the previous section, the About Box... and Data Entry... menu items referred to dialog box selections. Figure 20-11 shows a completed dialog box taken from an example that is developed in the next chapter.

Here is the resource script file for this dialog box:

```
PIEDLGBOX DIALOG DISCARDABLE  93, 37, 195, 159
STYLE DS_MODALFRAME|WS_POPUP|WS_VISIBLE|WS_CAPTION|WS_SYSMENU
CAPTION "Pie Chart Data"
FONT 8, "MS Sans Serif"
BEGIN
  GROUPBOX "Chart Title:",100,5,3,182,30,WS_TABSTOP
  GROUPBOX "Pie Wedge Sizes:",101,3,34,187,95,
           WS_TABSTOP
  LTEXT "Title: ",-1,10,21,30,8
  EDITTEXT DM_TITLE,40,18,140,12
  LTEXT "Wedge #1: ",-1,10,50,40,8,NOT WS_GROUP
  LTEXT "Wedge #2: ",-1,10,65,40,8,NOT WS_GROUP
  LTEXT "Wedge #3: ",-1,10,80,40,8,NOT WS_GROUP
  LTEXT "Wedge #4: ",-1,10,95,40,8,NOT WS_GROUP
  LTEXT "Wedge #5: ",-1,10,110,40,8,NOT WS_GROUP
  LTEXT "Wedge #6: ",-1,106,50,40,8,NOT WS_GROUP
  LTEXT "Wedge #7: ",-1,106,65,40,8,NOT WS_GROUP
```

```
    LTEXT "Wedge #8: ",-1,106,80,40,8,NOT WS_GROUP
    LTEXT "Wedge #9: ",-1,106,95,40,8,NOT WS_GROUP
    LTEXT "Wedge #10:",-1,102,110,45,8,NOT WS_GROUP
    EDITTEXT DM_P1,55,45,30,12
    EDITTEXT DM_P2,55,60,30,12
    EDITTEXT DM_P3,55,75,30,12
    EDITTEXT DM_P4,55,90,30,12
    EDITTEXT DM_P5,55,105,30,12
    EDITTEXT DM_P6,150,44,30,12
    EDITTEXT DM_P7,150,61,30,12
    EDITTEXT DM_P8,150,76,30,12
    EDITTEXT DM_P9,149,91,30,12
    EDITTEXT DM_P10,149,106,30,12
    PUSHBUTTON "OK",IDOK,39,135,24,14
    PUSHBUTTON "Cancel",IDCANCEL,122,136,34,14
END
```

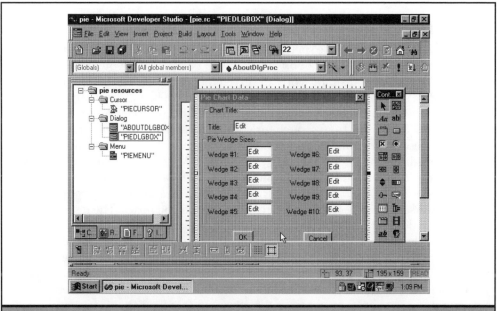

Figure 20-11.   *A completed dialog box for data entry*

The specifications that make up a dialog box are typically produced with the resource editor, which is designed to read and save dialog resource files in the text (.RC) and compiled format (.RES). Text files make it easy to combine several menu and dialog box specifications in one file.

DIALOG BOX CONCEPTS   Dialog boxes are actually "child" windows that pop up when selected from the user's menu. When various dialog box buttons, checkboxes, and so on are selected, Windows provides the means necessary for processing the message information.

Dialog boxes can be produced in two basic styles—modal and modeless. *Modal* dialog boxes are the most popular and are used for the example developed in the next chapter. When a modal dialog box is created, no other options within the current program will be available until the user ends the dialog box by clicking an OK or Cancel button. The OK button will process any new information selected by the user, while the Cancel button will return the user to the original window without processing new information. Windows expects the ID values for these push buttons to be 1 and 2, respectively.

Modeless dialog boxes are more closely related to ordinary windows. A pop-up window can be created from a parent window, and the user can switch back and forth between the two. The same thing is permitted with a modeless dialog box. Modeless dialog boxes are preferred when a certain option must remain on the screen, such as a color select dialog box.

Designing Dialog Boxes

There are two ways to enter the specifications for a dialog box. If you are entering information from a magazine or book listing, it will be easiest for you to use the compiler's text editor and simply copy the given menu and dialog box specifications into a resource script file, a file with a .RC file extension. When the resource script file is compiled, the resource compiler will create a file with a .RC file extension. If you are creating a new dialog box from scratch for your project, you should use the appropriate resource editor. The next few sections discuss the fundamentals of using the resource editor to create and modify a dialog box. Microsoft's online help utility will provide additional information for more advanced features and editing.

Reconsider the dialog box resource script file, shown earlier in this chapter, to convince yourself of the need of a resource editor for dialog boxes. The resource editor allows you to design the dialog box in a graphical environment.

Examine the dialog box resource script file, shown earlier. Ask yourself the following questions. Where do all those terms come from? What do all those numbers mean? How could I figure all of this out without the resource editor? I would have to create, size, and place dialog boxes and their associated controls on the screen experimentally. The resource editor, on the other hand, will do all this for you automatically. Except for being able to make the claim that you created a dialog box without the resource editor at least once in your life, there is no reason for design dialog boxes without the graphical environment of the editor.

Dialog Box Mechanics

If your dialog box information is entered in ASCII form from a book or magazine article, it must be compiled. This requires the use of the resource compiler, which works in conjunction with the resource editor. On the other hand, if you are creating a new dialog box for a project from scratch, use the resource editor by selecting the Insert | Resource menu from the compiler's main menu bar. Then select the dialog box option. A screen similar to the one in Figure 20-12 should appear.

The screen now contains the initial outline for the new dialog box. This initial dialog box can be moved about the screen and sized to fit your needs. The screen in Figure 20-13 shows the initial dialog box moved and sized with several controls in place.

PLACING CONTROLS WITH THE TOOLBOX   By far the most important aspect of using the resource editor when designing dialog boxes is an understanding of the various controls that are provided for the user in the toolbox. Figure 20-14 shows the toolbox used by the resource editor when designing dialog boxes.

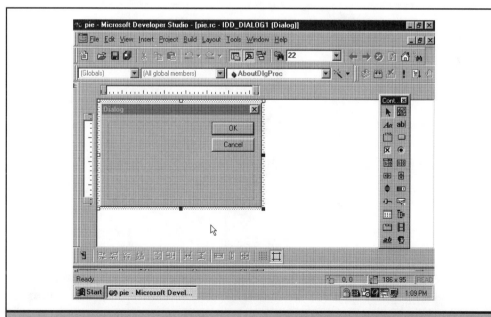

Figure 20-12.   *The resource editor's initial dialog box form*

WINDOWS
PROGRAMMING
FOUNDATIONS

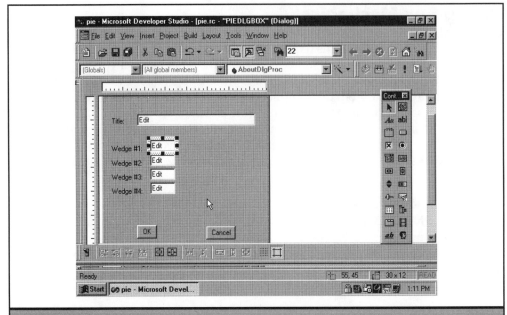

Figure 20-13. *A dialog box under construction in the resource editor*

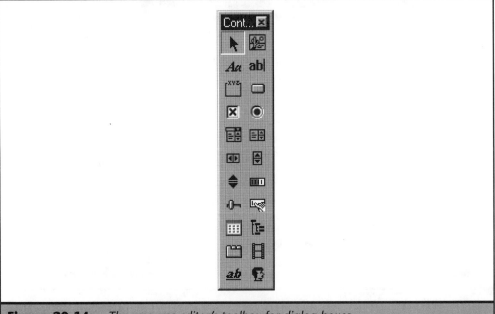

Figure 20-14. *The resource editor's toolbox for dialog boxes*

Here is a brief explanation of the toolbox controls.

■ The *Static Text control* allows the insertion of labels and strings within the dialog box. These can be used, for example, to label an edit box. Select this control using the toolbox icon with the upper- and lowercase characters.

■ The *Group Box control* creates a rectangular outline within a dialog box to enclose a group of controls that are to be used together. A group box contains a label on its upper-left edge. Select this control using the toolbox icon with the rectangular outline with text on the upper edge.

■ The *Check Box control* creates a small square box, called a *checkbox,* with a label to its right. Checkboxes are usually marked or checked by clicking with the mouse, but they can also be selected with the keyboard. Several checkboxes usually appear together in a dialog box; they allow the user to check one or more features at the same time. Select this control using the toolbox icon with the "x" or check mark located in a small rectangular region.

■ The *Combo Box control* is made up of two elements. It is a combination of a single-line edit field (also called a Static Text control) and a List Box control. With a combo box, the user has the ability to enter something into the edit box or scroll through the list box looking for an appropriate selection. Windows provides several styles of combo boxes. Select this control using the toolbox icon with three rectangular areas. This control is located under the Check Box control.

■ The *Horizontal Scroll Bar control* allows horizontal scroll bars to be created for the dialog box. These are normally used in conjunction with another window or control that contains text or graphics information. Select this control using the toolbox icon with the left and right directional arrows.

■ The *Spin control* creates two small rectangular areas, one on top of the other. The top area has an upward-pointing arrow and the bottom a downward-pointing arrow. This control functions like the thumb-wheel control on the new Microsoft mouse, allowing you to click selections up or down. Select this control using the toolbox icon with the two pyramid shapes (one upright and one upside down).

■ The *Slider control* initially creates a horizontal slider button and track; it can be changed to a vertical Slider control by changing the property of the control once it is placed in the dialog box. Slider controls are used frequently in place of scroll bars when simpler actions are required. Select this control using the toolbox icon with the slider button and horizontal track.

■ The *List control* contains a rectangular area for a list of items (these may be small iconic images) and a vertical scroll bar. This control is similar to the List Box control, but contains the vertical scroll bar. Select this control using the toolbox icon with the nine small images within the rectangular area.

■ The *Tab control* is used when a dialog box is to contain a large amount of information. Instead of creating a complicated dialog box with one screen, the tab control allows the user to flip to different pages within the dialog box. Each page then contains just a portion of the overall information. Select this control using the toolbox icon with the small tab folder.

■ The *Rich Edit control* allows the user to enter and edit multiple lines of text. Formatting can be applied as well as embedded OLE objects. Select this control using the toolbox icon with underlined "ab" characters.

■ The *Picture control* allows a rectangular area to be placed in the dialog box where a bitmapped image can be placed. Select this control using the toolbox icon with the small picture.

■ The *Edit Box control* creates a small interactive rectangle on the screen in which the user can enter string information. The edit box can be sized to accept short or long strings. This string information can be processed directly as character or numeric integer data and indirectly as real-number data in the program. The edit box is the most important control for data entry. Select this control using the toolbox icon with the lowercase "ab" characters.

■ The *Button control* is a small, slightly rounded, rectangular button that can be sized. The button contains a label within it. Buttons are used for an immediate choice such as accepting or canceling the dialog box selections made by the user. Select this control using the toolbox icon with the rounded rectangular shape.

■ The *Radio Button control* creates a small circle, called a *radio button,* with a label to its right. Radio buttons, like checkboxes, typically appear in groups. However, unlike checkboxes, only one radio button can be selected at a time in any particular group. Select this control using the toolbox icon with the small bull's-eye.

■ The *List Box control* creates a rectangular outline with a vertical scroll bar. List boxes are useful when scrolling is needed to allow the user to select a file from a long directory listing. Select this control using the toolbox icon with the rectangular area and an upward- and downward-facing arrow.

■ The *Vertical Scroll Bar control* allows vertical scroll bars to be created for the dialog box. These are normally used in conjunction with another window or control that contains text or graphics information. Select this control using the toolbox icon with the upward and downward-facing arrows.

■ The *Progress control* produces a small bar that an application can use to indicate the progress of an operation. The progress bar is filled from left to right. Select this control using the toolbox icon with the small progress bar image.

■ The *Hot Key control* enables the creation of a *hot key,* a key or key combination that allows the quick selection of menu items and so on. Select this control using the toolbox icon with the button and finger combination.

- The *Tree control* displays a list of data in a tree structure. This control is helpful when you wish to convey to the user a hierarchical structure. Select this control using the toolbox icon with the small tree structure image

- The *Animate control* supports the displays of an AVI clip (audio video interleaved). The clip is created as a short series of bitmap frames. This is the technique used for making animated cursors. Select this control using the toolbox icon with the two file frames.

- The *Custom Control control* allows the use of an existing custom or user control. This technique has been replaced by the use of ActiveX controls and is included to be backward compliant. Developers should elect to use ActiveX controls. Select this control using the toolbox icon with the image of a person.

You can place controls in the current dialog box outline by selecting the appropriate control from the toolbox, positioning the mouse pointer in the dialog box, and clicking the mouse button. If the placement is not where you desired, you can use the mouse for repositioning. It is also possible to size the controls once they are placed.

Creating a Dialog Box

In this section, a simple About dialog box is created. About dialog boxes are used to identify the project and developers, give a copyright date, and so on. They usually contain only one push button: OK. They are the easiest dialog boxes to design. Figure 20-15 shows a sized and positioned dialog box outline awaiting the final placement of the Static Text and Button controls.

In this dialog box example, only two types of controls will be used—the Static Text and Button controls. You can use the mouse to place, size, and position the Text Box control in the dialog window. Clicking the mouse within the box after positioning it will allow editing of the actual text string. Figure 20-16 shows several controls where the text has been edited.

The string to be printed is entered in the Text window, where the word "Text" now appears. The ID value is automatically supplied. Now position the OK push button in the about box. To delete an existing control, such as "Cancel," click on the control and press the DEL key. Clicking the mouse within the button allows you to enter the text for the button. In this case, it will be "OK". Figure 20-17 shows the placement of the push button and the final dialog box.

You can then save the dialog box information by selecting the Save option from the File menu. Remember that the resource editor will save this file in the text (.RC) or compiled resource (.RES) form. Using the resource editor to create dialog boxes is a skill learned with practice. Large dialog boxes, utilizing many controls, will initially take hours to design. Again, use the detailed information contained in the Help menu or your Microsoft user's manuals. Start with simple dialog boxes and work toward more complicated designs.

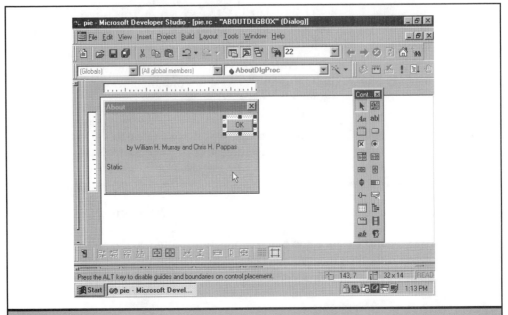

Figure 20-15. *A dialog box waiting the final placement of controls*

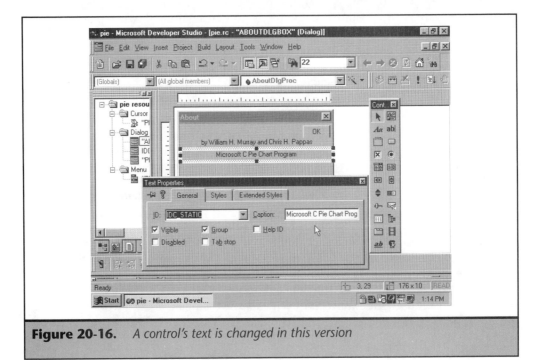

Figure 20-16. *A control's text is changed in this version*

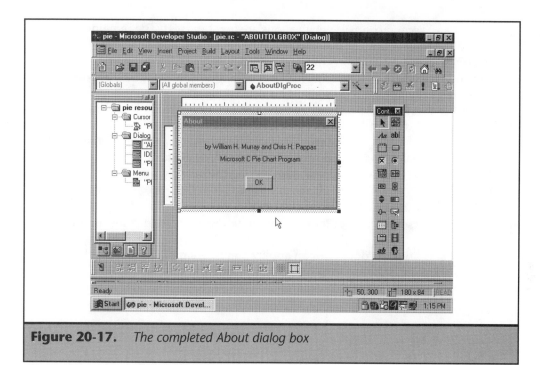

Figure 20-17. *The completed About dialog box*

EXAMINING THE RESOURCE SCRIPT   You can examine the script file information once the resource is saved as a .RC file. Use any ASCII text editor to see the text version of the About box description.

```
ABOUTDLGBOX DIALOG DISCARDABLE  50,300,180,84
STYLE DS_MODALFRAME|WS_POPUP|WS_VISIBLE|WS_CAPTION|WS_SYSMENU
CAPTION "About"
FONT 8, "MS Sans Serif"
BEGIN
  CTEXT "Microsoft C Pie Chart Program",-1,3,29,176,10
  CTEXT "by William H. Murray and Chris H. Pappas",-1,3,16,
        176,10
  PUSHBUTTON "OK",IDOK,74,51,32,14
END
```

The name of this dialog box is ABOUTDLGBOX. The editor has affixed various segment values along with size specifications for the box. The various style options further identify the dialog box as one that has a modal frame and is a pop-up type. Three controls are listed.

WINDOWS
PROGRAMMING
FOUNDATIONS

The first and second control specifications are for static text. The remaining specifications establish the text position and type.

The third control specifies an OK push button. The text within the first set of double quotes specifies what will appear within the push button. The labels for the ID values for the push button are a system default.

Remember that it is not necessary to view this information at all. The resource editor will convert the graphics dialog box you see on the screen directly into a compiled resource file (.RES). The only time you will need this information is when you are entering dialog box specifications from a book or magazine.

The About dialog box we just created is used in the next chapter.

A Look at Resource Statements

You can also use resource script files for combining menu and dialog resources in one file.

Defining additional resources for an application is as simple as naming the resource ID followed by a resource compiler keyword and then the actual filename. Suppose you've created a resource script file called MYRES.RC:

```
myicon ICON myicon.ico
mycursor CURSOR mycursor.cur
mybitmap BITMAP mybitmap.bmp
```

Remember that MYRES.RC is a resource script or text file that defines three new resources. The names of the three resources are myicon, mycursor, and mybitmap. ICON, CURSOR, and BITMAP are reserved keywords defining the type of the resource. These are followed by the actual filenames containing the resource information; for example: MYICON.ICO, MYCURSOR.CUR, and MYBITMAP.BMP.

There are five additional options that can be included with each single-line statement. These options follow the resource-type keyword and include PRELOAD, LOADONCALL, FIXED, MOVEABLE, and DISCARDABLE. The first two options define load options; the latter define memory options. For example:

```
resourceID resource-type [[load-option]] [[memory-option]]
            filename
```

The PRELOAD option automatically loads the resource whenever the application is run. LOADONCALL loads the resource only when it is called.

If a FIXED memory option is selected, the resource remains at a fixed memory address. Selecting MOVEABLE allows Windows to move the resource to compact and conserve memory. The last choice, DISCARDABLE, allows Windows to discard the resource if it is no longer needed. However, it can be reloaded should a call be made requesting the particular resource. For example, making mybitmap LOADONCALL and DISCARDABLE is as simple as entering the following modified single-line statement into the resource script:

```
myicon ICON myicon.ico
mycursor CURSOR mycursor.cur
mybitmap BITMAP LOADONCALL DISCARDABLE mybitmap.bmp
```

Compiling Resources

Resource script files must be compiled into resource files. The resource compiler, which is responsible for this operation, can be run from the command line or, preferably, with the use of the project utility.

The command to run the resource compiler includes the name of the resource script file, the name of the executable file that will receive the compiler's binary format output, and any optional instructions.

The syntax for using the resource compiler from the command line is simple. From the command line, type

```
rc [[compiler options]] filename.rc [[executable filename]]
```

For example, invoking the resource compiler with the example resource script described earlier would look like one of the following three lines:

```
rc myres
rc myres.rc
rc -r myres.rc
```

The first two examples read the MYRES.RC resource script file, create the compiled resource file MYRES.RES, and copy the resources into the executable file MYRES.EXE. The third command performs the same actions except that it does not put the resource into MYRES.EXE. If the third command were executed, the MYRES.RES binary file could be added to the MYRES.EXE file at a later date by using the following command structure:

```
rc myres.res
```

This causes the resource compiler to search for the compiled resource file (.RES) and places it into the executable file (.EXE) of the same filename.

Additional Resource Information

In addition to the information contained in this chapter, the Microsoft user's guides provide a wealth of data on each of these topics. While using the various resource editors, avail yourself of the extensive built-in help engine that is available. Details on the creation of actual Windows resources can be found in the books mentioned in this and earlier chapters and in various magazine articles. Developing serious Windows code is a major undertaking, but don't forget to have fun while learning.

The next chapter will put these programming concepts into practice as you learn how to develop traditional 32-bit procedure-oriented Windows 95 and NT applications.

The Complete Reference

Visual C++ 5

Chapter 21

Procedure-Oriented Windows Applications

Chapter 20 concentrated on Windows terms, definitions, and tools in order to prepare you for the applications you'll develop in this chapter. The most attractive features of Windows applications are the common visual interface, device independence, and concurrent execution. It is now time to put theory into practice and develop applications with these exciting features.

This chapter teaches you how to write 32-bit procedure-oriented Windows 95 and NT applications in C or C++. In Chapters 22 and 23 you will start writing 32-bit object-oriented Windows applications and incorporate the MFC library into your code. Even if you plan to do all of your development work in object-oriented C++, this is still an important chapter for you to study. By analyzing the applications developed in this chapter, you'll have a much better understanding of how the Foundation Class library aids in C++ code development.

A Framework for All Applications

In this section you will learn about the various components that make up a program called SWP.C (Simple Windows Program). The SWP.C program incorporates all of the Windows components minimally necessary to create and display a window (a main window with a border, a title bar, a system menu, and maximize/minimize boxes); draw a diagonal line; print a text message; and allow you to gracefully quit. You'll also learn that the SWP.C program and its related files can serve as templates for future C Windows applications you develop. Understanding code that is used over and over will save you time and help foster an understanding of how Windows applications are put together and why they work.

In Chapter 20, common Windows types were discussed. Table 21-1 summarizes frequently encountered types.

Type	Description
CALLBACK	Replaces FAR PASCAL in application's call back routine
HANDLE	A 32-bit unsigned integer that is used as a handle
HDC	A handle to a device context
HWND	A 32-bit unsigned integer that is used as the handle to a window
LONG	A 32-bit signed integer
LPARAM	Type used for declaration of lParam

Table 21-1. *Common Win32 Types*

Type	Description
LPCSTR	The same as LPSTR, but used for read-only string pointers
LPSTR	A 32-bit pointer
LPVOID	A generic pointer type, equivalent to (void *)
LRESULT	Used for the return value of a window procedure
NULL	An integral zero value, frequently used to trigger default parameters or actions for a function
UINT	An unsigned integer type whose size is determined by the host environment; 32 bits for Windows 95 and NT
WCHAR	A 16-bit UNICODE character used to represent all of the symbols for all of the world's languages
WINAPI	Replaces FAR PASCAL in API declarations
WPARAM	Used for the declaration of wParam

Table 21-1.   *Common Win32 Types* (continued)

There are a number of structures that are frequently encountered by Windows programmers. Table 21-2 will serve as a quick reference for these structures.

With these tools in hand, we're ready to examine the components of a Windows application.

Structure	Description
MSG	Defines the fields of an input message
PAINTSTRUCT	Defines the paint structure used when drawing inside a window
RECT	Defines a rectangle
WNDCLASS	Defines a window class

Table 21-2.   *Structures Common to Win32 Applications*

Components in a Windows Application

Windows 95 and NT applications contain two common and essential elements, the WinMain( ) function and a window function. The main body of your application is named *WinMain( )*. WinMain( ) serves as the entry-point for the Windows 95 and NT application and acts much like the main function in standard C programs.

The window function, not to be confused with WinMain( ), has a unique role. Recall that a Windows application never directly accesses any window functions. When a Windows application attempts to execute a standard window function, it makes a request to Windows to carry out the specified task. For this reason, all Windows applications must have a call back window function. This function is registered with Windows and is called back whenever Windows executes an operation on a window.

The WinMain( ) Function

A WinMain( ) function is required by all Windows 95 and NT applications. This is the point at which program execution begins and usually ends. The WinMain( ) function is responsible for:

- Registering the application's window class type
- Performing any required initializations
- Creating and initiating the application's message-processing loop (which accesses the program's message queue)
- Terminating the program, usually upon receiving a WM_QUIT message

Four parameters are passed to the WinMain( ) function from Windows. The following code segment illustrates these required parameters as they are used in the SWP.C application:

```
int WINAPI WinMain(HINSTANCE hInst,HINSTANCE hPreInst,
                   LPSTR lpszCmdLine,int nCmdShow)
```

The first formal parameter to WinMain( ) is hInst, which contains the instance handle of the application. This number uniquely identifies the program when it is running under Windows.

The second formal parameter, hPreInst, will always contain a NULL indicating that there is no previous instance of this application.

NOTE: *MS-DOS versions of Windows (Windows 3.3 and earlier) used hPreInst to indicate whether there were any previous copies of the program loaded. Under operating systems, such as Windows 95 and NT, each application runs in its own separate address space. For this reason, under Windows 95 and NT, hPreInst will never return a valid previous instance, just NULL.*

The third parameter, lpszCmdLine, is a long pointer to a null-terminated string that represents the application's command-line arguments. Normally, lpszCmdLine contains a NULL if the application was started using the Windows Run command.

The fourth and last formal parameter to WinMain( ) is nCmdShow. The int value stored in nCmdShow represents one of the many Windows predefined constants defining the possible ways a window can be displayed, such as SW_SHOWNORMAL, SW_SHOWMAXIMIZED, or SW_MINIMIZED.

WNDCLASS

WinMain( ) is responsible for registering the application's main window class. Every window class is based on a combination of user-selected styles, fonts, caption bars, icons, size, placement, and so on. The window class serves as a template that defines these attributes.

> **NOTE:** *Under earlier versions of Windows running over DOS, registered window classes became available to all programs running under Windows. For this reason, the programmer had to use caution when naming and registering classes to make certain that those names used did not conflict with any other application window classes. Windows 95 and NT require that every instance (each copy of an application) must register its own window class.*

Basically, the same standard C/C++ structure type is used for all Windows class definitions. The following example is taken directly from WINUSER.H, which is an #include file referenced in WINDOWS.H. The header file contains a typedef statement defining the structure type WNDCLASSW (a UNICODE-compatible definition), from which WNDCLASS is derived:

```
typedef struct tagWNDCLASSW {
    UINT        style;
    WNDPROC     lpfnWndProc;
    int         cbClsExtra;
    int         cbWndExtra;
    HANDLE      hInstance;
    HICON       hIcon;
    HCURSOR     hCursor;
    HBRUSH      hbrBackground;
    LPCWSTR     lpszMenuName;
    LPCWSTR     lpszClassName;
} WNDCLASSW, *PWNDCLASSW, NEAR *NPWNDCLASSW, FAR *LPWNDCLASSW;
```

Windows provides several predefined window classes, but most applications define their own window classes. To define a window class, your application must define a structure variable of the following type:

WINDOWS
PROGRAMMING
FOUNDATIOINS

```
WNDCLASS wcApp;
```

The wcApp structure is then filled with information about the window class. The following sections describe the various fields within the WNDCLASS structure. Some of the fields may be assigned a NULL, directing Windows to use predefined values, while others must be given specific values.

style   The style field names the class style. The styles can be combined with the bitwise OR operator. The style field is made up of a combination of the values shown in Table 21-3.

lpfnWndProc   lpfnWndProc receives a pointer to the window function that will carry out all of the tasks for the window.

cbClsExtra   cbClsExtra gives the number of bytes that must be allocated after the window class structure. It can be NULL.

Value	Meaning
CS_BYTEALIGNCLIENT	Aligns a client area on a byte boundary
CS_BYTEALIGNWINDOW	Aligns a window on the byte boundary
CS_CLASSDC	Provides the window class a display context
CS_DBLCLKS	Sends a double-click message to the window
CS_GLOBALCLASS	States that the window class is an application global class
CS_HREDRAW	Redraws the window when horizontal size changes
CS_NOCLOSE	Inhibits the close option from the system menu
CS_OWNDC	Each window receives an instance for its own display context (DC)
CS_PARENTDC	Sends the parent window's display context (DC) to the window class
CS_SAVEBITS	Saves that part of a screen that is covered by another window
CS_VREDRAW	Redraws the window when the vertical size changes

Table 21-3.   *Popular Windows Styles*

cbWndExtra   cbWndExtra gives the number of bytes that must be allocated after the window instance. It can be NULL.

hInstance   hInstance defines the instance of the application registering the window class. This must be an instance handle and cannot be NULL.

hIcon   hIcon defines the icon to be used when the window is minimized. This can be NULL.

hCursor   hCursor defines the cursor to be used with the application. This handle can be NULL. The cursor is valid only within the application's client area.

hbrBackground   hbrBackground provides the identification for the background brush. This can be a handle to the physical brush or it can be a color value. Color values must be selected from one of the standard colors in the following list. A value of 1 must be added to the selected color.

COLOR_ACTIVEBORDER
COLOR_ACTIVECAPTION
COLOR_APPWORKSPACE
COLOR_BACKGROUND
COLOR_BTNFACE
COLOR_BTNSHADOW
COLOR_BTNTEXT
COLOR_CAPTIONTEXT
COLOR_GRAYTEXT
COLOR_HIGHLIGHT
COLOR_HIGHLIGHTTEXT
COLOR_INACTIVEBORDER
COLOR_INACTIVECAPTION
COLOR_MENU
COLOR_MENUTEXT
COLOR_SCROLLBAR
COLOR_WINDOW
COLOR_WINDOWFRAME
COLOR_WINDOWTEXT

If hbrBackground is NULL, the application paints its own background.

lpszMenuName   lpszMenuName is a pointer to a null-terminated character string. The string is the resource name of the menu. This item can be NULL.

lpszClassName   lpszClassName is a pointer to a null-terminated character string. The string is the name of the window class.

WNDCLASSEX

Windows offers an expanded definition for WNDCLASS named WNDCLASSEX, which allows a small icon to be used for applications. Here is the WNDCLASSEX structure:

```
typedef struct _WNDCLASSEX {
    UINT    style;
    WNDPROC lpfnWndProc;
    int     cbClsExtra;
    int     cbWndExtra;
    HANDLE  hInstance;
    HICON   hIcon;
    HCURSOR hCursor;
    HBRUSH  hbrBackground;
    LPCTSTR lpszMenuName;
    LPCTSTR lpszClassName;
    HICON   hIconSm;
} WNDCLASSEX;
```

You can see that these two structures are identical, except that WNDCLASSEX includes the hIconSm member, which is the handle of the small icon associated with a window class.

Predefined window classes are available, but most programmers define their own window class.

Defining a Window Class

An application can define its own window class by defining a structure of the appropriate type and then filling the structure's fields with the information about the window class.

The following listing is from the SWP.C application and demonstrates how the WNDCLASS structure has been defined and initialized.

```
char szProgName[]="ProgName";
            .
            .
            .

WNDCLASS wcApp;
            .
            .
            .
```

```
wcApp.lpszClassName=szProgName;
wcApp.hInstance    =hInst;
wcApp.lpfnWndProc  =WndProc;
wcApp.hCursor      =LoadCursor(NULL,IDC_ARROW);
wcApp.hIcon        =NULL;
wcApp.lpszMenuName =szApplName;
wcApp.hbrBackground=GetStockObject(WHITE_BRUSH);
wcApp.style        =CS_HREDRAW|CS_VREDRAW;
wcApp.cbClsExtra   =0;
wcApp.cbWndExtra   =0;
if (!RegisterClass (&wcApp))
   return 0;
```

The SWP.C template application is assigned the generic name szProgName and is assigned to the window's wcApp.lpszClassName.

The second field in WNDCLASS, wcApp.hInstance, is assigned the value returned in hInst after WinMain( ) is invoked. This indicates the current instance of the application. lpfnWndProc is assigned the pointer address to the window function that will carry out all of the window's tasks. For the SWP.C application, the function is called WndProc( ).

NOTE: WndProc( ) is a user-defined, not a predefined, function name. The function must be prototyped before the assignment statement.

The wcApp.hCursor field is assigned a handle to the instance's cursor, which in this example is IDC_ARROW (representing the default tilted arrow cursor). This assignment is accomplished through a call to the LoadCursor( ) function. Since the SWP.C application has no default icon, wcApp.hIcon is assigned a NULL.

When wcApp.lpszMenuName is assigned a NULL, Windows understands that the class has no menu. If it did, the menu would have a name, which would appear within quotation marks. The GetStockObject( ) function returns a handle to a brush used to paint the background color of the client area of windows created from this class. For the SWP.C application, the function returns a handle to one of Windows' predefined brushes, WHITE_BRUSH.

The wcApp.style window class style has been set to CS_HREDRAW or CS_VREDRAW. All window class styles have identifiers in WINUSER.H that begin with "CS_". Each identifier represents a bit value. The bitwise OR operation | is used to combine these bit flags. The two parameters used (CS_HREDRAW and CS_VREDRAW) instruct Windows to redraw the entire client area whenever the horizontal or vertical size of the window is changed.

The last two fields, wcApp.cbClsExtra and wcApp.cbWndExtra, are frequently assigned zero. These fields are used to optionally indicate the count of extra bytes that may have been reserved at the end of the window class structure and the window data structure used for each window class.

From previous discussions about instances, you may recall that under earlier 16-bit versions of Windows, an application had to register a window class if it was the first instance of copy loaded. Here is a portion of code that was used for that purpose:

```
if (!hPreInst)
{
        .

        .

    .

  if (!RegisterClass (&wcApp))
    return FALSE;
}
```

Windows 95 and NT check the number of instances by examining the hPreInst parameter, which will always be NULL, and then register the class.

There are two if statements in the code segment. The first if takes care of filling the WNDCLASS structure when this is the first instance. The second if registers the new window class. It does this by sending RegisterClass( ) a long pointer to the window class structure. If Windows cannot register the window class, which can happen if sufficient memory is not available, RegisterClass( ) will return a zero, terminating the program.

Creating a Window

All windows are patterned after some predefined and registered class type. Defining and then registering a window class has nothing to do with actually displaying a window in a Windows application.

A window is created with a call to the CreateWindow( ) function. This process is common to all versions of Windows. While the window class defines the general characteristics of a window, allowing the same window class to be used for many different windows, the parameters for CreateWindow( ) specify more detailed information about the window. If the function call is successful, CreateWindow( ) returns the handle of the newly created window. Otherwise, the function returns NULL.

The parameter information for the CreateWindow( ) function falls under the following categories: the class, title, style, screen position, window's parent handle, menu handle, instance handle, and 32 bits of additional information. For the SWP.C application, this function would take on the following appearance:

```
hWnd=CreateWindow(szProgName,"Simple Windows Program",
                  WS_OVERLAPPEDWINDOW,CW_USEDEFAULT,
```

```
CW_USEDEFAULT, CW_USEDEFAULT,
CW_USEDEFAULT, (HWND)NULL, (HMENU)NULL,
(HANDLE)hInst, (LPSTR)NULL);
```

The first field, szProgName (assigned earlier), defines the window's class, followed by the title to be used for the window's title bar (Simple Windows Program). The style of the window is the third parameter (WS_OVERLAPPEDWINDOW). This standard Windows style represents a normal overlapped window with a caption bar; a system menu icon; minimize, maximize, and terminate icons; and a window frame.

The next six parameters (either CS_USEDEFAULT or NULL) represent the initial x and y positions and x and y size of the window, along with the parent window handle and window menu handle. Each of these fields has been assigned a default value. The hInst field contains the instance of the program, followed by no additional parameters (NULL).

Showing and Updating a Window

Under Windows, the ShowWindow( ) function is needed to actually display a window. The following portion of code, from the SWP.C application, demonstrates this:

```
ShowWindow(hWnd, nCmdShow);
```

The handle of the window created by the call to CreateWindow( ) is held in the hWnd parameter. The second parameter to ShowWindow( ), nCmdShow, determines how the window is initially displayed. This display mode is also referred to as the window's *visibility state.*

The nCmdShow parameter can specify that the window be displayed as a normal window (SW_SHOWNORMAL) or in several other possible forms. For example, substituting nCmdShow with the WINUSER.H constant SW_SHOWMINNOACTIVE, as shown in the following line of code, causes the window to be drawn as an icon.

```
ShowWindow(hWnd, SW_SHOWMINNOACTIVE);
```

Other display possibilities include SW_SHOWMAXIMIZED, which causes the window to be active and fill the entire display, along with its counterpart, SW_SHOWMINIMIZED.

The final step in displaying a window requires a call to the Windows UpdateWindow( ) function:

```
UpdateWindow(hWnd);
```

WINDOWS
PROGRAMMING
FOUNDATIONS

A call to ShowWindow( ) with a SW_SHOWNORMAL parameter causes the function to erase the window's client area with the background brush specified in the window's class. It is the call to UpdateWindow( ) that generates the familiar WM_PAINT message, causing the client area to be painted.

The Message Loop

With everything in place, the application is ready to perform its main task: processing messages. Recall that Windows does not send input from the mouse or keyboard directly to an application. Windows places all input into the application's message queue. The message queue can contain messages generated by Windows or messages posted by other applications.

The application needs a message-processing loop once the call to WinMain( ) has created and displayed the window. The most common approach is to use a standard while loop:

```
while (GetMessage(&lpMsg,NULL,0,0))
{
  TranslateMessage(&lpMsg);
  DispatchMessage(&lpMsg);
}
```

THE GETMESSAGE( ) FUNCTION   The next message to be processed from the application's message queue can be obtained with a call to the Windows GetMessage( ) function. GetMessage( ) copies the message into the message structure pointed to by the long pointer, lpMsg, and sends the message structure to the main body of the program.

The NULL parameter instructs the function to retrieve any of the messages for any window that belongs to the application. The last two parameters, 0 and 0, tell GetMessage( ) not to apply any message filters. Message filters can restrict retrieved messages to specific categories such as keystrokes or mouse moves. These filters are referred to as wMsgFilterMin and wMsgFilterMax, and specify the numeric filter extremes to apply.

Control can be returned to Windows at any time before the message loop is begun. For example, an application will normally make certain that all steps leading up to the message loop have executed properly. This can include making sure that each window class is registered and has been created. However, once the message loop has been entered, only one message can terminate the loop. Whenever the message to be processed is WM_QUIT, the value returned is FALSE. This causes the processing to proceed to the main loop's closing routine. The WM_QUIT message is the only way for an application to get out of the message loop.

THE TRANSLATEMESSAGE( ) FUNCTION   Virtual-key messages can be converted into character messages with the TranslateMessage( ) function. The function call is required only by applications that need to process character input from the keyboard. This ability can be very useful because it allows the user to make menu selections without having to use the mouse.

The TranslateMessage( ) function creates an ASCII character message (WM_CHAR) from a WM_KEYDOWN and WM_KEYUP message. As long as this function is included in the message loop, the keyboard interface will also be in effect.

THE DISPATCHMESSAGE( ) FUNCTION Windows sends current messages to the correct window procedures with the DispatchMessage( ) function. This function makes it easy to add additional windows and dialog boxes to your application. DispatchMessage( ) automatically routes each message to the appropriate window procedure.

The Window Function

Recall that all applications must include a WinMain( ) function and a Windows call back function. Since a Windows application never directly accesses any Windows function, each application must make a request to Windows to carry out any specified operation.

A call back function is registered with Windows and is called back whenever Windows executes an operation on a window. The length of the actual code for the call back function will vary with each application. The window function itself may be very small, processing only one or two messages, or it may be large and complex.

The following code segment (minus application-specific statements) shows the call back window function WndProc( ) as it is used in the SWP.C application:

```
LRESULT CALLBACK WndProc(HWND hWnd,UINT messg,
                         WPARAM wParam,LPARAM lParam)
{
  HDC hdc;
  PAINTSTRUCT ps;

  switch (messg)
  {
    case WM_PAINT:
      hdc=BeginPaint(hWnd,&ps);
            .
            .
            .
      ValidateRect(hWnd,NULL);
      EndPaint(hWnd,&ps);
      break;

    case WM_DESTROY:
```

```
        PostQuitMessage(0);
        break;

    default:
        return(DefWindowProc(hWnd,messg,wParam,lParam));
    }
    return(0);
}
```

Windows expects the name referenced by the wcApp.lpfnWndProc field of the window class structure definition to match the name used for the call back function. WndProc( ) will be the name used for the call back function for all subsequent windows created from this window class.

The following code segment reviews the placement and assignment of the call back function's name within the window class structure:

```
        .
        .
        .

wcApp.lpszClassName=szProgName;
wcApp.hInstance     =hInst;
wcApp.lpfnWndProc   =WndProc;
        .
        .
        .
```

Windows has several hundreds of messages that it can send to the window function. These messages are labeled with identifiers that begin with "WM_". For example, WM_CREATE, WM_SIZE, and WM_PAINT are used quite frequently. These identifiers are also known as symbolic constants.

The first parameter to WndProc( ) is hWnd. hWnd contains the handle to the window to which Windows will send the message. Since it is possible for one window function to process messages for several windows created from the same window class, this handle is used by the window function to determine which window is receiving the message.

The second parameter to the function, messg, specifies the actual message being processed as defined in WINUSER.H. The last two parameters, wParam and lParam, specify any additional information needed to process each specific message. Frequently, the value returned to each of these parameters is NULL. This means that they can be ignored. At other times, the parameters contain a 2-byte value and a pointer, or two word values.

The WndProc( ) function continues by defining two variables: hdc specifies the display context handle, and ps specifies a PAINTSTRUCT structure needed to store client area information.

The call back function is used to examine the type of message it is about to process and then select the appropriate action to be taken. This selection process usually takes place within a standard C switch statement.

Processing WM_PAINT Messages

The first message that WndProc( ) will process in this template is WM_PAINT. This message calls the Windows function BeginPaint( ), which prepares the specified window for painting and fills a PAINTSTRUCT (&ps) with information about the area to be painted. The BeginPaint( ) function also returns a handle to the device context for the given window.

Because Windows is a multitasking operating system, it is possible for one application to display its window or dialog box over another application's client area. This creates a problem whenever the window or dialog box is closed: a hole appears on the screen where the dialog box was displayed. Windows handles this problem by sending the active application a WM_PAINT message. In this case, Windows requests that the active application update its client area.

Except for the first WM_PAINT message, which is sent by the call to UpdateWindow( ) in WinMain( ), additional WM_PAINT messages are sent under the following conditions:

- When resizing a window
- Whenever a portion of a client area has been hidden by a menu or dialog box that has just been closed
- When using the ScrollWindow( ) function
- When forcing a WM_PAINT message with a call to the InvalidateRect( ) or InvalidateRgn( ) function

Here is how the process works. Any portion of an application's client area that has been corrupted by the overlay of a dialog box, for example, has that area of the client area marked as invalid. Windows makes the redrawing of a client area efficient by keeping track of the diagonal coordinates of this invalid rectangle. It is the presence of an invalid rectangle that prompts Windows to send the WM_PAINT message.

If several portions of the client area are invalidated, Windows will adjust the invalid rectangle coordinates to encapsulate all invalid regions. In other words, Windows does not send a WM_PAINT message for each invalid rectangle.

The call to InvalidateRect( ) allows Windows to mark the client area as invalid, thereby forcing a WM_PAINT message. An application can obtain the coordinates of the invalid rectangle by calling the GetUpdateRect( ) function. A call to the ValidateRect( ) function validates any rectangular region in the client area and deletes any pending WM_PAINT messages.

The EndPaint( ) function is called when the WndProc( ) function ends its processing of the WM_PAINT messages. This function is called whenever the application is finished outputting information to the client area. It tells Windows that the application has finished processing all paint messages and that it is now OK to remove the display context.

Processing the WM_DESTROY Message

When the Close option is selected by the user from an application's system menu, Windows posts a WM_DESTROY message to the application's message queue. The application terminates after it retrieves this message.

The DefWindowProc( ) Function

The DefWindowProc( ) function call, in the default section of WndProc( )'s switch statement, is needed to empty the application's message queue of any unrecognized and/or unprocessed messages. This function ensures that all of the messages posted to the application are processed.

A Module Definition File

As you learned earlier, LINK provides a command-line equivalent to the module definition files once required by all Windows applications. A *module definition file* can be used to provide the linker with definitions and descriptive information so that it knows how to organize the application's executable file for Windows. This information becomes part of the header section of the new executable file format.

 NOTE: Under Windows 95 and NT, it is very unlikely that you will have to create a module definition file. This information is provided for completeness and backward compatibility.

A module definition file for the SWP.C application might take on the following appearance:

```
NAME         swp
DESCRIPTION  'Simple Windows Program'
EXETYPE      WINDOWS
CODE         PRELOAD MOVEABLE DISCARDABLE
DATA         PRELOAD MOVEABLE MULTIPLE
HEAPSIZE     4096
EXPORTS      WndProc      @1
```

The NAME statement defines SWP.C as a Windows program (not a dynamic link library) and gives the module a name. This name should be the same name as the program's executable (.EXE) file.

The DESCRIPTION line copies the text into the executable file. Often this is used to embed added information such as a release date, version number, or copyright notice.

The EXETYPE refers to the type of executable file to create.

Both the CODE and DATA segments have been marked as preloadable and moveable, allowing Windows to relocate them for any dynamic memory allocation requests. The MULTIPLE statement also instructs Windows to create unique data segments for each instance of the application. The use of DISCARDABLE allows Windows to discard unused program code. This code can be automatically reloaded if necessary.

The HEAPSIZE statement specifies an amount of extra, expandable, local memory from within the application's data segment. The STACKSIZE has been set to 9216. You can experiment with various sizes. Larger values may be necessary for applications with large nonstatic variables or those applications using recursion.

Finally, the EXPORTS statement identifies the application's dynamic link entry-point and specifies the name of the procedure, in this case, WndProc.

Make or Project Utility?

There are two ways of putting your Windows applications together: from the command line or from within the integrated environment of the compiler. If you are building applications from the command line, you will need to write a make file. If you are building them from within the integrated environment, you will need to use the project utility. We strongly recommend the latter.

The NMAKE Utility

Microsoft provides a command-line program maintenance utility named NMAKE.EXE. The NMAKE utility is important when compiling command-line applications that use multiple source code or data segments. The use of the NMAKE utility requires the development of another text file, called the *make file*. Make files often do not have a file extension. Thus, for our first example, a command-line make file would be named SWP. The syntax for building an application from the command line is as simple as typing:

    nmake swp

The NMAKE utility is responsible for calling the Visual C++ compiler, linker, and resource compiler with the proper options. Make files also do partial builds of the application. For example, if the source code has changed but the resource code has not, the make file will just recompile the source code on subsequent operations.

A simple make file, such as one that could be used for the SWP.C application, will look something like this:

```
all : swp.exe

swp.obj: swp.c
  cl -c -AS -Gsw -Oas swp.c

swp.exe: swp.obj swp.def
  link /NOD swp,,,libw slibcew, swp.def
```

In a make file, the file named to the left of the colon is the file the NMAKE utility will update if any of the component files to the right of the colon have been updated. The action taken by the utility is restricted to the appropriate indented lines. Note that a command-line make file is a text file created in any text editor.

However, once again, we recommend the use of the project utility discussed in the next section as the preferred alternative to the command-line NMAKE utility.

Project Utility

Most users will choose to remain within the integrated environment of the Visual C++ compiler and compile and link their applications with the help of the project utility. This utility will create an additional file on your disk with a .DSP file extension. So, in this example, the project file would be named SWP.DSP. Project files are not text files, so we can't show you the contents of the file, only tell you how to create one. If a project is built within a unique workspace, another file with a .DSW file extension will be created on your disk. The process of using a project file to manage your files is so simple that you will probably never choose to build applications from the command line again!

To start a new project, use the compiler's File menu and select New to open the New dialog box. Use the Projects folder and select a Win32 Application, as shown in Figure 21-1.

The project name for this example is TestApp, as you can see in Figure 21-1. Click the OK button to arrive at an initially blank screen.

To write code for the project, use the compiler's Project menu then select Add To Project followed by the New… menu selection, as shown in Figure 21-2.

When this selection is made, a New dialog box appears. Using the Text File option, as shown in Figure 21-3, enter the name of the file. In this example, it is TESTAPP.C.

It is also possible to select the C++ Source File as the file type; just be sure to name the file TESTAPP.C.

It is now possible to type your source code into this file, as shown in Figure 21-4.

When the source code is complete, use the File menu to save the project.

If your application requires other files, such as resource files and so on, they can be added to the project at this point. Use the Project menu and select the Add menu item followed by the Files… menu selection to specify the filename.

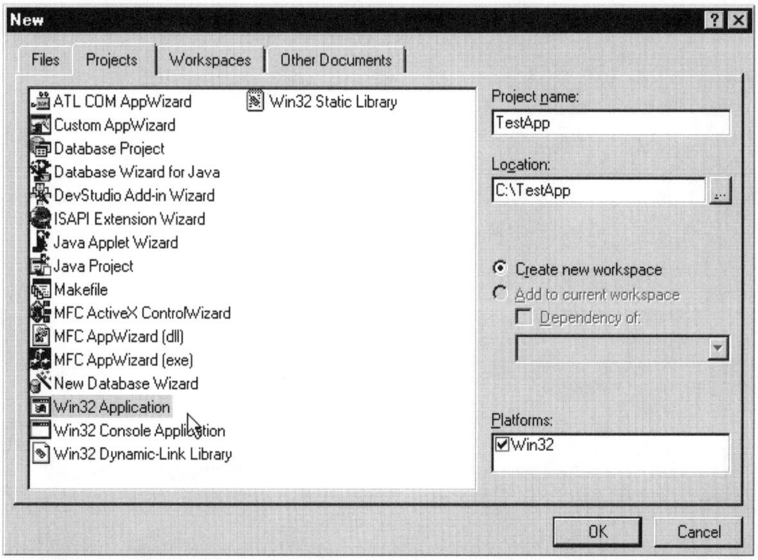

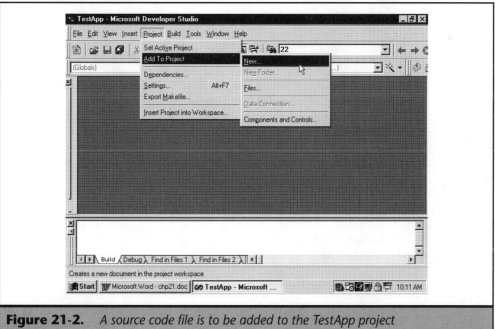

Figure 21-1. *A Win32 Application is selected for the new TestApp project*

Figure 21-2. *A source code file is to be added to the TestApp project*

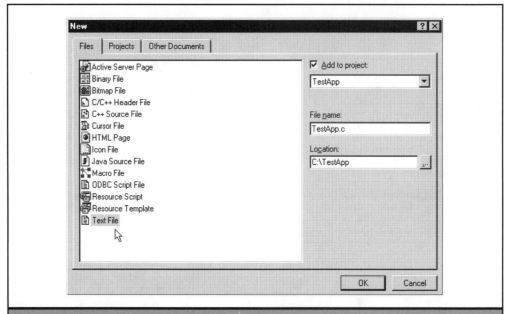

Figure 21-3. *A blank text file named TESTAPP.C will be the source code file for this example*

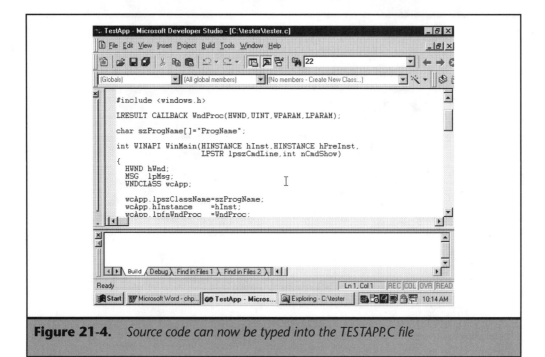

Figure 21-4. *Source code can now be typed into the TESTAPP.C file*

For all remaining applications in this book, we'll be developing our own project files and building our applications from within the integrated environment.

The next step in creating a new application is using the project utility to build an executable file. Before commencing, it is important that all switches are set properly to build a Windows application. The command-line make utility, NMAKE, allows you to specify this in text form within the file, but the project utility requires that these switches be set from within the integrated environment. They can be set from the Project menu by selecting the Settings... menu item. When the Project Settings dialog box is visible, you will be provided with a number of folders. From the General folder, make sure the Microsoft Foundation Class option is set to "Not Using MFC," as shown in Figure 21-5.

Files are created and saved in a DEBUG subdirectory by default. When you have completed the project and are ready to generate a release candidate, change to the Release option.

Switch to the C/C++ folder. If you have not changed the defaults, your folder should appear similar to Figure 21-6.

The default options are satisfactory for almost all applications. As a check, make sure your project options match those shown in the Project Options list in Figure 21-6.

Switch to the Link folder. It should appear similar to Figure 21-7.

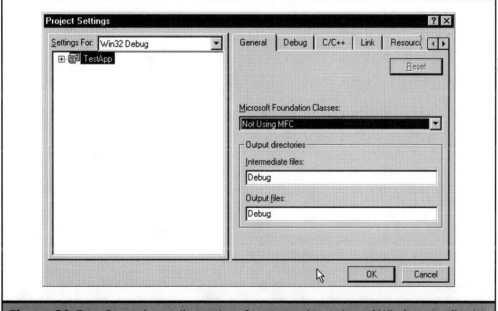

Figure 21-5. *General compiler settings for a procedure-oriented Windows application*

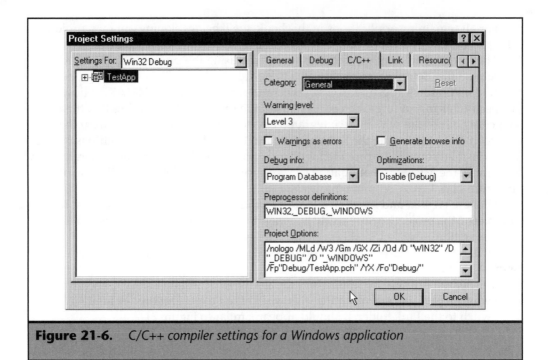

Figure 21-6. C/C++ compiler settings for a Windows application

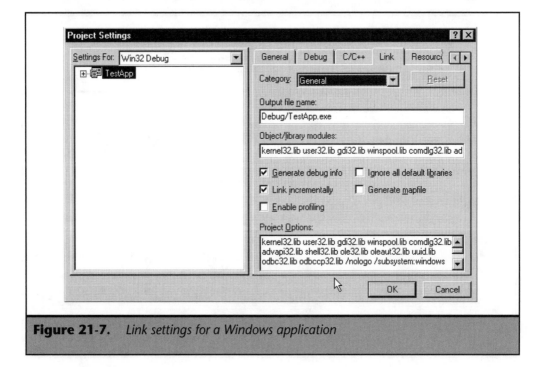

Figure 21-7. Link settings for a Windows application

Compare your project options with those shown in Figure 21-3. It is very important that the subsystem be set to /subsystem:windows and not to /subsystem:console. If it is not set in this manner, your application will compile but not link correctly.

A Simple Windows Program and Template

We have been discussing portions of a complete program throughout the previous sections of this chapter. For your convenience, the following is a complete listing of all the code necessary to create the Simple Windows Program.

The source code file, SWP.C, is straightforward. However, long listings warrant extra care when entering each line of code.

```
/*
 *  swp.c
 *  Simple Windows Program
 *  Copyright (c) William H. Murray and Chris H. Pappas, 1997
 */

#include <windows.h>

LRESULT CALLBACK WndProc(HWND,UINT,WPARAM,LPARAM);

char szProgName[]="ProgName";

int WINAPI WinMain(HINSTANCE hInst,HINSTANCE hPreInst,
                   LPSTR lpszCmdLine,int nCmdShow)
{
  HWND hWnd;
  MSG  lpMsg;
  WNDCLASS wcApp;

  wcApp.lpszClassName=szProgName;
  wcApp.hInstance     =hInst;
  wcApp.lpfnWndProc   =WndProc;
  wcApp.hCursor       =LoadCursor(NULL,IDC_ARROW);
  wcApp.hIcon         =0;
  wcApp.lpszMenuName =0;
  wcApp.hbrBackground=GetStockObject(WHITE_BRUSH);
  wcApp.style         =CS_HREDRAW|CS_VREDRAW;
  wcApp.cbClsExtra    =0;
```

```
     wcApp.cbWndExtra    =0;
     if (!RegisterClass (&wcApp))
       return 0;

     hWnd=CreateWindow(szProgName,"Simple Windows Program",
                     WS_OVERLAPPEDWINDOW,CW_USEDEFAULT,
                     CW_USEDEFAULT,CW_USEDEFAULT,
                     CW_USEDEFAULT,(HWND)NULL,(HMENU)NULL,
                     (HANDLE)hInst,(LPSTR)NULL);
     ShowWindow(hWnd,nCmdShow);
     UpdateWindow(hWnd);
     while (GetMessage(&lpMsg,0,0,0)) {
       TranslateMessage(&lpMsg);
       DispatchMessage(&lpMsg);
     }
     return(lpMsg.wParam);
   }

   LRESULT CALLBACK WndProc(HWND hWnd,UINT messg,
                           WPARAM wParam,LPARAM lParam)
   {
     HDC hdc;
     PAINTSTRUCT ps;

     switch (messg)
     {
       case WM_PAINT:
         hdc=BeginPaint(hWnd,&ps);

         MoveToEx(hdc,0,0,NULL);
         LineTo(hdc,639,429);
         MoveToEx(hdc,300,0,NULL);
         LineTo(hdc,50,300);

         TextOut(hdc,120,30,"<- a few lines ->",17);

         ValidateRect(hWnd,NULL);
         EndPaint(hWnd,&ps);
         break;
       case WM_DESTROY:
```

```
        PostQuitMessage(0);
        break;
    default:
        return(DefWindowProc(hWnd,messg,wParam,lParam));
        break;
    }
    return(0);
}
```

Recall, for earlier discussions, that the bulk of this code is required to define and register a window. The code that draws two lines and text in the client area is small in comparison.

```
MoveToEx(hdc,0,0,NULL);
LineTo(hdc,639,429);
MoveToEx(hdc,300,0,NULL);
LineTo(hdc,50,300);

TextOut(hdc,120,30,"<- a few lines ->",17);
```

It is at this location in the application's code that you can experiment with a wide variety of Windows GDI graphics drawing functions, which are called *drawing primitives.*

Compile and link your application by using the compiler's Build menu. You can choose the Build, Rebuild All, or Execute menu items. The Build menu item builds just the current file. The Rebuild All menu item rebuilds all project files (there is only one in this project). The Execute menu item attempts to run the application. When it finds no executable file, it will prompt you for permission to build and execute the application.

If everything goes okay during the build process, you'll end up with several additional files in your subdirectory. The executable file will be in the DEBUG subdirectory specified as a project default.

Figure 21-8 shows the application's window. This application draws two diagonal lines on the screen and prints a short text message.

You can experiment with other GDI graphics primitives such as ellipses, chords, pie wedges, and rectangles. Let's see how these GDI primitives work.

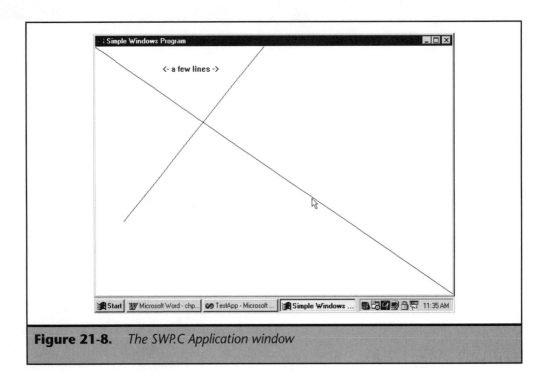

Figure 21-8. *The SWP.C Application window*

Drawing an Ellipse

The Ellipse( ) function is used for drawing an ellipse or a circle. The center of the ellipse is also the center of an imaginary rectangle described by the points *x1,y1* and *x2,y2*, as shown in Figure 21-9.

An ellipse is a closed figure and is filled with the current brush. The handle for the device context is given by hdc. All other parameters are of type int. This function returns a type BOOL.

The syntax for the command is

Ellipse(*hdc,x1,y1,x2,y2*)

For example, the following code draws a small ellipse in the user's window:

```
Ellipse(hdc,200,200,275,250);
TextOut(hdc,210,215,"<- an ellipse",13);
```

Figure 21-10 shows how the ellipse will appear on the screen.

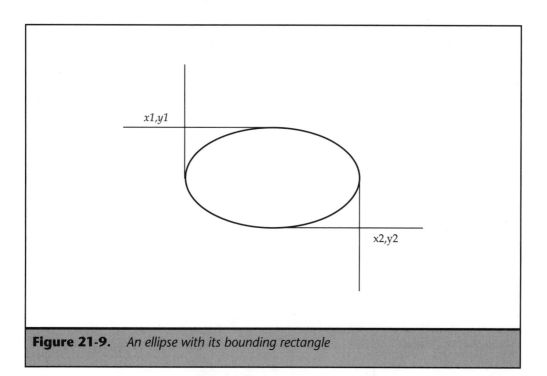

Figure 21-9. *An ellipse with its bounding rectangle*

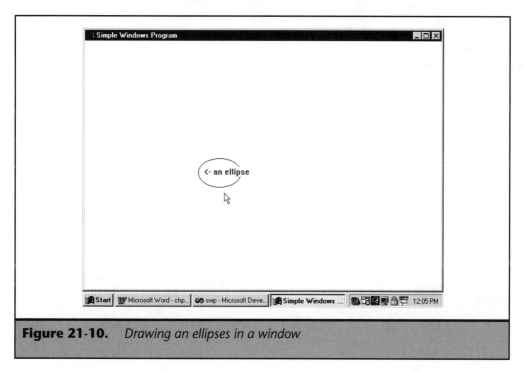

Figure 21-10. *Drawing an ellipses in a window*

Drawing a Chord

The Chord( ) function is a closed figure with a line between two arc points, *x3,y3* and *x4,y4*. Figure 21-11 shows these points. A chord is filled with the current brush.

The handle for the device context is given by hdc. All other parameters are of type int. This function returns a type BOOL.

The syntax for the command is

Chord(*hdc,x1,y1,x2,y2,x3,y3,x4,y4*)

For example, the following code draws a small chord in the user's window:

```
Chord(hdc,550,20,630,80,555,25,625,70);
TextOut(hdc,470,30," A Chord ->",11);
```

Figure 21-12 shows the chord section and its location on the user's screen.

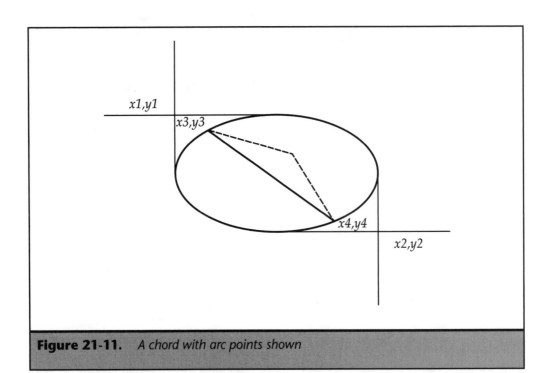

Figure 21-11. *A chord with arc points shown*

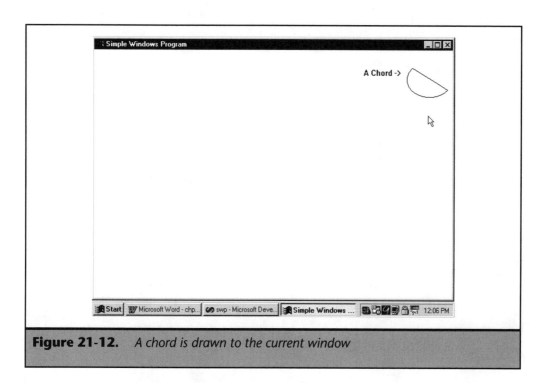

Figure 21-12. *A chord is drawn to the current window*

Drawing a Pie Wedge

Use the Pie( ) function for drawing pie-shaped wedges. The center of the elliptical arc is also the center of an imaginary rectangle described by the points *x1,y1* and *x2,y2*, as shown in Figure 21-13.

The starting and ending points of the arc are points *x3,y3* and *x4,y4*. Two lines are drawn from each end point to the center of the rectangle. Drawing is done in a counterclockwise direction. The pie wedge is filled because it is a closed figure. The handle for the device context is given by hdc. All other parameters are of type int. This function returns a type BOOL.

The syntax for the command is

Pie(*hdc,x1,y1,x2,y2,x3,y3,x4,y4*)

For example, the following code draws a small pie-shaped wedge in the window:

```
Pie(hdc,300,50,400,150,300,50,300,100);
TextOut(hdc,350,80,"<- A Pie Wedge",14);
```

Figure 21-14 shows the pie wedge on the screen.

WINDOWS
PROGRAMMING
FOUNDATIOINS

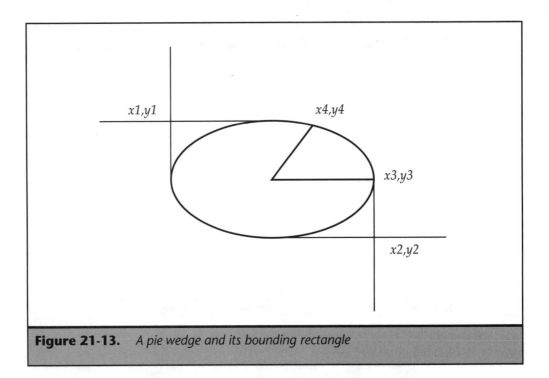

Figure 21-13. *A pie wedge and its bounding rectangle*

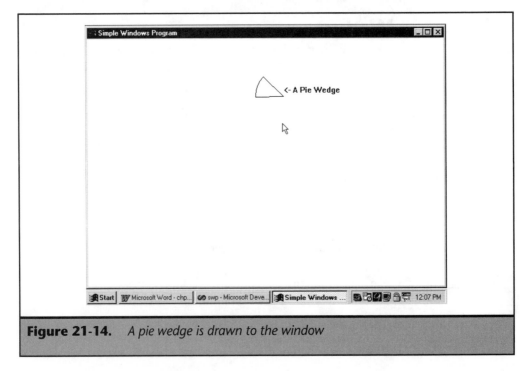

Figure 21-14. *A pie wedge is drawn to the window*

Drawing a Rectangle

The Rectangle( ) function draws a rectangle or box described by *x1,y1* and *x2,y2*. Again, the rectangle is filled because it is a closed figure. The values for the parameters cannot exceed 32,767 (7FFFH). The handle for the device context is given by hdc. All other parameters are of type int. This function returns a type BOOL.

The syntax for the command is

Rectangle(*hdc,x1,y1,x2,y2*)

As an example, the following code draws a rectangular figure in the user's window:

```
Rectangle(hdc,50,300,150,400);
TextOut(hdc,160,350,"<- A Rectangle",14);
```

Figure 21-15 shows the rectangle produced on the screen.

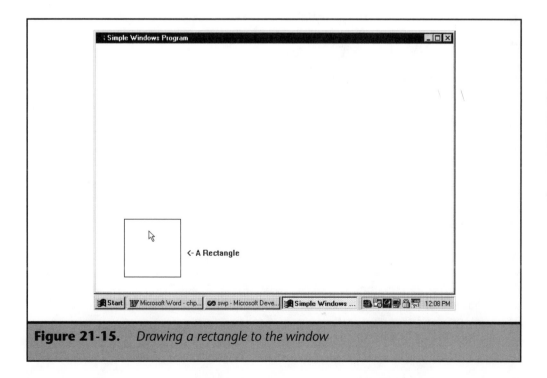

Figure 21-15. *Drawing a rectangle to the window*

Using the SWP.C as a Template

The previous section described the development of a simple application. That application can now serve as a template that will allow you to experiment with additional Windows functions. This template serves as the basis of many simple applications requiring only minor changes in coding. The next example illustrates how you can use the template to design a simple application that will draw a sine wave in the client area of a window.

Here is the SWP.C code modified to become the SINE.C application.

```c
/*
 * Sine.c
 * An application that draws a sine wave.
 * Developed using swp.c as a template.
 * Copyright (c) William H. Murray and Chris H. Pappas, 1997
 */

#include <windows.h>
#include <math.h>

#define pi 3.14159265359

LRESULT CALLBACK WndProc(HWND,UINT,WPARAM,LPARAM);

char szProgName[]="ProgName";

int WINAPI WinMain(HINSTANCE hInst,HINSTANCE hPreInst,
                   LPSTR lpszCmdLine,int nCmdShow)
{
  HWND hWnd;
  MSG  lpMsg;
  WNDCLASS wcApp;

  wcApp.lpszClassName=szProgName;
  wcApp.hInstance     =hInst;
  wcApp.lpfnWndProc   =WndProc;
  wcApp.hCursor       =LoadCursor(NULL,IDC_ARROW);
  wcApp.hIcon         =NULL;
  wcApp.lpszMenuName  =NULL;
  wcApp.hbrBackground=GetStockObject(WHITE_BRUSH);
  wcApp.style         =CS_HREDRAW|CS_VREDRAW;
  wcApp.cbClsExtra    =0;
  wcApp.cbWndExtra    =0;
```

```
    if (!RegisterClass (&wcApp))
      return 0;

    hWnd=CreateWindow(szProgName,"A Sine Wave",
                      WS_OVERLAPPEDWINDOW,CW_USEDEFAULT,
                      CW_USEDEFAULT,CW_USEDEFAULT,
                      CW_USEDEFAULT,(HWND)NULL,(HMENU)NULL,
                      (HANDLE)hInst,(LPSTR)NULL);
    ShowWindow(hWnd,nCmdShow);
    UpdateWindow(hWnd);
    while (GetMessage(&lpMsg,0,0,0)) {
      TranslateMessage(&lpMsg);
      DispatchMessage(&lpMsg);
    }
    return(lpMsg.wParam);
}

LRESULT CALLBACK WndProc(HWND hWnd,UINT messg,
                         WPARAM wParam,LPARAM lParam)
{
  HDC hdc;
  PAINTSTRUCT ps;

  double y;
  int i;

  switch (messg)
  {
    case WM_PAINT:
      hdc=BeginPaint(hWnd,&ps);

      /* draw the x & y coordinate axes */
      MoveToEx(hdc,100,50,NULL);
      LineTo(hdc,100,350);
      MoveToEx(hdc,100,200,NULL);
      LineTo(hdc,500,200);
      MoveToEx(hdc,100,200,NULL);

      /* draw the sine wave */
      for (i=0;i<400;i++) {
        y=120.0*sin(pi*i*(360.0/400.0)/180.0);
        LineTo(hdc,i+100,(int) (200.0-y));
```

```
        }

    ValidateRect(hWnd,NULL);
    EndPaint(hWnd,&ps);
    break;
  case WM_DESTROY:
    PostQuitMessage(0);
    break;
  default:
    return(DefWindowProc(hWnd,messg,wParam,lParam));
    break;
  }
  return(0);
}
```

In addition to the SINE.C file just shown, you will need a project file in order to compile and link the application within the integrated environment.

Examine the C source code and compare it with the previous SWP.C application. As you can see, this application makes only minor changes to the SWP.C template of the previous section.

Notice that new variables are declared in WndProc( ):

```
double y;
int i;
```

The actual sine wave plotting takes place under WM_PAINT. The coordinate axes are drawn with several calls to the MoveToEx( ) and LineTo( ) functions:

```
/* draw the x & y coordinate axes */
MoveToEx(hdc,100,50,NULL);
LineTo(hdc,100,350);
MoveToEx(hdc,100,200);
LineTo(hdc,500,200);
MoveToEx(hdc,100,200);
```

The sine wave is drawn and scaled in one operation. In this application, the waveform will extend 120 pixels above and below the horizontal axis. The sin( ) function from MATH.H is used to generate the sine values. The use of the constant PI is needed to convert angles from degrees to radians.

```
/* draw the sine wave */
for (i=0;i<400;i++) {
  y=120.0*sin(pi*i*(360.0/400.0)/180.0);
  LineTo(hdc,i+100,(int)(200.0-y));
}
```

Since this application was designed to work in the default drawing mode, the program draws directly in screen pixels. On a VGA monitor, the figure will fill the entire screen. Figure 21-16 shows the output of the program on a VGA screen. If a high-resolution monitor operating in 1024 x 768 graphics mode is used, the figure will be drawn in the upper-left corner of the monitor. Changes in figure size such as this are usually considered undesirable, and you'll see a technique for avoiding these variations in the PIE.C example that follows.

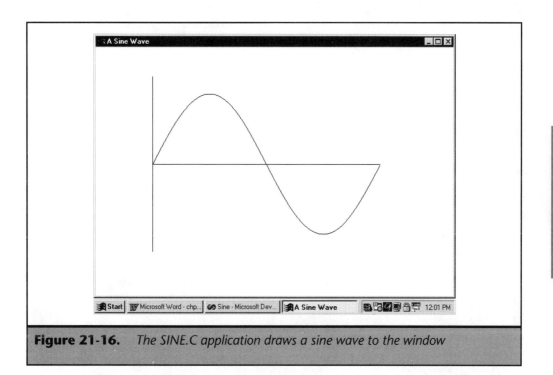

Figure 21-16. *The SINE.C application draws a sine wave to the window*

Creating a Windows Pie Chart Application

A *pie chart* is a useful business application that also allows you to incorporate many of the resources studied in the last chapter into a presentation-quality program. This particular pie chart will use a menu, an About dialog box, and a data entry dialog box for user input. All three items, you might recall, were designed in the previous chapter. The data entry dialog box will prompt the user to enter up to ten numbers that define the size of each pie wedge. These integer numbers are then scaled in order to make each pie slice proportional in the 360-degree pie chart. Slices are colored in a sequential manner. The sequence is defined by the programmer and contained in the global array lColor[]. The program also allows the user to enter a title for the pie chart that is centered below the pie figure. You may wish to continue the development of this example by adding a legend, label, or value for each pie slice.

Before compiling and linking, you will need to enter four separate files: PIE.H, PIE.RC, PIE.C, and PIE.CUR. The cursor was created with the resource editor, too.

Start this project by creating a new project file named PIE.DSP. If you are entering the code from the following listings, you will simply open several empty text files with the Project | Add | Files... menu selection and name them appropriately.

Here is the PIE.H header file containing unique identification numbers for menu, dialog, and other resource items.

```
#define IDM_ABOUT     10
#define IDM_INPUT     20
#define IDM_EXIT      30

#define DM_TITLE     160
#define DM_P1        161
#define DM_P2        162
#define DM_P3        163
#define DM_P4        164
#define DM_P5        165
#define DM_P6        166
#define DM_P7        167
#define DM_P8        168
#define DM_P9        169
#define DM_P10       170
```

The PIE.RC resource script file defines a menu and two dialog boxes (see Chapter 20 for additional details). See if you can identify this information in the following listing:

```
//Microsoft Developer Studio generated resource script.
//
#include "resource.h"

#define APSTUDIO_READONLY_SYMBOLS
/////////////////////////////////////////////////////////////////
//
// Generated from the TEXTINCLUDE 2 resource.
//
#include "pie.h"
#define APSTUDIO_HIDDEN_SYMBOLS
#include "windows.h"
#undef APSTUDIO_HIDDEN_SYMBOLS


/////////////////////////////////////////////////////////////////
#undef APSTUDIO_READONLY_SYMBOLS


/////////////////////////////////////////////////////////////////
// English (U.S.) resources

#if !defined(AFX_RESOURCE_DLL) || defined(AFX_TARG_ENU)
#ifdef _WIN32
LANGUAGE LANG_ENGLISH, SUBLANG_ENGLISH_US
#pragma code_page(1252)
#endif //_WIN32


/////////////////////////////////////////////////////////////////
//
// Cursor
//


PIECURSOR CURSOR DISCARDABLE "pie.cur"


/////////////////////////////////////////////////////////////////
//
// Menu
//


PIEMENU MENU DISCARDABLE
BEGIN
  POPUP "Pie_Chart_Data"
  BEGIN
```

```
      MENUITEM "About...",  IDM_ABOUT
      MENUITEM "Input...",  IDM_INPUT
      MENUITEM "Exit",      IDM_EXIT
   END
END


////////////////////////////////////////////////////////////
//
// Dialog
//

ABOUTDLGBOX DIALOG DISCARDABLE  50, 300, 180, 84
STYLE DS_MODALFRAME|WS_POPUP|WS_VISIBLE|WS_CAPTION|WS_SYSMENU
CAPTION "About"
FONT 8, "MS Sans Serif"
BEGIN
  CTEXT "Microsoft C Pie Chart Program",-1,3,29,176,10
  CTEXT "by William H. Murray and Chris H. Pappas",-1,3,16,
        176,10
  PUSHBUTTON "OK",IDOK,74,51,32,14
END

PIEDLGBOX DIALOG DISCARDABLE  93, 37, 195, 159
STYLE DS_MODALFRAME|WS_POPUP|WS_VISIBLE|WS_CAPTION|WS_SYSMENU
CAPTION "Pie Chart Data"
FONT 8, "MS Sans Serif"
BEGIN
  GROUPBOX "Chart Title:",100,5,3,182,30,WS_TABSTOP
  GROUPBOX "Pie Wedge Sizes:",101,3,34,187,95,WS_TABSTOP
  LTEXT "Title: ",-1,10,21,30,8
  EDITTEXT DM_TITLE,40,18,140,12
  LTEXT "Wedge #1: ",-1,10,50,40,8,NOT WS_GROUP
  LTEXT "Wedge #2: ",-1,10,65,40,8,NOT WS_GROUP
  LTEXT "Wedge #3: ",-1,10,80,40,8,NOT WS_GROUP
  LTEXT "Wedge #4: ",-1,10,95,40,8,NOT WS_GROUP
  LTEXT "Wedge #5: ",-1,10,110,40,8,NOT WS_GROUP
  LTEXT "Wedge #6: ",-1,106,50,40,8,NOT WS_GROUP
  LTEXT "Wedge #7: ",-1,106,65,40,8,NOT WS_GROUP
  LTEXT "Wedge #8: ",-1,106,80,40,8,NOT WS_GROUP
  LTEXT "Wedge #9: ",-1,106,95,40,8,NOT WS_GROUP
  LTEXT "Wedge #10:",-1,102,110,45,8,NOT WS_GROUP
```

```
    EDITTEXT DM_P1,55,45,30,12
    EDITTEXT DM_P2,55,60,30,12
    EDITTEXT DM_P3,55,75,30,12
    EDITTEXT DM_P4,55,90,30,12
    EDITTEXT DM_P5,55,105,30,12
    EDITTEXT DM_P6,150,44,30,12
    EDITTEXT DM_P7,150,61,30,12
    EDITTEXT DM_P8,150,76,30,12
    EDITTEXT DM_P9,149,91,30,12
    EDITTEXT DM_P10,149,106,30,12
    PUSHBUTTON "OK",IDOK,39,135,24,14
    PUSHBUTTON "Cancel",IDCANCEL,122,136,34,14
END


#ifdef APSTUDIO_INVOKED
/////////////////////////////////////////////////////////////
//
// TEXTINCLUDE
//

1 TEXTINCLUDE DISCARDABLE
BEGIN
    "resource.h\0"
END

2 TEXTINCLUDE DISCARDABLE
BEGIN
    "#include ""pie.h""\r\n"
    "#define APSTUDIO_HIDDEN_SYMBOLS\r\n"
    "#include ""windows.h""\r\n"
    "#undef APSTUDIO_HIDDEN_SYMBOLS\r\n"
    "\0"
END

3 TEXTINCLUDE DISCARDABLE
BEGIN
    "\r\n"
    "\0"
END

#endif    // APSTUDIO_INVOKED
```

```
#endif    // English (U.S.) resources
//////////////////////////////////////////////////////////////


#ifndef APSTUDIO_INVOKED
//////////////////////////////////////////////////////////////
//
// Generated from the TEXTINCLUDE 3 resource.
//


//////////////////////////////////////////////////////////////
#endif    // not APSTUDIO_INVOKED
```

Remember that the PIE.RC file is simply the text file equivalent to the menu and dialog boxes that were developed by the resource editors and discussed in the previous chapter.

The PIE.C source code is the last listing in this group of files. The length of this file has grown when compared to previous source code files because of the dialog box procedures. However, as you study the listing, you should still be able to locate elements of the SWP.C template.

```
/*
 *  PIE.C
 *  A Pie Chart Application with Resources
 *  Copyright (c) William H. Murray and Chris H. Pappas, 1997
 */

#include <windows.h>
#include <string.h>
#include <math.h>
#include "pie.h"

#define radius      180
#define maxnumwedge 10
#define pi          3.14159265359

LRESULT CALLBACK WndProc(HWND,UINT,WPARAM,LPARAM);
BOOL CALLBACK AboutDlgProc(HWND,UINT,WPARAM,LPARAM);
BOOL CALLBACK PieDlgProc(HWND,UINT,WPARAM,LPARAM);

char szProgName[]="ProgName";
```

```
char szApplName[]="PieMenu";
char szCursorName[]="PieCursor";

char szTString[80]="(bar chart title area)";
unsigned int iWedgesize[maxnumwedge]={5,20,10,15};
long lColor[maxnumwedge]={0x0L,0xFFL,0xFF00L,0xFFFFL,0xFF0000L,
                          0xFF00FFL,0xFFFF00L,0xFFFFFFL,
                          0x8080L,0x808080L};

int WINAPI WinMain(HINSTANCE hInst,HINSTANCE hPreInst,
                   LPSTR lpszCmdLine,int nCmdShow)
{
  HWND hWnd;
  MSG  lpMsg;
  WNDCLASS wcApp;

  wcApp.lpszClassName=szProgName;
  wcApp.hInstance     =hInst;
  wcApp.lpfnWndProc   =WndProc;
  wcApp.hCursor       =LoadCursor(hInst,szCursorName);
  wcApp.hIcon         =LoadIcon(hInst,szProgName);
  wcApp.lpszMenuName  =szApplName;
  wcApp.hbrBackground=GetStockObject(WHITE_BRUSH);
  wcApp.style         =CS_HREDRAW|CS_VREDRAW;
  wcApp.cbClsExtra    =0;
  wcApp.cbWndExtra    =0;
  if (!RegisterClass (&wcApp))
    return 0;

  hWnd=CreateWindow(szProgName,"C Pie Chart Program",
                    WS_OVERLAPPEDWINDOW,CW_USEDEFAULT,
                    CW_USEDEFAULT,CW_USEDEFAULT,
                    CW_USEDEFAULT,(HWND)NULL,(HMENU)NULL,
                    (HANDLE)hInst,(LPSTR)NULL);
  ShowWindow(hWnd,nCmdShow);
  UpdateWindow(hWnd);
  while (GetMessage(&lpMsg,0,0,0))
  {
    TranslateMessage(&lpMsg);
    DispatchMessage(&lpMsg);
  }
  return(lpMsg.wParam);
```

```
}

BOOL CALLBACK AboutDlgProc(HWND hdlg,UINT messg,
                           WPARAM wParam,LPARAM lParam)
{
  switch (messg)
  {
    case WM_INITDIALOG:
      break;
    case WM_COMMAND:
      switch (wParam)
      {
        case IDOK:
          EndDialog(hdlg,TRUE);
          break;
        default:
          return FALSE;
      }
      break;
    default:
      return FALSE;
  }
  return TRUE;
}


BOOL CALLBACK PieDlgProc(HWND hdlg,UINT messg,
                         WPARAM wParam,LPARAM lParam)
{
  switch (messg)
  {
    case WM_INITDIALOG:
      return FALSE;
    case WM_COMMAND:
      switch (wParam)
      {
        case IDOK:
          GetDlgItemText(hdlg,DM_TITLE,szTString,80);
          iWedgesize[0]=GetDlgItemInt(hdlg,DM_P1,NULL,0);
          iWedgesize[1]=GetDlgItemInt(hdlg,DM_P2,NULL,0);
          iWedgesize[2]=GetDlgItemInt(hdlg,DM_P3,NULL,0);
          iWedgesize[3]=GetDlgItemInt(hdlg,DM_P4,NULL,0);
          iWedgesize[4]=GetDlgItemInt(hdlg,DM_P5,NULL,0);
```

```
            iWedgesize[5]=GetDlgItemInt(hdlg,DM_P6,NULL,0);
            iWedgesize[6]=GetDlgItemInt(hdlg,DM_P7,NULL,0);
            iWedgesize[7]=GetDlgItemInt(hdlg,DM_P8,NULL,0);
            iWedgesize[8]=GetDlgItemInt(hdlg,DM_P9,NULL,0);
            iWedgesize[9]=GetDlgItemInt(hdlg,DM_P10,NULL,0);
            EndDialog(hdlg,TRUE);
            break;
          case IDCANCEL:
            EndDialog(hdlg,FALSE);
            break;
          default:
            return FALSE;
      }
      break;
    default:
      return FALSE;
  }
  return TRUE;
}

LRESULT CALLBACK WndProc(HWND hWnd,UINT messg,
                         WPARAM wParam,LPARAM lParam)
{
  HDC hdc;
  PAINTSTRUCT ps;
  HBRUSH hBrush;
  static FARPROC lpfnAboutDlgProc;
  static FARPROC lpfnPieDlgProc;
  static HWND hInst1,hInst2;
  static short xClientView,yClientView;

  unsigned int iTotalWedge[maxnumwedge+1];
  int i,iNWedges;

  iNWedges=0;
  for (i=0;i<maxnumwedge;i++) {
    if(iWedgesize[i]!=0) iNWedges++;
  }

  iTotalWedge[0]=0;

  for (i=0;i<iNWedges;i++)
```

```
  iTotalWedge[i+1]=iTotalWedge[i]+iWedgesize[i];

switch (messg)
{
  case WM_SIZE:
    xClientView=LOWORD(lParam);
    yClientView=HIWORD(lParam);
    break;
  case WM_CREATE:
    hInst1=((LPCREATESTRUCT) lParam)->hInstance;
    hInst2=((LPCREATESTRUCT) lParam)->hInstance;
    lpfnAboutDlgProc=MakeProcInstance(AboutDlgProc,
                                      hInst1);
    lpfnPieDlgProc=MakeProcInstance(PieDlgProc,hInst2);
    break;
  case WM_COMMAND:
    switch (wParam)
    {
      case IDM_ABOUT:
        DialogBox(hInst1,"AboutDlgBox",hWnd,
                  lpfnAboutDlgProc);
        break;
      case IDM_INPUT:
        DialogBox(hInst2,"PieDlgBox",
                  hWnd,lpfnPieDlgProc);
        InvalidateRect(hWnd,NULL,TRUE);
        UpdateWindow(hWnd);
        break;
      case IDM_EXIT:
        SendMessage(hWnd,WM_CLOSE,0,0L);
        break;
      default:
        break;
    }
    break;
  case WM_PAINT:
    hdc=BeginPaint(hWnd,&ps);

    SetMapMode(hdc,MM_ISOTROPIC);
    SetWindowExtEx(hdc,500,500,NULL);
    SetViewportExtEx(hdc,xClientView,-yClientView,NULL);
```

```
        SetViewportOrgEx(hdc,xClientView/2,yClientView/2,NULL);

        if (xClientView > 200)
          TextOut(hdc,strlen(szTString)*(-8/2),
                  240,szTString,strlen(szTString));

        for(i=0;i<iNWedges;i++) {
          hBrush=CreateSolidBrush(lColor[i]);
          SelectObject(hdc,hBrush);
          Pie(hdc,-200,200,200,-200,
              (short)(radius*cos(2*pi*iTotalWedge[i]/
                      iTotalWedge[iNWedges])),
              (short)(radius*sin(2*pi*iTotalWedge[i]/
                      iTotalWedge[iNWedges])),
              (short)(radius*cos(2*pi*iTotalWedge[i+1]/
                      iTotalWedge[iNWedges])),
              (short)(radius*sin(2*pi*iTotalWedge[i+1]/
                      iTotalWedge[iNWedges])));
        }


        ValidateRect(hWnd,NULL);
        EndPaint(hWnd,&ps);
        break;
      case WM_DESTROY:
        PostQuitMessage(0);
        break;
      default:
        return(DefWindowProc(hWnd,messg,wParam,lParam));
  }
  return(0);
}
```

In the next sections we'll look at the important components that make up the complete pie project.

The Project File

Use the project utility from within the integrated environment to build a project file for this application. Include the PIE.C and PIE.RC files in the project's file list.

The PIE.H Header File

The header file PIE.H contains identification information for various menu and dialog items. Additionally, note the ten unique identification numbers, which represent the ten values for wedge sizes. These values are eventually entered by the user.

The PIE.RC Resource File

The resource file PIE.RC contains information in script form for the pointer (PieCursor), menu (PieMenu), and two dialog boxes (AboutDlgBox and PieDlgBox). Figure 21-17 shows the About box, and Figure 21-18 shows the data entry dialog box.

The design of both of these dialog boxes was discussed in the previous chapter. This composite resource script file was created by the resource editor as each resource was added to the project. When using the resource editor to add dialog boxes, you must have a fairly clear idea of how you want to represent various data fields and other elements before starting the design. The control values are used to determine the position, size, and so on of dialog box items. These values are calculated by the resource editor. If you are entering this program, it will be easiest for you just to type this resource file as it appears in the listing.

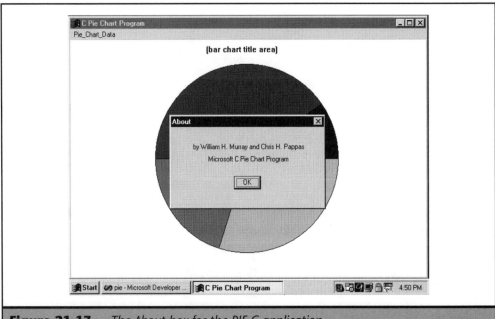

Figure 21-17. *The About box for the PIE.C application*

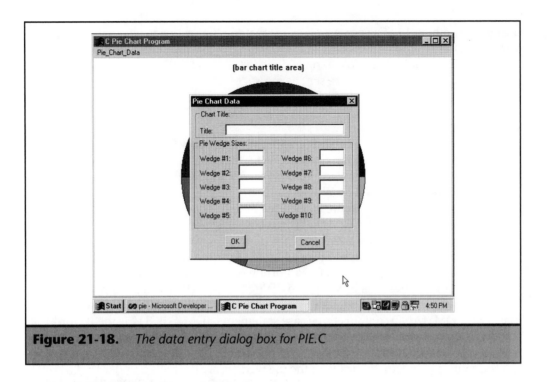

Figure 21-18. *The data entry dialog box for PIE.C*

The PIE.C Source Code

The C source code for PIE.C allows the user to develop a pie chart with as many as ten slices. An application will allow the user to input the data on pie-slice sizes directly to a dialog box. In addition to data on pie sizes, the user may enter the title of the pie chart. Don't let the size of this code listing scare you; much of the code is an extension of the SWP.C template code developed in the first example of this chapter. It would be a good idea to compare the SWP.C and PIE.C code at this time and discover the exact differences in the listings. This example concentrates on the new concepts for the application by extracting each important feature from the listing.

Dialog box information is processed with the case IDOK statement under the PieDlgProc. When the user selects the data entry item (a dialog box) from the program's menu, they will be allowed to enter a pie chart title and the data for up to ten pie slices. This data is accepted when the user selects the OK push button. The title is returned as a text string with the GetDlgItemText( ) function. Numeric information is returned with the GetDlgItemInt( ) function. This function translates the "numeric" string information entered by the user into an integer that can be a signed or unsigned number. The GetDlgItemInt( ) function requires four parameters. The handle and ID number are self-explanatory. The third parameter, which is NULL in this case, is used to flag a successful conversion. The fourth parameter is used to indicate signed and unsigned numbers. In this case, a zero states that the dialog box is returning unsigned numbers. These numbers are saved in the global array iWedgesize[ ] for future use.

The major work in this application is done in the WindowProc( ) function. Various pieces of information and data are sent as messages and examined by the five case statements. Study the code and make sure you can find these "message" case statements: WM_SIZE, WM_CREATE, WM_COMMAND, WM_PAINT, and WM_DESTROY.

Determining the size of the client or application window is achieved with the help of WM_SIZE. Windows sends a message to WM_SIZE any time the window is resized. In this case, the size will be returned in two variables, xClientView and yClientView. This information will be used by WM_PAINT to scale the pie chart to the window.

The program's instance handle is obtained and saved as hInst1 and hInst2 when processing messages to WM_CREATE. These values are used by the MakeProcInstance( ) function to create an instance thunk for each dialog box procedure or function. This is necessary because each dialog box procedure is a far procedure. The address returned by MakeProcInstance( ) points to a fixed portion of memory called the instance thunk. Two are required in this case because two dialog box procedures are being used.

Dialog boxes can be opened with messages sent to WM_COMMAND. Notice that WM_COMMAND contains three case statements. IDM_ABOUT is the ID for the About Box procedure, while IDM_INPUT is the ID for the data entry dialog box. IDM_EXIT allows a graceful exit from the application.

The routines for actually drawing the pie wedges are processed under WM_PAINT.

The mapping mode is changed to MM_ISOTROPIC from MM_TEXT. The default mapping mode is MM_TEXT. When in the MM_TEXT mapping mode, drawings are made in "pixel" coordinates with point 0,0 in the upper-left corner of the window. This is why the SINE.C example remained unchanged as the number of pixels changed in the client area.

```
SetMapMode(hdc,MM_ISOTROPIC);
SetWindowExtEx(hdc,500,500NULL);
SetViewportExtEx(hdc,xClientView,-yClientViewNULL);
SetViewportOrgEx(hdc,xClientView/2,yClientView/2NULL);
```

Table 21-4 shows additional mapping modes available under Windows.

MM_ISOTROPIC allows you to select the extent of both the x and y axes. The mapping mode is changed by calling the function SetMapMode( ). When the function SetWindowExt( ) is called, with both parameters set to 500, the height and width of the client or application area are equal. These are logical sizes, which Windows adjusts (scales) to fit the physical display device. The display size values are used by the SetViewportExt( ) function. The negative sign for the y coordinate specifies increasing y values from the bottom of the screen. It should be no surprise that these are the values previously obtained under WM_SIZE.

Value	Meaning
MM_ANISOTROPIC	Maps one logical unit to an arbitrary physical unit; x and y axes are scaled.
MM_HIENGLISH	Maps one logical unit to 0.001 inch; positive y is up.
MM_HIMETRIC	Maps one logical unit to 0.01 millimeter; positive y is up.
MM_ISOTROPIC	Maps one logical unit to an arbitrary physical unit; x and y unit lengths are equal.
MM_LOENGLISH	Maps one logical unit to 0.01 inch; positive y points up.
MM_LOMETRIC	Maps one logical unit to 0.1 millimeter; positive y points up.
MM_TEXT	Maps one logical unit to one pixel; positive y points down. This is the default mode.
MM_TWIPS	Maps one logical unit to 1/20 of a printer's point; positive y points up.

Table 21-4. *Windows Mapping Modes*

For this example, the pie chart will be placed on a traditional x,y coordinate system, with the center of the chart at 0,0. The SetViewportOrg( ) function is used for this purpose.

The pie chart title is printed to the screen using the coordinates for the current mapping mode. The program centers the title on the screen by estimating the size of the character font and knowing the string length. For really small windows, the title is not printed.

```
if (xClientView > 200) {
  TextOut(hdc,strlen(szTString)*(-8/2),
          240,szTString,strlen(szTString));
}
```

Before actually discussing how the pie wedges are plotted, let's return to the beginning of the WndProc procedure in order to gain an understanding of how the wedges are scaled to fit a complete circle. There are several pieces of code that are very important.

This code determines how many wedges have been requested by the user:

```
iNWedges=0;
for (i=0;i<maxnumwedge;i++) {
  if(iWedgesize[i]!=0) iNWedges++;
}
```

It is assumed that there is at least one wedge of some physical size, so the array iWedgesize[ ] can be scanned for the first zero value. For each nonzero value returned, iNWedges will be incremented. Thus, when leaving this routine, iNWedges will contain the total number of wedges for this plot.

A progressive total on wedge size values will be returned to the iTotalWedge[ ] array. These values will help determine where one pie slice ends and the next begins. For example, if the user entered 5, 10, 7, and 20 for wedge sizes, iTotalWedge[ ] would contain the values 0, 5, 15, 22, and 42. Study the following code to make sure you understand how these results are achieved:

```
iTotalWedge[0]=0;
for (i=0;i<iNWedges;i++)
  iTotalWedge[i+1]=iTotalWedge[i]+iWedgesize[i];
```

The values contained in iTotalWedge[ ] are needed in order to calculate the beginning and ending angles for each pie wedge. You might recall that the Pie( ) function accepts nine parameters. The first parameter is the handle, and the next four specify the coordinates of the bounding rectangle. In this case, for the mapping mode chosen, they are -200, 200, 200, and -200. The remaining four parameters are used to designate the starting x,y pair and the ending x,y pair for the pie arc. To calculate x values, the cosine function is used, and to calculate y values, the sine function is used. For example, the first x position is determined by multiplying the radius of the pie by the cosine of 2*pi*iTotalWedge[0]. The 2*pi value is needed in the conversion of degrees to radians. The y value is found with the sine function in an identical way. Those two values serve as the x,y starting coordinates for the first slice. The ending coordinates are found with the same equations, but using the next value in iTotalWedge[ ]. In order to scale each of these points to make all slices proportional and fit a 360-degree pie, each coordinate point is divided by the grand total of all individual slices. This total is the last number contained in iTotalWedge[ ]. Observe how this calculation is achieved in the next piece of code:

```
for(i=0;i<iNWedges;i++) {
  hBrush=CreateSolidBrush(lColor[i]);
  SelectObject(hdc,hBrush);
```

```
Pie(hdc,-200,200,200,-200,
    (short)(radius*cos(2*pi*iTotalWedge[i]/
            iTotalWedge[iNWedges])),
    (short)(radius*sin(2*pi*iTotalWedge[i]/
            iTotalWedge[iNWedges])),
    (short)(radius*cos(2*pi*iTotalWedge[i+1]/
            iTotalWedge[iNWedges])),
    (short)(radius*sin(2*pi*iTotalWedge[i+1]/
            iTotalWedge[iNWedges])));
}
```

In order to draw and fill all slices, a loop is used. This loop will index through all iNWedge values.

Figure 21-19 shows the default pie chart plot, and Figure 21-20 shows a unique pie chart application.

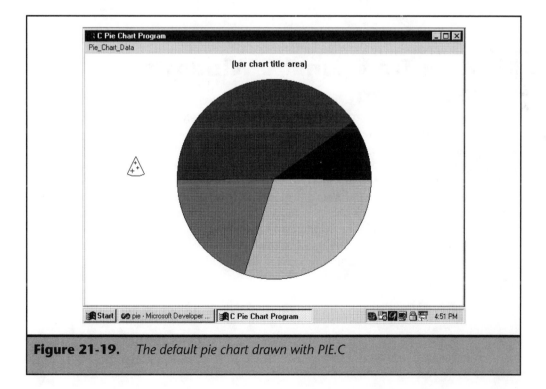

Figure 21-19. *The default pie chart drawn with PIE.C*

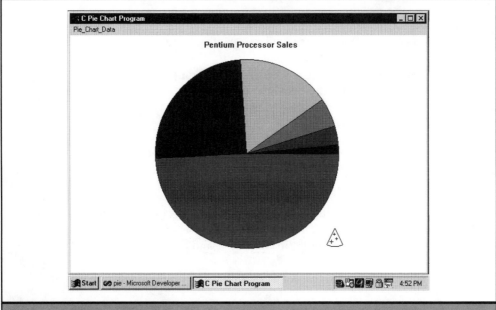

Figure 21-20.   *A unique pie chart created with PIE.C*

More on Traditional C Windows Programming

The procedure-oriented programming techniques presented in this chapter have been used by most C programmers, when developing Windows applications. You will find code similar to this C code in many books and magazine articles.

Applications developed in C++ can have a similar structure and appearance to the C code in this chapter. More importantly, however, C++ applications can take advantage of object-oriented concepts and include the advantages of Microsoft's Foundation Class' library. This library provides the programmer with access to reusable code—a chief advantage of C++. Many authors and programmers are suggesting that all Windows applications be developed with object-oriented programming techniques. These techniques will be the primary focus in the remainder of this book.

The
Complete
Reference

Visual
C++ 5

Chapter 22

Microsoft Foundation Class
Library: Concepts

In Chapter 21, you learned that even the simplest Windows applications, when created with the standard API function calls, are difficult and time consuming to develop. For example, the bare bones SWP.C template from Chapter 21 contains over two pages of C code and Windows function calls. You also learned that much of that code is used repeatedly from application to application. That base code is required just to establish a window on the screen. While Windows applications have been easy to use, procedure-oriented applications have certainly not been a joy to write.

Microsoft's Visual C++ compiler provides a 32-bit Foundation Class library containing a new set of object-oriented programming tools for the development of 32-bit Windows applications. The Microsoft Foundation Class (MFC) library provided with version 5 of Visual C++ encapsulates all normal procedure-oriented Windows functions and provides support for control bars, property sheets, OLEO, ActiveX controls, and more. In addition, database support is provided for a wide range of database sources, including DAO and ODBC. You'll also find that the MFC supports the development of Internet applications in C++.

This chapter examines the advantages of using the Microsoft Foundation Class library for Windows code development. The MFC library will make Windows application development easier. Also discussed are MFC terms, definitions, and techniques that are common across all Foundation Class versions. The material you learn in this chapter can be applied to all of the MFC application code developed in the remaining chapters of this book. You can determine the role of the MFC library when you realize that one chapter of this book was devoted to conventional procedure-oriented programming while all of the remaining chapters are devoted to object-oriented programming with the MFC!

You may want to take the time to review object-oriented terminology and programming techniques discussed earlier in Chapters 13 through 19 before tackling the MFC terminology presented in this chapter.

The MFC is a powerful toolkit for the object-oriented programmer. If conventional Windows developers have a hammer and crosscut saw in their toolkit, the C++ Windows developer, using the MFC, is equipped with a pneumatic hammer and circular power saw.

The Need for a Foundation Class Library

The Foundation Class library provides you with easy-to-use objects. From its very inception, Windows has followed many principles of object-oriented programming design, within the framework of a non-object-oriented language like C. These features were discussed in the previous two chapters. The marriage of C++ and Windows was a natural that can take full advantage of object-oriented features. The MFC development team designed a comprehensive implementation of the Windows Application Program Interface (API). This C++ library encapsulates the most important data structures and API function calls within a group of reusable classes.

Class libraries such as the MFC offer many advantages over the traditional function libraries used by C programmers and discussed in the previous two chapters. This list includes many of the usual advantages of C++ classes, such as

■ Encapsulation of code and data within the class

■ Inheritance

■ Elimination of function and variable name collisions

■ Resulting classes appearing to be natural extensions of the language

■ Often, reduced code size resulting from well-designed class libraries

With the use of the Foundation Class library, the code required to establish a window has been reduced to approximately one-third the length of a conventional application. This allows you, the developer, to spend less time communicating with Windows and more time developing your application's code.

MFC Design Considerations

The Foundation Class library design team set rigorous design principles that had to be followed in the implementation of the MFC library. These principles and guidelines include the following:

■ Utilize the power of C++ without overwhelming the programmer.

■ Make the transition from standard API function calls to the use of class libraries as simple as possible.

■ Allow the mixing of traditional function calls with the use of new class libraries.

■ Balance power and efficiency in the design of class libraries.

■ Produce a class library that can migrate easily to evolving platforms, such as Windows 95 and NT.

The design team felt that good code design had to start with the MFC library itself. The C++ foundation classes are designed to be small in size and fast in execution time. Their simplicity makes them very easy to use, and their execution speed is close to the bulkier function libraries of C.

These classes were designed in a way that requires minimal relearning of function names for seasoned Windows programmers. This feature was achieved by carefully naming and designing class features. As a matter of fact, Microsoft identifies this feature as the "single characteristic that sets the MFC apart from other class libraries…"

The MFC team also designed the Foundation Class library to allow a "mixed-mode" operation. That is, classes and traditional function calls can be intermixed in the same source code. Functions, such as SetCursor( ) and GetSystemMetrics( ), require direct calls, even when using the MFC.

Microsoft was also aware that class libraries should be usable. Some class libraries, provided by other manufacturers, are designed with too high a level of abstraction. These "heavy classes," as Microsoft calls them, tend to produce applications that are large in size and slow in execution. The MFC library provides a reasonable level of abstraction while keeping code sizes small.

The development team designed the original MFC library to be dynamic rather than static. The dynamic architecture has allowed the classes to be scaled to the growing Windows 95 and NT environments we now have.

Key MFC Library Features

Class libraries for Windows are available from other compiler manufacturers, but Microsoft claims a number of real advantages for its MFC library:

■ Complete support for all Windows functions, controls, messages, GDI (graphics device interface) graphics primitives, menus, and dialog boxes.

■ Use of the same naming convention as the conventional Windows API. Thus, the action of a class is immediately recognized by its name.

■ Elimination of many switch/case statements that are a source of error. All messages are mapped to member functions, within a class. This direct message-to-method mapping is available for all messages.

■ Better diagnostics support through the ability to send information about objects to a file. Also included is the ability to validate member variables.

■ An extensive exception-handling design that makes application code less subject to failure. Support for "out of memory" and other problems is provided.

■ Determination of a data object's type at run-time. This allows for a dynamic manipulation of a field when classes are instantized.

■ Small code with a fast implementation. As mentioned earlier, the MFC library adds only a small amount of object code overhead and executes almost as quickly as conventional C Windows applications.

■ Support for the Component Object Model.

The experienced Windows programmer will immediately appreciate two of these features: the familiar naming convention and the message-to-method mapping. If you reexamine the source code for the applications developed in Chapter 21, you will see extensive use of the error-prone switch/case statements. Also notice that these applications make extensive use of API function calls. Both groups of problems are eliminated or reduced when you use the MFC.

Professional developers will certainly appreciate Microsoft's dedication to better diagnostics and the small code overhead imposed by the MFC library. Now programmers can take advantage of the MFC library without gaining a size penalty on their application's code.

The bottom line is that the MFC library is the only real ball game in town!

It All Begins with CObject

Libraries such as the MFC library often start with a few parent classes. Additional classes are then derived from the parent classes. CObject is one parent class used extensively in developing Windows applications. The MFC library header files located in the MFC/INCLUDE subdirectory provide a wealth of information on defined classes.

Let's take a brief look at CObject, which is defined in the AFX.H header file.

```
//////////////////////////////////////////////////////////////
// class CObject is the root of all compliant objects

class CObject
{
public:

// Object model (types, destruction, allocation)
  virtual CRuntimeClass* GetRuntimeClass( ) const;
  virtual ~CObject( );   // virtual destructors are necessary

  // Diagnostic allocations
  void* PASCAL operator new(size_t nSize);
  void* PASCAL operator new(size_t, void* p);
  void PASCAL operator delete(void* p);

#if defined(_DEBUG) && !defined(_AFX_NO_DEBUG_CRT)
  // for file name/line number tracking using DEBUG_NEW
  void* PASCAL operator new(size_t nSize,
                            LPCSTR lpszFileName,
                            int nLine);
#endif

// Disable the copy constructor and assignment by default
// so you will get compiler errors instead of unexpected
// behavior if you pass objects by value or assign objects.

protected:
  CObject( );
```

```
private:
  CObject(const CObject& objectSrc);      //no implementation
  void operator=(const CObject& objectSrc);

// Attributes
public:
  BOOL IsSerializable( ) const;
  BOOL IsKindOf(const CRuntimeClass* pClass) const;

// Overridables
  virtual void Serialize(CArchive& ar);

  // Diagnostic Support
  virtual void AssertValid( ) const;
  virtual void Dump(CDumpContext& dc) const;

// Implementation
public:
  static const AFX_DATA CRuntimeClass classCObject;
#ifdef _AFXDLL
  static CRuntimeClass* PASCAL _GetBaseClass( );
#endif
};
```

This code has been edited slightly for clarity, but is essentially the same code you will find in the AFX.H header file.

Upon inspection of the CObject listing, notice the components that make up this class definition. First, CObject is divided into public, protected, and private parts. CObject also provides normal and dynamic type checking and serialization. Recall that dynamic type checking allows the type of object to be determined at run-time. The state of the object can be saved to a storage medium, such as a disk, through a concept called *persistence*. Object persistence allows object member functions to also be persistent, permitting retrieval of object data.

Child classes are derived from parent classes. CGdiObject is an example of a class derived from CObject. Here is the CGdiObject definition as found in AFXWIN.H. Again, this listing has been edited for clarity.

```
/////////////////////////////////////////////////////////////
// CGdiObject abstract class for CDC SelectObject

class CGdiObject : public CObject
{
  DECLARE_DYNCREATE(CGdiObject)
public:

// Attributes
  HGDIOBJ m_hObject;  // must be first data member
  operator HGDIOBJ( ) const;
  HGDIOBJ GetSafeHandle( ) const;

  static CGdiObject* PASCAL FromHandle(HGDIOBJ hObject);
  static void PASCAL DeleteTempMap( );
  BOOL Attach(HGDIOBJ hObject);
  HGDIOBJ Detach( );

// Constructors
  CGdiObject( ); // must create a derived class object
  BOOL DeleteObject( );

// Operations
  int GetObject(int nCount, LPVOID lpObject) const;
  UINT GetObjectType( ) const;
  BOOL CreateStockObject(int nIndex);
  BOOL UnrealizeObject( );
  BOOL operator==(const CGdiObject& obj) const;
  BOOL operator!=(const CGdiObject& obj) const;

// Implementation
public:
  virtual ~CGdiObject( );
#ifdef _DEBUG
  virtual void Dump(CDumpContext& dc) const;
  virtual void AssertValid( ) const;
#endif
};
```

CGdiObject and its member functions allow drawing items such as stock and custom pens, brushes, and fonts to be created and used in a Windows application. Classes, such as CPen, are further derived from the CGdiObject class.

Microsoft has provided complete source code for the MFC library in order to allow the utmost in programming flexibility and customization. However, for the beginner, it is not even necessary to know how the various classes are defined in order to use them efficiently.

For example, in traditional C Windows applications, the DeleteObject( ) function is called with the following syntax:

DeleteObject(hBRUSH); /*hBRUSH is the brush handle*/

In C++, with the MFC library, the same results will be achieved by accessing the member function with the following syntax:

newbrush.DeleteObject( ); //newbrush is current brush

As you can see, switching between C Windows function calls and class library objects can be intuitive. Microsoft has used this approach in developing all Windows classes, making the transition from traditional function calls to Foundation Class library objects very easy.

Important Foundation Library Classes

The following is an abbreviated list of important 32-bit MFC classes derived from CObject.

```
CObject
    CException
        CMemoryException
        CFileException
        CArchiveException
        CNotSupportedException
        CUserException
        COleException
            COleDispatchException
        CDBException
    CFile
        CStdioFile
        CMemFile
```

```
        COleStreamFile
CDC
    CClientDC
    CWindowDC
    CPaintDC
    CMetaFileDC
CGdiObject
    CPen
    CBrush
    CFont
    CBitmap
    CPalette
    CRgn
CMenu
CArray
CByteArray
CWordArray
CDWordArray
CPtrArray
CObArray
CStringArray
CUIntArray
CList
CPtrList
CObList
CStringList
CMap
CMapWordToPtr
CMapPtrToWord
CMapPtrToPtr
CMapWordToOb
CMapStringToPtr
CMapStringToOb
CMapStringToString
CDatabase
CRecordSet
CLongBinary
CCmdTarget
    CWinThread
        CWinApp
    CDocTemplate
```

```
            CSingleDocTemplate
            CMultiDocTemplate
        COleObjectFactory
            COleTemplateServer
        COleDataSource
        COleDropSource
        COleDropTarget
        COleMessageFilter
        CDocument
            COleDocument
                COleLinkingDoc
                    COleServerDoc
        CDocItem
            COleClientItem
            COleServerItem
    CWnd
        CFrameWnd
            CMDIChildWnd
            CMDIFrameWnd
            CMiniFrameWnd
            COleIPFrameWnd
        CControlBar
            CToolBar
            CStatusBar
            CDialogBar
            COleResizeBar
        CSplitterWnd
        CPropertySheet
        CDialog
            COleDialog
                COleInsertDialog
                COleChangeIconDialog
                COlePasteSpecialDialog
                COleConvertDialog
                COleBusyDialog
                COleLinksDialog
                    COleUpdateDialog
        CFileDialog
        CColorDialog
        CFontDialog
        CPrintDialog
```

```
CFindReplaceDialog
CPropertyPage
CView
    CScrollView
        CFormView
            CRecordView
CEditView
CStatic
CButton
    CBitmapButton
CListBox
CComboBox
CScrollBar
CEdit
```

From this list you can see and understand the general strategy in deriving one class or a group of classes from a parent class. Next is an abbreviated list of the 32-bit run-time object model support provided by the MFC.

```
CArchive
CDumpContext
CRuntimeClass
CString
CTime
CTimeSpan
CRect
CPoint
CSize
CFileStatus
CCreateContext
CPrintInfo
CMemoryState
CDataExchange
CFieldExchange
CCmdUI
COleDataObject
COleDispatchDriver
CRectTracker
CTypedPtrArray
CTypedPtrList
CTypedPtrMap
```

You'll want to put a bookmark at this spot. These tables will help you as you continue to study the MFC library in the remaining chapters of this book.

A Simplified Application

Before writing more complicated application code, let's see what is required to just establish a window on the screen. As mentioned earlier, to do this in C requires a program length of two pages. When you use the power of the MFC library, the initial program code can be reduced to one-third this size.

This section examines the simplest possible Windows application, SIMPLE.CPP. The simple application will establish a window on the screen and place a title in its title bar area.

Establishing a Window with SIMPLE.CPP

In order to compile this MFC application, you need to enter the source code that follows. The source code file, while initially strange in appearance, is certainly shorter than its procedure-oriented counterparts.

```
//
//   simple.cpp
//   The code needed to establish a window with
//   the Microsoft Foundation Class library
//   Copyright (c) William H. Murray and Chris H. Pappas, 1997
//

#include <afxwin.h>

class CTheApp : public CWinApp
{
public:
  virtual BOOL InitInstance( );
};

class CMainWnd : public CFrameWnd
{
public:
  CMainWnd( )
  {
    Create(NULL,"Hello MFC World",
           WS_OVERLAPPEDWINDOW,rectDefault,NULL,NULL);
  }
};
```

```
BOOL CTheApp::InitInstance( )
{
  m_pMainWnd=new CMainWnd( );
  m_pMainWnd->ShowWindow(m_nCmdShow);
  m_pMainWnd->UpdateWindow( );

  return TRUE;
}


CTheApp TheApp;
```

Once this C++ file is entered, you can compile this application from the integrated environment by creating a project file that includes the use of the MFC library.

The following sections examine how each piece of code works in establishing the window on the screen.

Using the AFXWIN.H

The AFXWIN.H header file is the gateway to Windows programming with the MFC library. This file calls all subsequent header files, including WINDOWS.H, as they are needed. Using one header file also aids in creating precompiled header files, which save time when repeated compilation is being done during application development.

It might be a good idea to print a copy of AFXWIN.H for your reference as you develop your own applications using the MFC library. However, be warned: this header file has grown to over 80 pages in the current version because of support for OLE features and so on.

Deriving a Class from CWinApp

This application starts by deriving a class, CTheApp, from the MFC parent class, CWinApp. This new object is defined by the programmer.

```
class CTheApp : public CWinApp
{
public:
  virtual BOOL InitInstance( );
};
```

The class CTheApp overrides the member function InitInstance( ) of CWinApp. You will find that overriding member functions occurs frequently. By overriding InitInstance( ), you can customize the initialization and execution of the application.

In CWinApp, it is also possible to override InitApplication( ), ExitInstance( ), and OnIdle( ), but for most applications this will not be necessary.

Here is an abbreviated portion of the CWinApp class description, as found in the AFXWIN.H header file:

```
/////////////////////////////////////////////////////////////
// CWinApp - the root of all Windows applications

class CWinApp : public CWinThread
{
  DECLARE_DYNAMIC(CWinApp)
public:

// Constructor
  CWinApp(LPCTSTR lpszAppName = NULL);   //app defaults
                                         //to EXE name

// Attributes
  // Startup args (do not change)
  HINSTANCE m_hInstance;
  HINSTANCE m_hPrevInstance;
  LPTSTR m_lpCmdLine;
  int m_nCmdShow;

  // Running args (can be changed in InitInstance)
  LPCTSTR m_pszAppName;
  LPCTSTR m_pszRegistryKey;   // used for registry entries
  CDocManager* m_pDocManager;

public:  // set in constructor to override default
  LPCTSTR m_pszExeName;       // executable name (no spaces)
  LPCTSTR m_pszHelpFilePath;  // default based on module path
  LPCTSTR m_pszProfileName;   // default based on app name

// Initialization Operations - should be done in InitInstance
protected:
  void LoadStdProfileSettings(UINT nMaxMRU = _AFX_MRU_COUNT);
  void EnableShellOpen( );

  void SetDialogBkColor(COLORREF clrCtlBk = RGB(192,192,192),
        COLORREF clrCtlText = RGB(0, 0, 0));
    // set dialog box and message box background color
```

```
  void SetRegistryKey(LPCTSTR lpszRegistryKey);
  void SetRegistryKey(UINT nIDRegistryKey);
    // enables app settings in registry instead of INI files
    //  (registry key is usually a "company name")

#ifdef _MAC
  friend void CFrameWnd::OnSysColorChange( );
  friend void CDialog::OnSysColorChange( );
#endif

  BOOL Enable3dControls( ); //use CTL3D32.DLL for 3D controls
#ifndef _AFXDLL
  BOOL Enable3dControlsStatic( );  //link CTL3D.LIB instead
#endif

  void RegisterShellFileTypes(BOOL bCompat=FALSE);
    // call after all doc templates are registered
  void RegisterShellFileTypesCompat( );
    // for backwards compatibility
  void UnregisterShellFileTypes( );

// Helper Operations - usually done in InitInstance
public:
  // Cursors
  HCURSOR LoadCursor(LPCTSTR lpszResourceName) const;
  HCURSOR LoadCursor(UINT nIDResource) const;
  HCURSOR LoadStandardCursor(LPCTSTR lpszCursorName) const;
  HCURSOR LoadOEMCursor(UINT nIDCursor) const;

  // Icons
  HICON LoadIcon(LPCTSTR lpszResourceName) const;
  HICON LoadIcon(UINT nIDResource) const;
  HICON LoadStandardIcon(LPCTSTR lpszIconName) const;
  HICON LoadOEMIcon(UINT nIDIcon) const;

      .
      .
      .

  // overrides for implementation
  virtual BOOL InitInstance( );
  virtual int ExitInstance( ); // return app exit code
  virtual int Run( );
  virtual BOOL OnIdle(LONG lCount);
```

WINDOWS PROGRAMMING FOUNDATIONS

```
   virtual LRESULT ProcessWndProcException(CException* e,
                                           const MSG* pMsg);

public:
  virtual ~CWinApp( );
     .
     .
     .
protected:
  //{{AFX_MSG(CWinApp)
  afx_msg void OnAppExit( );
  afx_msg void OnUpdateRecentFileMenu(CCmdUI* pCmdUI);
  afx_msg BOOL OnOpenRecentFile(UINT nID);
  //}}AFX_MSG
  DECLARE_MESSAGE_MAP( )
};
```

The CWinApp class is responsible for establishing and implementing the Windows message loop (discussed in Chapter 21). This action alone eliminates many lines of repetitive code.

CFrameWnd

The application's window, established by the CMainWnd class, is defined from the base class, CFrameWnd, as shown in the following segment of code:

```
class CMainWnd : public CFrameWnd
{
public:
  CMainWnd( )
  {
    Create(NULL,"Hello MFC World",
           WS_OVERLAPPEDWINDOW,rectDefault,NULL,NULL);
  }
};
```

The constructor for the class, CMainWnd( ), calls the Create( ) member function to establish initial window parameters. In this application, the window's style and caption are provided as parameters. You'll see in Chapter 23 that it is also possible to specify a menu name and an accelerator table when this member function is used.

Here is an abbreviated portion of CFrameWnd, also found in the AFXWIN.H header file:

```
//////////////////////////////////////////////////////////////
// CFrameWnd - base class for SDI and other frame windows

class CFrameWnd : public CWnd
{
  DECLARE_DYNCREATE(CFrameWnd)

// Constructors
public:
  static AFX_DATA const CRect rectDefault;
  CFrameWnd( );

  BOOL LoadAccelTable(LPCTSTR lpszResourceName);
  BOOL Create(LPCTSTR lpszClassName,
        LPCTSTR lpszWindowName,
        DWORD dwStyle = WS_OVERLAPPEDWINDOW,
        const RECT& rect = rectDefault,
        CWnd* pParentWnd = NULL,          // != NULL for popups
        LPCTSTR lpszMenuName = NULL,
        DWORD dwExStyle = 0,
        CCreateContext* pContext = NULL);

  // dynamic creation - load frame and associated resources
  virtual BOOL LoadFrame(UINT nIDResource,
        DWORD dwDefaultStyle = WS_OVERLAPPEDWINDOW |
                                FWS_ADDTOTITLE,
        CWnd* pParentWnd = NULL,
        CCreateContext* pContext = NULL);

  // special helper for view creation
  CWnd* CreateView(CCreateContext* pContext,
              UINT nID = AFX_IDW_PANE_FIRST);
   .
   .
   .
  // control bar docking
  void EnableDocking(DWORD dwDockStyle);
  void DockControlBar(CControlBar* pBar, UINT nDockBarID = 0,
    LPCRECT lpRect = NULL);
  void FloatControlBar(CControlBar* pBar, CPoint point,
    DWORD dwStyle = CBRS_ALIGN_TOP);
```

```
  CControlBar* GetControlBar(UINT nID);

    .
    .
    .
// Implementation
public:
  virtual ~CFrameWnd( );
  int m_nWindow;
  HMENU m_hMenuDefault;        // default menu resource
  HACCEL m_hAccelTable;        // accelerator table
  DWORD m_dwPromptContext;     // current help prompt
  BOOL m_bHelpMode;            // if TRUE, help mode is active
  CFrameWnd* m_pNextFrameWnd;  // CFrameWnd in app global list
  CRect m_rectBorder;          // OLE border space negotiation
  COleFrameHook* m_pNotifyHook;

  CPtrList m_listControlBars; // array of control bars that
                              // have this window as dock site
  int m_nShowDelay;           // SW_ command for delay show/hide


    .
    .
    .

  // Windows messages
  afx_msg int OnCreate(LPCREATESTRUCT lpCreateStruct);
  afx_msg void OnDestroy( );
  afx_msg void OnClose( );
  afx_msg void OnInitMenuPopup(CMenu*, UINT, BOOL);
  afx_msg void OnMenuSelect(UINT nItemID, UINT nFlags,
                            HMENU hSysMenu);
  afx_msg LRESULT OnPopMessageString(WPARAM wParam,
                                     LPARAM lParam);
  afx_msg LRESULT OnSetMessageString(WPARAM wParam,
                                     LPARAM lParam);
    .
    .
    .
protected:
#ifndef _MAC
  afx_msg LRESULT OnDDEInitiate(WPARAM wParam,
                                LPARAM lParam);
  afx_msg LRESULT OnDDEExecute(WPARAM wParam,
```

```
                                 LPARAM lParam);
  afx_msg LRESULT OnDDETerminate(WPARAM wParam,
                                 LPARAM lParam);
  afx_msg LRESULT OnRegisteredMouseWheel(WPARAM wParam,
                                         LPARAM lParam);
#endif
#ifdef _MAC
  afx_msg void OnActivateApp(BOOL bActive, HTASK hTask);
  afx_msg void OnPaint( );
#endif
  DECLARE_MESSAGE_MAP( )

  friend class CWinApp;
};
```

The first parameter in the Create( ) member function allows a class name to be specified in compliance with the traditional Windows API RegisterClass( ) function. Normally, this will be set to NULL in the applications you develop, and a class name will not be required.

Implementing the InitInstance( ) Member Function

Recall that the derived CTheApp class object overrode the InitInstance( ) member function. Here is how this application implements InitInstance( ):

```
BOOL CTheApp::InitInstance( )
{
  m_pMainWnd=new CMainWnd( );
  m_pMainWnd->ShowWindow(m_nCmdShow);
  m_pMainWnd->UpdateWindow( );

  return TRUE;
}
```

The new operator invokes the constructor CMainWnd( ), discussed in the previous section. The *m_pMainWnd* member variable (m_ indicates a member variable) holds the location for the application's main window. The ShowWindow( ) member function is required to display the window on the screen. The parameter, m_nCmdShow, is initialized by the application's constructor. UpdateWindow( ) displays and paints the window being sent to the screen.

The Constructor

The last piece of code invokes the application's constructor at startup:

```
CTheApp TheApp;
```

The application code for this example is very simple and straightforward. The application merely establishes a window; it does not permit you to draw anything in the window.

In the next chapter, you will create a more generalized template, as you did in Chapter 21. This template will allow you to use basically the same MFC code from one application to another. In addition, this template code will allow you to draw in the client area of the window.

Running the SIMPLE.CPP Application

Figure 22-1 shows a window similar to the one that will appear on your screen. While the application didn't draw anything in the client area of the window, it did give the application a new title!

Figure 22-1. *Establishing a window with the use of the MFC library*

This code forms the foundation for all Windows MFC library applications developed in this book. You might want to review the important details one more time, before going on to the applications created in Chapter 23.

A Simplified Design Ensures Easy Maintenance

Reusable classes are one of the main drawing cards in C++ for simplified design and application maintenance. The MFC library for Windows allows C++ to be extended in a natural way, making these classes appear to be part of the language itself. In the next chapter you'll explore many additional features of the MFC library as you develop applications that range from a simple program template to a robust charting program using menus and dialog boxes.

Chapter 23

Windows Applications
Using the MFC

In Chapters 20 through 21, you learned about various Windows building blocks such as menus, dialog boxes, keyboard accelerators, and so on. Then Chapter 22 described the theory and specifications of the Microsoft Foundation Class library. This chapter combines all of the previously discussed Windows building blocks while building programs for the 32-bit object-oriented MFC environment.

In this chapter you will find four complete MFC library Windows applications that will help you understand the MFC library even better. The examples in this chapter are graded; that is, each example builds upon the knowledge you gain from the previous example. It is imperative, therefore, that you study each application in the order in which they appear. By the time you get to the fourth application, you will be working with a complex Windows application that uses several Windows resources, depends heavily on the MFC library, and produces a useful, commercial-grade application.

The program listings for each application are quite long. If you are entering them from the keyboard, do so carefully. Remember, as you type, that these listings are still far shorter than their procedure-oriented counterparts from Chapter 21.

A Simple Application and Template

In Chapter 22, you learned how to establish a window on the screen by using the MFC library. That example serves as a gateway to all such Windows applications that utilize the client area for printing and drawing.

The first application in this chapter, MFCSWP, simply prints a message in the window's client area. The name of this program is derived from the acronym for "MFC simple windows program."

Before we begin our discussion of the important aspects of the application, let's examine a complete program listing. The listing that follows includes a header file and a C++ source code file. The information in the header file was essentially contained in the source code file in the previous chapter. The header file contains information on how our application's classes were derived from the MFC library. This is a style of coding that is promoted by Microsoft. Here is the MFCSWP.H header file listing:

```
class CMainWnd : public CFrameWnd
{
public:
  CMainWnd( );
  afx_msg void OnPaint( );
  DECLARE_MESSAGE_MAP( );
};

class CmfcswpApp : public CWinApp
{
public:
  BOOL InitInstance( );
};
```

The C++ source code file is straightforward. As you examine the following MFCSWP.CPP file, pay particular attention to the overall length of the listing.

```
//
// mfcswp.cpp
// A Simple Windows Program using the MFC.
// This code can serve as a template for the development
// of other MFC applications.
// Copyright (c) William H. Murray and Chris H. Pappas, 1997
//

#include <afxwin.h>
#include "mfcswp.h"

CmfcswpApp theApp;

CMainWnd::CMainWnd( )
{
  Create(NULL,"A MFC Windows Application",
         WS_OVERLAPPEDWINDOW,rectDefault,NULL,NULL);
}

void CMainWnd::OnPaint( )
{
  CPaintDC dc(this);
  dc.TextOut(200,200,"Using the MFC Library",21);
}

BEGIN_MESSAGE_MAP(CMainWnd,CFrameWnd)
  ON_WM_PAINT( )
END_MESSAGE_MAP( )

BOOL CmfcswpApp::InitInstance( )
{
  m_pMainWnd=new CMainWnd( );
  m_pMainWnd->ShowWindow(m_nCmdShow);
  m_pMainWnd->UpdateWindow( );

  return TRUE;
}
```

This composite listing gives you a chance to examine all of the code necessary to produce a working application. The next sections examine those details that are unique to this example.

The MFCSWP.H Header File

In this chapter you will find two types of header files. The first type, shown in this section, is used to indicate class definitions that are unique to the application. As a matter of style, this type of header file will always be identified by the filename and the .H extension—for example, MFCSWP.H. The second style of header file is the type used in Chapter 21. It can contain menu and dialog box resource identification values. When it is used, it is identified with an additional "r" (for "resource") at the end of the filename. For example, if the application in this section had used a resource ID header file, it would have been named MFCSWPR.H. You'll see this second style of header file used in the final two examples in this chapter.

The definitions for two classes are contained here: CMainWnd is derived from CWinApp, and CmfcswpApp is derived from CFrameWnd.

```
class CMainWnd : public CFrameWnd
{
public:
  CMainWnd( );
  afx_msg void OnPaint( );
  DECLARE_MESSAGE_MAP( );
};

class CmfcswpApp : public CWinApp
{
public:
  BOOL InitInstance( );
};
```

NOTE: *Recall that these classes were part of the body of the SIMPLE.CPP application and were explained in Chapter 21. Putting them in a separate header file is just a matter of style—one encouraged by Microsoft.*

Notice, in particular, that CMainWnd contains a member function declaration, OnPaint( ), and the addition of a message map. For member functions such as OnPaint( ), the afx_msg keyword is used instead of virtual. The OnPaint( ) member function belongs to the CWnd class that the CMainWnd class overrides. This allows the client area of the window to be altered. The OnPaint( ) function is automatically called when a WM_PAINT message is sent to a CMainWnd object.

DECLARE_MESSAGE_MAP is used in virtually all MFC Windows applications. This line states that the class overrides the handling of certain messages. (See the body of the application.) Microsoft uses message maps, instead of virtual functions, because it is more space efficient.

The MFCSWP.CPP Source Code File

The majority of this application's code is the same as the SIMPLE.CPP example from Chapter 21. However, notice the addition of the OnPaint( ) message handler function. Examine the portion of code shown here:

```
void CMainWnd::OnPaint( )
{
  CPaintDC dc(this);

  dc.TextOut(200,200,"Using the MFC Library",21);
}
```

A device context is created for handling the WM_PAINT message. Now any Windows GDI functions that are encapsulated in the device context can be used in this member function. This code is similar in concept to the procedure-oriented template created in Chapter 21. When the OnPaint( ) function has finished, the destructor for CPaintDC is called automatically.

This application uses a fairly short message map, as the following code indicates:

```
BEGIN_MESSAGE_MAP(CMainWnd,CFrameWnd)
  ON_WM_PAINT( )
END_MESSAGE_MAP( )
```

Two classes are specified by BEGIN_MESSAGE_MAP: CMainWnd and CFrameWnd. CMainWnd is the target class, and CFrameWnd is a class derived from CWnd. The ON_WM_PAINT( ) function handles all WM_PAINT messages and directs them to the OnPaint( ) member function just discussed. In upcoming applications, you'll see many additional functions added to the message map.

The biggest advantage of using a message map is the elimination of many error-prone switch/case statements that are so typical of procedure-oriented Windows applications.

Running MFCSWP

When you create your project file for your Visual C++ compiler, make sure that you mark this application as an MFC application. Otherwise, you will get a series of strange errors when compiling and linking. Once you have entered the application code and received an error-free compilation, run the program. The screen should be similar to the one shown in Figure 23-1.

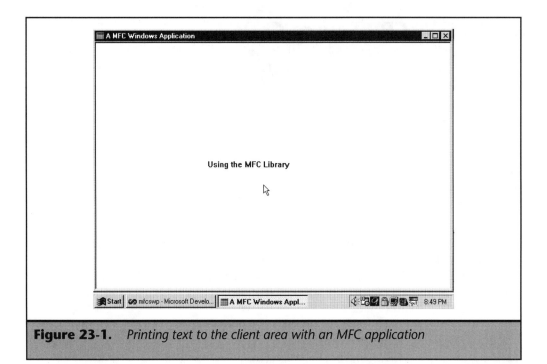

Figure 23-1. *Printing text to the client area with an MFC application*

If you want to experiment with other GDI primitives, just remove the TextOut( ) function call and insert the function of your choice into the template code. You can choose from such functions as Rectangle( ), Ellipse( ), LineTo( ), and so on. The next example will illustrate the use of several graphics functions that will draw a line, a chord, an arc, and more.

Drawing in the Client Area

The second application in this chapter, GDI, will draw several graphics shapes in the window's client area. These are the same GDI drawing primitives discussed (and used separately) in Chapter 21.

This application also requires two files: the header file, GDI.H and the source code file, GDI.CPP.

Enter each of the files carefully. When both files have been entered, the application can be compiled. Remember to state that this is an MFC application when building your application with the Project utility. The GDI.H header file, which follows, is similar in structure to the previous example.

```
class CMainWnd : public CFrameWnd
{
public:
  CMainWnd( );
  afx_msg void OnPaint( );
  DECLARE_MESSAGE_MAP( );
};

class CgdiAApp : public CWinApp
{
public:
  BOOL InitInstance( );
};
```

The source code file for the GDI.CPP application follows:

```
//
//  gdi.cpp
//  An extension of the mfcswp.cpp application
//  that allows experimentation with graphics
//  drawing primitives.
//  Copyright (c) William H. Murray and Chris H. Pappas, 1997
//

#include <afxwin.h>
#include "gdi.h"

CgdiAApp theApp;

CMainWnd::CMainWnd( )
{
  Create(NULL,"Experimenting With GDI Primitives",
         WS_OVERLAPPEDWINDOW,rectDefault,NULL,NULL);
}

void CMainWnd::OnPaint( )
{
  static DWORD dwColor[9]={RGB(0,0,0),          //black
                          RGB(255,0,0),        //red
```

```
                              RGB(0,255,0),        //green
                              RGB(0,0,255),        //blue
                              RGB(255,255,0),      //yellow
                              RGB(255,0,255),      //magenta
                              RGB(0,255,255),      //cyan
                              RGB(127,127,127),    //gray
                              RGB(255,255,255)};   //white
short xcoord;
POINT polylpts[4],polygpts[5];

CBrush newbrush;
CBrush* oldbrush;
CPen   newpen;
CPen*  oldpen;

CPaintDC dc(this);
// draws a wide black diagonal line
newpen.CreatePen(PS_SOLID,6,dwColor[0]);
oldpen=dc.SelectObject(&newpen);
dc.MoveTo(0,0);
dc.LineTo(640,430);
dc.TextOut(70,20,"<-diagonal line",15);
// delete pen objects
dc.SelectObject(oldpen);
newpen.DeleteObject( );

// draws a blue arc
newpen.CreatePen(PS_DASH,1,dwColor[3]);
oldpen=dc.SelectObject(&newpen);
dc.Arc(100,100,200,200,150,175,175,150);
dc.TextOut(80,180,"small arc->",11);
// delete pen objects
dc.SelectObject(oldpen);
newpen.DeleteObject( );

// draws a wide green chord
newpen.CreatePen(PS_SOLID,8,dwColor[2]);
oldpen=dc.SelectObject(&newpen);
dc.Chord(550,20,630,80,555,25,625,70);
dc.TextOut(485,30,"chord->",7);
// delete pen objects
```

```
dc.SelectObject(oldpen);
newpen.DeleteObject( );

// draws and fills a red ellipse
newpen.CreatePen(PS_SOLID,1,dwColor[1]);
oldpen=dc.SelectObject(&newpen);
newbrush.CreateSolidBrush(dwColor[1]);
oldbrush=dc.SelectObject(&newbrush);
dc.Ellipse(180,180,285,260);
dc.TextOut(210,215,"ellipse",7);
// delete brush objects
dc.SelectObject(oldbrush);
newbrush.DeleteObject( );
// delete pen objects
dc.SelectObject(oldpen);
newpen.DeleteObject( );

// draws and fills a blue circle with ellipse function
newpen.CreatePen(PS_SOLID,1,dwColor[3]);
oldpen=dc.SelectObject(&newpen);
newbrush.CreateSolidBrush(dwColor[3]);
oldbrush=dc.SelectObject(&newbrush);
dc.Ellipse(380,180,570,370);
dc.TextOut(450,265,"circle",6);
// delete brush objects
dc.SelectObject(oldbrush);
newbrush.DeleteObject( );
// delete pen objects
dc.SelectObject(oldpen);
newpen.DeleteObject( );

// draws a black pie wedge and fills with green
newpen.CreatePen(PS_SOLID,1,dwColor[0]);
oldpen=dc.SelectObject(&newpen);
newbrush.CreateSolidBrush(dwColor[2]);
oldbrush=dc.SelectObject(&newbrush);
dc.Pie(300,50,400,150,300,50,300,100);
dc.TextOut(350,80,"<-pie wedge",11);
// delete brush objects
dc.SelectObject(oldbrush);
newbrush.DeleteObject( );
// delete pen objects
```

```
dc.SelectObject(oldpen);
newpen.DeleteObject( );

// draws a black rectangle and fills with gray
newbrush.CreateSolidBrush(dwColor[7]);
oldbrush=dc.SelectObject(&newbrush);
dc.Rectangle(50,300,150,400);
dc.TextOut(160,350,"<-rectangle",11);
// delete brush objects
dc.SelectObject(oldbrush);
newbrush.DeleteObject( );

// draws a black rounded rectangle and fills with blue
newbrush.CreateHatchBrush(HS_CROSS,dwColor[3]);
oldbrush=dc.SelectObject(&newbrush);
dc.RoundRect(60,310,110,350,20,20);
dc.TextOut (120,310,"<------rounded rectangle",24);
// delete brush objects
dc.SelectObject(oldbrush);
newbrush.DeleteObject( );

// draws several green pixels
for(xcoord=400;xcoord<450;xcoord+=3)
  dc.SetPixel(xcoord,150,0L);
dc.TextOut(455,145,"<-pixels",8);

// draws several wide magenta lines with polyline
newpen.CreatePen(PS_SOLID,3,dwColor[5]);
oldpen=dc.SelectObject(&newpen);
polylpts[0].x=10;
polylpts[0].y=30;
polylpts[1].x=10;
polylpts[1].y=100;
polylpts[2].x=50;
polylpts[2].y=100;
polylpts[3].x=10;
polylpts[3].y=30;
dc.Polyline(polylpts,4);
dc.TextOut(10,110,"polyline",8);
// delete pen objects
dc.SelectObject(oldpen);
newpen.DeleteObject( );
```

```
  // draws a wide cyan polygon and
  // fills with diagonal yellow
  newpen.CreatePen(PS_SOLID,4,dwColor[6]);
  oldpen=dc.SelectObject(&newpen);
  newbrush.CreateHatchBrush(HS_FDIAGONAL,dwColor[4]);
  oldbrush=dc.SelectObject(&newbrush);
  polygpts[0].x=40;
  polygpts[0].y=200;
  polygpts[1].x=100;
  polygpts[1].y=270;
  polygpts[2].x=80;
  polygpts[2].y=290;
  polygpts[3].x=20;
  polygpts[3].y=220;
  polygpts[4].x=40;
  polygpts[4].y=200;
  dc.Polygon(polygpts,5);
  dc.TextOut(70,210,"<-polygon",9);
  // delete brush objects
  dc.SelectObject(oldbrush);
  newbrush.DeleteObject( );
  // delete pen objects
  dc.SelectObject(oldpen);
  newpen.DeleteObject( );
}

BEGIN_MESSAGE_MAP(CMainWnd,CFrameWnd)
  ON_WM_PAINT( )
END_MESSAGE_MAP( )

BOOL CgdiAApp::InitInstance( )
{
  m_pMainWnd=new CMainWnd( );
  m_pMainWnd->ShowWindow(m_nCmdShow);
  m_pMainWnd->UpdateWindow( );

  return TRUE;
}
```

This example uses a variety of pens and brushes, in addition to investigating various GDI graphics primitives. Let's look at the code in more detail.

The GDI.H Header File

Examine the GDI.H header file. Did you notice that only the name of the application has changed from the previous example? This feat is possible basically because of the simplicity of the example—no menus, dialog boxes, or other external resources.

The GDI.CPP Source Code File

Here is a portion of the source code listing contained in the OnPaint( ) message handler function. An array is created to hold the RGB values for nine unique brush and pen colors. You'll see shortly how colors are picked from this array.

```
static DWORD dwColor[9]={RGB(0,0,0),          //black
                        RGB(255,0,0),         //red
                        RGB(0,255,0),         //green
                        RGB(0,0,255),         //blue
                        RGB(255,255,0),       //yellow
                        RGB(255,0,255),       //magenta
                        RGB(0,255,255),       //cyan
                        RGB(127,127,127),     //gray
                        RGB(255,255,255)};    //white
```

The CBrush and CPen classes permit brush or pen objects to be passed to any CDC (base class for display context) member function. Brushes can be solid, hatched, or patterned, and pens can draw solid, dashed, or dotted lines. Here is the syntax that is required to create a new brush and pen object for this example:

CBrush newbrush;
CBrush* oldbrush;
CPen newpen;
CPen* oldpen;

Since each GDI primitive's code is somewhat similar to the others in the group, we'll only examine two typical sections. The first piece of code is used to draw a wide black diagonal line in the window:

```
// draws a wide black diagonal line
newpen.CreatePen(PS_SOLID,6,dwColor[0]);
oldpen=dc.SelectObject(&newpen);
dc.MoveTo(0,0);
dc.LineTo(640,430);
```

```
dc.TextOut(70,20,"<-diagonal line",15);
// delete pen objects
dc.SelectObject(oldpen);
newpen.DeleteObject( );
```

The pen object is initialized by the CreatePen( ) function to draw black solid lines six logical units wide. Once the pen is initialized, the SelectObject( ) member function is overloaded for the pen object class and attaches the pen object to the device context. The previously attached object is returned. The MoveTo( ) and LineTo( ) functions set the range for the diagonal line that is drawn by the selected pen. Finally, a label is attached to the figure with the use of the TextOut( ) function.

Brushes can be handled in a similar way. In the following code, the brush is initialized to be a hatched brush filled with blue crosses (HS_CROSS). The brush object is selected in the same way the pen object was selected.

```
// draws a black rounded rectangle and fills with blue
newbrush.CreateHatchBrush(HS_CROSS,dwColor[3]);
oldbrush=dc.SelectObject(&newbrush);
dc.RoundRect(60,310,110,350,20,20);
dc.TextOut (120,310,"<------rounded rectangle",24);
// delete brush objects
dc.SelectObject(oldbrush);
newbrush.DeleteObject( );
```

The RoundRect( ) function draws a rounded rectangle in black at the given screen coordinates. A label is also printed for this figure.

The remaining shapes are drawn to the screen using a similar technique.

Running the GDI Application

Build the application by creating a project file specifically requesting the inclusion of the MFC library. Run the application and note what you see on your screen.

This application has a minor drawback, as you might have observed! All coordinate points for the GDI functions are set to pixel values valid for VGA monitors. What happens if you are using an EGA or a Super VGA display? If you are using a monitor with a lower resolution, such as an EGA, you will get a partial image that seems magnified. If you are using a higher-resolution display, such as a Super VGA, the image will fill in only the upper-left part of your screen.

To eliminate this problem, your application must determine your display's characteristics and adjust accordingly. This adds an extra layer of complexity to the application code, which has been kept as simple as possible to this point. However, the final two examples in this chapter will teach you how to scale your figures to fit the current display type. All this can be done automatically if your program is properly written.

When you run this application, your screen should look something like Figure 23-2 if you are using a VGA monitor. The various GDI objects are displayed in very vivid colors.

A Fourier Series Application with Resources

The next application in this chapter, FOURIER.CPP, will draw a Fourier series waveform in the window's client area. This application uses two Windows resources: a menu and a dialog box. You may want to refer to Chapter 21 for details on the techniques for creating each of these resources.

As the complexity of each application grows, so does the list of files required for compiling and linking. This application requires a header file named FOURIER.H, a resource header file named FOURIERR.H (note the addition of the extra "R"), a

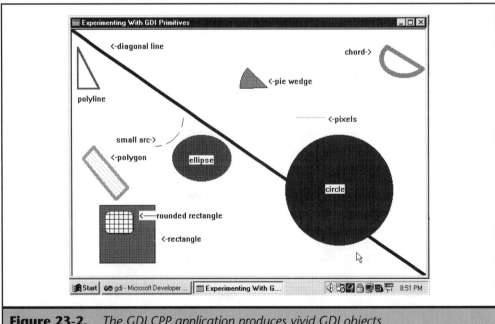

Figure 23-2. *The GDI.CPP application produces vivid GDI objects*

resource script file named FOURIER.RC, and the source code file named
FOURIER.CPP.

Enter each file carefully. When all the files have been entered, the application can
be compiled and linked. Also, remember to include FOURIER.RC, and FOURIER.CPP
in your project file's list of files needed for the build process.

One header file is used for class information, as you can see in the FOURIER.H file
that follows:

```
class CMainWnd : public CFrameWnd
{
public:
  CMainWnd( );
  afx_msg void OnPaint( );
  afx_msg void OnSize(UINT,int,int);
  afx_msg int  OnCreate(LPCREATESTRUCT cs);
  afx_msg void OnAbout( );
  afx_msg void OnFourierData( );
  afx_msg void OnExit( );
  DECLARE_MESSAGE_MAP( )
};


class CTheApp : public CWinApp
{
public:
  virtual BOOL InitInstance( );
};


class CFourierDataDialog : public CModalDialog
{
public:
  CFourierDataDialog(CWnd* pParentWnd=NULL)
                    : CModalDialog("FourierData",pParentWnd)
                    { }
  virtual void OnOK( );
};
```

Another header file contains the traditional ID values needed by menus and dialog
boxes. This file is named FOURIERR.H.

```
#define IDM_FOUR    100
#define IDM_ABOUT   110
#define IDM_EXIT    120
```

```
#define IDD_TERMS  200
#define IDD_TITLE  201
```

The resource script file, FOURIER.RC, for this example includes a description for a menu and two dialog box descriptions. The dialog box descriptions are for a simple About box and a data entry dialog box.

```
//Microsoft Developer Studio generated resource script.
//
#include "resource.h"

#define APSTUDIO_READONLY_SYMBOLS
/////////////////////////////////////////////////////////////////
//
// Generated from the TEXTINCLUDE 2 resource.
//
#define APSTUDIO_HIDDEN_SYMBOLS
#include "windows.h"
#undef APSTUDIO_HIDDEN_SYMBOLS
#include "afxres.h"


/////////////////////////////////////////////////////////////////
#undef APSTUDIO_READONLY_SYMBOLS


/////////////////////////////////////////////////////////////////
// English (U.S.) resources

#if !defined(AFX_RESOURCE_DLL) || defined(AFX_TARG_ENU)
#ifdef _WIN32
LANGUAGE LANG_ENGLISH, SUBLANG_ENGLISH_US
#pragma code_page(1252)
#endif //_WIN32


/////////////////////////////////////////////////////////////////
//
// Menu
//

FOURIERMENU MENU DISCARDABLE
BEGIN
  POPUP "Fourier Data"
```

```
    BEGIN
      MENUITEM "Fourier Data...", IDM_FOUR
      MENUITEM "Fourier About...", IDM_ABOUT
      MENUITEM "Exit", IDM_EXIT
    END
  END


  /////////////////////////////////////////////////////////
  //
  // Dialog
  //

  ABOUTBOX DIALOG DISCARDABLE  14, 22, 200, 75
  STYLE WS_POPUP | WS_CAPTION
  CAPTION "About Box"
  BEGIN
    CTEXT "A Fourier Series Waveform",-1,30,5,144,8
    CTEXT "A MFC Application",-1,30,17,144,8
    CTEXT "By William H. Murray and Chris H. Pappas",
          -1,28,28,144,8
    CTEXT "(c) Copyright 1997",201,68,38,83,8
    DEFPUSHBUTTON   "OK",IDOK,84,55,32,14,WS_GROUP
  END


  FOURIERDATA DIALOG DISCARDABLE  74, 21, 142, 70
  STYLE WS_POPUP | WS_CAPTION
  CAPTION "Fourier Data"
  BEGIN
    LTEXT "Title: ",-1,6,5,28,8,NOT WS_GROUP
    EDITTEXT IDD_TITLE,33,1,106,12
    LTEXT "Number of terms: ",-1,6,23,70,8,NOT WS_GROUP
    EDITTEXT IDD_TERMS,76,18,32,12
    PUSHBUTTON "OK",IDOK,25,52,24,14
    PUSHBUTTON "Cancel",IDCANCEL,89,53,28,14
  END


  #ifdef APSTUDIO_INVOKED
  /////////////////////////////////////////////////////////
  //
  // TEXTINCLUDE
  //
```

```
1 TEXTINCLUDE DISCARDABLE
BEGIN
  "resource.h\0"
END

2 TEXTINCLUDE DISCARDABLE
BEGIN
  "#define APSTUDIO_HIDDEN_SYMBOLS\r\n"
  "#include ""windows.h""\r\n"
  "#undef APSTUDIO_HIDDEN_SYMBOLS\r\n"
  "#include ""afxres.h""\r\n"
  "\0"
END

3 TEXTINCLUDE DISCARDABLE
BEGIN
  "\r\n"
  "\0"
END

#endif    // APSTUDIO_INVOKED


#endif    // English (U.S.) resources
/////////////////////////////////////////////////////////////

#ifndef APSTUDIO_INVOKED
/////////////////////////////////////////////////////////////
//
// Generated from the TEXTINCLUDE 3 resource.
//


/////////////////////////////////////////////////////////////
#endif    // not APSTUDIO_INVOKED
```

The source code file, FOURIER.CPP, is slightly more complicated than the previous example because it must handle a menu and two dialog box resources. See if you can find this additional code as you examine the following listing:

```
//
//   fourier.cpp
//   Drawing A Fourier Series with the use of
```

```
//   the MFC library.
//   Copyright (c) William H. Murray and Chris H. Pappas, 1997
//

#include <afxwin.h>
#include <string.h>
#include <math.h>
#include "fourierR.h"    // resource IDs
#include "fourier.h"

int m_cxClient,m_cyClient;
char mytitle[80]="Title";
int nterms=1;

CTheApp theApp;

CMainWnd::CMainWnd( )
{
  Create((AfxRegisterWndClass(CS_HREDRAW|CS_VREDRAW,
        LoadCursor(NULL,IDC_CROSS),
        (HBRUSH) (GetStockObject(WHITE_BRUSH)),NULL)),
        "Fourier Series Application with the MFC",
        WS_OVERLAPPEDWINDOW,rectDefault,NULL,"FourierMenu");
}

void CMainWnd::OnSize(UINT,int x,int y)
{
  m_cxClient=x;
  m_cyClient=y;
}

void CMainWnd::OnPaint( )
{
  CPaintDC dc(this);
  static DWORD dwColor[9]={RGB(0,0,0),        //black
                           RGB(245,0,0),      //red
                           RGB(0,245,0),      //green
                           RGB(0,0,245),      //blue
                           RGB(245,245,0),    //yellow
                           RGB(245,0,245),    //magenta
                           RGB(0,245,245),    //cyan
                           RGB(127,127,127),  //gray
```

```
                                   RGB(245,245,245)}; //white

int i,j,ltitle,ang;
double y,yp;
CBrush newbrush;
CBrush* oldbrush;
CPen newpen;
CPen* oldpen;

// create a custom drawing surface
dc.SetMapMode(MM_ISOTROPIC);
dc.SetWindowExt(500,500);
dc.SetViewportExt(m_cxClient,-m_cyClient);
dc.SetViewportOrg(m_cxClient/20,m_cyClient/2);

ang=0;
yp=0.0;

newpen.CreatePen(BS_SOLID,2,RGB(0,0,0));
oldpen=dc.SelectObject(&newpen);

// draw x & y coordinate axes
dc.MoveTo(0,240);
dc.LineTo(0,-240);
dc.MoveTo(0,0);
dc.LineTo(400,0);
dc.MoveTo(0,0);
// draw actual Fourier waveform
for (i=0; i<=400; i++) {
  for (j=1; j<=nterms; j++) {
    y=(150.0/((2.0*j)-1.0))*sin(((j*2.0)-1.0)*0.015708*ang);
    yp=yp+y;
  }
  dc.LineTo(i,(int) yp);
  yp-=yp;
  ang++;
}

// prepare to fill interior of waveform newbrush
newbrush.CreateSolidBrush(dwColor[7]);
oldbrush=dc.SelectObject(&newbrush);
dc.ExtFloodFill(150,10,dwColor[0],FLOODFILLBORDER);
```

```
    dc.ExtFloodFill(300,-10,dwColor[0],FLOODFILLBORDER);

    // print waveform title
    ltitle=strlen(mytitle);
    dc.TextOut(200-(ltitle*8/2),185,mytitle,ltitle);

    // delete brush objects
    dc.SelectObject(oldbrush);
    newbrush.DeleteObject( );
}

int CMainWnd::OnCreate(LPCREATESTRUCT)
{
    UpdateWindow( );
    return (0);
}

void CMainWnd::OnAbout( )
{
    CModalDialog about("AboutBox",this);
    about.DoModal( );
}

void CFourierDataDialog::OnOK( )
{
    GetDlgItemText(IDD_TITLE,mytitle,80);
    nterms=GetDlgItemInt(IDD_TERMS,NULL,0);
    CModalDialog::OnOK( );
}

void CMainWnd::OnFourierData( )
{
    CFourierDataDialog dlgFourierData(this);
    if (dlgFourierData.DoModal( )==IDOK) {
        InvalidateRect(NULL,TRUE);
        UpdateWindow( );
    }
};

void CMainWnd::OnExit( )
{
    DestroyWindow( );
```

```
}

BEGIN_MESSAGE_MAP(CMainWnd,CFrameWnd)
  ON_WM_PAINT( )
  ON_WM_SIZE( )
  ON_WM_CREATE( )
  ON_COMMAND(IDM_ABOUT,OnAbout)
  ON_COMMAND(IDM_FOUR,OnFourierData)
  ON_COMMAND(IDM_EXIT,OnExit)
END_MESSAGE_MAP( )

BOOL CTheApp::InitInstance( )
{
  m_pMainWnd=new CMainWnd( );
  m_pMainWnd->ShowWindow(m_nCmdShow);
  m_pMainWnd->UpdateWindow( );
  return TRUE;
}
```

The FOURIER.H Header File

As the next code segment shows, CMainWnd now contains several function declarations and a message map. The member functions include OnPaint( ), OnSize( ), OnCreate( ), OnAbout( ), OnFourierData( ), and OnExit( ). The afx_msg keyword is used instead of virtual. The OnPaint( ) member function is found in the CWnd class, which is overridden by the CMainWnd class. This allows the client area of the window to be altered.

```
afx_msg void OnPaint( );
afx_msg void OnSize(UINT,int,int);
afx_msg int  OnCreate(LPCREATESTRUCT cs);
afx_msg void OnAbout( );
afx_msg void OnFourierData( );
afx_msg void OnExit( );
```

The OnPaint( ) function is automatically called when a WM_PAINT message is sent to a CMainWnd object by Windows or the application. The OnSize( ) function is called whenever a WM_SIZE message is generated by a change in the size of the window. This information will be useful for scaling graphics to the window size. The

OnCreate( ) function points to a structure that contains information about the window being created. This structure contains information on the size, style, and other aspects of the window. The functions OnAbout( ), OnFourierData( ), and OnExit( ) are user-defined functions that respond to WM_COMMAND messages. WM_COMMAND messages are generated when the user selects an option from a menu or dialog box.

DECLARE_MESSAGE_MAP is used again to state that the class overrides the handling of certain messages. (See the body of the application.) Recall that this technique is more space efficient than the use of virtual functions.

The MFC library supports regular and modal dialog boxes with the CDialog and CModalDialog classes. For very simple dialog boxes such as About boxes, the MFC can be used directly. For data entry dialog boxes, however, the class will have to be derived. The dialog box for this example will permit the user to enter an optional graph title and an integer for the number of harmonics to be drawn in the window. The CFourierDataDialog class is derived from the CModalDialog foundation class. Modal dialog boxes must be dismissed before other actions can be taken in an application, as shown in the following portion of code.

```
class CFourierDataDialog : public CModalDialog
{
public:
  CFourierDataDialog(CWnd* pParentWnd=NULL)
                 : CModalDialog("FourierData",pParentWnd)
                   { }
  virtual void OnOK( );
};
```

In a derived modal dialog class, member variables and functions can be added to specify the behavior of the dialog box. Member variables can also be used to save data entered by the user or to save data for display. Classes derived from CModalDialog require their own message maps, with the exception of the OnInitDialog( ), OnOK( ), and OnCancel( ) functions.

In this simple example, the CFourierDataDialog( ) constructor supplies the name of the dialog box, "FourierData," and the name of the parent window that owns the dialog box. There is no owner for this modal dialog box.

The dialog box will actually return data to the application when the user clicks on the OK dialog box button. If either the OK or the Cancel button is clicked, the dialog box closes and is removed from the screen. When the dialog box closes, the member functions access its member variables to retrieve information entered by the user. Dialog boxes requiring initialization can override the OnInitDialog( ) member function for this purpose.

The Resource Files

The FOURIERR.H resource header file and the FOURIER.RC resource script file are used by the resource compiler to produce a single compiled Windows resource.

The FOURIERR.H resource header file contains five identification values. IDM_FOUR, IDM_ABOUT, and IDM_EXIT are used for menu selection choices, while IDD_TERMS and IDD_TITLE are for the data entry dialog box.

The resource script file also contains a description of the application's menu and dialog boxes. The menu is shown in Figure 23-3. Compare the menu title and features to the text used to create the menu in the resource file.

This application also uses two dialog boxes. Figure 23-4 shows the About dialog box for this application.

Figure 23-5 shows the data entry dialog box for this application.

Take a minute to compare the text file for each dialog box with the actual screen figures. Remember that the dialog box resources used the resource editor to construct both dialog boxes.

The FOURIER.CPP Source Code File

The complexity of the application file for this example has increased greatly because of the inclusion of menus and dialog boxes. Other features, which you might want to

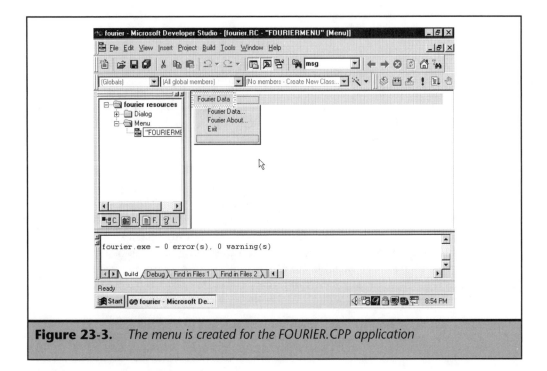

Figure 23-3.   *The menu is created for the FOURIER.CPP application*

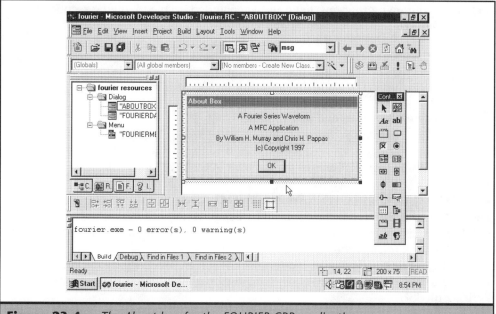

Figure 23-4. *The About box for the FOURIER.CPP application*

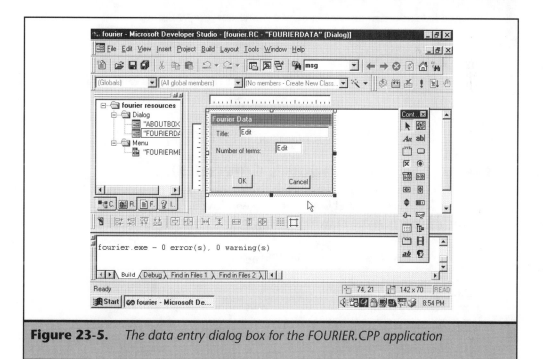

Figure 23-5. *The data entry dialog box for the FOURIER.CPP application*

include in your own programs, have also been added. In the following sections, you'll see how to:

- Select a new cursor
- Set the background color
- Determine the size of the current window
- Set a new viewport and origin for drawing
- Draw and fill an object in the window

Let's examine these features as they appear in the program.

Creating a Custom CMainWnd Class

The CMainWnd class can be customized by using AfxRegisterWndClass to create a registration class. A registration class has many fields, but four are easily altered: style, cursor, background, and the minimize icon.

The following small piece of code shows the syntax for changing the cursor to a stock cross shape (IDC_CROSS) and setting the brush that paints the background to a WHITE_BRUSH:

```
CMainWnd::CMainWnd( )
{
  Create((AfxRegisterWndClass(CS_HREDRAW|CS_VREDRAW,
        LoadCursor(NULL,IDC_CROSS),
        (HBRUSH) GetStockObject(WHITE_BRUSH),NULL)),
        " Fourier Series Application with the MFC",
        WS_OVERLAPPEDWINDOW,rectDefault,NULL,"FourierMenu");
}
```

Also note that the menu name is identified in the Create( ) member function.

Determining the Window's Current Size

The OnSize( ) member function returns the size of the current client window. A WM_SIZE message is generated whenever the window is resized. As shown here, the current window size is saved in two variables, *m_cxClient* and *m_cyClient*:

```
void CMainWnd::OnSize(UINT,int x,int y)
{
  m_cxClient=x;
  m_cyClient=y;
}
```

These values will be used to scale the graphics the application draws to fit the current window's dimensions.

Drawing the Fourier Waveform

In order to prevent the scaling problems described in the previous example, a scalable drawing surface is created. You may wish to review the purpose of these functions in Chapter 21.

As shown in the following code, the mapping mode is changed to MM_ISOTROPIC with the SetMapMode( ) function. The MM_ISOTROPIC mapping mode uses arbitrary drawing units.

```
dc.SetMapMode(MM_ISOTROPIC);
```

The next line of code shows the window's extent set to 500 units in both the x and y directions:

```
dc.SetWindowExt(500,500);
```

This simply means that the x and y axes will always have 500 units, regardless of the size of the window. The viewport extent is set to the currently reported window size, as shown here:

```
dc.SetViewportExt(m_cxClient,-m_cyClient);
```

In this case, you will see all 500 units in the window.

NOTE: *Using a negative value when specifying the* y *viewport extent forces* y *to increase in the upward direction.*

As the following code shows, the viewport origin is set midway on the y axis a short distance (a fifth of the length) from the left edge of the x axis:

```
dc.SetViewportOrg(m_cxClient/20,m_cyClient/2);
```

Next, x and y coordinate axes are drawn in the window. Compare the values shown here to the axes shown in screen shots later in this section:

```
// draw x & y coordinate axes
dc.MoveTo(0,240);
dc.LineTo(0,-240);
dc.MoveTo(0,0);
dc.LineTo(400,0);
dc.MoveTo(0,0);
```

The technique for drawing the Fourier wave, shown next, uses two for loops. The *s* variable controls the angle used by the sine function, and the *j* variable holds the value for the current Fourier harmonic. Each point plotted on the screen is a summation of all the Fourier harmonics for a given angle. Thus, if you request that the application draw 1,000 harmonics, 400,000 separate calculations will be made.

```
// draw actual Fourier waveform
for (i=0; i<=400; i++)
{
  for (j=1; j<=nterms; j++)
  {
    y=(150.0/((2.0*j)-1.0))*sin(((j*2.0)-1.0)*0.015708*ang);
    yp=yp+y;
  }
  dc.LineTo(i,(int) yp);
  yp-=yp;
  ang++;
}
```

The LineTo( ) function is used to connect each calculated point, forming a waveform drawn with a solid line. This waveform will have its interior region filled with a gray color by the ExtFloodFill( ) function. The ExtFloodFill( ) function requires the coordinates of a point within the fill region and the bounding color that the figure was drawn with. The FLOODFILLBORDER parameter fills to the boundary color. You can determine these values from the following code:

```
// prepare to fill interior of waveform newbrush.
  newbrush.CreateSolidBrush(dwColor[7]);
  oldbrush=dc.SelectObject(&newbrush);
  dc.ExtFloodFill(150,10,dwColor[0],FLOODFILLBORDER);
  dc.ExtFloodFill(300,-10,dwColor[0],FLOODFILLBORDER);
```

Before the figure is completed, a title is printed in the window and the brush object is deleted, as shown here:

```
// print waveform title
ltitle=strlen(mytitle);
dc.TextOut(200-(ltitle*8/2),185,mytitle,ltitle);

// delete brush objects
dc.SelectObject(oldbrush);
newbrush.DeleteObject( );
```

Remember that all objects drawn within the client area will be scaled to the viewport. This program eliminates the sizing problem of earlier examples and requires only a little additional coding.

The About Dialog Box

About boxes are very easy to create and implement. They are used to communicate information about the program, the program's designers, the copyright date, and so on.

A modal dialog box is created when the user selects the Fourier About... option from the application's menu. The OnAbout( ) command handler requires only a few lines of code:

```
void CMainWnd::OnAbout( )
{
  CModalDialog about("AboutBox",this);
  about.DoModal( );
}
```

The constructor for CModalDialog uses the current window as the parent window for the object. The *this* pointer is typically used here and refers to the currently used object. The DoModal( ) member function is responsible for drawing the About box in the client area. When the OK button in the About box is clicked, the box is removed and the client area is repainted.

The Data Entry Dialog Box

Dialog boxes that allow user input require a bit more programming than simple About boxes do. A data input dialog box can be selected from the application's menu by selecting Fourier Data.

An illustration of this dialog box was shown earlier. The user is permitted to enter a chart title and an integer representing the number of Fourier harmonics to draw. If the user clicks on the OK button, the data entry dialog box is removed from the window and the client area is updated, as shown in the following portion of code.

```
void CMainWnd::OnFourierData( )
{
  CFourierDataDialog dlgFourierData(this);
  if (dlgFourierData.DoModal( )==IDOK)
  {
    InvalidateRect(NULL,TRUE);
    UpdateWindow( );
  }
};
```

CFourierDataDialog was derived from CModalDialog in the header file, FOURIER.H, as discussed earlier. Notice, however, that it is at this point in the application that data is retrieved. This data was entered in the dialog box by the user. Here is a portion of code that returns this information when the dialog box's OK push button is clicked.

```
void CFourierDataDialog::OnOK( )
{
  GetDlgItemText(IDD_TITLE,mytitle,80);
  nterms=GetDlgItemInt(IDD_TERMS,NULL,0);
  CModalDialog::OnOK( );
}
```

The GetDlgItemText( ) function returns chart title information to mytitle in the form of a string. The dialog box location for this information is identified by IDD_TITLE. Integer information can be processed in a similar manner with the GetDlgItemInt( ) function. Its dialog box identification value is IDD_TERMS, and the integer retrieved by the function is returned to the variable *nterms*. The second parameter is used to report translation errors but is not used in this application. If the third parameter is nonzero, a check will be made for a signed number. In this application, only positive numbers are possible.

Responding to OnExit( )

The final application menu option is Exit. Exit will destroy the client window by calling the DestroyWindow( ) function:

```
void CMainWnd::OnExit( )
{
  DestroyWindow( );
}
```

This application menu option gives the user a method of exiting the application without using the system menu.

The Message Map

Two classes are specified in BEGIN_MESSAGE_MAP: CMainWnd and CFrameWnd. CMainWnd is the target class, and CFrameWnd is a class based on CWnd. The ON_WM_PAINT( ) function handles all WM_PAINT messages and directs them to the OnPaint( ) member function. ON_WM_SIZE( ) handles WM_SIZE messages and directs them to the OnSize( ) member function. The ON_WM_CREATE( ) function handles WM_CREATE messages and directs them to the OnCreate( ) member function. There is an ON_COMMAND( ) function for each application menu item. Message information on menu items is processed and then returned to the appropriate member function. Here is the message map for this example:

```
BEGIN_MESSAGE_MAP(CMainWnd,CFrameWnd)
  ON_WM_PAINT( )
  ON_WM_SIZE( )
  ON_WM_CREATE( )
  ON_COMMAND(IDM_ABOUT,OnAbout)
  ON_COMMAND(IDM_FOUR,OnFourierData)
  ON_COMMAND(IDM_EXIT,OnExit)
END_MESSAGE_MAP( )
```

As mentioned in an earlier example, the use of message maps has eliminated the need for error-prone switch/case statements.

Running FOURIER

Compile the application with the Project utility. When the FOURIER application is executed, a default waveform is drawn in the client area. A default value of one harmonic produces a sine wave, as shown in Figure 23-6. Figure 23-7 shows five harmonics, and Figure 23-8 shows 50 harmonics.

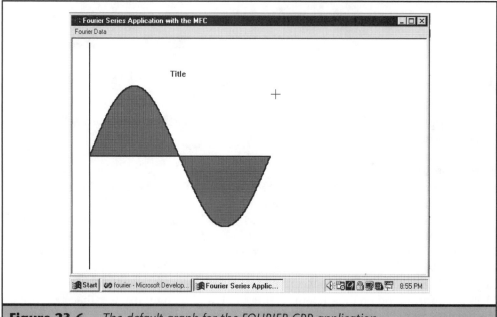

Figure 23-6. *The default graph for the FOURIER.CPP application*

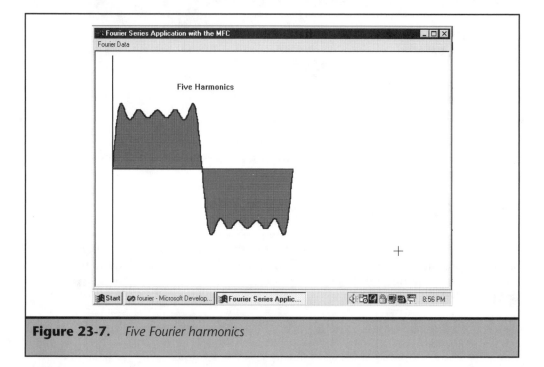

Figure 23-7. *Five Fourier harmonics*

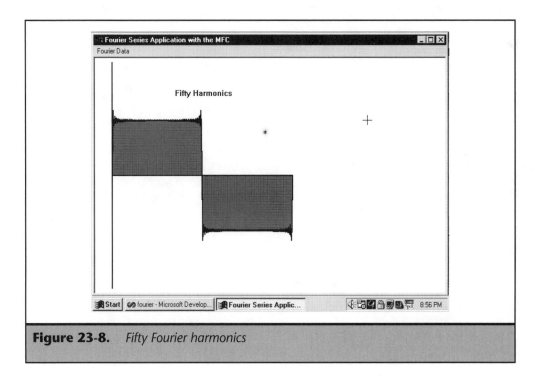

Figure 23-8. *Fifty Fourier harmonics*

As the number of harmonics increases, the figure drawn in the client area will approach a perfect square wave. You can experiment with various values and note how the drawing time increases for very large numbers of harmonics.

A Bar Chart with Resources

The final application in this chapter, BARCHART.CPP, will draw a presentation-quality bar chart in the window's client area. This application also makes use of several Windows resources, including a menu, an About dialog box, and a data entry dialog box.

The complete application is compiled and linked with four separate files. These include the header file, BARCHART.H; the resource header file, BARCHARTR.H; the resource script file, BARCHART.RC; and the source code file, BARCHART.CPP.

Enter each file carefully. You will also need to create a project file. Remember to mark this as an MFC application. The BARCHART.RC and BARCHART.CPP must be named in the project file's list of files to include for the build. When all files have been entered, the application can be compiled and linked.

The BARCHART.H header file gives our class descriptions for CMainWnd, CTheApp, and CBarDataDialog. These classes are children of MFC library classes:

```
class CMainWnd : public CFrameWnd
{
public:
  CMainWnd( );
  afx_msg void OnPaint( );
  afx_msg void OnSize(UINT,int,int);
  afx_msg int  OnCreate(LPCREATESTRUCT cs);
  afx_msg void OnAbout( );
  afx_msg void OnBarData( );
  afx_msg void OnExit( );
  DECLARE_MESSAGE_MAP( )
};

class CTheApp : public CWinApp
{
public:
  virtual BOOL InitInstance( );
};

class CBarDataDialog : public CModalDialog
{
public:
  CBarDataDialog(CWnd* pParentWnd=NULL)
                : CModalDialog("BarDlgBox",pParentWnd)
                { }
  virtual void OnOK( );
};
```

The BARCHARTR.H resource header file contains the ID values that will be used for the menu and two dialog boxes.

```
#define IDM_ABOUT    10
#define IDM_INPUT    20
#define IDM_EXIT     30
#define DM_TITLE     300
#define DM_XLABEL    301
#define DM_YLABEL    302
#define DM_P1        303
#define DM_P2        304
#define DM_P3        305
#define DM_P4        306
```

```
#define DM_P5        307
#define DM_P6        308
#define DM_P7        309
#define DM_P8        310
#define DM_P9        311
#define DM_P10       312
```

The BARCHART.RC resource script file defines the application's menu and dialog boxes.

```
//Microsoft Developer Studio generated resource script.
//
#include "resource.h"
#include "barchartr.h"

#define APSTUDIO_READONLY_SYMBOLS
/////////////////////////////////////////////////////////////////
//
// Generated from the TEXTINCLUDE 2 resource.
//
#define APSTUDIO_HIDDEN_SYMBOLS
#include "windows.h"
#undef APSTUDIO_HIDDEN_SYMBOLS
#include "afxres.h"


/////////////////////////////////////////////////////////////////
#undef APSTUDIO_READONLY_SYMBOLS


/////////////////////////////////////////////////////////////////
// English (U.S.) resources

#if !defined(AFX_RESOURCE_DLL) || defined(AFX_TARG_ENU)
#ifdef _WIN32
LANGUAGE LANG_ENGLISH, SUBLANG_ENGLISH_US
#pragma code_page(1252)
#endif //_WIN32


/////////////////////////////////////////////////////////////////
//
// Menu
//
```

```
BARMENU MENU DISCARDABLE
BEGIN
  POPUP "Bar_Chart"
  BEGIN
    MENUITEM "About Box...", IDM_ABOUT
    MENUITEM "Bar Values...", IDM_INPUT
    MENUITEM "Exit", IDM_EXIT
  END
END


/////////////////////////////////////////////////////////
//
// Dialog
//

ABOUTDLGBOX DIALOG DISCARDABLE  14, 22, 200, 75
STYLE WS_POPUP | WS_CAPTION
CAPTION "About Box"
BEGIN
  CTEXT "A Bar Chart Application",-1,30,5,144,8
  CTEXT "A Simple MFC Windows Application",-1,30,17,144,8
  CTEXT "By William H. Murray and Chris H. Pappas",
        -1,28,28,144,8
  CTEXT "(c) Copyright 1997",-1,68,38,83,8
  DEFPUSHBUTTON   "OK",IDOK,84,55,32,14,WS_GROUP
END

BARDLGBOX DIALOG DISCARDABLE  42, 65526, 223, 209
STYLE WS_POPUP | WS_CAPTION
CAPTION "Bar Chart Data"
BEGIN
  GROUPBOX "Bar Chart Title:",100,5,11,212,89,WS_TABSTOP
  GROUPBOX "Bar Chart Heights",101,5,105,212,90,WS_TABSTOP
  LTEXT "Title: ",-1,43,35,28,8,NOT WS_GROUP
  EDITTEXT DM_TITLE,75,30,137,12
  LTEXT "x-axis label:",-1,15,55,55,8,NOT WS_GROUP
  EDITTEXT DM_XLABEL,75,50,135,12
  LTEXT "y-axis label:",-1,15,75,60,8,NOT WS_GROUP
  EDITTEXT DM_YLABEL,75,70,135,12
  LTEXT "Bar #1: ",-1,45,125,40,8,NOT WS_GROUP
  LTEXT "Bar #2: ",-1,45,140,40,8,NOT WS_GROUP
  LTEXT "Bar #3: ",-1,45,155,40,8,NOT WS_GROUP
```

```
    LTEXT "Bar #4: ",-1,45,170,40,8,NOT WS_GROUP
    LTEXT "Bar #5: ",-1,45,185,40,8,NOT WS_GROUP
    LTEXT "Bar #6: ",-1,130,125,40,8,NOT WS_GROUP
    LTEXT "Bar #7: ",-1,130,140,40,8,NOT WS_GROUP
    LTEXT "Bar #8: ",-1,130,155,40,8,NOT WS_GROUP
    LTEXT "Bar #9: ",-1,130,170,40,8,NOT WS_GROUP
    LTEXT "Bar #10:",-1,130,185,45,8,NOT WS_GROUP
    EDITTEXT DM_P1,90,120,30,12
    EDITTEXT DM_P2,90,135,30,12
    EDITTEXT DM_P3,90,150,30,12
    EDITTEXT DM_P4,90,165,30,12
    EDITTEXT DM_P5,90,180,30,12
    EDITTEXT DM_P6,180,120,30,12
    EDITTEXT DM_P7,180,135,30,12
    EDITTEXT DM_P8,180,150,30,12
    EDITTEXT DM_P9,180,165,30,12
    EDITTEXT DM_P10,180,180,30,12
    PUSHBUTTON "OK",IDOK,54,195,24,14
    PUSHBUTTON "Cancel",IDCANCEL,124,195,34,14
END

#ifdef APSTUDIO_INVOKED
/////////////////////////////////////////////////////////////
//
// TEXTINCLUDE
//

1 TEXTINCLUDE DISCARDABLE
BEGIN
  "resource.h\0"
END

2 TEXTINCLUDE DISCARDABLE
BEGIN
  "#define APSTUDIO_HIDDEN_SYMBOLS\r\n"
  "#include ""windows.h""\r\n"
  "#undef APSTUDIO_HIDDEN_SYMBOLS\r\n"
  "#include ""afxres.h""\r\n"
  "\0"
END

3 TEXTINCLUDE DISCARDABLE
```

```
BEGIN
  "\r\n"
  "\0"
END


#endif    // APSTUDIO_INVOKED


#endif    // English (U.S.) resources
/////////////////////////////////////////////////////////////


#ifndef APSTUDIO_INVOKED
/////////////////////////////////////////////////////////////
//
// Generated from the TEXTINCLUDE 3 resource.
//


/////////////////////////////////////////////////////////////
#endif    // not APSTUDIO_INVOKED
```

It took a while to get here, but we're now ready to look at the source code for the BARCHART.CPP application. Examine this code and note the inclusion of various resources such as menus, dialog boxes, and so on.

```
//
//   barchart.cpp
//   A Presentation Quality Bar Chart Application
//   using the MFC Library.
//   Copyright (c) William H. Murray and Chris H. Pappas, 1997
//

#include <afxwin.h>
#include <string.h>
#include <math.h>
#include <stdlib.h>
#include "barchartr.h"    // resource IDs
#include "barchart.h"

#define maxnumbar 10
char szTString[80]="(bar chart title area)";
char szXString[80]="x-axis label";
char szYString[80]="y-axis label";
```

```
int iBarSize[maxnumbar]={20,10,40,50};
int m_cxClient,m_cyClient;

CTheApp theApp;

CMainWnd::CMainWnd( )
{
  Create((AfxRegisterWndClass(CS_HREDRAW|CS_VREDRAW,
        LoadCursor(NULL,IDC_CROSS),
        (HBRUSH) GetStockObject(WHITE_BRUSH),NULL)),
        "Bar Chart Application with the MFC",
        WS_OVERLAPPEDWINDOW,rectDefault,NULL,"BarMenu");
}

void CMainWnd::OnSize(UINT,int x,int y)
{
  m_cxClient=x;
  m_cyClient=y;
}

void CMainWnd::OnPaint( )
{
  CPaintDC dc(this);
  static DWORD dwColor[10]={RGB(0,0,0),         //black
                            RGB(245,0,0),       //red
                            RGB(0,245,0),       //green
                            RGB(0,0,245),       //blue
                            RGB(245,245,0),     //yellow
                            RGB(245,0,245),     //magenta
                            RGB(0,245,245),     //cyan
                            RGB(0,80,80),       //blend 1
                            RGB(80,80,80),      //blend 2
                            RGB(245,245,245)};  //white

  CFont newfont;
  CFont* oldfont;
  CBrush newbrush;
  CBrush* oldbrush;
  int i,iNBars,iBarWidth,iBarMax;
  int ilenMaxLabel;
  int x1,x2,y1,y2;
  int iBarSizeScaled[maxnumbar];
```

```
char sbuffer[10],*strptr;

iNBars=0;
for (i=0;i<maxnumbar;i++) {
  if(iBarSize[i]!=0) iNBars++;
}

iBarWidth=400/iNBars;

// Find bar with maximum height and scale
iBarMax=iBarSize[0];
for(i=0;i<iNBars;i++)
  if (iBarMax<iBarSize[i]) iBarMax=iBarSize[i];

// Convert maximum y value to a string
strptr=_itoa(iBarMax,sbuffer,10);
ilenMaxLabel=strlen(sbuffer);

// Scale bars in array.  Highest bar = 270
for (i=0;i<iNBars;i++)
  iBarSizeScaled[i]=iBarSize[i]*(270/iBarMax);

// Create custom viewport and map mode
dc.SetMapMode(MM_ISOTROPIC);
dc.SetWindowExt(640,400);
dc.SetViewportExt(m_cxClient,m_cyClient);
dc.SetViewportOrg(0,0);

// Draw text to window if large enough
if (m_cxClient > 200) {
newfont.CreateFont(12,12,0,0,FW_BOLD,
                   FALSE,FALSE,FALSE,OEM_CHARSET,
                   OUT_DEFAULT_PRECIS,
                   CLIP_DEFAULT_PRECIS,
                   DEFAULT_QUALITY,
                   VARIABLE_PITCH|FF_ROMAN,
                   "Roman");
oldfont=dc.SelectObject(&newfont);
dc.TextOut((300-(strlen(szTString)*10/2)),
           15,szTString,strlen(szTString));
dc.TextOut((300-(strlen(szXString)*10/2)),
           365,szXString,strlen(szXString));
```

```
dc.TextOut((90-ilenMaxLabel*12),70,strptr,ilenMaxLabel);
// delete font objects
dc.SelectObject(oldfont);
newfont.DeleteObject( );

newfont.CreateFont(12,12,900,900,FW_BOLD,
                    FALSE,FALSE,FALSE,
                    OEM_CHARSET,OUT_DEFAULT_PRECIS,
                    CLIP_DEFAULT_PRECIS,
                    DEFAULT_QUALITY,
                    VARIABLE_PITCH|FF_ROMAN,
                    "Roman");
oldfont=dc.SelectObject(&newfont);
dc.TextOut(50,200+(strlen(szXString)*10/2),
           szYString,strlen(szYString));
// delete font objects
dc.SelectObject(oldfont);
newfont.DeleteObject( );
}

// Draw coordinate axis
dc.MoveTo(99,49);
dc.LineTo(99,350);
dc.LineTo(500,350);
dc.MoveTo(99,350);

// Initial values
x1=100;
y1=350;
x2=x1+iBarWidth;

// Draw Each Bar
for(i=0;i<iNBars;i++) {
  newbrush.CreateSolidBrush(dwColor[i]);
  oldbrush=dc.SelectObject(&newbrush);
  y2=350-iBarSizeScaled[i];
  dc.Rectangle(x1,y1,x2,y2);
  x1=x2;
  x2+=iBarWidth;
  // delete brush objects
  dc.SelectObject(oldbrush);
  newbrush.DeleteObject( );
```

```
    }
  }

  int CMainWnd::OnCreate(LPCREATESTRUCT)
  {
    UpdateWindow( );
    return (0);
  }

  void CMainWnd::OnAbout( )
  {
    CModalDialog about("AboutDlgBox",this);
    about.DoModal( );
  }

  void CBarDataDialog::OnOK( )

  {
    GetDlgItemText(DM_TITLE,szTString,80);
    GetDlgItemText(DM_XLABEL,szXString,80);
    GetDlgItemText(DM_YLABEL,szYString,80);
    iBarSize[0]=GetDlgItemInt(DM_P1,NULL,0);
    iBarSize[1]=GetDlgItemInt(DM_P2,NULL,0);
    iBarSize[2]=GetDlgItemInt(DM_P3,NULL,0);
    iBarSize[3]=GetDlgItemInt(DM_P4,NULL,0);
    iBarSize[4]=GetDlgItemInt(DM_P5,NULL,0);
    iBarSize[5]=GetDlgItemInt(DM_P6,NULL,0);
    iBarSize[6]=GetDlgItemInt(DM_P7,NULL,0);
    iBarSize[7]=GetDlgItemInt(DM_P8,NULL,0);
    iBarSize[8]=GetDlgItemInt(DM_P9,NULL,0);
    iBarSize[9]=GetDlgItemInt(DM_P10,NULL,0);
    CModalDialog::OnOK( );
  }

  void CMainWnd::OnBarData( )
  {
    CBarDataDialog dlgBarData(this);
    if (dlgBarData.DoModal( )==IDOK) {
      InvalidateRect(NULL,TRUE);
      UpdateWindow( );
    }
  };
```

```
void CMainWnd::OnExit( )
{
  DestroyWindow( );
}

BEGIN_MESSAGE_MAP(CMainWnd,CFrameWnd)
  ON_WM_PAINT( )
  ON_WM_SIZE( )
  ON_WM_CREATE( )
  ON_COMMAND(IDM_ABOUT,OnAbout)
  ON_COMMAND(IDM_INPUT,OnBarData)
  ON_COMMAND(IDM_EXIT,OnExit)
END_MESSAGE_MAP( )

BOOL CTheApp::InitInstance( )
{
  m_pMainWnd=new CMainWnd( );
  m_pMainWnd->ShowWindow(m_nCmdShow);
  m_pMainWnd->UpdateWindow( );
  return TRUE;
}
```

When all of these files are entered, build the application with the Visual C++ Project Utility.

The BARCHART.H Header File

This application will use many of the features of the previous application. For example, note the similar function declarations in CMainWnd and the message map:

```
afx_msg void On Paint( );
afx_msg void OnSize(UINT,int,int);
afx_msg int  OnCreate(LPCREATESTRUCT cs);
afx_msg void OnAbout( );
afx_msg void OnBarData( );
afx_msg void OnExit( );
```

The creation of the About and data entry dialog boxes parallels the last example. In this application, however, the data entry dialog box will process more user input than in the previous example. You may want to review the information dealing with dialog boxes in the previous example at this time.

The Resource Files

The BARCHARTR.H and BARCHART.RC files are combined by the Microsoft Resource Compiler into a single compiled Windows resource, BARCHART.RES.

The BARCHARTR.H resource header file contains three menu identification values: IDM_ABOUT, IDM_INPUT, and IDM_EXIT.

Thirteen identification values are also included for use by the modal dialog box. Three are for the title and labels: DM_TITLE, DM_XLABEL, and DM_YLABEL. The remaining ten values, DM_P1 to DM_P10, are for retrieving the height of the individual bars. They will be represented with integer values.

The resource script file, BARCHART.RC, contains a description of the application's menu and dialog boxes. The menu is shown in Figure 23-9. Compare the menu title and features to the text used to create the menu in the resource file.

The application contains two dialog boxes. The About box is almost identical to that used in the previous application. The data entry dialog box is a bit more complex and is shown in Figure 23-10.

The resource editor was used to construct both the About and the data entry dialog boxes.

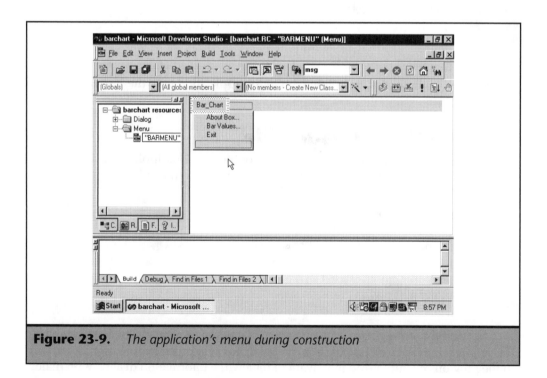

Figure 23-9. *The application's menu during construction*

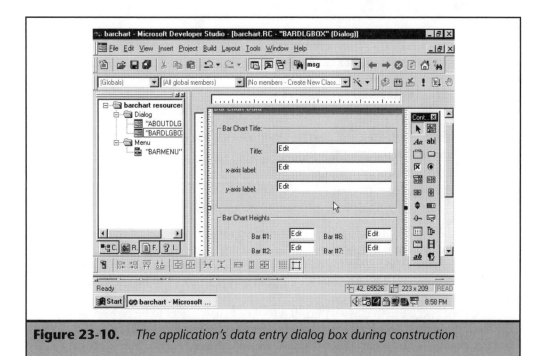

Figure 23-10. *The application's data entry dialog box during construction*

The BARCHART.CPP Source Code File

This section concentrates on those features of the bar chart application that were not addressed in the applications developed earlier in this chapter. The BARCHART.CPP application will allow the user to draw a presentation-quality bar chart in the client area of a window. With the use of a modal dialog box, the user can specify a chart title, axis labels, and the heights of up to ten bars. The chart will then be correctly scaled to the window, with each bar's color selected from an array of predefined values.

The maximum number of bars, maxnumbar, is set to ten at the start of the application:

```
#define maxnumbar 10
```

This value can be changed slightly, but remember that a good bar chart doesn't crowd too many bars onto a single chart.

As you can see in the following code, global data types hold initial bar chart values for titles, axis labels, and bar heights:

**WINDOWS
PROGRAMMING
FOUNDATIOINS**

```
char szTString[80]="(bar chart title area)";
char szXString[80]="x-axis label";
char szYString[80]="y-axis label";
int iBarSize[maxnumbar]={20,10,40,50};
```

The size of the client area will also be saved as a global value. These are the same variable names used in the previous example:

```
int m_cxClient,m_cyClient;
```

Because the application keeps track of the client area size, this bar chart can be scaled to fit the current window size.

Bar colors are selected from the *dwColor* array in a sequential manner. If the bar chart has three bars, they will be black, red, and green. Colors can be exchanged if you like.

The CFont and CBrush classes permit a font or brush object to be passed to any CDC (base class for display context) member function. New fonts will be needed to draw the chart title and axes labels. Brushes were discussed earlier in this chapter. Here is the syntax used to create a new font and brush object:

CFont newfont;
CFont* oldfont;
CBrush newbrush;
CBrush* oldbrush;

Manipulating Bar Data

Before plotting a bar chart, it is first necessary to determine how many bar values are being held in the global array *iBarSize*. This can be determined by counting values until the first zero value is encountered:

```
iNBars=0;
for (i=0;i<maxnumbar;i++)
{
   if(iBarSize[i]!=0) iNBars++;
}
```

Data values are returned to this array whenever the data entry dialog box is closed. The width of each bar drawn in the chart is dependent on the total number of bars. The chart will always be drawn to the same width. Individual bar width is determined with this calculation:

```
iBarWidth=400/iNBars;
```

The height of each bar is determined relative to the largest bar value entered by the user. The largest bar value is always drawn to the same chart height. The size of the largest bar value is easy to determine:

```
// Find bar with maximum height and scale
iBarMax=iBarSize[0];
for(i=0;i<iNBars;i++)
  if (iBarMax<iBarSize[i]) iBarMax=iBarSize[i];
```

This chart will also print the height of the largest bar value next to the vertical axis. The _itoa( ) function is used to convert this value to a string:

```
// Convert maximum y value to a string
strptr=_itoa(iBarMax,sbuffer,10);
ilenMaxLabel=strlen(sbuffer);
```

The remaining bars in the array are then scaled to the largest bar's value:

```
// Scale bars in array. Highest bar = 270
for (i=0;i<iNBars;i++)
  iBarSizeScaled[i]=iBarSize[i]*(270/iBarMax);
```

Preparing the Window

Before the application begins drawing in the window's client area, the mapping mode, window extent, viewport extent, and origin are set with the following portion of code:

```
// Create custom viewport and map mode
dc.SetMapMode(MM_ISOTROPIC);
dc.SetWindowExt(640,400);
dc.SetViewportExt(m_cxClient,m_cyClient);
dc.SetViewportOrg(0,0);
```

This same action was taken in the previous example to ensure that when the window changes size, the chart will remain proportional to the window size. See the previous application for additional details on these function calls.

Drawing Text to the Window

The previous application drew text to the screen using the Windows default font. When several fonts or orientations are required, various font functions must be used. This application requires several font sizes and orientations. Let's look at how these can be created. There are actually two ways to create and manipulate fonts in Windows: CreateFont( ) and CreateFontIndirect( ). This example uses the CreateFont( ) function.

WHAT IS A FONT?   A *font* can be defined as a complete set of characters of the same typeface and size. Fonts include letters, punctuation marks, and additional symbols. The size of a font is measured in points. For example, 12-point Arial, 12-point Times New Roman, 14-point Times New Roman, and 12-point Lucida Bright are all different fonts. A *point* is the smallest unit of measure used in typography. There are 12 points in a pica and 72 points (6 picas) in an inch.

A *typeface* is a basic character design that is defined by a stroke width and a *serif* (a smaller line used to finish off a main stroke of a letter, as you can see at the top and bottom of the uppercase letter "M"). As just mentioned, a font represents a complete set of characters from one specific typeface, all with a certain size and style, such as italics or bold. Normally, the system owns all of the font resources and shares them with application programs. Fonts are not usually compiled into the final executable version of a program.

Applications such as BARCHART.CPP treat fonts like other drawing objects. Windows supplies several fonts: System, Terminal, Courier, Helvetica, Modern, Roman, Script, and Times Roman, as well as several TrueType fonts. These are called GDI_supplied fonts.

THE CREATEFONT( ) FUNCTION SYNTAX   The CreateFont( ) function is defined in the WINDOWS.H header file. This function selects a logical font from the GDI's pool of physical fonts that most closely matches the characteristics specified by the developer in the function call. Once created, this logical font can be selected by any device. The syntax for the CreateFont( ) function is:

CreateFont(*Height,Width,Escapement,Orientation,Weight,*
        Italic,Underline,StrikeOut,CharSet,
        OutputPrecision,ClipPrecision,Quality,
        PitchAndFamily,Facename)

Using CreateFont( ), with its 14 parameters, requires quite a bit of skill. Table 23-1 gives a brief description of the CreateFont( ) parameters.

CreateFont( ) Parameters	Description
(LONG) Height	Desired font height in logical units
(LONG) Width	Average font width in logical units
(LONG) Escapement	Angle (in tenths of a degree) for each line written in the font
(LONG) Orientation	Angle (in tenths of a degree) for each character's baseline
(LONG) Weight	Weight of font (from 0 to 1,000); 400 is normal, 700 is bold
(BYTE) Italic	Italic font
(BYTE) Underline	Underline font
(BYTE) StrikeOut	Struck out fonts (redline)
(BYTE) CharSet	Character set (ANSI_CHARSET, OEM_CHARSET)
(BYTE) OutputPrecision	How closely output must match the requested specifications (OUT_CHARACTER_PRECIS, OUT_DEFAULT_PRECIS, OUT_STRING_PRECIS, OUT_STROKE_PRECIS)
(BYTE) ClipPrecision	How to clip characters outside of clipping range (CLIP_CHARACTER_PRECIS, CLIP_DEFAULT_PRECIS, CLIP_STROKE_PRECIS)
(BYTE) Quality	How carefully the logical attributes are mapped to the physical font (DEFAULT_QUALITY, DRAFT_QUALITY, PROOF_QUALITY)
(BYTE) PitchAndFamily	Pitch and family of font (DEFAULT_PITCH, FIXED_PITCH, PROOF_QUALITY, FF_ROMAN, FF_SCRIPT, FF_DECORATIVE, FF_DONTCARE, FF_MODERN, FF_SWISS)
(CHAR) Facename	A string pointing to the typeface name of the desired font

Table 23-1. *CreateFont( ) Parameters*

The first time the CreateFont( ) function is called by the application, the parameters are set to the following values:

Height = 12
Width = 12
Escapement = 0
Orientation = 0
Weight = FW_BOLD
Italic = FALSE
Underline = FALSE
StrikeOut = FALSE
CharSet = OEM_CHARSET
OutputPrecision = OUT_DEFAULT_PRECIS
ClipPrecision = CLIP_DEFAULT_PRECIS
Quality = DEFAULT_QUALITY
PitchAndFamily = VARIABLE_PITCH I FF_ROMAN
Facename = "Roman"

An attempt will then be made by Windows to find a font to match the preceding specifications. This font will be used to print a horizontal string of text in the window. The next time CreateFont( ) is called, the parameters are set to the following values:

Height = 12
Width = 12
Escapement = 900
Orientation = 900
Weight = FW_BOLD
Italic = FALSE
Underline = FALSE
StrikeOut = FALSE
CharSet = OEM_CHARSET
OutputPrecision = OUT_DEFAULT_PRECIS
ClipPrecision = CLIP_DEFAULT_PRECIS
Quality = DEFAULT_QUALITY
PitchAndFamily = VARIABLE_PITCH I FF_ROMAN
Facename = "Roman"

Again, an attempt will be made by Windows to find a match to the preceding specifications. Examine the listing and notice that only Escapement and Orientation were changed. Both of these parameters use angle values specified in tenths of a degree. Thus, 900 represents an angle of 90.0 degrees. The Escapement parameter rotates the line of text from horizontal to vertical. Orientation rotates each character in this application by 90.0 degrees. This font will be used to print a vertical axis label in the application.

Here is how the vertical axis label was printed in this application:

```
newfont.CreateFont(12,12,900,900,FW_BOLD,
                   FALSE,FALSE,FALSE,
                   OEM_CHARSET,
                   OUT_DEFAULT_PRECIS,
                   CLIP_DEFAULT_PRECIS,
                   DEFAULT_QUALITY,
                   VARIABLE_PITCH|FF_ROMAN,
                   "Roman");
oldfont=dc.SelectObject(&newfont);
dc.TextOut(50,200+(strlen(szXString)*10/2),
           szYString,strlen(szYString));
```

When you develop your own applications, be sure to examine the online documentation on the CreateFont( ) function and the additional typefaces that may be available for your use.

Drawing the Axes and Bars

Simple x and y coordinate axes are drawn with the use of the MoveTo( ) and LineTo( ) functions:

```
// Draw coordinate axis
dc.MoveTo(99,49);
dc.LineTo(99,350);
dc.LineTo(500,350);
dc.MoveTo(99,350);
```

The program then prepares for drawing each bar. As the following code shows, the first bar always starts at position 100,350 on the chart, as defined by $x1$ and $y1$. The width of the first bar and all subsequent bars is calculated from the last drawing position and the width of each bar. The second x value is defined by $x2$.

```
// Initial values
x1=100;
y1=350;
x2=x1+iBarWidth;
```

Bars are drawn (by the program) by retrieving the scaled bar height value from iBarSizeScaled. This scaled value, saved in *y2*, is used in the Rectangle( ) function. Since the Rectangle( ) function draws a closed figure, the figure will be filled with the current brush color. The color value selected from the array is incremented during each pass through the loop. Here is a portion of code to show how this is achieved:

```
// Draw Each Bar
for(i=0;i<iNBars;i++)
{
  newbrush.CreateSolidBrush(dwColor[i]);
  oldbrush=dc.SelectObject(&newbrush);
  y2=350-iBarSizeScaled[i];
  dc.Rectangle(x1,y1,x2,y2);
  x1=x2;
  x2+=iBarWidth;
}
```

After each bar is drawn, the values in *x1* and *x2* are updated to point to the next bar's position. This process is repeated in the for loop until all the bars are drawn.

Running BARCHART

Compile the BARCHART application within the Project utility. When you execute the application, a default bar chart similar to the one in Figure 23-11 will be drawn in the window. You can create a custom bar chart, as shown in Figure 23-12, by entering a chart title, axis labels, and unique bar values.

You can continue the development of this application by adding axis tick marks, a legend, and so on. Customization is limited only by your imagination.

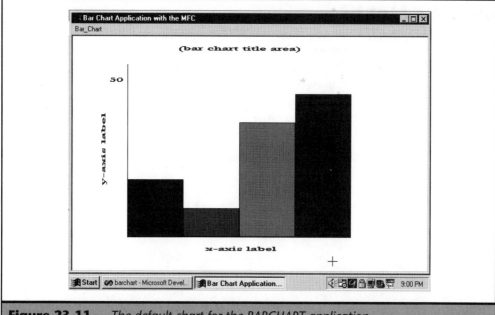

Figure 23-11.   *The default chart for the BARCHART application*

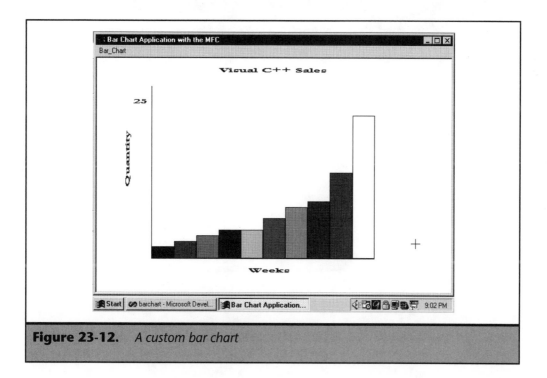

Figure 23-12.   *A custom bar chart*

What's Next?

The examples in this chapter were built on an MFC application (MFCSWP.CPP) that served as a template. This template was static in the sense that nothing in the template changed unless you changed it. In the next chapter you will learn how to produce dynamic templates using various wizards that work in conjunction with the MFC library. As you build applications using wizards, code will be generated to your specifications!

Part V

Wizards

The Complete Reference

Visual
C++ 5

Chapter 24

Application and Class Wizards

In the previous four chapters, you learned how to develop 32-bit Windows 95 and Windows NT applications with a procedure-oriented and object-oriented approach using Microsoft Foundation Class libraries. These chapters relied heavily on the use of templates for code development. Templates allow programmers to use redundant code over and over again, freeing them to concentrate on the new features of a particular application. We view these as static templates that you merely reused from one application to another.

Sometimes, however, static templates are not enough. Imagine an application where you want to incorporate file I/O capabilities, such as creating a new file, opening an existing file, saving a file, and so forth. Perhaps you'll also want to include editing capabilities, such as cutting, copying, pasting, and so on. Features such as these use a familiar menu style already incorporated in our static templates. Now extend your thinking a little farther and imagine creating applications with a multiple document interface (MDI) and object linking and embedding (OLE) features. No single static template will allow us to pick and choose from this extended list of programming features.

Microsoft's solution was to create a dynamic template generator called the *AppWizard*. The AppWizard depends heavily on the Microsoft Foundation Class library and generates object-oriented code. To select the AppWizard, when starting a new project, select the File menu in the Visual C++ Compiler. Then choose New and select the MFC AppWizard from the list of options. The AppWizard generates a code template that will allow you to select only those features you need for your application. However, as was the case with the static templates in this book, it is still up to you to write the remainder of the code for your unique application.

A close relative of the AppWizard is the *ClassWizard*. The ClassWizard allows you to add classes or customize existing classes. The ClassWizard can be used after the template code is created by the AppWizard. The ClassWizard is selected using the View menu and selecting the ClassWizard menu item.

This chapter will explore the use of these two wizards and help you understand how they can be put to work for you. Two applications will be developed as examples. The first will use the bare minimum AppWizard code to create an application with a client area that contains simple graphics. The second will use several wizard features. This application will be a simple text editor that can work with multiple documents (MDI), display a toolbar at the top of the application, and incorporate file I/O and editing capabilities.

Be warned, however, that there is a learning curve that you must overcome before you will become comfortable using these new tools. We strongly recommend that you review Chapters 22 and 23 before proceeding. These chapters deal with the MFC library. Wizards only generate object-oriented code; they rely on the MFC library for their power.

The Graph Application

In this section, you will learn all of the steps necessary to create a basic application using the AppWizard and ClassWizard tools. This is a mechanical process, requiring that certain steps be completed in a specific order. The steps discussed here will take you through the development of code that will be used to create the first program, named *Graph*.

If your compiler is up and running, follow the steps along with us as we create this application.

The AppWizard

From the Microsoft Visual C++ menu bar, select the File menu and then the New item from the menu list. As shown in Figure 24-1, a dialog box will appear that will allow you to start a new project by selecting the MFC AppWizard option.

Name the new project *Graph,* as shown in Figure 24-1. After you have named the project, you can start developing it using the AppWizard. Notice the project location shown in Figure 24-1. Now, simply click on OK to start the AppWizard.

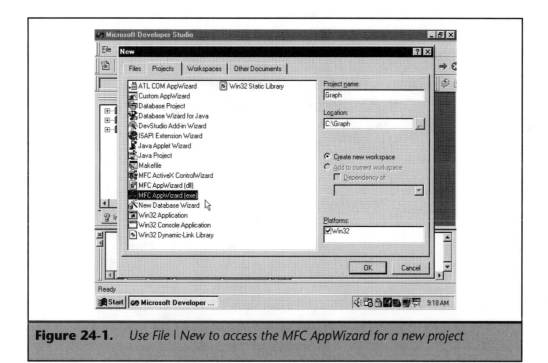

Figure 24-1. *Use File | New to access the MFC AppWizard for a new project*

The first step in generating a project with the AppWizard involves making a decision about whether the project will handle single, multiple, or dialog-based documents, as shown in Figure 24-2.

Single-document interfaces are the simplest, since multiple-document communications will not be required for this example. Accept the default for the resource language option. Click on the Next button to start Step 2, shown in Figure 24-3.

Step 2 is used only when you want to include database support. For this example, None is selected. Click on the Next button to start Step 3, shown in Figure 24-4.

Step 3 allows you to specify the type of OLE support: containers or servers. For this example, None is selected. You'll learn more about this option in Chapter 25. Click on the Next button to start Step 4, shown in Figure 24-5.

Step 4 gives you the opportunity to add special features to the project. For example, a toolbar or status bar could be added at this point. In our first example, however, no special features are needed. Click on the Next button to start Step 5, shown in Figure 24-6.

Step 6 gives you the opportunity to add comments and identify whether a shared DLL or statically linked MFC library is used. Click on the Next button to start Step 6, shown in Figure 24-7.

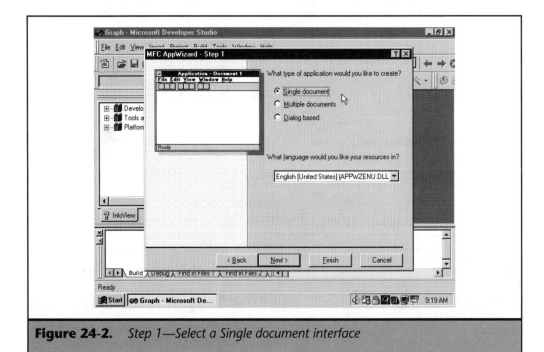

Figure 24-2. *Step 1—Select a Single document interface*

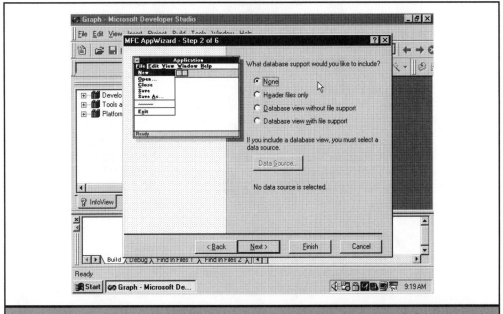

Figure 24-3.   *Step 2—Select None since no database support is needed*

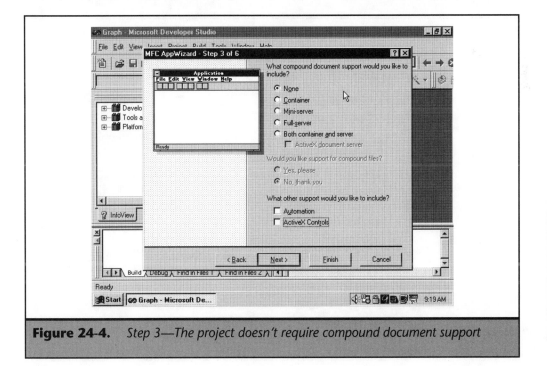

Figure 24-4.   *Step 3—The project doesn't require compound document support*

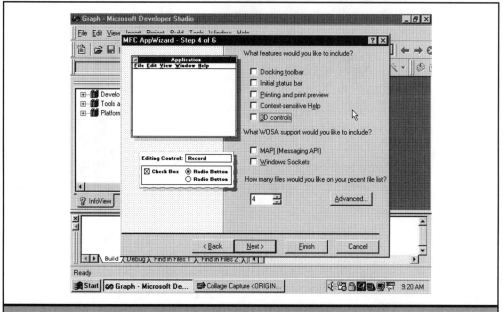

Figure 24-5.   *Step 4—Allows special application features to be added*

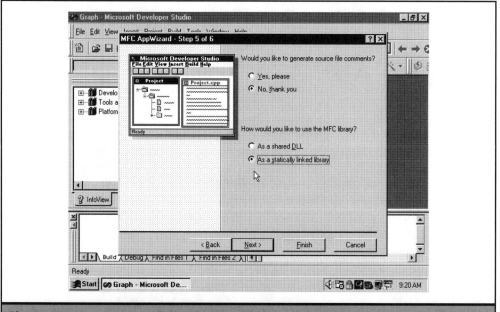

Figure 24-6.   *Step 5—Allows inclusion of source comments and the identification of the MFC library*

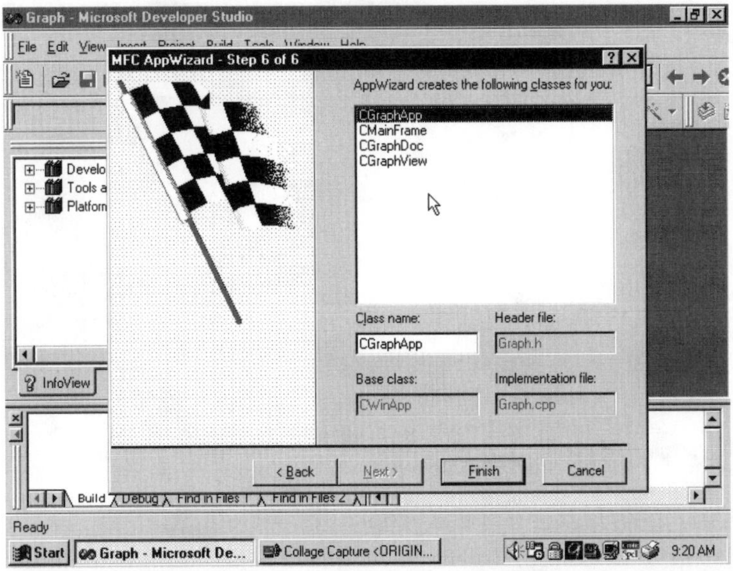

Figure 24-7. *Step 6—Allows a review of the classes to be generated by the AppWizard*

Step 6 is the final step used to specify project features. Here you will see a listing of the new classes that the AppWizard will automatically generate. The four classes that will be created for this application are CGraphApp, CMainFrame, CGraphDoc, and CGraphView.

If you select CGraphView in the list box, shown in Figure 24-7, the Base Class list box will expand so that you can specify whether you want the CGraphView class to be derived from the CEditView, CFormView, CScrollView, or CView base class.

The CView class, derived from the CWnd class, is used to create the base for user-defined view classes. A *view* serves as a buffer between the document and the user and is actually a child of a frame window. It produces an image of the document on the screen or on the printer and uses input from the keyboard or the mouse as an operation on the document.

Two of the classes just mentioned, CFormView and CEditView, are derived from the CView base class. CFormView describes a scrollable view that is based on a dialog template resource and includes dialog box controls. CEditView describes a text editor. CEditView is used in the second application developed in this chapter.

The Graph application will use CView as the base class. As a matter of fact, all of the default classes shown in the Base Class list box are acceptable. Click on the Finish button and see a description summary of what the AppWizard will create for this project. Figure 24-8 shows the information for this project.

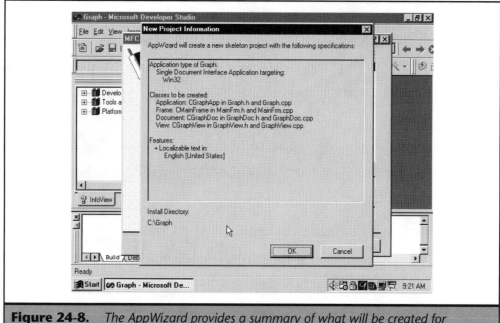

Figure 24-8.   *The AppWizard provides a summary of what will be created for the project*

The information displayed in this dialog box is a summary of your choices, and this box offers you one last chance to make alterations before the template code is generated. If the options are correct, click the OK button to generate the code.

The various files—and there seem to be quite a few of them—will be generated and stored in the subdirectory specified at the beginning of the project.

After the code has been generated, you can add additional features to the project code by selecting ClassWizard using the View menu and selecting the ClassWizard… menu item, as shown in Figure 24-9.

Our Graph example will eventually draw some simple graphics to the client area. Therefore, the application must be able to process WM_PAINT messages. The message handler can be added with the ClassWizard.

The ClassWizard

The ClassWizard generates additional code for the application. This code can be used to support the processing of messages such as WM_PAINT, WM_MOUSEMOVE, and so forth. The ClassWizard, as mentioned in the previous section, is started from the View menu by selecting the ClassWizard menu item. Figure 24-10 shows the initial ClassWizard dialog box.

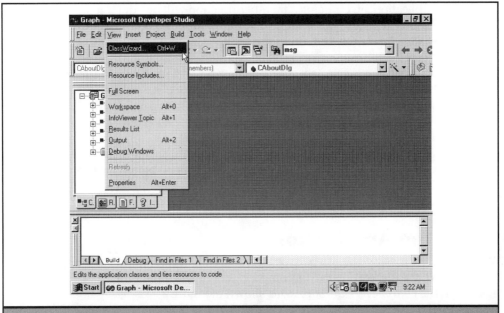

Figure 24-9. *The base code generated by the AppWizard can be customized by using the ClassWizard*

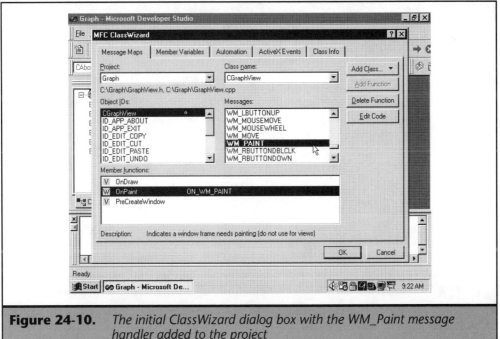

Figure 24-10. *The initial ClassWizard dialog box with the WM_Paint message handler added to the project*

In this application, an OnPaint( ) member function will be added to our program code to process WM_PAINT messages. To add this support code, select CGraphView in the Class Name text entry box. From the Object IDs list box, choose CGraphView, as shown in Figure 24-10.

When CGraphView is selected, a list of messages will be shown in the Messages list box. When the WM_PAINT message is selected from the Messages list box, the OnPaint( ) member function will be shown in the Member Functions list.

The GRAPHVIEW.CPP file will now contain this inserted code, as shown in Figure 24-11.

At this point various graphics functions can be added to this member function to make this application unique. You'll see how this is done before we conclude this example.

The next step is to compile and test the basic application.

Building the Application

When all of the message handlers have been added to the program's code with the ClassWizard, the application can be compiled and linked. Select the Rebuild All menu item from the compiler's Build menu, as shown in Figure 24-12.

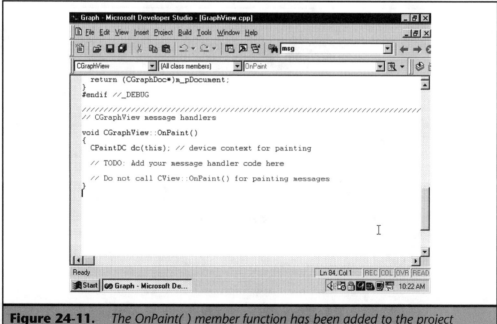

Figure 24-11. *The OnPaint( ) member function has been added to the project*

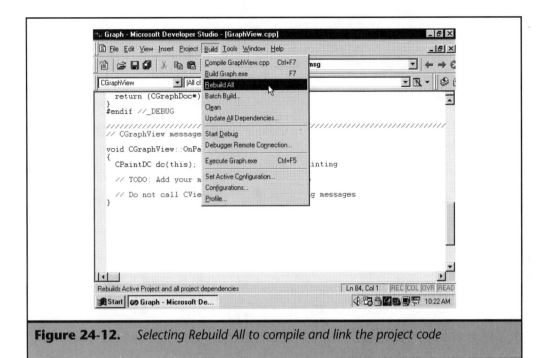

Figure 24-12. *Selecting Rebuild All to compile and link the project code*

During the build operation, details of the operation are displayed to the screen. Figure 24-13 shows the steps performed in the compile and link process for this application.

Notice in particular that four source code files—GRAPH.CPP, MAINFRM.CPP, GRAPHDOC.CPP, and GRAPHVIEW.CPP—will be compiled and then linked. In terms of sheer numbers, these four files are just the tip of the iceberg. When compilation is complete, examine the subdirectory in which these files are stored; you'll see more than 30 files stored there. Automation has its price!

An executable file is also present in the appropriate subdirectory. Execute the program. Your screen should look something like Figure 24-14.

The initial screen is empty because no graphics functions have been added at this point. Worse, none of the menu items work, with the exception of the About box from the Help menu. This is because the code for processing these messages must be added by you—it is not automatically generated. However, if you have gained a good understanding of the MFC library from previous chapters, developing this code will not be too difficult. The final example in this chapter will make use of all of these features.

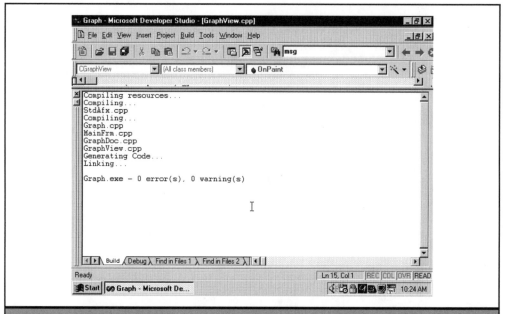

Figure 24-13. *During the build operation, the compile and link steps can be viewed*

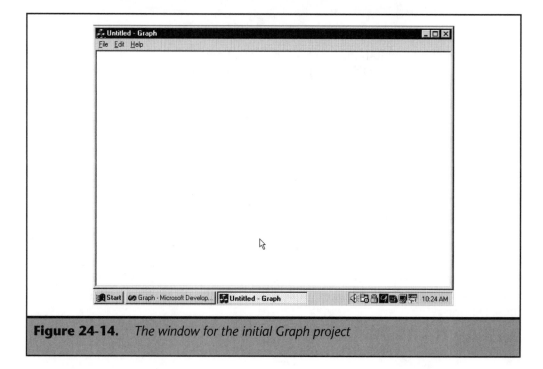

Figure 24-14. *The window for the initial Graph project*

Examining AppWizard Code

The AppWizard, with a little help from the ClassWizard, generated four important C++ files for the initial Graph application. These files were named GRAPH.CPP, MAINFRM.CPP, GRAPHDOC.CPP, and GRAPHVIEW.CPP. Each of these C++ files has an associated header file: GRAPH.H, MAINFRM.H, GRAPHDOC.H, and GRAPHVIEW.H. The header files contain the declarations of the specific classes in each C++ file. The purpose of each C++ file will be examined in the following sections.

THE GRAPH.CPP FILE   The GRAPH.CPP file, shown here, serves as the main file for the application. It contains the CGraphApp class.

```
// Graph.cpp : Defines the class behaviors for application.
//

#include "stdafx.h"
#include "Graph.h"

#include "MainFrm.h"
#include "GraphDoc.h"
#include "GraphView.h"

#ifdef _DEBUG
#define new DEBUG_NEW
#undef THIS_FILE
static char THIS_FILE[] = __FILE__;
#endif

/////////////////////////////////////////////////////////////
// CGraphApp

BEGIN_MESSAGE_MAP(CGraphApp, CWinApp)
  //{{AFX_MSG_MAP(CGraphApp)
  ON_COMMAND(ID_APP_ABOUT, OnAppAbout)
  //}}AFX_MSG_MAP
  // Standard file based document commands
  ON_COMMAND(ID_FILE_NEW, CWinApp::OnFileNew)
  ON_COMMAND(ID_FILE_OPEN, CWinApp::OnFileOpen)
END_MESSAGE_MAP( )

/////////////////////////////////////////////////////////////
// CGraphApp construction

CGraphApp::CGraphApp( )
```

```
{
}

//////////////////////////////////////////////////////////
// The one and only CGraphApp object

CGraphApp theApp;

//////////////////////////////////////////////////////////
// CGraphApp initialization

BOOL CGraphApp::InitInstance( )
{
  // Standard initialization

  // Change registry key under which our settings are stored.
  SetRegistryKey(_T("Local AppWizard-Generated Applications"));

  LoadStdProfileSettings( );  //Load standard INI file options

  // Register document templates

  CSingleDocTemplate* pDocTemplate;
  pDocTemplate = new CSingleDocTemplate(
    IDR_MAINFRAME,
    RUNTIME_CLASS(CGraphDoc),
    RUNTIME_CLASS(CMainFrame),          // main SDI frame window
    RUNTIME_CLASS(CGraphView));
  AddDocTemplate(pDocTemplate);

  // Parse command line for standard shell commands
  CCommandLineInfo cmdInfo;
  ParseCommandLine(cmdInfo);

  // Dispatch commands specified on the command line
  if (!ProcessShellCommand(cmdInfo))
    return FALSE;
  m_pMainWnd->ShowWindow(SW_SHOW);
  m_pMainWnd->UpdateWindow( );

  return TRUE;
}
```

```
/////////////////////////////////////////////////////////////
// CAboutDlg dialog used for App About

class CAboutDlg : public CDialog
{
public:
  CAboutDlg( );

// Dialog Data
  //{{AFX_DATA(CAboutDlg)
  enum { IDD = IDD_ABOUTBOX };
  //}}AFX_DATA

  // ClassWizard generated virtual function overrides
  //{{AFX_VIRTUAL(CAboutDlg)
  protected:
  virtual void DoDataExchange(CDataExchange* pDX);
  //}}AFX_VIRTUAL

// Implementation
protected:
  //{{AFX_MSG(CAboutDlg)
    // No message handlers
  //}}AFX_MSG
  DECLARE_MESSAGE_MAP( )
};

CAboutDlg::CAboutDlg( ) : CDialog(CAboutDlg::IDD)
{
  //{{AFX_DATA_INIT(CAboutDlg)
  //}}AFX_DATA_INIT
}

void CAboutDlg::DoDataExchange(CDataExchange* pDX)
{
  CDialog::DoDataExchange(pDX);
  //{{AFX_DATA_MAP(CAboutDlg)
  //}}AFX_DATA_MAP
}

BEGIN_MESSAGE_MAP(CAboutDlg, CDialog)
  //{{AFX_MSG_MAP(CAboutDlg)
```

```
    // No message handlers
  //}}AFX_MSG_MAP
END_MESSAGE_MAP( )

// App command to run the dialog
void CGraphApp::OnAppAbout( )
{
  CAboutDlg aboutDlg;
  aboutDlg.DoModal( );
}


//////////////////////////////////////////////////////////////
// CGraphApp commands
```

The message map, near the top of the listing, belongs to the CGraphApp class. This message map specifically links the ID_APP_ABOUT, ID_FILE_NEW, and ID_FILE_OPEN messages with their member functions: OnAppAbout( ), CWinApp::OnFileNew( ), and CWinApp::OnFileOpen( ). Also notice in the listing that a constructor, an initial instance InitInstance( ), and a member function OnAppAbout( ) are implemented.

The About dialog box is derived from the CDialog class. If you examine the lower portion of the code you will notice a message map, a constructor, and a member function CDialog::DoDataExchange( ) for this derived dialog class.

There are no initial CGraphApp commands, as you can see from the end of the listing.

THE MAINFRM.CPP FILE   The MAINFRM.CPP file, shown next, contains the frame class CMainFrame. This class is derived from CFrameWnd and is used to control all single document interface (SDI) frame features.

```
// MainFrm.cpp : implementation of the CMainFrame class
//

#include "stdafx.h"
#include "Graph.h"

#include "MainFrm.h"

#ifdef _DEBUG
#define new DEBUG_NEW
#undef THIS_FILE
```

```
static char THIS_FILE[] = __FILE__;
#endif

/////////////////////////////////////////////////////
// CMainFrame

IMPLEMENT_DYNCREATE(CMainFrame, CFrameWnd)

BEGIN_MESSAGE_MAP(CMainFrame, CFrameWnd)
  //{{AFX_MSG_MAP(CMainFrame)
  //}}AFX_MSG_MAP
END_MESSAGE_MAP( )

/////////////////////////////////////////////////////
// CMainFrame construction/destruction

CMainFrame::CMainFrame( )
{
}

CMainFrame::~CMainFrame( )
{
}

BOOL CMainFrame::PreCreateWindow(CREATESTRUCT& cs)
{
  return CFrameWnd::PreCreateWindow(cs);
}

/////////////////////////////////////////////////////
// CMainFrame diagnostics

#ifdef _DEBUG
void CMainFrame::AssertValid( ) const
{
  CFrameWnd::AssertValid( );
}

void CMainFrame::Dump(CDumpContext& dc) const
{
  CFrameWnd::Dump(dc);
}
```

```
#endif //_DEBUG

/////////////////////////////////////////////////////////////
// CMainFrame message handlers
```

When you examine this listing, you'll notice that the message map, constructor, and destructor initially contain no code. The member functions AssertValid( ) and Dump( ) use definitions contained in the parent class. Also note that CMainFrame initially contains no message handlers.

THE GRAPHDOC.CPP FILE   The GRAPHDOC.CPP file, shown here, contains the CGraphDoc class, which is unique to your application. This file is used to hold document data and to load and save files.

```
// GraphDoc.cpp : implementation of the CGraphDoc class
//

#include "stdafx.h"
#include "Graph.h"

#include "GraphDoc.h"

#ifdef _DEBUG
#define new DEBUG_NEW
#undef THIS_FILE
static char THIS_FILE[] = __FILE__;
#endif

/////////////////////////////////////////////////////////////
// CGraphDoc

IMPLEMENT_DYNCREATE(CGraphDoc, CDocument)

BEGIN_MESSAGE_MAP(CGraphDoc, CDocument)
  //{{AFX_MSG_MAP(CGraphDoc)
  //}}AFX_MSG_MAP
END_MESSAGE_MAP( )

/////////////////////////////////////////////////////////////
// CGraphDoc construction/destruction
```

```
CGraphDoc::CGraphDoc( )
{
}

CGraphDoc::~CGraphDoc( )
{
}

BOOL CGraphDoc::OnNewDocument( )
{
  if (!CDocument::OnNewDocument( ))
    return FALSE;

  return TRUE;
}

/////////////////////////////////////////////////////////
// CGraphDoc serialization

void CGraphDoc::Serialize(CArchive& ar)
{
  if (ar.IsStoring( ))
  {
  }
  else
  {
  }
}

/////////////////////////////////////////////////////////
// CGraphDoc diagnostics

#ifdef _DEBUG
void CGraphDoc::AssertValid( ) const
{
  CDocument::AssertValid( );
}

void CGraphDoc::Dump(CDumpContext& dc) const
{
  CDocument::Dump(dc);
}
```

```
#endif //_DEBUG

/////////////////////////////////////////////////////////
// CGraphDoc commands
```

Examine this listing and you will again notice that the message map, constructor, and destructor contain no code. Four member functions can be used to provide vital document support. OnNewDocument( ) uses the definition provided by the parent class. Serialize( ) supports persistent objects. Our second programming example will use this member function to help with file I/O. The member functions AssertValid( ) and Dump( ) use definitions contained in the parent class. There are no initial CGraphDoc commands.

THE GRAPHVIEW.CPP FILE   The GRAPHVIEW.CPP file, shown here, provides the view of the document. In this implementation, CGraphView is derived from the CView class. CGraphView objects are used to view CGraphDoc objects.

```
// GraphView.cpp : implementation of the CGraphView class
//

#include "stdafx.h"
#include "Graph.h"

#include "GraphDoc.h"
#include "GraphView.h"

#ifdef _DEBUG
#define new DEBUG_NEW
#undef THIS_FILE
static char THIS_FILE[] = __FILE__;
#endif


/////////////////////////////////////////////////////////
// CGraphView

IMPLEMENT_DYNCREATE(CGraphView, CView)

BEGIN_MESSAGE_MAP(CGraphView, CView)
  //{{AFX_MSG_MAP(CGraphView)
  ON_WM_PAINT( )
  //}}AFX_MSG_MAP
```

```
END_MESSAGE_MAP( )

//////////////////////////////////////////////////////////////
// CGraphView construction/destruction

CGraphView::CGraphView( )
{
}

CGraphView::~CGraphView( )
{
}

BOOL CGraphView::PreCreateWindow(CREATESTRUCT& cs)
{
  return CView::PreCreateWindow(cs);
}

//////////////////////////////////////////////////////////////
// CGraphView drawing

void CGraphView::OnDraw(CDC* pDC)
{
  CGraphDoc* pDoc = GetDocument( );
  ASSERT_VALID(pDoc);
}

//////////////////////////////////////////////////////////////
// CGraphView diagnostics

#ifdef _DEBUG
void CGraphView::AssertValid( ) const
{
  CView::AssertValid( );
}

void CGraphView::Dump(CDumpContext& dc) const
{
  CView::Dump(dc);
}

CGraphDoc* CGraphView::GetDocument( ) // non-debug ver inline
```

```
{
  ASSERT(m_pDocument->IsKindOf(RUNTIME_CLASS(CGraphDoc)));
  return (CGraphDoc*)m_pDocument;
}
#endif //_DEBUG

/////////////////////////////////////////////////////////////////
// CGraphView message handlers

void CGraphView::OnPaint( )
{
  CPaintDC dc(this); // device context for painting

  // TODO: Add your message handler code here

  // Do not call CView::OnPaint( ) for painting messages
}
```

Normally, the message map would be empty, but remember that we used the ClassWizard to add ON_WM_PAINT message-handling abilities. The constructor and destructor are empty.

The OnDraw( ) member function uses the pointer pDoc to point to the document. The member functions AssertValid( ) and Dump( ) use definitions contained in the parent class.

The message handler, OnPaint( ), is described at the end of this listing. Simple graphics commands, such as those shown in earlier chapters, can be inserted here.

Drawing in the Client Area

In the initial design phase of the Graph application, a single-document interface (SDI) application was created using the AppWizard and the ClassWizard. The view class was derived from the parent class, CView. Recall that the ClassWizard allowed us to add the WM_PAINT message handler to this code.

This is the perfect platform from which to draw simple graphics to the client area with very little additional work. To see how easy this can be, add the following code to the OnPaint( ) message handler shown in the previous listing.

```
// CGraphView message handlers

void CGraphView::OnPaint( )
{
```

```
static DWORD dwColor[9]={RGB(0,0,0),           //black
                         RGB(255,0,0),          //red
                         RGB(0,255,0),          //green
                         RGB(0,0,255),          //blue
                         RGB(255,255,0),        //yellow
                         RGB(255,0,255),        //magenta
                         RGB(0,255,255),        //cyan
                         RGB(127,127,127),      //gray
                         RGB(255,255,255)};     //white

POINT polylpts[4],polygpts[5];
int xcoord;

CBrush newbrush;
CBrush* oldbrush;
CPen newpen;
CPen* oldpen;

CPaintDC dc(this); // device context for painting

// draws and fills a red ellipse
newpen.CreatePen(PS_SOLID,1,dwColor[1]);
oldpen=dc.SelectObject(&newpen);
newbrush.CreateSolidBrush(dwColor[1]);
oldbrush=dc.SelectObject(&newbrush);
dc.Ellipse(275,300,200,250);
dc.TextOut(220,265,"ellipse",7);
dc.SelectObject(oldbrush);
newbrush.DeleteObject( );
dc.SelectObject(oldpen);
newpen.DeleteObject( );

// draws and fills a blue circle with ellipse function
newpen.CreatePen(PS_SOLID,1,dwColor[3]);
oldpen=dc.SelectObject(&newpen);
newbrush.CreateSolidBrush(dwColor[3]);
oldbrush=dc.SelectObject(&newbrush);
dc.Ellipse(375,75,525,225);
dc.TextOut(435,190,"circle",6);
dc.SelectObject(oldbrush);
newbrush.DeleteObject( );
dc.SelectObject(oldpen);
```

```
newpen.DeleteObject( );

// draws several green pixels
for(xcoord=400;xcoord<450;xcoord+=5)
  dc.SetPixel(xcoord,350,0L);
dc.TextOut(460,345,"<- pixels",9);

// draws a wide black diagonal line
newpen.CreatePen(PS_SOLID,6,dwColor[0]);
oldpen=dc.SelectObject(&newpen);
dc.MoveTo(20,20);
dc.LineTo(100,100);
dc.TextOut(60,20,"<- diagonal line",16);
dc.SelectObject(oldpen);
newpen.DeleteObject( );

// draws a blue arc
newpen.CreatePen(PS_DASH,1,dwColor[3]);
oldpen=dc.SelectObject(&newpen);
dc.Arc(25,125,175,225,175,225,100,125);
dc.TextOut(50,150,"small arc ->",12);
dc.SelectObject(oldpen);
newpen.DeleteObject( );

// draws a wide green chord
newpen.CreatePen(PS_SOLID,8,dwColor[2]);
oldpen=dc.SelectObject(&newpen);
dc.Chord(125,125,275,225,275,225,200,125);
dc.TextOut(280,150,"<- chord",8);
dc.SelectObject(oldpen);
newpen.DeleteObject( );

// draws a black pie slice and fills with green
newpen.CreatePen(PS_SOLID,1,dwColor[0]);
oldpen=dc.SelectObject(&newpen);
newbrush.CreateSolidBrush(dwColor[2]);
oldbrush=dc.SelectObject(&newbrush);
dc.Pie(200,0,300,100,200,50,250,100);
dc.TextOut(260,80,"<- pie wedge",12);
dc.SelectObject(oldbrush);
newbrush.DeleteObject( );
dc.SelectObject(oldpen);
```

```
newpen.DeleteObject( );

// draws a black rectangle and fills with gray
newbrush.CreateSolidBrush(dwColor[7]);
oldbrush=dc.SelectObject(&newbrush);
dc.Rectangle(25,300,150,375);
dc.TextOut(50,325,"rectangle",9);
dc.SelectObject(oldbrush);
newbrush.DeleteObject( );

// draws a black rounded rectangle and fills with blue
newbrush.CreateHatchBrush(HS_CROSS,dwColor[3]);
oldbrush=dc.SelectObject(&newbrush);
dc.RoundRect(350,250,400,290,20,20);
dc.TextOut(410,270,"
rectangle",20);
dc.SelectObject(oldbrush);
newbrush.DeleteObject( );

// draws several wide magenta lines with polyline
newpen.CreatePen(PS_SOLID,3,dwColor[5]);
oldpen=dc.SelectObject(&newpen);
polylpts[0].x=10;
polylpts[0].y=30;
polylpts[1].x=10;
polylpts[1].y=100;
polylpts[2].x=50;
polylpts[2].y=100;
polylpts[3].x=10;
polylpts[3].y=30;
dc.Polyline(polylpts,4);
dc.TextOut(10,110,"polyline",8);
dc.SelectObject(oldpen);
newpen.DeleteObject( );

// draws a wide cyan polygon and
// fills with diagonal yellow
newpen.CreatePen(PS_SOLID,4,dwColor[6]);
oldpen=dc.SelectObject(&newpen);
newbrush.CreateHatchBrush(HS_FDIAGONAL,dwColor[4]);
oldbrush=dc.SelectObject(&newbrush);
polygpts[0].x=40;
```

```
polygpts[0].y=200;
polygpts[1].x=100;
polygpts[1].y=270;
polygpts[2].x=80;
polygpts[2].y=290;
polygpts[3].x=20;
polygpts[3].y=220;
polygpts[4].x=40;
polygpts[4].y=200;
dc.Polygon(polygpts,5);
dc.TextOut(80,230,"<- polygon",10);
dc.SelectObject(oldbrush);
newbrush.DeleteObject( );
dc.SelectObject(oldpen);
newpen.DeleteObject( );

// Do not call CView::OnPaint( ) for painting messages
}
```

This should be familiar code, since it employs simple GDI graphics functions. Compile and execute the revised version of this application. Your screen should be similar to the one shown in Figure 24-15.

The AppWizard generated a template with a menu bar containing the File, Edit, and Help menus, along with the various graphics shapes. The default About box is viewed from the Help menu, as shown in Figure 24-16.

Remember that the other menus and menu items are not functional. Why? Because no additional code was added to the template to handle those responses.

If you diligently went through the AppWizard's template and removed code not used by this application, you would arrive at a static template very similar to the one we created and used in Chapter 23.

The next example will use an entirely new AppWizard template to generate a simple text editor. Enhancements will be made to the template code to add additional functionality to the application.

The Word Processor Application

Here is an application that will allow you to do simple text editing. From the Microsoft Visual C++ main menu bar, select the File menu then the New menu item. The list box in the New dialog box will allow you to select the MFC AppWizard option to generate a new project. Remember to enter the name of the project, as shown in Figure 24-17.

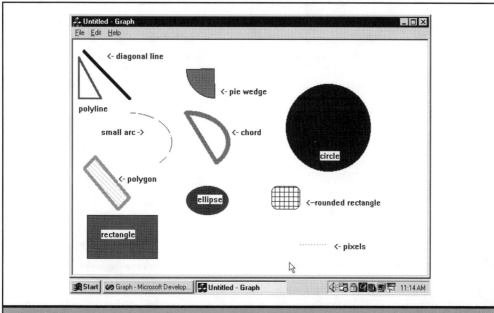

Figure 24-15. *Graphics shapes are drawn in the client area of the Graph application*

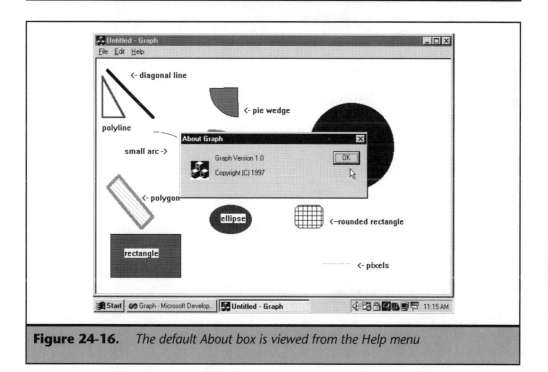

Figure 24-16. *The default About box is viewed from the Help menu*

Figure 24-17. *Starting the Editor project using the AppWizard*

The AppWizard will simultaneously create a new subdirectory by the same name beneath the currently selected directory and path. Now you can begin the six-step process that the AppWizard uses to build new applications. In Step 1, shown in Figure 24-18, you can see that this application will permit the user to work with multiple documents.

Figures 24-19 and 24-20 show that no database or compound document support will be included with this project.

In Step 4, shown in Figure 24-21, select options that allow this application to include a toolbar, a status bar, 3-D controls, and the ability to print the documents.

In Step 5, shown in Figure 24-22, no source code comments were requested and this project's library option was set to a statically linked library.

Step 6 shows the five classes that will be created for this application: CEditorApp, CMainFrame, CChildFrame, CEditorDoc, and CEditorView. This final dialog box can be seen in Figure 24-23.

When CEditorView is selected in the list box, the Base Class list box will expand so that you can specify whether you want the CEditorView class to be derived from the CEditView, CFormView, CListView, CRichEditView, CScrollView, CTreeView, or CView base class.

In this example the CEditorView class, derived from the CEditView class, is used to create the base for this application's user-defined view classes. CEditView describes

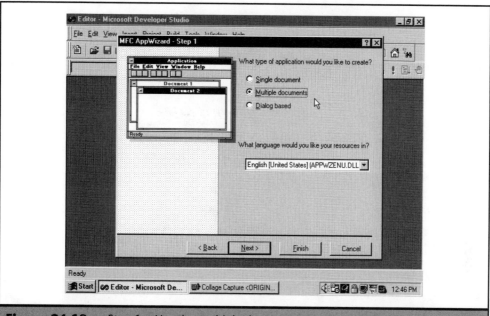

Figure 24-18.   *Step 1—Use the multiple document interface for this project*

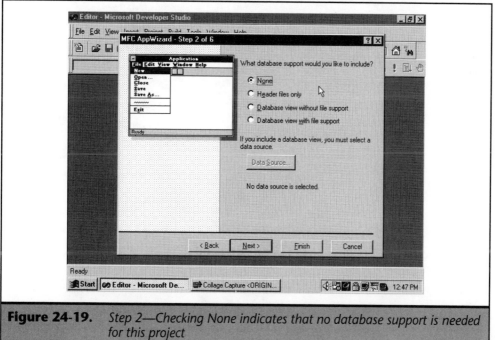

Figure 24-19.   *Step 2—Checking None indicates that no database support is needed for this project*

WIZARDS

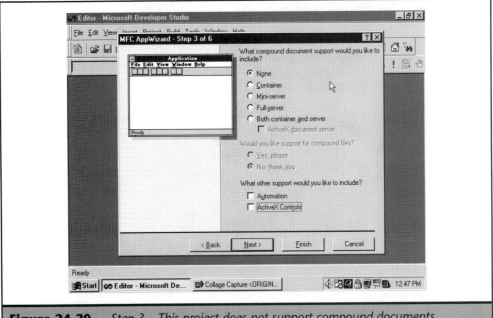

Figure 24-20. Step 3—This project does not support compound documents

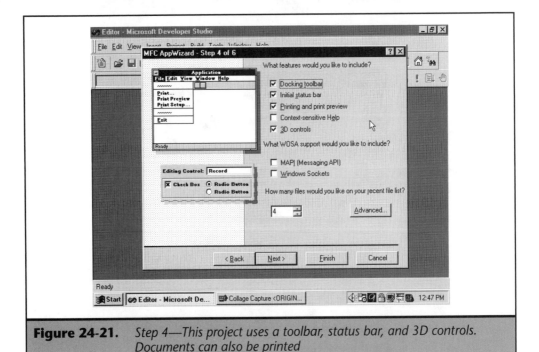

Figure 24-21. Step 4—This project uses a toolbar, status bar, and 3D controls. Documents can also be printed

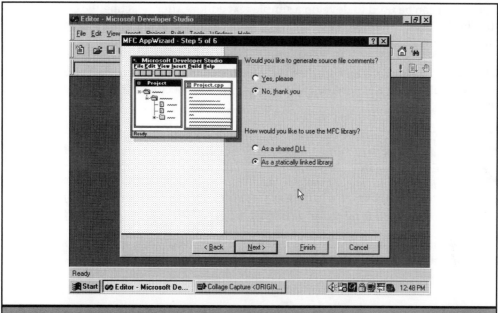

Figure 24-22. *Step 5—No comments are requested in the source code. A statically linked library is requested*

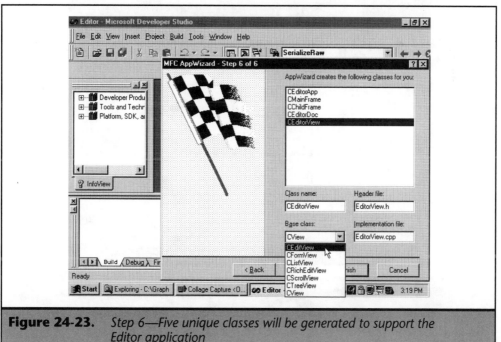

Figure 24-23. *Step 6—Five unique classes will be generated to support the Editor application*

a class that can be used to develop a simple text editor. After selecting the class, select the Finish button. A summary of the AppWizard's development process is then shown. Figure 24-24 shows the summary for this example application.

Select the OK button in this dialog box to start the code-generation process. Figure 24-25 shows the project file list when the AppWizard's build process is complete.

These files will be generated and stored in the subdirectory specified at the start of the project.

NOTE: *The CEditView class supplies the necessary functionality of an edit control. Now your template can print, find and replace, cut, copy, paste, clear, and undo. Since the CEditView class is derived from the CView class, its objects can be used with documents and document templates. By default, this class handles ID_FILE_PRINT, ID_EDIT_CUT, ID_EDIT_COPY, ID_EDIT_PASTE, ID_EDIT_CLEAR, ID_EDIT_UNDO, ID_EDIT_SELECT_ALL, ID_EDIT_FIND, ID_EDIT_REPLACE, and ID_EDIT_REPEAT.*

The Editor application, currently being built, will eventually use one message handler, but we're saving the details on that message handler for later!

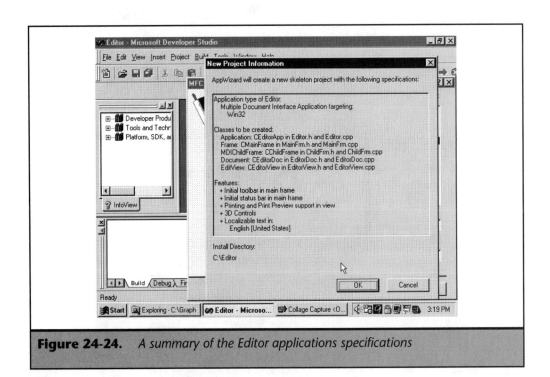

Figure 24-24. *A summary of the Editor applications specifications*

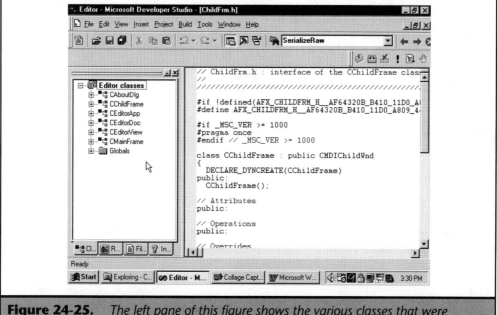

Figure 24-25. *The left pane of this figure shows the various classes that were generated by the AppWizard to support this project*

Building the Application

This application can now be compiled and linked in the normal manner. When the compile and link process has been completed, an executable file will be present in the appropriate subdirectory. Run the application from the Build menu. You should be able to open existing text files or create new files.

Let's examine the code produced by the AppWizard and discuss several additions we're going to make to the project.

Examining AppWizard Code

The AppWizard generates five C++ files for the initial Editor application. These files are named EDITOR.CPP, MAINFRM.CPP, EDITORDOC.CPP, CHILDFRM.CPP, and EDITORVIEW.CPP. Each of these C++ files has an associated header file: EDITOR.H, MAINFRM.H, EDITORDOC.H, CHILDFRM.H, and EDITORVIEW.H. The header files contain the declarations of the specific classes in each C++ file. The C++ files will be examined in the following sections.

THE EDITOR.CPP FILE   The EDITOR.CPP file serves as the main file for the application. It contains the CEditorApp class.

```cpp
// Editor.cpp : Defines the class behaviors.
//

#include "stdafx.h"
#include "Editor.h"

#include "MainFrm.h"
#include "ChildFrm.h"
#include "EditorDoc.h"
#include "EditorView.h"

#ifdef _DEBUG
#define new DEBUG_NEW
#undef THIS_FILE
static char THIS_FILE[] = __FILE__;
#endif

/////////////////////////////////////////////////////////////////
// CEditorApp

BEGIN_MESSAGE_MAP(CEditorApp, CWinApp)
  //{{AFX_MSG_MAP(CEditorApp)
  ON_COMMAND(ID_APP_ABOUT, OnAppAbout)
  //}}AFX_MSG_MAP
  // Standard file based document commands
  ON_COMMAND(ID_FILE_NEW, CWinApp::OnFileNew)
  ON_COMMAND(ID_FILE_OPEN, CWinApp::OnFileOpen)
  // Standard print setup command
  ON_COMMAND(ID_FILE_PRINT_SETUP, CWinApp::OnFilePrintSetup)
END_MESSAGE_MAP( )

/////////////////////////////////////////////////////////////////
// CEditorApp construction

CEditorApp::CEditorApp( )
{
}

/////////////////////////////////////////////////////////////////
// The one and only CEditorApp object

CEditorApp theApp;
```

```cpp
/////////////////////////////////////////////////////////////
// CEditorApp initialization

BOOL CEditorApp::InitInstance( )
{
  COLORREF clrCtlBk, clrCtlText;

  // Set dialog background color to blue, text to white
  SetDialogBkColor(clrCtlBk=RGB(0,0,255),
                   clrCtlText=RGB(255,255,255));

  // Standard initialization

#ifdef _AFXDLL
  Enable3dControls( );        // when using MFC in a shared DLL
#else
  Enable3dControlsStatic( ); // when linking to MFC statically
#endif

  // Change the registry key where settings are stored.
  SetRegistryKey(_T("Local AppWizard-Generated Applications"));

  LoadStdProfileSettings( );  // Load standard INI file options

  // Register document templates

  CMultiDocTemplate* pDocTemplate;
  pDocTemplate = new CMultiDocTemplate(
    IDR_EDITORTYPE,
    RUNTIME_CLASS(CEditorDoc),
    RUNTIME_CLASS(CChildFrame), // custom MDI child frame
    RUNTIME_CLASS(CEditorView));
  AddDocTemplate(pDocTemplate);

  // create main MDI Frame window
  CMainFrame* pMainFrame = new CMainFrame;
  if (!pMainFrame->LoadFrame(IDR_MAINFRAME))
    return FALSE;
  m_pMainWnd = pMainFrame;

  // Parse command line for standard shell commands
  CCommandLineInfo cmdInfo;
```

```
  ParseCommandLine(cmdInfo);

  // Dispatch commands specified on the command line
  if (!ProcessShellCommand(cmdInfo))
    return FALSE;
  pMainFrame->ShowWindow(m_nCmdShow);
  pMainFrame->UpdateWindow( );

  return TRUE;
}


/////////////////////////////////////////////////////////////////
// CAboutDlg dialog used for App About

class CAboutDlg : public CDialog
{
public:
  CAboutDlg( );

// Dialog Data
  //{{AFX_DATA(CAboutDlg)
  enum { IDD = IDD_ABOUTBOX };
  //}}AFX_DATA

  // ClassWizard generated virtual function overrides
  //{{AFX_VIRTUAL(CAboutDlg)
  protected:
  virtual void DoDataExchange(CDataExchange* pDX);
  //}}AFX_VIRTUAL

// Implementation
protected:
  //{{AFX_MSG(CAboutDlg)
    // No message handlers
  //}}AFX_MSG
  DECLARE_MESSAGE_MAP( )
};

CAboutDlg::CAboutDlg( ) : CDialog(CAboutDlg::IDD)
{
  //{{AFX_DATA_INIT(CAboutDlg)
  //}}AFX_DATA_INIT
```

```
}

void CAboutDlg::DoDataExchange(CDataExchange* pDX)
{
  CDialog::DoDataExchange(pDX);
  //{{AFX_DATA_MAP(CAboutDlg)
  //}}AFX_DATA_MAP
}

BEGIN_MESSAGE_MAP(CAboutDlg, CDialog)
  //{{AFX_MSG_MAP(CAboutDlg)
    // No message handlers
  //}}AFX_MSG_MAP
END_MESSAGE_MAP( )

// App command to run the dialog
void CEditorApp::OnAppAbout( )
{
  CAboutDlg aboutDlg;
  aboutDlg.DoModal( );
}

/////////////////////////////////////////////////////////////
// CEditorApp commands
```

The message map, near the top of the listing, belongs to the CEditorApp class. This message map specifically links the ID_APP_ABOUT, ID_FILE_NEW, ID_FILE_OPEN, and ID_FILE_PRINT_SETUP messages with their member functions OnAppAbout( ), CWinApp::OnFileNew( ), CWinApp::OnFileOpen( ), and CWinAppOnFilePrintSetup( ). Also notice in the listing that a constructor, an initial instance InitInstance( ), and a member function OnAppAbout( ) are implemented.

One change that has been made to the AppWizard's code is a change in the background and foreground colors for all dialog boxes used by this application. The portion of code required for this change is shown in bold in the previous listing.

Also, as the following code shows, this application will use a multiple document interface instead of the single-document interface used in the previous example.

```
// Register document templates
CMultiDocTemplate* pDocTemplate;
pDocTemplate = new CMultiDocTemplate(
  IDR_EDITORTYPE,
```

```
      RUNTIME_CLASS(CEditorDoc),
      RUNTIME_CLASS(CChildFrame), // custom MDI child frame
      RUNTIME_CLASS(CEditorView));
   AddDocTemplate(pDocTemplate);
```

The About dialog box is derived from the CDialog class just as in the previous example. There are no initial CEditorApp commands, as you can see from the end of the listing.

THE MAINFRM.CPP FILE   The MAINFRM.CPP file, shown here, contains the frame class CMainFrame. This class is derived from CFrameWnd and is used to control all multiple document interface (MDI) frame features.

```
// MainFrm.cpp : implementation of the CMainFrame class
//

#include "stdafx.h"
#include "Editor.h"

#include "MainFrm.h"

#ifdef _DEBUG
#define new DEBUG_NEW
#undef THIS_FILE
static char THIS_FILE[] = __FILE__;
#endif

/////////////////////////////////////////////////////////////////
// CMainFrame

IMPLEMENT_DYNAMIC(CMainFrame, CMDIFrameWnd)

BEGIN_MESSAGE_MAP(CMainFrame, CMDIFrameWnd)
  //{{AFX_MSG_MAP(CMainFrame)
  ON_WM_CREATE( )
  //}}AFX_MSG_MAP
END_MESSAGE_MAP( )

static UINT indicators[] =
{
  ID_SEPARATOR,              // status line indicator
```

```
    ID_INDICATOR_CAPS,
    ID_INDICATOR_NUM,
    ID_INDICATOR_SCRL,
};

/////////////////////////////////////////////////////////////////
// CMainFrame construction/destruction

CMainFrame::CMainFrame( )
{
}

CMainFrame::~CMainFrame( )
{
}

int CMainFrame::OnCreate(LPCREATESTRUCT lpCreateStruct)
{
  if (CMDIFrameWnd::OnCreate(lpCreateStruct) == -1)
    return -1;

  if (!m_wndToolBar.Create(this) ||
    !m_wndToolBar.LoadToolBar(IDR_MAINFRAME))
  {
    TRACE0("Failed to create toolbar\n");
    return -1;      // fail to create
  }

  if (!m_wndStatusBar.Create(this) ||
    !m_wndStatusBar.SetIndicators(indicators,
      sizeof(indicators)/sizeof(UINT)))
  {
    TRACE0("Failed to create status bar\n");
    return -1;      // fail to create
  }

  m_wndToolBar.SetBarStyle(m_wndToolBar.GetBarStyle( ) |
    CBRS_TOOLTIPS | CBRS_FLYBY | CBRS_SIZE_DYNAMIC);

  m_wndToolBar.EnableDocking(CBRS_ALIGN_ANY);
  EnableDocking(CBRS_ALIGN_ANY);
  DockControlBar(&m_wndToolBar);
```

```
  return 0;
}

BOOL CMainFrame::PreCreateWindow(CREATESTRUCT& cs)
{
  return CMDIFrameWnd::PreCreateWindow(cs);
}

/////////////////////////////////////////////////////////////
// CMainFrame diagnostics

#ifdef _DEBUG
void CMainFrame::AssertValid( ) const
{
  CMDIFrameWnd::AssertValid( );
}

void CMainFrame::Dump(CDumpContext& dc) const
{
  CMDIFrameWnd::Dump(dc);
}

#endif //_DEBUG

/////////////////////////////////////////////////////////////
// CMainFrame message handlers
```

When you examine this listing, you will notice that the message map does handle ON_WM_CREATE messages. The constructor and destructor, however, still contain no code.

However, notice the inclusion of this small portion of code:

```
static UINT indicators[] =
{
  ID_SEPARATOR,           // status line indicator
  ID_INDICATOR_CAPS,
  ID_INDICATOR_NUM,
  ID_INDICATOR_SCRL,
};
```

Recall that the AppWizard was asked to generate a template with an initial toolbar and status bar. This group of custom controls will require ID values for the various status-line indicators.

The inclusion of the toolbar and status bar is handled by the second portion of bolded code, shown in the MAINFRM.CPP listing.

The member functions AssertValid( ) and Dump( ) use definitions contained in the parent class. CMainFrame initially contains no message handlers.

THE EDITORDOC.CPP FILE   The EDITORDOC.CPP file, shown here, contains the CEditorDoc class, which is unique to this application. This file is used to hold document data and to load and save files.

```
// EditorDoc.cpp : implementation of the CEditorDoc class
//

#include "stdafx.h"
#include "Editor.h"

#include "EditorDoc.h"

#ifdef _DEBUG
#define new DEBUG_NEW
#undef THIS_FILE
static char THIS_FILE[] = __FILE__;
#endif

/////////////////////////////////////////////////////////////////
// CEditorDoc

IMPLEMENT_DYNCREATE(CEditorDoc, CDocument)

BEGIN_MESSAGE_MAP(CEditorDoc, CDocument)
  //{{AFX_MSG_MAP(CEditorDoc)
  //}}AFX_MSG_MAP
END_MESSAGE_MAP( )

/////////////////////////////////////////////////////////////////
// CEditorDoc construction/destruction

CEditorDoc::CEditorDoc( )
{
}
```

```
CEditorDoc::~CEditorDoc( )
{
}

BOOL CEditorDoc::OnNewDocument( )
{
  if (!CDocument::OnNewDocument( ))
    return FALSE;

  return TRUE;
}

/////////////////////////////////////////////////////////////
// CEditorDoc serialization

void CEditorDoc::Serialize(CArchive& ar)
{
  ((CEditView*)m_viewList.GetHead( ))->SerializeRaw(ar);
}

/////////////////////////////////////////////////////////////
// CEditorDoc diagnostics

#ifdef _DEBUG
void CEditorDoc::AssertValid( ) const
{
  CDocument::AssertValid( );
}

void CEditorDoc::Dump(CDumpContext& dc) const
{
  CDocument::Dump(dc);
}
#endif //_DEBUG

/////////////////////////////////////////////////////////////
// CEditorDoc commands
```

When you examine this listing, you will again notice that the message map, constructor, and destructor contain no code. Several member functions can be used to provide vital document support. OnNewDocument( ) uses the definition provided by the parent class. Serialize( ) supports persistent objects. This line of code, set in bold type in the previous listing, provides the functionality to the file I/O menu commands, allowing text files to be created, opened, and saved.

The member functions AssertValid( ) and Dump( ) use definitions contained in the parent class. There are no initial CEditorDoc commands.

THE EDITORVIEW.CPP FILE   The EDITORVIEW.CPP file, shown next, provides the view of the document. In this implementation, CEditorView is derived from the CEditView class.

```cpp
// EditorView.cpp : implementation of the CEditorView class
//

#include "stdafx.h"
#include "Editor.h"

#include "EditorDoc.h"
#include "EditorView.h"

#ifdef _DEBUG
#define new DEBUG_NEW
#undef THIS_FILE
static char THIS_FILE[] = __FILE__;
#endif

/////////////////////////////////////////////////////////
// CEditorView

IMPLEMENT_DYNCREATE(CEditorView, CEditView)

BEGIN_MESSAGE_MAP(CEditorView, CEditView)
  //{{AFX_MSG_MAP(CEditorView)
  ON_WM_RBUTTONDOWN( )
  //}}AFX_MSG_MAP
  // Standard printing commands
  ON_COMMAND(ID_FILE_PRINT, CEditView::OnFilePrint)
  ON_COMMAND(ID_FILE_PRINT_DIRECT, CEditView::OnFilePrint)
  ON_COMMAND(ID_FILE_PRINT_PREVIEW,
             CEditView::OnFilePrintPreview)
END_MESSAGE_MAP( )

/////////////////////////////////////////////////////////
// CEditorView construction/destruction
```

```
CEditorView::CEditorView( )
{
}


CEditorView::~CEditorView( )
{
}


BOOL CEditorView::PreCreateWindow(CREATESTRUCT& cs)
{
  BOOL bPreCreated = CEditView::PreCreateWindow(cs);
  cs.style &= ~(ES_AUTOHSCROLL|WS_HSCROLL);

  return bPreCreated;
}


/////////////////////////////////////////////////////////////
// CEditorView drawing

void CEditorView::OnDraw(CDC* pDC)
{
  CEditorDoc* pDoc = GetDocument( );
  ASSERT_VALID(pDoc);
}


/////////////////////////////////////////////////////////////
// CEditorView printing

BOOL CEditorView::OnPreparePrinting(CPrintInfo* pInfo)
{
  // default CEditView preparation
  return CEditView::OnPreparePrinting(pInfo);
}


void CEditorView::OnBeginPrinting(CDC* pDC,CPrintInfo* pInfo)
{
  CEditView::OnBeginPrinting(pDC, pInfo);
}


void CEditorView::OnEndPrinting(CDC* pDC, CPrintInfo* pInfo)
{
  CEditView::OnEndPrinting(pDC, pInfo);
```

```
}

/////////////////////////////////////////////////////////////
// CEditorView diagnostics

#ifdef _DEBUG
void CEditorView::AssertValid( ) const
{
  CEditView::AssertValid( );
}

void CEditorView::Dump(CDumpContext& dc) const
{
  CEditView::Dump(dc);
}

CEditorDoc* CEditorView::GetDocument( )
{
  ASSERT(m_pDocument->IsKindOf(RUNTIME_CLASS(CEditorDoc)));
  return (CEditorDoc*)m_pDocument;
}
#endif //_DEBUG

/////////////////////////////////////////////////////////////
// CEditorView message handlers

void CEditorView::OnRButtonDown(UINT nFlags, CPoint point)
{
  char szTimeStr[20];
  CTime tm=CTime::GetCurrentTime( );

  sprintf(szTimeStr, "It's now  %02d:%02d:%02d",
          tm.GetHour( ),tm.GetMinute( ),
          tm.GetSecond( ));

  MessageBox(szTimeStr, "Is it time to quit yet?",
            MB_OK);


  CEditView::OnRButtonDown(nFlags, point);
}
```

When you examine the message map, you will see that it contains ON_WM_RBUTTONDOWN, which was added by the ClassWizard, and ID_FILE_PRINT and ID_FILE_PREVIEW, which are provided when the CEditorView class is used. The constructor and destructor are empty.

The OnDraw( ) member function uses the pointer pDoc to point to the document. CEditorView handles document printing with OnPreparePrinting( ), OnBeginPrinting( ), and OnEndPrinting( ). The member functions AssertValid( ) and Dump( ) use definitions contained in the parent class.

The message handler code for OnRButtonDown( ) is an easy enhancement to the application. Use the ClassWizard, shown in Figure 24-26, to add WM_RBUTTONDOWN message capabilities and the OnRButtonDown class.

Double-click the mouse on the OnRButtonDown member function, shown in Figure 24-26, to move directly to the CEditorView message handler section of EDITORVIEW.CPP. Figure 24-27 shows the point where the code was inserted.

Now, if the user clicks the right mouse button while using the text editor, a small dialog box will pop-up on the screen and displays the current time.

Figure 24-28 shows the application running with two text files opened for inspection.

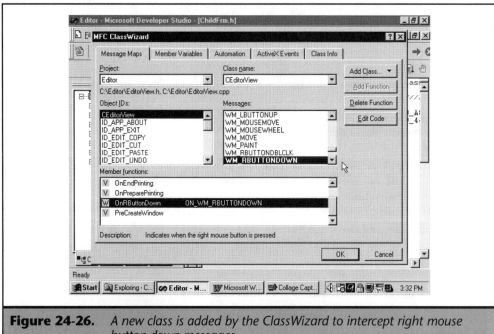

Figure 24-26. *A new class is added by the ClassWizard to intercept right mouse button down messages*

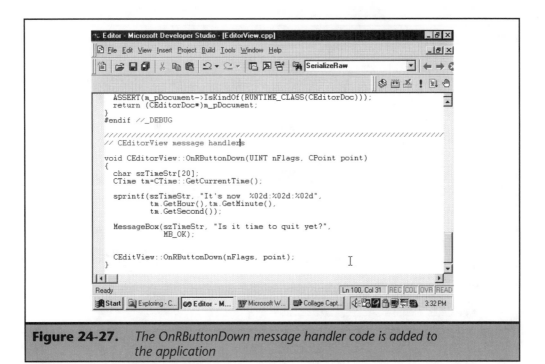

Figure 24-27.   *The OnRButtonDown message handler code is added to the application*

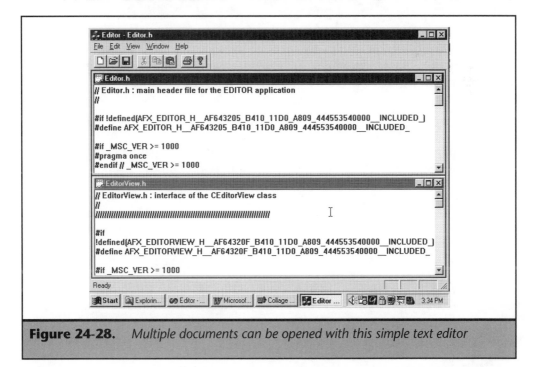

Figure 24-28.   *Multiple documents can be opened with this simple text editor*

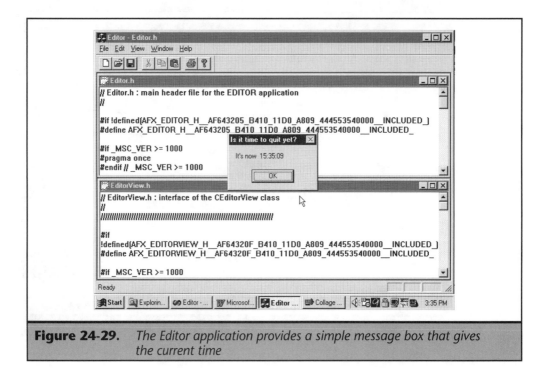

Figure 24-29. *The Editor application provides a simple message box that gives the current time*

Want to know what time it is while you are working? Maybe it's time to quit? Depress the right mouse button while over a document to pop-up a message box with the current time. Figure 24-29 shows an example of this message box.

What's Coming?

The next chapter uses the knowledge you have gained in this chapter about the AppWizard and the ClassWizard to develop applications that deal with compound document support.

The Complete Reference

Visual
C++ 5

Chapter 25

An Introduction to OLE

This chapter will introduce you to the concepts and definitions used with the tools in Microsoft OLE. At its inception, OLE stood simply for Object Linking and Embedding. However, as Microsoft expanded its power and features, its abilities exceeded this definition. Microsoft no longer refers to this product as anything but OLE. By definition, OLE is an object-based technology for sharing information and services across process and machine boundaries.

OLE tools allow the programmer to develop interconnected applications—*compound documents*—that are dynamically linked together. These compound documents include linked or embedded objects in addition to data.

Developing OLE-compliant containers and servers without the use of Microsoft's Wizards and the Foundation Class library is foolish, because you will have to write literally thousands of lines of code, much of it redundant from application to application.

This chapter will discuss how to build OLE-compliant applications with the AppWizard. This tool, discussed in Chapter 24, is great for developing applications with OLE features. The program developer can transcend the mundane tasks of repetitive programming code by using the AppWizard's dynamic templates. The AppWizard also allows you, the programmer, to introduce features into your applications without having to worry about the details of the implementation. With the AppWizard, implementing OLE in an application has become very, very simple!

A container application is developed in this chapter with the use of the AppWizard. The information you learn from this application can be applied to a server application that you can develop on your own.

OLE Features and Specifications

OLE offers additional features that are not directly related to compound documents. These features specify methods for handling drag-and-drop, data transfer, file management, and so on. This section contains an overview of these concepts.

Objects

Procedure-oriented Windows programming makes extensive use of API function calls. Sometimes it is difficult to see the implementation language (C or C++) because these applications seem to contain nothing but function calls!

In Chapters 22 and 23 you observed a movement away from a procedure-oriented programming approach and toward an object-oriented approach. The MFC library provides the tools for this transition. With OLE, additional tools for object-oriented programming have become available.

The object-oriented *component object model* is a binary specification or standard that allows two unrelated applications to communicate with each other. The communication takes place through interfaces implemented on the object. When an object conforms to this standard, it is called a component object model or COM object.

A component object can be instantiated through a component object library—which contains functions that support this instantiation. A *component object* is a Windows object with a unique class ID. The object's functions, contained in the library and referred to as an *interface*, can be called via a returned pointer. This process allows the creation of objects that are not dependent upon the programming language. The library also *marshals* how function calls and function parameters are handled between processes.

Files

OLE allows the use of stream and storage objects—*compound files*—that streamline file manipulation. The stream object most closely resembles a single file, and the storage object resembles a file directory. This structured storage concept shields you from the actual location of data on a disk.

Microsoft's long-range plans include the development of a common file structure so that all files can be easily browsed.

Data

Uniform data transfers are made through a *data object*. OLE uses pointers to a data object. This helps connect the data source to the data receiver. The data object, in turn, handles how data is actually exchanged. Thus, to the programmer, data transfers that use the Clipboard will be handled in the same manner as those that use drag-and-drop.

Embedding

Compound documents can hold information from a variety of unrelated sources. For example, a Microsoft Word document can contain an Excel chart and a Paint bitmap.

Before OLE, items such as charts and bitmaps could be copied to other documents via the Clipboard. Once the objects were "pasted" into the receiving document, they retained no knowledge of their former life. They were static, dead images. If changes eventually had to be made to these objects, the user had to return to the application that originally generated the object, make the changes on the original, and go through the cut-and-paste transfer process once again.

In this case, the Word document would be called the *container*, and Excel and Paint would be called the servers. A container holds an object or objects created by other applications, whereas a server is the source of an object or objects used by other applications.

An Embedded Object

As an example, this section will teach you how to embed a Paint object into a Microsoft Word document. Word will be the container, and Paint will be the server.

Open Microsoft Word. Figure 25-1 shows a typical Word screen with a small amount of text written in the window. From the Microsoft Word Insert menu, select the Object... menu item, as shown in Figure 25-2. Once the menu item is selected, the Object dialog box will appear, as shown in Figure 25-3.

From the Object dialog box, choose Paintbrush Picture as the object to embed. Paint will be opened automatically, as shown in Figure 25-4, and the drawing surface will float over the top of the Word document. You will now be in the Page Layout view mode of Word.

The next step is to use Paint to draw the object that you wish to embed in the Word document. In this example, a little text and several simple graphics shapes were drawn in the Paint drawing area, as shown in Figure 25-5. When you are done creating the object, select the Save menu item in Paint's File menu, as shown in Figure 25-6. Now click on the Word document to return to Microsoft Word, and close the Paint application. Figure 25-7 shows the Word document containing the embedded object while in the Page Layout mode.

Now here is the magic. Suppose you decide that the object isn't exactly what you wanted. Because the transfer is OLE compliant, you can simply double-click on the object to block it for editing, as shown in Figure 25-8. When the object is selected in Word, Paint is immediately opened again with the currently selected object ready for editing. Figure 25-9 shows this process.

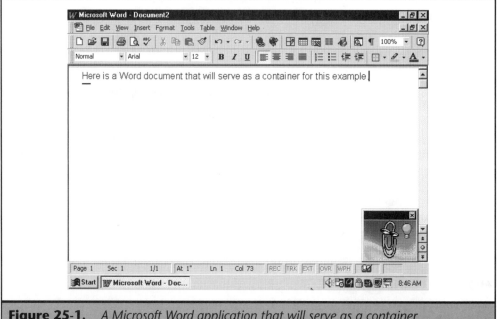

Figure 25-1. *A Microsoft Word application that will serve as a container*

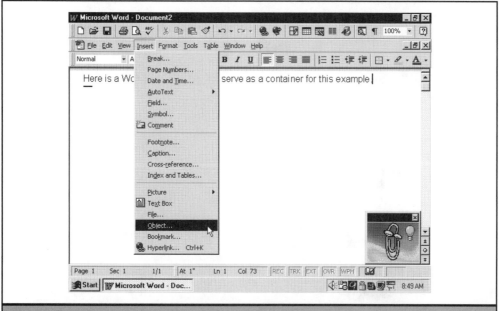

Figure 25-2.   *Use the Insert menu to select the Object... menu item*

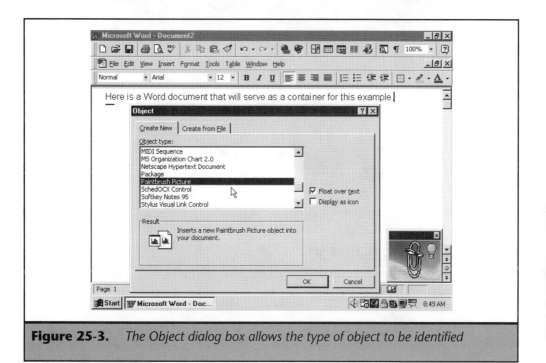

Figure 25-3.   *The Object dialog box allows the type of object to be identified*

WIZARDS

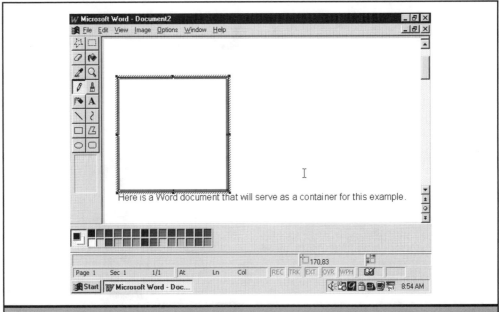

Figure 25-4. *Paint has been identified as the object to be embedded in the Word document*

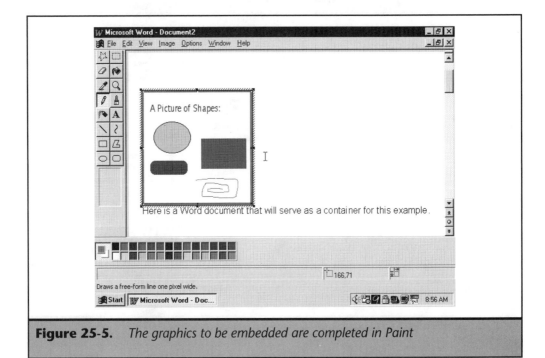

Figure 25-5. *The graphics to be embedded are completed in Paint*

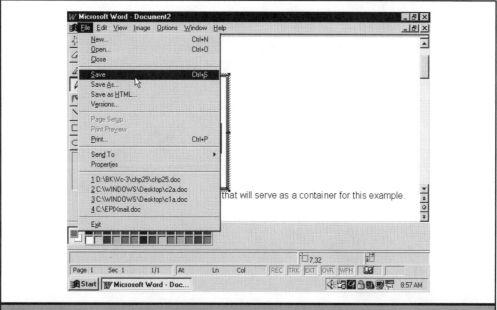

Figure 25-6.   *A new object is saved while within the Paint application*

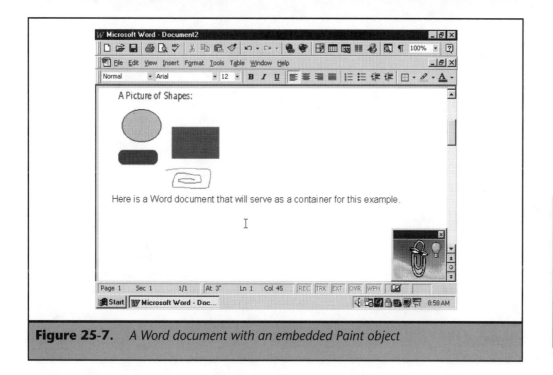

Figure 25-7.   *A Word document with an embedded Paint object*

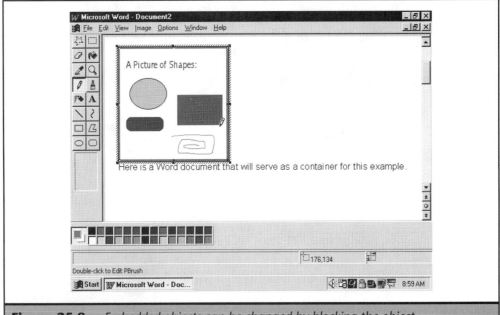

Figure 25-8. Embedded objects can be changed by blocking the object

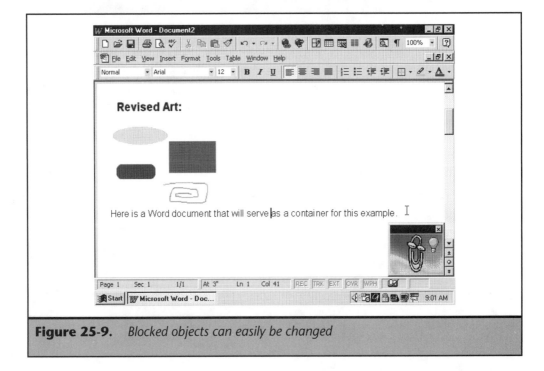

Figure 25-9. Blocked objects can easily be changed

Linking

OLE supports a dynamic linking process between applications. When applications are linked, data can be shared instantaneously between the applications. In the past, linking was difficult because it was too easy for users to break the links. With OLE, *file monikers* prevent most of the link breakage problems. File monikers, based on a path in the file system, are used to identify COM objects that are saved in their own files.

Building a Container Application

In Chapter 24, a simple single-document interface (SDI) application named "Graph" was developed. The container application in this chapter will be patterned closely after that example. We'll call this application "Cnt."

This application uses two important OLE classes, COleClientItem and COleDocument. COleDocument manages a list of COleClientItem items. COleClientItem itself manages the embedded or linked objects and the required communications.

The important thing to remember as you view the container code in the next sections is that the code is completely generated by the AppWizard. This container template code can be enhanced with your specific application features to turn it into a full-blown product. In this chapter, however, no additional features were added to the basic template.

Using the AppWizard

The AppWizard is used here in the same way it was used in Chapter 24. You might want to review that chapter for a more detailed explanation of each step in the creation process. This section will examine the most important steps, in an abbreviated form, for building the container application, Cnt.

- Use the Microsoft Visual C++ File menu to start a new project.
- Select the MFC AppWizard (exe) to start the 6-step process.
    1. Create a single-document interface.
    2. Do not include database support.
    3. Select a container as the OLE compound document. Include support for AcitveX controls.
    4. Include all of the default features for the container application.
    5. Request source code comments. Use a statically linked library.
    6. Examine the list of classes to be generated, making any necessary changes. Click on the Finish button to complete the specification process.

- The AppWizard will generate a summary screen. If this information is correct, click on the OK button to generate the project's code.

- The panel, to the left of your display, should now show the various classes and files created for the project.

Finally, build the executable file by selecting the Rebuild All option from the compiler's Build menu. When the process is complete, the appropriate subdirectory will contain an executable file named CNT.EXE. We will test this container in another section of this chapter.

The AppWizard Files

The files generated by the AppWizard produce a fully operable container application named Cnt. When the files have been generated by the AppWizard, your subdirectory will contain the following unique C++ files: CNT.CPP, MAINFRM.CPP, CNTDOC.CPP, CNTVIEW.CPP, and CNTRITEM.CPP. Also in this subdirectory will be a host of supporting header files, resource files, and so on.

The Container File: CNT.CPP

The code used in the container CNT.CPP file is almost identical to that used in the Graph example in Chapter 24. Compare the two files and notice the similarities. You might also want to return to Chapter 24 if you need more details on the message map and the classes used in this file.

The file is listed here, so the application's code for this chapter will be complete.

```
// Cnt.cpp : Defines the class behaviors for the application.
//

#include "stdafx.h"
#include "Cnt.h"

#include "MainFrm.h"
#include "CntDoc.h"
#include "CntView.h"

#ifdef _DEBUG
#define new DEBUG_NEW
#undef THIS_FILE
static char THIS_FILE[] = __FILE__;
#endif


/////////////////////////////////////////////////////////////////////
// CCntApp
```

```
BEGIN_MESSAGE_MAP(CCntApp, CWinApp)
  //{{AFX_MSG_MAP(CCntApp)
  ON_COMMAND(ID_APP_ABOUT, OnAppAbout)
    // The ClassWizard will add/remove mapping macros here.
    // DO NOT EDIT these blocks of generated code!
  //}}AFX_MSG_MAP
  // Standard file based document commands
  ON_COMMAND(ID_FILE_NEW, CWinApp::OnFileNew)
  ON_COMMAND(ID_FILE_OPEN, CWinApp::OnFileOpen)
  // Standard print setup command
  ON_COMMAND(ID_FILE_PRINT_SETUP, CWinApp::OnFilePrintSetup)
END_MESSAGE_MAP( )

/////////////////////////////////////////////////////////////
// CCntApp construction

CCntApp::CCntApp( )
{
  // TODO: add construction code here,
  // Place all significant initialization in InitInstance
}

/////////////////////////////////////////////////////////////
// The one and only CCntApp object

CCntApp theApp;

/////////////////////////////////////////////////////////////
// CCntApp initialization

BOOL CCntApp::InitInstance( )
{
  // Initialize OLE libraries
  if (!AfxOleInit( ))
  {
    AfxMessageBox(IDP_OLE_INIT_FAILED);
    return FALSE;
  }

  AfxEnableControlContainer( );
```

```
  // Standard initialization
  // If not used these features can be removed.
#ifdef _AFXDLL
  Enable3dControls( ); //Call when using MFC in a shared DLL
#else
  Enable3dControlsStatic( ); //Call when linking statically
#endif

  // Change the registry key under which settings are stored.
  // Modify this string to be something appropriate
  // such as the name of your company or organization.
  SetRegistryKey(_T("Local AppWizard-Generated Applications"));

  LoadStdProfileSettings( ); //Load INI file options with MRU

  // Register the App's document templates.  Document templates
  // are the connection between documents, frame windows, etc.

  CSingleDocTemplate* pDocTemplate;
  pDocTemplate = new CSingleDocTemplate(
    IDR_MAINFRAME,
    RUNTIME_CLASS(CCntDoc),
    RUNTIME_CLASS(CMainFrame),          // main SDI frame window
    RUNTIME_CLASS(CCntView));
  pDocTemplate->SetContainerInfo(IDR_CNTR_INPLACE);
  AddDocTemplate(pDocTemplate);

  // Parse command line for standard shell commands, DDE, etc.
  CCommandLineInfo cmdInfo;
  ParseCommandLine(cmdInfo);

  // Dispatch commands specified on the command line
  if (!ProcessShellCommand(cmdInfo))
    return FALSE;

  // The only window has been initialized.  Show and update.
  m_pMainWnd->ShowWindow(SW_SHOW);
  m_pMainWnd->UpdateWindow( );

  return TRUE;
}
```

```
/////////////////////////////////////////////////////////////
// CAboutDlg dialog used for App About

class CAboutDlg : public CDialog
{
public:
  CAboutDlg( );

// Dialog Data
  //{{AFX_DATA(CAboutDlg)
  enum { IDD = IDD_ABOUTBOX };
  //}}AFX_DATA


  // ClassWizard generated virtual function overrides
  //{{AFX_VIRTUAL(CAboutDlg)
  protected:
  virtual void DoDataExchange(CDataExchange* pDX);
  //}}AFX_VIRTUAL

// Implementation
protected:
  //{{AFX_MSG(CAboutDlg)
    // No message handlers
  //}}AFX_MSG
  DECLARE_MESSAGE_MAP( )
};

CAboutDlg::CAboutDlg( ) : CDialog(CAboutDlg::IDD)
{
  //{{AFX_DATA_INIT(CAboutDlg)
  //}}AFX_DATA_INIT
}

void CAboutDlg::DoDataExchange(CDataExchange* pDX)
{
  CDialog::DoDataExchange(pDX);
  //{{AFX_DATA_MAP(CAboutDlg)
  //}}AFX_DATA_MAP
}

BEGIN_MESSAGE_MAP(CAboutDlg, CDialog)
  //{{AFX_MSG_MAP(CAboutDlg)
```

```
    // No message handlers
  //}}AFX_MSG_MAP
END_MESSAGE_MAP( )

// App command to run the dialog
void CCntApp::OnAppAbout( )
{
  CAboutDlg aboutDlg;
  aboutDlg.DoModal( );
}


/////////////////////////////////////////////////////////////
// CCntApp commands
```

There is an interesting section of code in this file that deserves a mention. Under OLE, in-place editing is supported. *In-place editing* means that when an object is embedded in a container, such as our Cnt application, its menu replaces the container's menu. For example, if an Excel spreadsheet object is embedded in Cnt, Cnt's menu will change to that of Excel's!

This menu change is handled by MFC, via OLE, almost automatically. MFC makes this possible by having three menu sources available: IDR_MAINFRAME, IDR_DOCTYPE, and IDR_CNTR_INPLACE (the name of the last IDR is specific to your application). When no object is embedded in the container application, IDR_MAINFRAME is used. When a document is opened, IDR_DOCTYPE is used. Finally, when an object has been embedded in the container, IDR_CNTR_INPLACE is used.

The Container File: MAINFRM.CPP

The code used in the container MAINFRM.CPP file is the same as that used in the Graph example in Chapter 24. Again, return to Chapter 24 if you need more details on the message map and classes used in this file.

For completeness, the file is listed here.

```
// MainFrm.cpp : implementation of the CMainFrame class
//

#include "stdafx.h"
#include "Cnt.h"


#include "MainFrm.h"
```

```
#ifdef _DEBUG
#define new DEBUG_NEW
#undef THIS_FILE
static char THIS_FILE[] = __FILE__;
#endif

/////////////////////////////////////////////////////////////
// CMainFrame

IMPLEMENT_DYNCREATE(CMainFrame, CFrameWnd)

BEGIN_MESSAGE_MAP(CMainFrame, CFrameWnd)
  //{{AFX_MSG_MAP(CMainFrame)
    // The ClassWizard will add/remove mapping macros here.
    //    DO NOT EDIT these blocks of generated code !
  ON_WM_CREATE( )
  //}}AFX_MSG_MAP
END_MESSAGE_MAP( )

static UINT indicators[] =
{
  ID_SEPARATOR,            // status line indicator
  ID_INDICATOR_CAPS,
  ID_INDICATOR_NUM,
  ID_INDICATOR_SCRL,
};

/////////////////////////////////////////////////////////////
// CMainFrame construction/destruction

CMainFrame::CMainFrame( )
{
  // TODO: add member initialization code here

}

CMainFrame::~CMainFrame( )
{
}
```

```
int CMainFrame::OnCreate(LPCREATESTRUCT lpCreateStruct)
{
  if (CFrameWnd::OnCreate(lpCreateStruct) == -1)
    return -1;

  if (!m_wndToolBar.Create(this) ||
    !m_wndToolBar.LoadToolBar(IDR_MAINFRAME))
  {
    TRACE0("Failed to create toolbar\n");
    return -1;      // fail to create
  }

  if (!m_wndStatusBar.Create(this) ||
    !m_wndStatusBar.SetIndicators(indicators,
      sizeof(indicators)/sizeof(UINT)))
  {
    TRACE0("Failed to create status bar\n");
    return -1;      // fail to create
  }

  //Remove code to remove tool tips & resizeable toolbar
  m_wndToolBar.SetBarStyle(m_wndToolBar.GetBarStyle( ) |
    CBRS_TOOLTIPS | CBRS_FLYBY | CBRS_SIZE_DYNAMIC);

  //Delete if you don't want the toolbar to
  //  be dockable
  m_wndToolBar.EnableDocking(CBRS_ALIGN_ANY);
  EnableDocking(CBRS_ALIGN_ANY);
  DockControlBar(&m_wndToolBar);

  return 0;
}

BOOL CMainFrame::PreCreateWindow(CREATESTRUCT& cs)
{
  // Modify the Window class or styles here by modifying
  //  the CREATESTRUCT cs

  return CFrameWnd::PreCreateWindow(cs);
}
```

```
/////////////////////////////////////////////////////
// CMainFrame diagnostics

#ifdef _DEBUG
void CMainFrame::AssertValid( ) const
{
  CFrameWnd::AssertValid( );
}

void CMainFrame::Dump(CDumpContext& dc) const
{
  CFrameWnd::Dump(dc);
}

#endif //_DEBUG


/////////////////////////////////////////////////////
// CMainFrame message handlers
```

The Container File: CNTDOC.CPP

The code used in the container CNTDOC.CPP file, shown here, contains some
additional code that does not appear in the Graph application in Chapter 24.
Compare the two files and notice the differences.

```
// CntDoc.cpp : implementation of the CCntDoc class
//

#include "stdafx.h"
#include "Cnt.h"

#include "CntDoc.h"
#include "CntrItem.h"

#ifdef _DEBUG
#define new DEBUG_NEW
#undef THIS_FILE
static char THIS_FILE[] = __FILE__;
#endif
```

```
/////////////////////////////////////////////////////
// CCntDoc

IMPLEMENT_DYNCREATE(CCntDoc, COleDocument)

BEGIN_MESSAGE_MAP(CCntDoc, COleDocument)
  //{{AFX_MSG_MAP(CCntDoc)
    // The ClassWizard will add/remove mapping macros here.
    // DO NOT EDIT these blocks of generated code!
  //}}AFX_MSG_MAP
  // Enable default OLE container implementation
  ON_UPDATE_COMMAND_UI(ID_EDIT_PASTE,
                       COleDocument::OnUpdatePasteMenu)
  ON_UPDATE_COMMAND_UI(ID_EDIT_PASTE_LINK,
                       COleDocument::OnUpdatePasteLinkMenu)
  ON_UPDATE_COMMAND_UI(ID_OLE_EDIT_CONVERT,
                       COleDocument::OnUpdateObjectVerbMenu)
  ON_COMMAND(ID_OLE_EDIT_CONVERT,
             COleDocument::OnEditConvert)
  ON_UPDATE_COMMAND_UI(ID_OLE_EDIT_LINKS,
                       COleDocument::OnUpdateEditLinksMenu)
  ON_COMMAND(ID_OLE_EDIT_LINKS,
             COleDocument::OnEditLinks)
  ON_UPDATE_COMMAND_UI(ID_OLE_VERB_FIRST,
                       COleDocument::OnUpdateObjectVerbMenu)
END_MESSAGE_MAP( )

/////////////////////////////////////////////////////
// CCntDoc construction/destruction

CCntDoc::CCntDoc( )
{
  // Use OLE compound files
  EnableCompoundFile( );

  // TODO: add one-time construction code here

}

CCntDoc::~CCntDoc( )
{
}
```

```
BOOL CCntDoc::OnNewDocument( )
{
  if (!COleDocument::OnNewDocument( ))
    return FALSE;

  // TODO: add reinitialization code here
  // (SDI documents will reuse this document)

  return TRUE;
}


//////////////////////////////////////////////////////////
// CCntDoc serialization

void CCntDoc::Serialize(CArchive& ar)
{
  if (ar.IsStoring( ))
  {
    // TODO: add storing code here
  }
  else
  {
    // TODO: add loading code here
  }

  // The base class COleDocument enables serialization
  //  of the container document's COleClientItem objects.
  COleDocument::Serialize(ar);
}


//////////////////////////////////////////////////////////
// CCntDoc diagnostics

#ifdef _DEBUG
void CCntDoc::AssertValid( ) const
{
  COleDocument::AssertValid( );
}

void CCntDoc::Dump(CDumpContext& dc) const
{
  COleDocument::Dump(dc);
```

```
}
#endif //_DEBUG


/////////////////////////////////////////////////////////
// CCntDoc commands
```

The most significant change in this file comes with the expansion of the message map, as shown in bold type.

The message map will now allow the implementation of the default OLE container. You can also see that the constructor calls the EnableCompoundFile( ) function. This is required for a container application.

The Container File: CNTVIEW.CPP

The container CNTVIEW.CPP file also has some major changes in comparison to the Graph application in Chapter 24. Examine the following file and note the additions to the message map.

```
// CntView.cpp : implementation of the CCntView class
//

#include "stdafx.h"
#include "Cnt.h"

#include "CntDoc.h"
#include "CntrItem.h"
#include "CntView.h"

#ifdef _DEBUG
#define new DEBUG_NEW
#undef THIS_FILE
static char THIS_FILE[] = __FILE__;
#endif


/////////////////////////////////////////////////////////
// CCntView

IMPLEMENT_DYNCREATE(CCntView, CView)

BEGIN_MESSAGE_MAP(CCntView, CView)
  //{{AFX_MSG_MAP(CCntView)
```

```
      // The ClassWizard will add/remove mapping macros here.
      // DO NOT EDIT these blocks of generated code!
   ON_WM_DESTROY( )
   ON_WM_SETFOCUS( )
   ON_WM_SIZE( )
   ON_COMMAND(ID_OLE_INSERT_NEW, OnInsertObject)
   ON_COMMAND(ID_CANCEL_EDIT_CNTR, OnCancelEditCntr)
   //}}AFX_MSG_MAP
   // Standard printing commands
   ON_COMMAND(ID_FILE_PRINT, CView::OnFilePrint)
   ON_COMMAND(ID_FILE_PRINT_DIRECT, CView::OnFilePrint)
   ON_COMMAND(ID_FILE_PRINT_PREVIEW,
               CView::OnFilePrintPreview)
END_MESSAGE_MAP( )

/////////////////////////////////////////////////////////
// CCntView construction/destruction

CCntView::CCntView( )
{
   m_pSelection = NULL;
   // TODO: add construction code here


}

CCntView::~CCntView( )
{
}

BOOL CCntView::PreCreateWindow(CREATESTRUCT& cs)
{
   // Modify the Window class or styles here by modifying
   //   the CREATESTRUCT cs

   return CView::PreCreateWindow(cs);
}

/////////////////////////////////////////////////////////
// CCntView drawing

void CCntView::OnDraw(CDC* pDC)
{
```

```
    CCntDoc* pDoc = GetDocument( );
    ASSERT_VALID(pDoc);

    // TODO: add draw code for native data here
    // TODO: also draw all OLE items in the document

    // Draw the selection at an arbitrary position.  This code
    // should be removed once your real drawing code is
    // implemented.  This position corresponds exactly to the
    // rectangle returned by CCntCntrItem, to give the effect
    // of in-place editing.

    // TODO: remove this code when final draw code is complete.

    if (m_pSelection == NULL)
    {
      POSITION pos = pDoc->GetStartPosition( );
      m_pSelection=(CCntCntrItem*)pDoc->GetNextClientItem(pos);
    }
    if (m_pSelection != NULL)
      m_pSelection->Draw(pDC, CRect(10, 10, 210, 210));
}

void CCntView::OnInitialUpdate( )
{
  CView::OnInitialUpdate( );

  // Remove when final selection model code is written
  m_pSelection = NULL;    // initialize selection

}

/////////////////////////////////////////////////////////////
// CCntView printing

BOOL CCntView::OnPreparePrinting(CPrintInfo* pInfo)
{
  // default preparation
  return DoPreparePrinting(pInfo);
}

void CCntView::OnBeginPrinting(CDC* /*pDC*/,
```

```
                                CPrintInfo* /*pInfo*/)
{
  // TODO: add extra initialization before printing
}

void CCntView::OnEndPrinting(CDC* /*pDC*/,
                             CPrintInfo* /*pInfo*/)
{
  // TODO: add cleanup after printing
}

void CCntView::OnDestroy( )
{
  // Deactivate the item on destruction; this is important
  // when a splitter view is being used.
  CView::OnDestroy( );
  COleClientItem* pActiveItem = GetDocument( )-> \
                                GetInPlaceActiveItem(this);
  if (pActiveItem != NULL && pActiveItem-> \
                   GetActiveView( ) == this)
  {
    pActiveItem->Deactivate( );
    ASSERT(GetDocument( )-> \
           GetInPlaceActiveItem(this) == NULL);
  }
}


/////////////////////////////////////////////////////////////
// OLE Client support and commands

BOOL CCntView::IsSelected(const CObject* pDocItem) const
{
  // The implementation below is adequate if your selection
  // consists of only CCntCntrItem objects.  To handle
  // different selection mechanisms, the implementation here
  // should be replaced.

  // Implement function - that tests a selected OLE client

  return pDocItem == m_pSelection;
}
```

```
void CCntView::OnInsertObject( )
{
  // Invoke Insert Object dialog box to obtain information
  //  for new CCntCntrItem object.
  COleInsertDialog dlg;
  if (dlg.DoModal( ) != IDOK)
    return;

  BeginWaitCursor( );

  CCntCntrItem* pItem = NULL;
  TRY
  {
    // Create new item connected to this document.
    CCntDoc* pDoc = GetDocument( );
    ASSERT_VALID(pDoc);
    pItem = new CCntCntrItem(pDoc);
    ASSERT_VALID(pItem);

    // Initialize the item from the dialog data.
    if (!dlg.CreateItem(pItem))
      AfxThrowMemoryException( );  // any exception will do
    ASSERT_VALID(pItem);

    // If item created from class list, launch
    //  the server to edit the item.
    if (dlg.GetSelectionType( ) ==  \
        COleInsertDialog::createNewItem)
      pItem->DoVerb(OLEIVERB_SHOW, this);

    ASSERT_VALID(pItem);

    // This sets the selection to the last item inserted.

    // TODO: reimplement selection for your application
    m_pSelection = pItem;   // set to last inserted item
    pDoc->UpdateAllViews(NULL);
  }
  CATCH(CException, e)
  {
    if (pItem != NULL)
    {
```

```
      ASSERT_VALID(pItem);
      pItem->Delete( );
    }
    AfxMessageBox(IDP_FAILED_TO_CREATE);
  }
  END_CATCH

  EndWaitCursor( );
}


// The following command handler provides the standard
// keyboard user interface to cancel an in-place editing
// session.  Here, the container causes the deactivation.
void CCntView::OnCancelEditCntr( )
{
  // Close any in-place active item on this view.
  COleClientItem* pActiveItem = GetDocument( )-> \
                                GetInPlaceActiveItem(this);
  if (pActiveItem != NULL)
  {
    pActiveItem->Close( );
  }
  ASSERT(GetDocument( )->GetInPlaceActiveItem(this) == NULL);
}


// Special handling of OnSetFocus and OnSize are required
//  when an object is being edited in-place.
void CCntView::OnSetFocus(CWnd* pOldWnd)
{
  COleClientItem* pActiveItem = GetDocument( )-> \
                                GetInPlaceActiveItem(this);
  if (pActiveItem != NULL &&
    pActiveItem->GetItemState( ) == \
              COleClientItem::activeUIState)
  {
    // need to set focus to this item if in the same view
    CWnd* pWnd = pActiveItem->GetInPlaceWindow( );
    if (pWnd != NULL)
    {
      pWnd->SetFocus( );   // don't call the base class
      return;
```

```
    }
  }

  CView::OnSetFocus(pOldWnd);
}

void CCntView::OnSize(UINT nType, int cx, int cy)
{
  CView::OnSize(nType, cx, cy);
  COleClientItem* pActiveItem = GetDocument( )-> \
                                GetInPlaceActiveItem(this);
  if (pActiveItem != NULL)
    pActiveItem->SetItemRects( );
}

/////////////////////////////////////////////////////////////
// CCntView diagnostics

#ifdef _DEBUG
void CCntView::AssertValid( ) const
{
  CView::AssertValid( );
}

void CCntView::Dump(CDumpContext& dc) const
{
  CView::Dump(dc);
}

CCntDoc* CCntView::GetDocument( ) // non-debug is inline
{
  ASSERT(m_pDocument->IsKindOf(RUNTIME_CLASS(CCntDoc)));
  return (CCntDoc*)m_pDocument;
}
#endif //_DEBUG

/////////////////////////////////////////////////////////////
// CCntView message handlers
```

So that it can handle drawing (i.e., inserted objects) for the CCntView container, the OnDraw( ) member function has to be altered by the AppWizard. This portion of code was shown in bold type in the file. Here is just a small portion of that code.

```
if (m_pSelection != NULL)
    m_pSelection->Draw(pDC, CRect(10, 10, 210, 210));
}
```

This code places the object at a prearranged location designated by CRect( ) at 10,10 and 210,210. These values can be changed manually or automatically.

Other additions include OnInitialUpdate( ), IsSelected( ), OnInsertObject( ), OnCancelEdit( ), OnSetFocus( ), and OnSize( ). These signal when an OLE object is selected or otherwise being manipulated. OnInsertObject( ) runs COleInsertDialog. Any additional code for these functions must be supplied by you, the programmer.

The Container File: CNTRITEM.CPP

The container CNTRITEM.CPP file, shown here, is responsible for the implementation of the CCntCntrItem class.

```
// CntrItem.cpp : implementation of the CCntCntrItem class
//

#include "stdafx.h"
#include "Cnt.h"

#include "CntDoc.h"
#include "CntView.h"
#include "CntrItem.h"

#ifdef _DEBUG
#define new DEBUG_NEW
#undef THIS_FILE
static char THIS_FILE[] = __FILE__;
#endif


/////////////////////////////////////////////////////////////////
// CCntCntrItem implementation

IMPLEMENT_SERIAL(CCntCntrItem, COleClientItem, 0)
```

WIZARDS

```
CCntCntrItem::CCntCntrItem(CCntDoc* pContainer)
  : COleClientItem(pContainer)
{
  // TODO: add one-time construction code here

}

CCntCntrItem::~CCntCntrItem( )
{
  // TODO: add cleanup code here

}

void CCntCntrItem::OnChange(OLE_NOTIFICATION nCode,
                            DWORD dwParam)
{
  ASSERT_VALID(this);

  COleClientItem::OnChange(nCode, dwParam);

  // When an item is being edited it sends OnChange
  //  notifications for changes in the state of the
  //  item or visual appearance of its content.

  // TODO: invalidate the item by calling UpdateAllViews
  //  (with hints appropriate to your application)

  GetDocument( )->UpdateAllViews(NULL);
    // for now just update ALL views/no hints
}

BOOL CCntCntrItem::OnChangeItemPosition(const CRect& rectPos)
{
  ASSERT_VALID(this);

  // In-place activation CCntCntrItem::OnChangeItemPosition
  //  is called by the server to change the position of the
  //  in-place window.  This is a result of the data in the
  //  server document changing such that the extent has
  //  changed or as a result of in-place resizing.
```

```
    // The default is to call the base class, which will call
    //   COleClientItem::SetItemRects to move the item
    //   to the new position.

    if (!COleClientItem::OnChangeItemPosition(rectPos))
      return FALSE;
    // TODO: update any cache of the item's rectangle/extent

    return TRUE;
}

void CCntCntrItem::OnGetItemPosition(CRect& rPosition)
{
    ASSERT_VALID(this);

    // In-place activation, CCntCntrItem::OnGetItemPosition
    //   will be called to determine the location of this item.
    //   The default implementation created from AppWizard
    //   simply returns a hard-coded rectangle.  Usually, this
    //   rectangle would reflect the current position of the
    //   item relative to the view used for activation.
    //   Obtain the view by calling CCntCntrItem::GetActiveView.

    // TODO: return correct rectangle (in pixels) in rPosition

    rPosition.SetRect(10, 10, 210, 210);
}

void CCntCntrItem::OnActivate( )
{
    // Allow only one in-place activate item per frame
    CCntView* pView = GetActiveView( );
    ASSERT_VALID(pView);
    COleClientItem* pItem = GetDocument( )-> \
                          GetInPlaceActiveItem(pView);
    if (pItem != NULL && pItem != this)
        pItem->Close( );

    COleClientItem::OnActivate( );
}
```

```
void CCntCntrItem::OnDeactivateUI(BOOL bUndoable)
{
  COleClientItem::OnDeactivateUI(bUndoable);

    // Hide the object if it is not an outside-in object
    DWORD dwMisc = 0;
    m_lpObject->GetMiscStatus(GetDrawAspect( ), &dwMisc);
    if (dwMisc & OLEMISC_INSIDEOUT)
        DoVerb(OLEIVERB_HIDE, NULL);
}

void CCntCntrItem::Serialize(CArchive& ar)
{
  ASSERT_VALID(this);

  // Call base class first to read in COleClientItem data.
  // Since this sets up the m_pDocument pointer returned from
  //  CCntCntrItem::GetDocument, it is a good idea to call
  //  the base class Serialize first.
  COleClientItem::Serialize(ar);

  // now store/retrieve data specific to CCntCntrItem
  if (ar.IsStoring( ))
  {
    // TODO: add storing code here
  }
  else
  {
    // TODO: add loading code here
  }
}

/////////////////////////////////////////////////////////////
// CCntCntrItem diagnostics

#ifdef _DEBUG
void CCntCntrItem::AssertValid( ) const
{
  COleClientItem::AssertValid( );
}
```

```
void CCntCntrItem::Dump(CDumpContext& dc) const
{
  COleClientItem::Dump(dc);
}
#endif
```

The main purpose of this file is to help monitor the position and size of the item in the drawing. Examine the portion of code set in bold type. Have you seen these coordinates before?

In the next section you'll see how to use the container application to accept an object from a server.

Testing the Container Application

The container application can now be tested. Remember that the container application was produced as a template, without additional functionality added. However, what you will see in the next few pages is a very complete and functioning application.

The container application can be started by typing **Cnt** at the command line or run directly from the integrated environment of the Visual C++ compiler. Figure 25-10 shows the initial container window.

This container can use objects from any server. For this example we'll insert an Excel spreadsheet into the container. To select Excel as the server, open the container's Edit menu and use the Insert New Object… menu option. This will open the Insert Object dialog box, as shown in Figure 25-11.

From the Insert Object dialog box, choose Microsoft Excel Worksheet as the object to embed in the container.

Figure 25-12 shows the initial insertion of the object into the container document with data entered in various cells.

Remember, you gained all of this functionality without writing one line of code. The AppWizard has made it very easy to develop OLE container and server applications. As a little project, why not create your own server application. Then to test your skills further, insert a server object from this application into the Cnt container.

Figure 25-10. *The initial window for the Cnt container application*

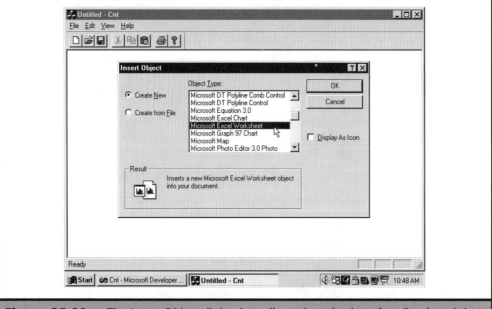

Figure 25-11. *The Insert Object dialog box allows the selection of an Excel worksheet*

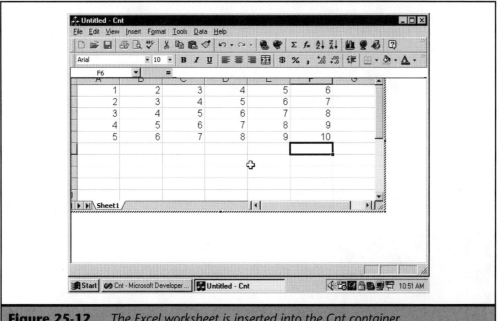

Figure 25-12. *The Excel worksheet is inserted into the Cnt container*

What's Coming?

OLE is truly a complicated subject, but one worthy of your attention. The smart money is on building OLE applications with the help of the AppWizard and the MFC library.

We recommend studying articles on OLE and COM that can be found in the *Microsoft Systems Journal*.

In the next chapter we will examine another exciting subject: ActiveX controls.

The Complete Reference

Visual
C++ 5

Chapter 26

ActiveX Controls with
the MFC Library

W indows provides a wide variety of controls such as radio buttons, checkboxes, list boxes, and so on. Many developers also design their own controls, known as ActiveX or custom controls. As Windows evolved from 3.*x* to Windows 95 and Windows NT, so have custom controls. Custom controls really had their beginning with Microsoft's Visual Basic. Visual Basic made it easy to implement new controls that were not part of the standard group of Windows controls. These custom controls, also known as VBXs (after their file extension .VBX), are specialty items. They are actually small dynamic link libraries (DLLs) with VBX file extensions. A good example of a custom control is a custom slide bar that might be used to control the volume in a CD-ROM player application. However, custom controls developed commercially can also be much more complicated. Some include complete spreadsheet, image, and database capabilities within the control!

Many C/C++ programmers have developed custom controls using Visual Basic and then incorporated them into their C/C++ applications. Obviously, the C/C++ language has needed its own mechanism for creating custom controls. At the same time Microsoft was developing a solution, they began the migration from (16-bit) Windows 3.1 to (32-bit) Windows 95 and NT. As it turns out, the hardware-specific 16-bit VBX controls will not serve the new 32-bit multiple platform environments as well as programmers desired. Thus, Microsoft decided that rather than expand the VBX specifications, it would redesign the custom control architecture to include the 32-bit platforms. Under Windows 95 and Windows NT, OLE controls will be the natural replacement for the older VBX custom controls of Visual Basic. These new custom controls will also serve container applications such as Microsoft Access, Excel, Word, PowerPoint, and so on. The term "custom control" has largely been replaced with "ActiveX control."

The good news about OLE controls, for the C++ developer, is that ActiveX controls have a Microsoft C++ wizard that helps build the control. This wizard is officially called the *MFC ActiveX ControlWizard*. It develops object-oriented C++ code, taking full advantage of the Microsoft Foundation Class library (MFC).

During development, your controls can be tested with the ActiveX Test Container tool. Once the ActiveX control is complete, it can be incorporated into any application that supports OLE objects. Microsoft Word, Excel, and Access are typical applications that support ActiveX controls.

OLE ActiveX Controls

ActiveX controls can be placed alongside standard controls such as radio buttons, push buttons, checkboxes, and so on. Therefore, you might find a dialog box containing a few radio buttons, checkboxes, and an ActiveX control. ActiveX controls, however, are inherently more difficult to implement.

Unless an ActiveX control has been supplied by a commercial vendor, you, the programmer, will be responsible for the design and complete implementation of the control and its properties. The problem is now twofold. First, during the design phase you must create, write, and compile the code that draws the control and implements all of the control's, methods, and so on. This code eventually becomes a tiny dynamic link library (see Appendix C for more information on DLLs) with an OCX file extension. Second, the application that is to use the ActiveX control must now interface with the control's methods, data, and so on. You also must properly design this interface.

A properly designed ActiveX control must be independent from the application in which it is used. In other words, it must be completely re-entrant. Remember that an ActiveX control is really a separate dynamic link library that is not linked to any particular application. A separate instance for data for each use of the control is required for re-entrance in a DLL. The only communications allowed between an application and an ActiveX control are via messages. Hence, an ActiveX control must be defined in a dynamic link library.

ActiveX Control Design Criterion

When entering the design phase for an ActiveX control, several decisions must be made to create an ActiveX control as appealing and functional as possible.

First, you must decide how the ActiveX control will be drawn and displayed. Here, some talent will be required to produce ActiveX controls that are both functional and attractive.

Next, the ActiveX control should be designed to take advantage of changes in control properties resulting from the automation interface of the control. Note that for ActiveX controls, so designed, property pages will allow the user to change properties at run-time. Arguments should be assigned ActiveX controls in order to control events, set their names, and determine when they should be fired. A control's methods should be defined in terms of arguments and return types.

Finally, the persistence of a control's various property states must be determined and implemented.

The COleControl Class

ActiveX controls are derived from MFC's COleControl class. Examine the code in the next listing. This listing contains an edited portion of the AFXCTL.H header file. If you are interested in examining the full header file, you should be able to locate it in the MFC's INCLUDE subdirectory. Be warned, this file is approximately 30 pages in length.

```
// Part of the Microsoft Foundation Classes C++ library.
// Copyright (C) 1992-1997 Microsoft Corporation
// All rights reserved.
//
// This source code is only intended as a supplement to the
```

```
// Microsoft Foundation Classes Reference and related
// electronic documentation provided with the library.
// See these sources for detailed information regarding the
// Microsoft Foundation Classes product.

// AFXCTL.H - MFC OLE Control support
   .
   .
   .

// Stock properties
#define DISP_PROPERTY_STOCK(theClass, szExternalName, dispid, \
                            pfnGet, pfnSet, vtPropType) \
  { _T(szExternalName), dispid, NULL, vtPropType, \
    (AFX_PMSG)(void (theClass::*)(void))&pfnGet, \
    (AFX_PMSG)(void (theClass::*)(void))&pfnSet, 0, \
    afxDispStock }, \

#define DISP_STOCKPROP_APPEARANCE( ) \
  DISP_PROPERTY_STOCK(COleControl, "Appearance", \
                      DISPID_APPEARANCE, \
                      COleControl::GetAppearance, \
                      COleControl::SetAppearance, \
                      VT_I2)

#define DISP_STOCKPROP_BACKCOLOR( ) \
  DISP_PROPERTY_STOCK(COleControl, "BackColor", \
                      DISPID_BACKCOLOR, \
                      COleControl::GetBackColor, \
                      COleControl::SetBackColor, VT_COLOR)

#define DISP_STOCKPROP_BORDERSTYLE( ) \
  DISP_PROPERTY_STOCK(COleControl, "BorderStyle", \
                      DISPID_BORDERSTYLE, \
                      COleControl::GetBorderStyle, \
                      COleControl::SetBorderStyle, VT_I2)

#define DISP_STOCKPROP_CAPTION( ) \
  DISP_PROPERTY_STOCK(COleControl, "Caption", DISPID_CAPTION, \
                      COleControl::GetText, \
                      COleControl::SetText, VT_BSTR)
   .
   .
   .
```

```
// Stock methods
#define DISP_FUNCTION_STOCK(theClass, szExternalName, \
                            dispid, pfnMember, vtRetVal, \
                            vtsParams) \
  { _T(szExternalName), dispid, vtsParams, vtRetVal, \
    (AFX_PMSG)(void (theClass::*)(void))&pfnMember, \
    (AFX_PMSG)0, 0, afxDispStock }, \

#define DISP_STOCKFUNC_REFRESH( ) \
  DISP_FUNCTION_STOCK(COleControl, "Refresh", DISPID_REFRESH, \
      COleControl::Refresh, VT_EMPTY, VTS_NONE)

#define DISP_STOCKFUNC_DOCLICK( ) \
  DISP_FUNCTION_STOCK(COleControl, "DoClick", DISPID_DOCLICK, \
      COleControl::DoClick, VT_EMPTY, VTS_NONE)

  .
  .
  .

// Firing functions for stock events
void FireKeyDown(USHORT* pnChar, short nShiftState);
void FireKeyUp(USHORT* pnChar, short nShiftState);
void FireKeyPress(USHORT* pnChar);
void FireMouseDown(short nButton, short nShiftState,
  OLE_XPOS_PIXELS x, OLE_YPOS_PIXELS y);
void FireMouseUp(short nButton, short nShiftState,
  OLE_XPOS_PIXELS x, OLE_YPOS_PIXELS y);
void FireMouseMove(short nButton, short nShiftState,
  OLE_XPOS_PIXELS x, OLE_YPOS_PIXELS y);
void FireClick( );
void FireDblClick( );
void FireError(SCODE scode, LPCTSTR lpszDescription, UINT nHelpID = 0);
void FireReadyStateChange( );

  .
  .
  .

// Type library
BOOL GetDispatchIID(IID* pIID);

// Stock events
void KeyDown(USHORT* pnChar);
void KeyUp(USHORT* pnChar);
```

WIZARDS

```
void ButtonDown(USHORT iButton, UINT nFlags, CPoint point);
void ButtonUp(USHORT iButton, UINT nFlags, CPoint point);
void ButtonDblClk(USHORT iButton, UINT nFlags, CPoint point);
    .
    .
    .

// Stock properties
OLE_COLOR m_clrBackColor;              // BackColor
OLE_COLOR m_clrForeColor;              // ForeColor
CString m_strText;                     // Text/Caption
CFontHolder m_font;                    // Font
HFONT m_hFontPrev;                     // Previously selected font object
short m_sAppearance;                   // Appearance
short m_sBorderStyle;                  // BorderStyle
BOOL m_bEnabled;                       // Enabled
long m_lReadyState;                    // ReadyState
    .
    .
    .

// Message maps
protected:
    //{{AFX_MSG(COleControl)
    afx_msg void OnKeyDown(UINT nChar, UINT nRepCnt, UINT nFlags);
    afx_msg void OnKeyUp(UINT nChar, UINT nRepCnt, UINT nFlags);
    afx_msg void OnChar(UINT nChar, UINT nRepCnt, UINT nFlags);
    afx_msg void OnMouseMove(UINT nFlags, CPoint point);
    afx_msg void OnLButtonDown(UINT nFlags, CPoint point);
    afx_msg void OnLButtonUp(UINT nFlags, CPoint point);
    afx_msg void OnLButtonDblClk(UINT nFlags, CPoint point);
    afx_msg void OnMButtonDown(UINT nFlags, CPoint point);
    afx_msg void OnMButtonUp(UINT nFlags, CPoint point);
    afx_msg void OnMButtonDblClk(UINT nFlags, CPoint point);
    afx_msg void OnRButtonDown(UINT nFlags, CPoint point);
    afx_msg void OnRButtonUp(UINT nFlags, CPoint point);
    afx_msg void OnRButtonDblClk(UINT nFlags, CPoint point);
    .
    .
    .

// IPersistStreamInit
    BEGIN_INTERFACE_PART(PersistStreamInit, IPersistStreamInit)
      INIT_INTERFACE_PART(COleControl, PersistStreamInit)
```

```
  STDMETHOD(GetClassID)(LPCLSID);
  STDMETHOD(IsDirty)( );
  STDMETHOD(Load)(LPSTREAM);
  STDMETHOD(Save)(LPSTREAM, BOOL);
  STDMETHOD(GetSizeMax)(ULARGE_INTEGER *);
  STDMETHOD(InitNew)( );
END_INTERFACE_PART(PersistStreamInit)
  .
  .
  .
```

Our intention in showing this partial listing was not to explain each section of the listing in detail, but to provide you with a reference as we introduce some new terms used with ActiveX controls. You'll find the captions for those sections set in a bold font.

Events

Events are actions or responses that are triggered by the control's reaction to an action on the control—for example, a keypress or mouse button click. KeyUp and KeyDown are examples of stock events.

Since your class will be derived from Microsoft's COleControl class, it will be able to use a new map that enables messages. These messages or events are sent to the application using the control. This application is called the *control container*. The application or container will receive information about an event when something happens to the control. This event could be as simple as clicking the mouse within the control. Additional information can be provided by using event parameters. Examine the message maps area of the previous listing.

A control communicates with its application (container) by firing events. ActiveX provides stock and custom events to be used by your control. See the sections marked stock events in the previous listing. Stock events are handled by the COleControl as a default. Custom events might be used to signal the application (container) when a control event occurs, such as receiving a message.

Methods and Properties

The control must expose a set of methods (functions) and properties (interface) to the application using the control in order to make an ActiveX control interactive. Methods are control functions that permit external code to alter characteristics of the control. Typical characteristics include appearance, properties, or behavior. Control properties, on the other hand, include the color, text, font, and other elements used in the control. Methods and properties form the basic mechanism whereby the application (container) communicates with the control. This communication allows the appearance and values of the control to be changed. Methods and properties are defined by the developer while using Microsoft's ClassWizard. Find the section defining stock methods in the previous listing. Stock methods are implemented automatically by the COleControl class. Custom methods can be added by the programmer if additional custom features are needed by the control.

A primary interface to the control allows early bound access to the control's methods and properties. Here, object methods are exposed as methods, and properties as get/set method pairs. IDispatch is used for late bound access. The application using the control (container) decides which type of binding is provided the user. IProvideClassInfo returns a CoClass TypeInfo, which describes the control.

ActiveX controls also provide extended properties, methods, and events. Usually this is control-specific information needed only by the application (container).

Persistence

Controls support persistence to streams through IPersistStream and persistence to storage through IPersistStorage. Both implementations can be found in the interface maps section of the previous listing. IPersistStorage is necessary for continued support of compound document applications (containers). IPersistStream allows embedded controls to be saved to streams, where feasible.

Persistence permits the ActiveX control to read or write property values to and from a file or stream. An application (container) can use persistence to store property values for the control. These values can then be retrieved if a new instance of the control is created.

An example, not shown in the previous listing, is the parameter PX_Blob that is used to exchange a control property that stores Binary Large Object (BLOB) data. In a similar manner, PX_Bool is used to exchange a control property of type BOOL.

Control Containers

The standard compound document interface required for an in-place embedding container has the attributes necessary for a control container. In addition to the container attributes inherent in this type of container, the container must also provide two additional items: events and ambient properties.

An ActiveX control actually serves as a converter when dealing with events. As such, a control must convert events from the user into events that are meaningful to the container. For each event so converted, the container must supply an entry point in order to respond to the event.

Ambient properties refers to container properties that typically apply to all controls in the container. These include default colors and fonts.

Creating a Control with the MFC ActiveX ControlWizard

In this section, you will learn the step-by-step approach to creating a simple ActiveX control template. Then we will modify the template to create a unique control for our use.

Remember that all of Microsoft's wizards generate Microsoft Foundation Class (MFC) library code. If you need to review object-oriented coding techniques using the MFC, study the material in Chapters 22 through 25.

From this point on, the MFC ActiveX ControlWizard will be referred to simply as the ControlWizard.

A Basic ActiveX Control

From the Microsoft Visual C++ menu bar, select the File | New menu item. From the New dialog box, select the MFC ActiveX ControlWizard, as shown in Figure 26-1. Name this project TDCtrl.

Step 1, in the two-step process, allows you to select a variety of options including the number of controls, source code comments, and so on. Accept the default settings, as shown in Figure 26-2.

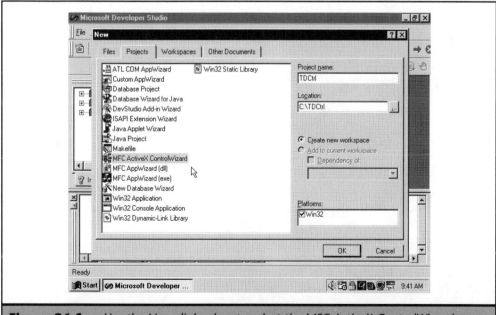

Figure 26-1.   *Use the New dialog box to select the MFC ActiveX ControlWizard*

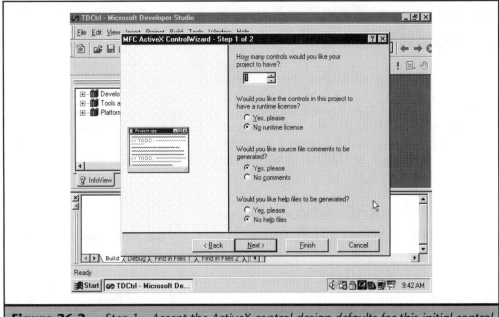

Figure 26-2. *Step 1—Accept the ActiveX control design defaults for this initial control*

Step 2 allows additional design features to be added to the control. Again, accept the default settings—with one exception. Check the box that allows the control to be added to the Insert Object dialog box, as shown in Figure 26-3.

Figure 26-4 shows a summary of the new control's specifications just prior to generating the code.

When the OK button is clicked in the New Project Information dialog box, the ControlWizard will generate the files necessary to create the basic control. Figure 26-5 shows a list of classes and global values for this control.

The TDCtrl control can now be built using the Build | Build or Build | Rebuild All menu selection. When this operation is complete, a new control with the filename TDCTRL.OCX will be located in the appropriate subdirectory.

ActiveX controls are small DLL files that can be tested in the appropriate container. Until the control is complete, it is best to use a test container to examine your control's operation. Microsoft provides the ActiveX Control Test Container. This container is accessed from the Tools menu, as shown in Figure 26-6.

When you start the test container, you will have to select the TDCtrl control from the test container's Edit | Insert OLE Control menu. When this selection is made, the Insert OLE Control dialog box will display a list of registered controls. Scroll down the list till you find the TDCtrl control, as shown in Figure 26-7.

The registered control list will vary as you increase and decrease registered controls on your system. You should find the TDCtrl, however.

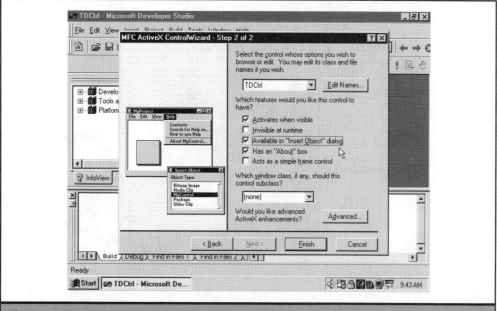

Figure 26-3.   *Step 2—Accept the default settings and add "Insert Object" support*

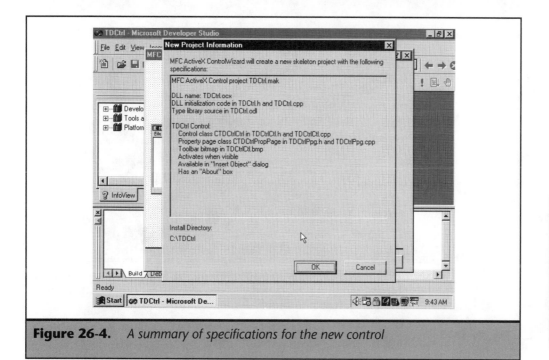

Figure 26-4.   *A summary of specifications for the new control*

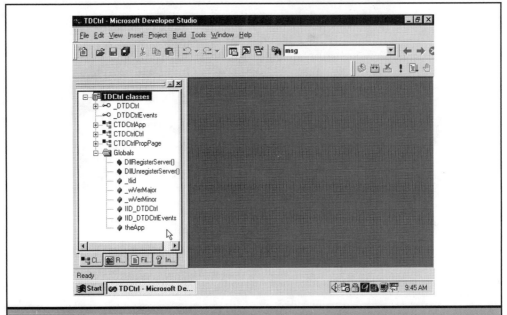

Figure 26-5. *A list of classes and globals for the TDCtrl ActiveX control*

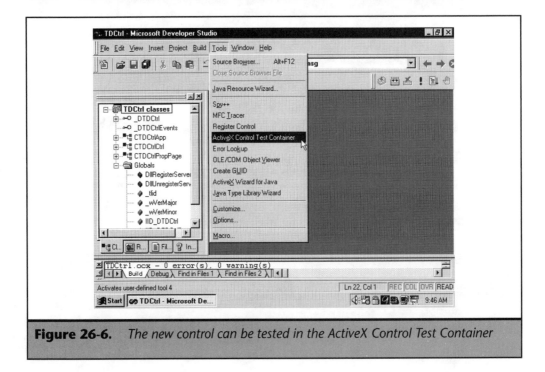

Figure 26-6. *The new control can be tested in the ActiveX Control Test Container*

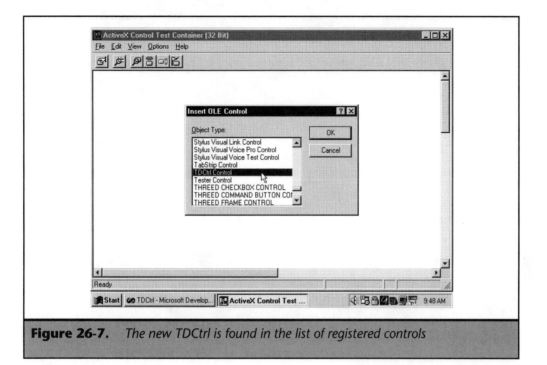

Figure 26-7. *The new TDCtrl is found in the list of registered controls*

When you click the mouse on the OK button in the Insert OLE Control dialog box, the control will be brought into the test container, as you can see in Figure 26-8.

The actual control is graphically just the ellipse shape that you see surrounded by a design frame. At this point the control is not really functional. We will have to add some code to this template to create a unique control for our purposes.

Before we modify the template code, let's look at the code generated by the ControlWizard. We'll examine the code specifically related to the changes we're about to make to the template.

A Look at Important Code

A detailed analysis of the code for the whole TDCtrl project is beyond the scope of this book. Actually, it would probably require a whole book itself. However, you don't have to be an automobile mechanic to drive a car, and you certainly don't have to understand every nuance of program code to build effective ActiveX controls. You have learned the basics of how the MFC combines object-oriented objects into complete applications.

The ControlWizard generates four C++ files for most ActiveX controls. In this example they are named STDAFX.CPP, TDCTRL.CPP, TDCTRLCTL.CPP, and

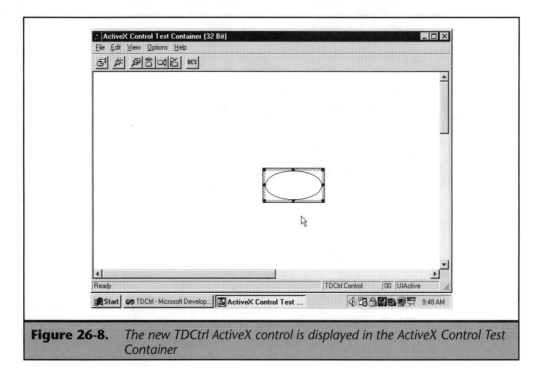

Figure 26-8. *The new TDCtrl ActiveX control is displayed in the ActiveX Control Test Container*

TDCTRLPPG.CPP. These files are supported with their appropriate support header files.

The STDAFX.CPP file is used to include all the standard header files that your ActiveX control will need. The TDCTRL.CPP file is responsible for the implementation of the CTDCtrlApp class and the registration of the subsequent DLL file.

In the following sections we examine the role of the TDCTRLCTL.CPP and TDCTRLPPG.CPP files in more detail.

The TDCTRLCTL.CPP File

The TDCTRLCTL.CPP file provides the actual implementation of the ActiveX control's OLE class. In this example, that class is CTDCtrlCtrl. This is the file you will most likely spend most of your time editing. In this file, you will be able to create unique implementations of your ActiveX control from the default ActiveX control created by the ControlWizard.

Let's examine the specific code allotted to the default ActiveX control. Study the following listing.

```cpp
// TDCtrlCtl.cpp : Implementation of the Control class.

#include "stdafx.h"
#include "TDCtrl.h"
#include "TDCtrlCtl.h"
#include "TDCtrlPpg.h"


#ifdef _DEBUG
#define new DEBUG_NEW
#undef THIS_FILE
static char THIS_FILE[] = __FILE__;
#endif

IMPLEMENT_DYNCREATE(CTDCtrlCtrl, COleControl)


/////////////////////////////////////////////////////////
// Message map

BEGIN_MESSAGE_MAP(CTDCtrlCtrl, COleControl)
  //{{AFX_MSG_MAP(CTDCtrlCtrl)
  // NOTE - ClassWizard will add/remove message map entries
  //    DO NOT EDIT these blocks of generated code !
  //}}AFX_MSG_MAP
  ON_OLEVERB(AFX_IDS_VERB_EDIT, OnEdit)
  ON_OLEVERB(AFX_IDS_VERB_PROPERTIES, OnProperties)
END_MESSAGE_MAP( )


/////////////////////////////////////////////////////////
// Dispatch map

BEGIN_DISPATCH_MAP(CTDCtrlCtrl, COleControl)
  //{{AFX_DISPATCH_MAP(CTDCtrlCtrl)
  // NOTE - ClassWizard will add/remove dispatch map entries
  //    DO NOT EDIT these blocks of generated code !
  //}}AFX_DISPATCH_MAP
  DISP_FUNCTION_ID(CTDCtrlCtrl, "AboutBox", DISPID_ABOUTBOX,
                   AboutBox, VT_EMPTY, VTS_NONE)
END_DISPATCH_MAP( )
```

```
//////////////////////////////////////////////////////////
// Event map

BEGIN_EVENT_MAP(CTDCtrlCtrl, COleControl)
  //{{AFX_EVENT_MAP(CTDCtrlCtrl)
  // NOTE - ClassWizard will add/remove event map entries
  //     DO NOT EDIT these blocks of generated code !
  //}}AFX_EVENT_MAP
END_EVENT_MAP( )


//////////////////////////////////////////////////////////
// Property pages

// TODO: Add more property pages as needed.
// Remember to increase the count!
BEGIN_PROPPAGEIDS(CTDCtrlCtrl, 1)
  PROPPAGEID(CTDCtrlPropPage::guid)
END_PROPPAGEIDS(CTDCtrlCtrl)


//////////////////////////////////////////////////////////
// Initialize class factory and guid

IMPLEMENT_OLECREATE_EX(CTDCtrlCtrl, "TDCTRL.TDCtrlCtrl.1",
  0x45233889, 0xb705, 0x11d0, 0xa8, 0x9, 0x44, 0x45, 0x53,
  0x54, 0, 0)


//////////////////////////////////////////////////////////
// Type library ID and version

IMPLEMENT_OLETYPELIB(CTDCtrlCtrl, _tlid, _wVerMajor,
                     _wVerMinor)


//////////////////////////////////////////////////////////
// Interface IDs

const IID BASED_CODE IID_DTDCtrl =
    { 0x45233887, 0xb705, 0x11d0, { 0xa8, 0x9, 0x44, 0x45,
      0x53, 0x54, 0, 0 } };
const IID BASED_CODE IID_DTDCtrlEvents =
    { 0x45233888, 0xb705, 0x11d0, { 0xa8, 0x9, 0x44, 0x45,
                                    0x53, 0x54, 0, 0 } };
```

```
//////////////////////////////////////////////////////////
// Control type information

static const DWORD BASED_CODE _dwTDCtrlOleMisc =
  OLEMISC_ACTIVATEWHENVISIBLE |
  OLEMISC_SETCLIENTSITEFIRST |
  OLEMISC_INSIDEOUT |
  OLEMISC_CANTLINKINSIDE |
  OLEMISC_RECOMPOSEONRESIZE;

IMPLEMENT_OLECTLTYPE(CTDCtrlCtrl, IDS_TDCTRL,
                     _dwTDCtrlOleMisc)


//////////////////////////////////////////////////////////////
// CTDCtrlCtrl::CTDCtrlCtrlFactory::UpdateRegistry -
// Adds or removes system registry entries for CTDCtrlCtrl

BOOL CTDCtrlCtrl::CTDCtrlCtrlFactory::UpdateRegistry(BOOL \
                                    bRegister)
{
  // TODO: Verify the control follows apartment-model
  // threading rules.
  // Refer to MFC TechNote 64 for more information.
  // If your control does not conform to the apartment-model
  // rules, then you must modify the code below, changing the
  // 6th parameter from afxRegInsertable |
  // afxRegApartmentThreading to afxRegInsertable.

  if (bRegister)
    return AfxOleRegisterControlClass(
      AfxGetInstanceHandle( ),
      m_clsid,
      m_lpszProgID,
      IDS_TDCTRL,
      IDB_TDCTRL,
      afxRegInsertable | afxRegApartmentThreading,
      _dwTDCtrlOleMisc,
      _tlid,
      _wVerMajor,
      _wVerMinor);
  else
    return AfxOleUnregisterClass(m_clsid, m_lpszProgID);
```

```
}

/////////////////////////////////////////////////////////
//CTDCtrlCtrl::CTDCtrlCtrl - Constructor

CTDCtrlCtrl::CTDCtrlCtrl( )
{
  InitializeIIDs(&IID_DTDCtrl, &IID_DTDCtrlEvents);

  // TODO: Initialize your control's instance data here.
}

/////////////////////////////////////////////////////////
// CTDCtrlCtrl::~CTDCtrlCtrl - Destructor

CTDCtrlCtrl::~CTDCtrlCtrl( )
{
  // TODO: Cleanup your control's instance data here.
}

/////////////////////////////////////////////////////////
// CTDCtrlCtrl::OnDraw - Drawing function

void CTDCtrlCtrl::OnDraw(
    CDC* pdc, const CRect& rcBounds, const CRect& rcInvalid)
{
  // TODO: Replace the code with your own drawing code.
  pdc->FillRect(rcBounds,
    CBrush::FromHandle((HBRUSH)GetStockObject(WHITE_BRUSH)));
  pdc->Ellipse(rcBounds);
}

/////////////////////////////////////////////////////////
// CTDCtrlCtrl::DoPropExchange - Persistence support

void CTDCtrlCtrl::DoPropExchange(CPropExchange* pPX)
{
  ExchangeVersion(pPX, MAKELONG(_wVerMinor, _wVerMajor));
  COleControl::DoPropExchange(pPX);

  // TODO: Call PX_ functions for persistent custom property.
}
```

```
///////////////////////////////////////////////////////////
// CTDCtrlCtrl::OnResetState - Reset control to default state

void CTDCtrlCtrl::OnResetState( )
{
  COleControl::OnResetState( );  // Resets defaults

  // TODO: Reset any other control state here.
}


///////////////////////////////////////////////////////////
// CTDCtrlCtrl::AboutBox - Display an "About" box to the user

void CTDCtrlCtrl::AboutBox( )
{
  CDialog dlgAbout(IDD_ABOUTBOX_TDCTRL);
  dlgAbout.DoModal( );
}


///////////////////////////////////////////////////////////
// CTDCtrlCtrl message handlers
```

The message map, dispatch map, and event map are automatically created and edited by the Microsoft's wizards. Under most circumstances, you will not edit these maps directly.

Recall that message maps are important because they provide an alternative to the switch statement used in procedure-oriented programs to handle messages. OLE automation includes techniques to call methods and access properties across several applications. These requests are dispatched via the dispatch map. The event map helps process ActiveX control events.

Examine the listing and notice the section of code used to implement the OLE type library. In general, OLE ActiveX controls need to exchange information concerning various properties and methods. The best way to provide this information is through a type library.

As you continue reading down the listing, you will see code for updating the system registry as well as constructor code for initializing instances of the control.

The OnDraw member function is going to be of immediate interest to us, because it is this section of code that draws the graphics for the control. In the default control provided by the ControlWizard, the default shape is an Ellipse( ).

WIZARDS

```
/////////////////////////////////////////////////////////
// CTDCtrlCtrl::OnDraw - Drawing function

void CTDCtrlCtrl::OnDraw(
    CDC* pdc, const CRect& rcBounds, const CRect& rcInvalid)
{
  // TODO: Replace the code with your own drawing code.
  pdc->FillRect(rcBounds,
    CBrush::FromHandle((HBRUSH)GetStockObject(WHITE_BRUSH)));
  pdc->Ellipse(rcBounds);
}
```

The ControlWizard also designed a default About box for this project. The contents of this simple dialog box can be edited to suit your project's needs or used as is. You'll find the resource information in the TDCTRL.RC resource file. The About dialog box is brought to the screen with the following portion of code.

```
/////////////////////////////////////////////////////////
// CTDCtrlCtrl::AboutBox - Display an "About" box to the user

void CTDCtrlCtrl::AboutBox( )
{
  CDialog dlgAbout(IDD_ABOUTBOX_TDCTRL);
  dlgAbout.DoModal( );
}
```

Notice that the default About box is a standard modal dialog box of the type we have been using since Chapter 22.

The TDCTRLPPG.CPP File

This file derives the CTDCtrlPropPage class from Microsoft's COlePropertyPage class. Examine the following listing.

```
// TDCtrlPpg.cpp : Implementation of the CTDCtrlPropPage

//   property page class.

#include "stdafx.h"
#include "TDCtrl.h"
#include "TDCtrlPpg.h"
```

```
#ifdef _DEBUG
#define new DEBUG_NEW
#undef THIS_FILE
static char THIS_FILE[] = __FILE__;
#endif

IMPLEMENT_DYNCREATE(CTDCtrlPropPage, COlePropertyPage)

/////////////////////////////////////////////////////////////
// Message map

BEGIN_MESSAGE_MAP(CTDCtrlPropPage, COlePropertyPage)
  //{{AFX_MSG_MAP(CTDCtrlPropPage)
  // NOTE - ClassWizard will add/remove message map entries
  //    DO NOT EDIT these blocks of generated code !
  //}}AFX_MSG_MAP
END_MESSAGE_MAP( )

/////////////////////////////////////////////////////////////
// Initialize class factory and guid

IMPLEMENT_OLECREATE_EX(CTDCtrlPropPage,

                 "TDCTRL.TDCtrlPropPage.1",

                 0x4523388a, 0xb705, 0x11d0, 0xa8, 0x9,

                 0x44, 0x45, 0x53, 0x54, 0, 0)

/////////////////////////////////////////////////////////////
// CTDCtrlPropPage::CTDCtrlPropPageFactory::UpdateRegistry -
// Adds/removes system registry entries for CTDCtrlPropPage

BOOL CTDCtrlPropPage::CTDCtrlPropPageFactory::UpdateRegistry \

                                      (BOOL bRegister)
{
  if (bRegister)
    return AfxOleRegisterPropertyPageClass \

        (AfxGetInstanceHandle( ),
      m_clsid, IDS_TDCTRL_PPG);
```

```
      else
        return AfxOleUnregisterClass(m_clsid, NULL);
    }


    /////////////////////////////////////////////////////////////////
    // CTDCtrlPropPage::CTDCtrlPropPage - Constructor

    CTDCtrlPropPage::CTDCtrlPropPage( ) :
      COlePropertyPage(IDD, IDS_TDCTRL_PPG_CAPTION)
    {
      //{{AFX_DATA_INIT(CTDCtrlPropPage)
      // NOTE: ClassWizard will add member initialization here
      //     DO NOT EDIT these blocks of generated code !
      //}}AFX_DATA_INIT
    }


    /////////////////////////////////////////////////////////////////
    // CTDCtrlPropPage::DoDataExchange - Moves data between page

    // and properties

    void CTDCtrlPropPage::DoDataExchange(CDataExchange* pDX)
    {
      //{{AFX_DATA_MAP(CTDCtrlPropPage)
      // NOTE: ClassWizard will add DDP, DDX, and DDV calls here
      //     DO NOT EDIT these blocks of generated code !
      //}}AFX_DATA_MAP
      DDP_PostProcessing(pDX);
    }


    /////////////////////////////////////////////////////////////////
    // CTDCtrlPropPage message handlers
```

The AfxOleRegisterPropertyPageClass( ) function is used to register the property page class with the registration database. This permits the property page to be used by other OLE containers that are made aware of ActiveX controls. The registry, with the property page name and its location on the system, will be updated after this function is called.

Notice in this file that COlePropertyPage, from which our CTDCtrlPropPage class is derived, can use the constructor to identify the dialog-template resource on which the property page is based and also the string resource containing the caption.

The DoDataExchange( ) function is generally used by the framework to exchange and validate dialog data. Here the specific job is to move data between the page and properties of the control.

Customizing the Initial ActiveX Control

The ClassWizard can be used to modify the default custom control produced by the ControlWizard. To modify the default custom control described in the previous section, the following features will be added to the project.

■ The TDCtrl control will always draw a rectangle instead of the default ellipse.

■ The TDCtrl surface will be a unique color.

■ The TDCtrl control will respond to a mouse event within the control and print the current system time and date within the control.

All of these new features can be added to the control by just working with the TDCTRLCTL.CPP and TDCTRLCTL.H files. In the next section, we'll add several of the new features.

Changing the Shape, Size, and Colors of the TDCtrl

From within the C++ compiler, use the View menu to select the ClassWizard menu item. The following modifications allow the shape and color properties of the control to be modified:

1. Select the OLE Automation tab from within the ClassWizard dialog box.

2. Select CTDCtrlCtrl from the Class name list box.

3. Use the Add Property button to display the Add Property dialog box. See Figure 26-9.

4. Enter the name "TDShape" as the External name.

5. Select Member variable as the implementation.

6. Choose BOOL from the drop-down Type list box. Notice that the Notification function edit control contains OnTDShapeChanged. The member variable is *m_tDShape*.

7. Accept these values with the OK button, and return to the OLE Automation tab.

8. Select the Add Property button again, and display the Add Property dialog box.

9. In the edit control of the External name combo box, select BackColor from the drop-down list of available items.

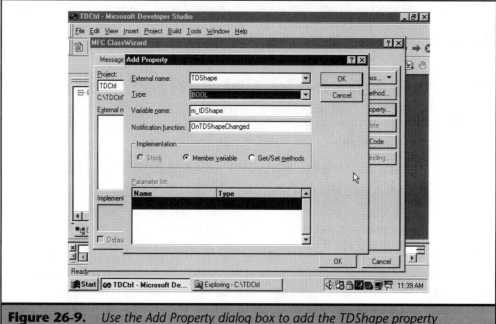

Figure 26-9. *Use the Add Property dialog box to add the TDShape property*

10. For an Implementation, select Stock.

11. Accept these values with the OK button, and return to the OLE Automation tab. The MFC ClassWizard dialog box should be similar to Figure 26-10.

12. Use the OK push button to accept the choices and close the ClassWizard.

The ClassWizard will create the code to add the TDShape and BackColor properties to the CTDCtrlCtrl class. The CTDCtrlCtrl class's dispatch map will be altered to accommodate the TDShape property. A declaration for the OnTDShapeChanged( ) function is added to the TDCTRLCTL.H header file.

The previous changes are added automatically by the ClassWizard. Now it becomes our job to write the code that reacts to these changes.

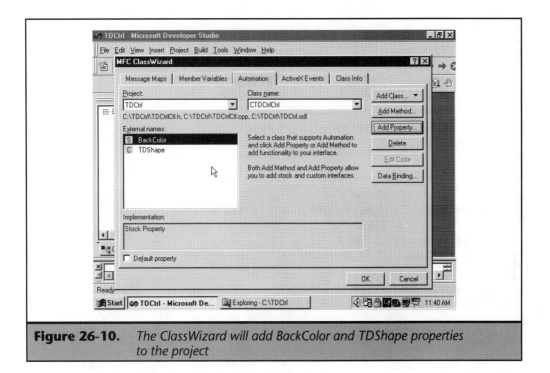

Figure 26-10. *The ClassWizard will add BackColor and TDShape properties to the project*

Back to the TDCTRLCTL.CPP File

The following listing shows the code we've modified in the TDCTRLCTL.CPP file. This file is identical to the default file returned by the ControlWizard, except for the lines of code set in a bold font. Make these changes to your file, too.

```
///////////////////////////////////////////////////////////
// CTDCtrlCtrl::OnDraw - Drawing function

void CTDCtrlCtrl::OnDraw(CDC* pdc, const CRect& rcBounds,
                         const CRect& rcInvalid)
{
  CBrush* pOldBrush;
  CBrush NewBrush;
  CPen* pOldPen;
```

```
      CPen NewPen;

      pdc->FillRect(rcBounds,CBrush::FromHandle((HBRUSH) \
                  GetStockObject(WHITE_BRUSH)));

      NewPen.CreatePen(PS_SOLID,3,RGB(0,0,0));
      pOldPen=(CPen*)pdc->SelectObject(&NewPen);

      // Create a yellow brush
      NewBrush.CreateSolidBrush(RGB(255,255,0));
      pOldBrush=(CBrush*)pdc->SelectObject(&NewBrush);

      // Draw and fill the rectangle
      pdc->Rectangle(rcBounds);

      pdc->SelectObject(pOldPen);
      pdc->SelectObject(pOldBrush);
}
```

The modified control is drawn with the Rectangle( ) function and filled with a yellow brush.

Mouse Events

In this section, you'll learn how to make the TDCtrl control respond to a mouse event. If the cursor is on the TDCtrl control when the left mouse button is depressed, the TDCtrl will change to a light gray color and report the system date and time to the control. The color change, date, and time information are indicators that a control "hit" has occurred.

Here are a list of steps needed to implement the "hit" features:

1. Select the OLE Automation tab from the MFC ClassWizard dialog box.

2. Select CTDCtrlCtrl from the Class name list box.

3. Select the Add Property button and display the Add Property dialog box.

4. In the edit control of the External name combo box, type **HitTDCtrl**.

5. For an Implementation, check to make sure Member variable is selected.

6. Select OLE_COLOR from the Type list box, and clear the Notification function edit control.

7. Close the Add Property dialog box by selecting the OK button, and return to the OLE Automation tab. Your screen should look similar to Figure 26-11.

8. Select the Message Maps tab.

9. Select CTDCtrlCtrl from the Class name list box.

10. From the Object IDs list box, select CTDCtrlCtrl and then view a list of messages in the Messages list box.

11. Select WM_LBUTTONDOWN from the Messages list box.

12. Choose the Add Function button.

13. Repeat this process by selecting WM_LBUTTONUP. Your screen should look similar to Figure 26-12.

14. Select the OK push button to accept the choices and close the ClassWizard.

The ClassWizard will automatically create the code to add the HitTDCtrl property and the outlines for the previous function implementations for the CTDCtrlCtrl class.

These changes are added by the ClassWizard, but we must now write the code that reacts to these events.

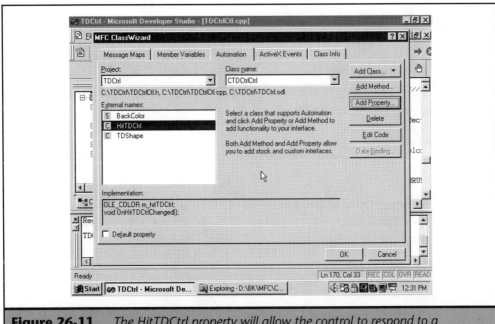

Figure 26-11. *The HitTDCtrl property will allow the control to respond to a mouse event*

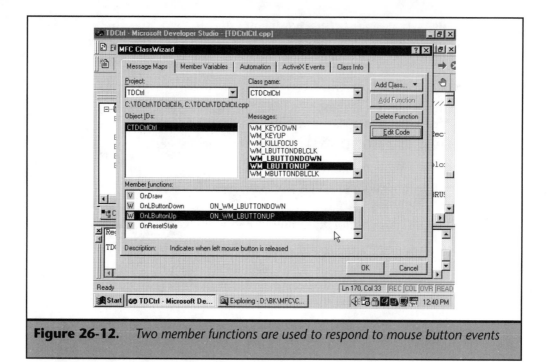

Figure 26-12.   *Two member functions are used to respond to mouse button events*

The TDCTRLCTL.H Header File

Two additional insertions must be made in the header file to accommodate two functions. The first function is used to determine if a mouse event occurred within the control. The second is used to change the control's color when a hit occurs. Insert the function prototypes, InTDCtrl( ) and HitTDCtrl( ), just under the destructor shown in the following partial listing of the TDCTRLCTL.H header file.

```
// Implementation
protected:
  ~CTDCtrlCtrl( );

  BOOL InTDCtrl(CPoint& point);      // Hit the control?
  void HitTDCtrl(CDC* pdc);          // Blink the color
    .
    .
    .
```

The code will now be added for detecting mouse clicks within the control.

Back to the TDCTRLCTL.CPP File

The control's face will change color when the user clicks the left mouse button within the rectangular area. The event notification, in part, is handled by the DoPropExchange( ) function. Here is the DoPropExchange( ) function and modification showing the new line in a bold font.

```
/////////////////////////////////////////////////////////////
// CTDCtrlCtrl::DoPropExchange - Persistence support

void CTDCtrlCtrl::DoPropExchange(CPropExchange* pPX)
{
  ExchangeVersion(pPX, MAKELONG(_wVerMinor, _wVerMajor));
  COleControl::DoPropExchange(pPX);

  // TODO: Call PX_ functions for persistent custom property.

  // Use a light-gray color to show a hit
  PX_Long(pPX,_T("HitTDCtrl"), (long &)m_hitTDCtrl,
        RGB(200, 200, 200));
}
```

This function is responsible for initializing the *m_hitTDCtrl* member variable to a light gray color. The variable *m_hitTDCtrl* must be cast to a long since it is an unsigned long value. The ClassWizard added the OnLButtonDown( ) and OnLButtonUp( ) function outlines.

This code checks to make sure the left mouse button was clicked within the face of the clock. If it was, the HitTDCtrl( ) function will be called to change the color of the clock face from yellow to light gray.

When the left mouse button is released, the OnLButtonUp( ) function merely invalidates the control, forcing a repaint in the face to yellow.

The InFace( ) function is used to determine if the left mouse button was depressed within the clock face. All of the following code must be added to the end of the CLOCKCTL.CPP listing.

```
void CTDCtrlCtrl::OnLButtonDown(UINT nFlags, CPoint point)
{
  // TODO: Add message handler code here and/or call default

  CDC* pdc;
```

```
//Blink a color change for control
if(InTDCtrl(point)) {
  pdc = GetDC( );
  HitTDCtrl(pdc);
  ReleaseDC(pdc);
}

COleControl::OnLButtonDown(nFlags, point);
}

void CTDCtrlCtrl::OnLButtonUp(UINT nFlags, CPoint point)
{
  // TODO: Add message handler code here and/or call default

  if (InTDCtrl(point))
    InvalidateControl( );

  COleControl::OnLButtonUp(nFlags, point);
}
```

This function first locates the center of the TDCtrl control and then determines if the hit occurred within the rectangle.

If the point falls within the rectangle, the HitTDCtrl( ) function is called. All of the code in the following function must be added to the end of the TDCTRLCTL.CPP listing.

```
void CTDCtrlCtrl::HitTDCtrl(CDC* pdc)
{

  CBrush* pOldBrush;
  CBrush hitBrush(TranslateColor(m_hitTDCtrl));
  CRect rc;
  TEXTMETRIC tm;
  struct tm *date_time;
  time_t timer;

  // Background mode to transparent
  pdc->SetBkMode(TRANSPARENT);
```

```
GetClientRect(rc);

pOldBrush=pdc->SelectObject(&hitBrush);

// Draw and fill the rectangle
pdc->Rectangle(rc);

// Get time and date
time(&timer);
date_time=localtime(&timer);
const CString& strtime = asctime(date_time);

// Get Font information then print
pdc->GetTextMetrics(&tm);
pdc->SetTextAlign(TA_CENTER | TA_TOP);
pdc->ExtTextOut((rc.left + rc.right) / 2,
                (rc.top + rc.bottom - tm.tmHeight) /2,
                ETO_CLIPPED, rc, strtime,
                strtime.GetLength( ) - 1, NULL);
pdc->SelectObject(pOldBrush);
}
```

The code in this function selects the light gray brush, defined earlier, and repaints the entire TDCtrl control area. The time and date information is accessed with normal C functions.

Testing the TDCtrl ActiveX Control

The Test Container can be used to test the final version of the TDCtrl control, or the control can be inserted in an application such as Microsoft Word, Excel, or Access.

For this example, let's insert it in a Microsoft Word document. Open Microsoft Word and use the Insert | Object... menu item. From the list of registered controls, select TDCtrl Control. The new control will be inserted into Word, as shown in Figure 26-13.

Now position the cursor over the control and click the left mouse button to see the current time and date information, as shown in Figure 26-14.

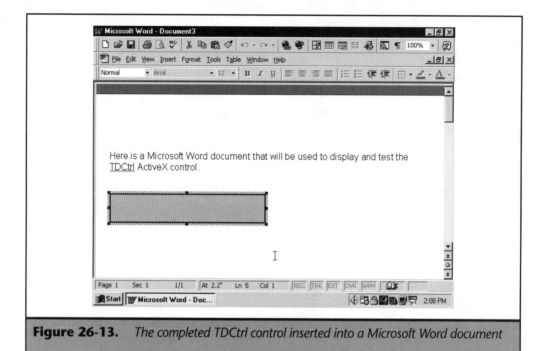

Figure 26-13. The completed TDCtrl control inserted into a Microsoft Word document

Figure 26-14. The time and date are displayed when a mouse hit occurs

More ActiveX Controls?

If the topic of ActiveX controls is of real interest to you, you'll want to read additional sources of information. The *Microsoft Systems Journal* contains a wealth of material on ActiveX controls.

ActiveX controls can also be designed in Microsoft's Visual Basic 5. Some programmers prefer the use of Visual Basic when designing ActiveX controls because of its drag-and-drop design capabilities.

WIZARDS

Part VI

Appendixes

The Complete Reference

Visual
C++ 5

Appendix A

Extended ASCII Table

Decimal	Hexadecimal	Symbol	Decimal	Hexadecimal	Symbol
0	0	(blank)	32	20	(blank)
1	1	☺	33	21	!
2	2	☻	34	22	"
3	3	♥	35	23	#
4	4	♦	36	24	$
5	5	♣	37	25	%
6	6	♠	38	26	&
7	7	✚	39	27	'
8	8	◘	40	28	(
9	9	○	41	29	)
10	A	◙	42	2A	*
11	B	♂	43	2B	+
12	C	♀	44	2C	,
13	D	♪	45	2D	-
14	E	♫	46	2E	.
15	F	☼	47	2F	/
16	10	►	48	30	0
17	11	◄	49	31	1
18	12	↕	50	32	2
19	13	‼	51	33	3
20	14	¶	52	34	4
21	15	§	53	35	5
22	16	▬	54	36	6
23	17	↨	55	37	7
24	18	↑	56	38	8
25	19	↓	57	39	9
26	1A	→	58	3A	:
27	1B	←	59	3B	;
28	1C	∟	60	3C	<
29	1D	↔	61	3D	=
30	1E	▲	62	3E	>
31	1F	▼	63	3F	?

Decimal	Hexadecimal	Symbol	Decimal	Hexadecimal	Symbol
64	40	@	96	60	`
65	41	A	97	61	a
66	42	B	98	62	b
67	43	C	99	63	c
68	44	D	100	64	d
69	45	E	101	65	e
70	46	F	102	66	f
71	47	G	103	67	g
72	48	H	104	68	h
73	49	I	105	69	i
74	4A	J	106	6A	j
75	4B	K	107	6B	k
76	4C	L	108	6C	l
77	4D	M	109	6D	m
78	4E	N	110	6E	n
79	4F	O	111	6F	o
80	50	P	112	70	p
81	51	Q	113	71	q
82	52	R	114	72	r
83	53	S	115	73	s
84	54	T	116	74	t
85	55	U	117	75	u
86	56	V	118	76	v
87	57	W	119	77	w
88	58	X	120	78	x
89	59	Y	121	79	y
90	5A	Z	122	7A	z
91	5B	[	123	7B	{
92	5C	\	124	7C	|
93	5D	]	125	7D	}
94	5E	^	126	7E	~
95	5F	_	127	7F	⌂

Decimal	Hexadecimal	Symbol	Decimal	Hexadecimal	Symbol
128	80	Ç	160	A0	á
129	81	ü	161	A1	í
130	82	é	162	A2	ó
131	83	â	163	A3	ú
132	84	ä	164	A4	ñ
133	85	à	165	A5	Ñ
134	86	å	166	A6	ª
135	87	ç	167	A7	º
136	88	ê	168	A8	¿
137	89	ë	169	A9	⌐
138	8A	è	170	AA	¬
139	8B	ï	171	AB	½
140	8C	î	172	AC	¼
141	8D	ì	173	AD	¡
142	8E	Ä	174	AE	«
143	8F	Å	175	AF	»
144	90	É	176	B0	░
145	91	æ	177	B1	▒
146	92	Æ	178	B2	▓
147	93	ô	179	B3	│
148	94	ö	180	B4	┤
149	95	ò	181	B5	╡
150	96	û	182	B6	╢
151	97	ù	183	B7	╖
152	98	ÿ	184	B8	╕
153	99	Ö	185	B9	╣
154	9A	Ü	186	BA	║
155	9B	¢	187	BB	╗
156	9C	£	188	BC	╝
157	9D	¥	189	BD	╜
158	9E	Pt	190	BE	╛
159	9F	ƒ	191	BF	┐

Decimal	Hexadecimal	Symbol	Decimal	Hexadecimal	Symbol
192	C0	└	224	E0	α
193	C1	┴	225	E1	β
194	C2	┬	226	E2	Γ
195	C3	├	227	E3	π
196	C4	─	228	E4	Σ
197	C5	┼	229	E5	σ
198	C6	╞	230	E6	μ
199	C7	╟	231	E7	τ
200	C8	╚	232	E8	ϕ
201	C9	╔	233	E9	θ
202	CA	╩	234	EA	Ω
203	CB	╦	235	EB	δ
204	CC	╠	236	EC	∞
205	CD	═	237	ED	$\varnothing$
206	CE	╬	238	EE	$\in$
207	CF	╧	239	EF	$\cap$
208	D0	╨	240	F0	$\equiv$
209	D1	╤	241	F1	$\pm$
210	D2	╥	242	F2	$\geq$
211	D3	╙	243	F3	$\leq$
212	D4	╘	244	F4	$\lceil$
213	D5	╒	245	F5	$\rfloor$
214	D6	╓	246	F6	$\div$
215	D7	╫	247	F7	$\approx$
216	D8	╪	248	F8	$\circ$
217	D9	┘	249	F9	•
218	DA	┌	250	FA	•
219	DB	█	251	FB	$\sqrt{}$
220	DC	▄	252	FC	^{n}
221	DD	▌	253	FD	^{2}
222	DE	▐	254	FE	■
223	DF	▀	255	FF	(blank)

The
Complete
Reference

Visual
C++ 5

Appendix B

DOS 10H, 21H, and 33H

Interrupt Parameters

This appendix contains the most popular DOS, BIOS, and Mouse interrupts and parameters.

Screen Control with BIOS-Type 10H Interrupts

Syntax: INT 10H (when the following parameters are set to the required values).

Interface Control of the CRT

AH Value	Function	Input	Output
AH = 0	Set the mode of display	AL = 0	40x25 color text
		AL = 1	40x25 color text
		AL = 2	80x25 color text
		AL = 3	40x25 color text
		AL = 4	320x200 4-color graphics
		AL = 5	320x420 4-color graphics
		AL = 6	640x200 2-color graphics
		AL = 7	80x25 monochrome text
		AL = 13	320x200 16-color graphics
		AL = 14	640x200 16-color graphics
		AL = 15	640x350 monochrome graphics
		AL = 16	640x350 16-color graphics
		AL = 17	640x480 2-color graphics
		AL = 18	640x480 16-color graphics
		AL = 19	320x200 256-color graphics
AH = 1	Set cursor type	CH =	Bits 4–0 start of line for cursor
		CL =	Bits 4–0 end of line for cursor
AH = 2	Set cursor position	DH =	Row
		DL =	Column
		BH =	Page number of display (0 for graphics)

AH Value	Function	Input	Output
AH = 3	Read cursor position		DH = row
			DL = column
			CH = cursor mode
			CL = cursor mode
			BH = page number of display
AH = 4	Get light pen position		AH = 0, switch not down/triggered
			AH = 1, valid answers as follows:
			DH = row
			DL = column
			CH = graph line (0 to 99)
			BX = graph column (0 to 319/639)
AH = 5	Set active display page	AL =	New page value
			(0 to 7) modes 0 and 1
			(0 to 3) modes 2 and 3
AH = 6	Scroll active page up	AL =	Number of lines, 0 for entire screen
		CH =	Row, upper-left corner
		CL =	Column upper-left corner
		DH =	Row, lower-right corner
		DL =	Column, lower-right corner
		BH =	Attribute to be used
AH = 7	Scroll active page down	AL =	Number of lines, 0 for entire screen
		CH =	Row, upper-left corner
		CL =	Column, upper-left corner

AH Value	Function	Input	Output
		DH =	Row, lower-right corner
		DL =	Column, lower-right corner
		BH =	Attribute to be used

Handling Characters

AH Value	Function	Input	Output
AH = 8	Read attribute/character at cursor position	BH =	Display page
		AL =	Character read
		AH =	Attribute of character
AH = 9	Write attribute/character at cursor position	BH =	Display page
		CX =	Count of characters to write
		AL =	Character to write
		BL =	Attribute of character
AH = 10	Write character at cursor position	BH =	Display page
		CX =	Count of characters to write
		AL =	Character to write

Graphics Interface

AH Value	Function	Input	Output
AH = 11	Select color palette	BH =	Palette ID (0 to 127)
		BL =	Color for above ID
			0—background (0 to 15)
			1—palette
			0—green(1), red(2), yellow(3)

AH Value	Function	Input	Output
			1—cyan(1), magenta(2), white(3)
AH = 12	Draw dot on screen	DX =	Row (0 to 199)
		CX =	Column (0 to 319/639)
		AL =	Color of dot
AH = 13	Read dot information	DX =	Row (0 to 199)
		CX =	Column (0 to 319/639)
		AL =	Value of dot

ASCII Teletype Output

AH Value	Function	Input	Output
AH = 14	Write to active page	AL =	Character to write
		BL =	Foreground color
AH = 15	Get video state	AL =	Current mode
		AH =	Number of screen columns
		BH =	Current display page
AH = 16	(Reserved)		
AH = 17	(Reserved)		
AH = 18	(Reserved)		
AH = 19	Write string	ES:BP =	Point to string
		CX =	Length of string
		DX =	Cursor position for start
		BH =	Page number
		AL = 0	BL = attribute (char, char, char,...char) cursor not moved
		AL = 1	BL = attribute (char, char, char,...char) cursor is moved
		AL = 2	(char, attr, char, attr...) cursor not moved

AH Value	Function	Input	Output
		AL = 3	(char, attr, char, attr...) cursor is moved
AH = 1A	R/W display combination code		
AH = 1B	Return functionality state information		
AH = 1C	Save/restore video state		

Specifications and Requirements for the DOS 21H Interrupt

Syntax: INT 21H (when the following parameters are set to the required values).

AH Value	Function	Input	Output
AH = 0	End of program		(similar to INT 20H)
AH = 1	Wait and display keyboard character with CTRL-BREAK check		AL = character entered
AH = 2	Display character with CTRL-BREAK check	DL =	Character to display
AH = 3	Asynchronous character input		AL = character entered
AH = 4	Asynchronous character output	DL =	Character to send
AH = 5	Character to write	DL =	Character to write
AH = 6	Input keyboard character	DL =	0FFH if character entered, 0 if none
AH = 7	Wait for keyboard character (no display)		AL = character entered
AH = 8	Wait for keyboard character (no display—CTRL-BREAK check)		AL = character entered

AH Value	Function	Input	Output
AH = 9	String displayed	DS:DX	Address of string; must end with $ sentinel
AH = A	Keyboard string to buffer	DS:DX =	Address of buffer. First byte = size, second = number of characters read

AH = B	Input keyboard status		AL–no character
			    = 0FFH
			    character = 0

AH = C	Clear keyboard buffer and call function	AL =	1,6,7,8,0,A (function #)
AH = D	Reset default disk drive	None	None
AH = E	Select default disk drive		Al = number of drives DL–0 = A drive 1 = B drive, etc.
AH = F	Open file with unopened FCB	DS:DX =	Location AL = 0FFH if not found AL = 0H if found
AH = 10	Close file with FCB	DS:DX =	Location (same as AH = OFH)
AH = 11	Search directory for match of unopened FCB	 DS:DX =	AL = 0FFH if not found 00000AL = 0H if found Location DTA contains directory entry
AH = 12	Search (after AH = 11) for other files that match wildcard specifications		(Same as AH = 11H)
AH = 13	Delete file named by FCB	DS:DX =	Location (same as AH = 11H)
AH = 14	Sequential read of open file. Number of bytes in FCB (record size)	DS:DX =	Location AL = 0 transfer OK AL = 1 end of file AL = 2 overrun DTA segment AL = 3 EOF/partial read

AH Value	Function	Input	Output
AH = 15	Sequential write of open file. Transfer from DTA to file, with FCB update of current record	DS:DX =	Location AL = 0 transfer OK AL = 1 disk full/ROF AL = 2 overrrun DTA segment
AH = 16	Create file (length set to zero)	DS:DX =	Location (same as AH = 11H)
AH = 17	Rename file	DS:DX	Location AL = 0 rename OK AL = 0FFH no match found
AH = 18	(DOS internal use)		
AH = 19	Drive code (default)		AL–0 = A drive 1 = B drive, etc.
AH = 1A	Set Data Transfer Add	DS:DX =	Points to location
AH = 1B	File Allocation Table	DS:DX =	Address of FAT DX = number of units AL = record/alloc. unit CX = sector size (same as AH = 1B)
AH = 1C	Disk drive FAT information	DL =	Drive number: 0 = default, 1 = A, 2 = B
AH = 1D	(DOS internal use)		
AH = 1E	(DOS internal use)		
AH = 1F	(DOS internal use)		
AH = 20	(DOS internal use)		
AH = 21	Random read file	DS:DX =	Location of FCB (same as AH = 14H)
AH = 22	Random write file	DS:DX =	(same as AH = 21H)
AH = 23	Set file size	DS:DX =	Location of FCB AL = 0 if set AL = 0FFH if not set

AH Value	Function	Input	Output
AH = 24	Random record size	DS:DX =	Location of FCB
AH = 25	Set interrupt vector (change address)	DS:DX = AL =	Address of vector table Interrupt number
AH = 26	Create program segment	DX =	Segment number
AH = 27	Random block read	DS:DX =	Address of FCB AL–0 read OK 1 EOF 2 wrap around 3 partial record
AH = 28	Random block write	DS:DX =	Address of FCB AL–0 write OK 1 lack of space
AH = 29	Parse file name	DS:SI = DS:DI =	Point to command line Memory location for FCB AL = bits to set options
AH = 2A	Read date		CX = year (80 to 99) DH = month (1 to 12) DL = day (1 to 31)
AH = 2B	Set date		CX and DX (same as previous) AL0 if valid 0FF if not valid
AH = 2C	Read time		CH = hours (0 to 23) CL = minutes (0 to 59)
AH = 2D	Set time		CX and DX (same as previous) AL0 if valid 0FF if not valid
AH = 2E	Set verify state	DL = AL =	0 0 = verify off 1 = verify on
AH = 2F	Get DTA	ES:BX =	Get DTA into ES

AH Value	Function	Input	Output
AH = 30	Get DOS version		AL = version number AH = sub number
AH = 31	Terminate and remain resident		AL = exit code DX = memory size in paragraphs
AH = 32	(DOS internal use)		
AH = 33	CTRL-BREAK check	AL = AL =	0 = request state 1 = set the state DL = 0 for off DL = 1 for on
AH = 34	(DOS internal use)		
AH = 35	Read interrupt address	AL =	Interrupt number ES:BX point to vector address
AH = 36	Disk space available	DL =	Drive (0 = default, 1 = A, 2 = B, etc.) AX = sectors/cluster (FFFF if invalid) BX = number of free clusters CX = bytes per sector DX = total number of clusters
AH = 37	(DOS internal use)		
AH = 38	Country-dependent information (32-byte block)	DS:DX =	Location of memory Date/time Currency symbol Thousands separator Decimal separator
AH = 39	Make directory	DS:DX =	Address of string for directory
AH = 3A	Remove directory	DS:DX =	Address of string for directory
AH = 3B	Change directory	DS:DX =	Address of string for new directory
AH = 3C	Create a file	DS:DX = CX =	Address of string for file AX = file handle File attribute

AH Value	Function	Input	Output
AH = 3D	Open a file	DS:DX = AL =	Address of string for file 0 = open for reading 1 = open for writing 2 = open for both AX returns file handle
AH = 3E	Close a file handle	BX =	File handle
AH =3F	Read a file or device	BX = CX = DS:DX =	File handle Number of bytes to read Address of buffer AX = number of bytes read
AH = 40	Write a file or device	BX = CX = DS:DX =	File handle Number of bytes to read Address of buffer AX = number of bytes written
AH = 41	Delete a file	DS:DX =	Address of file string
AH = 42	Move file pointer	BX = AL = CX:DX DX:AX	File handle Pointer's starting location Number of bytes Current file pointer
AH = 43	Set file attribute	AL = 1 CX = DS:DX =	 Attribute Address of file string
AH = 45	Duplicate file handle	BX	File handle AX = returned file handle
AH = 46	Force duplicate file handle	BX	File handle CX = second file handle
AH = 47	Current directory	DL = DS:SI =	Drive number (0 = default, 1 = A drive, 2 = B drive) Buffer address DS:SI returns address of string
AH = 48	Allocate memory	BX	Number of paragraphs AX = allocated blocks
AH = 49	Free allocated memory	ES	Segment of returned block
AH = 4A	Set block	ES BX	Segment block New block size

AH Value	Function	Input	Output
AH = 4B	Load/execute program	DS:DX	Location of ASCIIZ string (drive/path/filename) AL0 = load and execute 3 = load/no execute
AH = 4C	Terminate (exit)	AL	Binary return code (all files closed)
AH = 4D	Retrieve return code		AX returns exit code of another program
AH = 4E	Find first matching file	DS:DX	Location of ASCIIZ string (drive/path/filename) CX = search attribute DTA completed
AH = 4F	Next matching file		(AH = 4EH called first)
AH = 50	(DOS internal use)		
AH = 51	(DOS internal use)		
AH = 52	(DOS internal use)		
AH = 53	(DOS internal use)		
AH = 54	Verify state	None	AL0 if verify off 1 if verify on
AH = 55	(DOS internal use)		
AH = 56	Rename file	DS:DX = ES:DI =	Address of string for old information Address of string for new information
AH = 57	Get/set file date/time	AL BX DX and CX	00 (return) 01 (set) File handle Date and time information
AH = 59	Extended error code	BX =	DOS version (3.0 = 0) AX = error code BH = class of error BL = suggested action CH = where error occurred

AH Value	Function	Input	Output
AH = 5A	Create temporary file		CX = file attribute
			CF = Set on error
			AX = error code
		DS:DX =	Points to string
AH = 5B	Create a new file		(same as previous)

NOTE: For DOS versions above 2.0, use AH = 36H for file management.

Mouse Control Functions Accessed Through Interrupt 33H

Syntax: INT 33H (when the following parameters are set to the required values)

AH Value	Function	Input	Output
AX = 0	Install flag and reset	BX =	If AX = 0 and BX = 1
		CX =	Mouse support not available
		DX =	AX = 1, then BX = number of supported mouse buttons
AX = 1	Show pointer	BX =	Does nothing if already visible, otherwise
		CX =	increments the pointer-draw flag by 1
		DX =	Shows pointer image when pointer-draw flag = 0
AX = 2	Hide pointer	BX =	Does nothing if already hidden, otherwise
		CX =	decrements the pointer-draw flag
		DX =	Value of 1 hides image

AH Value	Function	Input	Output
AX = 3	Get position and button status	BX = CX = DX =	For 2- or 3-button mice, BX returns which button pressed: 0 = leftmost, 1 = rightmost, 2 = center button. Button 3 to 15 reserved. CX = x coordinate; DX = y coordinate of pointer in pixels
AX = 4	Set pointer position	CX = DX =	New horizontal position in pixels New vertical position in pixels For values that exceed screen boundaries, screen maximum and minimum are used

AX = 5	Get button press information	BX =	Button status requested, where 0 = leftmost, 1 = rightmost, 2 = center button.
			AXbit 0 (leftmost) = 0 or 1
			    bit 1 (rightmost) = 0 or 1
			    bit 2 (center) = 0 or 1
			If 0 button up, and if 1 button down. BX = number of times button pressed since last call
			CX = horizontal coordinate of mouse
			DX = vertical coordinate of mouse

AX = 6	Get button release information	BX =	Button status requested, same format as for AX = 5 previosly described. AX, BX, CX, and DX as previously described. If 0, button up,; 1 if button down

AH Value	Function	Input	Output
AX = 7	Set minimum and maximum horizontal position	CX =	Minimum virtual-screen horizontal coordinate in pixels
		DX =	Maximum virtual-screen horizontal coordinate in pixels
AX = 8	Set minimum and maximum vertical position	DX =	Maximum virtual-screen vertical coordinate in pixels
AX = 9	Set graphics pointer block	BX=	Pointer hot-spot horizontal coordinate in pixels
		CX =	Pointer hot-spot vertical coordinate in pixels
		DX =	Address of screen/pointer masks
		ES =	Segment of screen/pointer masks
AX = 10	Set text pointer	BX =	Pointer select value
		CX =	Screen mask value/hardware cursor start scan line
		DX =	Pointer mask value/ hardware cursor stop scan line
			BX = 0 select software text pointer
			BX = 1 select hardware cursor CX and DX bit map to:
			0 to 7 character
			8 to 10 foreground color
			11 intensity
			12 to 14 background color
			15 blinking
AX = 11	Read mouse motion counters	BX =	CX = horizontal count
		CX =	DX = vertical count
		DX =	Range 32,768 read in mickeys

AH Value	Function	Input	Output
AX = 12	Set user-defined subroutine	CX = DX = ES =	Call mask Offset of subroutine Segment of subroutine CX word bit map: 0 pointer position changed 1 leftmost button pressed 2 leftmost button released 3 rightmost button pressed 4 rightmost button released 5 center button pressed 6 center button released 7 to 15 reserved = 0 Following values loaded when subroutine is called: AX = condition of mask BX = button status CX = pointer horizontal coordinate DX = pointer vertical coordinate SI = last vertical mickey count read DI = last horizontal mickey count read
AX = 13	Light pen emulation on	BX = CX = DX =	Instructs mouse driver to emulate a light pen Vertical mickey/pixel ratio Ratios specify number of mickeys per 8 pixels
AX = 14	Light pen emulation off	BX = CX = DX =	Disables mouse driver light pen emulation (Same as AX = 13)
AX = 15	Set mickey/pixel ratio	CX = DX =	Horizontal mickey/pixel ratio (Same as AX = 13)

AH Value	Function	Input	Output
AX = 16	Conditional off	CX = DX = SI = DI =	Left column coordinate in pixels Upper row coordinate in pixels Right column coordinate in pixels Lower row coordinate in pixels Defines an area of the screen for updating
AX = 19	Set double speed threshold	BX = DX =	Doubles pointer motion Threshold speed in mickeys/second

AX = 20	Swap user-defined
	subroutine
		CX =
		DX = ES =
			Call mask Offset subroutine
			Segment of subroutine
			Sets hardware interrupts for
			call mask and subroutine
			address, returns previous
			values CX word call mask:
			0 pointer position changed
			1 leftmost button pressed
			2 leftmost button released
			3 rightmost button pressed
			4 rightmost button released
			5 center button pressed
			6 center button released
			7 to 12 reserved = 0
			Following values loaded
			when subroutine is called:
			  AX = condition of mask
			  BX = button status
			  CX = pointer horizontal
			  coordinate
			  DX = pointer vertical
			  coordinate
			  SI = last vertical mickey
			  count read
			  DI = last horizontal mickey
			  count read

AH Value	Function	Input	Output
AX = 21	Get mouse state storage requirements	BX = CX = DX =	Gets size of buffer in bytes needed to store state of the mouse driver BX = size of buffer in bytes
AX = 22	Save mouse driver state	BX = CX = DX = ES =	Saves the mouse driver state Offset of buffer Segment of buffer
AX = 23	Restore mouse driver state	BX = CX = DX = ES =	Restores the mouse driver state from a user buffer Offset of buffer Segment of buffer

Appendix C

Dynamic Link Libraries

Dynamic link libraries (DLLs), like other Visual C++ libraries, give programmers an easy way to distribute new functions and other resources. DLLs are different from other libraries because they are linked to the application at run time rather than during the compile/link cycle. This process could be described as *dynamic linking* rather than *static linking*. Static linking occurs when linking C or C++ run-time libraries to an application at compile/link time. DLLs also offer the advantage, in a multitasking environment, of sharing both functions and resources.

DLLs can be divided into two distinct groups: conventional API-based DLLs written in C or C++ (without objects) and MFC object-based DLLs. API DLLs have the advantage of being portable from one compiler to another. DLLs based on the MFC are, of course, restricted to compilers using a licensed version of the MFC.

Since our focus has been on the MFC, we'll demonstrate the development of a simple DLL with the use of the MFC library.

An MFC-Based Dynamic Link Library

This type of DLL can be created and compiled in a manner similar to the MFC Windows applications of Chapters 23 through 26 in this book, but with some subtle differences. To build the FRAMER.DLL dynamic link library, use the AppWizard to create all necessary header, resource, and source code files. Follow these steps to complete the Framer project.

1. Use the Visual C++ File | New menu option to bring up the New dialog box, as shown in Figure C-1.

2. Name the new DLL project *Framer*. Create a new workspace.

3. Click OK to start the MFC AppWizard.

4. Step 1 of 1 for the DLL AppWizard is shown in Figure C-2. Use all defaults suggested by the AppWizard.

5. Click Finish, review the options, and generate the base code for the project.

When the AppWizard creates the base code for the Framer project, your subdirectory should contain the files shown in Figure C-3.

Like other AppWizard templates, the code that was generated is functional—it just doesn't do anything for us until we add our own unique code.

The two files that are of greatest interest to us are the FRAMER.H and FRAMER.CPP files.

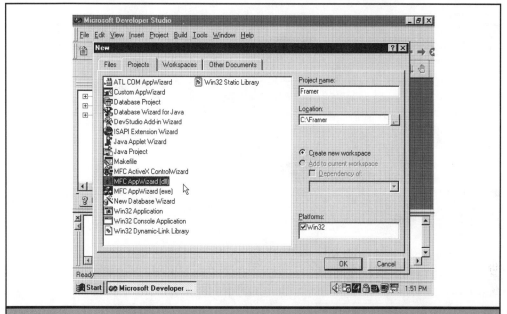

Figure C-1. *The New dialog box allows you to create an MFC AppWizard (dll) project*

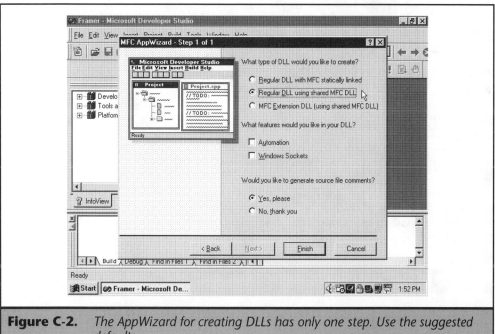

Figure C-2. *The AppWizard for creating DLLs has only one step. Use the suggested defaults.*

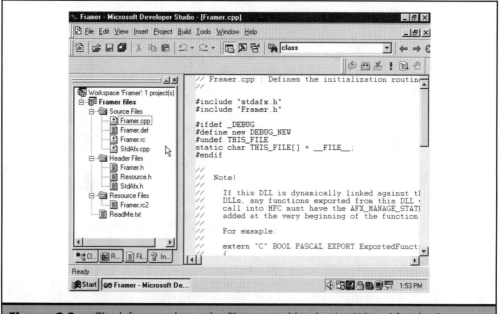

Figure C-3. *The left pane shows the files created by the AppWizard for the Framer DLL project*

The FRAMER.H Header File

The FRAMER.H header file is used to hold any function prototypes that we wish to export. In this example, DateAndTime( ) is the only function we've included in this code. Here is a partial listing of this file.

```
// Framer.h : main header file for the FRAMER DLL
//
   .
   .
   .
#ifndef __AFXWIN_H__
  #error include 'stdafx.h' before including this file for PCH
#endif

#include "resource.h"    // main symbols


__declspec( dllexport ) void WINAPI DateAndTime( );
```

```
//////////////////////////////////////////////////////////////////
//////////
// CFramerApp

// See Framer.cpp for the implementation of this class
//

class CFramerApp : public CWinApp
    .
    .
    .
```

Microsoft uses the extended attribute syntax—for example, __declspec—for simplifying and standardizing Microsoft-specific extensions to the C++ language. Here the __declspec keyword indicates that an instance of the type will be stored with a Microsoft-specific storage-class attribute.

The explicit use of the dllexport keyword has eliminated the need for EXPORT statements in the module definition file (FRAMER.DEF). Developers of C-based DLLs are familiar with the practice of identifying all exported functions in the module definition file. That practice is now outdated.

The FRAMER.CPP Source Code File

The specific DLL code is added to the FRAMER.CPP file. In the following complete listing, that code is shown in a bold font.

```
// Framer.cpp : The initialization routines for the DLL.
//

#include "stdafx.h"
#include "Framer.h"

#ifdef _DEBUG
#define new DEBUG_NEW
#undef THIS_FILE
static char THIS_FILE[] = __FILE__;
#endif
```

```
//
//   Note!
//
//     If this DLL is dynamically linked against the MFC
//     DLLs, any functions exported from this DLL which
//     call into MFC must have the AFX_MANAGE_STATE macro
//     added at the very beginning of the function.
//
//     It is very important that this macro appear in each
//     function, prior to any calls into MFC.  This means that
//     it must appear as the first statement within the
//     function, even before any object variable declarations,
//     as their constructors may generate calls into the MFC
//     DLL.
//
//     Please see MFC Technical Notes 33 and 58 for additional
//     details.
//


/////////////////////////////////////////////////////////////

// CFramerApp

BEGIN_MESSAGE_MAP(CFramerApp, CWinApp)
  //{{AFX_MSG_MAP(CFramerApp)
    // NOTE - ClassWizard adds/removes mapping macros here.
    //     DO NOT EDIT blocks of generated code!
  //}}AFX_MSG_MAP
END_MESSAGE_MAP( )

/////////////////////////////////////////////////////////////
// CFramerApp construction

CFramerApp::CFramerApp( )
{
  // TODO: add construction code here,
  // Place all significant initialization in InitInstance
}


/////////////////////////////////////////////////////////////
// The one and only CFramerApp object
```

```
CFramerApp theApp;


__declspec( dllexport ) void WINAPI DateAndTime( )
{
  AFX_MANAGE_STATE(AfxGetStaticModuleState( ));

  // get current date and time information
  struct tm *date_time;
  time_t timer;

  time(&timer);
  date_time=localtime(&timer);

  const CString& strtime = asctime(date_time);

  // Draw a message box to the window
  AfxMessageBox(strtime, MB_OK, 0);
}
```

As you learned while examining this listing, if this DLL is dynamically linked against the MFC DLLs, certain considerations must be made. Specifically, all exported functions that call into the MFC must have the AFX_MANAGE_STATE macro added at the start of the function.

The next six lines of code are used to retrieve the date and time information from the system. This information is then placed in a string, *strtime*.

When a call is made to this DLL, the DLL will in turn draw a message box to the window. The message box reports the date and time that the DLL was called. The message box can be canceled by clicking on the OK button.

Building the FRAMER.DLL

Build the DLL by selecting the appropriate build option from the compiler's Build menu. When the build cycle is complete, the DEBUG subdirectory will contain several important files.

The FRAMER.DLL is the dynamic link library, and FRAMER.LIB is the associated library. Both files must be placed in specific locations.

- Copy FRAMER.DLL to your Windows subdirectory containing system DLLs. This is usually C:\WINDOWS\SYSTEM.

- Copy FRAMER.LIB to the DEBUG subdirectory of the application that will use the DLL. The subdirectory for this example will be named C:\DLLDEMO\DEBUG.

In order to test the DLL, we will have to build a standard MFC application and call the DLL.

An Application That Calls a DLL

In this section, you will build an application designed to take advantage of the FRAMER.DLL dynamic link library. This application, named DLLDemo, will make a single call to the DateAndTime( ) function in the DLL created in the previous section.

Use the following steps to create the DLLDemo base code with the AppWizard.

1. Use the Visual C++ File | New menu option to bring up the New dialog box, as shown in Figure C-4.

2. Name the project DLLDemo. Click OK to start the MFC AppWizard.

3. Create an application with a single-document interface.

4. Choose no database support.

5. Select no compound documents.

6. Add no additional features.

7. Select source code comments and build as a shared DLL.

8. Review and accept the classes as shown in the review list. Click the Finish button to generate the project files.

It is now up to us to add the application-specific code to the previous base code. As you will recall from Chapters 24 through 26, the AppWizard generated numerous files to support each application. In this case there will be five source code files and their associated header files.

There are two files that are of interest to us. The first is DLLDEMOVIEW.H and the second is DLLDEMOVIEW.CPP.

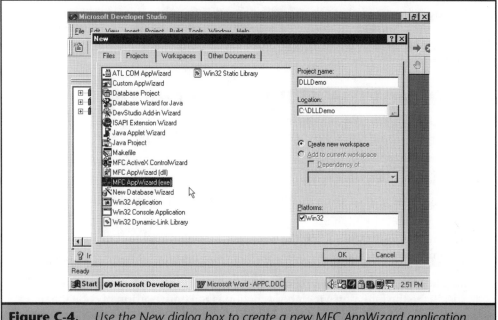

Figure C-4. *Use the New dialog box to create a new MFC AppWizard application named DLLDemo*

The DLLDEMOVIEW.H Header File

The DLLDEMOVIEW.H header file is used to hold any function prototypes that we wish to import. In this example, DateAndTime( ) is the only function we wish to use. Here is a partial listing of this file.

```
// DLLDemoView.h : interface of the CDLLDemoView class
//
/////////////////////////////////////////////////////////////////
        .
        .
        .

extern void WINAPI DateAndTime( );

class CDLLDemoView : public CView
{
        .
        .
        .
```

The extern keyword alerts the compiler that this function is external to the body of the current program. During the build process, the linker will look for this function. If the linker cannot find DateAndTime( ) in an appropriate library, you will receive a short but sweet error message.

The DLLDEMOVIEW.CPP Source Code File

In order to handle WM_PAINT messages, you'll want to add the OnPaint( ) member function and associated message handlers. To do this, follow these steps:

1. Use the View | ClassWizard... menu selection to open the MFC ClassWizard dialog box, as shown in Figure C-5.
2. Select WM_PAINT from the Messages list box. This will add the OnPaint( ) member function.
3. Double-click the mouse on the OnPaint( ) member function to add and edit the member-specific code.

The following is a partial listing of the DLLDEMOVIEW.CPP source code file. The code specific to the OnPaint( ) member function is the only portion of code that is

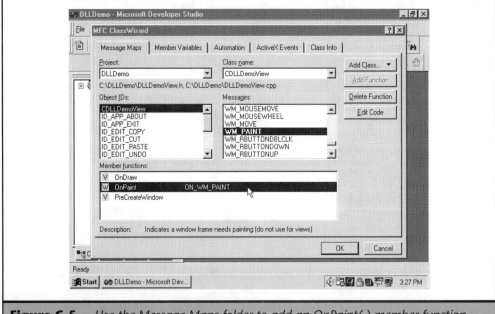

Figure C-5.   *Use the Message Maps folder to add an OnPaint( ) member function*

altered from the original listing. This is the location where the DateAndTime( ) DLL function is called.

```
// DLLDemoView.cpp : implementation of CDLLDemoView
//

    .

    .

    .

/////////////////////////////////////////////////////////////
// CDLLDemoView message handlers

void CDLLDemoView::OnPaint( )
{
  CPaintDC dc(this); // device context for painting

  dc.TextOut(280,100,"Send a little text to the Window",32);

  // Call the DLL
  DateAndTime( );

  // Do not call CView::OnPaint( ) for painting messages
}
```

Before building this project, there is one more critical step that must be taken. The DLL FRAME.LIB must be identified so the linker can resolve the external functions. This is done using the compiler's Project | Settings... menu selection to open the Project Settings dialog box. Figure C-6 shows this dialog box and the Link folder selected.

You can now build the application by making the appropriate build selection from the compiler's Build menu.

Run the program from within the IDE. You should see a screen similar to Figure C-7.

The DLLDemo application will draw the message box on the screen anytime a WM_MOUSE message is received. This action allowed us to keep the application as simple as possible yet demonstrate all of the steps necessary in incorporating a DLL.

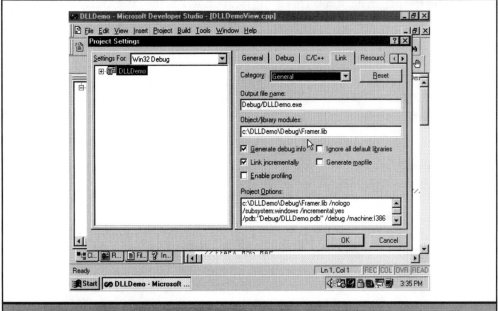

Figure C-6. *Use the Link folder to identify the FRAME.LIB in the linker's object/library module*

Figure C-7. *The DLLDemo shows a client screen with the DateAndTime message box*

More DLLs?

DLLs are considered an advanced programming topic by most developers. We included this appendix because of our discussion of ActiveX controls, which are really small DLLs.

If you are interested in expanding your knowledge of DLLs, we can only recommend one book. It is Steve Holzner's *Advanced Visual C++ 4.0 Programming*, published by M&T Books, 1996. Steve devotes a whole chapter to this advanced but important topic.

Index

G

H

I